The Self in Relationships

The Self in Relationships

Social-Personality Theory, Research, and New Directions

STANLEY O. GAINES JR.

OXFORD
UNIVERSITY PRESS

Oxford University Press is a department of the University of Oxford. It furthers
the University's objective of excellence in research, scholarship, and education
by publishing worldwide. Oxford is a registered trade mark of Oxford University
Press in the UK and certain other countries.

Published in the United States of America by Oxford University Press
198 Madison Avenue, New York, NY 10016, United States of America.

© Oxford University Press 2023

All rights reserved. No part of this publication may be reproduced, stored in
a retrieval system, or transmitted, in any form or by any means, without the
prior permission in writing of Oxford University Press, or as expressly permitted
by law, by license, or under terms agreed with the appropriate reproduction
rights organization. Inquiries concerning reproduction outside the scope of the
above should be sent to the Rights Department, Oxford University Press, at the
address above.

You must not circulate this work in any other form
and you must impose this same condition on any acquirer.

Library of Congress Cataloging-in-Publication Data
Names: Gaines Jr., Stanley O., 1961– author.
Title: The self in relationships : social-personality theory, research,
and new directions / Stanley O. Gaines, Jr.
Description: New York, NY : Oxford University Press, [2023] |
Includes bibliographical references and index.
Identifiers: LCCN 2022060548 (print) | LCCN 2022060549 (ebook) |
ISBN 9780197687635 (hardcover) | ISBN 9780197687659 (epub) | ISBN 9780197687642
Subjects: LCSH: Self. | Personality. | Field theory (Social psychology)
Classification: LCC BF697 .G28 2023 (print) | LCC BF697 (ebook) |
DDC 155.2—dc23/eng/20230109
LC record available at https://lccn.loc.gov/2022060548
LC ebook record available at https://lccn.loc.gov/2022060549

DOI: 10.1093/oso/9780197687635.001.0001

Printed by Integrated Books International, United States of America

To my son, Luther Gaines-White: You exist; therefore, I am.

Contents

Preface   ix
Acknowledgments   xvii

SECTION I: PROLOGUE

1. The Self in Relationships: An Introduction   3

SECTION II: CONCEPTUAL ISSUES REGARDING THE SELF IN RELATIONSHIPS

2. Self-Esteem (and Narcissism) as Reflected in Conflict
   Resolution Behaviors   23

3. Gender-Related Traits as Reflected in Conflict Resolution
   Behaviors   56

4. The "Big Five" Traits as Reflected in Conflict Resolution
   Behaviors   89

SECTION III: FROM CONCEPTUAL TO METHODOLOGICAL ISSUES REGARDING THE SELF IN RELATIONSHIPS

5. Conceptualization of Dominance and Nurturance as
   Interpersonal Traits   123

SECTION IV: METHODOLOGICAL ISSUES REGARDING THE SELF IN RELATIONSHIPS

6. Measurement of Dominance and Nurturance as
   Interpersonal Traits I   159

7. Measurement of Dominance and Nurturance as
   Interpersonal Traits II   191

8. Interpersonal Traits as Predictors of Accommodation   222

viii CONTENTS

SECTION V: EPILOGUE

9. The Self in Relationships: Concluding Thoughts   253

Postscript   265
Appendices   273
Bibliography   379
Index   419

Preface

Within the field of relationship science, a *close relationship* is defined as an ongoing pattern of interactions between two persons in which "(1) the individuals *have frequent* impact on each other; (2) the degree of impact per each occurrence is *strong*; (3) the impact involves *diverse* kinds of activities for each person; and (4) all of these properties characterize the interconnected activity series for a relatively long *duration* of time" (Kelley et al. 1983/2002, p. 13; emphasis in original). Drawing upon a wide array of disciplines (e.g., psychology, sociology) and multidisciplinary fields (e.g., family studies, communication studies), relationship science has flourished since the early 1980s, having created its own conferences, journals, and professional identity (Berscheid & Reis, 1998). Along the way, relationship science has matured from "greening" (Berscheid, 1999), to "ripening" (Reis, 2007), to "blossoming" (L. Campbell & Simpson, 2013) stages of development. This is not to say that relationship science is progressing along a preordained trajectory; like many of the patterns of human interaction that constitute its subject matter (Eastwick et al., 2019a, 2019b), relationship science is a work in progress (Finkel et al., 2017).

During the mid-1990s, Hazan and Shaver (1994a, 1994b) argued that relationship science would benefit from adopting John Bowlby's (1969/1997, 1973/1998, 1980/1998) *attachment theory* as a primary organizational framework among academicians and practitioners alike (Gaines, 2016/2018). According to attachment theory, all humans enter the world with a need to bond emotionally with other persons; the extent to which individuals have been able to fulfill this need from infancy onward exerts a continuing influence upon individuals' personality and social development (Gaines, 2020). Given Hazan and Shaver's (1987) enormous success in galvanizing the field of relationship science with their conceptually elegant (yet methodologically simple) research on the categorical construct of *adult attachment style*, their optimism regarding the prospects of an attachment theory foundation for the field is understandable in retrospect (see also J. A. Feeney & Noller, 1996). When one considers the ascendancy of adult attachment style (originally comprising a typology of *secure, anxious-ambivalent,* and *[fearful-]avoidant* categories) as an individual-difference variable throughout relationship science (Clark & Lemay, 2010), one might well conclude that Hazan and Shaver were right to promote attachment theory in such a robust manner.

Many relationship scientists greeted Hazan and Shaver's (1987) operationalization of attachment-related constructs from Bowlby's (1969/1997, 1973/1998, 1980/1998) attachment theory and Ainsworth's (e.g., Ainsworth et al., 1978) earlier study of infant attachment style with enthusiasm during the late 1980s (Clark & Reis, 1988). However, by the time that Hazan and Shaver (1994a, 1994b) advocated the wholesale adoption of attachment theory, some relationship scientists' enthusiasm had begun to wane (Berscheid, 1994). Perhaps the most challenging critique over the short term was the view (e.g., Bartholomew, 1994) that prevailing methods for measuring adult attachment style—including a continuous-item survey that added a fourth, *dismissing-avoidant* style (Bartholomew & Horowitz, 1991)—might be *too* simple, although the number and sophistication of assessment tools had grown substantially by the late 1990s (as noted jointly by Bartholomew & Shaver, 1998). Shaver and colleagues (Brennan et al., 1998) ultimately created an omnibus continuous-item measure of two *attachment orientations* (i.e., anxiety and avoidance) known as the Experiences in Close Relationships (ECR) survey, the current "gold standard" within the adult attachment literature (Mikulincer & Shaver, 2007a, 2016).

From the standpoint of the present author, important conceptual as well as methodological problems remain unresolved with regard to continuous attachment orientations. Conceptually speaking, attachment theorists in the tradition of Bowlby (1969/1997, 1973/1998, 1980/1998) generally have not specified where attachment-related anxiety and attachment-related avoidance fit within the "grand pantheon" of dispositional constructs within personality psychology (e.g., traits, values, attitudes, motives; Gaines, 2016/2018). Methodologically speaking, although Bartholomew's writings (e.g., Bartholomew, 1990; Bartholomew & Horowitz, 1991; Griffin & Bartholomew, 1994a, 1994b) hint that attachment orientations can be (re)cast as *interpersonal attitudes* (i.e., attachment anxiety = individuals' negative attitude toward self in relation to significant others; attachment avoidance = individuals' negative attitude toward significant others in relation to the self), no survey has been published that can assess those interpersonal attitudes in their full complexity (i.e., in accordance with a *circumplex model of attitudes within the interpersonal domain*; see Wiggins, 2003/2005). Thus, notwithstanding revisions (e.g., Fraley et al., 2000; Wei et al., 2007), the ECR is not optimal for our purposes.

Perhaps the biggest conceptual problem underlying classic attachment theory (e.g., Bowlby, 1969/1997, 1973/1998, 1980/1998) and contemporary adult attachment research (e.g., Brennan et al., 1998; Fraley et al., 2000; Wei et al., 2007) is the lack of a clear statement regarding the construct of *the self*. Of course, attachment theory is by no means the only psychodynamic personality theory that frequently invokes the term *self* without explaining the construct (Redfearn, 1983). Nevertheless, given the centrality of self in Bartholomew's (1990) (re)conceptualization of continuous adult attachment styles (i.e., dismissing-avoidant = positive internal working model of self + negative internal working model of other; fearful-avoidant = negative working models of self + other; preoccupied/anxious-ambivalent = negative working model of self + positive working model of other; secure = positive working models of self and other), an overt definition of the self would be useful within attachment theory and accompanying research on adult attachment style/orientations (Gaines, 2016/2018). Although Baumeister (1997) had a different psychodynamic theory in mind (i.e., *ego psychology*; Erikson, 1959/1980, 1968/1994, 1963/1995), we believe that Baumeister's definition of self is serviceable:

> The term *self* corresponds to its everyday usage in colloquial speech. As such, it encompasses the direct feeling each person has of privileged access to his or her own thoughts and feelings and sensations. It begins with the awareness of one's own body and is augmented by the sense of being able to make choices and initiate action. It also encompasses the more complex and abstract constructions that embellish the self. In everyday speech, the familiar expressions "to find yourself" or "to know yourself" do not ordinarily mean to locate one's body and be able to recognize it; rather, those expressions refer to some difficult act regarding complex, abstract knowledge. (p. 681; emphasis in original)

Obviously, one cannot hope to do justice to such a multifaceted construct as self within the confines of a single theory (Baumeister, 1998)—not even Bowlby's (1969/1997, 1973/1998, 1980/1988) attachment theory. Nonetheless, if our interpretation of continuous adult attachment orientations as interpersonal attitudes is correct (consistent with Bartholomew, 1990; Bartholomew & Horowitz, 1991; Griffin &

xii PREFACE

Bartholomew, 1994a, 1994b), then attachment theory may offer considerable insight into the self as a fundamentally relational construct (see also Gaines, 2016/2018). Unlike *global self-esteem* (i.e., individuals' overall attitude toward themselves; e.g., Rosenberg, 1965) or *social self-esteem* (i.e., individuals' attitude toward themselves *in relation to other persons in general*, but not necessarily significant others in particular; e.g., Spence & Helmreich, 1978), attachment orientations/interpersonal attitudes position the self *as inextricably bound with close or personal relationships* (see J. G. Holmes, 2000). In principle, even if global self-esteem is not consistently related to individuals' pro-relationship behaviors (Baumeister, 1998), one might expect the negative interpersonal attitudes of attachment anxiety and attachment avoidance to consistently inhibit individuals' pro-relationship behaviors (Berscheid & Reis, 1998).

For proponents of Bowlby's (1969/1997, 1973/1998, 1980/1998) attachment theory, the good news is that attachment *avoidance* consistently is a negative predictor of individuals' pro-relationship behaviors; the not-so-good news is that attachment *anxiety* is not consistently related to individuals' pro-relationship behavior, in a positive *or* negative direction (Berscheid & Reis, 1998). Perhaps attachment anxiety truly reflects the "ambivalence" that Hazan and Shaver (1987) initially anticipated when they operationalized attachment style as a categorical variable (J. G. Holmes, 2000). Alternatively, it is possible that existing measures of continuous attachment orientations are not sufficiently "fine-tuned" to detect genuine effects of attachment anxiety on individuals' pro-relationship behavior (Gaines, 2016/2018). In fact, even if appropriate psychometric techniques (e.g., exploratory and confirmatory factor analyses; B. Thompson, 2004) have been applied, surveys in which items are expected to "load" on a single factor (e.g., original and revised versions of the ECR; Brennan et al., 1998; Fraley et al., 2000; Wei et al., 2007) might demonstrate satisfactory *construct validity* without demonstrating commensurate *predictive validity* (or, more accurately, *criterion-related validity*; see Nunnally & Bernstein, 1994).

J. G. Holmes (2000) expressed hope that results of research by Klohnen and John (1998) would yield a psychometrically sound measure of attachment orientations as akin to (if not synonymous with) interpersonal attitudes. However, inspection of the items from Klohnen and John's study by the present author suggests that Klohnen and John were measuring individuals' prototypes of interpersonal traits—*not* individuals' self-reported interpersonal attitudes (for a similar conclusion, see Onishi et al.,

2001). One additional set of researchers (Gallo et al., 2003) cited Klohnen and John in passing but did not use Klohnen and John's measure of interpersonal trait prototypes; instead, the researchers in question attempted to place scores on anxiety and avoidance as measured by the Adult Attachment Scale (AAS; Collins & Read, 1990) within a circular grid but ended up plotting men's and women's anxiety and avoidance within one narrow portion of the grid (corresponding to low scores on both *agentic* and *communal* aspects of personality, even though anxiety and avoidance should have been orthogonal or independent dimensions; see Wiggins & Broughton, 1991). Overall, we are unaware of any direct or indirect evidence that would support Klohnen and John's circumplex operationalization of attachment orientations.

So far, we have considered attachment orientations (Brennan et al., 1998; Fraley et al., 2000; Wei et al., 2007) as interpersonal attitudes that are not quite the same as "global self-esteem" or "social self-esteem" (the latter of which also is known as *social competence*; Blascovich & Tomaka, 1991). However, attachment orientations may not be totally disconnected from global self-esteem (or, for that matter, social self-esteem): Just as global self-esteem composes the evaluative aspect of the *self-concept* in general (defined in part as "the totality of inferences that a person has made about himself or herself"; Baumeister, 1997, p. 681), so too may attachment orientations make up evaluative aspects of the *relational self-concept* in particular (see J. G. Holmes, 2000). In turn, assuming that the relational self-concept includes nonevaluative (e.g., motivational) as well as evaluative aspects (extrapolating from Collins et al., 2011), one might contend that individuals' current relational self-concept not only bears the influence of individuals' past interactions with significant others (e.g., caregivers) but also goes on to influence individuals' current interactions with significant others (e.g., romantic partners)—which subsequently influence individuals' future relational self-concept (extrapolating from B. C. Feeney, 2006).

The relational self-concept, including attachment orientations as interpersonal attitudes, may be associated with particular *relational schemas* (i.e., relationship-specific cognitive frameworks; J. G. Holmes, 2000). However, we do not wish to imply that the self-concept as a whole can be understood solely as a composite of relational schemas, or that the self-concept as a whole is limited to relational and nonrelational schemas (see S. L. Murray, 2008/2016). Continuing his definition of the self-concept, Baumeister (1997) argued that the totality of individuals' inferences about themselves

xiv PREFACE

"refer centrally to one's personality traits and schemas, but they may also involve an understanding of one's social roles and relationships" (p. 681). Although Baumeister applied the term *trait* to all dispositional personality constructs (i.e., a variety of stable individual-difference variables outside the domain of presumed cognitive abilities or intelligence), we limit our use of the term *trait* to individuals' answer to the question "How would you describe yourself?" (following Allport, 1937/1951)—a construct that is not synonymous with *attitude*, or individuals' answer to the question "How would you evaluate that entity?" (following Allport, 1935). In our view, attachment orientations qualify as attitudes, not traits (Gaines, 2016/2018).

All in all, John Bowlby's (1969/1997, 1973/1998, 1980/1998) attachment theory goes a long way toward identifying those aspects of personality that are especially likely to be reflected in individuals' behavior toward significant others (Shaver & Mikulincer, 2011). Nevertheless, attachment theory is but one of many interpersonally oriented personality theories (S. Strack & Horowitz, 2011); rather than rely exclusively upon attachment theory, relationship scientists would be well-advised to draw upon multiple personality theories that offer complementary perspectives on relevant aspects of personality within the interpersonal domain (see Horowitz & Strack, 2011). One of the most promising choices as a complement to attachment theory is Harry Stack Sullivan's (1953, 1954, 1956) *interpersonal theory of personality*, which not only posits that dispositions are best understood as manifested in individuals' behavior toward significant others but also inspired the earliest attempts by researchers to operationalize certain pairs of higher-order traits and other aspects of personality as combinations of a larger number of lower-order dimensions along two-dimensional, circular grids (thus giving rise to various *interpersonal circumplex models*; Fournier et al., 2011).

Unlike Bowlby's (1969/1997, 1973/1998, 1980/1998) attachment theory, Sullivan's (1953, 1954, 1956) interpersonal theory of personality has directly stimulated research on particular traits within the interpersonal domain— namely, the interpersonal traits of *dominance and nurturance*—in a manner that conforms to circumplex models (Millon, 1996). The most relevant model for the purposes of the present book is Wiggins and Holzmuller's (1978) model, which focused on the nonclinical or "normal" range of interpersonal traits (see also Wiggins & Holzmuller, 1981). Afterward, Wiggins (1979) proposed an *interpersonal circumplex theory of traits and social behavior* that linked dominance and nurturance to individuals' giving versus denial of affection and respect toward themselves and other persons (incorporating key constructs from the *resource exchange theory* of U. G. Foa & Foa, 1974). Subsequently, Wiggins (1991) proposed an *interpersonal circumplex theory of personality and social behavior* that established *agency and communion* as modes of being-in-the-world that included, but were not limited to, the traits of dominance and nurturance (incorporating key constructs from several neo-Freudian, "social-psychological" personality theories; see C. S. Hall & Lindzey, 1970).

In terms of conceptual content, the present book was influenced substantially by Wiggins's interpersonal circumplex theory of personality and social behavior as elaborated in *Paradigms of Personality Assessment* (2003/2005), which in turn was influenced largely by Sullivan's interpersonal theory of personality as articulated in a series of posthumously published books (1953, 1954, 1956). However, in terms of methodological content, the present book departs substantially from Wiggins's book (for a recently published book that hews closer to Wiggins's preferred methodology, see the edited volume by Hopwood & Waugh, 2020). Wiggins's book clearly was written for personality and *clinical* psychologists, with its emphasis on analyses of an enormous amount of quantitative and qualitative personality data from one participant (the same observation would apply to the edited book by Hopwood & Waugh, in which the authors literally followed the same participant who had provided so much raw data for Wiggins's book, 20 years later), whereas the present book was written for personality and *social* psychologists, with its focus on analyses of a relatively small amount of quantitative personality *and behavioral* data from hundreds of participants in multiple samples (albeit at a single point in time).

Above all else, the present book was written for relationship scientists—a fact that makes the present book a logical successor to Stanley O. Gaines Jr's *Personality and Close Relationship Processes* (2016/2018), keeping in mind the debt that the present book also owes to Wiggins (2003/2005). Moreover, the nucleus of the present book originated in an invited talk that Gaines (2021) presented at the Close Relationships Preconference of the on-line 2021 Convention of the Society for Personality and Social Psychology (SPSP). Gaines's 45-minute talk had been accompanied by an ambitiously crafted manuscript that could not be presented in full and greatly exceeded the customary page length of most journal manuscripts! As it happens, Nadina Persaud (editor, *Social Psychology and Neuropsychology*, Oxford University Press) had been perusing the list of speakers and topics for the

xvi PREFACE

SPSP convention; following discussions with the present author (and insightful comments from reviewers), a full-fledged book gradually took shape. Hopefully, the present book will chart new territory for followers of Sullivan (1953, 1954, 1956) who famously called for a "science of interpersonal relations" more than a generation before the modern-day field of relationship science was formally launched (Gaines, 2007a, 2007b).

Acknowledgments

To Nadina Persaud, Katharine Pratt, Kamala Palaniappan, several anonymous reviewers, and the entire team at Oxford University Press and Newgen Knowledge Works, my deepest thanks.

SECTION I
PROLOGUE

1

The Self in Relationships

An Introduction

Synopsis: In this chapter, we delve into Kurt Lewin's field theory as an overarching framework for conceptualizing the self and the psychological environment (including significant others) as interrelated aspects of individuals' life space; we consider individuals' potential exercise of self-control via conflict-reducing behaviors within close relationships; we comment on Thibaut and Kelley's interdependence theory as a major Lewin-inspired theory within relationship science (notwithstanding its frequent use of personality-friendly terminology that actually refers to social-psychological, rather than individual-difference, phenomena); we provide an overview of the present book (including a list of the major sections); and we offer a prelude to Chapter 2, which covers Sullivan's interpersonal theory of personality as an additional Lewin-inspired theory, albeit distinctive in its focus on self-esteem as an outcome of individuals' experience of (low) interpersonal anxiety over the long term.

> Nothing helps a child more than being able to express hostile and jealous feelings candidly, directly, and spontaneously, and there is no parental task more valuable, I believe, than being able to accept with equanimity such expressions of filial piety as "I hate you, mummy" or "Daddy, you're a beast." By putting up with these outbursts we show our children that we are not afraid of hatred and that we are confident it can be controlled; moreover, we provide for the child the tolerant atmosphere in which self-control can grow.
>
> —John Bowlby,
> *The Making and Breaking of Affectional Bonds*
> (1979/2005, pp. 19–20)

Within parent–offspring relationships, not every parent is equally adept at providing a *secure base* (Ainsworth, 1969) for his or her son or daughter (Bowlby, 1988/2005). Nevertheless, as the preceding quote from Bowlby (1979/2005) illustrates, one of the most important functions that a parent can fulfill is to "be there" emotionally when his or her offspring is distressed—even when the offspring expresses negative emotions toward the parent along the way (see J. Holmes, 2004). Furthermore, by displaying restraint in the midst of receiving negativity from his or her own offspring, the parent not only promotes the development of a positive working model of other in the mind of the offspring (Dozier & Bernard, 2021) but also models conflict resolution behavior that may serve the offspring well in a variety of close relationships that do not necessarily involve the parent (R. A. Thompson et al., 2021). In turn, throughout childhood and beyond, the offspring may take the parent's implicit and explicit conflict resolution messages to heart when interacting with significant others (J. P. Allen, 2021). One overarching message may be that offspring need not forsake their need for emotional intimacy in the process of exercising self-control (Marvin et al., 2016).

Given the primacy of parent-offspring relationships as influences on individuals' social and personality development within Bowlby's (1969/1997, 1973/1998, 1980/1998) *attachment theory*, it is not surprising that Bowlby's (1979/2005) quote alludes to the complementarity between the parent's caregiving system and the offspring's attachment system, *during the offspring's childhood* (Hazan & Shaver, 1994a, 1994b). However, the offspring's journey from childhood to adulthood is likely to be accompanied by the dual realization that (1) significant others (including immediate and extended family members, but especially friends and romantic partners) also need attachment over time, and (2) the offspring himself or herself will be increasingly placed in the position of caregiver over time (Mikulincer & Shaver, 2012; Shaver & Mikulincer, 2012). In any event, Bowlby's attachment theory suggests that individuals' development of self-control within their earliest relationships with parents and other caregivers can help enable individuals to attain a stable (yet adaptable), coherent (yet multifaceted) sense of self across relationship contexts and across time (Shaver & Mikulincer, 2011). As individuals progress toward the end of life's journey, the maintenance of self-control may become particularly salient within intact relationships (Antonucci, 1994).

The present book is not intended to be a treatise on Bowlby's (1969/1997, 1973/1998, 1980/1998) attachment theory per se, given that excellent authored books already provide comprehensive coverage of Bowlby's theory as applied to adult relationships (most notably Mikulincer & Shaver, 2007, 2016). By the same token, Bowlby's (1979/2005) quote from the beginning of the present chapter arguably represents one of the most eloquent statements that one will find in print concerning the adaptiveness of self-control within close relationships (whether interacting with offspring or interacting with other persons who may not be quite as dependent upon individuals as providers of emotional intimacy), regardless of one's theoretical perspective (see Steele, 2010, regarding the eclectic nature of the 1956 lecture that eventually served as Chapter 1 for Bowlby's 1979/2005 book). More generally, Bowlby's comments regarding the interpersonal ramifications of self-control are consistent with the predominant theme in the present book that *understanding various manifestations of the self can help relationship researchers account for substantial variance in individuals' behavior toward significant others*—a theme that surfaces repeatedly in research on *conflict resolution behaviors* within close relationships (Rusbult, 1993).

A Conceptual Starting Point: Lewin's Field Theory

According to Kurt Lewin's (1951/1976) *field theory*, individuals' behavior is a function of individuals' *life space*, which comprises "the person and the psychological environment as it exists for [that person]" (p. 57). Although Lewin has been hailed as a "master of social psychology" (Schellenberg, 1978), Lewin's emphasis on individual-difference variables within the life space—including unstable aspects of personality (e.g., moods) alongside stable or dispositional aspects of personality (e.g., motives)—simultaneously distinguishes field theory as a classic theory of personality (C. S. Hall & Lindzey, 1970). Although one will not find an explicit definition of *self* within field theory, one might contend that Lewin's construct of *person* (i.e., "the more complex, higher order processes that are responsive to the broad patterning of the geo-behavioral environment and that generate individual differences in response to it"; Kelley, 1991, p. 232) implicitly defines the self. In the Preface of the present book, we cited Baumeister's (1997) definition of the self; we propose a working definition of self as *individuals' experience as separate from, yet interconnected with, various aspects of their social and physical environments* (based on Gaines, 2016/2018) that integrates Lewin's and Baumeister's respective views.

6 THE SELF IN RELATIONSHIPS

Just as Lewin's (1951/1976) field theory lacks an explicit definition of the self, so too does Lewin's theory lack an overt definition of the *self-concept*. In *The Conceptual Representation and the Measurement of Psychological Forces*, Lewin (1938/2013) did refer briefly to *self-consciousness* as a possible mediator of "the effect of a psychological force on locomotion" (p. 98). However, that acknowledgment is not accompanied by further commentary; and it is not clear whether readers should regard self-consciousness as more versus less important than "language defects" or "a broken leg" as a mediator(!). Notwithstanding the importance of language defects or a broken leg to individuals' personalities and behavior, the executive-function aspect of self-consciousness or self-concept in mediating personality–behavior covariance is not addressed within Lewin's field theory (see Baumeister, 1998, regarding the pivotal role of the self-concept in maintaining individuals' selfhood). Keeping in mind Baumeister's (1997) attempts to define self-concept (as noted in the Preface to the present book), we offer a working definition of self-concept as *individuals' reflection upon their experience as separate from, yet interconnected with, various aspects of their social and physical environments* (based on Gaines, 2016/2018), thus incorporating Baumeister's perspective.

Finally, like the constructs of self and self-concept, Lewin's (1951/1976) field theory does not define *self-esteem*. Tesser (2000) cited Lewin's *A Dynamic Theory of Personality* (1935) in support of the view that individuals' resumption of work on tasks following interruption by experimenters provides insight into individuals' maintenance of self-esteem, although a careful reading of Lewin's book does not uncover any allusion to self-esteem. In any event, Tesser inferred that individuals' willingness to (1) undertake a task, (2) endure distractions from that task, and (3) re-engage with the task when permitted to do so illustrates individuals' goal strivings—not just to complete tasks that experimenters have assigned to them, but also to fulfill their own need for esteem—an inference that requires a leap of faith for readers but could be construed as consistent with Lewin's view on the antecedents of success (see also McClelland, 1985/1987). With Baumeister's (1997) definition of self-esteem in mind (as cited in the Preface of the present book), we submit a working definition of self-esteem as *the thoughts and feelings that result from individuals' reflection upon their experience as separate from, yet interconnected with, various aspects of their social and physical environments* (based on Gaines, 2016/2018), thus channeling Baumeister.

Self-Control of Behavior Following Within- and Between-Person Conflict

Now that we have defined the term *self*, let us consider individuals' self-control of behavior following *conflict*, which Lewin (1935) defined as "the opposition of approximately equally strong field forces" (p. 88). Lewin regarded the term *psychological field* as interchangeable with *life space* (as noted earlier in the present chapter, encompassing person and psychological environment). Thus, conflict may occur (1) within individuals, (2) between individuals in the same group, and (3) between groups (at least one of which may include the individuals in question; Schellenberg, 1978). Although Lewin commented at length upon intergroup conflict in *Resolving Social Conflicts* (1948/1967), we shall confine our review to Lewin's writings on intraindividual and interindividual conflict (e.g., as emphasized in *Field Theory in Social Science: Selected Theoretical Papers*; Lewin, 1951/1976). We note in passing that the topic of *interethnic relationships* (i.e., ongoing interactions, characterized by high levels of interdependence, between individuals who are members of different racial, religious, and/or national groups) lends itself well to the exploration of overlap between interpersonal conflict and intergroup conflict but is so under-researched that we would not be able to reach many firm conclusions (Gaines, 2017/2018).

When reading Lewin's (1935, 1948/1967, 1951/1976) field theory, one is struck by the extent to which Lewin emphasizes the interior world of young children—not in terms of emotional intimacy with caregivers (as one would expect from the attachment theory of Bowlby, 1969/1997, 1973/1998, 1980/1998), but rather in terms of children's success versus failure in reconciling their own "approach" and "avoidance" motives (McClelland, 1985/1987). Such reconciliation is complicated by the prospects of competing "approach" motives or competing "avoidance" motives within children, in addition to the expected conflicts between an "approach" motive and an "avoidance" motive that children may need to resolve within a particular situation (C. S. Hall & Lindzey, 1970). From Lewin's vantage point, parents—and, more often than not, *mothers*—seem almost oblivious to their offspring's need for emotional intimacy; resulting analyses of social interactions within field theory tend to focus on parents' giving versus denial of rewards and costs that do not necessarily involve love or affection (somewhat akin to the perspective of operant reinforcement theory; Skinner, 1938). In the end, children are left largely to

8 THE SELF IN RELATIONSHIPS

their own devices to summon the self-control that is required to get what they want from their psychological environment (Schellenberg, 1978).

In the process of shifting his attention from parent-offspring relationships to adult marital relationships, Lewin (1935, 1948/1967, 1951/1976) noted that adults' experience of selfhood is more complex in its own right *and* is more clearly distinct from adults' experience of the psychological environment within their life space, compared to children's experience of selfhood (C. S. Hall & Lindzey, 1970). Consequently, Lewin's field theory deals with (1) the intraindividual conflict of husbands (or, more generally, Partner A), (2) the intraindividual conflict of wives (or, more generally, Partner B), and (3) the interpersonal conflict that arises between the partners during everyday social interaction (Kelley, 1991). In their major revision of *interdependence theory* (Thibaut & Kelley, 1959), Kelley and Thibaut (1978) highlighted Lewin's dyadic approach to conflict in adult relationships, viewing intrapersonal and interpersonal conflict as resulting primarily from clashes over conscious goal strivings (instead of clashes over unconscious motives; Van Lange & Balliet, 2015). Nevertheless, according to Lewin's field theory as well as Kelley and Thibaut's interdependence theory, individuals' exercise of self-control over their own behavior remains crucial in the de-escalation of conflict, within and between persons (Agnew & VanderDrift, 2015).

Conceptualizing Between-Person Conflict Resolution Behaviors

In a chapter on conflict resolution in close relationships, Rusbult (1993) identified *responses to relationship dissatisfaction* (Rusbult et al., 1982) as one interrelated set of behaviors that individuals might pursue in order to de-escalate versus escalate interpersonal as well as intrapersonal conflict. Inspired by Hirschman's (1970) exit-voice-loyalty typology of individuals' responses to organizational decline, Rusbult et al. distinguished among four responses to conflict resolution: (1) *Exit* (active, destructive behavior); (2) *voice* (active, constructive behavior); (3) *loyalty* (passive, constructive behavior); and (4) *neglect* (passive, destructive behavior). Following the logic of interdependence theory (Thibaut & Kelley, 1959) as revised by Kelley and Thibaut (1978), Rusbult and colleagues reasoned that most individuals are capable of refraining from acting in their self-interest over the short term (i.e., opting to "cut bait"), instead acting in a manner that promotes their relationships over the long term (i.e., continuing to "fish"; VanderDrift & Agnew, 2020). Rusbult et al.'s construct of responses to dissatisfaction highlights one set of self-controlling behaviors that individuals may enact in situations where no one necessarily is to blame for current relationship difficulties (see Columbus et al., 2020).

In addition to responses to relationship dissatisfaction, Rusbult (1993) identified *accommodation following anger or criticism by partners* (Rusbult et al., 1991) as an interrelated set of behaviors that individuals might pursue in order to de-escalate versus escalate interpersonal as well as intrapersonal conflict. Unlike responses to relationship dissatisfaction, accommodation occurs in response to particular situations in which individuals have experienced hostility from their partners (Rusbult & Buunk, 1993). Furthermore, given that individuals may experience such direct negativity from their partners as unwarranted, the resulting internal conflict for individuals may be especially high; this "accommodative dilemma" places individuals in the position of deciding whether to turn the other cheek rather than simply fish or cut bait (Berscheid, 1994). Nonetheless, the exit-voice-loyalty-neglect (EVLN) typology that Rusbult and colleagues (e.g., Rusbult et al., 1982) had applied to responses to dissatisfaction likewise can be applied to accommodation following partners' anger/criticism (Rusbult et al., 1994). Overall, accommodation clearly qualifies as a self-controlling behavior in situations where the individuals' partners are to blame (Berscheid, 2010).

At the time that Rusbult's (1993) chapter on conflict resolution in close relationships was published, Rusbult and colleagues had not undertaken research on *forgiveness following betrayal by partners* (Finkel et al., 2002). In a subsequent review article, Rusbult and Van Lange (2003) identified forgiveness as a third interrelated set of behaviors that individuals might pursue in order to de-escalate versus escalate interpersonal as well as intrapersonal conflict. Given that betrayal undermines individuals' *relational trust* (see W. H. Jones et al., 1997), one might expect forgiveness to present even more challenges for individuals than does accommodation (for a discussion of the importance of relational trust to close relationships, see Kelley et al., 2003). However, betrayal as operationalized by Rusbult and colleagues has focused on partners' norm-violating behaviors that stop short of the worst-case scenario that "betrayal" brings to mind (i.e., sexual infidelity; e.g., Hannon et al., 2010). All in all, using the EVLN typology, Rusbult and colleagues concluded that forgiveness reflects self-controlling behavior in situations where individuals' partners are to blame (see also Raj & Wiltermuth, 2016).

10 THE SELF IN RELATIONSHIPS

A Social-Psychological Aside: "Investment Model" Variables as Influences on Conflict Resolution Behaviors

Probably the most influential, empirically supported model to emerge directly from the tradition of Thibaut and Kelley's (1959; Kelley, 1979; Kelley & Thibaut, 1978) interdependence theory and indirectly from the tradition of Lewin's (1935, 1948/1967, 1951/1976) field theory is Caryl Rusbult's (1980) *investment model*, which proposes that *commitment* (i.e., individuals' conscious decision to remain in a particular close relationship) reflects the influence of no fewer than three social-psychological variables: (1) *satisfaction* (i.e., individuals' experience of a preponderance of rewards over costs within the relationship), (2) *perception of alternatives to the relationship* (i.e., individuals' belief that being with someone else *or* being with no one else would be preferable to remaining in their current relationship), and (3) *investment size* (i.e., the extent to which individuals stand to lose resources that they have devoted to their relationship, if that relationship were going to end; see Finkel et al., 2017). Given our emphasis on individual differences in conflict resolution behaviors in the present book, we will provide a brief review of social-psychological, "investment model" influences (for more definitive reviews, see Kelley et al., 1983/2002, 2003).

We note that, when Rusbult and colleagues measured satisfaction, alternatives, and investment along with conflict resolution behaviors (e.g., Rusbult et al., 1982, 1991), the "investment model" variables were hypothesized as *predictors* (with satisfaction and investment as significant positive predictors, and with alternatives as a significant negative predictor, of voice and loyalty; the valences for all predictions were reversed for exit and neglect). However, when Rusbult et al. measured commitment alongside conflict resolution variables, the responses to *partners behaving badly* (i.e., accommodation and forgiveness; e.g., Finkel et al., 2002; Rusbult et al., 1991) were cast as *outcomes* of commitment; but the responses to partner-nonspecific dissatisfaction (e.g., Rusbult et al., 1982; Rusbult, Johnson, & Morrow, 1986a) were cast as *predictors* of commitment. In terms of results, satisfaction and commitment were more likely to be significantly associated with conflict resolution behaviors (and in the expected direction) than were alternatives or investment. However, commitment was not examined as an *outcome* of responses to partners behaving badly; and commitment was not examined as a *predictor* of responses to partner-nonspecific dissatisfaction (but see Rusbult & Buunk, 1993, regarding possible "feedback loops").

On the basis of field theory (Lewin, 1935, 1948/1967, 1951/1976) and interdependence theory (Kelley, 1979; Kelley & Thibaut, 1978; Thibaut & Kelley, 1959), we are not aware of any a priori reason to expect conflict resolution behaviors—whether operationalized as responses to partner-nonspecific dissatisfaction (e.g., Rusbult et al., 1982) or operationalized as responses to partners behaving badly (e.g., Finkel et al., 2002; Rusbult et al., 1991)—to serve as predictors of personality variables *at one point in time* (Gaines, 2016/2018). Nevertheless, we acknowledge that results of longitudinal research may uncover effects of conflict resolution behaviors enacted at one point in time, upon individuals' personalities *at a later point in time* (not to mention effects upon individuals' "investment model" variables at a later point in time; see C. T. Hill, 2019). In the present book, we will focus upon results of cross-sectional research in which personality variables have been examined as predictors of conflict resolution behaviors, combining summaries of previous analyses from several sets of studies (i.e., Rusbult, Johnson, & Morrow, 1986a, 1986b; Rusbult et al., 1987; Rusbult et al., 1991, Study 4; Rusbult, Zembrodt, & Iwaniszek, 1986) with new analyses from one additional set of studies (i.e., Gaines, 2021, Main Studies 1 and 2).

Commitment: A Motive That Influences Certain Conflict Resolution Processes(?)

So far, we have described commitment (e.g., as conceptualized and measured by Rusbult et al., 1998) as a consciously experienced, social-psychological construct. In much of the research by Rusbult and colleagues (e.g., Rusbult et al., 1991; Wieselquist et al., 1999), commitment is framed clearly as a social-psychological predictor of accommodation and other "pro-relationship" behaviors (assuming that conflict resolution behaviors such as accommodation promote relationship maintenance; see Dindia & Canary, 1993). However, in various reviews of their own work, Rusbult and colleagues (e.g., Rusbult & Agnew, 2010; Rusbult & Buunk, 1993; Rusbult & Van Lange, 2003) refer to commitment as a "motive"—a term that, within personality psychology, raises the prospect of individual differences (Gaines, 2020). The issue is not simply semantic; Rusbult and colleagues have concluded that individual-difference variables—including adult attachment style (e.g., Hazan & Shaver, 1987), which some of Rusbult's own previous studies had associated with accommodation (e.g., Gaines, Reis, et al., 1997)—accounted

12 THE SELF IN RELATIONSHIPS

for a small proportion of interindividual variance in "pro-relationship behaviors," *compared to commitment* (Gaines, 2016/2018).

In the present book, we shall adopt the working definition that a *motive* is individuals' answer to the question, "What compels you to do what you do?" (with the caveat that individuals may not be aware of the impact that their own motives exert upon their behavior; Gaines, 2016/2018). Therefore, in our view, commitment as operationalized by Rusbult et al. (1998) does *not* qualify as a motive. However, we believe that commitment *might* qualify as a *goal*—which we shall define as individuals' answer to the question, "What are you seeking to accomplish?" (inspired by McAdams & Olson, 2010)—that can mediate the impact of motives on accommodation (Rusbult et al., 1991), forgiveness (Finkel et al., 2002), and additional conflict resolution behaviors within close relationships (Crocker & Canevello, 2015). Indeed, Strachman and Gable (2006) postulated that commitment mediates the impact of individuals' "approach" and "avoidance" motives upon individuals' behavior in close relationships; such a distinction is not apparent from the writings of Rusbult and colleagues (e.g., Rusbult & Buunk, 1993). Then again, Strachman and Gable's multidimensional conceptualization of commitment contradicts the argument by Rusbult et al. (e.g., Rusbult et al., 2006) that commitment is a unidimensional construct.

One additional point regarding motives within Rusbult's (1980) investment model is that—consistent with the broader interdependence theory as presented initially by Thibaut and Kelley (1959) and revised subsequently by Kelley and Thibaut (1978)—Rusbult's model took it for granted that all human beings possess a *need for self-interest* (Crocker & Canevello, 2015). Given that Rusbult and colleagues proceeded on the assumption of individual *similarities* in the self-interest need, it should come as no surprise that commitment and its social-psychological precursors (especially satisfaction) tended to receive priority over individual-difference variables when Rusbult et al. attempted to predict conflict resolution behaviors (e.g., Rusbult et al., 1991; Wieselquist et al., 1999). Crocker et al. (2017) applied the term *selfishness motivation* to this oft-presumed "universal" need for self-interest (although, like Rusbult and colleagues, Crocker et al. have not always maintained a distinction between the terms *motive* and *goal*). At any rate, Crocker and colleagues have contended that (1) humans also possess a "universal" *otherishness motivation* and (2) commitment as operationalized by Rusbult et al. can reflect selfishness *and* otherishness motives (see also Canevello & Crocker, 2015).

"Transformation of Motivation": *Not* a Change in Stable Motives Over Time

Perhaps the most striking example regarding the potential misuse of personality-related terminology within interdependence theory (Kelley, 1979; Kelley & Thibaut, 1978; Thibaut & Kelley, 1959) is the gradual adoption of the phrase *transformation of motivation*—a phrase that has been popularly associated with Lewin's (1935, 1948/1967, 1951/1976) field theory, even though the phrase appeared around the same time within Gordon Allport's (1937/1951, 1961/1963) *psychology of the individual* (which proposes that the construct of *trait* should be the predominant construct throughout personality psychology; C. S. Hall & Lindzey, 1970). According to Allport's concept of *functional autonomy*, (1) not only are most of the prevailing motives underlying behavior during adulthood fundamentally different from most of the prevailing motives underlying behavior during childhood, but also (2) formerly prevailing needs from childhood may be *extinguished* during adulthood (Bertocci, 1940). Therefore, within Allport's psychology of the individual, "transformation of motivation" implies that the need for self-interest that individuals presumably possessed as children might vanish during adulthood—surely not the scenario that interdependence theorists envision when they use the term (Karremans et al., 2015).

Some advocates of Allport's (1937/1951, 1961/1963) psychology of the individual have contended that "transformation of motivation" might be (re)interpreted as *sublimation* of motivation (e.g., Winter, 1997)—an interesting possibility for relationship scientists in general, given the implication that the need for self-interest may not be inherently adaptive (notwithstanding the argument that the self-interest motive is important to interpersonal attraction from acquaintanceship onward; e.g., Montoya & Horton, 2020). However, Allport had famously rejected Freudian motivation-related concepts, such as defense mechanisms (including sublimation; see Ewen, 1998). Moreover, for interdependence theorists in particular (following Kelley, 1979; Kelley & Thibaut, 1978; Thibaut & Kelley, 1959), the *psychic determinism* that is central to Freud's (1923/1927) psychoanalytic theory might seem like anathema to their Lewinian emphasis on the psychological environment as no less important (and possibly *more* important) than personality processes in shaping individuals' behavior (see Schellenberg, 1978). In any event, the need for self-interest does not appear to be one of the motives that individuals retain from childhood to adulthood within

14 THE SELF IN RELATIONSHIPS

Allport's psychology of the individual (though the *need for esteem* survives the cut; Redfearn, 1983).

In all fairness to proponents of interdependence theory (Thibaut & Kelley, 1959) as revised by Kelley and Thibaut (1978), Lewin (1935, 1948/1967, 1951/1976) *did* argue that the successful exercise of self-control might require that individuals either (1) refrain from acting upon their current goals (if not their motives) or (2) *change* their current goals (if not their motives; see Karniol & Ross, 1996). Assuming that goals are more consistently accessible to consciousness than are motives, one might reasonably expect that individuals are likely to find it easier to change goals (or, at least, refrain from acting upon goals) in comparison to motives (see Kuper et al., 2021). If interdependence theorists have such a well-delineated version of "transformation of motivation" in mind, then it might be worth amending the term to "transformation of *goals*" (Gaines, 2016/2018). Otherwise, interdependence theorists run the risk of conveying the inaccurate impression that motives as experienced by individuals in everyday life (and outside social-psychological experimental settings) are more malleable than actually is the case (Gaines, 2020).

Before We Proceed: Prospects for Individual Differences in Motives

Owing to the legacy of Lewin's (1935, 1948/1967, 1951/1976) field theory and Kelley's (1979; Kelley & Thibaut, 1978; Thibaut & Kelley, 1959) interdependence theory, Rusbult's (1980) investment model does not offer much insight into the ways that individuals might differ in motives as stable, cross-situational dispositions (Gaines, 2016/2018). Probably the most systematic account of individual differences in motives within personality psychology can be found in Henry Murray's (1938) *personology*, a psychodynamic theory that lists more than two dozen motives (although the *needs for power, intimacy, and achievement* have received the most attention from researchers over the years; McClelland, 1985/1987). Unlike most psychodynamic personality theories, personology assumes that most motives are acquired over time, rather than inborn (an assumption that may help explain the existence of individual differences in motives at a particular point in time; Ewen, 1998). By the same token, according to H. Murray's theory, different situations that individuals encounter within their psychological environments on a daily basis—collectively known as *press*—will interact with motives to produce particular behavioral patterns or *thema* (C. S. Hall & Lindzey, 1970).

Both H. Murray's (1938) personology and Lewin's (1935) field theory acknowledge that individuals' behavior reflects a complex interaction between within-person and outside-person influences, although the two theories differ in their relative emphases (i.e., personology prioritizes the impact of motives as aspects of individuals' personalities, whereas field theory places equal or greater priority upon the impact of individuals' psychological environment as an aspect of the total environment; Rosenzweig, 1944). We do not wish to overstate the degree of overlap between H. Murray's personology and Lewin's field theory: Personology embraces the personality structure of id, ego, and superego that is a hallmark of Freud's (1923/1927) *psychoanalytic theory* and is implicated in personality and behavior from childhood, whereas field theory focuses on individuals' immediate past, without invoking a particular structure of personality (C. S. Hall & Lindzey, 1970). Nevertheless, modern-day readers might be surprised to discover the extent to which Lewin (1936) respected Freud's (1924) motive-oriented theoretical contributions to personality psychology, even though Lewin criticized Freud's single-case-oriented methodological innovations as unscientific (Schellenberg, 1978).

Kelley (1991) credited Lewin's (1935, 1948/1967, 1951/1976) field theory with providing much of the individual-difference and social-psychological foundation for Thibaut and Kelley's (1959, Kelley, 1979; Kelley & Thibaut, 1978) interdependence theory. For instance, both field theory and interdependence theory regard significant others as important actors within individuals' psychological environment, keeping in mind that individuals *and their partners* possess motives that may be communicated directly or indirectly within close relationships (Rusbult & Van Lange, 2003). However, Kelley (1997) looked primarily to McClintock's *game theory* (e.g., McClintock, 1972; McClintock & Liebrand, 1988)—especially McClintock's list of *social motives* (i.e., *own, relative, joint,* and *other gain maximization*)—for details regarding *which* motives were most likely to be reflected in individuals' behavior toward relationship partners. Unfortunately, neither field theorists nor interdependence theorists have focused on the effects of "social motives" upon individuals' behavior within ongoing relationships (see Berscheid, 2010). Instead, field theorists and interdependence theorists alike have tended to infer motives from covariances among individuals' scores on purely social-psychological variables (see Finkel et al., 2017).

16   THE SELF IN RELATIONSHIPS

Overview of the Present Book

The main text of the present book is organized into five sections that, hopefully, will enable readers to gain a clear understanding of the ways in which each chapter builds upon key conceptual and empirical points from the chapter(s) that preceded it:

(I) *Prologue*, consisting of a Preface (briefly acquainting readers with the subject matter of relationship science, including an ode to the attachment theory of Bowlby, 1969/1997) and Chapter 1: The Self in Relationships: An Introduction (identifying the field theory of Lewin, 1935, as a meta-theory that serves as a broad conceptual and methodological foundation for the rest of the book).

(II) *Conceptual Issues Regarding the Self in Relationships*, consisting of Chapter 2: Self-Esteem (and Narcissism) as Reflected in Conflict Resolution Behaviors (identifying the interpersonal theory of Sullivan [1953] as an intellectual descendant of field theory that is relevant to research on self-esteem); Chapter 3: Gender-Related Traits as Reflected in Conflict Resolution Behaviors (identifying the feminine psychology of Horney [1967] as another "social-psychological" personality theory, alongside Sullivan's interpersonal theory, that is relevant to research on gender-related traits); and Chapter 4: The "Big Five" Traits as Reflected in Conflict Resolution Behaviors (identifying the analytical psychology of Jung [1921/1971] and the factor-analytic trait theory of McCrae and Costa [2003/2006] as relevant to research on "universal" traits, with the latter theory informed by Spence's [1993] multifactorial gender identity theory).

(III) *From Conceptual to Methodological Issues Regarding the Self in Relationships*, consisting of Chapter 5: Conceptualization of Dominance and Nurturance as Interpersonal Traits (identifying Wiggins's [2003/2005] interpersonal circumplex theory as relevant to research on interpersonal traits, keeping in mind the lack of previously published research that might bear directly upon the implications of interpersonal traits for conflict resolution behaviors).

(IV) *Methodological Issues Regarding the Self in Relationships*, consisting of Chapter 6: Measurement of Dominance and Nurturance as Interpersonal Traits I (applying geometric and psychometric analyses to actual data from Gaines, Panter, et al., 1997, Study 2; Hofsess & Tracey,

2005; Sodano & Tracey, 2006, Adult Sample; and DeYoung et al., 2013, Sample 2), using the Interpersonal Adjective Scales-Revised version (IAS-R; Wiggins et al., 1988); Chapter 7: Measurement of Dominance and Nurturance as Interpersonal Traits II (applying geometric and psychometric analyses to actual data from Barford et al., 2015; P. M. Markey & Markey, 2009, Study 1, Samples 1 and 2; and DeYoung et al., 2013, Sample 3), using the International Personality Item Pool–Interpersonal Circle (IPIP-IPC; P. M. Markey & Markey, 2009); and Chapter 8: Interpersonal Traits as Predictors of Accommodation (applying geometric and psychometric analyses to actual data from Gaines, 2021, Main Studies 1 and 2, using the IPIP-IPC alongside accommodation items based on Rusbult et al., 1991).

(V) *Epilogue*, consisting of Chapter 9, The Self in Relationships: Concluding Thoughts (addressing strengths and limitations of the studies for which new analyses were reported in Chapters 6 through 8); directions for future research and applications concerning the self in relationships, including summaries of preliminary findings that offer grounds for guarded optimism regarding the circumplexity of interpersonal motives as linked to the prediction of accommodation (Rusbult et al., 1991) on the basis of data from Gaines (2021, Main Study 2) using the former Circumplex Scales of Interpersonal Values (Locke, 2000; reinterpreted by Locke, 2015); and a Postscript (returning briefly to the attachment theory of Bowlby [1969/1997], with special attention given to the prospect of conceptualizing and measuring attachment orientations as interpersonal attitudes [Gaines et al., 2013], using a combination of the Experiences in Close Relationships Scale [ECR; Brennan et al., 1998] and the Relationship Scales Questionnaire [RSQ; Griffin & Bartholomew, 1994b]).

Prelude to Chapter 2

In *Principles of Topological Psychology*, Lewin (1936) elaborated upon his field theory (initially presented in book-length form by Lewin, 1935) by pointing the way toward a metaphorically mathematics-based approach within personality and social psychology (Back, 1992). Lewin was concerned primarily with the *psychological* space, rather than the physical space, that demarcates individuals from the psychological field within which they are situated

18 THE SELF IN RELATIONSHIPS

(Skowron & Wojtowicz, 2021). To the extent that individuals have not succeeded in fulfilling their psychological needs or motives, individuals experience *tension,* or "a state of a region relative to that of another region" (Lewin, 1936, p. 175) within those individuals. The default response of individuals to tension, which is affective in nature (i.e., manifested in heightened levels of negative moods and emotions), is to try and exert increased self-control over their own behavior (Koch, 1941). However, given that part of individuals' psychological environment frequently includes significant others, self-control is most likely to reduce individuals' internal tension when the behavior results in conflict resolution (1) *within the individuals in question* and (2) *between the individuals and their partners* (who may or may not be experiencing comparable levels of tension; Burnes & Cooke, 2013).

Harry Stack Sullivan (1953, 1954, 1956) arguably was the first psychodynamically oriented personality theorist to embrace Lewin's (1935, 1948/1967, 1951/1976) field theory to an appreciable degree (Tubert-Oklander, 2007). Sullivan's interpersonal theory builds upon Lewin's field theory, even as it recasts the psychological field as an *interpersonal field* (Conci, 2013). According to Sullivan, even when individuals physically are alone, the social and psychological effects of previous interactions with significant others continue to reverberate through individuals' current patterns of behavior (and, one may infer, continue to shape individuals' personalities; Stern, 2013). In fact, Sullivan contended that individuals' experience of selfhood from birth onward cannot be understood properly without taking individuals' histories of interactions with significant others into account (Gaines, 2007a, 2007b). Finally, Sullivan's interpersonal theory follows the lead of Lewin's field theory—which, in turn, follows the lead of Freud's (1921/1922) psychoanalytic theory—in highlighting the free-floating fear of *anxiety* as an important affective manifestation of tension (although Sullivan and other neo-Freudian, "social-psychological" personality theorists viewed anxiety as inherently *interpersonal*; Kanter, 2013).

To a greater extent than one finds within Lewin's (1935, 1948/1967, 1951/1976) field theory, Sullivan's (1953, 1954, 1956) interpersonal theory addresses the implications of interpersonal anxiety for individuals' self-esteem over time (M. Cortina, 2020). Furthermore, interpersonal theory poses intriguing questions regarding the extent to which realistically high self-esteem (as distinct from *narcissism,* or individuals' inflated evaluation of themselves) enables individuals to reduce interpersonal anxiety within themselves by defusing conflict with their partners at a given point in time (see Kernis, 2003a, 2003b). In turn, Sullivan's theory asserts that individuals' reduction of interpersonal anxiety within themselves (via conflict resolution behavior or other forms of "pro-relationship behavior") may promote *felt security* as well as self-esteem within individuals over the long term (J. G. Holmes, 2002). In Chapter 2, we shall consider interpersonal theory as a means toward understanding whether (and how) self-esteem and the possibly related construct of narcissism are manifested in individuals' conflict resolution behaviors toward significant others. Along the way, we shall learn that Sullivan's interpersonal theory is not limited in scope to the "good-me" and "bad-me" evaluations that constitute self-esteem (Cooper & Guynn, 2006).

SECTION II
CONCEPTUAL ISSUES REGARDING THE SELF IN RELATIONSHIPS

2

Self-Esteem (and Narcissism) as Reflected in Conflict Resolution Behaviors

Synopsis: In the present chapter, we explore Harry Stack Sullivan's interpersonal theory of personality as partly descended from Kurt Lewin's field theory, acknowledging that certain similarly named constructs within the two theories (e.g., the self-system) convey markedly different meanings; we consider additional constructs that clearly represent a progression from Lewin's theory to Sullivan's theory (e.g., Sullivan's construct of the interpersonal force field); we examine constructs in Sullivan's interpersonal theory that have no obvious counterparts in Lewin's field theory (e.g., "good-me," "bad-me," and "not-me" aspects of individuals' personality structure); we scrutinize Sullivan's assumption that high levels of interpersonal anxiety as communicated by caregivers to individuals in infancy and childhood place individuals at risk for developing low levels of self-esteem during adolescence and adulthood; we learn that self-esteem generally tends to promote intrapersonal functioning, although the extent to which self-esteem promotes interpersonal functioning in general remains a matter of debate; we review correlational evidence that self-esteem is associated with "relationship quality" in friendships and romantic relationships at various points in individuals' lifespan; we report contradictory findings regarding the magnitude and direction of self-esteem as covarying with relationship maintenance processes, including the conflict resolution processes of responses to dissatisfaction, accommodation following partners' anger/criticism, and forgiveness following partners' betrayal; we discover that the covariance between the potentially related personality construct of narcissism and accommodation in particular tends to be negative; we take stock of Sullivan's legacy within relationship science (especially with regard to understanding possible links among interpersonal anxiety, self-esteem, and conflict resolution behaviors); and we provide a prelude to Chapter 3, which covers Horney's feminine psychology as a second

The Self in Relationships. Stanley O. Gaines, Jr., Oxford University Press. © Oxford University Press 2023.
DOI: 10.1093/oso/9780197687635.003.0002

24 THE SELF IN RELATIONSHIPS

"neo-Freudian" or "social-psychological" personality theory after Sullivan's interpersonal theory.

> It would be natural from Gestalt theoretical considerations to understand the self in terms of the psychical totality perhaps as its structural individuality. As a matter of fact, some such notion is basic to the concept of character, for the adequate conception of which one must start, not from the presence of certain isolated properties (traits), but from the whole of the person. If from this beginning one comes to the problem of the psychical dynamic systems, the attempt will in all probability be made to identify the self with the whole of the psychical totality.
>
> A number of facts, however, drive one in the opposite direction to the view that a special region, within the psychical totality, must be defined as the self in the narrower sense. Not every psychically existent system would belong to this central self. Not every one to whom I say "Du," not all the things, men, and environmental regions which I know and which may perhaps be very important to me, belong to my self. This self-system would also have in functional respects—this is most important—a certain unique position. Not every tense psychical system would stand in communication with this self. Tensions which have to do with the self would also have functionally a special significance in the total psychical organism . . . , and it is possible that within this region differently directed tensions would tend to equilibrium considerably more strongly and that relatively isolated dynamic systems within it could much less readily occur.
>
> —Kurt Lewin,
> *A Dynamic Theory of Personality* (1935, pp. 61–62)

Lewin's (1951/1976) field theory arose from the tradition of Gestalt psychology that is associated with Koffka (1935) and Kohler (1938/1976), among others (Fiske & Taylor, 1991). Like other Gestalt-oriented theories, field theory is based on the premise that individuals' interpretation of events in their environment is inherently subjective (i.e., not easily reducible to "objective" properties of particular targets within that world; Schellenberg, 1978). However, Lewin's field theory is set apart by its emphasis on events within individuals' *social* environment, instead of events within individuals' *physical* environment (Kelley & Thibaut, 1978). In *Principles of Topological Psychology*, Lewin (1936) defined *environment* as "everything . . . in which, toward which, or away from which the person as a whole can perform locomotion" (p. 167), with the term *locomotion* referring to individuals' psychological (as distinct from geographic) movement (C. S. Hall & Lindzey, 1970). Interestingly, one will not find a comparable definition of *self* within field theory; as the above quote from Lewin's *A Dynamic Theory of Personality* (1935) indicates, one must infer the existence of a self from the presumed functioning of a *self-system* that manages individuals' conscious and nonconscious goal-seeking behavior on a daily basis (see McClelland, 1985/1987).

Like Lewin's (1935, 1948/1967, 1951/1976) field theory, Sullivan's (1953, 1954, 1956) interpersonal theory of personality invokes the term *self-system* to refer collectively to a set of processes that are tasked with lessening (if not eliminating) tension within individuals, as well as conflict between and within individuals (see C. S. Hall & Lindzey, 1970). However, unlike Lewin's version of the self-system, Sullivan's version is described in detail and is akin to a variety of executive function constructs that one encounters in personality psychology—from the ego in Freud's (1923/1927) psychoanalytic theory, to the proprium in Allport's (1937/1951) psychology of the individual, to the self-concept in Rogers's (1961) version of self-actualization theory (see Ewen, 1998). Despite Sullivan's rejection of Freud's proposed personality structure of id, ego, and superego, the self-system in interpersonal theory functions much like the ego in psychoanalytic theory, employing *security operations* (Sullivan's analog to ego defense mechanisms) that ideally bring about anxiety reduction (thus placing Sullivan's theory within the psychodynamic school of thought; Gaines, 2020). In Sullivan's theory, individuals' anxiety initially reflects "mothering ones'" transmission of their own anxiety, thus activating the self-system for the first time (McClelland, 1985/1987).

In the present chapter, we examine Sullivan's (1953, 1954, 1956) interpersonal theory of personality in detail. First, we consider the "good-me," "bad-me," and "not-me" aspects of the self-system in Sullivan's theory—terms that sound compatible with the *Empirical Me* or self-as-known construct in William James's (1890/2010) seminal version of self-theory, though it would be more accurate to say that Sullivan's terminology was intended to capture the *Pure Ego* or "I"/self-as-knower function of the self-system in terms of *organizing* bits and pieces of individuals' biological, social, and psychological data into a more or less coherent whole (i.e., fragments of autobiographical data undergo active interpretation rather than passive encoding, storage, and retrieval processes; C. S. Hall & Lindzey, 1970). Afterward, we explore the implications of interpersonal theory—especially the distinction between

26   THE SELF IN RELATIONSHIPS

(1) individuals' realistic appraisal of "good-me" versus "bad-me" information about themselves and (2) individuals' unrealistic redirection of "bad-me" information into the "not-me" of the unconscious (Ewen, 1998)—and self-esteem as a predictor of individuals' conflict resolution behaviors. As a bonus, we consider narcissism (see Raskin & Hall, 1979) as relevant to Sullivan's theory *and* as relevant to predicting conflict resolution behaviors.

Lewin and Beyond: Sullivan's Interpersonal Theory of Personality

In Lewin's (1935, 1948/1967, 1951/1976) field theory, the life space comprises varied forces that operate (1) within individuals, (2) within psychological environments, and (3) between individuals and their psychological environment; one can speak of a *force field* that gives rise to individuals' behavior at a given point in time (Kelley & Thibaut, 1978). Also, in Sullivan's (1953, 1954, 1956) interpersonal theory of personality, one may refer to an *interpersonal force field* (including forces that operate within and between individuals and psychological environments) that gives rise to individuals' behavior *in a particular relationship* at a given point in time (Wiggins, 2003/2005). Field theory increasingly addressed relationship pairs or dyads through successive developments of Lewin's ideas, whereas Sullivan's theory began with the relationship dyad—including the client-therapist pair—as the primary focal point (Gaines, 2016/2018). Sullivan proclaimed that individuals' personalities could be ascertained only through their observable behavior toward significant others, although followers from T. Leary (1957) onward have expanded the boundaries of "observable behavior" to include results of personality assessments (including self-reported aspects of personality within the interpersonal domain; Millon, 1996).

According to Sullivan's (1953, 1954, 1956) interpersonal theory of personality, due to the multitude of forces that may converge within individuals and their psychological environments at any given moment, individuals may be bombarded with incoming information about (1) themselves, (2) their significant others, and (3) their relationships with the significant others in question (Tubert-Oklander, 2007). Furthermore, in Sullivan's theory, not all of that incoming information is flattering to individuals' selves (though the information may or may not be accurate from individuals' own perspective; Mitchell & Harris, 2004). To the extent that incoming information not only is negative but also is accurate, interpersonal theory proposes that individuals engage in *selective inattention*, such that the self-system banishes the information from consciousness—not exactly preventing the information from entering individuals' memory or even wiping that information from memory, but rather making it difficult for individuals to gain access to that information in the absence of psychotherapy (Kanter, 2013). The net effect of such a security operation on the part of individuals' self-system, Sullivan argues, is that the self-system's redirection of "bad-me-destined" information to the "not-me" inflates individuals' self-esteem (M. Cortina, 2020).

We do not mean to imply that all (or even most) individuals unconsciously set aside negative information about themselves, or that narcissism (rather than realistically high self-esteem) is a default outcome of the self-system's "security operations," within Sullivan's (1953, 1954, 1956) interpersonal theory of personality. Among nonclinical populations, Sullivan's theory would lead one to expect that most individuals not only tend to be aware of negative as well as positive aspects of themselves but also are capable of embarking on efforts to *change* themselves, possibly deciding to seek professional help toward that end (Ewen, 1998). In fact, viewed from an interpersonal theory perspective, one should not dismiss the potential for some individuals within clinical populations to use constructive criticism from significant others (including therapists as relationship partners over the short term) as an impetus for behavioral and personality change (Millon, 1996). At a minimum, Sullivan's interpersonal theory alerts relationship scientists and other social scientists to the possibility that the need to reduce anxiety is such a powerful motive that individuals' self-system may engage in selective inattention and other security operations to a dysfunctional degree, intrapersonally and interpersonally speaking (Gaines, 2016/2018).

Fulfillment of the Anxiety Reduction Motive, Leading to High Self-Esteem: A Matter of Faith(?)

Sullivan's (1953, 1954, 1956) interpersonal theory of personality hypothesizes that, to the extent that individuals experience *low* levels of interpersonal anxiety (thus fulfilling their anxiety reduction motive), those individuals subsequently will experience *high* levels of self-esteem (M. Cortina, 2020). On the one hand, Sullivan's hypothesis concerning the effect of interpersonal anxiety on self-esteem has not been tested via experimental studies (see

Alicke et al., 2020). On the other hand, at least one qualitative case study (i.e., J. P. Schwartz & Waldo, 2003) has yielded results that are consistent with Sullivan's assumptions regarding the association between interpersonal anxiety and self-esteem. Even if one accepts this premise on the basis of insight that Sullivan had obtained from his own clients in psychotherapy across many years (Cooper & Guynn, 2006), one's confidence regarding the generalizability of Sullivan's conclusions could be bolstered by results of additional research, especially findings from quantitative studies (whether correlational or experimental). Unfortunately, we are not aware of such research—at least regarding studies that were explicitly designed with interpersonal theory in mind (although a variation on Sullivan's hypothesis has been supported by research on *terror management theory*; Greenberg, 2008).

Saribay and Andersen (2007) contended that results of experimental studies on *security priming* from the standpoint of Bowlby's (1969/1997, 1973/1998, 1980/1998) attachment theory, and reviewed by Mikulincer and Shaver (2007b), implicitly support Sullivan's (1953, 1954, 1956) hypothesis concerning the positive effects of achieved reduction in interpersonal anxiety upon individuals' self-esteem. In their response to Saribay and Andersen, Mikulincer and Shaver (2007c) acknowledged that attachment theorists and interpersonal theorists share a keen interest in individuals' felt security within caregiver-offspring and other types of close relationships. However, Mikulincer and Shaver drew a contrast between the perspectives of (1) Bowlby and other attachment theorists (e.g., Ainsworth et al., 1978) and (2) Sullivan and other neo-Freudian theorists who emphasized the potentially negative effects of interpersonal anxiety on individuals' social and psychological functioning (e.g., Horney, 1937) as they explained that attachment theorists use the term *security* to refer simultaneously to attachment figures "providing a safe haven and a secure base" to individuals (2007c, p. 198). (It is worth noting that Horney was concerned about the implications of interpersonal anxiety for individuals' feelings of helplessness and danger, rather than loss of self-esteem; Zerbe, 1990.)

Quoting Sullivan's *Conceptions of Modern Psychiatry* (1947/1966), J. G. Allen (2012) concluded that Sullivan's (1953, 1954, 1956) interpersonal theory of personality anticipated subsequent developments in Bowlby's (1969/1997, 1973/1998, 1980/1998) attachment theory, especially regarding the role of caregivers in communicating *empathy* to individuals. Also, citing Sullivan (1947/1966), Kay (2012) surmised that the propositions of interpersonal theory and attachment theory overlap in many respects (although Kay believed that attachment theory offered a more comprehensive account of individuals' psychic structures beyond the self-system than did interpersonal theory). Lastly, citing Sullivan (1947/1966), M. Cortina (2020) credited Sullivan with articulating one of the earliest relationally oriented critiques of Freud's (1923/1927) psychoanalytic theory long before Bowlby had done so (although Cortina added that Bowlby's innovation in tying infants' *separation anxiety* to the survival of *Homo sapiens* sets attachment theory apart from interpersonal theory). Overall, in-depth reading of the only full-length book that Sullivan published during his lifetime (1947/1966) indicates that security priming studies provide reasonable approximations to tests of Sullivan's hypothesis concerning interpersonal anxiety and self-esteem.

High Self-Esteem: Good for *Intra*personal Functioning, in Principle and in Practice

From the vantage point of Sullivan's (1953, 1954, 1956) interpersonal theory of personality, every waking day presents new opportunities and new challenges for individuals to minimize interpersonal anxiety and thus maximize self-esteem (Conci, 2009). Although Sullivan's interpersonal theory does not propose specific stages of personality development beyond individuals' late teens/early 20s, Sullivan's view of the self as an aggregate of *reflected appraisals* from other persons (following the psychologically oriented self-theory of James, 1890/2010, and the sociologically oriented self-theory of Mead, 1934/1967) nonetheless hints that individuals continue to accumulate feedback from significant others (and, hence, gain additional insight into their strengths and limitations) throughout the lifespan (Pizer, 2019). As we noted earlier in the present chapter, it does not necessarily follow that individuals attend to all (or most) of the feedback that they receive from other persons; Sullivan used the term *personified self* to designate those attributes of which individuals are aware at a given moment, including "good-me" and "bad-me" (with "not-me" existing outside consciousness, possibly containing information about individuals' unacknowledged shortcomings; see M. Cortina, 2020).

Although Sullivan's (1953, 1954, 1956) interpersonal theory of personality does not assume that all individuals are conscious of their intentions at all times, Sullivan's theory nonetheless assumes that most individuals possess the capacity to strive toward achieving conscious as well as nonconscious goals in the future (Shahar, 2011). Indeed, according to interpersonal theory,

30 THE SELF IN RELATIONSHIPS

high levels of self-esteem (presumably fostered by low levels of interpersonal anxiety) enable individuals to plan and pursue behavior that makes it possible to achieve short-term and long-term goals (J. P. Schwartz & Waldo, 2003). Consequently, Sullivan believed that individuals' success in achieving various goals can lead individuals to experience improved mental health over time (Conci, 2009). Sullivan expressed confidence that even among individuals who contend with moderate-to-severe psychological difficulties within psychotherapy settings, it is possible for individuals to marshal their internal resources and ultimately bolster their intrapersonal functioning (Korsbek, 2016). Sullivan's own experience with schizophrenia during adolescence informed his optimism regarding the prospect that individuals within clinical populations may be sufficiently resourceful to attain high self-esteem and "normal" mental health (Frank & Davidson, 2014).

By the early 1990s, it was clear that—consistent with Sullivan's (1953, 1954, 1956) interpersonal theory of personality—high self-esteem was associated with a variety of positive mental health outcomes in correlational studies (e.g., low overall anxiety, low depression; for a review, see Blascovich & Tomaka, 1991). However, it is *not* clear that Sullivan's proposed causal process (i.e., a decrease in interpersonal anxiety leading directly to an increase in self-esteem and indirectly to an increase in intrapersonal functioning) is responsible for the observed covariance between self-esteem and mental health outcomes (see Baumeister, 1997). For example, some personality psychologists have argued that high levels of genuine self-esteem as well as narcissism reflect a *self-enhancement bias* (i.e., a combination of individuals' oversampling of positive information and undersampling of negative information about themselves); such anrgumentt seemingly implies that most individuals' self-system redirects negative information to the "not-me" after all (see Robins & John, 1997). If most individuals really are that unreceptive to incoming negative information about themselves, then one could question whether Sullivan's optimism about the prospective functionality of the self-system was misplaced (Gaines, 2020).

Is High Self-Esteem Good for *Inter*personal Functioning in Principle?

We will consider the distinction between genuine self-esteem (Rosenberg, 1965) and narcissism (Raskin & Terry, 1988) in greater detail near the end of the present chapter. For now, we return to the point that high self-esteem is linked to positive mental health outcomes (e.g., significantly and negatively associated with clinical depression; Shaver & Brennan, 1991). Without a doubt, Sullivan's (1953, 1954, 1956) interpersonal theory of personality anticipates that high self-esteem will promote positive *intra*personal functioning (Gaines, 2020). Moreover, interpersonal theory predicts that—as long as one sets aside narcissism as a grandiose variation on self-esteem—high self-esteem will promote positive *inter*personal functioning (Gaines, 2016/2018). Nevertheless, critics of the "self-esteem is good" literature (e.g., Baumeister, 1997) pose a question for which the answer from Sullivan's theory may not be straightforward: Will high self-esteem lead to *selfishness* (rather than selflessness) regarding individuals' behavior within social and personal relationships? Interestingly, Baumeister (1998) cited interpersonal theory as compatible with the view (e.g., Swann, 1987) that persons with high self-esteem are more likely than persons with low self-esteem to hold unfavorable evaluations toward other persons who have given them negative feedback.

In the process of contending that Sullivan's (1953) interpersonal theory of personality supported the perspective that individuals tend to hold favorable attitudes toward other persons whose feedback supports individuals' pre-existing self-concept (with high-self-esteem persons preferring positive feedback and low-self-esteem persons preferring negative feedback), Baumeister (1998) drew a parallel between Sullivan's theory and Swann's (1987) *self-verification theory*, the latter of which hails from the tradition of *cognitive consistency theories* within social psychology (paying homage to the cognitive dissonance theory of Festinger, 1954; see Robins & John, 1997). Customarily, interpersonal theory tends to be classified as part of the tradition of "social-psychological" theories within personality psychology (owing a debt to the individual psychology of Adler, 1927) that advocate probing individuals' unconscious, rather than cognitive consistency theories that prioritize individuals' conscious experience (C. S. Hall & Lindzey, 1970). Nevertheless, in *The Interpersonal Theory of Personality*, Sullivan (1953, pp. 350–359) alludes to a subgroup of persons with "customarily low self-esteem" who *expect* to receive negative feedback from significant others yet manage to maintain close relationships (see also Sullivan, 1947/1966).

Some reviews of Sullivan's (1953, 1954, 1956) interpersonal theory of personality (e.g., Millon, 1996) have cited Sullivan as support for the diagnosis of a "masochistic personality disorder" among some chronically low-self-esteem persons. However, a direct reading of Sullivan (e.g., Sullivan, 1953, pp. 352–352) reveals that interpersonal theory argues *against* such a diagnosis. Overall, Sullivan's theory encourages therapists (in their time-limited role of significant others) to facilitate the building of clients' self-esteem as a means toward the end of improving the quality and maintenance of clients' close relationships outside the context of psychotherapy (Gaines, 2020). More generally, interpersonal theory predicts that individuals within nonclinical as well as clinical populations will be well prepared for success in close relationships to the extent that they have developed high levels of self-esteem (Gaines, 2016/2018). Therefore, the predictions that one would derive from Sullivan's theory concerning positive interpersonal consequences of high self-esteem do not fit neatly within prevailing modes of metaphors of self-perception (e.g., Scientist, Egoist, Consistency Seeker, Politician) that are commonplace in personality psychology (see Robins & John, 1997).

An Additional Process to Consider: Emergence of the Need for Interpersonal Intimacy During Individuals' Preteen Years

Earlier in the present chapter, we briefly alluded to similarities and differences between the assumptions that underlie Sullivan's (1953, 1954, 1956) interpersonal theory versus Bowlby's (1969/1997, 1973/1998, 1980/1988) attachment theory. One of the most striking differences is that, unlike Bowlby's theory (which posits a need for emotional intimacy or *attachment* that individuals experience from birth onward), Sullivan's theory proposes that individuals do not begin to experience a need for emotional intimacy or *interpersonal intimacy* until they are approximately 8 to 10 years of age (see von Salisch, 1997). Furthermore, according to interpersonal theory, individuals experience the need for interpersonal intimacy most intensely from puberty onward, when an emerging desire for *physical* intimacy accompanies the need for *emotional* intimacy (Reis & Shaver, 1988). Lastly, from the standpoint of Sullivan's theory, it stands to reason that *depression*—which, as we have already learned, can be a major negative *intrapersonal* outcome when individuals' interpersonal anxiety has not been alleviated and individuals' self-esteem has not been boosted—may end up exerting a substantial negative effect upon individuals' *interpersonal* functioning by the time that individuals reach adulthood, if not sooner (Segrin, 2011).

Writing and lecturing several years *before* the advent of the *Diagnostic and Statistical Manual of Mental Disorders* (DSM; American Psychiatric Association, 1952), Sullivan (1953, 1954, 1956) postulated that major mental disorders by their very nature were reflected in individuals' destructive patterns of behavior within close relationships (Pincus & Wright, 2011). Thus, Sullivan's interpersonal theory of personality was far ahead of the curve in terms of proposing an inherently relational aspect to mental health (or lack thereof; Levenson, 2011). The possibly negative role of high depression, alongside the potentially positive role of high self-esteem, in influencing individuals' behavior toward (1) best friends or "chums" from the preteen years onward *and* (2) romantic partners from the teenage years onward highlights the links between nonfamilial peer relationships and individuals' social and psychological functioning from the perspective of Sullivan's theory (Reis & Shaver, 1988). Additionally, the importance that Sullivan granted to individuals' friendships from prepuberty onward distinguishes interpersonal theory from attachment theory (which has tended to focus to a greater extent upon prospective continuity between attachment in childhood and attachment in adulthood; Shaver & Mikulincer, 2011).

One issue for which Bowlby's (1969/1997, 1973/1998, 1980/1998) attachment theory might hold an advantage over Sullivan's (1953, 1954, 1956) interpersonal theory is the ease with which *loneliness* can be understood as a significant, positive covariate of depression (Shaver & Brennan, 1991). Ironically, compared to Sullivan's interpersonal theory, Bowlby's attachment theory initially was not embraced by many members of the psychoanalytic community (possibly because of Bowlby's emphasis on "normal" social and personality development; M. Cortina & Marrone, 2004). By the same token, given that both loneliness and depression covary significantly and negatively with self-esteem (Blascovich & Tomaka, 1991), interpersonal theory can help relationship scientists account for loneliness as a potential antecedent and consequence of disordered interpersonal functioning (see Pincus & Wright, 2011). In any event, as we review the results of studies concerning self-esteem and conflict resolution behaviors within adult romantic relationships later in the present chapter, we will keep in mind the possibility that low self-esteem may serve as a de facto proxy for depression and loneliness (neither of which has been included in relevant studies by Rusbult or her followers; for representative reviews, see Rusbult, 1993; Rusbult & Van Lange, 2003).

Children's Self-Esteem: Reflected in Children's Friendship Quality in Practice(?)

Consistent with Sullivan's (1953, 1954, 1956) interpersonal theory of personality, Berndt and colleagues (e.g., Berndt, 1996, 2002; Berndt et al., 1999; Keefe & Berndt, 1996) obtained significant positive correlations between children's self-esteem and friendship quality at a given time (for a summary of results, see Berndt, 2005). However, Berndt and colleagues did *not* find a longitudinal effect of friendship quality on children's self-esteem—a null effect that Berndt (2004) interpreted as lack of support for Sullivan's theory. Interestingly, it does not appear that Berndt and colleagues tested the hypothesis that children's self-esteem exerts a positive effect on children's friendship quality over time; our reading of interpersonal theory suggests that *this* hypothesis is the one that follows directly from Sullivan's writings (for a comparable interpretation concerning self-esteem as a potentially positive influence on the quality of adolescents' friendships, see Mufson & Dorta, 2000). After all, Sullivan had proposed that "mothering ones" (not peers) introduced interpersonal anxiety into individuals' lives; unless children's experience of affection from friends successfully counteracts a *lack* of affection from caregivers, it might be unreasonable to expect friendship quality to boost children's self-esteem over time (see Bukowski, 2001).

Also, in keeping with Sullivan's (1953, 1954, 1956) interpersonal theory of personality, results of a qualitative study by Azmitia and colleagues (2005) indicated that self-esteem was reflected in the "health" or quality of boys' and girls' friendships (Bukowski & Sippola, 2005). However, Azmitia et al. did not discount the possibility that the observed link could reflect a bidirectional pattern over time (e.g., children's affirmation of their own self-esteem may occur hand in hand with children's behaving in ways that affirm their friends' self-esteem; see Kanter, 2013). For that matter, one could interpret the aforementioned correlations that Berndt and colleagues had reported (e.g., Berndt, 1996, 2002; Berndt et al., 1999; Keefe & Berndt, 1996) as compatible with a bidirectional perspective on children's self-esteem and friendship quality. Ultimately, given that Sullivan's interpersonal theory specified a developmental sequence whereby the quality of individuals' "chumships" during the preteen years carries important implications for the subsequent quality of individuals' romantic relationships during adolescence (Paul & White, 1990), quantitatively oriented longitudinal studies will be needed for relationship scientists to put Sullivan's theory to a proper test.

One additional aspect of Sullivan's (1953, 1954, 1956) interpersonal theory of personality that is worth considering within the realm of children's friendships yet has not been examined empirically (as far as we know) is the hypothesis that self-esteem will promote *relational trust*—which, as we learned in Chapter 1 of the present book, is central to Thibaut and Kelley's (1959; Kelley, 1979; Kelley & Thibaut, 1978) interdependence theory—within children's relationships (including, but not limited to, friendships). In *Conceptions of Modern Psychiatry*, Sullivan (1947/1966) proposed that the development of normal self-esteem involves individuals' self-system accurately distinguishing between "good-me" and "bad-me" bits of information, whereas "abnormal" development of self-esteem may involve individuals' self-system misinterpreting objectively negative, "bad-me" information instead as "good-me," a *malevolent transformation* that can lead individuals to become distrustful toward significant others (Cooper & Guynn, 2006). In principle, one should be able to explore the role that relational trust might play in mediating the effects of individuals' self-esteem during childhood upon the quality of individuals' romantic relationships during adolescence, even though such research may not exist in practice (see W. H. Jones et al., 1997).

Developmental- and Social-Psychological Asides: "Relationship Quality" in Children's Friendships, Adolescents' Romances, and Adults' Romances

Although we have spent the past few paragraphs discussing studies of children's friendship quality (e.g., Azmitia et al., 2005; Berndt, 1996, 2002; Berndt et al., 1999; Keefe & Berndt, 1996), we have not stated exactly what we mean by "friendship quality." As it turns out, within developmental psychology, children's friendship quality typically has been operationalized in terms of one or more of the following attributes: (1) *number of friendships*, (2) *positive features of a particular friendship*, and (3) *negative features of a particular friendship* (Schwartz-Mette et al., 2020). Despite the availability of published surveys that were designed to measure children's friendship quality, such as the Friendship Quality Questionnaire (FQQ; Parker & Asher, 1993) and the Friendship Qualities Scale (FQS; Bukowski et al., 1994), no consensus currently exists regarding the conceptualization or measurement of that particular construct. Moreover, even the influence of Sullivan's (1953,

1954, 1956) interpersonal theory of personality varies widely across studies of children's friendship quality (notwithstanding the fact that Sullivan's theory stands as an early testament to the importance of "chumships" in children's lives; Berndt, 2004).

Just as one encounters the term *friendship quality* in studies of children's friendships (Schwartz-Mette et al., 2020), so too does one find the term *relationship quality* in studies of adolescents' and adults' romantic relationships (Mirsu-Paun & Oliver, 2017). Within developmental psychology, positive and negative features tend to be examined in adolescents' romantic relationships, although the question of number of friendships for children tends to be replaced by the question of whether adolescents have or have not been involved in romantic relationships (Kochendorfer & Kerns, 2020). Similarly, within social psychology, positive and negative features are commonly examined among adults' romantic relationships (sometimes with further distinctions among cognition, affect, and behavior; Li & Chan, 2012). Developmental psychologists are more likely to use the Network of Relationships Inventory (NRI; Furman & Buhrmester, 1985), whereas social psychologists are more likely to use the Perceived Relationship Quality Components inventory (PRQC; Fletcher et al., 2000). However, no consensus exists regarding those surveys in developmental *or* social psychology; and Sullivan's (1953, 1954, 1956) interpersonal theory of personality is not usually cited (B. B. Brown et al., 1999).

All things considered, the phrase *relationship quality* is applied so freely to so many aspects of children's friendships, adolescents' romantic relationships, and adults' romantic relationships that one cannot assume consistency in the meaning with which researchers invest the term across (or within) different age groups (see Laursen & Jensen-Campbell, 1999). When one adds the understandable but regrettable lack of longitudinal studies that might link (1) individuals' self-esteem as shaped by significant others during childhood (yet amenable to change over time), (2) individuals' relationship quality within friendships during childhood, (3) individuals' relationship quality within romances during adolescence, and (4) individuals' relationship quality within romances during adulthood, one can appreciate the difficulty of identifying research that tests hypotheses from Sullivan's (1953, 1954, 1956) interpersonal theory regarding personality and social development (B. B. Brown et al., 1999). Going forward, we will focus on the results of cross-sectional and longitudinal studies in which adults' self-esteem has been examined as a predictor of adults' relationship quality, noting that

(1) self-esteem can change dramatically from childhood to adulthood, and (2) *relationship quality* can be a vague term (see Mallinckrodt, 1997).

Adults' Self-Esteem: Reflected in Adults' Relationship Quality, in Principle and in Practice

Historically, reviewers of Sullivan's (1953, 1954, 1956) interpersonal theory of personality have emphasized Sullivan's proposed stages of children's personality development (i.e., *infancy, childhood, juvenile, preadolescent, early adolescent*, and *late adolescent*), generally neglecting Sullivan's personality typology (although reviewers often alluded to Sullivan's therapeutic interventions with individuals who were diagnosed with the "abnormal" trait of schizophrenia; Carson, 1969). However, in *Conceptions of Modern Psychiatry*, Sullivan (1947/1966) presented a clinical taxonomy (i.e., *nonintegrative, self-absorbed, incorrigible, negativistic, stammerer, ambition-ridden, asocial, inadequate, homosexual*, and *chronically adolescent*) that is not very interpersonal in orientation at first glance but includes an *asocial* type that is characterized by low social competence and a recurrent pattern of problems with establishing and maintaining close relationships (Millon, 1996). Of course, certain dubious aspects of Sullivan's taxonomy are highly offensive by modern standards (e.g., "stammerer"? "homosexual"?), although one might be surprised by the pervasiveness of the offending types in the psychodynamic school of personality psychology as recently as the late 20th century (e.g., McClelland, 1985/1987).

A key point within Sullivan's (1953, 1954, 1956) interpersonal theory of personality is the adaptiveness of individuals' conscious or nonconscious updating of their self-concept (and, consequently, individuals' experience of change in self-esteem) as they enter, maintain, and possibly exit various close relationships throughout their lives (Paul & White, 1990). In turn, according to Sullivan, individuals' *changes* in self-esteem may be expressed via *changes* in behavior across current and subsequent relationships (Champion, 2012). Consistent with interpersonal theory, within the domain of adult romantic relationships, the evidence from several longitudinal studies generally suggests that self-esteem is a significant positive predictor of relationship quality over time (whereas the reverse hypothesis of relationship quality predicting self-esteem over time is *not* generally supported; Erol & Orth, 2016). Even though Sullivan's theory tends not to

38 THE SELF IN RELATIONSHIPS

be mentioned in longitudinal studies (or in cross-sectional studies) of adult romantic relationships, such findings directly or indirectly invoke the broad theme of self-in-relationships that Sullivan and many other "relational psychoanalysts" (including Bowlby, 1969/1997, 1973/1998, 1980/1998) have articulated (Mitchell & Harris, 2004).

Aron and Nardone (2012) noted the results of some experiments that qualify the effects of self-esteem on individuals' behavior toward romantic partners, although they acknowledged the oft-replicated finding that self-esteem influences relationship quality over time within longitudinal studies. Also, G. MacDonald and Leary (2012) pointed out that certain rival theories (e.g., the *sociometer theory* of M. R. Leary & Baumeister, 2000) are distinguished by positing an explicitly evolutionary basis for the development of self-esteem in the first instance, although some of the assumptions that underlie rival theories (e.g., the existence of a "self-esteem system" in sociometer theory) bear more than a passing resemblance to assumptions that underlie Sullivan's (1953, 1954, 1956) interpersonal theory of personality. Nevertheless, even some of the proponents regarding alternative theories (e.g., Pyszczynski et al., 2012; promoting the briefly aforementioned *terror management theory* of Greenberg et al., 1986) not only have cited Sullivan's theory as part of their inspiration but also concur with Sullivan that self-esteem originates in response to individuals' experience of anxiety from infancy onward (with the caveat that the type of anxiety is *existential* in terror management theory).

From "Relationship Quality" to Relationship Maintenance: Focusing on Overt Behavior in Close Relationships

Before we delve into self-esteem as reflected in specific aspects of relationship maintenance, we wish to comment further upon the meaning of "relationship quality" (Mirsu-Paun & Oliver, 2017). We have already mentioned the PRQC (Fletcher et al., 2000) as one omnibus survey of relationship quality. As it turns out, the PRQC is a composite of items that previous sets of researchers had designed to measure (1) *satisfaction* (S. S. Hendrick, 1988), (2) *commitment* (Lund, 1985), (3) *intimacy* (Sternberg, 1986, 1988), (4) *relational trust* (Boon & Holmes, 1990), (5) *passion* (Sternberg, 1986, 1988), and (6) *love* (Rubin, 1973). On the one hand, the PRQC was inspired by varied conceptual models, such as Rusbult's (1980, 1983) investment model and Sternberg's (1986, 1988) triangular model of love. On the other hand, it is not clear why items that originally were developed with a relevant theory or model in mind were not used (e.g., satisfaction and commitment items from the Investment Model Scale of Rusbult et al., 1998, were excluded). Furthermore, the term *relationship quality* could be interpreted as implying that one or more aspects of individuals' *behavior* would be assessed; yet all of the items within the PRQC are cognitive or affective, rather than behavioral (Sakaluk et al., 2021).

In the remainder of the present chapter, we will limit our attention to the potential influence of self-esteem on relationship *maintenance*, or the words and deeds that individuals employ in an attempt to keep their relationships intact (Dindia & Canary, 1993). As we noted in Chapter 1, conflict resolution behaviors such as responses to dissatisfaction (Rusbult et al., 1982), accommodation following anger/criticism by partners (Rusbult et al., 1991), and forgiveness following betrayal by partners (Finkel et al., 2002) all qualify as relationship maintenance behaviors (Rusbult & Van Lange, 2003). Notwithstanding the conceptual appeal of interdependence-oriented constructs regarding "relationship well-being" (Sakulak et al., 2021)—including aspects of relationship quality (Fletcher et al., 2000) and investment model variables (Rusbult et al., 1998)—we are interested primarily in the consequences of individuals' self-esteem for *what people say and do* to maintain their relationships (Rusbult & Buunk, 1993). The exit-voice-loyalty-neglect (EVLN) scheme for classifying conflict resolution behaviors, which we likewise encountered in Chapter 1, will assist us in understanding which behaviors are likely to be positively related, negatively related, or unrelated to self-esteem (see Rusbult et al., 1994).

One additional point is noteworthy regarding terminology: Within communication studies, the term *relational maintenance* has been applied to several behavioral strategies that individuals might pursue (e.g., *positivity, assurances, openness, sharing tasks*, and *engaging with social and personal networks*; Stafford & Canary, 1991). Dindia and Canary (1993) contended that "relational maintenance" not only covers those particular strategies but also covers various "pro-relationship behaviors" that Rusbult and colleagues have measured, such as responses to dissatisfaction (Rusbult et al., 1982) and accommodation following partners' anger/criticism (Rusbult et al., 1991). Nonetheless, Rusbult and Buunk (1993) opted to use the slightly different term *relationship maintenance* when referring specifically to Rusbult's

40 THE SELF IN RELATIONSHIPS

social-psychological constructs. Consistent with Rusbult and Buunk's terminology, we shall use the term *relationship maintenance* in the present chapter and throughout the book. We acknowledge that some relationship scientists (e.g., Stafford, 2011) use the terms as if they were synonymous, although we have not been able to find any studies in which "relational maintenance" strategies as measured by Stafford and colleagues (see also Stafford et al., 2000) have been examined as consequences of self-esteem.

Self-Esteem as Reflected in Responses to Dissatisfaction

If one were going to use Sullivan's (1953, 1954, 1956) interpersonal theory of personality as the basis for predictions about the effects of self-esteem on individuals' responses to dissatisfaction in romantic relationships, then one might begin with Sullivan's (1947/1966) speculation that "asocial" persons (i.e., individuals who may or may not be high in personal self-esteem but definitely are low in social self-esteem) find it difficult to establish or maintain close relationships. By Sullivan's estimation, such a deficit in self-esteem might lead individuals to disengage from romantic relationships when they and/or their partners are unhappy with those relationships (S. Strack & Millon, 2013). Thus, at least when self-esteem is conceptualized in terms of prosociality versus asociality, one might expect low self-esteem to lead individuals to respond to dissatisfaction with high levels of destructive (i.e., exit and neglect) behaviors plus low levels of constructive (i.e., voice and loyalty) behaviors (see also Kingery et al., 2010). However, in a series of studies examining self-esteem as a predictor of responses to dissatisfaction in romantic relationships, Rusbult and colleagues (1987) did not address the possible relevance of interpersonal theory to their studies.

Rusbult and colleagues (1987) were influenced by Thibaut and Kelley's (1959; Kelley, 1979; Kelley & Thibaut, 1978) interdependence theory, rather than any particular theory of personality, in predicting that high self-esteem would promote high levels of active (i.e., exit and voice) responses plus low levels of passive (i.e., loyalty and neglect) responses to dissatisfaction in romantic relationships. Rusbult et al. obtained a pattern of results that did not provide clear support for their hypotheses *or* the post hoc hypotheses that we would have anticipated via Sullivan's (1953, 1954, 1956) interpersonal theory: Self-esteem was associated with *high* levels of exit, *low* levels of neglect, and (to some extent) *high* levels of loyalty (but unrelated to voice). On the basis of Rusbult et al.'s results, one might wonder whether the logic underlying the choice of self-esteem as a predictor of any of the responses to dissatisfaction (whether one subscribes to interdependence theory and/or interpersonal theory) was fundamentally flawed. Before we embrace such a sweeping conclusion, though, it might be prudent for us to ask whether the methodology underlying Rusbult et al.'s studies was problematic, especially since Rusbult and colleagues did not use the "gold standard" Rosenberg Self-Esteem Scale (RSES; Rosenberg, 1965) as their measure of self-esteem.

According to D. N. Jackson (1976), a subscale within the Jackson Personality Inventory (JPI) measures social self-esteem. Moreover, results of a "multitrait-multimethod" analysis by van Tuinen and Ramanaiah (1979) indicated that the JPI subscale performed in a manner consistent with (other) measures of self-esteem. Therefore, Rusbult and colleagues (1987) appeared to be on solid methodological ground when they decided to use the JPI subscale in their studies of self-esteem and individuals' responses to dissatisfaction in romantic relationships. Nevertheless, we view it as noteworthy that a subsequent review of nearly a dozen self-esteem inventories (Blascovich & Tomaka, 1991) did not mention the JPI. Therefore, we wonder whether the inclusion of global self-esteem such as the RSES (Rosenberg, 1965) or a more widely used measure of social competence such as the Texas Social Behavior Inventory (TSBI; Spence & Helmreich, 1978) might have led to more conclusive results in Rusbult et al.'s studies. In any event, the fact that Rusbult and colleagues obtained consistent results across heterosexual, gay male, and lesbian female samples was impressive during an era when the nascent field of relationship science overwhelmingly focused on heterosexual samples (see Clark & Reis, 1988).

Self-Esteem as a Predictor of Accommodation Following Partners' Anger/Criticism

In Chapter 1, we noted that Rusbult et al.'s (1982) construct of responses to dissatisfaction refers to individuals' sense that they and/or their partners are unhappy with their relationships—*not* individuals' sense that they or their partners necessarily have done anything wrong. In contrast, Rusbult et al.'s (1991) construct of accommodation following partners' anger/criticism is quite specific in pointing to partners having "behaved badly" as the instigation for individuals' behavioral responses. From the standpoint of

42 THE SELF IN RELATIONSHIPS

Sullivan's (1953, 1954, 1956) interpersonal theory of personality, perhaps we should expect self-esteem to emerge as a more unequivocal predictor of accommodation-related responses, given that partners' anger or criticism poses a more direct threat to the long-term stability of relationships than does individuals' generic sense that their relationships are not going well (Gaines, 2016/2018). Additionally, the main prediction that can be derived from Sullivan's interpersonal theory (i.e., self-esteem will be a significant positive predictor of accommodation) is identical to the prediction that Rusbult et al. proposed, although Rusbult and colleagues drew exclusively upon Thibaut and Kelley's (1959; Kelley, 1979; Kelley & Thibaut, 1978) interdependence theory in making their prediction.

Between the publication of Rusbult et al.'s (1982) initial research on responses to dissatisfaction and Rusbult et al.'s (1991) initial research on accommodation following partners' anger/betrayal, an empirical critique by Goodwin (1991) challenged the assumption that the active/passive dichotomy is as salient as the constructive/destructive dichotomy that participants use when distinguishing among exit (active, destructive), voice (active, constructive), loyalty (passive, constructive), and neglect (passive, destructive) behaviors. Although Rusbult et al.'s (1991) research on accommodation was not undertaken in response to Goodwin's critique, Rusbult and colleagues *did* de-emphasize the active/passive dichotomy in their work going forward (see Berscheid, 1994). In the present section, we summarize results of (1) one study in which Rusbult and colleagues (1991, Study 4) calculated separate scores for constructive and destructive responses, (2) one study in which Overall and Sibley (2010, Samples 1 and 2) calculated one score for accommodation as a whole (albeit with separate scores for self-reported and diary-coded versions), and (3) one related study in which Kumashiro et al. (2002) created a composite score of "pro-relationship behaviors" that included accommodation, forgiveness, and conciliation.

Initial research: Rusbult et al. (1991, Study 4). In Study 4 of their multistudy paper, Rusbult et al. (1991) reported that global self-esteem and social self-esteem (both of which were measured via subscales within the Multifaceted-Evaluation-of-Self Inventory [MESI]; Hoyle, 1987) were unrelated to individuals' quantitative self-reports of constructive or destructive responses to partners' anger/criticism. The nonsignificant (and nonmarginal) effects for global or social self-esteem as individual-difference predictors of accommodation-related behaviors stand in contrast to the significant effects of the social-psychological construct of commitment (Rusbult, 1980,

1983) on constructive responses (positive) and destructive responses (negative) in that particular study. Unfortunately, given that Rusbult et al. (1991) did not report separate results for exit, voice, loyalty, and neglect responses, we do not know whether their results were similar across voice versus loyalty, or across exit versus neglect. Nevertheless, it is clear that Rusbult et al.'s results concerning global and social self-esteem did not provide direct support for Thibaut and Kelley's (1959; Kelley, 1979; Kelley & Thibaut, 1978) interdependence theory *or* indirect support for Sullivan's (1953, 1954, 1956) interpersonal theory.

Like the JPI social self-esteem subscale (D. N. Jackson, 1976) that Rusbult et al. (1987) had used in their study of self-esteem as a predictor of individuals' responses to dissatisfaction, the MESI global and social self-esteem subscales (Hoyle, 1987) that Rusbult et al. (1991) used in their study of aspects of self-esteem as a set of predictors of individuals' constructive and destructive responses to partners' anger/criticism did not appear in the review of self-esteem scales by Blascovich and Tomaka (1991) that we cited earlier in the present chapter. Once again, we have to wonder whether the choice of self-esteem measure in research by Rusbult and colleagues played a role in the unexpected (and, in this instance, nonsignificant) results for aspects of self-esteem as predictors of relationship maintenance behaviors (Gaines, 2016/ 2018). Without heaping excessive criticism upon the individual-difference portion of Rusbult et al.'s methodology in the studies that we have reviewed thus far, we are struck by the seemingly ad hoc approach to measuring self-esteem (arguably the most ubiquitous of all individual-difference variables; see Gaines, 2020). Then again, the erratic performance of self-esteem so far raises the possibility that the problem lies in personality researchers' operationalization of this key construct (see C. T. Hill, 2019).

Subsequent research: Overall and Sibley (2010, Samples 1 and 2). Outside the program of research by Rusbult and colleagues (1991), Overall and Sibley (2010) included self-esteem as a covariate of individuals' self-reported and diary-coded accommodation toward romantic partners (Sample 1) and family members (Sample 2). Overall and Sibley were interested primarily in the correlations between total scores on individuals' self-reported and diary-coded versions of accommodation. Thus, for Overall and Sibley's purposes, self-esteem (measured via the RSES; Rosenberg, 1965) served as an individual-difference control variable, whereas relationship satisfaction (measured by the Investment Model Scale, or IMS; Rusbult et al., 1998) served as a social-psychological control variable. Although Overall and Sibley did

44 THE SELF IN RELATIONSHIPS

not state hypotheses and limited their results concerning self-esteem and satisfaction to zero-order correlations, results were consistent with Sullivan's (1953, 1954, 1956) interpersonal theory and Thibaut and Kelley's (1959; Kelley, 1979; Kelley & Thibaut, 1978) interdependence theory: Self-esteem and satisfaction were significant positive covariates of self-reported accommodation toward romantic partners and family members (plus diary-coded accommodation toward family members, but not romantic partners).

As far as accommodation toward romantic partners was concerned, Overall and Sibley's (2010, Sample 1) results vindicated their choice of the RSES (Rosenberg, 1965) as the measure of self-esteem, regardless of the manner with which accommodation was assessed. However, as far as accommodation toward family members was concerned, Overall and Sibley's (2010, Sample 2) results were mixed (with self-esteem covarying significantly with accommodation only when the latter was self-reported). By the same token, satisfaction performed in a similar manner to self-esteem as a covariate, in both samples. Therefore, the measurement of self-esteem per se did not surface as a problem. All things covered, Overall and Sibley's results suggest that—when the "go to" measure of self-esteem is employed—self-esteem is positively related to accommodation after all (at least for self-reported accommodation). Unfortunately, Overall and Sibley did not report separate scores for exit, voice, loyalty, and neglect, thus making it impossible for us to determine whether all or most of the four behaviors are correlated with self-esteem in the direction that Sullivan's (1953, 1954, 1956) interpersonal theory of personality would have led us to anticipate.

Related research ("pro-relationship behaviors"): Kumashiro et al. (2002). Returning to the program of research by Rusbult and colleagues, we consider a study by Kumashiro et al. (2002) in which global self-esteem was measured alongside *self-respect*, which Kumashiro and colleagues defined as "the tendency to perceive the self as a principled person who is worthy of honor and high regard and is argued to rest on moral integrity" (p. 1009) as predictors of "pro-relationship behaviors" comprising (1) individuals' accommodation following partners' anger/criticism, (2) individuals' forgiveness following partners' betrayal, and (3) individuals' *and* partners' conciliation (including victims' forgiveness, plus perpetrators' atonement, following perpetrators' betrayal). Kumashiro et al. described self-respect as a cognitively oriented aspect of global self-esteem (presumably in contrast to a more affectively oriented aspect; Gaines, 2016/2018). In this particular study, Kumashiro and colleagues used the RSES (Rosenberg, 1965) as a measure of overall self-esteem, whereas they created their own measure of self-respect. Kumashiro et al. found that individuals' self-respect was a significant positive predictor of their own *and their partners'* pro-relationship behaviors, whereas global self-esteem was unrelated to such behaviors.

On the one hand, Kumashiro et al.'s (2002) study represents one instance in which Rusbult and colleagues employed the RSES (Rosenberg, 1965) as a measure of self-esteem. On the other hand, Kumashiro and colleagues did not indicate the extent to which scores on self-respect and global self-esteem covaried (thus raising the prospect of multicollinearity in regression analyses that pitted the two variables against each other as predictors of pro-relationship behaviors; see Cohen et al., 2002). Furthermore, even though Kumashiro and colleagues defined self-respect as the cognitive dimension of global self-esteem, the content of the two items that they reported from their five-item self-respect scale (i.e., "I have a lot of respect for myself" and "I should treat myself better than I do") suggests that the scale actually measures the *affective* dimension of self-esteem that Tafarodi and Swann (1995) labeled as *self-liking* (which, in turn, complements Tafarodi and Swann's cognitive dimension of *self-competence*; see also Tafarodi & Swann, 2001). Thus, although Kumashiro et al. were justified in advocating a multidimensional perspective on self-esteem, their efforts might have been better spent adopting Tafarodi and Swann's Self-Liking/Self-Competence (SL/SC) pre-existing inventory, rather than crafting their own survey.

BONUS: Narcissism as Reflected in Accommodation Following Partners' Anger/Criticism

At first glance, Sullivan's (1953, 1954, 1956) interpersonal theory of personality seems to be tailor-made for generating predictions about narcissism (Raskin & Hall, 1979) as a negative predictor of accommodation following partners' anger/criticism (Rusbult et al., 1991), among other conflict resolution behaviors (Gaines, 2016/2018). For example, clinical narcissism qualifies as a form of psychopathology that may be formed and maintained via individuals' unconscious yet excessive reliance upon the self-system to reallocate contents of "bad-me" to the "not-me" domain of personality (I. Hirsch, 2014). However, in *Personal Psychopathology*, Sullivan (1965/ 1972) cast doubt upon the assumption that narcissism (possibly at subclinical levels) inevitably would lead to dysfunctional behavior within

46   THE SELF IN RELATIONSHIPS

close relationships (Blechner, 2006). (In that same book, Sullivan made the ahead-of-the-curve declaration that "homosexuality" only becomes problematic for an individual when that person's society treats sexual orientation as "normal" versus "abnormal.") Furthermore, some critics (e.g., Kafka, 2006) have contended that Sullivan's optimism regarding human nature led Sullivan to misunderstand the origins of narcissism, such as postulating "malevolent transformations" that are not necessary from the perspective of Freud's (1923/1927) psychoanalytic theory.

In the present section, we will review two sets of studies in which W. K. Campbell and colleagues (i.e., W. K. Campbell et al., 2004, Study 8; W. K. Campbell & Foster, 2002, Studies 1 and 2) examined narcissism as a covariate of accommodation (Rusbult et al., 1991) in close relationships. At the outset, we note that W. K. Campbell and Foster (2002) cited Freud's (1914/1953) psychoanalytic theory as well as Thibaut and Kelley's (1959) interdependence theory—*not* Sullivan's (1953) interpersonal theory—as part of the inspiration for their research. Nevertheless, if we assume that the self-system in Sullivan's theory is analogous to the ego in Freud's theory as a manager of individuals' anxiety (e.g., M. Cortina, 2020), then we would argue that both theories predict a negative effect of narcissism on accommodation. Although one could argue that Freud's psychoanalytic theory overemphasizes narcissism as a personality type (e.g., Reisner, 2001), one likewise could contend that psychoanalytic theory is unique in the extent to which it anticipates the manifestation of narcissism in individuals' efforts toward pursuing social and personal relationships in the service of self-fulfillment, at the expense of other persons' welfare (Blatt, 2007).

Initial research: W. K. Campbell & Foster (2002, Studies 1 and 2). In an initial set of studies, W. K. Campbell and Foster (2002) examined subclinical narcissism (measured via the Narcissistic Personality Inventory, or NPI; Raskin & Hall, 1979) as a predictor of commitment and accommodation in romantic relationships (sexual orientation was not mentioned as a criterion for including or excluding participants). In Study 1, the zero-order correlation between narcissism and self-reported total accommodation was nonsignificant and negative. As for Study 2, W. K. Campbell and Foster reported that results for two samples (A and B) yielded significant negative zero-order correlations between narcissism and self-reported accommodation, yet no regression analysis was performed with narcissism and commitment as predictors of self-reported accommodation for the Study 2 samples. However, the association between narcissism and commitment in the two studies turned out to be indirect, mediated by individuals' perception of alternatives (i.e., narcissism was a significant positive predictor of individuals' perception of alternatives, which subsequently was a significant negative predictor of commitment). W. K. Campbell and Foster interpreted their results as consistent with Rusbult's (1980, 1983) investment model.

To their credit, W. K. Campbell and Foster (2002) used the best-known measure of narcissism (i.e., the NPI; Raskin & Hall, 1979) in their studies (see Millon, 1996). However, a careful reading of the text indicates that W. K. Campbell and Foster shifted among regression analyses involving (1) self-reported accommodation, (2) individuals' reports of partners' accommodation, and (3) combined self-reported/individuals' reports of partners' accommodation score (even though only one member of a given couple took part) in Study 1; and their regression analyses apparently were limited to the combined self-reported/individuals' reports of partners' accommodation score in the Study 2 samples. Unfortunately, such caveats are not obvious from Figures 1 and 2 in the Campbell/Foster paper; casual readers are likely to reach the incorrect conclusion that the figures are based solely on self-reported accommodation (which was the focus of the original measure by Rusbult et al., 1991). If we are left with the zero-order correlations to interpret, then the results of W. K. Campbell and Foster's studies are consistent with the views of Freud's (1932/1933) psychoanalytic theory and Sullivan's (1953) interpersonal theory concerning narcissism as negatively associated with self-reported accommodation.

Subsequent research: W. K. Campbell et al. (2004, Study 8). Responding to Raskin and Terry's (1988) conclusion that the NPI (Raskin & Hall, 1979) contains *seven* subdimensions (i.e., *authority, exhibitionism, superiority, vanity, exploitativeness, entitlement,* and *self-sufficiency*), W. K. Campbell and colleagues (2004) focused on the subdimension of entitlement. More specifically, W. K. Campbell et al. designed their own inventory (i.e., the Psychological Entitlement Scale, or PES) as an alternative to the NPI entitlement subscale. In Study 8, W. K. Campbell and colleagues reported that their entitlement dimension was significantly and negatively correlated with individuals' overall accommodation score; this correlation could be attributed to the significant negative correlation between their entitlement dimension and the two constructive behaviors (i.e., voice and loyalty). However, W. K. Campbell et al. also reported that all correlations except the negative correlation between their entitlement dimension and loyalty were rendered nonsignificant after controlling statistically for scores on the NPI

48 THE SELF IN RELATIONSHIPS

entitlement subdimension. W. K. Campbell and colleagues did not state whether overall accommodation or any of its four aspects (exit, voice, loyalty, neglect) were correlated with NPI entitlement.

W. K. Campbell and colleagues (2004) concluded that their PES scale was psychometrically sound and displayed criterion-related validity across nine studies, one of which (i.e., Study 8) is relevant to the present chapter. The PES seems to be aligned with the grandiosity aspect (rather than the vulnerability aspect) of entitlement, a fact that may distinguish the PES from original and revised versions of the NPI entitlement subscale (which, in turn, may be aligned with the vulnerability aspect, rather than the grandiosity aspect; e.g., Ackerman & Donnellan, 2013; B. K. Miller, 2021). However, for the purposes of the present review, the criterion-related validity of the PES has not been established to a sufficient degree; W. K. Campbell et al. did not report any results of regression analysis with PES and NPI versions of entitlement as predictors of accommodation as a whole (or exit, voice, loyalty, and neglect in particular). Given that even W. K. Campbell and colleagues (e.g., J. D. Miller et al., 2012) have recommended that researchers proceed cautiously before attempting to replace any of the NPI subscales with completely different (and narrowly conceptualized) inventories, we believe that both the PES and NPI entitlement surveys would benefit from further investigation in studies of accommodation.

The Story So Far: Genuine Self-Esteem and Subclinical Narcissism as Differentially Related to Accommodation(?)

The literature on self-esteem and narcissism as covariates of accommodation in close relationships is considerably more fragmented, and less extensive, than one might expect from modern-day relationship science (Gaines, 2016/ 2018). In our experience, several years of reviewing relevant library databases such as APA PsycINFO and Academic Search Complete (with the most recent search conducted on March 28, 2022) have yet to uncover a single paper in which a multiple regression analysis has been performed with genuine self-esteem (e.g., as measured via the RSES; Rosenberg, 1965) and subclinical narcissism (e.g., as measured via the NPI; Raskin & Terry, 1988) together as predictors of self-reported accommodation or its four interrelated behaviors of exit, voice, loyalty, and neglect (keeping in mind that no "official" accommodation survey currently exists; readers are referred to Rusbult et al., 1991, for sample items). Although one paper (W. K. Campbell & Foster, 2002, Studies 1 and 2) included measures of all three of the constructs in question, that particular paper dealt primarily with the link between narcissism and *commitment* (i.e., in regression analyses, narcissism was a significant negative predictor of commitment, whereas self-esteem was unrelated to commitment).

Thus far, it appears that (1) global self-esteem is significantly and *positively* correlated with self-reported accommodation (Overall & Sibley, 2010) but (2) global narcissism is significantly and *negatively* correlated with self-reported accommodation (W. K. Campbell & Foster, 2002). These divergent valences for correlations involving self-esteem (Rosenberg, 1965) versus narcissism (Raskin & Terry, 1988) are fully consistent with Sullivan's (1953, 1954, 1956) interpersonal theory, especially when one accounts for the presumed role of individuals' self-system in (1) correctly interpreting negative intrapersonal information as "bad-me," as opposed to (2) incorrectly interpreting that information as "not-me" (Gaines, 2020). Nevertheless, no published paper has provided results of regression analyses that might enable relationship scientists to make definitive statements regarding the utility of interpersonal theory in explaining between-person variance in the self-reported accommodation construct (Rusbult et al., 1991) that is steeped in Thibaut and Kelley's (1959; Kelley, 1979; Kelley & Thibaut, 1978) interdependence theory (Gaines, 2016/2018). Such a lack of inferential tests is especially puzzling in light of decades-old arguments for examining attitudes as predictors of interdependence processes (e.g., J. G. Holmes, 2002; Kelley, 1983).

One reason for the dearth of empirical research with the modest aim of directly pitting unidimensional versions of two attitudes toward the self (i.e., global self-esteem and global narcissism) against each other in regression analyses of accommodation—not to mention more ambitious aims of expanding the predictor variables to include *multivariate* versions—may be the fact that Thibaut and Kelley's (1959; Kelley, 1979; Kelley & Thibaut, 1978) interdependence theory historically has been regarded as a theory of *behavior* (see Kelley, 1997). Despite the acknowledgment that *interdependence* encompasses mutual influence of partners' thoughts and feelings (not just mutual influence of behavior) upon each other, interdependence theorists have tended to emphasize "external" phenomena (from the vantage point of the target person) such as partners' responsiveness to the self (Reis, 2007), without addressing this *self* as a coherent entity to which partners respond in

50 THE SELF IN RELATIONSHIPS

the first instance (Reis et al., 2002). As successive generations of interdependence theorists (following the lead of Kelley et al., 1983/2002, 2003) gradually incorporate more so-called "person" factors into their model-building and hypothesis-testing efforts, perhaps greater acknowledgment concerning the coherence of the self will occur (see Gaines, 2016/2018).

If we were to recommend a direction for future research, then that direction would be toward explicit hypothesis tests with self-esteem (Rosenberg, 1965) and narcissism (Raskin & Terry, 1988) as competing predictors of accommodation-related behaviors (i.e., exit, voice, loyalty, and neglect; Rusbult et al., 1991) in close relationships. Although some type of multiple regression analysis would be appropriate, we suggest that researchers initially examine the matrix of correlations among self-esteem, narcissism, and the four accommodation-related behaviors (Gaines, 2016/2018). If the intercorrelations among the accommodation-related behaviors generally are significant (as likely will be the case), then a multivariate multiple regression analysis would be particularly useful (i.e., begin by examining whether self-esteem and narcissism predict accommodation in general; afterward, for any significant multivariate effect, one could subsequently examine univariate effects to see which particular accommodation-related behaviors are responsible for the overall effect; see R. J. Harris, 2001). Although self-esteem and narcissism might be significantly correlated as well, the correlation probably will not be sufficiently high to evoke concerns about multicollinearity in the regression analysis (see Cohen et al., 2002).

Self-Esteem and Forgiveness Following Partners' Betrayal: Is Self-Esteem the *Outcome* Equivalent to *Self-Respect*?

Earlier in the present chapter, we discussed Kumashiro et al.'s (2002) research on self-esteem and "self-respect" as predictors of pro-relationship behaviors (i.e., accommodation following partners' anger/criticism, forgiveness following partners' betrayal, and conciliation following partners' betrayal). In that study, Kumashiro and colleagues concluded that "self-respect"—but *not* self-esteem—served as a significant positive predictor of pro-relationship behaviors. However, we noted that the distinction between "self-respect" (measured by a scale that Kumashiro et al. created) and self-esteem (measured by the RSES; Rosenberg, 1965) was blurred. In four follow-up studies,

Luchies and colleagues (2010) rebranded self-esteem (again, measured by the RSES) as *self-respect* and identified various conditions under which forgiveness (Finkel et al., 2002) *predicts* self-esteem—in a *negative* direction. Thus, Luchies and colleagues upended multiple aspects of the rationale that Kumashiro and colleagues previously applied to "self-respect" and its covariance with forgiveness. Given the decades of research that preceded Luchies et al.'s studies concerning the RSES as a measure of self-esteem (Blascovich & Tomaka, 1991), we will use the term *self-esteem* for the rest of the present section.

Drawing upon Kelley and Thibaut's (1978) heavily revised version of Thibaut and Kelley's (1959) interdependence theory within social psychology, and mentioning the entire field of evolutionary psychology (but *not* mentioning the field of personality psychology), Luchies et al. (2010) reasoned that individuals' forgiveness following partners' betrayal will bolster individuals' self-esteem (as well as individuals' *self-concept clarity*, or the stability of individuals' beliefs about their attributes; J. D. Campbell, 1990) if partners make amends in a manner that affirms individuals' safety and value as persons, whereas individuals' forgiveness will undermine individuals' self-esteem and self-concept clarity if partners fail to make amends. Results of Luchies et al.'s four studies, which supported their hypotheses, have been cited by some reviewers as evidence that therapists should refrain from encouraging clients to forgive transgressing partners as a matter of course (e.g., Martens, 2013). Therefore, despite the status of forgiveness following partners' betrayal as a conflict resolution process in particular (Rusbult, 1993) and as a pro-relationship behavior more generally (Rusbult & Van Lange, 2003), findings by Luchies and colleagues cast doubt upon the functionality of forgiveness as a relationship maintenance process.

The lack of overt references to Sullivan's (1953, 1954, 1956) interpersonal theory of personality, or *any* theory of personality theory for that matter, by Luchies et al. (2010) helps explain how self-esteem—which had been depicted as a lesser competitor to "self-respect" in explaining pro-relationship behaviors (including forgiveness following partners' betrayal) by Kumashiro et al. (2002)—could be transformed into "self-respect" without explanation. By the same token, Luchies and colleagues' finding that self-esteem may be a *consequence* (and not necessarily positive in valence)—rather than invariably a positive *antecedent*—of forgiveness is worth keeping in mind (Martens, 2013). In any event, considering the paucity of research concerning personality constructs as predictors of forgiveness

52 THE SELF IN RELATIONSHIPS

(Finkel et al., 2002) compared to research on personality predictors of accommodation following partners' anger/criticism (Rusbult et al., 1991), Luchies et al.'s results lead us to wonder whether forgiveness should continue to be viewed as a prototypical post–"transformation of motivation" interdependence process alongside accommodation (see Gaines, 2016/2018). Lastly, like the paper by Kumashiro and colleagues, we believe that the paper by Luchies and colleagues would have benefited from delving into Sullivan's interpersonal theory.

The Legacy of Sullivan's Interpersonal Theory of Personality: Interpersonal Anxiety, Self-Esteem, and Conflict Resolution

In *Psychiatrist of America: The Life of Harry Stack Sullivan*, biographer Helen Swick Perry (1982) pointed out that Sullivan was one of the first psychiatrists to emphasize the ramifications of self-esteem for individuals' mental health. Perry credited Edward Kempf's *Psychopathology* (1921) with steering Sullivan toward conceptualizing self-esteem as an interpersonal construct. However, Perry's annotated notes in Sullivan's *Personal Psychopathology* (1965/1972)—written during Sullivan's lifetime yet published more than a decade after Sullivan's death—indicate that the term *interpersonal* did not appear in Kempf's book. At any rate, a close reading of *Personal Psychopathology* attests to Sullivan's belief that both the anticipation and the experience of social disapproval may be sufficient to damage individuals' self-esteem over the long term, depending on the potential sources of such disapproval (e.g., individuals' self-esteem may be affected most adversely by significant others whose behavior conveys the impression that individuals are not properly understood, let alone valued, as persons; see also Reis et al., 2017). Furthermore, Sullivan highlighted the role of spouses (as distinct from other relationship partners) in validating versus undermining individuals' self-esteem (see also Reis & Shaver, 1988).

In turn, *Conceptions of Modern Psychiatry* (1947/1966)—which Sullivan wrote after *Personal Psychopathology* (1965/1972), notwithstanding the earlier publication date—represents a maturation in Sullivan's thinking with regard to anxiety as an interpersonal phenomenon that carries important implications for individuals' self-esteem (see Perry, 1982). The logic that emerges from Sullivan's later thought can be summarized as follows: To the extent that individuals anticipate or experience social disapproval from significant others, individuals may experience anxiety that harks back to individuals' earliest (albeit preverbal) anxiety as communicated by caregivers during infancy; such anxiety can exert a negative effect on individuals' self-esteem over time, making it increasingly likely that individuals will engage in pre-emptive as well as retaliatory attempts to derogate the potentially offending significant others (see also J. G. Holmes, 2002). In Sullivan's interpersonal theory of personality, the psychological (if not physical) survival of individuals' selves may be at stake during such negative interactions; if individuals experience their sense of self primarily *in relation to significant others*, then individuals may not take perceived threats to their selfhood lightly (J. G. Holmes, 2000).

Finally, in the posthumous collection of Sullivan's mid-to-late-career articles that was published as *The Fusion of Psychiatry and Social Science* (1964/1971), Sullivan incorporated the constructs of interpersonal anxiety, self-esteem, and conflict resolution within a unifying framework of interpersonal fields (see Perry, 1982). Without referring specifically to Lewin's (1935, 1948/1967, 1951/1976) field theory, Sullivan alluded to within-person conflict (manifested as heightened anxiety and, possibly, diminished self-esteem) as well as between-person conflict (manifested as individuals' efforts toward "getting back" at significant others who are perceived as disrespectful toward them, accurately or not) in a manner that is compatible with Lewin's theory. However, throughout relationship science, Sullivan's interpersonal theory of personality has been regarded mainly as a neo-Freudian theory that presaged Bowlby's (1969/1997, 1973/1998, 1980/1998) attachment theory—not as a neo-Lewinian theory that presaged Thibaut and Kelley's (1959; Kelley, 1979; Kelley & Thibaut, 1978) interdependence theory (Gaines, 2016/2018). Overall, we believe Sullivan's interpersonal theory has been tacitly influential (though often unrecognized) within relationship science (see also Gaines, 2007a, 2007b).

Prelude to Chapter 3

Earlier in the present chapter, we found that Sullivan's (1953, 1954, 1956) interpersonal theory of personality depicted individuals' need for interpersonal intimacy as a distinct motive that initially is expressed via preteen children's behavior toward "chums" and subsequently is expressed in a more fully developed form via teenagers' behavior toward romantic partners (see also

Kanter, 2013). However, Sullivan's depiction of individuals' unconsciously expressed need for interpersonal intimacy was highly gendered, with preteen friendships described as exclusively *same sex* and teenage (as well as adult) romantic relationships described as exclusively *opposite sex* in nature (Paul & White, 1990). Interestingly, a perusal of *Personal Psychopathology* (1965/1972)—which, we noted in the preceding section, was the first book that Sullivan wrote (but the last book to be published posthumously)—reveals that Sullivan reserved the term *chumship* for male-male friendships, as if those relationships warranted special consideration. In contrast, a perusal of *Conceptions of Modern Psychiatry* (1947/1966)—which, as noted above, was the only book by Sullivan to be published while he was alive—indicates that Sullivan eventually expanded his use of the term *chumship* to cover female-female as well as male-male friendships.

As McLaughlin (1998) pointed out, Harry Stack Sullivan's (1953) interpersonal theory of personality is known for its insight regarding the dynamics of interpersonal relations (and not necessarily gender relations within marriage or other relational contexts), whereas another neo-Freudian personality theory—namely, Karen Horney's (1967) *feminine psychology*—is known for its insight concerning the confluence between gender and personality. (Although McLaughlin referred to the neo-Freudianism of Sullivan, Horney, and others as a "failed" school of thought, other reviewers not only dispute such a negative description but also note that "neo-Freudian" or "social-psychological" personality theories gave rise to the *psychocultural analysis* movement; e.g., Gitre, 2011.) Moreover, A. J. Stewart and McDermott (2004) contended that Horney's feminine psychology addressed gender relations as *intergroup* relations (within and beyond the context of marriage and other types of close relationships) to a greater extent than Sullivan's interpersonal theory had done. Lastly, Mitchell and Harris (2004) observed that—notwithstanding Sullivan's innovations, such as conceptualizing the interpersonal field—Horney made singular contributions to personality theorists' understanding of gender and sexuality.

Both Sullivan's (1953) interpersonal theory of personality and Horney's (1967) feminine psychology viewed individuals' need for sex as *less* important, and individuals' need for anxiety reduction as *more* important, than Freud's (1923/1927) version of psychoanalytic theory had assumed (C. S. Hall & Lindzey, 1970). Furthermore, both Sullivan's theory and Horney's theory emphasized the interpersonal (rather than intrapersonal) basis of individuals' anxiety (May, 1950/1996). However, Sullivan's interpersonal theory focused on the implications of interpersonal anxiety for individuals' self-esteem, whereas Horney's feminine psychology focused on the implications of interpersonal anxiety for individuals' helplessness and danger (T. Leary, 1957). In Chapter 3, we turn our attention to feminine psychology, particularly the role that Horney's theory played in challenging the androcentric assumptions behind Freud's psychoanalytic theory (which Horney criticized as "masculine psychology"; Gaines, 2020). We will be particularly interested in the broad influence that Horney's theory exerted upon Sandra Bem's (1981) *gender schema theory*, which in turn was developed after Bem and others (most notably Spence & Helmreich, 1978) had conducted pioneering research on the *gender-related traits* of positive masculinity and positive femininity.

3

Gender-Related Traits as Reflected in Conflict Resolution Behaviors

Synopsis: In the present chapter, we examine Karen Horney's feminine psychology as derived partly from Alfred Adler's individual psychology (especially with regard to the individual-level effects of male-oriented sexism in "Western" societies), and as diverging markedly from Freud's version of psychoanalytic theory (particularly regarding the applicability of constructs from Freud's "masculine psychology," such as "castration anxiety," to girls and women); we compare and contrast Horney's and Freud's respective views of the so-called masculinity complex in women; we cover Horney's unique perspective on the so-called femininity complex in men; we discuss the meanings of *masculinity* and *femininity* in Horney's feminine psychology; we delve into the eventual evolution of Horney's feminine psychology to introduce "universal" constructs (e.g., interpersonal anxiety in its non-neurotic and neurotic forms) that nonetheless can be interpreted as extensions of Horney's original theory; we elaborate upon Horney's moving toward, moving against, and moving away from other persons; we explain the progression from Horney's feminine psychology to Sandra Bem's gender schema theory, especially regarding (proto-)feminists' understanding of positive aspects of masculinity and femininity among individuals in "normal" or nonclinical populations; we examine Bem's construct of psychological androgyny, including controversies regarding its conceptualization and measurement; we provide an overview of the early literature on psychological androgyny and its lack of impact on "pro-relationship behaviors" (despite hints by Bem's gender schema theory that androgyny might promote relationship maintenance); we review details regarding the impact of positive masculinity and (especially) positive femininity on individuals' responses to relationship dissatisfaction, as well as the effects of positive femininity on individuals' responses to partners' anger or criticism, in close relationships; and we offer a prelude to Chapter 4, which covers Carl Jung's analytical psychology and the version of factor-analytic trait theory by Robert McCrae and

The Self in Relationships. Stanley O. Gaines, Jr., Oxford University Press. © Oxford University Press 2023.
DOI: 10.1093/oso/9780197687635.003.0003

Paul Costa (the latter of which may be informed by Spence's multifactorial gender identity theory).

> We have considered the stage of personality development in which the other fellow, the chum, someone of the same sex and approximately the same age, becomes highly significant, and by this very fact acts as the final binding agency to commit the growing individual with the full force and control action of the cultural environment. One can follow certain autistic courses, certain individualized highly personal courses of development, giving lip service to the requirements of one social environment as long as nobody in that environment has more than instrumental meaning to one. One can for instance do homage to people who are afflicted with a sense of greatness without feeling any sympathy with what they regard as important. It pays; it gives something that is repaid with what one wants— satisfactions or security. But when somebody else begins to matter as much as I do, then what this other person values must receive some careful consideration from me. So it is in the preadolescent that the great control-ling power of the cultural, social, forces is finally inescapably written into the human personality.
>
> —Harry Stack Sullivan,
> *Conceptions of Modern Psychiatry* (1947/1966, p. 23)

As Wake (2019) noted (and as we learned in Chapter 2), Sullivan re-ferred to "homosexuality" as a disordered personality type in *Conceptions of Modern Psychiatry* (1947/1966). However, Wake (2008) also pointed out that—in a posthumously published set of articles entitled *Schizophrenia as a Human Process* (1962)—Sullivan contended that the issue was *not* sexual orientation, but rather the effect of negative societal prohibitions upon individuals' desire toward persons of the same sex. Of course, as the above quote from Sullivan (1947/1966) indicates, societal influences upon per-sonality are not uniformly negative (e.g., in encouraging "chumships"). Nonetheless, Waugaman (2012) concluded that societal agents such as re-ligious institutions may provoke conflict between individuals' acceptance and rejection of their own sexuality (a predicament that even Sullivan may have experienced; see also Hansen, 2002). Also, as Blechner (2006) observed, Sullivan's (1953, 1954, 1956) interpersonal theory reminds us that societal norms grant privilege to male–female romantic relationships as contexts for sexual relations. Finally, as Blechner (2008) emphasized, Sullivan was ahead

58 THE SELF IN RELATIONSHIPS

of his time in advocating social equality for gay men (if not lesbian women), in psychotherapeutic institutions and throughout societies.

If Sullivan's (1962) interpersonal theory of personality was ahead of the curve in challenging heterosexist attitudes and behaviors from agents of societies (including mental health institutions), then Horney's (1967) feminine psychology similarly was ahead of the curve in challenging *sexist* attitudes and behaviors at the societal and institutional levels (McLaughlin, 1998). Indeed, both Sullivan and Horney ascended to leadership positions within professional associations (i.e., the William Alanson White Institute and the American Institute for Psychoanalysis, respectively) that served as platforms for them to offer their own visions of mental health in opposition to the viewpoints that emanated from orthodox Freudian psychoanalytic institutions (see Stern, 2015). However, Horney's theory was singularly countercultural in positing that—notwithstanding Freud's (1912, 1923/1927, 1959) dubious claim that females are afflicted by a biologically based, psychologically dysfunctional "penis envy" toward males in general—males are socialized to harbor an equally dysfunctional "womb envy" toward women of reproductive age in particular (Semmelhack et al., 2011). Moreover, according to Horney's feminine psychology, neither "penis envy" nor "womb envy" is inevitable (Goldscheider, 2014).

In the present chapter, we explore Horney's (1967) feminine psychology in further detail. At the outset, we acknowledge that some reviewers have criticized the version of Horney's theory that appears in the posthumously published collections of lectures from 1922 to 1937 bearing the name *Feminine Psychology* as too dependent upon its contrast with Freud's (1923/ 1927) version of psychoanalytic theory to be considered a standalone theory (e.g., C. S. Hall & Lindzey, 1970). However, we also note that other reviewers (e.g., Ewen, 1998) have credited *The Neurotic Personality of Our Time* (1937)—an authored book that Horney published during her lifetime—with providing a viable personality typology of neurotic responses to interpersonal anxiety (i.e., *moving toward, moving against,* and *moving away* from other persons) that may covary with gender (i.e., women as more likely to be socialized to move toward other persons, and men as more likely to be socialized to move against and away from other persons, than is the case for the opposite gender). Subsequently, we highlight the influence of Horney's feminine psychology upon Bem's (1981) *gender schema theory* (see also Bem, 1993) as we ponder the impact of positive masculinity and positive femininity on individuals' conflict response behaviors in close relationships.

Sullivan and Beyond: Horney's Feminine Psychology

In the quote from *Conceptions of Modern Psychiatry* (1947/1966) with which we began the present chapter, Sullivan described an almost idyllic process by which preteens begin to think in terms of their "chums'" welfare as much as they think in terms of their own welfare. In fact, Sullivan went so far as to proclaim that voluntary same-sex friendships could be so effective in reducing interpersonal anxiety that children may experience fewer negative effects of dysfunctional relationships with parents and other family members (Bukowski, 2001). However, in *The Interpersonal Theory of Psychiatry* (1953), Sullivan commented upon the potential for rivalry and competition as well as camaraderie and cooperation in same-sex friendships, before and during the preadolescent era (Berndt, 2004). Thus, socialization of preadolescents can lead to individuals' internalization of societal-level messages such as "it's a dog-eat-dog world" within the context of their relationships with best friends, even as preadolescents ostensibly experience genuine emotional intimacy for the first time within those relationships (although the largely positive impact of socialized competition upon the quality of "chumships" that Sullivan had presumed may be limited to boys, with a *negative* impact emerging for girls; Paul & White, 1990).

Unlike Sullivan's (1953) interpersonal theory of personality, Horney's (1967) feminine psychology posits that—even if boys stand to benefit by engaging in competition with their friends—girls stand to benefit by pursuing *cooperation* with their friends (see Powell, 2004). Thus, Horney's theory raises the possibility that girls and women (as well as boys and men) possess distinct social and psychological strengths by virtue of their gendered socialization—a possibility that is not articulated within Sullivan's theory (e.g., Paul & White, 1990). However, the empirical evidence regarding the differentially positive effects of socialization on girls' versus boys' friendships as envisioned by Horney's feminine psychology is equivocal, with results of some studies indicating that friendships generally are more important to boys than to girls (see Bukowski, 2001). Furthermore, some of Horney's followers caution against the temptation to interpret feminine psychology as promoting girls' socialization in cooperation over boys' socialization in competition as a desired norm (e.g., Westkott, 1990). Perhaps the most balanced assessment that we can offer is that boys and girls may thrive differentially within friendships (e.g., boys within larger groups versus girls within dyads; Kingery et al., 2010).

60 THE SELF IN RELATIONSHIPS

Despite differences in their attention to gender differences in children's social and psychological experiences within friendships, Horney's (1967) feminine psychology and Sullivan's (1953) interpersonal theory are more aligned with each other than they are aligned with Freud's (1923/1927) psychoanalytic theory, which focuses to a greater extent upon the individuals' experiences within pre-school-age relationships with same-sex and opposite-sex parents (see LeVine, 2001). Horney's theory in particular takes aim at the devaluation of girls' and women's psychosexual development within Freud's theory (Rendon, 2008). On the one hand, Freud's psychoanalytic theory casts girls and women as "not-male," psychologically and biologically speaking (e.g., lacking positive or socially desirable masculinity; see W. B. Smith, 2007). On the other hand, Freud's theory depicts girls and women as "female to a fault," psychologically and biologically speaking (e.g., even positive or socially desirable femininity, which females presumably possess, is treated as a lesser personality trait when compared to positive masculinity; see Semmelhack et al., 2011). Moreover, consistent with Adler's (1927) individual psychology, Horney's feminine psychology rejects the Freudian dichotomy between positive masculinity and positive femininity (P. Hirsch, 2005).

A Theoretical Point of Reference: Adler's Individual Psychology as Questioning Male-Oriented Sexism in Society

Horney's (1967) feminine psychology simultaneously represents a repudiation of Freud's (1923/1927) version of psychoanalytic theory and an embrace of Adler's (1927) individual psychology with regard to assumptions about the functionality of traditional gender roles (Janssen, 2020). In Freud's theory, gender roles serve as effective means by which societies direct individuals toward behavior that is congruent with their biological sex, whereas in Adler's theory, gender roles unnecessarily constrain individuals' behavior to conform to societal demands, especially where girls and women are concerned (P. Hirsch, 2005). Although Adler's individual psychology resembled Freud's psychoanalytic theory in terms of an overarching emphasis on early childhood experiences (rather than children's friendships) as shaping women's as well as men's personalities, Adler rejected Freud's belief that women were psychologically inferior to men (Chandler, 1991). Adler's theory is distinguished especially for promoting the construct of *masculine protest* (originally denoting individuals' pattern of responding to feelings of inferiority toward male role models by engaging in stereotypically masculine behavior and eschewing stereotypically feminine behavior, later recast as *striving for superiority* in response to patriarchy; Nelson, 1991).

Interestingly, Adler's name does not appear in the index of Horney's posthumous collection of 1920s- and 1930s-era lectures that were published a generation later as *Feminine Psychology* (1967). Nonetheless, inspection of Horney's authored books that were published after the 1922–1937 lectures—but before *Feminine Psychology* was made available in print—confirms that Horney credited Adler's (1927) individual psychology with helping to shape her ideas regarding gender and personality. Consider the following passage from *New Ways in Psychoanalysis* (1939), which was published during Horney's lifetime: "Here we come to see cultural factors. The [woman's] wish to be a man, as Alfred Adler has pointed out, may be the expression of a wish for all those qualities or privileges which in our culture are regarded as masculine, such as strength, courage, independence, success, sexual freedom, right to choose a partner" (p. 108). In turn, Horney elaborated upon Adler's critique of "penis envy" in the process of reframing this key construct from Freud's (1933) version of psychoanalytic theory (P. Hirsch, 2005). According to Horney's feminine psychology as well as Adler's individual psychology, to the extent that one can find any merit in the construct of "penis envy," the construct is a function of culture rather than biology (Janssen, 2020).

Unlike "penis envy," the construct of "womb envy" originated within Horney's (1967) feminine psychology and has no direct counterpart in Adler's (1927) individual psychology, let alone Freud's (1923/1927) version of psychoanalytic theory (see Semmelhack et al., 2011). According to Horney's theory, boys and men are intimidated by the sexual and/or maternal powers that girls and women may wield against them (Maguire & Dewing, 2007). Moreover, like "penis envy," Horney's feminine psychology views "womb envy" as a function of culture, *not* as a function of biology (J. Benjamin, 2015). Furthermore, progressing beyond debates over which sex harbors more versus less intense envy toward members of the opposite sex, Horney's theory suggests that—among women and men alike—individuals' self-concept is linked to individuals' experience of their own sexuality, including their awareness of their sex organs (Notman, 2003). Horney's seemingly straightforward argument, at least when evaluated several decades after the fact, that women are as likely as men to incorporate the physical attributes that they possess (instead of the physical attributes that they lack) serves to

62   THE SELF IN RELATIONSHIPS

highlight the overt male-oriented sexism of Freud's theory (see Bhugra & Bhui, 2002).

"Castration Anxiety": Contrasting Views in Freud's Psychoanalytic Theory Versus Horney's Feminine Psychology

In Freud's (1900/1965) version of psychoanalytic theory, *all* infants (whether male or female) are assumed to suckle their mothers' breasts in order to satisfy their need for sexual gratification as well as nourishment (Krausz, 1994). Moreover, boys' sexual desire toward their mothers ostensibly leads them to view their fathers as competitors (and, hence, as objects of boys' need for aggression)—an anxiety-provoking situation that gives rise to the *Oedipus complex* (Bhugra & Bhui, 2002). In Freud's theory, the anxiety in question is intrapersonal in nature, involving mixed messages that boys' ego receives from the id (i.e., "I want to express sexuality toward my mother and aggression toward my father") versus the superego (i.e., "I should not express sexuality toward my mother or aggression toward my father"; Horne et al., 2000). However, Freud struggled to account for girls' psychosexual experiences, eventually concluding that girls redirect their sexual desire toward their fathers and recast their mothers (with whom they identify yet regard as competitors) as would-be objects of aggression (Bernstein, 2004). Nonetheless, the anxiety that girls experience is similarly intrapersonal within Freud's psychoanalytic theory, supposedly arising from id-superego conflicts that are mediated by girls' ego (see Pillay & Pillay, 2017).

The closest that Freud's (1933/1965) version of psychoanalytic theory comes to conceptualizing anxiety as interpersonal (as distinct from intrapersonal) is to propose (1) "*castration anxiety*" as boys' vague dread that their seemingly omnipotent fathers will take away the boys' external genitalia in a literal sense, or will render the boys powerless in a figurative sense, and (2) "*female castration anxiety*" as girls' vague dread that their seemingly all-powerful mothers have already taken away their external genitalia in a literal sense, or will render the girls powerless in a figurative sense (Balsam, 2018). However, as Horney's (1967) feminine psychology points out, Freud's psychoanalytic theory begins with the false premise that one can readily generalize from the default male "castration anxiety" to female "castration anxiety" (Notman, 2003). Additionally, Horney's theory notes that Freud's "masculine psychology" is silent with regard to the possibility that girls may experience anticipation as well as anxiety over the prospect that they will eventually undergo the same processes of biological maturation associated with reproduction that their mothers have undergone (e.g., menstruation, insemination, pregnancy, childbirth, breastfeeding; Balsam, 2018).

Departing substantially from Freud's (1933/1965) version of psychoanalytic theory, Horney's (1967) feminine psychology recasts female "castration anxiety" as an interrelated set of *female genital anxieties* (Rudden, 2018). In Horney's theory, such anxieties are rooted partly in girls' sense of their own femininity, including awareness that they possess a vagina (rather than obsession over a disembodied penis that they do not possess; McEnery-West, 2019). Furthermore, in Horney's feminine psychology, female genital anxieties are grounded partly in girls' awareness of *their mothers'* possession of a vagina as well as secondary sex characteristics (Balsam, 2018). Controversially, Horney's theory posits that female genital anxieties also are based partly upon girls' unconscious reaction to their sexual attraction toward their fathers (Donmall, 2013). However, some contemporary reviewers interpret Horney's feminine psychology broadly as a theory about female genital anxieties concerning sexuality (without dwelling upon the prospect of incestuous desires from childhood onward; e.g., Santamaria, 2018). All in all, Horney's theory emphasizes the social and psychological difficulties that girls and women may experience as a result of constant bombardment by societal messages that they are deemed inferior to boys and men (Pillay & Pillay, 2017).

The Masculinity Complex in Women: Contrasting Views in Freud's Psychoanalytic Theory Versus Horney's Feminine Psychology

Freud's (1933/1965) version of psychoanalytic theory does not presuppose that all girls are destined to follow a single psychosexual path of development toward womanhood (Chodorow, 2004). Nonetheless, Freud's theory *does* presuppose that the "normal" or nonclinical developmental path is for girls to accept their "penis envy" and female "castration anxiety," thereby enabling girls to renounce their masculinity and instead come to terms with their (lesser) femininity along the way to womanhood (see Maguire & Dewing, 2007). Otherwise, according to Freud's psychoanalytic theory, girls may end

64 THE SELF IN RELATIONSHIPS

up cultivating personality characteristics that are (stereo)typically associated with the opposite sex (e.g., ambitiousness)—an "abnormal" or clinical
developmental path that culminates in the *masculinity complex* in women
(Salberg, 2008). (Freud's theory also posits that girls' simultaneous failure to
reject their masculinity *and* accept their femininity could lead to an "ascetic"
or sexuality-denying stance; Young-Bruehl & L. Wexler, 1992.) Therefore, on
the basis of Freud's psychoanalytic theory, it is not clear how girls and women
might embrace masculine as well as feminine aspects of themselves in an
adaptive manner (Williamson, 2004).

In the process of refining her feminine psychology over the years, Horney
(1967) repudiated the inherent sexism in Freud's (1933/1965) version of psychoanalytic theory for proclaiming that girls and women necessarily harbor
"penis envy" or act on the basis of female "castration anxiety" (Semmelhack
et al., 2011). Even in her earlier incarnation of feminine psychology, Horney
questioned Freud's assumption that "penis envy" was normative among
females (Kieffer, 2004). However, in later years, Horney concluded that—
among those girls and women who experienced "penis envy"—the envy in
question was directed toward male *privilege* (and females were not destined
to experience such envy; Young-Bruehl & Wexler, 1992). Horney's latter-
day feminine psychology offered a comparable critique of Freud's psychoanalytic theory regarding the universality of female "castration anxiety" (or,
more accurately, female genital anxieties) and resulting behavior (Balsam,
2018). Lastly, just as Adler's (1927) individual psychology highlighted societal influences on the *inferiority complex* among females (beyond the developmental aspects of that complex among males and females alike), so too did
Horney's feminine psychology emphasize societal influences on the masculinity complex among females (Salberg, 2008).

In contrast to Freud's (1933/1965) version of psychoanalytic theory,
Horney's (1967) feminine psychology comprehended the female body on
its own terms (Balsam, 2018). Accordingly, Horney's theory regards "primary femininity" as the default psychological orientation for girls, leading
to the wish to emulate their mothers by becoming pregnant themselves (and
not typically as the result of insemination by their fathers, even though girls
may feel attracted to their fathers; see Bernstein, 2004). Therefore, within
Horney's feminine psychology, one need not postulate a developmental sequence in which girls (1) initially are attracted to their mothers but (2) subsequently identify with mothers once the girls have gravitated toward fathers
as objects of attraction (Corbett, 2008). Moreover, Horney's theory notes that

girls become aware of their own vaginas and accompanying sensations *before* they become aware that other sex organs exist, and *before* they entertain any thoughts about what it must be like to possess other sex organs (or to contemplate copulation with persons who possess those sex organs; Young-Bruehl & Wexler, 1992). In the aftermath, even critiques of Horney's feminine psychology (e.g., within the version of psychoanalytic theory by Lacan, 1973/1977) admitted that Freud's "masculine psychology" was misinformed (see Rae, 2020).

The Femininity Complex in Men: Acknowledged by Horney's Feminine Psychology, Unacknowledged by Freud's Psychoanalytic Theory

Is it useful for psychodynamic theorists to contemplate a separate *Electra complex* or "female Oedipus complex" when attempting to understand the psychosexual development of girls and women? Some reviewers (e.g., Bahroun, 2018) answer yes to this question, referring broadly to the psychoanalytic theories of Freud (1920/1961) and Lacan (1973/1977) as support for their response. Other reviewers (e.g., Bernstein, 2004) answer no to the same question, quoting passages directly from Freud to refute the invocation of an Electra complex for females. Still other reviewers (e.g., Katz, 2018) do not provide a simple yes or no response, instead contending that the Electra complex should be interpreted as a pre-Oedipal complex for *all* persons, regardless of gender. Overall, despite advocacy for the concept of the Electra complex (at least for females) within certain psychodynamic theories (e.g., the *analytical psychology* of Jung, 1921/1971, and the *object relations theory* of Klein, 1975), inspection of the books that presented Horney's feminine psychology in the greatest detail reveals that (1) Horney did not refer to the Electra complex at all in *New Ways in Psychoanalysis* (1939) and (2) the index to *Feminine Psychology* (1967) listed the Electra complex only as a term to redirect readers toward the concept of the Oedipus complex.

What, exactly, *does* Horney's (1967) feminine psychology offer that Freud's (1933/1965) version of psychoanalytic theory fails to offer regarding gender and personality? In addition to revamping Freud's concept of the masculinity complex in women, Horney postulated the *femininity complex for men*— that is, responding to their "womb envy" toward (and corresponding fear of humiliation at the hands of) seemingly omnipotent mothers by acquiring

66   THE SELF IN RELATIONSHIPS

personality characteristics that are (stereo)typical of the opposite sex (such as subordination; see Maguire & Dewing, 2007). According to Horney's theory, a glaring omission in Freud's (1909/1955) account of "Little Hans" (who actually was psychoanalyzed by his own father) was the missed opportunity to interpret Hans's desire to *be* a procreating mother through a lens other than castration anxiety (Knafo, 2018). In fact, Horney's feminine psychology speculates that mothers' pivotal role as caregivers in boys' lives might make their fear of mothers' omnipotence *greater* than their fear of fathers' omnipotence (Hamman, 2017). Furthermore, Horney's theory suggests that the femininity complex may arise when men's fear of female relationship partners in general is so debilitating that it undermines men's "normal" sense of masculinity (see Kierski & Blazina, 2009).

In Horney's (1967) feminine psychology, men's vulnerability is at odds with men's tendency to fall prey to a *superiority complex* (following the individual psychology of Adler, 1927) within their relationships with women (see Gough, 2004). Although male privilege may afford men ample opportunities to humiliate women (as well as other men), Horney's theory proposes that revealing their vulnerability to women may lead men to develop an inferiority complex, such that they endure humiliation from women (Chodorow, 2015). Some reviewers (e.g., Maguire & Dewing, 2007) surmise that Horney's feminine psychology regards the resulting femininity complex in men as a stronger influence on behavior than the aforementioned masculinity complex in women. However, other reviewers (e.g., Pillay & Pillay, 2017) observe that Horney refrained from assuming differences between the influence of the femininity complex in men and the influence of the masculinity complex in women, concluding instead that men's advantaged status in various societies provides men with more numerous and more constructive avenues to compensate for their fear toward women's perceived omnipotence, compared to the avenues that societies offer women to compensate for their fear toward men's perceived omnipotence.

On the Meanings of *Masculinity* and *Femininity* in Horney's Feminine Psychology

So far, we have noted major contributions of Horney's (1967) feminine psychology as a complement and challenge to Freud's (1933/1965) "masculine psychology" (i.e., psychoanalytic theory). However, the standalone terms *masculine/masculinity* and *feminine/femininity* do not appear in the index of Horney's *New Ways in Psychoanalysis* (1939) or Horney's posthumously published *Feminine Psychology* (1967). Thus, one might ask whether Horney's theory differs substantially from Freud's theory with regard to formal definitions of masculinity and femininity (considering that Freud famously refrained from providing such definitions, notwithstanding Freud's overt stance that men's and women's conformity to traditional "sex roles" should be *encouraged*—whereas nonconformity to pre-existing "sex roles" should be *discouraged*—by societal agents; Margolis, 1984). On a related note, one could ask whether Horney's feminine psychology departs from Freud's version of psychoanalytic theory with respect to the unidimensionality versus multidimensionality of masculinity and/or femininity (keeping in mind that Freud acknowledged bidimensionality as possible in principle but promoted unidimensionality as "normal" in practice; Bem, 1993).

In *New Ways in Psychoanalysis*, Horney (1939) implicitly suggested that *masculinity* denotes seeking, possessing, and attempting to hold onto power and authority over other persons; historically (at least in so-called Western nations), such behaviors—which are products of socialization by various agents of society, manifested by way of society's influence upon individuals' personality characteristics—have been (stereo)typically associated with men (who are far more likely to be rewarded by societal agents for such personality attributes and corresponding behavior than are women; A. J. Stewart & McDermott, 2004). However, an in-depth reading of *New Ways in Psychoanalysis* indicates that Horney did not explicitly define masculinity; such an observation applies to *Feminine Psychology* (1967) as well. Rather, Horney emphasized the implications of male advantage within "Western" societies for men's and (especially) women's psychosexual development (Salberg, 2008). Additionally, Horney argued that Freud (1933/1965) need not have concerned himself so obsessively with the notion that girls as well as boys start life with a masculine orientation toward themselves and the world (supposedly placing girls on a developmental path along which they are destined to regret the discovery that they are not "little men"; Newbigin, 2013).

In *Feminine Psychology*, Horney (1967) implied that *femininity* denotes seeking, possessing, and attempting to hold onto close or personal relationships with other persons; throughout the history of "Western" nations, such behaviors—which, in a manner that is analogous to the behaviors that represent masculinity, are products of socialization by societal agents and

68 THE SELF IN RELATIONSHIPS

reflected in societal influence upon individuals' personality characteristics—
have been (stereo)typically associated with women (who are considerably
more likely to be rewarded by agents of society for such personality attributes
and corresponding behavior than are men; Enns, 1989). Nevertheless, a close
reading of *Feminine Psychology* indicates that Horney did not overtly define
femininity; such an observation is true of *New Ways in Psychoanalysis* (1939)
as well. Instead, Horney focused on the ramifications of female disadvantage in "Western" societies—in spite of (or possibly *because of*) the fact that
boys and men are dependent upon women's role as relationship managers—
for men's and (especially) women's psychosexual development (see Knafo,
2018). Moreover, Horney contended that Freud (1933/1965) was wrong
to assume that femininity could be understood solely as not-masculinity
(Gough, 2004).

One of the more contentious aspects of Horney's (1967) feminine psychology is the lack of differentiation between psychological and sexual
aspects of masculinity and femininity in her earlier writings (Elise, 2002).
Such a lack of differentiation leads Horney to make certain claims about
women's femininity that contradict her proto-feminist stance regarding
women as deserving the same respect as men (e.g., menstruation as inevitably associated with passivity and pain among women, as individuals and as
partners in heterosexual relationships; Donmall, 2013). By the same token,
Horney's later writings represent a conscious effort to decouple psychological from sexual aspects of masculinity and femininity (Enns, 1989). For example, in the process of articulating a culturally informed view regarding
gender and personality, Horney increasingly prioritized the impact that societal devaluation of women may exert directly upon mothers' psychological
development and indirectly upon their daughters' psychological development (by way of mothers' communication of such gendered devaluation to
daughters; Marcus, 2004). Furthermore, Horney (1939) surmised that objectification of women need not be sexual in order to convey the impression that
women exist to satisfy others' needs (Westkott, 1990).

From *Feminine Psychology* to *Neurosis and Human Growth*: Evolution in Horney's Theory Over Time

Some reviewers (e.g., C. S. Hall & Lindzey, 1970) have argued that
Horney's enduring legacy as a "neo-Adlerian" psychodynamic theorist

is evident from the collection of post–World War I–era papers that later generations of social scientists and laypersons would know as *Feminine Psychology* (1967). Other reviewers (e.g., Ewen, 1998) have contended that Horney's enduring legacy as a "neo-Freudian" psychodynamic theorist is evident from the trilogy of books on anxiety and neuroses that she published before, during, and after World War II—namely, *The Neurotic Personality of Our Time* (1937), *Our Inner Conflicts* (1945), and *Neurosis and Human Growth* (1950). At first glance, one might think that Horney ultimately abandoned her theory of feminine psychology (Paris, 1994). However, Horney never gave up her keen interest in gender and personality (Westkott, 1986). Indeed, further inspection of Horney's World War II–era scholarship reveals that Horney postulated societally influenced gender differences in neurotic responses to interpersonal anxiety (Gaines, 2020). Unfortunately, within relationship science, the relevance of Horney's theory (which we shall continue to designate as *feminine psychology*) to conflict resolution behaviors in close relationships has not always been recognized (e.g., Gaines, 2016/2018).

On the one hand, Horney's *New Ways in Psychoanalysis* (1939) is positioned outside the trilogy of books (Horney, 1939, 1945, 1950) that commonly are regarded as Horney's essential works on anxiety and neuroses (e.g., Westkott, 1986). On the other hand, in *The Meaning of Anxiety*, Rollo May (1950/1996) credited Horney's *New Ways in Psychoanalysis* with fleshing out the concept of *basic anxiety* as children's free-floating fear that arises from a conflict between (1) dependence upon parents for their security and (2) hostility toward parents for holding so much power over them. Just as Adler (1927) had argued that all children experience an inferiority complex in relation to parents, so too did Horney contend that all children experience basic anxiety in relation to parents (see Ewen, 1998). However, unlike Adler (who proposed a *need for social interest* as the master motive that underlies human behavior), Horney proposed a *need for anxiety reduction* as the master motive (as we noted in Chapter 2). Furthermore, unlike other "neo-Adlerian" psychodynamic theorists who emphasized the need for anxiety reduction (e.g., Fromm, 1956; Sullivan, 1953), Horney surmised that basic anxiety is triggered by children's hostility *in response to parents' arbitrary or capricious exertion of power over them* (see McClelland, 1985/1987).

Additionally, May (1950/1996) credited Horney's *New Ways in Psychoanalysis* (1939) with distinguishing between (1) the basic anxiety that

70 THE SELF IN RELATIONSHIPS

all children experience in response to actual hostility toward parents and (2) the *neurotic anxiety* that some (but not most, let alone all) adults experience in response to anticipated hostility from other persons within close relationships. Just as Adler (1927) had contended that some individuals (disproportionately women) have been socialized in such a manner that they continue to experience an inferiority complex throughout adulthood, so too did Horney argue that some individuals (disproportionately women) have been socialized in such a way that they continue to experience a conflict between (1) dependency upon significant others and (2) hostility toward significant others for holding power over them—*even when no objective basis exists for such a conflict within current voluntary relationships* (see C. S. Hall & Lindzey, 1970). However, unlike Adler (who proposed a *styles of life typology* including manifestations of an inferiority complex, superiority complex, or no complex), Horney proposed a *typology of neurotic responses to interpersonal difficulties* that emphasizes patterns of social-psychological dysfunctionality among some persons (detailed below; see also Gaines, 2020).

Horney's Neurotic Responses: Moving Toward, Moving Against, and Moving Away From Others

In *The Feminist Legacy of Karen Horney*, Marcia Westkott (1986) noted that Horney's (1937, 1945, 1950) trilogy of books on anxiety and neuroses identified three to four categories of behavioral responses to the neurotic form of interpersonal anxiety, although the specific number and (especially) terminology associated with the typology varied considerably across the trilogy. First, within *The Neurotic Personality of Our Time* (1937), Horney listed four types: (1) *indiscriminately seeking affection*; (2) *engaging in submissive or compliant behavior*; (3) *seeking power, prestige, and possession*; and (4) *withdrawal*. Second, within *Our Inner Conflicts* (1945), Horney consolidated the former categories of indiscriminately seeking affection and engaging in submissive/compliant behavior en route to creating a new, threefold typology: (1) *moving toward others*, (2) *moving against others*, and (3) *moving away from others*. Lastly, within *Neurosis and Human Growth* (1950), Horney provided yet another threefold typology: (1) *self-effacing solution(s)*, (2) *expansive solution*, and (3) *resigned solution*. Westkott synthesized Horney's various typologies as reflecting (1) *dependent*,

(2) *domineering*, and (3) *detached* behavioral tendencies—a list that sounds decidedly trait-like (see Allport, 1937/1951, 1961/1963).

Notwithstanding the virtues of Westkott's (1986) synthesis of Horney's (1937, 1945, 1950) shifting typologies regarding individuals' behavioral responses to neurotic anxiety, we shall use the terms *moving toward, moving against*, and *moving away from others* that Horney proposed in *Our Inner Conflicts* (1945). We believe that this version of Horney's typology strikes the optimal balance between (1) highlighting the interpersonal aspects of personality, which was not the case in *Neurosis and Human Growth* (Horney, 1950), and (2) limiting the number to three types, which was not the case in *The Neurotic Personality of Our Time* (Horney, 1937). Also, the moving toward/moving against/moving away from others typology has emerged as the default Horneyan classification scheme among clinical practitioners (see Millon, 1996). By the same token, some personality researchers have opted to use still other terms, such as the *compliant, aggressive*, and *detached* distinctions within the continuous-item Horney-Coolidge Tridimensional Inventory (HCTI; Coolidge et al., 2001). All in all, we are swayed by Horney's expectations that (1) women are more likely to be classified as moving toward others, whereas men are more likely to be classified as (2) moving against and (3) moving away from others (Gaines, 2020).

As Westkott (1986) pointed out, Horney's (1945) neurotic personality types of moving toward others and moving against others can be interpreted as individuals' attempts to engage in problem-solving behavior, whereas moving away from others can be interpreted as individuals' refusal to engage in problem-solving behavior. In addition, one of the most relevant social/personality theories for the purposes of the present book—that is, Jerry Wiggins's (1991) interpersonal circumplex theory of personality and social behavior (which will be our leading theory from Chapter 5 onward)—focuses on the implications of moving toward and moving against others for individuals' giving of interpersonal resources (i.e., affection and respect within social and personal relationships; see also Gaines, 2016/2018). Given that Wiggins viewed the Horneyan types of moving toward and moving against others as analogous to the respective continuous dimensions of *positive aspects of masculinity and femininity*, which appear in Sandra Bem's (1981) gender schema theory (which we will cover to some extent in the present chapter) as well as Janet Spence's (1993) multifactorial gender identity theory (which we will cover to a lesser extent in the present chapter), we will put aside Horney's category of moving away from others for the time being.

72 THE SELF IN RELATIONSHIPS

From Horney's Feminine Psychology to Bem's Gender Schema Theory: Positive Aspects of Masculinity and Femininity Among Nonclinical Populations

Horney (1945) proposed her typology of behavioral responses to the neurotic version of interpersonal anxiety largely as a means toward guiding psychotherapists in their work with clients (Paris, 1994). Indeed, Horney's typology is compatible with many neo-Freudian practitioners' goal of helping clients resolve interpersonal difficulties within social and personal relationships (Millon, 1996). Nonetheless, Horney's (1967) overarching theory of feminine psychology is depicted as applicable to women (and men) outside as well as within clinical settings (Westkott, 1986). Therefore, one might expect the neurotic responses of moving toward and moving against others among individuals in clinical populations to be complemented by non-neurotic behavioral tendencies of moving toward and moving against others among individuals in nonclinical populations (see Gaines, 2020). Unfortunately, even the neo-Adlerian personality theory that offers the most overtly non-neurotic typology of behavior in close relationships—that is, Erich Fromm's (1956) didactic humanism (which not only emphasizes the implications of interpersonal anxiety for individuals' experiences of isolation and weakness but also proposes a *ways of loving* typology)—bears little resemblance to Horney's typology (see Ewen, 1998).

In *The Lenses of Gender*, Bem (1993) credited Horney and several other feminist or proto-feminist psychodynamic theorists with influencing the development of the Bem Sex Role Inventory (BSRI; Bem, 1974), although Bem did not cite specific works such as Horney's *Feminine Psychology* (1967). Consistent with Horney's theory of feminine psychology—which, as we learned earlier in the present chapter, presupposes that (1) the (stereo)typical male possesses a set of socially desirable or positive personality characteristics that are worthy of envy by the (stereo)typical female and (2) the (stereo)typical female possesses a separate set of socially desirable or positive personality characteristics that are worthy of envy by the (stereo)typical male—Bem designed the BSRI to measure positive (but not negative) aspects of masculinity and femininity (Lenney, 1991). Notwithstanding her interest in clinical applications of the BSRI, Bem is best known for her research on positive masculinity and positive femininity among large nonclinical samples (see Donnelly & Twenge, 2017). Subsequently, Bem (1981) proposed her gender schema theory in an attempt to explain the impact of society on children's adoption of gender-related traits (Starr & Zurbriggen, 2017).

A *schema* is a cognitive framework in general (see R. Brown, 1965). In turn, a *gender schema* is a cognitive framework that is based upon individuals' psychological "maleness" or "femaleness" in particular (see R. Brown, 1986). Bem's (1981) gender schema theory places the construct of gender schema on par with the construct of *self-schema* (i.e., cognitive frameworks that are based upon individuals' knowledge that they are separate from—yet interconnected with—other aspects of their physical and social environments; Markus, 1977) in terms of importance among social cognition processes (Fiske & Taylor, 1991). Furthermore, Bem's theory posits that individuals differ in the extent to which they are *gender schematic* (i.e., tending to organize information about self and the world along rigid boundaries of masculinity and femininity) versus *gender aschematic* (i.e., tending *not* to organize information about self in the world along such inflexible boundaries; Gaines, 2020). Despite the emphasis on the unconscious in Horney's (1967) feminine psychology and other (proto-)feminist psychodynamic theories that helped pave the way for Bem's gender schema theory, Bem's musings on "schematic" versus "aschematic" individuals reflect Bem's interest in cognitive development alongside social and personality development (e.g., Bem, 1993).

Psychological Androgyny: Evidence of "Gender Aschematicity"(?)

Following Constantinople's (1973) landmark critique of previous surveys that purportedly measured masculinity and femininity as a single bipolar dimension (going as far back as the Attitude-Interest Analysis Test, or AIST; Terman & Miles, 1936), Bem's publication of the BSRI (1974) revolutionized research on gender-related traits by providing separate scales to measure the positive aspects of masculinity and femininity (Lenney, 1991). Bem was one of the first researchers to demonstrate that, when resulting positive masculinity scores are calculated separately from positive femininity scores, the two constructs often are uncorrelated with each other (Hoffman & Pasley, 1998). Additionally, by obtaining orthogonal scores on positive aspects of masculinity and femininity, Bem was in a position to propose that some men and some women possess high levels of both gender-related traits—in other words, some individuals might be *androgynous* (Hoffman, 2001).

74 THE SELF IN RELATIONSHIPS

Subsequently, Bem elaborated upon the construct of psychological androgyny as a centerpiece of her gender schema theory (1981), contending that androgynous individuals are especially likely to possess high levels of mental wellness and to navigate a wide range of interpersonal situations with relative ease (Leaper, 2017).

Even more revolutionary than Bem's (1974) conceptualization and measurement of androgyny was Bem's (1981) view that, not only do parents and other societal agents actively seek to teach their offspring to think of self and the world in terms of masculinity and femininity (thus reflecting the pervasive influence of *gender-schematic nations*), but also societal agents should *refrain* from socializing children in this manner, instead enabling children to develop as *gender-aschematic individuals* (Starr & Zurbriggen, 2017). During her early work on the BSRI, Bem (1974) operationalized gender-aschematic individuals as those men and women who scored equally high *or* equally low on positive masculinity and positive femininity (Hoffman & Pasley, 1998). However, following an empirical critique from Spence and colleagues (1975), Bem (1977) began to operationalize gender-aschematic individuals more narrowly as individuals who scored above the median for their gender on positive masculinity as well as positive femininity (Hoffman, 2001). In any event, having reoperationalized gender-aschematic individuals solely in terms of high positive masculinity plus high positive femininity, Bem (1981) eventually incorporated aschematicity into her gender schema theory (see also Bem, 1983).

Although Bem (1981) ultimately agreed with Spence et al. (1975) regarding the operationalization of androgyny (and, hence, gender aschematicity), Bem's gender schema theory retained another assumption that raised questions in its own right—namely, Bem operationalized gender schematicity as a single construct that encompassed (1) above-median scores on positive masculinity (but not positive femininity) among men *and* (2) above-median scores on positive femininity (but not positive masculinity) among women (Starr & Zurbriggen, 2017). In contrast, in their revision of Markus's (1977) *self-schema theory*, Hazel Markus and colleagues (1982) not only argued that (1) sex-typing on positive masculinity among men was *not* functionally equivalent to sex-typing on positive femininity among women but also argued that (2) separate schemas existed in *all* individuals regarding positive masculinity and positive femininity, with the important implication that aschematicity on positive masculinity must be assessed separately from aschematicity on positive femininity (see also Crane & Markus, 1982). As it turns out, Bem (1982) opted not to debate aschematicity or schematicity with Markus and colleagues, declaring that the lack of a shared definition for such constructs precluded further discussion.

Key Controversies Surrounding Bem's Conceptualization and Measurement of Psychological Androgyny

Not only did the would-be debate between Bem (1981) and Markus et al. (1982; see also Crane & Markus, 1982) regarding the proper conceptualization and measurement of gender aschematicity versus schematicity fizzle due to lack of engagement from Bem (1982), but also Bem subsequently opted not to mention Markus (let alone the point of controversy that Markus and colleagues had raised) in *The Lenses of Gender* (1993). Based on the nondebate between Bem and Markus with respect to aschematicity, one might be tempted to conclude that Bem's underlying construct of psychological androgyny emerged relatively unscathed (see Starr & Zurbriggen, 2017). However, a more accurate conclusion may be that the disparate theories of Bem, Markus, and other cognitively oriented psychologists concerning gender and social/personality development simply ended up coexisting over time (see Leaper, 2017). At any rate, Bem's construct of psychological androgyny has attained a status of venerability within the literature on gender and personality, due in large part to its association with feminist scholarship within the United States and other "Western" nations (Donnelly & Twenge, 2017). By the same token, certain controversies persist regarding psychological androgyny (Golden & McHugh, 2017).

Earlier in the present chapter, we observed that Bem (1974) originally operationalized psychological androgyny as little to no difference between individuals' scores on positive masculinity and femininity but subsequently reoperationalized androgyny as the combination of above-median scores for positive masculinity and positive femininity in comparison to other persons of the same gender (thus bringing the scoring procedure for the BSRI in line with scoring procedures for other post—women's rights movement—era inventories of gender-related traits; see also Sedney, 1981). However, scoring procedures for the BSRI *and* the other inventories that were published afterward have been criticized on the grounds that categories such as "androgynous," "masculine sex-typed," and "feminine sex-typed" (not to mention "masculine reverse sex-typed," "feminine reverse sex-typed," and

76   THE SELF IN RELATIONSHIPS

"undifferentiated") never should have been created on the basis of continuous scale scores for positive masculinity or positive femininity (Hoffman, 2001). Although some researchers have proposed the calculation of psychological androgyny by multiplying standardized scores for positive masculinity by standardized scores for positive femininity (e.g., J. Hall & Taylor, 1985), Bem never endorsed this option for the BSRI (e.g., Bem, 1993, 1998).

Also, earlier in the present chapter, we pointed out that Bem's (1981) gender schema theory touted psychological androgyny as conducive to individuals' mental wellness (see also Lips, 2017). Although we are not aware of any instance in which Bem explicitly drew a parallel between (1) her recommendation (e.g., Bem, 1983) that parents in particular teach children to be gender aschematic by cultivating positive aspects of masculinity *and* femininity as personality characteristics (thus promoting children's mental wellness) and (2) Horney's (1967) recommendation that societal agents in general make it possible for children to develop behavioral repertoires that are not subject to traditional gender role constraints (thus reducing children's helplessness and sense of danger in interpersonal relations with societal agents), one could argue that Bem's embrace of Horney's feminine psychology in the career-retrospective *The Lenses of Gender* (Bem, 1993) creates an opening for followers of Horney and Bem to integrate their respective theories in this manner (see Gaines, 2020). Unfortunately, results of studies using the BSRI (Bem, 1974) reveal that positive masculinity in itself—*not* androgyny (or positive femininity in itself)—is significantly associated with indices of mental wellness (e.g., high self-esteem, low depression; Golden & McHugh, 2017).

Lastly, although we have focused upon psychological androgyny throughout the present chapter, Bem's (1981) gender schema theory proposes that individuals' renouncing traditional assumptions about their possession of gender-related traits ideally should co-occur with individuals' renouncing traditional assumptions about their sexual orientation. We hasten to add that Bem's 1990s-era books—specifically, the aforementioned *The Lenses of Gender* (1993) and the autobiographical *An Unconventional Family* (1998)—encourage individuals and societies to let go of preconceptions concerning fixed categories of sexual orientation (Golden & McHugh, 2017). Nonetheless, according to some reviewers (e.g., R. Brown, 1986), Bem's writings during the late 1970s and early 1980s hinted that *psychological* androgyny covaried with *sexual* androgyny (e.g., Bem, 1978). By and large, Bem's followers sidestepped the controversy over hypothesized links between psychological androgyny and sexual androgyny; in a review of the literature on gender-related traits during the early 1990s, Lenney (1991) did not identify a single study using the BSRI (Bem, 1974) that addressed the issue, even though other controversies that we have mentioned in the preceding paragraphs (e.g., trait categorization, links to mental wellness) *were* addressed.

Psychological Androgyny: *Not* Optimal for Pro-Relationship Behaviors in General(!)

In the Preface to *The Lenses of Gender*, Bem (1993) made the following observation regarding her own marriage at the time: "Living in a heterosexual marriage and rearing two children have ... contributed to my feminist politics by prompting me to theorize about, and experiment with, both egalitarian relationships and gender-liberated child-rearing" (p. viii). Notwithstanding the lack of any acknowledgment regarding the importance of emotional intimacy as distinct from sexual intimacy within her own marriage, this observation suggests that Bem's (1974) construct of psychological androgyny and Bem's (1981) gender schema theory influenced (and were influenced by) the interpersonal dynamics underlying her relationship (see also Bem, 1998, reflecting on her since-ended marriage). In the absence of formal predictions from Bem's gender schema theory, we draw upon Bem's anecdotal account of her marital relationship dynamics in particular, as we speculate that psychological androgyny ideally should promote individuals' efforts toward pro-relationship behaviors in close relationships (see also Gaines, 2016/ 2018). We are unaware of comparable hypotheses regarding psychological androgyny and pro-relationship behaviors that might be derived, directly or indirectly, from Horney's (1967) feminine psychology (see Gaines, 2020).

By the mid-1980s, results of studies on gender-related traits (as measured by the BSRI; Bem, 1974) and close relationship processes repeatedly revealed a null effect for psychological androgyny (Ickes, 1985). Rather, the cumulative evidence suggested that positive femininity in itself—*not* androgyny (or positive masculinity in itself)—promotes individuals' pro-relationship behavior (see also Spence et al., 1985). At first glance, the positive effect for socially desirable/positive femininity on pro-relationship behavior stands in contrast to the null effect for positive femininity on individuals' mental wellness (as described earlier in the present chapter). By the same token, the null effect for socially desirable/positive masculinity on pro-relationship behavior

78 THE SELF IN RELATIONSHIPS

seems to be at odds with the aforementioned positive effect of socially de-
sirable/positive masculinity on individuals' mental wellness. Throughout
the remainder of the present chapter, we shall keep in mind the possibility
that positive femininity is more likely to emerge as a consistent covariate of
individuals' conflict resolution behaviors within close relationships (e.g.,
responses to dissatisfaction, responses to partners' anger/criticism; see
Rusbult, 1993) than is positive masculinity.

In a review of the literature on links between gender roles and relationship dynamics, Ickes (1993) proposed a twist on the androgyny-promotes-
relationships premise: Perhaps it is not a matter of the extent to which
psychological androgyny per se promotes pro-relationship behavior, but
rather a matter of the extent to which pairings of "sex-typed" partners
(i.e., men who score high on positive masculinity, but not positive femininity, compared to other men, paired with women who score high on positive femininity, but not positive masculinity, compared to other women)
yield short-term benefits but long-term costs, at least within heterosexual
relationships (see also Huston, 2009). As it happens, Ickes did not mention
Horney's (1967) feminine psychology or Bem's (1981) gender schema theory
regarding the possible consequences of "sex-typed" pairings. However, Ickes
did cite a series of studies by Bem (i.e., Bem, 1974; Bem & Lenney, 1976; Bem
& Lewis, 1975) in proposing that (1) "sex-typed" pairings may seem attrac-
tive to partners during the establishment of heterosexual relationships, yet
(2) those pairings may create social-psychological contexts in which partners engage in stereotypical behavioral patterns that foster incompatibility,
thus threatening the stability of heterosexual relationships over time (J.
G. Holmes, 2000).

Positive Masculinity and Positive Femininity (but *Not* Psychological Androgyny): Relevant to Responses to Dissatisfaction

In their major revision of Timothy Leary's (1957) *interpersonal circumplex
model of traits*, Jerry Wiggins and Ana Holzmuller (1978) equated Bem's
(1974) gender-related trait of positive masculinity with the agentic
or intrapersonally oriented trait of *dominance*, whereas Wiggins and
Holzmuller equated Bem's gender-related trait of positive femininity with
the communal or interpersonally oriented trait of *nurturance* (see also

Wiggins & Holzmuller, 1981). At the time that Wiggins and Holzmuller originally published their version of the interpersonal circumplex model, the article in which Bem formally presented gender schema theory (1981) had not been published. Nonetheless, Wiggins and Holzmuller agreed with Bem's premise that positive masculinity and positive femininity are conceptually and empirically orthogonal constructs (Gaines, 2020). The major point of divergence between the respective views of Wiggins and Holzmuller versus Bem is that Wiggins and Holzmuller operationalized positive masculinity and positive femininity as the positive ends of Y and X axes, in that order, along a circular or circumplex model of *interpersonal traits*, whereas Bem operationalized positive masculinity and positive femininity as the building blocks of categorical *sex-role orientations* (Gaines, 2016/2018).

Building upon Wiggins and Holzmuller's (1978) interpersonal circumplex model of traits, Wiggins (1979) proposed an *interpersonal circumplex theory of traits and social behavior* that combines elements of Sullivan's (1953) interpersonal theory of personality (as interpreted by T. Leary, 1957) with elements of Uriel G. Foa and Edna B. Foa's (1974) *resource exchange theory* (a theory of behavior within social and personal relationships; see also Wiggins, 1980). U. G. Foa and E. B. Foa had posited that (1) both social/not-close and personal/close relationships frequently involve partners' reciprocity of *tangible commodities* (i.e., money, information, goods, and services), whereas (2) personal/close relationships (but *not* social/not-close relationships) routinely involve partners' reciprocity of *intangible commodities* (i.e., love and status; see also E. B. Foa & Foa, 1980). Having integrated Sullivan's theory with the Foas' theory, Wiggins hypothesized that (1) dominance/positive masculinity will be reflected in (a) individuals' *giving* of love (i.e., *affection*, or emotional acceptance) and (b) individuals' *denying* of status (i.e., *respect*, or social acceptance) toward other persons, whereas (2) nurturance/positive femininity will be reflected in (a) individuals' *giving* of love and (b) individuals' *giving* of status to other persons (see also Wiggins, 1991).

Drawing upon Wiggins and Holzmuller's (1978) interpersonal circumplex model of traits, Rusbult, Zembrodt, and Iwaniszek (1986) examined positive masculinity and positive femininity (measured via the BSRI; Bem, 1974) as predictors of responses to dissatisfaction (Rusbult et al., 1982) among individuals in romantic relationships (see also Rusbult, 1993). Rusbult et al. did not allude to any other theory that seemingly would be relevant to their set of studies (e.g., the gender schema theory of Bem, 1974; the interpersonal theory of Thibaut & Kelley, 1959). Instead, Rusbult and colleagues

80 THE SELF IN RELATIONSHIPS

used Wiggins's theory as the basis for predicting that (1) positive masculinity would be reflected in (a) *high* levels of *active* (i.e., exit and voice) responses and (b) *low* levels of *passive* (i.e., loyalty and neglect) responses, whereas (2) positive femininity would be reflected in (a) *high* levels of *constructive* (i.e., voice and loyalty) responses and (b) *low* levels of *destructive* (i.e., exit and neglect) responses. Also, Rusbult et al. predicted that (3) gender would be a significant predictor of responses to dissatisfaction, whereby (a) women would tend to score higher in constructive responses than men, whereas (b) men would tend to score higher in destructive responses than women.

In partial support of their hypotheses across three studies, Rusbult, Zembrodt, and Iwaniszek (1986) found that (1) positive masculinity was (a) a marginal-to-significant positive predictor of active responses and (b) a marginal-to-significant negative predictor of passive responses, in two studies, whereas (2) positive femininity was (a) a marginal-to-significant positive predictor of constructive responses in all three studies but (b) virtually unrelated to destructive responses (with the exception of a significant negative effect for exit in one study). Additionally, concluding that gender was an inconsistent predictor, Rusbult and colleagues reported that (3) gender was (a) completely unrelated to constructive responses but (b) somewhat related to destructive responses (i.e., men scored marginally higher on neglect than did women in all three studies, and men scored significantly higher on exit than did women in one study). Finally, although sexual orientation was not a focal point in Rusbult et al.'s article, we note in passing that results for Studies 1 and 2 (in which all participants classified themselves as heterosexual) resembled each other to a greater degree than which they resembled results for Study 3 (in which roughly equal numbers classified themselves as heterosexual men, heterosexual women, gay men, and lesbian women).

The limited marginal-to-significant effects for gender on individuals' responses to dissatisfaction that Rusbult, Zembrodt, and Iwaniszek (1986) obtained across their three studies differ from the unequivocally nonsignificant results that Rusbult, Johnson, and Morrow (1986a, 1986b) obtained in two separate studies, at least for self-reported quantitative measures of dissatisfaction responses. Taking the results of Rusbult et al.'s additional studies into account, we recommend that relationship researchers avoid placing undue importance upon gender as a predictor of individuals' responses to dissatisfaction (e.g., making the unsupported assumption that women take on the role of "relationship managers" when interacting with male partners; for a discussion regarding the nuances of gender as reflected in close relationship processes, see C. Hendrick, 1988). Moreover, we encourage relationship researchers to quantify (if possible) what exactly gender as a separate construct is meant to explain that gender-related traits do not already explain regarding individuals' responses to dissatisfaction (e.g., if *gender-role attitudes* are presumed to be the operative constructs, then measuring gender-role attitudes alongside gender-related traits should be preferred over inferring gender-role attitudes solely on the basis of gender; see Spence & Helmreich, 1978).

The most consistent results in Rusbult, Johnson, and Morrow's (1986b) studies were the effects of positive femininity on constructive (i.e., voice and loyalty) responses to dissatisfaction. Perhaps it is not coincidental that Rusbult et al.'s most consistent findings also were the most overtly grounded in Wiggins and Holzmuller's (1978) interpersonal circumplex model of traits—specifically, positive femininity/nurturance is a communal trait that should be reflected positively in giving *socioemotional behaviors* (e.g., love and status as interpersonal resources; see E. B. Foa & Foa, 1980). Conversely, it might not be coincidental that Rusbult et al.'s least consistent findings also were the *least* overtly grounded in Wiggins and Holzmuller's model—namely, the model does *not* predict that gender will explain significant variance in socioemotional behaviors beyond the variance that gender-related/interpersonal traits explain (although one might be able to make such predictions from the gender schema theory of Bem, 1981). Lastly, we were surprised that Rusbult et al. obtained support for their predictions concerning positive masculinity/dominance as a predictor of *active* responses (rather than *constructive* responses) on the basis of Wiggins and Holzmuller's model (although, once again, one might be able to make such predictions from Bem's theory).

One set of unproposed hypotheses in Rusbult, Johnson, and Morrow's (1986b) studies that would not be logically derived from Wiggins and Holzmuller's (1978) interpersonal circumplex model of traits but *would* be logically derived from Bem's (1981) gender schema theory have to do with psychological androgyny: Androgynous individuals should score highest on constructive (i.e., voice and loyalty) responses and lowest on destructive (i.e., exit and neglect) responses (see Ickes, 1985). Although we have described results *as if* Rusbult et al. had retained the continuous scores for positive masculinity/dominance and positive femininity/nurturance (which is the way Rusbult et al. described the results in their abstract on p. 1), Rusbult and colleagues actually performed median splits on scores for the gender-related/

82 THE SELF IN RELATIONSHIPS

interpersonal traits. Nevertheless, Rusbult et al. *did* examine interaction effects between positive masculinity and positive femininity, obtaining virtually no advantage for androgyny (with the exception of androgynous men scoring especially high on loyalty, compared to other men, in one study). All things considered, psychological androgyny was irrelevant to Rusbult et al.'s pattern of results with regard to individuals' responses to dissatisfaction across the three studies.

Lastly, in Study 3 of Rusbult, Johnson, and Morrow's (1986b) article, results were reported concerning sexual orientation as a predictor of individuals' responses to dissatisfaction (although no hypotheses had been specified). With the exception of neglect (for which heterosexual men and heterosexual women scored significantly *higher* than did gay men and lesbian women, contrary to negative societal stereotypes against same-sex relationships), sexual orientation was unrelated to dissatisfaction responses. Moreover, Rusbult and colleagues did not obtain any interaction effects between gender and sexual orientation in Study 3, and gender-related traits (or, alternatively, categories of "sex-role orientation"; Bem, 1974) did not interact with gender or sexual orientation in predicting responses to dissatisfaction. In retrospect, Study 3 of Rusbult et al.'s article is noteworthy for the fact that it examined links between sexual orientation and responses to dissatisfaction; we are not aware of any previous studies that examined such links, although the aforementioned study by Rusbult et al. (1987) concerning self-esteem and responses to dissatisfaction included a footnote reporting a similar lack of association for any behavior except neglect (again, with heterosexual men and heterosexual women scoring *higher* in neglect than did gay men or lesbians; Jowett, 2020).

Beyond Psychological Androgyny: Positive Femininity (but *Not* Positive Masculinity) as a Predictor of Accommodation-Related Behaviors

In Chapter 2 of the present book, we covered Rusbult et al.'s (1991) initial set of studies on individuals' accommodation-related responses to partners' anger/criticism. Despite our emphasis on self-esteem as a (non)predictor of accommodation-related responses in Study 4 of Rusbult et al.'s article, it turns out that self-esteem was one of several individual-difference variables that Rusbult and colleagues measured. In the present chapter, we will review

Rusbult et al.'s results for positive masculinity and positive femininity (measured via the BSRI; Bem, 1974) as predictors of accommodation-related behaviors. At the outset, we note that Rusbult et al.'s research on gender-related/interpersonal traits and accommodation in close relationships was informed considerably by Thibaut and Kelley's (1959) interdependence theory as revised by Kelley and Thibaut (1978), but *not* by Bem's (1981) gender schema theory or Wiggins and Holzmuller's (1978) interpersonal circumplex model of traits as expanded into Wiggins's (1979) interpersonal circumplex theory of traits and social behavior. Thus, the theoretical grounding for Rusbult et al.'s research on gender-related traits and accommodation reflects a social-psychological perspective, rather than an individual-differences perspective (Gaines, 2016/2018).

Ironically, even though Rusbult and colleagues (1991) did not mention any personality theories in their Introduction, they made predictions regarding gender-related traits—in particular, that (1) positive masculinity will be *negatively* associated with accommodation, whereas (2) positive femininity will be *positively* associated with accommodation. These hypotheses are highly compatible with Bem's (1981) gender schema theory, as well as Wiggins and Holzmuller's (1978) interpersonal circumplex model of traits as expanded into Wiggins's (1979) interpersonal circumplex theory of traits and social behavior. However, Rusbult et al. described positive masculinity and positive femininity alongside self-esteem as "self-centeredness factors" (p. 1991, p. 57)—a description that evokes images of the self-aggrandizing attitude of narcissism (Raskin & Terry, 1988), instead of interpersonal traits (see Gaines, 2016/2018). Furthermore, Rusbult and colleagues included gender as an individual-difference, "self-centeredness factor" (predicting that women would score higher on accommodation than would men)—even though gender is a socially defined *group* variable (rather than an individual-difference variable; Wiggins, 1991).

Unlike the scores for positive masculinity and positive femininity in Rusbult et al.'s (1986) research on gender-related traits and responses to dissatisfaction, the scores for all continuous variables in Rusbult et al.'s (1991, Study 4) research on gender-related traits and accommodation were kept in their original (i.e., continuous) form. Subsequently, Rusbult et al.'s (1991) correlation and regression analyses were based on continuous scores for positive masculinity and positive femininity (as was the case for self-esteem, which we covered in Chapter 2). In terms of zero-order correlations, Rusbult and colleagues found that (1) positive masculinity was (a) a marginal *negative*

84 THE SELF IN RELATIONSHIPS

correlate of individuals' constructive (i.e., voice and loyalty) responses to partners' anger/criticism and (b) a marginal *positive* correlate of individuals' destructive (i.e., exit and neglect) responses to partners' anger and criticism, whereas (2) positive femininity was (a) a significant *positive* correlate of constructive responses and (b) a significant *negative* correlate of destructive responses. As for regression beta weights (with a total accommodation score as the criterion variable), (1) consistent with hypotheses, positive femininity was a significant *positive* predictor of accommodation, whereas (2) contrary to hypotheses, positive masculinity was unrelated to accommodation.

Although the abstract of Rusbult et al.'s (1991, p. 53) article does not mention gender, Rusbult and colleagues made the additional prediction that gender would be a significant predictor of individuals' responses to partners' anger/criticism, with women expected to display significantly *higher* levels of constructive (i.e., voice and loyalty) responses and significantly *lower* levels of destructive (i.e., exit and neglect) responses. (Rusbult et al. apparently did not ask participants to disclose their sexual orientation.) Drawing upon Kelley and Thibaut's (1978) revised version of Thibaut and Kelley's (1959) interdependence theory, Rusbult and colleagues reasoned that gender is simultaneously a "commitment factor" (i.e., women as more likely to commit themselves to long-term relationships than are men) *and* an "importance factor" (i.e., women as more likely to place importance upon close relationships than do men). However, across all six studies, Rusbult et al. concluded that gender was *not* a consistent predictor of individuals' constructive or destructive responses to partners' anger or criticism. In fact, across Studies 2 through 4 (the latter of which also included gender-related traits as predictors), women scored significantly lower that men on destructive *and* constructive accommodation-related responses(!).

Summarizing across (1) Rusbult et al.'s (1991, Study 4) research on gender-related traits and individuals' responses to partners' anger/criticism, combined with (2) Rusbult, Zembrodt, and Iwaniszek's (1986, Studies 1 through 3) previously mentioned research on gender-related traits and individuals' responses to relationship dissatisfaction, positive femininity consistently emerges as a significant positive predictor of individuals' conflict responses, whereas positive masculinity is not a consistent predictor of individuals' conflict responses. In turn, results from Rusbult's studies extend the narrative that emerged from the early years of relationship science regarding covariance between gender-related traits and "pro-relationship behaviors"—specifically, positive femininity as a positive influence on those behaviors (see Ickes, 1985). Interestingly, not only are Horney's (1967) feminine psychology and Bem's (1981) gender schema theory relevant to understanding links between positive femininity and "pro-relationship behaviors," but also the respective theorists' differing experiences in marriage helped to inform their theories (i.e., Horney's husband as reputedly low versus Bem's husband as reputedly high in stereotype-defying positive femininity; see also Makosky, 1990; McConnell, 1990).

The Legacy of Horney's Feminine Psychology (and Bem's Gender Schema Theory): Interpersonal Anxiety, Gender-Related Traits, and Conflict Resolution

In *Feminist Foremothers in Women's Studies, Psychology, and Mental Health*, editors Phyllis Chesler, Esther Rothblum, and Ellen Cole (1995) paid homage to the impact of Bem's (1981) gender schema theory in the aftermath of the "second wave" of feminism (associated with the latter-day women's rights movement of the late 1960s and early 1970s) by including a selected reading from Bem (1995). In turn, although Bem made only passing comments about Horney in *The Lenses of Gender* (1993), it is clear that Bem considered Horney's (1967) feminine psychology to be an important influence following the "first wave" of feminism (associated with the original women's rights movement of the late 19th century and early 20th century; see Westkott, 1986). Consistent with Bem's appreciation for Horney's proto-feminist perspective, in *Karen Horney: A Psychoanalyst's Search for Self-Understanding*, biographer Bernard Paris (1994) hailed Horney as a pioneering feminist-leaning psychodynamic theorist. In particular, Horney's challenge to Freud's (1933/1965) version of psychoanalytic theory offered a panoramic view of gender and personality (including positive and negative aspects of masculinity and femininity, among men and women) that proved to be remarkably prescient (see Walsh et al., 2014).

On a related note, in *New Ways in Psychoanalysis*, Horney (1939) argued that the experience of neurotic and non-neurotic versions of interpersonal anxiety may prompt individuals to respond on the basis of perceived threats to core aspects of themselves (Paris, 1994). Consequently, if any threatened aspects of individuals' selves involve individuals' set of self-conceptions regarding gender, then Horney's (1967) feminine psychology would lead one to expect the development of positive and negative aspects of masculinity and

86   THE SELF IN RELATIONSHIPS

femininity to reflect individuals' responses to interpersonal anxiety across an extended interval of time (Westkott, 1986). For instance, the chronic experience of *non-neurotic* anxiety might be especially likely to become manifested in individuals' development of *positive* aspects of masculinity and femininity, whereas the chronic experience of *neurotic* anxiety might be especially likely to become manifested in individuals' development of *negative* aspects of masculinity and femininity (Ewen, 1998). Bem's decision to focus on the implications of child-rearing for children's development of positive aspects of masculinity and femininity in her own research (Bem, 1974) and theorizing (Bem, 1981) is consistent with Horney's theory (even though Bem did not make that connection explicit; Gaines, 2020).

Lastly, in *The Lenses of Gender*, Bem (1993) identified gender schema as cognitive structures that might help account for the roles of positive masculinity and positive femininity in mediating the impact of non-neurotic interpersonal anxiety on individuals' behavior within close relationships (see Gaines, 2016/2018). To the extent that individuals conceive of themselves and their social environments regarding degrees of compliance with societally prescribed gender norms, Bem's (1981) gender schema theory suggests that parents not only tend to play an active role in encouraging offspring to think of self and the world in terms of masculinity versus femininity but also may impose psychological and other sanctions against offspring who exhibit reluctance to engage in gender-stereotypical cognitive and behavioral processes (thus increasing the likelihood that offspring will experience neurotic anxiety, though offspring might not necessarily cultivate *negative* aspects of masculinity or femininity; see Fiske & Taylor, 1991). All things considered, the contributions of Horney's feminine psychology and Bem's gender schema theory to relationship science have been substantial, though often unheralded (a critique that could be applied to the influence of proto-feminist and feminist theories in general within relationship science; see Duck, 1994).

Prelude to Chapter 4

As one reads the latter portion of Horney's *Feminine Psychology* (1967), and as one reads the entirety of Bem's *The Lenses of Gender* (1993), one notices the emphasis that both (proto)feminist perspectives place upon the impact of culture upon individuals' social and personality development (Gaines,

2020). Some followers of Horney and Bem (e.g., Gaines, 2016/2018) regard the prioritization of cultural influences on individuals' personality characteristics and accompanying behavior toward significant others as entirely appropriate for relationship science, in which the incorporation of cultural constructs into theoretically informed models of personality and interpersonal dynamics has not proceeded at a pace that one might expect for such a young and vibrant field (especially in the midst of breathtaking cultural change around the world; see Goodwin, 2009). However, not all relationship scientists would necessarily agree with such a positive evaluation of culturally oriented theorizing and research on personality and interpersonal dynamics (see Gaines, 2017/2018). Additionally, not all relationship scientists would necessarily agree with the assumption that gender-related traits mediate the effects of culture upon individuals' behavior toward their partners (see C. T. Hill, 2019).

Despite the "classic" status of Horney's (1967) feminine psychology and the "modern classic" status of Bem's (1981) gender schema theory within personality psychology, both culturally oriented theories are not mentioned in *The Oxford Handbook of Personality and Social Psychology* (edited by Deaux & Snyder, 2012); the only indirect acknowledgment of their influence comes from Pettigrew and Cherry's (2012) chapter, which briefly alludes to post-1960s/1970s-era feminist scholarship on gender and personality. In contrast, biologically oriented theories (which go back at least as far as the version of psychoanalytic theory by Freud, 1900/1965) are well represented within that same handbook, such as Jung's (1921/1971) analytical psychology and the version of factor-analytic trait theory by Robert McCrae and Paul Costa (2003/2006) within Fleeson's (2012) chapter—complete with the claim that the *"Big Five" traits* of McCrae and Costa are up to 50% heritable(!). Even more relevant to the present book, within *The Oxford Handbook of Close Relationships* (edited by Simpson & Campbell, 2013), the chapter by McNulty (2013) regarding personality and close relationships devotes considerable attention to McCrae and Costa's "Big Five" model, whereas gender-related traits as conceptualized by Bem are nowhere to be found.

The version of factor-analytic trait theory that McCrae and Costa (2003/2006) developed is so popular within personality psychology than an entire edited volume—namely, *The Oxford Handbook of the Five Factor Model* (edited by Widiger, 2017)—was devoted to McCrae and Costa's theory. Consequently, in Chapter 4 of the present book, we will delve into McCrae and Costa's version of factor-analytic trait theory with the goal of identifying studies of the "Big Five" traits as predictors of conflict resolution behavior in close relationships. Along the way, we will also consider Jung's (1921/1971) analytical psychology, for which the trait of extraversion has been subsumed by McCrae and Costa's version of factor-analytic trait theory (as well as the versions of factor-analytic trait theory by Cattell, 1943, and Eysenck, 1970) but remains popular within personality psychology (Gaines, 2020). Notwithstanding the ubiquitous nature of McCrae and Costa's "Big Five" model in particular, we will also examine the claim by McCrae and Costa that the respective sets of traits are relatively impervious to cultural and other environmental influences—a claim that has been vigorously challenged by some personality psychologists (e.g., Munafo, 2009).

4

The "Big Five" Traits as Reflected in Conflict Resolution Behaviors

Synopsis: In the present chapter, we examine Jung's analytical psychology as derived largely from Freud's version of psychoanalytic theory (especially regarding the id, ego, and superego as constituents of personality structure, reconstrued respectively as personal unconscious, personal conscious, and personal/collective unconscious) and as diverging greatly from Freud's theory by introducing the collective unconscious and its manifestations, whether direct (e.g., the *Self* and *Anima/Animus* as archetypes that are common to all humans) or indirect (e.g., mother and father complexes that are unique to individuals); Jung's construct of libido, a form of psychic energy that was de-sexualized in comparison to Freud's construct of the same name; Jung's construct of introversion versus extraversion (described as "attitudes" or, more correctly, directions of libido flowing inward versus outward) as a typology, which subsequently was recast as the continuous trait of extraversion that routinely appears in versions of factor-analytic trait theory by Eysenck, Cattell, McCrae/Costa, and Lee/Ashton, among others; research yielding inconsistent results with regard to extraversion as a predictor of "pro-relationship" behaviors; spotlight on McCrae and Costa's version of factor-analytic trait theory, perhaps the best-known theory that includes a "five-factor model" (comprising the "universal" traits of openness to experience, conscientiousness, extraversion, agreeableness, and neuroticism) at its core; controversy over McCrae and Costa's increasing emphasis on the presumed "heritability" of all "Big Five" traits, with a corresponding lack of acknowledgment regarding familial, cultural, and other "external" influences on individuals' personality development; our proposal of a "gender-plus" variation on McCrae's factor-analytic trait theory, incorporating elements of Spence's multifactorial gender identity theory in order to develop the construct of the gendered self-concept (and, in the process, to reintroduce the prospect of "external" influences on individuals' personality and social development); research on "Big Five" traits in

The Self in Relationships. Stanley O. Gaines, Jr., Oxford University Press. © Oxford University Press 2023.
DOI: 10.1093/oso/9780197687635.003.0004

90 THE SELF IN RELATIONSHIPS

addition to extraversion as predictors of "pro-relationship" behaviors, with consistently negative effects for neuroticism, (somewhat) consistently positive effects for extraversion, and no effects for conscientiousness or openness to experience; and research on two of the "Big Five" traits as predictors of "automatic accommodation," with agreeableness emerging as a positive influence (and conscientiousness as a noninfluence); and we provide a prelude to Chapter 5, which details Wiggins's conceptualization of dominance and nurturance as interpersonal traits.

[Women's] discontentment [with the traditional female gender role] has two main reasons. One is that in a culture in which human relationships are so generally disturbed it is difficult to attain happiness in love life (by that I do not mean sexual relations). The other is that this situation is likely to create inferiority feelings. Sometimes the question is raised whether in our culture men or women suffer more from inferiority feelings. It is difficult to measure psychic quantities, but there is this difference: [A]s a rule man's feeling of inferiority does not arise from the fact that he is a man; but woman often feels inferior merely because she is a woman.

—Karen Horney,
New Ways in Psychoanalysis (1939, p. 116)

In addition to putting females at risk for giving themselves too little priority in relationships with others, [an] androcentric and gender-polarizing way of looking at the self also puts males at risk for giving themselves too much priority in relationships with others. Specifically, it predisposes males to reject any ways of being and behaving that put them in a subordinate position—a predisposition that is exaggerated whenever the more dominant position is to be held by a woman. It also predisposes males to elaborate any ways of being or behaving that put them in a more dominant or powerful position.

—Sandra L. Bem,
The Lenses of Gender (1993, p. 158)

As Rendon (2008) noted, in *Neurosis and Human Growth*, Horney (1950) proposed that all individuals possess a *real self* that is accessible to consciousness and can be fully realized under optimal social and psychological conditions (e.g., receiving consistent social support from family members and other societal agents over time). However, as Shabad (2020) pointed out,

Horney added that repeated exposure to excesses of power (and shortages of love) from societal agents can lead individuals to develop an unconscious *ideal self* that consists of unfulfilled fantasies that cannot be attained. Regarding gender, Westkott (1990) emphasized Horney's view that girls are more likely than boys to be socialized in such a way that they pursue the neurotic solution of moving toward others in the absence of assurances of safety or security from the other persons in question. On a related note, O'Connell (1990) concluded that Horney's evolving views on the self had remained gender aware, given Horney's belief that patriarchal societies often require that girls and women (rather than boys or men) seek solace from precisely the persons who pose the gravest threats to physical and psychological selfhood. Thus, it is little wonder that (as indicated by the quote from Horney [1939] cited above) females may be made to feel inferior to men.

According to Horney's (1967) feminine psychology, if girls and women are socialized to respond to societal agents' unbridled exertion of power to *move toward* others (even when those "others" are dangerous and may cause girls and women to feel even more helpless in the process), then boys and men are socialized to respond to analogous displays of power from societal agents by pursuing the neurotic solutions of *moving against* or *moving away* from others (E. Jordan, 1995). Consequently, males' as well as females' social and personality development may be shaped negatively by external forces within families and within societies at large—a theme that also emerges in Bem's (1981) gender schema theory (as reflected in the quote from Bem [1993] cited above). Although Bem's theory does not comment as extensively upon the self as does Horney's theory, one notices an emphasis on gender as more central to the self-concepts of some individuals (i.e., "masculine sex-typed" boys and men, "feminine sex-typed" girls and women) compared to other persons (i.e., gender-aschematic boys, girls, men, and women) within Bem's theory (Makosky, 1990). Of course, as we observed in Chapter 3, many individuals do not fit neatly within the categories of "sex-typed" and "androgynous" (see also Hoffman, 2001).

In contrast to Horney's (1967) psychodynamically oriented feminine psychology, Carl Jung's (1921/1971) similarly psychodynamic analytical psychology has been criticized by some reviewers (e.g., Barone-Chapman, 2014) as "masculine psychology" (like the version of psychoanalytic theory by Freud (1900/1965). Additionally, in contrast to Bem's (1981) trait-leaning gender schema theory, Robert McCrae and Paul Costa's (2003/2006) more thoroughly trait-oriented version of factor-analytic trait theory has been

92   THE SELF IN RELATIONSHIPS

criticized by some reviewers (e.g., W. Wood & Eagly, 2002) for failing to take differing socialization experiences of males versus females into account. Accordingly, in the process of reviewing the literature on extraversion in particular (as championed by Jung) and the "Big Five" traits in general (as promoted by McCrae and Costa) as predictors of conflict resolution behavior, we will keep in mind critiques of Jung's analytical psychology and McCrae/Costa's version of factor-analytic trait theory as less "universal" than the respective theorists might have believed. Advance notice: "Big Five" traits have been examined in only one study (Perunovic & Holmes, 2008) concerning an experimenter-induced simulation of conflict resolution behavior (i.e., *automatic accommodation*; Yovetich & Rusbult, 1994, Study 2).

Horney and Beyond: Jung's Analytical Psychology

In *Neurosis and Human Growth*, Horney (1950) identified the *actual self* as the self that exists in individuals' consciousness at the present time, which is not necessarily synonymous with the real self (which *could* exist in consciousness but may be submerged within the unconscious) *or* the ideal self (an illusion that is responsible for submerging the real self within the unconscious among neurotic persons; Alvarez-Segura et al., 2015). According to Horney, when neurotic individuals fail to meet the unspoken yet overwhelming demands of the ideal self, those individuals frequently respond by developing narcissistic tendencies that inflate self-esteem over the short term (even while glossing over felt inadequacies over the long term; Neff, 2003). In turn, narcissistic tendencies often lead neurotic individuals to reject efforts at intervention by therapists (Britton, 2004). Via formal psychoanalysis by clinicians or via informal self-analysis, individuals' path toward non-neurotic responses to interpersonal anxiety lies in the re-emergence of the real self into consciousness (and subsequent alignment of the actual self with the real self; Rendon, 2008). Fortunately, as is evident from Horney's *Self-Analysis* (1942), some individuals need not enter into therapy in order to obtain such insight (Westkott, 1990).

A perusal of several books by Horney (1937, 1939, 1942, 1945, 1950) reveals that Horney was a proto-humanist, influencing *self-actualization theorists* such as Carl Rogers (1961) and Abraham Maslow (1968; see O'Connell, 1990). However, Horney's focus on anxiety reduction as a master motive has led to the widespread (mis)perception that Horney was comparatively less concerned about the fulfillment of human potential (see DeRobertis, 2008). As time progressed, Horney wrote increasingly about *self-realization*—a construct that, labeled as *individuation*, also was part and parcel of Carl Jung's (1921/1971) *analytical psychology* (Horne et al., 2000). Like Horney, Jung contended that theories about the psychology of women (or men) likely will be influenced by the theorists' own gender-relevant social and psychological experiences (Hubback, 1978). Nonetheless, some reviewers (e.g., Young-Bruehl, 2009) have argued that both Jung's and Horney's theories contain elements of feminist-leaning insight into self-realization for women and men alike. For example, Jung's construct of the *true self* (analogous to Horney's construct of the real self) as distinct from the *false self* (analogous to the *ideal self*) acknowledges the possibility of "masculine" and "feminine" qualities in all persons (see Schlegel & Hicks, 2011).

To a greater extent than one finds in neo-Freudian psychodynamic personality theories (e.g., the interpersonal theory of Sullivan [1953]; the feminine psychology of Horney [1967]), Jung's (1921/1971) analytical psychology largely retains the Freudian personality constructs of id (renamed as the *personal unconscious*), ego (sometimes renamed as the *personal conscious*), and superego (renamed as the *persona* or *collective conscious*) but adds the *collective unconscious* to account for species-wide lessons in life that ostensibly have been transmitted across generations (Gaines, 2020). Jung's theory is unique in its separation between presumed building blocks of the collective unconscious (i.e., the *archetype*, or "a universal thought form [idea] which contains a large element of emotion"; C. S. Hall & Lindzey, 1970, p. 84) and id/personal unconscious (i.e., the *complex*, or "an organized group or constellation of feelings, thoughts, perceptions, and memories"; C. S. Hall & Lindzey, 1970, p. 82). In the present chapter, we shall focus upon one archetype (i.e., the species-level *Self*, with a capital "S" to distinguish it from the individual-level self) and two complexes (i.e., the *anima* and the *animus*, respectively representing the "feminine" qualities in every man and the "masculine" qualities in every woman; Ewen, 1998) in Jung's analytical psychology.

The Self as an Archetype

The construct of archetype may be the most controversial construct within Jung's (1921/1971) analytical psychology (Mills, 2019). According to Jung's theory, archetypes are transmitted biologically (rather than socially) from

94   THE SELF IN RELATIONSHIPS

ancestors to descendants within *Homo sapiens*; yet Jung did not offer any plausible explanation regarding *how* such image-based transmissions of species-wide information might occur, except to assert that metaphysical events likely are involved (Smythe & Baydala, 2012). In all fairness, Jung's "evidence" for the existence of archetypes ultimately is phenomenological, based largely on "data" such as the symbols and themes that have recurred in mythology across the millennia (Laughlin & Tiberia, 2012). Nevertheless, Jung's belief that archetypes transcend time and place leads one to wonder if biology is meant to be interpreted as a mediator of spiritual influences on individuals' acquisition of archetypes (and, hence, major aspects of individuals' personalities) within analytical psychology (Wollman, 1982). All things considered, Jung's theory implies that an entity akin to a "World-Soul" is responsible for the existence and accumulation of archetypes across time, as well as the appearance of those archetypes in the psyches of all living human beings (Brooks, 2013).

Among the multitude of archetypes that one finds within Jung's (1921/ 1971) analytical psychology, the uppercase-"S" *Self* archetype (also known as the *God-image archetype* or *central archetype*) is especially important to understanding individuals' personality development (Coward, 1989). For example, in Jung's view, the *Self* archetype serves an essential organizing function by offering a cohesive core of meaning that binds all other archetypes (e.g., Great Mother, Old Wise Man) within the collective unconscious of each individual (Henderson, 1985). As the primary conduit for individual souls (as derived from the World-Soul) to be manifested in all persons, according to Jung's analytical psychology, the *Self* archetype opens a window from the collective unconscious into individuals' personal conscious or ego (Anderson, 2021). In turn, during the first 30 years of individuals' lives, the development of the ego gradually paves the way for the emergence of individuals' consciousness regarding the lowercase-"s" self (i.e., the totality of individuals' psyches; see Redfearn, 1977). Lastly, to the extent that the *Self* enables individuals to attain their own sense of selfhood, those individuals will be in a position to appreciate "otherness" and to develop intimate relationships with fellow human beings (Urban, 2008).

In *Aion: Researches into the Phenomenology of the Self*, Jung (1959/1975) described the divinely given, uppercase-"S" *Self* as an entity that is worthy of individuals' awe, immortal and beyond humans' comprehension (Anderson, 2021). Conversely, in *Psychological Types*, Jung (1921/1971) depicted the lowercase-"s" self as not necessarily comprehensible in its full complexity, but at least existing as an inner entity toward which individuals may seek fulfillment or realization (Zinkin, 2008). Nevertheless, throughout *Aion* and *Psychological Types* (among other works), even understanding of the lowercase-"s" self may be hindered by individuals' lack of acknowledgment regarding the presence of the *shadow* (i.e., the "dark side" of individuals' psyches; Casement, 2003). Just as the ego may block individuals' access to awareness concerning the role of sexual and aggressive motives in their own behavior within Freud's (1923/1927) version of psychoanalytic theory, so too may the personal conscious or ego block individuals' access to awareness regarding the mere existence of the shadow within the unconscious (including collective as well as personal aspects; Moore, 1984). Fortunately, through the process of psychoanalysis (possibly including self-analysis), individuals may gain insight into their shadow (Gordon, 1987).

Child, Mother, and Father: Family-Related Archetypes Bound Together by the Self

As Driver (2013) pointed out, in *Aion: Researches into the Phenomenology of the Self*, Jung (1959/1975) identified Child, Mother, and Father as family-related archetypes that the Self binds together. Additionally, as Kradin (2009) noted, Jung's analytical psychology maintains that such organization of (other) archetypes by the Self or central archetype helps explain the evergreen nature of the family myth that has captured the imaginations of human beings throughout (and prior to) eras of civilization. Granted that the construct of archetype already is controversial, Merchant (2019) observed that an especially contentious belief within Jung's theory is the conviction that the archetypes composing the family myth are part of individuals' species-wide inheritance, existing prior to individuals' birth. At any rate, as Fordham (1977) observed, Jung's perspective on the role of archetypes in general (and family-related archetypes in particular) in facilitating the developmental process of individuation or lowercase-"s" self-realization—including individuals' encounters with the "bright"/positive and "dark"/negative sides of uppercase-"S" Self, Mother, and Father over time—is most fully articulated in *Symbols of Transformation* (1956).

Within the essays that were published together as *Psyche and Symbol*, Jung (1958) devoted special attention to the uppercase-"C" Child archetype (also known as the child motif or Divine Child; Fortune, 2003). According to

96   THE SELF IN RELATIONSHIPS

Jung's analytical psychology, the magical/mythical Child is present within the collective unconscious of all persons from birth onward, potentially available to the personal conscious or ego during major crossroads in individuals' lives, from chronological childhood through elderly adulthood (Wesley, 2019). However, in Jung's theory, individuals' accessibility to the Child is unsystematic, occurring without (or despite) any active effort on individuals' part (although therapists ostensibly can play a part in bringing the Child into individuals' consciousness; see Merchant, 2019). In any event, within Jung's analytical psychology, the Child may assume various forms (e.g., Hero/Savior, Orphan, Little Big [Wo]Man) at the societal level (e.g., folklore) and individual level (e.g., dreams; see Mercer, 2003). Regardless of the particular form or context in which the Child appears, this archetype frequently involves the possession of omnipotence/supernatural abilities (presumably bestowed by a Creator) and may seem indistinguishable from the Self archetype in individuals' conscious experience (Ekstrom, 2018).

Taking into account the distinction between "bright" and "dark" aspects of all family role archetypes as rendered by Jung in *Symbols of Transformation* (1956), particularly when one considers the overall positivity of the uppercase-"C" Child archetype, one is struck by the starkness of the duality between the Good Mother and the Terrible Mother aspects of the uppercase-"M" Mother or Great Mother archetype (Fordham, 1977). From the standpoint of Jung's analytical psychology, the Good Mother portion of the Mother archetype can be very positive (e.g., Divine Mother/Holy Mother), whereas the Terrible Mother portion of the Mother archetype can be quite negative (e.g., Death Mother/Devouring Mother; see Griessel & Kotze, 2009). Like the Child archetype, the Mother archetype presumably is present in the collective unconscious of all persons at birth; according to Jung's theory, the archetypes cumulatively prepare all individuals to (1) form images of their in-the-flesh mothers and (2) display particular behaviors toward their in-the-flesh mothers during infancy, such as crying and sucking (see Weitz, 1976). However, Jung's analytical psychology implies that the Mother archetype must recede in importance over time in order for the Child archetype to give way to the Self archetype (thus enabling individuation to proceed; Norby, 2021).

Just as one detects a bipolarity between the Good Mother and Terrible Mother aspects of the uppercase-"M" Mother or Great Mother archetype, so too does one notice a bipolarity between the Good Father and Bad Father aspects of the uppercase-"F" Father or Great Father archetype in Jung's analytical psychology (Griessel & Kotze, 2009). In *Answer to Job* (Jung,

1955) and (to a lesser extent) *The Structure and Dynamics of the Psyche* (Jung, 1972), Jung alluded to extreme versions of the Good Father (e.g., Divine/ Holy Father) and the Terrible Father (e.g., Death Father/Devouring Father; Driver, 2013). Although the *Father* archetype (like the *Child* and *Mother* archetypes) supposedly is contained within the collective unconscious of all human beings from birth onward, the degree to which individuals are predisposed to (1) form images of their actual fathers and (2) manifest specific behaviors toward their actual fathers is not clear from Jung's theory, possibly because of the depiction of *Father* as instrumental provider of tangible resources such as money and goods (as distinct from *Mother* as expressive provider of intangible resources such as affection/love and respect/status; Kradin, 2009). Nonetheless, Jung's theory suggests that the *Father* archetype must eventually recede in order for individuation to occur (Colman, 2000).

All in all, Jung's (1955, 1956, 1972) analytical psychology offers a less-than-flattering portrait of family-related archetypes (Kradin, 2009). On the one hand, if an individual's in-the-flesh father is present (both physically and psychologically speaking), then Jung's theory suggests that the specter of the Terrible Father portion of the uppercase-"F" *Father* archetype—which may loom even larger than the specter of the Terrible Mother part of the uppercase-"M" *Mother* archetype—may result in the individual seeking refuge in the relative comfort of the individual's in-the-flesh mother (Colman, 2000). On the other hand, if an individual's in-the-flesh father is absent (either physically or psychologically speaking), then Jung's analytical psychology suggests that the specter of the Terrible Mother portion of the *Mother* archetype may lead the individual to become overly dependent upon the in-the-flesh mother (notwithstanding the prospect that the actual mother may become domineering; Kullberg, 2019). Then again, Jung's theory implies that—in situations where actual mothers and actual fathers are absent (both physically and psychologically speaking)—individuals may be confronted by the variant of the uppercase-"C" *Child* archetype known as the Orphan, which (unless supplanted by the Hero variant) may reign supreme (Rothenberg, 2013).

Anima and *Animus*: Gender-Related Archetypes Bound Together by the *Self*

To the extent that the family myth within Jung's (1955, 1956, 1972) analytical psychology provides insight into the interpersonal relations of actual families,

98 THE SELF IN RELATIONSHIPS

that insight arguably is most enlightening with regard to the coexistence of the Child and Mother archetypes; less enlightening with respect to the coexistence of the Child and Father archetypes; and least enlightening with regard to the co-existence of the Mother and Father archetypes (see Kradin, 2009). Even when one takes into account the limitations that are inherent to the applicability of Jung's family myth beyond relational contexts that involve a nuclear family with one child, Jung's tendency to prioritize the understanding of sons' social and personality development over the understanding of daughters' social and per-sonality development means that the family myth cannot provide a balanced account of gendered development during infancy or childhood, let alone ado-lescence or adulthood (although neo-Jungian feminist perspectives have helped to counteract this imbalance; Rybak et al., 2000). At most, Jung's family myth offers a glimpse into the relational dynamics of individuals' actual families of origin but does not yield a comparable glimpse into the relational dynamics of individuals' actual families of procreation (Byock, 2015).

In order to comprehend the development of heterosexual male-female relationships on their own terms (and as the close relationships that serve as the bases for establishing families of procreation), one must examine the role of *syzygy*, a multifaceted construct that Jung (1956) described as "consist[ing] of three elements: the femininity pertaining to the man and the mascu-linity pertaining to the woman; the experience which man has of woman and vice versa; and, finally, the masculine and feminine archetypal image" (p. 21). Some reviewers (e.g., Allain-Dupre, 2005) have interpreted syzygy as a Hermaphrodite archetype in its own right that can emerge during child-hood with the effect of impeding individuals' "natural" sexual development in certain instances, although a direct reading of Jung does not support the view that syzygy can be reduced to a single archetype (e.g., Jung [1956, p. 21] also referred to a "divine syzygy" consisting of Jesus Christ and the Catholic Church). Other reviewers (e.g., McKenzie, 2006) have interpreted syzygy as a field within which the "contrasexual" archetypes of the Anima (a "feminine" archetype that is present in men but not women) and Animus (a "masculine" archetype that is present in women but not men) are located; in the present chapter, we will adopt the latter interpretation (see also Stein, 2008).

As von Raffay (2000) pointed out, the Anima archetype is second only to the Self archetype in terms of importance within Jung's (1956) analytical psy-chology. Moreover, as Colman (2018) noted, Jung described the Anima arche-type as exerting such a powerful influence in men's lives that the projection of the Anima upon particular in-the-flesh women outside the family of origin can fuel men's desire to conceive offspring and thus start a family of procreation. In addition, McKenzie (2006) observed that Jung's theory leads to the conclusion that men *must* project the Anima upon actual women outside the family of origin, lest men run the risk of "becoming" gay by projecting the Anima upon women within the family of origin (especially in-the-flesh mothers). If Jung's analytical psychology strikes one as heterosexist in light of such a sentiment (even when taking into account the era in which it was expressed), then Karaban's (1992) question about the construct of Anima (as well as the construct of Animus) as enlightening versus frightening is not as alarmist as one might otherwise think. However, Jung's theory ultimately contends that—putting aside sexuality—a reconciliation between the ego and the Anima is necessary for men to achieve self-realization or individuation (Rybak et al., 2000).

Unlike men's response to the unconsciously experienced allure of the Anima archetype, Jung's (1956) perspective on women's response to the unconsciously experienced demands of the Animus archetype can be summarized essentially as "damned if you do, damned if you don't" (see Karaban, 1992). To the degree that women are ruled by the Animus, according to Jung's analytical psychology, they may fall prey to an archetype that is characterized by numerous negative attributes (e.g., domineering, strident; Enns, 1994). Unfortunately, to the degree that women are *not* ruled by the Animus, Jung's theory suggests that women may end up alone and feeling bitter about themselves and other persons (Moreno, 1965). Therefore, just as Jung's analytical psychology emphasizes the desirability of men seeking a reconciliation between their ego and the Anima, so too does Jung's theory highlight the desirability of women seeking a reconciliation between their ego and the Animus in order for individuation to occur (Laughlin & Tiberia, 2012). Such a conclusion on Jung's part indicates that women may be able to channel positive aspects of the Animus after all (TePaske, 2017). For example, some feminists who seek to retain key features of Jung's theory (e.g., Liotta, 1997) have argued that the Animus inspires creativity in women.

We would be remiss at this juncture if we did not acknowledge the critique (e.g., Lindenfeld, 2009) that Jung's writings are littered with instances of anti-Semitism as well as heterosexism, and racism as well as sexism. Indeed, first-hand inspection of Jung's autobiographical *Memories, Dreams, Reflections* (1973) uncovers several passages in which Jung's stereotyping (if not prejudice) is on full display. By the same token, Jung's autobiography offers examples of Jung's willingness to figuratively venture outside his privileged self to try and understand how other persons who are not so privileged

100 THE SELF IN RELATIONSHIPS

might view him (and the "Western" worldview that he literally embodied). Additionally, Jung's autobiography provides instances in which Jung is willing to figuratively venture deep within his own psyche—not coincidentally, the source of such novel constructs as the *Anima* and *Animus* archetypes that appear in *Aion* (Jung, 1959/1975) and make up the subject matter of the present section. In retrospect, it is little wonder that the *Anima* archetype in particular occupies such a prominent role in Jung's analytical psychology; Jung was reflecting partly on his own unconscious as manifested in his relationships with specific in-the-flesh women (e.g., Helene Preiswerk, Sabina Spielrein, Toni Wolff; see Roberts, 2020).

From Collective Archetypes to Personal Complexes: Anima and *Animus* as Prime Examples

Despite the conviction with which Jung (1955, 1956, 1972) promoted the construct of archetypes, the notion that human beings inherit particular mental representations (or, at least, the propensity to form such representations) from their species-wide ancestors has been problematic from the outset (Merchant, 2019). However, if one conceives of species-wide *archetypes* broadly as presumed influences on the development of individual-specific *complexes*, then one need not agree with Jung's premise concerning the metaphysical or biological origins of archetypes in order to accept the possibility that cognitively accessible complexes in adolescence and adulthood result from largely unconscious processes that date back to individuals' infancy and childhood (Saunders & Skar, 2001). In effect, Jung's analytical psychology presents an elaborate origin story regarding the complexes that therapists can readily observe in their clients' words and deeds; that origin story is unnecessary for 21st-century followers of Jung (Skar, 2004). We hasten to add that some reviewers (e.g., Vaughn Becker & Neuberg, 2019) have argued that "internal representation systems" identified by modern-day cognitive neuroscientists and evolutionary psychologists may well serve the same "origin" function that Jung had hypothesized about archetypes.

Just as one may speak of *Mother, Father, Anima,* and *Animus* archetypes within the collective unconscious, so too may one speak of mother, father, anima, and animus complexes within the personal unconscious or id in Jung's (1955, 1956, 1972) analytical psychology (Saunders & Skar, 2001). However, the potential paths from archetypes to complexes in Jung's theory are varied in scope: *Mother* and *Father* archetypes likely influence the development of mother and father complexes; *Anima* and *Animus* archetypes probably influence the development of anima and animus complexes; *Anima* and *Animus* archetypes might influence the development of mother and father complexes; and mother and father complexes may influence the development of anima and animus complexes (among other possibilities; Rybak et al., 2000). Some reviewers (e.g., Griessel & Kotze, 2009) have contended that superordinate Masculine and Feminine archetypes subsume the *Mother*, *Father*, *Anima*, and *Animus* archetypes that we have kept separate in the present chapter. However, even if we do not adopt Masculinity and Femininity archetypes, we can interpret anima and animus complexes as reflecting individuals' expressions of positive and/or negative aspects of masculinity and/or femininity toward significant others (Colman, 1996).

Chow and Jeffery's (2018) Anima-Animus Continuum Scale (AACS) purportedly measures individual differences in the anima and animus complexes. The AACS is projective *and* quantitative, such that individuals are asked to indicate the extent to which particular relationship *Partners* strike them as "masculine," "feminine," or somewhere in between. The six-item AACS asks participants "where they thought P should be, where they thought P would place themself, how P looks, how P feels, what P does, and what P's interests are" (p. 267). Chow and Jeffery interpreted results of a principal component analysis concerning the AACS items (which yielded one higher-order dimension) as evidence for more than two sexes(!). Notwithstanding the fact that (as noted in Chapter 3) unifactorial masculinity-femininity surveys (e.g., the Attitude-Interest Analysis Test [AIST]; Terman & Miles, 1936) have been out of favor since the early 1970s, Chow and Jeffery (mis)interpreted the AACS as a replacement for self-reported gender-related trait surveys such as the Bem Sex Role Inventory (BSRI; Bem, 1974) and the Personal Attributes Questionnaire (PAQ; Spence & Helmreich, 1974; misattributed to Palan et al., 1999). In any event, we are unaware of any studies in which anima and animus complexes have been examined as predictors of "pro-relationship" behaviors.

From Archetypes to a De-Sexed "Libido": Psychic Energy as Ostensibly Reflected in Introversion/Extraversion

In the set of works that were published together as *The Structure and Dynamics of the Psyche*, Jung (1972) speculated that *libido* (i.e., psychic

102 THE SELF IN RELATIONSHIPS

energy) may be generated via conflicts between archetypes (as mentioned above, located within the collective unconscious) and *instincts* (i.e., biological needs, located within the personal conscious or id; see B. Hill, 2015). However, for several decades before *The Structure and Dynamics of the Psyche* was published, Jung had written extensively about libido, de-sexualizing this Freudian construct in the process (a departure from orthodox psychoanalytic theory that earned criticism as well as praise over the years; e.g., Burrow, 1917). Especially pertinent to the present chapter, in *Psychological Types*, Jung (1921/1971) contended that libido flows throughout conscious as well as unconscious aspects of individuals' lowercase-"s" selves (see Marshall, 1967). Nevertheless, like archetypes and instincts, libido can be regarded as originating in the unconscious within Jung's theory (Pylkko, 2019). Even during infancy, according to Jung's analytical psychology, the effects of (nonsexual) libido on individuals' behavior are evident (e.g., play as sparked by individuals' experience of joy or ecstasy; curiosity as sparked by individuals' interest or excitement; L. H. Stewart, 1987).

Psychological Types (Jung, 1921/1971) stands as Jung's most influential work, due to its popularization of *introversion* (reflecting an inward flow of psychic energy or libido) versus *extraversion* (reflecting an outward flow of libido) as a major personality construct (Gaines, 2020). Jung referred to introversion and extraversion as opposing "attitudes," although Jung's use of the term *attitude* varied markedly from most post–World War I–era uses of the term (see Gaines, 2016/2018). Rather, Jung equated "attitude" with a perceptual "orientation," such that he defined introversion as individuals' tendency to interpret events from a vantage point outside themselves, whereas he defined extraversion as a tendency to interpret events from a viewpoint within themselves (Millon, 1996). Jung assumed that such perceptual orientations are relatively stable at a given point in time, yet capable of change over the long term (Ewen, 1998). Although some clinicians have contended that introversion and extraversion *as described in general terms by Jung* are best understood as *motives*, academicians generally have argued that introversion and extraversion *as described in specific terms by Jung* (i.e., detailed psychological types) actually are best understood as *traits* (McClelland, 1985/1987).

As Jung acknowledged in *Psychological Types* (1921/1971, p. 147), he did not invent the personality dimension of introversion versus extraversion; Jung cited Furneaux Jordan's *Character as Seen in Body and Parentage* (1896) as invoking the introversion/extraversion dichotomy much earlier. Initial inspection reveals that Jordan's general definitions regarding introversion as a reflection-oriented tendency versus extraversion as an activity-oriented tendency are not far removed from contemporary definitions of the two poles (Gaines, 2020). However, further inspection indicates that Jordan viewed introversion as denoting *passion* (alongside reflection) versus extraversion as denoting *lack of passion* (alongside activity), whereas the added assumptions concerning passion (or lack thereof) are not commonly included in Jung's post–World War I–era account of the two poles (C. S. Hall & Lindzey, 1970). Moreover, Jordan made further distinctions between male and female introverts and extraverts, based largely on the premise that women were naturally more spontaneous than were men, whereas Jung's introversion/ extraversion distinction was expanded to take individual-level differences in *functions* or processes of thinking, feeling, sensation, and intuition (rather than a group-level difference in gender) into account (see Ewen, 1998).

Extraversion as Reflected in "Pro-Relationship" Behaviors

The Myers-Briggs Type Indicator (MBTI; Myers, 1962)—purportedly the most widely used personality inventory of all time—was based on Jung's (1921/1971) analytical psychology, especially Jung's constructs of "attitudes" (i.e., introversion and extraversion) and "functions" (i.e., thinking, feeling, sensation, and intuition; C. S. Hall & Lindzey, 1970). However, the MBTI classification scheme departs from Jung's theory by designating fourfold individual profiles as (1) introverted versus extraverted, (2) thinking versus feeling, (3) sensation versus intuition, *or* (4) perception versus judgment (Ewen, 1998). Notwithstanding the popularity of the MBTI outside academia, a variety of surveys that include continuous items measuring introversion versus extraversion among other constructs are more commonly used within academia; these surveys include the Eysenck Personality Inventory (EPI; Eysenck & Eysenck, 1968) as a measure of the "Big Two" traits; the Big Five Inventory (BFI; John et al., 1991) as a measure of the "Big Five" traits; and the *H*onesty/humility, *E*motionality/Neuroticism, e*X*traversion, *A*greeableness, *C*onscientiousness, and *O*penness to experience Questionnaire (HEXACO; Lee & Ashton, 2004) as a measure of the "Big Six" traits, just to name a few examples (Gaines, 2020).

In *Psychological Types*, Jung (1921/1971) contended that all individuals possess elements of introversion as well as extraversion; at one point in time, an individual's conscious experience of inward- versus outward-flowing libido is

104 THE SELF IN RELATIONSHIPS

the experience that clinical and personality psychologists would interpret as "traited" (Marshall, 1967). Moreover, in the posthumously published *The Red Book*, Jung (2009) argued that neither introversion nor extraversion signifies mental health (or lack thereof); ideally, individuals should be encouraged to reach a middle ground between the conscious and unconscious aspects of their personalities (Galipeau, 2013). Interestingly, Jung's *The Red Book*—portions of which subsequently were published in *Psychological Types*—reveals Jung's attempts to balance the introverted (for him, conscious) and extraverted (for him, unconscious) dimensions of his own personality (Odajynk, 2013). At any rate, Jung's analytical psychology suggests that most individuals' personality development includes a preponderance of conscious extraversion over unconscious introversion from childhood through early adulthood, followed by a preponderance of conscious introversion over unconscious extraversion from middle age through old age (Cochrane et al., 2014).

Notwithstanding Jung's (1921/1971) cautious stance regarding mental health implications of introversion versus extraversion, studies of individuals' *subjective well-being* (see Diener, 2000) indicate that extraversion (rather than introversion) not only promotes *positive affect* (Watson et al., 1988) but also is associated with higher levels of social activity and engagement within social and personal relationships (Lucas & Dyrenforth, 2006). However, to the extent that extraversion covaries with *narcissism* (Raskin & Terry, 1988), extraversion may be involved in promoting individuals' *establishment* of social and personal relationships over the short term while threatening the *maintenance* of social and (especially) personal relationships over the long term (W. K. Campbell & Green, 2008/2016). This "double-edged sword" that extraversion might confer to close or personal relationships could explain why empirical results concerning extraversion as a predictor of pro-relationship behaviors are mixed (i.e., exerting a positive effect in some studies, exerting no effect in other studies, and exerting a *negative* effect in still other studies; see McNulty, 2013). Unfortunately, we are unaware of any research directly addressing extraversion as reflected in conflict resolution behaviors (see W. K. Campbell et al., 2006).

From Jung's Analytical Psychology to McCrae and Costa's Factor-Analytic Trait Theory: (Additional) "Big Five" Traits

In a chapter from the *Handbook of Personality Psychology* (edited by R. Hogan et al., 1997), Watson and Clark (1997) pointed out that Jung's

Psychological Types (1921/1971) describes extraversion as encompassing sociability (which frequently is adaptive) alongside impulsivity (which frequently is *mal*adaptive). However, the personality inventory that was derived most directly from Jung's analytical psychology—that is, the MBTI (Myers, 1962)—yields a two-category typology (i.e., individualism versus extraversion) that makes it impossible for researchers to evaluate Jung's implicit assumption that sociability and impulsivity tend to covary among individuals (see Wiggins & Trapnell, 1997). Moreover, in a chapter from *The Oxford Handbook of the Five Factor Model* (edited by Widiger, 2017), Wilt and Revelle (2017) concluded that (1) H. J. Eysenck's (e.g., Eysenck, 1957; Eysenck & Himmelweit, 1947) research in general had established a solid empirical base that Jung's clinical insight had lacked, and (2) H. J. Eysenck's trait surveys (e.g., the Eysenck Personality Inventory [EPI] of Eysenck & Eysenck, 1964, and the Eysenck Personality Questionnaire [EPQ] of Eysenck & Eysenck, 1975) set the standard for operationalizing extraversion as a continuous construct.

Hans Eysenck's (1951) version of *factor-analytic trait theory* (which proposed that extraversion and *neuroticism*/emotional instability are two constructs that ought to be included in any comprehensive survey of traits) was directly influenced by Jung's (1921/1971) analytical psychology (C. S. Hall & Lindzey, 1970). Conversely, Raymond Cattell's (1946) version of *factor-analytic trait theory* (which proposed that the *16* traits of *warmth, emotional stability, dominance, liveliness, rule-consciousness, social boldness, sensitivity, vigilance, abstractedness, privateness, apprehension, openness to change, self-reliance, perfectionism,* and *tension* should be included in any comprehensive survey) was directly influenced by Allport's (1937/1951) *psychology of the individual*, rather than H. J. Eysenck's theory (Ewen, 1998). The debates between H. J. Eysenck and Cattell concerning the minimum number of required traits for any omnibus survey are the stuff of legend; suffice it to say that a consensus view ultimately emerged within the trait school of personality psychology, concluding that no fewer than five traits (i.e., *openness to experience, conscientiousness, extraversion, agreeableness,* and *neuroticism*) should be part and parcel of a comprehensive survey (Hampson, 1988).

Among the theories that have been infused with a five-factor model of traits, Robert McCrae and Paul Costa's (2003/2006) version of *factor-analytic trait theory* is especially well known within and beyond personality psychology (Gaines, 2016/2018). McCrae and Costa cited several personality theories (e.g., Jung's [1921/1971] analytical psychology, Allport's [1937/1951]

106 THE SELF IN RELATIONSHIPS

psychology of the individual, H. J. Eysenck's [1951] version of factor-analytic trait theory, and Cattell's [1943] version of factor-analytic trait theory) en route to developing their own theory (see Gaines, 2020). Like Eysenck's and Cattell's respective versions of factor-analytic trait theory, McCrae and Costa's version not only presumes stability of traits across situations and across time but also goes beyond Jung's analytical psychology and Allport's psychology of the individual by making strong assumptions about the "heritability" of traits (see Ewen, 1998). Such assumptions, which have persisted in the absence of research that might clarify *which* genes or *which* chromosomes ostensibly are responsible for stability in traits, have been questioned throughout the history of McCrae and Costa's research using the Neuroticism-Extraversion-Openness Personality Inventory (NEO-PI; Costa & McCrae, 1985, 1992; for an early review, see Hampson, 1988).

Evolution of McCrae and Costa's Version of Factor-Analytic Theory: Increasing Emphasis on "Heritability" of Traits

McCrae and Costa (1985) did not initially make strong assumptions about the "heritability" of the "Big Five" traits (Piekkola, 2011). However, as they gradually developed a formal theory (based on results of studies using the NEO-PI; Costa & McCrae, 1985, 1992), McCrae and Costa (2003/2006) concluded that traits were relatively impervious to change, even among clients within clinical and counseling settings (which could offer the potential for individuals to reflect upon their characteristic ways of thinking and behaving; see Cervone, 2005). According to McCrae and Costa's version of factor-analytic trait theory, laypersons and psychologists alike are interested in knowing where individuals stand on the "Big Five"; laypersons presumably count on other individuals' hardwired trait stability when deciding whether to embrace them as friends or to keep them at arm's length as foes (Funder & Fast, 2010). However, McCrae and Costa's theory does not explain why individuals' scores on all of the "Big Five" traits tend to change significantly over time, except to speculate that unspecified biological maturation processes must be involved (McAdams & Olson, 2010). Unfortunately (as alluded to in the preceding paragraph), it is not clear which genes or chromosomes would be involved in such processes (see also Deary, 2009).

Inspection of several chapters from *The Oxford Handbook of the Five Factor Model* (edited by Widiger, 2017) indicates that adherents of McCrae and Costa's (2003/2006) version of factor-analytic trait theory sometimes make broad assertions about "heritability" without providing details about the genes (or, at least, chromosomes) that supposedly are implicated. In a chapter on extraversion, Wilt and Revelle (2017) claimed "heritability" of 45% to 50% for that trait; yet they did not specify any genes or chromosomes that might be involved. Also, in a chapter on neuroticism, Tackett and Lahey (2017) claimed roughly 50% "heritability" for that trait; a 5-HTTLPR repeat polymorphism apparently makes the serotonin transporter gene an especially promising candidate, though substantiated evidence for the role of that gene has not materialized. Additionally, in a chapter on openness to experience, Sutin (2017) claimed approximately 50% "heritability" for that trait; a link between the dopamine D4 receptor gene and the catechol-methyltransferase gene seems to be promising, yet substantiated evidence regarding the roles of those genes has not surfaced. (In the chapters on conscientiousness [J. J. Jackson & Roberts, 2017] and agreeableness [Graziano & Tobin, 2017], the respective authors did not make particular claims about "heritability" or genes that might be implicated.)

The chasm between (1) the assertions of McCrae and Costa's (2003/2006) version of factor-analytic trait theory regarding genetic influences on the development of traits and (2) the paucity of corroborated evidence pointing to specific genes (or, at least, chromosomes) is striking across chapters within *The Oxford Handbook of the Five Factor Model*. On the one hand, according to Costa and McCrae (2017), "What does shape personality? Genes, which contribute to traits at all levels of the hierarchy [among other biological factors]" (p. 28). On the other hand, according to Jarnecke and South (2017), "It has been very difficult to identify specific polymorphisms that are associated with any behavioral or health-related outcome, let alone personality" (p. 314). When one considers that debates persist regarding the unidimensionality of "Big Five" traits such as extraversion (e.g., should sociability and impulsivity be grouped together; Wilt & Revelle, 2017), openness to experience (e.g., should lowercase-"c" culture and intellect be grouped together; Sutin, 2017), and especially agreeableness (e.g., should friendliness and humility be grouped together; Graziano & Tobin, 2017), proponents of the five-factor model might wish to refine their operationalization of traits before making unsubstantiated claims about "heritability" (see also Munafo, 2009).

108 THE SELF IN RELATIONSHIPS

A Disconnect Between McCrae/Costa's Factor-Analytic Trait Theory and Bem's Gender Schema Theory Concerning the "Heritability" of Traits

In Chapter 3, we learned that Bem's (1981) gender schema theory emphasizes societal and familial influences on the development of gender-related traits in particular. Bem's focus on environmental influences regarding individuals' positive masculinity and positive femininity is consistent with a simple fact regarding genes and personality: *No study has ever demonstrated a link between (1) individuals' possession of XX versus XY (or other) "sex chromosome" combinations and (2) individuals' levels of gender-related traits* (notwithstanding pronouncements concerning the near-universality of gender differences in gender-related traits that have not acknowledged generational changes in such differences; e.g., Allik & Realo, 2017). Given that empirical associations between the "Big Five" trait of extraversion and the forced-choice version of "masculinity-femininity" were established long before McCrae and Costa (2003/2006) developed their version of factor-analytic trait theory (e.g., Marshall, 1967), one might wonder how McCrae and Costa regard Bem's prioritization of culture over biology in shaping gender-related traits (and, presumably, extraversion). We do not know the answer, because McCrae and Costa did not cite Bem's theory in the second edition of *Personality in Adulthood: A Five-Factor Theory Perspective* (2003/2006).

Results of searches in APA PsycINFO and Academic Search Complete (conducted on May 29, 2022) yielded two "hits" (i.e., Lockenhoff et al., 2014; McCrae et al., 1986) in which McCrae and Costa cited Bem's writings. In both articles, McCrae and Costa (with their colleagues) mentioned the BSRI (Bem, 1974)—specifically, their interpretation of Wiggins and Broughton's (1985) results concerning the alignment of Bem's positive aspects of masculinity and femininity with Costa and McCrae's (1985) "Big Five" traits of extraversion and agreeableness (i.e., positive masculinity as a combination of high extraversion and low agreeableness, and positive femininity as a combination of high extraversion and high agreeableness). If any genes or (at a higher level) chromosomes should be linked to extraversion and agreeableness, then the literature on gender and personality would lead one to expect "sex chromosomes" to provide that link; yet (as we have seen) no such links have been established (see also Allik & Realo, 2017). Moreover, McCrae and Costa's (2003/2006) factor-analytic trait theory does not explain why women tend to score higher than men on *all* of the "Big Five" traits (or why gender differences in "Big Five" traits are less pronounced prior to adulthood; see De Fruyt et al., 2017).

Although McCrae and Costa (2003/2006) did not refer to Bem's (1981) gender schema theory, they *did* mention Alice Eagly's (1987) *social role theory* (which posits that individuals observe physical differences in biological sex contributing to other persons' and their own choice of occupational and other roles, which in turn influences individuals' self-perceived personality traits; for a meta-analytic review, see Hsu et al., 2021) in passing. Specifically, McCrae and Costa took issue with a presumed emphasis on cultural over biological influences on individuals' personality development within Eagly's theory, even though Eagly stated clearly over the years that social role theory places equal weight upon biological *and* cultural influences (e.g., Eagly & Wood, 2013). It seems that McCrae and Costa were objecting to the prospect of *any* cultural influences on individuals' gender-related personality development as anticipated by Eagly's theory (e.g., Costa et al., 2001). Thus, it comes as no surprise that McCrae and Costa omitted any acknowledgment of Bem's socioculturally informed gender schema theory in the second edition of *Personality in Adulthood: A Five-Factor Theory Perspective* (2003/2006).

Toward a "Gender-Plus" Factor-Analytic Trait Theory: Incorporating Spence's Multifactorial Gender Identity Theory Within McCrae/Costa's Theory

So far, we have seen that McCrae and Costa's (2003/2006) version of factor-analytic trait theory occasionally acknowledges the BSRI (Bem, 1974) but never explicitly acknowledges Bem's (1981) gender schema theory. However, an even more glaring set of omissions in McCrae and Costa's theory is the lack of any mention concerning empirical or theoretical contributions of Janet Spence and colleagues to the literature on gender and personality (Wiggins, 1991). Especially relevant to the present book, with regard to empirical contributions, Spence and colleagues developed the PAQ (Spence & Helmreich, 1978) to measure positive aspects of masculinity and femininity; and Spence et al. developed the Expanded Personality Attributes Questionnaire (EPAQ; Spence et al., 1979) to measure negative as well as positive aspects of masculinity and femininity (Lenney, 1991). Furthermore, Spence (1993) proposed a *multifactorial gender identity theory* that transcends traits, incorporating *gender-role attitudes* among other

110   THE SELF IN RELATIONSHIPS

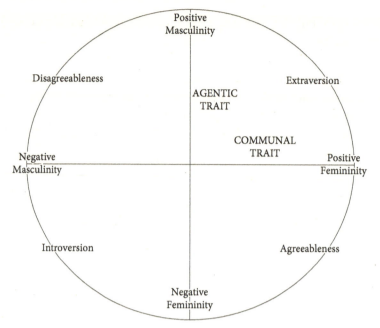

Figure 4.1. Proposed Circumplex Model of Extraversion and Agreeableness as Blends of Positive and Negative Aspects of Masculinity and Femininity.

gendered personality constructs (Deaux & LaFrance, 1998). We believe that, by drawing upon Spence's theory, McCrae and Costa would be in a position to flesh out a circular or circumplex model of gender-related traits, as shown in Figure 4.1.

Inspired by Wiggins's (1991) *interpersonal circumplex theory of personality and social behavior* (to be covered in detail from Chapter 5 onward), we would conceptualize the "Big Five" traits of extraversion (versus introversion) and agreeableness (versus disagreeableness) as blends of the gender-related traits of *positive masculinity, positive femininity, negative masculinity,* and *negative femininity* (rather than the other way around). Afterward, we would designate a higher-order intrapersonally oriented or *agentic trait* as the Y axis (with positive masculinity at the positive end and negative femininity at the negative end), and we would designate a higher-order interpersonally oriented or *communal trait* as the X axis (with positive femininity at the positive end and negative masculinity at the negative end) around which the lower-order gender-related traits of *disagreeableness* (high agentic trait plus low communal trait), *introversion* (low agentic trait plus low communal trait), *agreeableness* (low agentic trait plus high communal trait), and *extraversion* (high agentic trait plus high communal trait) may be plotted along midpoints between the Y and X axes. The result is a two-dimensional circular model for which a survey could be constructed to measure the eight lower-order traits, at least in principle (see also Gaines, 1991/1992).

We hasten to add that we are not aware of a published survey that is designed to measure extraversion and agreeableness as blends of gender-related traits in practice (Gaines, 2020). Nevertheless, the conceptual logic that underlies Figure 4.1 suggests a mix of hypotheses and research questions that might be posed regarding the impact of agentic and communal traits on individuals' "pro-relationship" behaviors (see Gaines, 2016/2018). For example, inspired by the expanded version of Wiggins's (2003/2005) interpersonal circumplex theory, we would predict that (1) positive masculinity will be reflected in individuals' giving of affection and denial of respect to others, (2) disagreeableness will be reflected in individuals' denial of affection and respect to others, (3) negative masculinity will be reflected in individuals' denial of affection and respect to others, (4) introversion will be reflected in individuals' denial of affection and respect to others, (5) negative femininity will be reflected in individuals' denial of affection and giving of respect to others, (6) agreeableness will be reflected in individuals' giving of affection and respect to others, (7) positive femininity will be reflected in individuals' giving of affection and respect to others, and (8) extraversion will be reflected in individuals' giving of affection and respect to others.

As McCrae and Costa (2003/2006) pointed out, one could generate a different circumplex model for any of the 10 potential pairings of "Big Five" traits. However, the full ramifications of "Big Five" traits for interpersonal behavior have been articulated most extensively for a circumplex model that includes extraversion and agreeableness, rather than other "Big Five" pairings (Wiggins, 2003/2005). Although it might be possible to use H. J. Eysenck's (1947) version of factor-analytic trait theory to construct a circumplex model that pairs extraversion with neuroticism, we are unaware of any efforts to progress beyond a four-category typology regarding those "Big Five" traits (Hampson, 1988). In contrast, Wiggins's (1991) conceptualization of extraversion and agreeableness allows personality psychologists to progress beyond a corresponding four-group typology of gender-related traits (e.g., Spence & Helmreich, 1978). Thus, notwithstanding the inconsistent results that relationship scientists have obtained concerning extraversion as a predictor, we would expect extraversion and agreeableness to promote individuals' "pro-relationship" behaviors on theoretical

112 THE SELF IN RELATIONSHIPS

grounds, whereas we would simply ask whether the other "Big Five" traits are manifested in individuals' "pro-relationship behaviors" (and, if so, in what direction; Gaines, 2016/2018).

In order for McCrae and Costa's (2003/2006) version of factor-analytic theory to be made fully compatible with Spence's (1993) multifactorial gender identity theory, we believe that it would behoove McCrae, Costa, and followers to acknowledge the likelihood that—*at least where extraversion and agreeableness are concerned*—gender role socialization continues to exert a substantial influence on individuals' development of one or more "Big Five" traits, long after the 1970s-era heyday of the women's rights movement in so-called Western nations and around the world (see Wood & Eagly, 2010). Societal institutions (e.g., governments, organized religions, families) are not nearly as change oriented as "Big Five" theorists might wish to believe; those same institutions still play an active role in shaping individuals' selves—including, but not limited to, gendered selves—according to traditional norms (A. J. Stewart & McDermott, 2004). Furthermore, gender relations within social and personal relationships remain marked by power differentials that tend to favor men over women (whether the relationships are romantic or platonic); such power differentials can serve to reinforce pre-existing gender stereotypes and gender-related traits, even in the midst of modest social change in the public and private spheres (see Finkel et al., 2017).

Gendered Self-Concept: A Potentially Unifying Construct Within a "Gender-Plus" Factor-Analytic Trait Theory(?)

We do not wish to convey the impression that Spence's (1993) multifactorial gender identity theory should be adopted without modification as part of a "gender-plus" factor-analytic trait theory. In a key chapter that served as part of the basis for her theory, Spence (1985, p. 79) alluded to *self-concepts* of masculinity and femininity, as if one's gendered self-concept is equivalent to one's gender identity. However, the constructs of self-concept and identity are *not* identical, as Baumeister (1997) explained:

> The term *identity* refers to the definitions that are created for and superimposed on the self. These definitions refer to concepts about who the person is and what the person is like. Identity can be analyzed as consisting

of an interpersonal aspect (a set of roles and relationships), a potentiality aspect (a concept of who the person might become), and a values aspect (a set of values and priorities). . . . Identity differs from self-concept in that it is socially defined. That is, the self-concept is wholly contained in the person's own mind, whereas identity is often created by the larger society, although individuals typically have some opportunity to refine or negotiate the identities that society gives them. (p. 682)

Spence (1985) criticized Bem (1981) for interpreting the BSRI (Bem, 1974) as a measure of *gender identity* (which we shall define as individuals' answer to the question "Who am I?" as a function of individuals' presumed biological and/or psychological sex), given that the content of the BSRI is confined to certain self-described traits (i.e., *instrumentality and expressivity*; see Bussey, 2011). However, by Spence's standard, her own surveys— including the PAQ (Spence & Helmreich, 1978) and the EPAQ (Spence et al., 1979) regarding gender-related traits, as well as the Attitudes toward Women Scale (AWS; Spence & Helmreich, 1978) regarding gender-role attitudes— should not be regarded as measures of gender identity (see Helgeson, 2015). Ironically, Bem's (1985) distinction between (1) individuals' classification regarding "sex-role orientation" and (2) societies' promotion of gender schemas may offer a better fit with Baumeister's (1997, p. 682) definition of identity than does Spence's distinction between (1) gender-related traits and (2) gender-role attitudes (see M. R. Leary & Toner, 2015). Conversely, Spence's trait-attitude distinction fits Baumeister's (1997, p. 681) definition of self-concept as "a loose combination of the many ideas and inferences that the person has about him- or herself."

Ironically, one potential obstacle to our suggested use of the gendered self-concept as a means toward developing a "gender-plus" version of factor-analytic trait theory (thus incorporating the multifactorial gender identity theory of Spence, 1993) is McCrae and Costa's (2003/2006) definition regarding the self-concept as a global construct. Keeping in mind that McCrae and Costa did not provide a definition of the self as a whole, it strikes us as odd that McCrae and Costa (following Epstein, 1973) would define the self-concept as "what we believe we are like" immediately after defining personality (which, for them, is reducible to traits) as "what we are really like" (2003/2006, p. 119). Paraphrasing Robins and John's (1997) modes or metaphors of self-perception, it seems to us that McCrae and Costa depicted individuals' self-concept as a reflection of the *Consistency Seeker* mode

114 THE SELF IN RELATIONSHIPS

(prioritizing stability), whereas McCrae and Costa depicted individuals' traits as reflections of the *Scientist* mode (prioritizing accuracy). Exactly why individuals' self-reported traits, but *not* individuals' self-reported self-concept, can be accepted as accurate reports of aspects of the self within McCrae and Costa's version of factor-analytic trait theory is unclear (see also Baumeister, 1997).

Even more problematic is McCrae and Costa's (2003/2006) definition of identity as "those aspects of the Self-Concept that are particularly salient or definitional—characteristics which, if they were taken from us, would lead us at least briefly to wonder if we were still ourselves" (p. 228). This latter definition leads us to wonder whether McCrae and Costa view the terms *self* and *self-concept* as identical, given Baumeister's (1997) framing of identity as an aggregate of definitions about the self. Paradoxically, McCrae/Costa's lack of distinction between *self* and *self-concept* enables us to incorporate Spence's (1993) multifactorial gender identity theory into their factor-analytic trait theory: Neither Spence nor McCrae/Costa provided an adequate definition of self-concept. Hence, we retain Baumeister's definitions of self, self-concept, and identity as we argue that the gendered self-construct represents sets of inferences about those attributes that individuals regard as relevant to their presumed biological and/or psychological sex (see also Robins & John, 1997). Unlike Spence *or* McCrae/Costa, we contend that individual choice regarding the gendered self-concept is reflected in many of the individual differences in gender-related and "Big Five" traits that can be observed, within and across genders (Banaji & Prentice, 1994).

Agreeableness, Sometimes Related; Neuroticism, Consistently Related; and Openness and Conscientiousness, Unrelated to "Pro-Relationship" Behaviors

As noted earlier in the present chapter, the magnitude and direction of extraversion as a predictor of individuals' "pro-relationship" behaviors are inconsistent across studies. The emerging pattern regarding the effects of agreeableness on such behaviors is complicated as well, though for different reasons: Agreeableness tends to be a significant positive predictor of "pro-relationship" behaviors among men, but not among women (McNulty, 2013). Exactly why gender should be implicated as a moderator of the impact of agreeableness on relationship-promoting (versus relationship-threatening) behaviors is unclear, keeping in mind that we are unaware of any studies that have formally tested the significance of differences in those effects across genders (see J. Cohen et al., 2003, concerning significance tests for differences in beta weights across subsamples). Although it is tempting to speculate about gender as a moderator (e.g., agreeableness as a blend of positive and negative aspects of femininity might be salient in the "pro-relationship" behaviors of men, who are not stereotypically expected to embrace agreeableness or to behave in a manner that maintains relationships over the long term), we urge caution in forming such after-the-fact hypotheses (such moderating effects are uncommon; see M. S. Clark & Lemay, 2010).

Despite Wiggins's (2003/2005) focus on extraversion and agreeableness as the "Big Five" traits that should be especially relevant to understanding why individuals differ in their "pro-relationship behaviors," it turns out that neuroticism is the most consistent and (perhaps not coincidentally) most dependably negative predictor of such behaviors (McNulty, 2013). As the most unambiguously maladaptive "Big Five" trait, neuroticism is associated with a variety of negative social and psychological outcomes (Tackett & Lahey, 2017). Putting aside issues of circumplexity for the moment, the factor-analytic trait theories of Cattell (1943), H. J. Eysenck (1947), and McCrae and Costa (2003/2006) all highlight neuroticism as the subclinical trait that is most likely to be linked to psychopathology—a fact that might help explain the lack of a chapter on neuroticism within the *Handbook of Personality Psychology* (edited by R. Hogan et al., 1997), which emphasizes the "normal" range of traits and other aspects of personality. In any event, just as individuals are particularly attuned to partners' relationship-threatening (as opposed to relationship-promoting) behaviors, so too may individuals be especially attuned to their own emotional *in*stability as an impediment to the stability of their relationships (see De Pauw, 2017).

Finally, openness to experience and conscientiousness are consistently *un*related to individuals' "pro-relationship" behaviors (McNulty, 2013). Given that (1) Wiggins's (2003/2005) interpersonal circumplex theory does not predict significant effects for those traits and (2) results indicate null effects for those traits, the lack of relevance for openness to experience or conscientiousness within the context of relationship maintenance underscores an important point for personality psychologists to consider: Despite the salutary efforts of McCrae and Costa as theorists (e.g., McCrae & Costa, 1990, 2003/2006) and as researchers (e.g., Costa & McCrae, 1985, 1989, 1992) in helping to consolidate the consensus view that five major traits compose a

116　THE SELF IN RELATIONSHIPS

relatively comprehensive taxonomy, it does not necessarily follow that all (or most) of the "Big Five" traits are important to individual differences in relationship-promoting versus relationship-threatening behaviors toward significant others (see Winterheld & Simpson, 2018). As M. Snyder and Ickes (1985) noted around the time that McCrae and Costa began their programmatic research on the "Big Five" traits, a basic question for personality psychologists to answer is which traits conceptually make sense as potential predictors of social behavior in general (see also Ickes et al., 1997).

Agreeableness (but Not Conscientiousness) as Related to "Automatic Accommodation"

We are unaware of any previous studies in which the "Big Five" traits have been examined as predictors of actual conflict resolution behaviors (i.e., responses to relationship dissatisfaction, responses to partners' anger/criticism, and responses to partners' betrayal; see Rusbult, 1993) that we covered in previous chapters. However, we *are* aware of one study (i.e., Perunovic & Holmes, 2008) in which two of the "Big Five" traits—specifically, agreeableness and conscientiousness—were examined as predictors of "*automatic accommodation*" (i.e., responses to partners' *hypothetical* anger/criticism, with the caveat that individuals provide responses under experimentally imposed time constraints; Yovetich & Rusbult, 1994). Perunovic and Holmes (2008) offered an empirical (rather than theoretical) rationale for choosing agreeableness and conscientiousness as predictors (e.g., those two traits, but *not* the other "Big Five" traits, had been shown to influence individuals' self-regulatory behaviors; conscientiousness was significantly and positively associated with agreeableness). Nevertheless, Perunovic and Holmes surmised that the weight of the evidence from previous studies was sufficient to hypothesize that agreeableness (and possibly conscientiousness) would significantly and positively predict "automatic accommodation."

Perunovic and Holmes (2008) used 10-item scales, drawn from the International Personality Item Pool (IPIP; Goldberg, 1993), to measure agreeableness and conscientiousness. Consistent with predictions, agreeableness was a significant predictor of "automatic accommodation" (i.e., high-agreeableness individuals reported significantly higher levels of constructive rather than destructive responses to partners' anger/criticism in hypothetical scenarios, compared to low-agreeableness individuals, under time constraints). However, contrary to (tentative) predictions, conscientiousness was unrelated to "automatic accommodation." Perunovic and Holmes speculated that, unlike agreeableness, conscientiousness is not associated with self-regulation within hypothetical accommodation-related scenarios. Moreover, although Perunovic and Holmes briefly alluded to Kelley and Thibaut's (1978) revision of Thibaut and Kelley's (1959) interdependence theory in the process of interpreting their results, Kelley's (1983) conceptual analysis of "transformational tendencies" might provide the strongest rationale in hindsight: Interpersonal warmth—which presumably is part and parcel of agreeableness (as well as extraversion; Trapnell & Wiggins, 1990)—predisposes individuals to de-escalate conflict (Gaines, 2016/2018).

The results that Perunovic and Holmes (2008) obtained regarding agreeableness as a significant predictor of "automatic accommodation" were especially impressive in light of the fact that their study also included the *attachment orientations* of anxiety and avoidance (as measured by the 17-item Adult Attachment Questionnaire, or AAQ; Simpson et al., 1996). As it turns out, attachment avoidance (but *not* attachment anxiety) was a significant negative predictor of "automatic accommodation." Perunovic and Holmes's results concerning attachment orientations are consistent with a broader body of results with regard to attachment avoidance (rather than attachment anxiety) as a significant negative predictor of actual "pro-relationship" behaviors (a set of findings that we mentioned briefly in the Preface). Given that attachment theorists (in the tradition of Bowlby, 1969/1997) have not consistently made it clear whether attachment orientations are best conceptualized as traits, attitudes, or other aspects of personality, we have not commented at length upon attachment orientations thus far (for details concerning attachment orientations and "pro-relationship behaviors, see Mikulincer & Shaver, 2007, 2016). However, in Chapter 9, we will have more to say about attachment orientations as interpersonal attitudes (following Gaines, 2016/2018).

The Legacies of Jung's Analytical Psychology and McCrae/Costa's Version of Factor-Analytic Theory: Gendered Self-Concept, "Big Five" Traits, and Conflict Resolution

Historically speaking, personality psychologists have tended to credit Jung's analytical psychology, especially as articulated in *Psychological Types* (Jung,

1921/1971), with introducing the introversion/extraversion dichotomy (eventually reimagined as the continuous trait of extraversion; Watson & Clark, 1997). However, the extent to which Jung's theory implicitly or explicitly addresses gender—for example, in *Aion* (Jung, 1959/1975)—has not been fully appreciated within personality psychology (although part of the problem may lie in Jung's oft-unsystematic, androcentric discussions of gender and personality; Barone-Chapman, 2014). For example, Bem (1985) did not comment upon the overlap between Jung's construct of extraversion and Bem's own construct of psychological androgyny (both of which can be interpreted as a combination of positive aspects of masculinity and femininity; Moraglia, 1994). Also, even though Spence (1985) criticized the masculinity/femininity dichotomy within Jung's analytical psychology, Spence did not mention that her own conceptualization of negative as well as positive aspects of masculinity and femininity opens the possibility that individuals may score in one direction on the two masculine traits *and* in the opposite direction on the two feminine traits (see Lenney, 1991).

Unlike Jung's (1921/1971) analytical psychology, McCrae and Costa's (1990, 2003/2006) factor-analytic trait theory is a modern classic for which the legacy is still in the making (Widiger, 2017). Nevertheless, as noted earlier in the present chapter, McCrae and Costa have settled into such an absolutist stance regarding the "heritability" of the "Big Five" traits that they not only speculate (with zero evidence) about the role of "sex chromosomes" in determining individuals' traits but also make it a point to refer only to *biological sex* (thus avoiding the prospect of non-hardwired, psychological maleness and femaleness that composes much of the basis for gender in individuals' everyday lives; for an example, see Costa & McCrae, 2017). Moreover, McCrae and Costa view the self-concept as an aspect of individuals' psyches that is less a consequence of active construction than it is a consequence of faulty reflectiveness—a view that even adherents of their theory do not endorse in a wholehearted manner (e.g., Wilt & Revelle, 2017). Unfortunately, McCrae and Costa's depiction of the self-concept as a passive and less-than-accurate byproduct of inherited traits does not explain why one of the "Big Five" traits—that is, agreeableness—has emerged as an especially promising predictor of accommodation (Graziano & Tobin, 2017).

Among the theories in the present chapter, Spence's (1993) multifactorial gender identity theory may have left the most underappreciated legacy within personality psychology—specifically, the realization that gender-related constructs are only loosely interrelated (see Frable, 1997). As we have made clear in the present chapter, we believe that a shift of focus from gender identity to gendered self-construct can simultaneously reignite interest in Spence's theory *and* make McCrae and Costa's (2003/2006) version of factor-analytic trait theory responsive to gender as a construct that encompasses biological sex and more. In fact, if we interpret agreeableness as the combination of positive and negative aspects of femininity, then Perunovic and Holmes's (2008) finding that agreeableness promotes "automatic accommodation" (Yovetich & Rusbult, 1994) literally represents the gendered self-concept in action. Thus, regardless of XX versus XY chromosomal makeup, individuals' active reflection upon their separateness from (and connectedness to) their physical and social environments may lead them to embrace femininity in all of its complexity and consequently recognize the relationship-bolstering effects of quickly de-escalating conflict with partners (albeit at the risk of exposing themselves to further verbal attacks; see Wiggins, 1991).

Prelude to Chapter 5

In the present chapter, we have seen how Spence's (1993) multifactorial gender identity theory allows us to interpret the "Big Five" traits of extraversion and agreeableness (e.g., as measured by Costa & McCrae, 1985) as blends of the gender-related traits of positive masculinity, positive femininity, negative masculinity, and/or negative femininity (e.g., as measured by Spence et al., 1979). So far, however, we have not explicitly stated the role that Wiggins's (1991) interpersonal circumplex theory can play in "connecting the dots" between the "Big Five" traits and gender-related traits in question. If Wiggins's theory is correct, then (1) both of the interpersonal traits represent the bipolarities between (a) positive masculinity and negative femininity (in the case of dominance) and (b) between positive femininity and negative masculinity (in the case of nurturance), and (2) in turn, two of the "Big Five" traits represent blends of (a) high dominance and high nurturance (in the case of extraversion) and (b) low dominance and high nurturance (in the case of agreeableness; Gaines, 2016/2018). Moreover, an earlier version of Wiggins's interpersonal circumplex theory (1979) implies that extraversion—but *not* agreeableness—contains *positive emotionality* at its core (see Watson & Clark, 1997).

Particularly in its most fully developed version, Wiggins's (2003/2005) interpersonal circumplex theory attends to geometrics and psychometrics as much as it attends to personality constructs and conceptual models (see Gaines, 2020). Although Wiggins is best known for his operationalization of lower-order traits that represent blends of the higher-order interpersonal traits of dominance and nurturance (measured via the original and revised versions of the IAS; Wiggins, 1979; Wiggins et al., 1988), Wiggins also advocated the identification of those interpersonal behaviors that might reflect the influence of interpersonal traits (Gaines, 2016/2018). Overall, Wiggins's theory is sufficiently rich to serve as the main conceptual and empirical framework for the remainder of the present book (see also Hopwood & Waugh, 2020, for a single-case, single-study counterpart to the $n = 100+$, multiple-study approach that we take in exploring the nuances of Wiggins's theory). Finally, although interpersonal circumplex theorists have tended to de-emphasize the ramifications of Wiggins's personality constructs for understanding interpersonal behavior, we shall treat the operationalization of interpersonal traits as a means toward the end of predicting accommodation (thus incorporating interdependence theory; see Kelley et al., 2003).

In Chapter 5, we will make the transition from mostly theoretical material to primarily empirical material, as we delve deeper into Wiggins and Holzmuller's (1978) conceptualization of dominance and nurturance as interpersonal traits. Along the way, we will learn about the influence of Bakan's (1966) overarching constructs of agency and communion, which may be manifested in various interpersonal aspects of personality (including, but not limited to, traits; Wiggins, 1991), upon Spence's (1993) multifactorial gender identity theory as well as Wiggins's (2003/2005) interpersonal circumplex theory. Subsequently, we shall learn about geometric analyses (especially circulant correlation analyses; Gurtman & Pincus, 2000) and psychometric analyses (especially confirmatory factor analyses; Gaines, Panter, et al., 1997) that have been applied to lower-order interpersonal trait correlation matrices, using (1) a "simulated" set of correlations from Wiggins (1979) concerning the subclinical range of traits and (2) a corresponding "simulated" set of correlations from Gurtman (1992) regarding the clinical range of traits. We will be interested particularly in the extent to which results of "simulated" geometric and psychometric analyses complement each other (following Fabrigar et al., 1997).

SECTION III

FROM CONCEPTUAL TO METHODOLOGICAL ISSUES REGARDING THE SELF IN RELATIONSHIPS

5

Conceptualization of Dominance and Nurturance as Interpersonal Traits

Synopsis: In the present chapter, we examine Wiggins's interpersonal circumplex theory of personality and social behavior (which evolved from Wiggins and Holzmuller's circumplex model of subclinical traits) as influenced directly by Sullivan's interpersonal theory of personality and T. Leary's initial circumplex model of subclinical and clinical traits (and indirectly by Jung's analytical psychology); Bakan's superordinate constructs of agency and communion as ways of being-in-the-world, as crucial to the development of Wiggins's theory; the geometrics of Wiggins's interpersonal circumplex theory (as exemplified by an equal-spacing, equal-communality model of correlations among lower-order subclinical and clinical interpersonal traits; ideal matrices of reproduced correlations among lower-order subclinical and clinical interpersonal traits; and "simulated" matrices of subclinical and clinical trait correlations that can be entered into a circulant correlation analysis via the maximum likelihood method in LISREL); and the psychometrics of Wiggins's theory (as exemplified by comparing and contrasting a two-factor model that is limited to the higher-order circumplex axes of dominance and nurturance versus a three-factor model that adds a noncircumplex "acquiescence" factor; ideal matrices of higher-order factor loadings for lower-order subclinical and clinical interpersonal traits; and "simulated" matrices of lower-order subclinical and clinical interpersonal traits that can be entered into confirmatory factor analyses via the maximum likelihood method in LISREL); and we offer a prelude to Chapter 6, in which we evaluate the geometric and psychometric properties of the best-known survey of subclinical interpersonal traits—namely, the Interpersonal Adjective Scales—Revised Version (IAS-R; Wiggins et al., 1988).

What we understand by the concept "individual" is a relatively recent acquisition in the history of the human mind and human culture. It is no wonder, therefore, that the earlier all-powerful collective attitude prevented almost

The Self in Relationships. Stanley O. Gaines, Jr., Oxford University Press. © Oxford University Press 2023.
DOI: 10.1093/oso/9780197687635.003.0005

124 THE SELF IN RELATIONSHIPS

completely an objective psychological evaluation of individual differences, or any scientific objectification of individual psychological processes. It was owing to this very lack of psychological thinking that knowledge became "psychologized," i.e., filled with projected psychology. We find striking examples of this in man's first attempts at a philosophical explanation of the cosmos. The development of individuality, with the consequent psychological differentiation of man, goes hand in hand with the de-psychologizing work of objective science.

—Carl Jung,
Psychological Types (1921/1971, p. 10)

What all of this suggests to us is that the unconscious level of personality either cannot be measured by projective techniques or does not have much influence on human conduct. No one who has read Freud or Jung could fail to appreciate the marvelous insight that there are levels of the mind that operate by a logic different from that of our waking consciousness; that these are more characteristic of children than of adults; that they appear in dreams, in artistic productions, in psychotic delusions, and in culturally shared myths; and that the primitive ways of thinking we have inherited from our evolutionary ancestors often appear in them in undisguised form. The data collected over the past 70 years, however, have convinced us that these curious relics of our past have relatively little to do with our daily life or with such important outcomes as happiness, response to stress, or political beliefs.

—Robert R. McCrae and Paul T. Costa Jr.,
Personality in Adulthood: A Five-Factor Theory Perspective
(2003/2006, p. 156)

Despite Jung's role in pioneering the construct of introversion versus extraversion, not one of Jung's writings—including *Psychological Types* (Jung, 1921/1971)—is cited in the *Handbook of Interpersonal Psychology* (edited by Horowitz & Strack, 2011). Nevertheless, the relevance of extraversion to understanding traits within the interpersonal domain of personality is clear from inspection of the chapters by Simpson et al. (2011), Costa and McCrae (2011), and Clarkin et al. (2011), among others. The chapter by Simpson and colleagues devotes the most extensive coverage to extraversion within the *Handbook of Interpersonal Psychology*, offering the insightful observation that extraversion may be associated with interpersonal benefits

CONCEPTUALIZATION OF DOMINANCE AND NURTURANCE   125

and costs—an observation that may help explain the sometimes-positive, sometimes-negative, and sometimes-null effects of extraversion on "pro-relationship" behaviors that we summarized in Chapter 4 (see also K. Harris & Vazire, 2016). However, all of the chapters in the *Handbook of Interpersonal Psychology* repeat the controversial assertion—promoted by McCrae and Costa's (2003/2006) version of factor-analytic trait theory, as we learned in Chapter 4—concerning the "heritability" of extraversion, with estimates *exceeding* 50%(!).

One reason for the lack of acknowledgment concerning *Psychological Types* (Jung, 1921/1971) in the *Handbook of Personality Psychology* (edited by Horowitz & Strack, 2011) may be the overall omission of Jung's analytical psychology from Sullivan's (1953, 1954, 1956) interpersonal theory of personality. When Sullivan *did* mention Jung, the citation tended to be fleeting, yet disparaging—for example, the dismissal of Jung's collective unconscious as a construct that does *not* accurately depict the human psyche, in *Conceptions of Modern Psychiatry* (Sullivan, 1947/1966). Within that same book, Sullivan briefly affirmed Freud's (1900/1965) sexualized conceptualization of libido but neglected to mention Jung's de-sexualized conceptualization of libido; such an oversight helped guarantee that Sullivan would fail to recognize the construct of introversion/extraversion (which, as we noted in Chapter 4, Jung postulated as a byproduct of libido). In any event, one can draw a conceptual line from (1) Jung's analytical psychology through (2) Sullivan's interpersonal theory to (3) Wiggins's (1991) interpersonal circumplex theory regarding the metamorphosis from (a) extraversion as one-half of a typology to (b) extraversion as a continuous trait that combines high dominance and high nurturance (e.g., Wiggins & Trapnell, 1997).

In his initial outline of an interpersonal circumplex theory that encompassed traits and other personality constructs, Wiggins (1991) did not mention Jung's analytical psychology in general or *Psychological Types* (Jung, 1921/1971) in particular. However, in his extended presentation of interpersonal circumplex theory, Wiggins (2003/2005) *did* allude to Jung's *Psychological Types* in passing. Unlike Sullivan (1947/1965), Wiggins not only found value in Jung's analytical psychology (keeping in mind that this acknowledgment was brief) but also noted that interpretation of results from the projective Rorschach Inkblot Test (see Rorschach, 1924) had yielded an "experience balance" construct that bears a strong resemblance to Jung's introversion/extraversion construct. Wiggins's appreciation for Jung's analytical psychology is emblematic of the eclecticism that one notices within

126 THE SELF IN RELATIONSHIPS

Wiggins's theory, which draws upon every major theory that we have covered so far in the present book (see also Gaines, 2016/2018). Accordingly, throughout the next several chapters, we shall explore Wiggins's interpersonal circumplex theory as the conceptual perspective that is most widely associated with the constructs of dominance and nurturance as interpersonal traits (Gaines, 2020).

Jung and Beyond: Wiggins's Interpersonal Circumplex Theory of Personality and Social Behavior

As we noted in Chapter 4, within Jung's (1921/1971) analytical psychology, both introversion and extraversion may be combined with one or more of the "functions" or modes of adaptation (i.e., thinking, feeling, sensing, and intuiting; Millon, 1996). According to Jung's theory, just as individuals possess the capacity for introversion as well as extraversion yet tend to consciously experience one of those "attitudes" at a given point in time, so too do individuals possess the capacity for all four "functions" yet tend to consciously experience one of those "functions" to a greater extent than the other three "functions" at a particular point in time (C. S. Hall & Lindzey, 1970). Depending upon the situation, Jung reasoned, any of the eight "attitude"/"function" types might be adaptive in terms of its consequences for individuals' behavior (Ewen, 1998). However, in Jung's view, individuals' rigidity in adhering to a single psychological type may prove to be *mal*adaptive in a specific situation (T. Leary, 1957). Fortunately, from the vantage point of Jung's analytical psychology, the process of striving toward individuation or self-realization can lead individuals to learn from previous unsuccessful behavioral outcomes and subsequently draw upon differing aspects of their personalities over time (McClelland, 1985/1987).

Despite Sullivan's (1947/1965) disparagement of Jung's (1921/1971) analytical psychology regarding the construct of the collective unconscious, T. Leary (1957) pointed out that Jung's attempt to establish a continuum from "normality" to "abnormality" regarding individuals' personalities (and, presumably, accompanying behaviors) not only represented a conceptual advance beyond Freud's (1900/1965) psychoanalytic theory but also helped to lay the groundwork for a more clearly articulated "normality"–"abnormality" continuum within Sullivan's own interpersonal theory of personality. Indeed, Carson's (1969) elaboration of Sullivan's theory suggests that

CONCEPTUALIZATION OF DOMINANCE AND NURTURANCE 127

judgments of "normality" and "abnormality" of targets' personalities and behavior ultimately are influenced by perceivers' cultural context. Interestingly, C. S. Hall and Lindzey (1970) noted that Sullivan's interpersonal theory emphasizes the role of culture (rather than biology) in shaping individuals' personality development. Ewen (1998) concluded that, to the extent that individuals are deemed "abnormal" within a given society, Sullivan's theory indicates that one ideally should acknowledge the role that society may have played in promoting precisely those intrapersonal and interpersonal characteristics that are judged to be "abnormal" in particular individuals.

As Pincus and Wright (2011) noted, T. Leary's (1957) early *circumplex model of interpersonal traits* elaborated upon Sullivan's (1953) normality-abnormality continuum, subsuming maladaptive and adaptive lower-order traits within a single two-dimensional diagram. M. Snyder and Ickes (1985) provided details regarding Leary's model, comprising eight pairs of lower-order traits whereby "normal" versions were paired with presumably "abnormal" variations (i.e., *managerial-autocratic, competitive-exploitive, blunt-aggressive, skeptical-distrustful, modest–self-effacing, docile-dependent, cooperative-overconventional,* and *responsible-overgenerous*) and placed at 45-degree angles. As Gurtman (2011) observed, modern-day interpretations of Leary's interpersonal circumplex model depict the eight "normal" and "abnormal" pairs of lower-order traits as combinations of the higher-order traits of dominance and nurturance. However, Kiesler (1983) pointed out that Leary described the lower–order traits as circling the higher-order *motives* of "dominance-submission" and "love-hate." Carson (1969) resolved this discrepancy by explaining that Freud's (1900/1965) psychoanalytic theory linked the higher-order motives in question with positive aspects of masculinity and femininity (i.e., the traits of dominance and nurturance).

Evolution from a model of traits to a theory of various aspects of personality and social behavior. As we indicated in Chapter 3, Wiggins and Holzmuller's (1978) version of an interpersonal circumplex model of traits retained certain elements of T. Leary's (1957) earlier model. Specifically, as noted by Pincus and Wright (2011), Wiggins and Holzmuller discarded the combined "normal" and "abnormal" forms of lower-order traits that had been associated with Leary's circumplex model, replacing the lower-order traits (which had been measured via the Interpersonal Check List, or ICL; LaForge & Suczek, 1955) with purely "normal" versions. Having described Wiggins and Holzmuller's (1978, p. 41) model explicitly in Chapter 3 (and implicitly in Chapter 4),

128 THE SELF IN RELATIONSHIPS

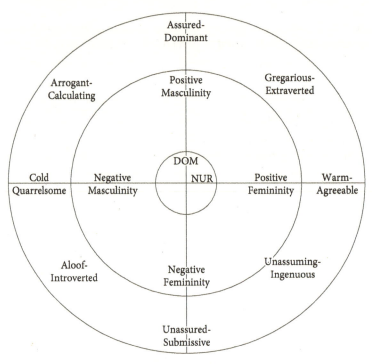

Figure 5.1. Circumplex Model of Lower-Order Subclinical Interpersonal Traits.

we unveil our adapted version of their model in Figure 5.1. We retain Wiggins and Holzmuller's eight lower-order traits (i.e., starting at the 12 o'clock position and moving counterclockwise, *ambitious-dominant, arrogant-calculating, cold-quarrelsome, aloof-introverted, unassured-submissive, unassuming-ingenuous, warm-agreeable,* and *gregarious-extraverted*) and two higher-order traits (i.e., dominance and nurturance as the Y and X axes, respectively), and we add gender-related traits (i.e., negative and positive aspects of masculinity and femininity) along the poles of the higher-order traits.

Following the publication of the first version of Wiggins's (1979) interpersonal circumplex theory of personality and social behavior (which was limited to coverage of traits at that time) as well as the original version of Wiggins's Interpersonal Adjective Scales (IAS), Alden and colleagues (Alden et al., 1990) published a circumplex model of *maladaptive* interpersonal traits alongside the Inventory of Interpersonal Problems-Circumplex version (IIP-C; see Pincus & Wright, 2011). The maladaptive versions of dominance and nurturance are listed (beginning at the 12 o'clock position,

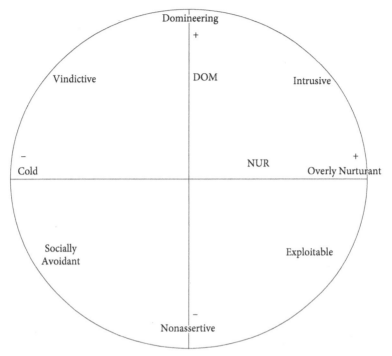

Figure 5.2. Circumplex Model of Lower-Order Clinical Interpersonal Traits (adapted from Alden et al., 1990, p. 529).

then proceeding in a counterclockwise manner along 45-degree intervals) as *domineering, vindictive, cold, socially avoidant, nonassertive, exploitable, overly nurturant,* and *intrusive* (Gurtman, 2009). We present Alden et al.'s (1990, p. 529) maladaptive-trait version of the interpersonal circumplex model in Figure 5.2. Unlike Wiggins and Holzmuller's (1978) adaptive-trait version of the interpersonal circumplex model (in which "polar opposite" lower-order traits are expected to be negatively correlated), Alden et al.'s maladaptive-trait version holds that "polar opposite" lower-order traits are *less positively correlated* than are lower-order traits that are adjacent to each other (but still positively correlated; Gurtman, 1993).

Finally, Wiggins (1991) presented the basics of his expanded interpersonal circumplex theory of personality and social behavior, transcending traits (but still focusing on implications for individuals' giving versus denial of love/affection and status/respect; Gurtman, 2009). The most fully articulated version of Wiggins's expanded theory was presented in *Paradigms of Personality Assessment* (Wiggins, 2003/2005), which alluded to Wiggins's

130   THE SELF IN RELATIONSHIPS

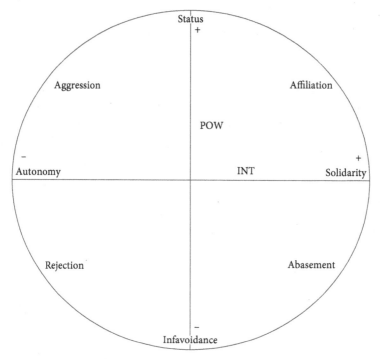

Figure 5.3. Circumplex Model of Interpersonal Motives (adapted from Wiggins, 1997, p. 1072). Adapted from "Circumnavigating Dodge Morgan's Interpersonal Style," by J. S. Wiggins, 1997, *Journal of Personality, 65*, p. 1072. Copyright 1997 by John Wiley & Sons. Reproduced and adapted with permission.

(1997) *circumplex model of interpersonal motives*—a separate model that identifies the agentic motive of *power* and the communal motive of *intimacy* from H. A. Murray's (1938) personology as the higher-order axes around which eight lower-order motives (starting from the 12 o'clock position and proceeding at 45-degree intervals, *status, aggression, autonomy, rejection, infavoidance, abasement, solidarity,* and *affiliation*) can be plotted. (In the present book, we substitute the terms of *status and solidarity* for the terms of *dominance and nurturance* in order to mitigate confusion over the nature of those respective higher-order motives, as distinct from the higher-order traits that Wiggins and colleagues have studies across several decades; see R. Brown, 1965.) We present our version of Wiggins's (1997, p. 1072) circumplex model of interpersonal motives in Figure 5.3.

Like Bem's (1981) gender schema theory and Spence's (1993) multifactorial gender identity theory—and unlike versions of factor-analytic trait theory by Cattell (1943), H. J. Eysenck (1970), and McCrae and Costa (2003/

2006), among others—Wiggins's (2003/2005) interpersonal circumplex theory ultimately does *not* rely upon possibly inflated "heritability" estimates or otherwise make a strident argument for biology as largely determining individual differences in interpersonal traits (Gaines, 2020). By the same token, Wiggins's theory only hints at the role that specific "environmental" influences (e.g., societal, cultural, familial) might play in individuals' personality and social development—a critique that also applies to Sullivan's (1953) interpersonal theory of personality (see Gaines, 2016/2018). In any event, judging from the case study approach to "Madeline G." that one finds in *Paradigms of Personality Assessment* (Wiggins, 2003/2005) and the follow-up *Personality Assessment Paradigms and Methods: A Collaborative Reassessment of Madeline G* (edited by Hopwood & Waugh, 2020), "environment" matters more—and "biology" matters less—to the presumed origins of individuals' personalities from the standpoint of Wiggins's interpersonal circumplex theory than one would expect from certain factor-analytic trait theories.

A Point of Departure: Superordinate Constructs of Agency and Communion as Conceptualized by Bakan

In the process of expanding his interpersonal circumplex theory beyond traits, Wiggins (1991) drew upon David Bakan's *The Duality of Human Existence* (1966) as the source of the rationale that agency and communion are broadly conceived ways of being-in-the-world that encompass various pairs of subclinical personality constructs (e.g., the agentic trait of dominance and the communal trait of nurturance; the agentic motive of power and the communal motive of intimacy) that might strike one as bipolar ends of one dimension apiece but actually are orthogonal or independent dimensions (Gurtman, 2009). Bakan proposed that agency and communion are products of human evolution, with agency in particular (over) emphasized in postindustrial societies during the past several hundred years (see S. Strack & Horowitz, 2011). Furthermore, just as Sullivan (1953) had viewed individuals' seeking self-esteem and security as potentially complementary goals that can facilitate individuals' adaptive personality and social development, so too did Bakan view individuals' pursuit of agency and communion as potentially complementary ways of being-in-the-world that can promote the well-being of individuals and the societies in which they live (Fournier et al., 2011).

132 THE SELF IN RELATIONSHIPS

En route to developing her multifactorial gender identity theory (which would be presented in Spence, 1993), Spence (1985) referred to Bakan (1966) alongside Jung (1921/1971) as advocating a typology of masculinity versus femininity. However, a careful reading of *The Duality of Human Existence* (Bakan, 1966) reveals that Bakan had distinguished between (1) individuals' and societies' tendency to cast agency (including, but not limited to, masculinity) and communion (including, but not limited to, femininity) and (2) the adaptiveness of individuals' and societies' efforts to *refrain* from invoking a dichotomous view of agency versus communion (and, specifically, masculinity versus femininity; Bem, 1978). Nevertheless, Spence et al.'s (1979) construction of the Expanded Personality Attributes Questionnaire (EPAQ) to include negative and positive aspects of masculinity and femininity builds upon Bakan's insight in framing negative masculinity as a form of "unmitigated agency" and negative femininity as a form as "unmitigated communion" (see Lenney, 1991). In turn, the content of the EPAQ makes it possible for individuals to attain a socially undesirable type of "androgyny" by combining negative aspects of masculinity and femininity, thus turning Bem's (1981) gender schema theory on its head (Woodhill & Samuels, 2004).

One additional theory that acknowledges the impact of Bakan's (1966) constructs of agency and communion is Helgeson and Fritz's (1998) *theory of unmitigated communion,* which holds that gender differences in depression (with women consistently scoring higher than men) can be traced to gender differences in socialization (i.e., women as having been taught to prioritize other persons' needs over their own needs, thus leading to a greater likelihood of experiencing psychological distress than men; see also Helgeson, 2015). Part of Helgeson and Fritz's rationale for developing a new theory regarding gender and personality was that the Bem Sex Role Inventory (Bem, 1974) and the original Personal Attributes Questionnaire (Spence & Helmreich, 1978) did not operationalize negative aspects of masculinity or femininity, although such an argument neglects to mention the EPAQ (Spence et al., 1979), which *does* measure negative as well as positive aspects of masculinity and femininity (as noted by Helgeson, 1994; Helgeson & Fritz, 2000). One of the most noteworthy features of Helgeson and Fritz's theory of unmitigated communion for our purposes is the assumption that positive masculinity (i.e., the positive pole of dominance) is irrelevant to relationship maintenance processes, though Wiggins's (1991) interpersonal circumplex theory would not anticipate such a null result (see Gurtman, 2009).

The Geometrics of Wiggins's Interpersonal Circumplex Theory

By the time that Wiggins (1991) had proposed Bakan's (1966) constructs of agency and communion as the conceptual foundation for an interpersonal circumplex theory of personality and social behavior that transcends traits, Wiggins and colleagues (e.g., Wiggins et al., 1989) already had developed a set of strong geometric assumptions regarding correlations among lower-order interpersonal traits that presumably reflect the higher-order agentic trait of dominance and the higher-order communal trait of nurturance (Digman, 1990). Foremost among the assumptions underlying Wiggins's theory is the following pattern of lower-order trait correlations: (1) the set of freed correlations along the first diagonal below the fixed elements of 1.00s will be equal to each other, and "more positive" than the set of freed correlations immediately below it; (2) the set of freed correlations along the second diagonal below the fixed elements will be equal to each other, and "more positive" than the set of freed correlations immediately below it; (3) the set of freed correlations along the third diagonal below the fixed elements will be equal to each other, and "more positive" than the set of freed correlations immediately below it; (4) the set of freed correlations along the fourth diagonal below the fixed elements will be equal to each other, and "*less* positive" than the set of freed correlations immediately below it; (5) the set of freed correlations along the fifth diagonal below the fixed elements will be equal to each other, and "*less* positive" than the set of freed correlations immediately below it; and (6) the set of freed correlations along the sixth diagonal below the fixed elements will be equal to each other, and "*less* positive" than the single correlation immediately below it (Gurtman, 2011, p. 302). Also, as Table 5.1 indicates, Wiggins's interpersonal circumplex theory predicts that (a) the first and seventh sets of freed correlations will be equal to each other, (b) the second and sixth sets of freed correlations will be equal to each other, and (c) the third and fifth sets of freed correlations will be equal to each other. The resulting pattern of expected intercorrelations can be applied to various interpersonal aspects of personality, not just traits (Locke, 2011).

Furthermore, Wiggins et al. (1989) proposed that—in an ideal world—the magnitudes of correlations among lower-order *subclinical interpersonal traits* (if not other interpersonal aspects of personality) will conform to a sine-cosine matrix (Gurtman, 1993). Such an ideal matrix of lower-order intercorrelations, reported by Gurtman (2009, p. 608), is shown in Table 5.2.

134   THE SELF IN RELATIONSHIPS

Table 5.1 Expected Pattern of Intercorrelations Among Lower-Order Interpersonal Aspects of Personality in General (Gurtman, 2011, p. 302)

Var.	Correlations							
	PA	BC	DE	FG	HI	JK	LM	NO
PA	1.00							
BC	a	1.00						
DE	b	a	1.00					
FG	c	b	a	1.00				
HI	d	c	b	a	1.00			
JK	c	d	c	b	a	1.00		
LM	b	c	d	c	b	a	1.00	
NO	a	b	c	d	c	b	a	1.00

Note: The structure of expected intercorrelations (shown below the diagonal) can be applied to various personality constructs, including (but not limited to) subclinical and clinical traits. For subclinical traits, PA = ambitious-dominant, BC = arrogant-calculating, DE = cold-quarrelsome, FG = aloof-introverted, HI = unassured-submissive, JK = unassuming-ingenuous, LM = warm-agreeable, NO = gregarious-extraverted.

Summarizing across (1) the general expected pattern of lower-order personality intercorrelations in Table 5.1 and (2) the specific expected magnitudes and directions of intercorrelations among lower-order subclinical interpersonal traits in Table 5.2, one may hypothesize that the extent of

Table 5.2 Ideal Pattern of Intercorrelations Among Lower-Order Subclinical Interpersonal Traits in Particular (Gurtman, 2009, p. 608)

Var.	Correlations							
	PA	BC	DE	FG	HI	JK	LM	NO
PA	1.00							
BC	.71	1.00						
DE	.00	.71	1.00					
FG	−.71	.00	.71	1.00				
HI	−1.00	−.71	.00	.71	1.00			
JK	−.71	−1.00	−.71	.00	.71	1.00		
LM	.00	−.71	−1.00	−.71	.00	.71	1.00	
NO	.71	.00	−.71	−1.00	−.71	.00	.71	1.00

Note: The values of expected intercorrelations (shown above the diagonal) can be applied to *traits*, at least within the subclinical range. For subclinical traits, PA = ambitious-dominant, BC = arrogant-calculating, DE = cold-quarrelsome, FG = aloof-introverted, HI = unassured-submissive, JK = unassuming-ingenuous, LM = warm-agreeable, NO = gregarious-extraverted.

correspondence between (a) the matrix of ideal correlations that have been estimated by a given model and (b) the matrix of actual intercorrelations against which the model has been tested will serve as the basis for goodness-of-fit tests (including chi-square and many of its derivative statistics) that enable researchers to reject or fail to reject Wiggins's circumplex model for a particular data set (see Fabrigar et al., 1997). However, an actual set of lower-order subclinical interpersonal trait intercorrelations need not provide a perfect or near-perfect match to idealized sine or cosine values in order to yield acceptable fit to the circumplex model (Gurtman & Pincus, 2000).

In order to evaluate the geometric properties of a lower-order matrix of correlations among interpersonal aspects of personality (whether subclinical or clinical, and whether traits or other constructs), one likely will find it advantageous to conduct a *circulant correlation analysis* upon the correlation matrix (whereby goodness-of-fit statistics concerning the correspondence between ideal and actual correlation matrices are generated via maximum likelihood or other estimation methods; Gurtman, 2011). For instance, Wiggins and colleagues (1981) conducted circulant correlation analyses of data from one sample in which the original IAS was administered (Wiggins, 1979, Sample C), using three estimation methods (i.e., ordinary least squares, maximum likelihood, and generalized least squares) that generated nearly identical—albeit significant—chi-square values (which one does *not* want in such analyses). Also, Gurtman and Pincus (2000) conducted circulant correlation analyses of data from Wiggins (1995) and one sample from Gaines et al. (1997, Study 2) in which the IAS-R (Wiggins et al., 1998) was administered, using maximum likelihood estimation. However, the sample sizes were so different that the chi-square values were quite different as well (and significant, indicating "badness-of-fit").

"Simulated" Example 1: Lower-order subclinical interpersonal trait intercorrelations. In addition to offering an ideal matrix of lower-order subclinical interpersonal trait intercorrelations, Wiggins's (2003/2005) interpersonal circumplex theory provides "simulated" correlation matrices that can be evaluated via circulant correlation analyses (Gurtman, 2011). We present an example of a "simulated" matrix, from Gurtman (2011, p. 302), in Table 5.3. Inspection of Tables 5.2 and 5.3 reveals that the magnitudes of the correlations along the first, third, fifth, and seventh diagonals below the 1.00s at the top of the "simulated" matrix are approximately half the magnitudes of the corresponding correlations in the ideal matrix, sharing 25% (versus nearly 50%) of variance. At any rate, the correspondence between "simulated" matrices and model-generated estimates of matrices can be evaluated

136   THE SELF IN RELATIONSHIPS

Table 5.3 "Simulated" Matrix of Intercorrelations Among Lower-Order Subclinical Interpersonal Traits (Gurtman, 2011, p. 302)

Var.	Correlations							
	PA	BC	DE	FG	HI	JK	LM	NO
PA	1.00							
BC	.50	1.00						
DE	.00	.50	1.00					
FG	−.50	.00	.50	1.00				
HI	−1.00	−.50	.00	.50	1.00			
JK	−.50	−1.00	−.50	.00	.50	1.00		
LM	.00	−.50	−1.00	−.50	.00	.50	1.00	
NO	.50	.00	−.50	−1.00	−.50	.00	.50	1.00

Note: With an n of 120, all nonzero correlations would be significant ($p < .01$). For subclinical traits, PA = ambitious-dominant, BC = arrogant-calculating, DE = cold-quarrelsome, FG = aloof-introverted, HI = unassured-submissive, JK = unassuming-ingenuous, LM = warm-agreeable, NO = gregarious-extraverted.

via linear structural relations (LISREL; Joreskog & Sorbom, 2019), following Rosen (1992). We evaluated the goodness-of-fit concerning a circulant correlation model with *equal spacing* (i.e., the eight lower-order traits are assumed to be aligned at 45-degree angles around a circle) and *equal communality* (i.e., common variance associated with each lower-order trait is assumed to be equal; Gurtman & Pincus, 2000).

The syntax file for LISREL 10.20 (Joreskog & Sorbom, 2019) that we used for the circulant correlation analysis of the "simulated" matrix of lower-order subclinical interpersonal trait correlations from Gurtman (2011, p. 302) is shown in Table 5.4. Within the syntax file, the first line (i.e., Title, or TI) is arbitrary; the second line (i.e., Data, or DA) states that the number of input variables is eight (NI = 8), the number of observations is 120 (NO = 120, or 10 times the number of parameters [12] that must be estimated), and the type of data matrix to be analyzed is a correlation matrix (DA = KM); and the third line states the format of data to be analyzed (i.e., correlation matrix, or KM). Next, the eight lines of the "simulated" matrix are entered. Afterward, the 12th line (i.e., Model, or MO) lists the number of observed variables as eight (NY = 8), number of latent variables as eight (NE = 8), observed variable error variance-covariance matrix (i.e., Theta

CONCEPTUALIZATION OF DOMINANCE AND NURTURANCE 137

Table 5.4 Syntax File Used as Input for Circulant Correlation Analysis of "Simulated" Matrix From Gurtman (2011, p. 302)

```
HYPOTHETICAL DATA FROM GURTMAN (2011) EQUAL SPACING, EQUAL
COMMUNALITY MODEL
DA NI=8 NO=120 MA=KM
KM
  1.00
   .50    1.00
   .00     .50    1.00
  -.50     .00     .50    1.00
 -1.00    -.50     .00     .50    1.00
  -.50   -1.00    -.50     .00     .50    1.00
   .00    -.50   -1.00    -.50     .00     .50    1.00
   .50     .00    -.50   -1.00    -.50     .00     .50    1.00
```

```
MO NY=8 NE=8 TE=SY,FI LY=FU,FI PS=SY,FR
LA
PA BC DE FG HI JK LM NO
FR TE 1 1 TE 2 2 TE 3 3 TE 4 4 TE 5 5 TE 6 6 TE 7 7 TE 8 8
ST 1.00 LY 1 1 LY 2 2 LY 3 3 LY 4 4 LY 5 5 LY 6 6 LY 7 7 LY 8 8
FI PS 1 1 PS 2 2 PS 3 3 PS 4 4 PS 5 5 PS 6 6 PS 7 7 PS 8 8
ST 1.00 PS 1 1 PS 2 2 PS 3 3 PS 4 4 PS 5 5 PS 6 6 PS 7 7 PS 8 8
EQ PS 2 1 PS 3 2 PS 4 3 PS 5 4 PS 6 5 PS 7 6 PS 8 7 PS 8 1
ST .71 PS 2 1
EQ PS 3 1 PS 4 2 PS 5 3 PS 6 4 PS 7 5 PS 8 6 PS 7 1 PS 8 2
ST .00 PS 3 1
EQ PS 4 1 PS 5 2 PS 6 3 PS 7 4 PS 8 5 PS 6 1 PS 7 2 PS 8 3
ST -.71 PS 4 1
EQ PS 5 1 PS 6 2 PS 7 3 PS 8 4
ST -1.00 PS 5 1
OU ALL ME=ML RO RC AD=OFF
```

Epsilon, or TE) as symmetrical with fixed parameters across the top and bottom halves (SY,FI), the latent-observed variable matrix (i.e., Lambda Y, or LY) as full with fixed parameters (FU,FI), and the latent variable error-covariance matrix (i.e., Psi, or PS) as symmetrical with freed parameters (SY,FR). In turn, the 13th line provides labels (LA) for the input variables, which are listed on the 14th line (PA, BC, DE, FG, HI, JK, LM, and NO, which are standard for interpersonal circumplex theorists in the tradition of Wiggins, 2003/2005). Subsequently, the 15th line frees the elements along the top diagonal of the TE matrix (FR, thus allowing error variances associated with the eight lower-order trait scores to vary). Next, the 16th through 26th lines instruct LISREL to free correlations other than 1.00, −1.00, or .00,

138 THE SELF IN RELATIONSHIPS

yet subjecting the correlations to equality constraints and starting values as required by Table 5.2. Lastly, the 27th line requests output (OU) with all options (ALL), method of maximum likelihood estimation applied to all freed parameters (ME = ML), ridge option and ridge constant (RO RC) that controls statistically for expected correlations reaching or approaching −1.00 in magnitude between lower-order traits that are placed directly opposite each other within the circumplex model, and admissibility check turned off (AD = OFF).

Results of the circulant correlation analysis for the "simulated" matrix from Gurtman (2011, p. 302) indicate that the discrepancy between the "simulation" and the model-generated matrix of lower-order trait correlations was nonsignificant (chi-square = .00, 24 degrees of freedom [df], NS). Given that the fit of the model to the "data" was perfect, no other goodness-of-fit indicators were produced. Interestingly, the matrix of reproduced correlations (shown in Table 5.5) reveals that the estimated correlations were identical to the "simulated" correlations, rather than the ideal sine-cosine correlations that one would have expected on the basis of Wiggins's (2003/2005) interpersonal circumplex theory (and that we entered as initial, nonfixed values). Overall, results of the circulant correlation analysis for the "simulated" matrix give us a "gold standard" for evaluating results from actual data.

Table 5.5 Reproduced Correlation Matrix for "Simulated" Data From Gurtman (2011, p. 302)

Var.	PA	BC	DE	FG	HI	JK	LM	NO
PA	1.00							
BC	.50	1.00						
DE	.00	.50	1.00					
FG	−.50	.00	.50	1.00				
HI	−1.00	−.50	.00	.50	1.00			
JK	−.50	−1.00	−.50	.00	.50	1.00		
LM	.00	−.50	−1.00	−.50	.00	.50	1.00	
NO	.50	.00	−.50	−1.00	−.50	.00	.50	1.00

Note: For subclinical traits, PA = ambitious-dominant, BC = arrogant-calculating, DE = cold-quarrelsome, FG = aloof-introverted, HI = unassured-submissive, JK = unassuming-ingenuous, LM = warm-agreeable, NO = gregarious-extraverted.

CONCEPTUALIZATION OF DOMINANCE AND NURTURANCE 139

"Simulated" Example 2: Lower-order clinical interpersonal trait intercorrelations. Just as Gurtman (2011, p. 302) constructed a "simulated" matrix of lower-order *subclinical* interpersonal trait correlations, so too did Gurtman (1993, p. 241) create a "simulated" matrix of lower-order *clinical* interpersonal trait intercorrelations (Wiggins & Trobst, 1997). Gurtman's "simulated" matrix of clinical interpersonal trait correlations is shown in Table 5.6. As was the case for circulant correlation analyses of subclinical interpersonal trait correlations, circulant correlation analyses of clinical interpersonal trait correlations can be conducted readily via LISREL (Joreskog & Sorbom, 2019; see Tracey, 2000). Therefore, with relatively minor modifications, the syntax file that we presented in Table 5.4 regarding Wiggins's "simulated" subclinical trait matrix can be repurposed for Gurtman's "simulated" clinical trait matrix. The required modifications in question involve tweaking the title, replacing the correlations from Wiggins's matrix with correlations from Gurtman's matrix, and changing the labels to emphasize the switch from subclinical to clinical traits. The resulting syntax file for Gurtman's "simulated" clinical trait intercorrelation matrix is shown in Table 5.7.

Results of the circulant correlation analysis for Gurtman's (1993, p. 241) "simulated" matrix of clinical interpersonal trait correlations indicated that, as we reported for Gurtman's (2011, p. 302) "simulated" matrix of subclinical interpersonal trait correlations, the model fit was perfect

Table 5.6 "Simulated" Matrix of Intercorrelations Among Lower-Order Clinical Interpersonal Traits (Gurtman, 1993, p. 241)

	Correlations							
Var.	*DO*	*VI*	*CO*	*SO*	*NA*	*EX*	*ON*	*IT*
DO	1.00							
VI	.85	1.00						
CO	.50	.85	1.00					
SO	.15	.50	.85	1.00				
NA	.00	.15	.50	.85	1.00			
EX	.15	.00	.15	.50	.85	1.00		
ON	.50	.15	.00	.15	.50	.85	1.00	
IT	.85	.85	.15	.00	.15	.50	.85	1.00

Note: With an *n* of 120, all correlations with absolute values greater than .16 would be significant ($p < .05$ or lower). For clinical traits, DO = domineering, VI = vindictive, CO = cold, SO = socially avoidant, NA = nonassertive, EX = exploitable, ON = overly nurturance, IT = intrusive.

140 THE SELF IN RELATIONSHIPS

Table 5.7 Syntax File Used as Input for Circulant Correlation Analysis of "Simulated" Matrix From Gurtman (1993, p. 241)

```
HYPOTHETICAL DATA FROM GURTMAN (1993) EQUAL SPACING, EQUAL
COMMUNALITY
DA NI=8 NO=120 MA=KM
KM
1.00
 .85    1.00
 .50     .85    1.00
 .15     .50     .85    1.00
 .00     .15     .50     .85    1.00
 .15     .00     .15     .50     .85    1.00
 .50     .15     .00     .15     .50     .85    1.00
 .85     .50     .15     .00     .15     .50     .85    1.00
```

```
MO NY=8 NE=8 TE=SY,FI LY=FU,FI PS=SY,FR
LA
DO VI CO SO NA EX ON IT
FR TE 1 1 TE 2 2 TE 3 3 TE 4 4 TE 5 5 TE 6 6 TE 7 7 TE 8 8
ST 1.00 LY 1 1 LY 2 2 LY 3 3 LY 4 4 LY 5 5 LY 6 6 LY 7 7 LY 8 8
FI PS 1 1 PS 2 2 PS 3 3 PS 4 4 PS 5 5 PS 6 6 PS 7 7 PS 8 8
ST 1.00 PS 1 1 PS 2 2 PS 3 3 PS 4 4 PS 5 5 PS 6 6 PS 7 7 PS 8 8
EQ PS 2 1 PS 3 2 PS 4 3 PS 5 4 PS 6 5 PS 7 6 PS 8 7 PS 8 1
ST .71 PS 2 1
EQ PS 3 1 PS 4 2 PS 5 3 PS 6 4 PS 7 5 PS 8 6 PS 7 1 PS 8 2
ST .00 PS 3 1
EQ PS 4 1 PS 5 2 PS 6 3 PS 7 4 PS 8 5 PS 6 1 PS 7 2 PS 8 3
ST -.71 PS 4 1
EQ PS 5 1 PS 6 2 PS 7 3 PS 8 4
ST -1.00 PS 5 1
OU ALL ME=ML RO RC AD=OFF
```

(chi-square = .00, 24 *df, NS*). Moreover, the reproduced correlation matrix was identical to the input matrix for Gurtman's "simulation" (rather than the sine-cosine correlations that we had entered as starting yet nonfixed values)—a finding that parallels the complete convergence between the reproduced correlation matrix and input matrix for Wiggins's "simulation." The reproduced correlation matrix from the circulant correlation analysis of Gurtman's "simulated" matrix of clinical interpersonal trait correlations is shown in Table 5.8.

Given that (1) roughly half of the correlations in the ideal matrix of correlations among interpersonal aspects of personality (whether sub-clinical or clinical) are negative, yet (2) *all* of the correlations in Gurtman's

CONCEPTUALIZATION OF DOMINANCE AND NURTURANCE 141

Table 5.8 Reproduced Correlation Matrix for "Simulated" Data From Gurtman (1993, p. 241)

Var.	Correlations							
	DO	VI	CO	SO	NA	EX	ON	IT
DO	1.00							
VI	.85	1.00						
CO	.50	.85	1.00					
SO	.15	.50	.85	1.00				
NA	.00	.15	.50	.85	1.00			
EX	.15	.00	.15	.50	.85	1.00		
ON	.50	.15	.00	.15	.50	.85	1.00	
IT	.85	.85	.15	.00	.15	.50	.85	1.00

Note: For clinical traits, DO = domineering, VI = vindictive, CO = cold, SO = socially avoidant, NA = nonassertive, EX = exploitable, ON = overly nurturance, IT = intrusive.

(1993, p. 241) "simulated" matrix of clinical interpersonal trait correlations were *positive* in direction, why were we unable to reject the equal-spacing, equal-communality model for Gurtman's "simulation"? The answer to this question may lie within a fundamental premise of so-called structural equation modeling (SEM) programs, including LISREL (Joreskog & Sorbom, 2019): The "best" or optimal combination of fixed and freed parameters is the combination that maximizes the extent to which the hypothesized model recreates the matrix of observed correlations, with the assumption that the recreated or reproduced correlation matrix can be applied to a larger population (Schumacker & Lomax, 2016). Therefore, if the nonfixed starting values (provided by the ideal correlation matrix in the circulant correlation analyses that we have conducted so far) do not enable the hypothesized model to recreate the observed correlations in an essentially faithful manner, then LISREL ultimately may set aside those starting values (Kline, 2016).

The Psychometrics of Wiggins's Interpersonal Circumplex Theory

In *Paradigms of Personality Assessment* (Wiggins, 2003/2005) and *Personality Assessment Paradigms and Methods: A Collaborative Reassessment of*

142   THE SELF IN RELATIONSHIPS

Madeline G (edited by Hopwood & Waugh, 2020), Wiggins and other inter-personal circumplex theorists have tended to approach geometric analyses (e.g., circulant correlation analysis) as ends in themselves or, alternatively, as means toward creating profiles for individual participants on eight lower-order traits (whether subclinical or clinical in nature). However, it is clear from the *Handbook of Interpersonal Psychology: Theory, Research, Assessment, and Therapeutic Implications* (edited by Horowitz & Strack, 2011) that inter-personal circumplex theory—like earlier theories that influenced it directly (e.g., the interpersonal theory of Sullivan, 1953) or indirectly (e.g., the at-tachment theory of Bowlby, 1969/1997)—possibly could explain substantial variance in individuals' behavior within social and personal relationships, using samples numbering in the hundreds or more, in addition to samples numbering in the dozens or less. In *Personality and Close Relationship Processes*, Gaines (2016/2018) concluded that researchers would find it diffi-cult to fulfill the potential of interpersonal circumplex theory unless they add underutilized *psychometric* analyses, such as confirmatory factor analysis.

Throughout the development of the original IAS (Wiggins, 1979), IAS-R (Wiggins et al., 1988) surveys, as well as the noncircumplex IAS-Big Five survey (Trapnell & Wiggins, 1990), Wiggins and colleagues have relied pri-marily upon *principal component analysis* (an empirically driven data reduc-tion procedure for creating linear composites of measured variables) as their default psychometric analysis (for details concerning the logic behind prin-cipal component analysis, see Fabrigar et al., 1999). Unfortunately, principal component analysis—which interpersonal circumplex theorists often de-scribe (inaccurately) as if it were synonymous with *exploratory factor analysis* (an empirically driven latent variable extraction procedure for interpreting the patterns of correlations among measured variables)—often generates a noncircumplex "acquiescence" dimension that represents more strongly positive correlations (even among lower-order aspects of personality that ostensibly are negative in direction) than Wiggins's (1991) theory would predict, in addition to expected agentic and communal dimensions such as dominance and nurturance (Fabrigar et al., 1997). Nevertheless, many in-terpersonal circumplex theorists continue to embrace principal component analysis (Gurtman, 2009).

Gaines, Panter, et al. (1997) contended that *confirmatory factor analysis* (a conceptually driven latent variable extraction procedure that, unlike ex-ploratory factor analysis, allows researchers to test hypotheses regarding the loadings from specific latent variables to specific measured variables) was conspicuously missing from previous studies that had employed geometric and psychometric analyses of correlations among lower-order traits and other aspects of personality (see also Fabrigar et al., 1997). Furthermore, Gaines and colleagues expressed concern that previous studies of the circumplexity of correlations among lower-order aspects of personality had not employed LISREL (for which the most current version at the time was Version 7; see Joreskog & Sorbom, 1989) as the statistical package of choice for confirmatory factor analysis, even though LISREL was (and remains) unique in enabling researchers to control for perfect or near-perfect "nonpositive definite" matrices (i.e., ridge option and ridge constant; Kline, 2016; Wothke, 1993). Consistent with Gaines et al., we shall apply confirmatory factor analyses— whether on their own (from the present chapter through Chapter 7) or integrated within more complex types of covariance structure analyses (in Chapter 8)—to matrices of subclinical interpersonal trait correlations.

Combining circumplex and noncircumplex factors. Although we generally followed the lead of Gaines, Panter, et al. (1997) in applying confirmatory factor analyses to "simulated" matrices of correlations among lower-order subclinical and clinical interpersonal traits (in the present chapter) and actual matrices of correlations among lower-order subclinical interpersonal traits (in Chapters 6 through 8), we have made major as well as minor changes to the analyses that Gaines and colleagues conducted on data from the original IAS (Wiggins, 1979) and the IAS-R (Wiggins et al., 1988). First, instead of using weighted least squares estimation (as Gaines et al. had done in portions of analyses for their Study 2), we used the default of maximum likelihood estimation as the method for extracting higher-order factors. Second, rather than constrain uncorrelated measurement error to be equal across the lower-order traits, we allowed the error terms to vary across those traits. Lastly (and most important), instead of limiting ourselves to two higher-order circumplex factors, we added a noncircumplex "acquiescence" factor on which the loadings were freed but constrained to be equal across the eight lower-order traits. The final modification indicates that confirmatory factor analysis is amenable to noncircumplex factors (contrary to Tracey, 2000).

Unlike the circulant correlation analyses that we reported earlier in the present chapter (whereby we evaluated the goodness-of-fit regarding a single model to "simulated" data), we will compare and contrast the goodness-of-fit regarding pairs of models (one of which excludes a noncircumplex "acquiescence" factor, and one of which includes such a factor) in our confirmatory factor analyses from the present chapter

144 THE SELF IN RELATIONSHIPS

onward. For the two higher-order circumplex factors, we adopted Gaines, Panter, et al.'s (1997, Study 2) "quasi-circumplex" model, which specifies (1) freed loadings, constrained to be equal, for the lower-order traits at the positive poles of the agentic and communal axes; (2) freed loadings, constrained to be equal, for the lower-order traits at the negative poles of the agentic and communal axes; (3) freed loadings, constrained to be equal, across (a) the second lower-order trait on the agentic axis, (b) the eighth lower-order trait on the agentic axis, (c) the sixth lower-order trait on the communal axis, and (d) the eighth lower-order trait on the communal axis (with starting values); (4) freed loadings, constrained to be equal, across (a) the second lower-order trait on the communal axis, (b) the fourth lower-order trait on the communal axis, (c) the fourth lower-order trait on the agentic axis, and (d) the sixth lower-order trait on the agentic axis; and (5) fixed loadings of .00 for all other lower-order traits on the agentic and communal axes. The competing models regarding circumplex and noncircumplex factor loadings are shown in Table 5.9.

In the preceding section, we learned that Gurtman (1993) presented an ideal matrix of correlations among lower-order subclinical traits (if not other aspects of personality). Similarly, Wiggins and Broughton (1991) presented an ideal matrix of higher-order factor loadings on agentic and communal axes for lower-order subclinical traits (and, perhaps, other aspects of personality) based on sine-cosine functions, following Wiggins et al. (1989). Notably, Wiggins and Broughton did *not* acknowledge that a third, noncircumplex "acquiescence" factor might be extracted in addition to the two circumplex factors. In Table 5.10, we present *two* ideal factor matrices (one without the noncircumplex factor and one with that factor) that include Wiggins and Broughton's hypothesized loadings—namely, (1) starting values of 1.00 for the lower-order traits at the positive poles of the agentic and communal axes; (2) starting values of −1.00 for the lower-order traits at the negative poles of the agentic and communal axes; (3) starting values of .71 across (a) the second lower-order trait on the agentic axis, (b) the eighth lower-order trait on the agentic axis, (c) the sixth lower-order trait on the communal axis, and (d) the eighth lower-order trait on the communal axis (with starting values); (4) starting values of −.71 across (a) the second lower-order trait on the communal axis, (b) the fourth lower-order trait on the communal axis, (c) the fourth lower-order trait on the agentic axis, and (d) the sixth lower-order trait on the agentic axis; and (5) fixed loadings of .00 for all other lower-order traits on the agentic and communal axes.

CONCEPTUALIZATION OF DOMINANCE AND NURTURANCE 145

Table 5.9 Expected Patterns of Factor Loadings Among Lower-Order Interpersonal Aspects of Personality in General for "Simulated" Matrix From Gurtman (2011, p. 302)

Two-factor solution			
Var.	*Factor*		
	DOM	*NUR*	*AQC*
PA	c	.00	.00
BC	a	b	.00
DE	.00	d	.00
FG	b	b	.00
HI	d	.00	.00
JK	b	a	.00
LM	.00	c	.00
NO	a	a	.00

Three-factor solution			
Var.	*Factor*		
	DOM	*NUR*	*AQC*
PA	c	.00	[e]
BC	a	b	[e]
DE	.00	d	[e]
FG	b	b	[e]
HI	d	.00	[e]
JK	b	a	[e]
LM	.00	c	[e]
NO	a	a	[e]

Note: The structure of expected higher-order factor loadings can be applied to various personality constructs, including (but not limited to) traits. Regarding higher-order factors, DOM = dominance, NUR = nurturance, ACQ = acquiescence. Regarding lower-order interpersonal traits, PA = ambitious-dominant, BC = arrogant-calculating, DE = cold-quarrelsome, FG = aloof-introverted, HI = unassured-submissive, JK = unassuming-ingenuous, LM = warm-agreeable, NO = gregarious-extraverted.

Return to "Simulated" Example 1: Lower-order subclinical interpersonal trait intercorrelations. Also, in the preceding section, we encountered Gurtman's (2011, p. 302) "simulated" matrix of correlations among lower-order interpersonal subclinical traits. We shall enter that correlation matrix into two competing confirmatory factor analyses (again, one without a noncircumplex

146 THE SELF IN RELATIONSHIPS

Table 5.10 Expected Patterns of Factor Loadings Among Lower-Order Subclinical Interpersonal Traits in Particular for "Simulated" Matrix From Gurtman (2011, p. 302)

Two-factor solution			
Var.	*Factor*		
	DOM	*NUR*	*AQC*
PA	1.00	.00	.00
BC	.71	−.71	.00
DE	.00	−1.00	.00
FG	−.71	−.71	.00
HI	−1.00	.00	.00
JK	−.71	.71	.00
LM	.00	1.00	.00
NO	.71	.71	.00
Three-factor solution			
Var.	*Factor*		
	DOM	*NUR*	*AQC*
PA	1.00	.00	[e]
BC	.71	−.71	[e]
DE	.00	−1.00	[e]
FG	−.71	−.71	[e]
HI	−1.00	.00	[e]
JK	−.71	.71	[e]
LM	.00	1.00	[e]
NO	.71	.71	[e]

Note: The values of expected higher-order factor loadings can be applied to *traits*, at least within the subclinical range (similar logic should apply to clinical traits as well). Regarding higher-order factors, DOM = dominance, NUR = nurturance, ACQ = acquiescence. Regarding lower-order interpersonal traits, PA = ambitious-dominant, BC = arrogant-calculating, DE = cold-quarrelsome, FG = aloof-introverted, HI = unassured-submissive, JK = unassuming-ingenuous, LM = warm-agreeable, NO = gregarious-extraverted.

"acquiescence" factor, followed by one with the noncircumplex factor, alongside the circumplex factors of dominance and nurturance). In both confirmatory factor analyses using LISREL 10.20 (Joreskog & Sorbom, 2019), we entered the combination of fixed and freed parameters (as well as starting values for freed parameters where appropriate) that we had listed in Table 5.10.

CONCEPTUALIZATION OF DOMINANCE AND NURTURANCE   147

The syntax files that we used as input for the confirmatory factor analyses of Wiggins's "simulation" are shown in Table 5.11. The syntax files for the two confirmatory factor analyses differ from the syntax file for the single circulant correlation analysis (Table 5.7) as follows: (1) in the Model (MO) line, the number of latent variables or factors (NE) is two in the first syntax file and three in the second syntax file; (2) in the latent-observed or Lambda Y (LY) lines, the fixed and freed parameters refer to loadings for the eight lower-order traits on the two/three higher-order traits (rather than correlations among the eight lower-order traits); and (3) in the latent variable covariance or Psi (PS) line, the fixed and freed parameters refer to the correlations among the two/

Table 5.11 Syntax Files Used as Input for Confirmatory Factor Analyses of "Simulated" Matrix From Gurtman (2011, p. 302)

Two-factor model

```
HYPOTHETICAL DATA FROM GURTMAN (2011) DOM NUR
DA NI=8 NO=120 MA=KM
KM
 1.00
  .50    1.00
  .00     .50    1.00
 -.50     .00     .50    1.00
-1.00    -.50     .00     .50    1.00
 -.50   -1.00    -.50     .00     .50    1.00
  .00    -.50   -1.00    -.50     .00     .50    1.00
  .50     .00    -.50   -1.00    -.50     .00     .50    1.00
```

```
MO NY=8 NE=2 TE=SY,FI LY=FU,FI PS=SY,FI
LA
PA BC DE FG HI JK LM NO
FR TE 1 1 TE 2 2 TE 3 3 TE 4 4 TE 5 5 TE 6 6 TE 7 7 TE 8 8
FR LY 1 1 LY 7 2
FR LY 2 1 LY 8 1 LY 6 2 LY 8 2
FR LY 5 1 LY 3 2
FR LY 4 1 LY 6 1 LY 2 2 LY 4 2
EQ LY 1 1 LY 7 2
EQ LY 2 1 LY 8 1 LY 6 2 LY 8 2
EQ LY 5 1 LY 3 2
EQ LY 4 1 LY 6 1 LY 2 2 LY 4 2
ST 1.00 LY 1 1
ST .71 LY 2 1
ST -.71 LY 4 1
ST -1.00 LY 5 1
ST 1.00 PS 1 1 PS 2 2
OU ALL ME=ML RO RC AD=OFF
```

(continued)

148 THE SELF IN RELATIONSHIPS

Table 5.11 Continued

```
Three-factor model
HYPOTHETICAL DATA FROM GURTMAN (2011) DOM NUR ACQ
DA NI=8 NO=120 MA=KM
KM
 1.00
  .50    1.00
  .00     .50    1.00
 -.50     .00     .50    1.00
-1.00    -.50     .00     .50    1.00
 -.50   -1.00    -.50     .00     .50    1.00
  .00    -.50   -1.00    -.50     .00     .50    1.00
  .50     .00    -.50   -1.00    -.50     .00     .50    1.00
```

```
MO NY=8 NE=3 TE=SY,FI LY=FU,FI PS=SY,FI
LA
PA BC DE FG HI JK LM NO
FR TE 1 1 TE 2 2 TE 3 3 TE 4 4 TE 5 5 TE 6 6 TE 7 7 TE 8 8
FR LY 1 1 LY 7 2
FR LY 2 1 LY 8 1 LY 6 2 LY 8 2
FR LY 5 1 LY 3 2
FR LY 4 1 LY 6 1 LY 2 2 LY 4 2
EQ LY 1 1 LY 7 2
EQ LY 2 1 LY 8 1 LY 6 2 LY 8 2
EQ LY 5 1 LY 3 2
EQ LY 4 1 LY 6 1 LY 2 2 LY 4 2
ST 1.00 LY 1 1
ST .71 LY 2 1
ST -.71 LY 4 1
ST -1.00 LY 5 1
FR LY 1 3 LY 2 3 LY 3 3 LY 4 3 LY 5 3 LY 6 3 LY 7 3 LY 8 3
EQ LY 1 3 LY 2 3 LY 3 3 LY 4 3 LY 5 3 LY 6 3 LY 7 3 LY 8 3
ST 1.00 PS 1 1 PS 2 2 PS 3 3
OU ALL ME=ML RO RC AD=OFF
```

three latent variables (rather than correlations among the eight lower-order traits).

Results of the initial confirmatory factor analysis of Gurtman's (2011, p. 302) "simulated" matrix of correlations among lower-order subclinical interpersonal traits indicated that a two-factor model (i.e., dominance and nurturance as circumplex factors, without the addition of a "noncircumplex" acquiescence factor) provided satisfactory fit to the data (chi-square = 17.76, df = 24, NS; root mean square error of approximation [RMSEA] = .00, comparative fit index [CFI] = .96). Furthermore, the matrix

CONCEPTUALIZATION OF DOMINANCE AND NURTURANCE 149

Table 5.12 Obtained Patterns of Factor Loadings Among Lower-Order Subclinical Interpersonal Traits in Particular for "Simulated" Matrix From Gurtman (2011, p. 302), Two- and Three-Factor Solutions

Var.	Factor		
	DOM	NUR	ACQ
PA	.90	.00	.00
BC	.63	−.63	.00
DE	.00	−.90	.00
FG	−.63	−.63	.00
HI	−.90	.00	.00
JK	−.63	.63	.00
LM	.00	.90	.00
NO	.63	.63	.00

Note: Regarding higher-order factors, DOM = dominance, NUR = nurturance, ACQ = acquiescence. Regarding lower-order interpersonal traits, PA = ambitious-dominant, BC = arrogant-calculating, DE = cold-quarrelsome, FG = aloof-introverted, HI = unassured-submissive, JK = unassuming-ingenuous, LM = warm-agreeable, NO = gregarious-extraverted.

of loadings on the dominance and circumplex axes conformed to a "quasi-circumplex" pattern, with freed parameters achieving significance ($p < .01$) in the expected magnitude and direction. As was the case for estimated correlations in the circulant correlation analysis, estimated factor loadings in the initial confirmatory factor analysis of Wiggins's "simulation" were not as high as Wiggins and Broughton's (1991) ideal loadings but nonetheless were impressive. The matrix of higher-order loadings for the first confirmatory factor analysis of Wiggins's "simulated" correlation matrix are shown in Table 5.12.

Results of the final confirmatory factor analysis of Gurtman's (2011, p. 302) "simulated" matrix of correlations among lower-order subclinical interpersonal traits indicated that a three-factor model (i.e., dominance and nurturance as circumplex factors, with the addition of a "noncircumplex" acquiescence factor) likewise provided satisfactory fit to the data (chi-square = 17.76, $df = 23$, *NS*; RMSEA = .00, CFI = .96). Indeed, a direct comparison yielded literally zero gain for the three-factor model over the two-factor model (difference in chi-square = .00, difference in $df = 1$, *NS*). As Table 5.12 demonstrates, even when

150 THE SELF IN RELATIONSHIPS

loadings on the noncircumplex "acquiescence" factor were allowed to vary, the loadings remained steady at .00. Therefore, results for Gurtman's (2011, p. 302) "simulation" suggest that a two-factor model provides more parsimonious fit than does a three-factor model (see T. A. Brown, 2015, regarding comparisons of models in confirmatory factor analyses).

Return to "simulated" example 1: Lower-order clinical interpersonal trait intercorrelations. Finally, in the preceding section, we encountered Gurtman's (1993, p. 241) "simulated" matrix of correlations among lower-order interpersonal clinical traits. We will enter that correlation matrix into two competing confirmatory factor analyses (one without a noncircumplex "acquiescence" factor, followed by one with the noncircumplex factor, alongside the circumplex factors of dominance and nurturance). The syntax files that we used as input for the confirmatory factor analyses of Gurtman's "simulation," which are virtually identical to the syntax files that we used for the confirmatory factor analyses of Wiggins's "simulation" (except for the title and the correlations), are shown in Table 5.13.

Results of the initial confirmatory factor analysis of Gurtman's (1993, p. 241) "simulated" matrix of correlations among lower-order subclinical interpersonal traits indicated that a two-factor model (i.e., dominance and nurturance as circumplex factors, without the addition of a "noncircumplex" acquiescence factor) did *not* provide satisfactory fit to the data (chi-square = 174.71, $df = 24$, $p < .01$; RMSEA = .23, CFI = .63). Given the "badness-of-fit," we do not present factor loadings for the two-factor model. We concluded that a two-factor model was insufficient to explain the correlations within Gurtman's "simulation."

Conversely, results of the final confirmatory factor analysis of Gurtman's (1993, p. 241) "simulated" matrix of correlations among lower-order subclinical interpersonal traits indicated that a three-factor model (i.e., dominance and nurturance as circumplex factors, with the addition of a "noncircumplex" acquiescence factor) provided satisfactory fit to the data (chi-square = .01, $df = 23$, NS; RMSEA = .00, CFI = 1.00). Moreover, the three-factor model yielded significantly better fit to the data than did the two-factor model (chi-square difference = 174.70, difference in $df = 1$, $p < .01$). In addition, as Table 5.14 indicates, the magnitude and direction of loadings of lower-order traits on the dominance and nurturance factors within the three-factor solution were fully consistent with (though lower in magnitude than) Wiggins and Broughton's (1991) hypothesized loadings for lower-order aspects of personality in general. The major surprise regarding

CONCEPTUALIZATION OF DOMINANCE AND NURTURANCE 151

Table 5.13 Syntax Files Used as Input for Confirmatory Factor Analyses of "Simulated" Matrix From Gurtman (1993, p. 241)

Two-factor model

```
HYPOTHETICAL DATA FROM GURTMAN (1993) DOM GEN
DA NI=8 NO=120 MA=KM
KM
```

```
1.00
 .85    1.00
 .50     .85    1.00
 .15     .50     .85    1.00
 .00     .15     .50     .85    1.00
 .15     .00     .15     .50     .85    1.00
 .50     .15     .00     .15     .50     .85    1.00
 .85     .50     .15     .00     .15     .50     .85    1.00
```

```
MO NY=8 NE=2 TE=SY,FI LY=FU,FI PS=SY,FI
LA
DO VI CO SO NA EX ON IT
FR TE 1 1 TE 2 2 TE 3 3 TE 4 4 TE 5 5 TE 6 6 TE 7 7 TE 8 8
FR LY 1 1 LY 7 2
FR LY 2 1 LY 8 1 LY 6 2 LY 8 2
FR LY 5 1 LY 3 2
FR LY 4 1 LY 6 1 LY 2 2 LY 4 2
EQ LY 1 1 LY 7 2
EQ LY 2 1 LY 8 1 LY 6 2 LY 8 2
EQ LY 5 1 LY 3 2
EQ LY 4 1 LY 6 1 LY 2 2 LY 4 2
ST 1.00 LY 1 1
ST .71 LY 2 1
ST -.71 LY 4 1
ST -1.00 LY 5 1
ST 1.00 PS 1 1 PS 2 2
OU ALL ME=ML RO RC AD=OFF
```

Three-factor model

```
HYPOTHETICAL DATA FROM GURTMAN (1993) DOM NUR GEN
DA NI=8 NO=120 MA=KM
KM
1.00
 .85    1.00
 .50     .85    1.00
 .15     .50     .85    1.00
 .00     .15     .50     .85    1.00
 .15     .00     .15     .50     .85    1.00
```

(continued)

152 THE SELF IN RELATIONSHIPS

Table 5.13 Continued

Three-factor model							
.50	.15	.00	.15	.50	.85	1.00	
.85	.50	.15	.00	.15	.50	.85	1.00

```
MO NY=8 NE=3 TE=SY,FI LY=FU,FI PS=SY,FI
LA
DO VI CO SO NA EX ON IT
FR TE 1 1 TE 2 2 TE 3 3 TE 4 4 TE 5 5 TE 6 6 TE 7 7 TE 8 8
FR LY 1 1 LY 7 2
FR LY 2 1 LY 8 1 LY 6 2 LY 8 2
FR LY 5 1 LY 3 2
FR LY 4 1 LY 6 1 LY 2 2 LY 4 2
EQ LY 1 1 LY 7 2
EQ LY 2 1 LY 8 1 LY 6 2 LY 8 2
EQ LY 5 1 LY 3 2
EQ LY 4 1 LY 6 1 LY 2 2 LY 4 2
ST 1.00 LY 1 1
ST .71 LY 2 1
ST -.71 LY 4 1
ST -1.00 LY 5 1
FR LY 1 3 LY 2 3 LY 3 3 LY 4 3 LY 5 3 LY 6 3 LY 7 3 LY 8 3
EQ LY 1 3 LY 2 3 LY 3 3 LY 4 3 LY 5 3 LY 6 3 LY 7 3 LY 8 3
ST 1.00 PS 1 1 PS 2 2 PS 3 3
OU ALL ME=ML RO RC AD=OFF
```

Table 5.14 Obtained Patterns of Factor Loadings
Among Lower-Order Clinical Interpersonal Traits
in Particular for "Simulated" Matrix from Gurtman
(1993, p. 241), Three-Factor Solution

Var.	Factor		
	DOM	*NUR*	*ACQ*
DO	.71	.00	.71
VI	.50	−.50	.71
CO	.00	−.71	.71
SO	−.50	−.50	.71
NA	−.71	.00	.71
EX	−.50	.50	.71
ON	.00	.71	.71
IT	.71	.50	.71

Note: Regarding higher-order factors, DOM = dominance, NUR =
nurturance, GEN = general distress. Regarding lower-order interpersonal traits, DO = domineering, VI = vindictive, CO = cold,
SO = socially avoidant, NA = nonassertive, EX = exploitable, ON =
overly nurturance, IT = intrusive.

results for the three-factor model was the magnitude of the loadings for lower-order traits on the noncircumplex "acquiescence" factor, which exceeded the magnitude of loadings for all of the lower-order traits on the two circumplex factors. Therefore, we concluded that—after controlling for "acquiescence"—the "simulated" data for clinical traits conformed to a "quasi-circumplex" model.

The Legacy of Wiggins's Interpersonal Circumplex Theory I: Higher-Order Traits, Lower-Order Traits, and Circumplexity

In a 1990s-era critique of circumplex models of interpersonal traits (apparently including the model by Wiggins & Holzmuller, 1978), Millon (1996) concluded, "As with other circumplex models in which only two or three dimensions are employed to characterize the many variations of personality disorder, these models fall short of completeness in their formal derivations" (p. 58). However, by that time, Wiggins (1991) already had established the conceptual foundation for a standalone theory that linked multiple (though mostly adaptive) aspects of personality with certain aspects of social behavior (i.e., individuals' giving versus denial of respect to other persons) on a preliminary basis (Gaines, 2020). Also, by the early 2000s, the field of interpersonal psychology had been built largely on the basis of the conceptual and methodological innovations that were associated with Wiggins's (2003/2005) most detailed exposition of interpersonal circumplex theory (see edited book by Horowitz & Strack, 2011). As is evident from the results of circulant correlation analyses and confirmatory factor analyses concerning "simulated" data sets by Gurtman (2011, p. 302) and Gurtman (1993, p. 241) in the present chapter, Wiggins's legacy includes laser-focused attention to theoretical and empirical detail (see edited book by Hopwood & Waugh, 2020).

In order to appreciate the scope of Wiggins's influence upon interpersonal psychology, one need only consider the extent to which Wiggins and Holzmuller's (1978) circumplex model of interpersonal traits supplanted T. Leary's (1957) earlier model. Not only did Wiggins and Holzmuller's set of eight lower-order trait terms replace T. Leary's previous set of eight lower-order trait terms (as we noted earlier in the present chapter), but also the specific items and resulting subscales from Wiggins's (1979) original IAS—which was developed in conjunction with Wiggins and Holzmuller's model—similarly replaced the particular items and resulting subscales

154 THE SELF IN RELATIONSHIPS

from the ICL (LaForge & Suczek, 1955) within the literature on interpersonal circumplexes (Gurtman & Pincus, 2000). Moreover, even seemingly "dissenting" perspectives on the original IAS and the IAS-R (Wiggins et al., 1988)—for example, the paper by Gaines et al. (1997) that applied confirmatory factor analyses to both inventories yielded factor loadings that were slightly lower in magnitude than one would have anticipated from Wiggins's (e.g., Wiggins, 1995; Wiggins et al., 1981) principal component loadings—did not go so far as to recommend revising or replacing Wiggins's lower-order trait terms or specific items within subscales.

Despite the impact of Wiggins's (2003/2005) interpersonal circumplex theory upon interpersonal psychology, Wiggins's theory is relatively underappreciated within relationship science (possibly because of the role that social psychologists, as distinct from personality psychologists, historically played in the development of relationship science; see Berscheid, 1999). For instance, one will not find any coverage of Wiggins's theory in the latest editions of *The Oxford Handbook of Close Relationships* (edited by Simpson & Campbell, 2013) or *The Cambridge Handbook of Personal Relationships* (edited by Vangelisti & Perlman, 2018). Additionally, in spite of our contention that Wiggins's interpersonal circumplex theory (having been informed by the interpersonal theory of Sullivan, 1953) can serve as a conceptual bridge between attachment theory (Bowlby, 1969/1997) and interdependence theory (Thibaut & Kelley, 1959), Wiggins's theory receives little to no coverage in the latest edition of the attachment-focused *Attachment in Adulthood* (Mikulincer & Shaver, 2016) or the interdependence-focused *An Atlas of Interpersonal Situations* (Kelley et al., 2003). All in all, the process of cementing Wiggins's legacy within relationship science remains a work in progress (Gaines, 2016/2018).

Prelude to Chapter 6

Several decades before Wiggins (1979) published the original IAS as a measure of dominance and nurturance, Allport (1928) published the Ascendance-Submission inventory essentially as a measure of dominance (see Ewen, 1998). At the time that Allport published his dominance survey, exploratory factor analysis (popularized by Cattell, 1943) was not a widely used tool within personality psychology, and Allport was not "sold" on that statistical technique (e.g., Allport, 1937/1951). Nonetheless, Cattell's groundbreaking exploratory factor analyses of Allport and Odbert's (1936) exhaustive taxonomy of more than 3,000 trait terms led Allport to embrace Cattell's research (albeit without conducting his own exploratory factor analyses; e.g., Allport, 1961/1963). Suffice it to say that confirmatory factor analysis—which was developed by Joreskog and Sorbom (1979) more than a decade after Allport had passed away—similarly was not a part of Allport's methodological toolkit. Finally, although Wiggins was inspired conceptually by Allport's trait theory (part of Allport's psychology of the individual), Wiggins's use of principal component analysis as a technique for creating linear composites of lower-order trait scores was unrelated to Allport's methodology (which did not emphasize construct validity; see Hall & Lindzey, 1970).

In the process of developing the original IAS, Wiggins (1979) cited Allport's *Personality: A Psychological Interpretation* (1937/1951), which argued that the construct of trait should be the primary construct within personality psychology (Gaines, 2020). However, Wiggins did not draw upon Allport's subsequent *Pattern and Growth in Personality* (1961/1963), which articulated the construct of the *proprium* (analogous to the self-concept; Ewen, 1998). The proprium may help us understand the relevance of traits to the self in a manner that unites Wiggins's interpersonal circumplex theory with Allport's psychology of the individual: Although not all aspects of the self are necessarily experienced at a conscious level at a given point in time, individuals' traits—which are implicated in individuals' active efforts to respond to, and to shape, their environments—are among the most readily accessible aspects of personality (indicative of a capacity for selective reflection that is a hallmark of the proprium; see C. S. Hall & Lindzey, 1970). The role of the proprium in bringing certain aspects of personality to the fore might explain individuals' tendency to spontaneously mention their levels of extraversion and agreeableness (i.e., blends of dominance and nurturance), but not other "Big Five" traits (McCrae & Costa, 2003/2006).

At this point, we complete our transition from conceptual to methodological issues regarding the self in relationships by turning in Chapter 6 to new analyses of previously published lower-order subclinical trait correlations that were derived from the IAS-R (Wiggins et al., 1988). Specifically, we reanalyze correlation matrices from three studies (i.e., Gaines, Panter, et al., 1997, Study 2; Hofsess & Tracey, 2005; and Sodano & Tracey, Adult Sample, 2006) plus a bonus study from DeYoung et al. (2013, Sample 2) in which sample sizes exceeded the recommended minimum (i.e., 10 participants/freed parameter

× 12 freed parameters = 120 participants) but were not so large as to inflate all chi-square values to significant levels (e.g., 50 participants/freed parameter × 12 freed parameters = 600 participants; see Schumacker & Lomax, 2016). We will be interested especially in testing Wiggins's (1995) claim that lower-order trait correlations as derived from the IAS-R (unlike the original IAS; Wiggins, 1979) do not yield a "noncircumplex" factor of acquiescence alongside the circumplex factors of dominance and nurturance. Also, not only will we examine the geometric and psychometric properties of the IAS-R within each of the first three samples, but also we will attempt to summarize results *across* those samples (using multiple-group analyses; see Kline, 2016).

SECTION IV
METHODOLOGICAL ISSUES REGARDING THE SELF IN RELATIONSHIPS

6

Measurement of Dominance and Nurturance as Interpersonal Traits I

Synopsis: In the present chapter, we evaluate the geometric and psychometric properties of the Interpersonal Adjective Scales-Revised Version (IAS-R) by reanalyzing data sets from journal articles by Gaines, Panter, et al. (1997, Study 2), Hofsess and Tracey (2005), and Sodano and Tracey (2006, Adult Sample); we report the results of single-group and multiple-group versions of circulant correlation analyses (i.e., consistent with predictions, an equal-spacing, equal-communality model yields satisfactory fit across the three data sets in general); we report the results of single-group and multiple-group versions of confirmatory factor analyses (i.e., contrary to predictions, a three-factor model with the circumplex latent variables of dominance and nurturance augmented by a noncircumplex latent variable of "acquiescence" not only provides satisfactory fit but also yields significantly better fit than does a two-factor model limited to dominance and nurturance across the three data sets in general); we supplement the aforementioned analyses with a circulant correlation analysis and a pair of confirmatory factor analyses of ipsatized data from DeYoung et al. (2013, Sample 2), finding that (consistent with predictions) an equal-spacing, equal-communality model offers satisfactory fit to the ipsatized data, whereas (contract to predictions) neither a two-factor nor a three-factor model provides satisfactory fit to the ipsatized data (and the "badness-of-fit" of those models is identical for that data set); and we provide a prelude to Chapter 7, in which we segue from the IAS-R to the International Personality Item Pool-Interpersonal Circle (IPIP-IPC) as a possible go-to survey for measuring subclinical interpersonal traits.

As Wiggins et al. (1981) acknowledged, the original 128-item Interpersonal Adjective Scales (IAS; Wiggins, 1979) measured dominance as one circumplex principal component (reflecting an agentic trait), nurturance as the other circumplex principal component (reflecting a communal trait), "general" (or, as we have labeled it, "acquiescence") as one noncircumplex principal component, and five additional noncircumplex principal components (i.e., two

The Self in Relationships. Stanley O. Gaines, Jr., Oxford University Press. © Oxford University Press 2023.
DOI: 10.1093/oso/9780197687635.003.0006

160   THE SELF IN RELATIONSHIPS

"polarity" principal components, two "orthogonality" principal components, and one "specificity" principal component). Afterward, even though Wiggins et al. (1988) cited the need for relative brevity (rather than the need for an "acquiescence"-free survey of interpersonal traits) when they dropped half of the items from the original IAS in the process of developing the 64-item IAS-R, we noted in Chapter 5 that Wiggins (1995) eventually proclaimed the IAS-R as "general"- or "acquiescence"-free (and, presumably, the IAS-R did not measure other noncircumplex principal components that warranted interpretation). Nevertheless, to our knowledge, no published study has scrutinized Wiggins's proclamation about the IAS-R (although an unpublished master's thesis by Hoessler, 2009, alluded to the IAS-R as one interpersonal trait survey that does not measure a "nuisance" or "acquiescence" dimension).

Wiggins et al.'s (1988) decision to publish a reduced-length, ostensibly "acquiescence"-free IAS-R is all the more noteworthy in light of the absence of any concerns regarding the geometric (as distinct from psychometric) properties of the original IAS (Wiggins, 1979). In fact, based on the reproduced correlation matrix that we obtained via our circulant correlation analysis of Wiggins's (1979, p. 399) "simulated" matrix in Chapter 5, we would argue that Wiggins et al.'s (1981) actual IAS data (or, more accurately, Wiggins's [1979, Sample C] actual IAS data) conform closely to a circular or circumplex pattern. Therefore, the conceptual rationale that Wiggins et al. (1988) appear to have embraced (judging from Wiggins's [1995] later comments on the shift from the original IAS to the IAS-R) was that the *psychometric* properties of the original IAS were suboptimal (e.g., a survey of interpersonal traits ideally should *not* measure a noncircumplex "acquiescence" dimension). Ironically, the default technique for evaluating the psychometric properties of the IAS-R (i.e., principal component analysis) also happens to be suboptimal (Gurtman, 2009). Overall, interpersonal circumplex theorists have devoted the bulk of their attention to evaluating the geometric (instead of psychometric) properties of the IAS-R (Acton & Revelle, 2002, 2004).

In the present chapter, we take a new look at lower-order subclinical interpersonal trait correlations from three published studies that used Wiggins et al.'s (1988) IAS-R (i.e., Gaines, Panter, et al., 1997, Study 2; Hofsess & Tracey, 2005; Sodano & Tracey, Adult Sample, 2006). We will conduct the same geometric analysis (i.e., circulant correlation analysis, testing a circulant correlation model) and the same psychometric analyses (i.e., confirmatory factor analyses, testing a model that is limited to the two circumplex factors of dominance and nurturance, as compared to a model that adds a third noncircumplex factor of "acquiescence") that we conducted on "simulated" data in Chapter 5. All three studies fall within the "Goldilocks zone" that we described in Chapter 5 regarding desired sample size on the basis of number of participants per estimated parameter (i.e., ns of 120 or higher, but preferably not above 600, when the number of estimated or freed parameters equals 12; Schumacker & Lomax, 2016). In the process, we have omitted three published studies (i.e., Wiggins, 1995; Martinez-Arias et al., 1999, Samples B and C) for which the number of participants/number of freed parameters ratio was greater than 50:1 (and, thus, likely to yield significant chi-square values).

Goals of Study 1

In Study 1, we tested the following hypotheses regarding the geometric and psychometric properties of the IAS-R (Wiggins et al., 1988): (1) With regard to geometric properties, an equal-spacing, equal-communality model will provide satisfactory fit to the data (i.e., such a circular or circumplex model cannot be rejected when applied to a matrix of correlations among lower-order subclinical interpersonal traits). (2) With regard to psychometric properties, (a) a model that is limited to two circumplex factors (i.e., dominance and nurturance as higher-order axes that are reflected in scores on the eight lower-order traits) will provide satisfactory fit to the data, whereas (b) a model that adds a third, noncircumplex factor (i.e., "acquiescence") similarly will provide satisfactory fit on its own but will *not* yield a significant or marginal improvement in fit when compared to the two-factor model. Hypothesis 1 was tested via circulant correlation analysis, while Hypotheses 2a and b were tested via confirmatory factor analyses, using maximum likelihood estimation in LISREL 10.20 (Joreskog & Sorbom, 2019).

Study 1

Method

Participants
Sample 1. In the present Study 1, Sample 1 (Gaines, Panter, et al., 1997, Study 2) consisted of 401 participants (111 men and 290 women). Gaines, Panter,

162   THE SELF IN RELATIONSHIPS

et al. (1997, Study 2) did not report descriptive statistics regarding age or ethnic group membership for their participants.

Sample 2. Also, in the present Study 1, Sample 2 (Hofsess & Tracey, 2005) consisted of 206 participants (101 men, 105 women). Hofsess and Tracey (2005) reported an age range from 17 to 22 years of age for their participants. In terms of ethnic group membership, Hofsess and Tracey did not report descriptive statistics for their participants.

Sample 3. Finally, in the present Study 1, Sample 3 (Sodano & Tracey, 2006, Adult Sample) consisted of 194 participants (reported as percentages, 19.6% male, 80.4% female). Sodano and Tracey (2006, Adult Sample) reported an age range from 17 to 50 years of age ($M = 20.80$ years, $SD = 3.19$ years). Furthermore, in terms of ethnic group membership, Sodano and Tracey reported that 1.5% of the sample classified themselves as Asian or Asian American, 3.5% as Black or African American, 10.7% as Hispanic or Latin American, 0.5% as Native American, 82.8% as White or European American, and 1.0% as "Other."

Materials

Sample 1. Participants in the present Study 1, Sample 1 (Gaines et al., 1997, Study 2) completed the 64-item IAS-R (Wiggins et al., 1988), which was designed to measure eight lower-order traits (i.e., ambitious-dominant, arrogant-calculating, cold-quarrelsome, aloof-introverted, unassured-submissive, unassuming-ingenuous, warm-agreeable, and gregarious-extraverted) as blends of two higher-order traits (i.e., the agentic trait of dominance and the communal trait of nurturance). As reported by Gaines, Panter, et al. (1997, Study 2), results of reliability analyses indicated that all eight IAS-R subscales were internally consistent (Cronbach's alphas ranged from .75 to .90; separate Cronbach's alphas for the eight subscales were not reported).

Sample 2. Additionally, participants in the present Study 1, Sample 2 (Hofsess & Tracey, 2005) completed the IAS-R (Wiggins et al., 1988; credited as the IAS by Wiggins, 1995). As reported by Hofsess and Tracey (2005), results of reliability analyses indicated that—with the exception of the unassuming-ingenuous subscale—the IAS-R subscales were internally consistent (Cronbach's alphas ranged from .49 to .83; separate Cronbach's alphas = .79 for ambitious-dominant, .72 for arrogant-calculating, .70 for cold-quarrelsome, .81 for aloof-introverted, .74 for unassured-submissive, .49 for unassuming-ingenuous, .83 for warm-agreeable, and .73 for gregarious-extraverted).

Sample 3. Lastly, participants in the present Study 1, Sample 3 (Sodano & Tracey, 2006, Adult Sample) completed the IAS-R (Wiggins et al., 1988; credited as the IAS by Wiggins, 1995). As reported by Sodano and Tracey

(2006, Adult Sample), results of reliability analyses indicated that all eight IAS-R subscales were internally consistent (Cronbach's alphas ranged from .71 to .87; separate Cronbach's alphas = .78 for ambitious-dominant, .77 for arrogant-calculating, .82 for cold-quarrelsome, .87 for aloof-introverted, .82 for unassured-submissive, .71 for unassuming-ingenuous, .87 for warm-agreeable, and .83 for gregarious-extraverted.

Procedure

Sample 1. Prior to conducting the present Study 1, Sample 1, Gaines and colleagues (Gaines, Panter, 1997, Study 2) obtained ethics approval from the Psychology Ethics Committees at two academic institutions (one small liberal arts college and one large research university). Participants read and signed an informed consent sheet that explained the purpose of the study in general terms, completed a "Dispositions Questionnaire" that included the IAS-R (Wiggins et al., 1988) and additional surveys that are not directly relevant to the present book, read a debriefing form that explained the purpose of the study in detail, and received research participant credit for completing the study.

Sample 2. Also, prior to conducting the present Study 1, Sample 2, Hofsess and Tracey (2005) obtained ethics approval from their academic institution (a large research university). Participants read and signed an informed consent sheet that explained the purpose of the study in general terms, completed the IAS-R (Wiggins et al., 1988) and additional surveys that are not directly relevant to the present book, and read a debriefing form that explained the purpose of the study in detail (participants did not receive compensation for taking part in the study).

Sample 3. Lastly, prior to conducting the present Study 1, Sample 3, Sodano and Tracey (2006, Adult Sample) obtained ethics approval from their academic institution (a large research university). Participants read and signed an informed consent sheet that explained the purpose of the study in general terms, completed the IAS-R (Wiggins et al., 1988) and additional surveys that are not directly relevant to the present book, and read a debriefing form that explained the purpose of the study in detail (it appears that participants did not receive compensation for taking part in the study, though this point is not made explicit).

Results and Discussion

Matrices of zero-order correlations among the eight subclinical interpersonal traits that were measured by the IAS-R (Wiggins et al., 1988) among

164 THE SELF IN RELATIONSHIPS

the three samples in the present Study 1 (i.e., Gaines, Panter, et al., 1997, Study 2, p. 616; Hofsess & Tracey, 2005, p. 143; Sodano & Tracey, 2006, Adult Sample, p. 325) are presented in Table 6.1. First, each of the correlation matrices was entered into a separate circulant correlation analysis, in which we tested goodness-of-fit concerning the equal-spacing, equal-communality model that we described in Chapter 5. Afterward, each of the correlation matrices was entered into a pair of confirmatory factor analyses, in which we tested goodness-of-fit regarding the two-factor (i.e., dominance and nurturance) and three-factor (i.e., dominance, nurturance, and "acquiescence") models that we described in Chapter 5.

Table 6.1 Matrices of Zero-Order Correlations Among Lower-Order Subclinical Interpersonal Traits, Study 1 Samples[a,b,c]

Gaines, Panter, et al. (1997, Study 2, p. 616, n = 401)

Var.	Correlations							
	PA	BC	DE	FG	HI	JK	LM	NO
PA	1.00							
BC	.41	1.00						
DE	.21	.63	1.00					
FG	−.20	.22	.54	1.00				
HI	−.64	−.18	.04	.49	1.00			
JK	−.43	−.64	−.29	.07	.46	1.00		
LM	−.13	−.38	−.65	−.43	.12	.37	1.00	
NO	.33	−.06	−.35	−.76	−.38	.01	.49	1.00

Hofsess & Tracey (2005, p. 143, n = 206)

Var.	Correlations							
	PA	BC	DE	FG	HI	JK	LM	NO
PA	1.00							
BC	.29	1.00						
DE	.13	.60	1.00					
FG	−.19	.20	.53	1.00				
HI	−.36	.14	.29	.54	1.00			
JK	−.09	−.52	−.21	.05	.06	1.00		
LM	−.01	−.41	−.54	−.28	−.10	.51	1.00	
NO	.48	.09	−.12	−.43	−.37	.04	.30	1.00

MEASUREMENT OF DOMINANCE AND NURTURANCE I   165

Table 6.1 Continued

Sodano & Tracey (2006, Adult Sample, p. 325, *n* = 194)

Var.	Correlations							
	PA	BC	DE	FG	HI	JK	LM	NO
PA	1.00							
BC	.22	1.00						
DE	.08	.69	1.00					
FG	.07	.38	.42	1.00				
HI	−.47	.19	.27	.35	1.00			
JK	−.29	−.45	−.28	.03	.25	1.00		
LM	.06	−.43	−.58	−.48	−.19	.23	1.00	
NO	.15	−.22	−.38	−.59	−.38	−.06	.60	1.00

[a]Adapted from "Evaluating the Circumplexity of Interpersonal Traits and the Manifestation of Interpersonal Traits in Interpersonal Trust," by S. O. Gaines, Jr., A. T. Panter, M. D. Lyde, W. N. Steers, C. E. Rusbult, et al., 1997, *Journal of Personality and Social Psychology, 73*, p. 616. Copyright 1997 by American Psychological Association. Reproduced and adapted with permission.
[b]Adapted from "The Interpersonal Circumplex as a Model of Interpersonal Capabilities," by C. D. Hofsess & T. J. G. Tracey, 2005, *Journal of Personality Assessment, 84*, p. 143. Copyright 2005 by Taylor & Francis. Reproduced and adapted with permission.
[c]Adapted from "Interpersonal Traits in Childhood: Development of the Child and Adolescent Interpersonal Survey," by S. M. Sodano & T. J. G. Tracey, 2006, *Journal of Personality Assessment, 87*, p. 325. Copyright 2006 by Taylor & Francis. Reproduced and adapted with permission.

Note: PA = ambitious-dominant, BC = arrogant-calculating, DE = cold-quarrelsome, FG = aloof-introverted, HI = unassured-submissive, JK = unassuming-ingenuous, LM = warm-agreeable, NO = gregarious-extraverted.

Circulant Correlation Analyses

In order to conduct circulant correlation analyses on the matrices of correlations from the three samples (i.e., Gaines, Panter, et al., 1997, Study 2, p. 616; Hofsess & Tracey, 2005, p. 143; Sodano & Tracey, 2006, Adult Sample, p. 325) in the present Study 1, we used the same templates (i.e., equal-spacing, equal communality model; maximum likelihood estimation via LISREL 10.20 [Joreskog & Sorbom, 2019], using the ridge option and ridge constant) that we described in Chapter 5. The syntax files for the three samples are presented in Table 6.2. Results of circulant correlation analyses indicated that, consistent with hypotheses, an equal-spacing, equal-communality model provided satisfactory fit to the data for Sample 1 (chi-square = 18.61, degrees of freedom [*df*] = 24, *NS*; root mean square error of approximation [RMSEA] = .00; comparative fit index [CFI] = 1.00), Sample 2 (chi-square = 21.24, *df* = 24, *NS*; RMSEA = .00; CFI = 1.00), and Sample 3 (chi-square = 31.37, *df* = 24, *NS*; RMSEA = .04; CFI = .94). Moreover, in-spection of reproduced correlation matrices (shown in Table 6.3) revealed

166 THE SELF IN RELATIONSHIPS

Table 6.2 Syntax Files Used as Input for Circulant Correlation Analyses of Lower-Order Subclinical Interpersonal Traits, Study 1 Samples

Gaines, Panter, et al. (1997, Study 2, *n* = 401)

```
GAINES ET AL. (1997, STUDY 2) EQUAL SPACING, EQUAL COMUNALITY
DA NI=8 NO=401 MA=KM
KM

1.00
 .41     1.00
 .21      .63     1.00
-.20      .22      .54     1.00
-.64     -.18      .04      .49     1.00
-.43     -.64     -.29      .07      .46     1.00
-.13     -.38     -.65     -.43      .12      .37     1.00
 .33     -.06     -.35     -.76     -.38      .01      .49     1.00
```

```
MO NY=8 NE=8 TE=SY,FI LY=FU,FI PS=SY,FR
LA
PA BC DE FG HI JK LM NO
FR TE 1 1 TE 2 2 TE 3 3 TE 4 4 TE 5 5 TE 6 6 TE 7 7 TE 8 8
ST 1.00 LY 1 1 LY 2 2 LY 3 3 LY 4 4 LY 5 5 LY 6 6 LY 7 7 LY 8 8
FI PS 1 1 PS 2 2 PS 3 3 PS 4 4 PS 5 5 PS 6 6 PS 7 7 PS 8 8
ST 1.00 PS 1 1 PS 2 2 PS 3 3 PS 4 4 PS 5 5 PS 6 6 PS 7 7 PS 8 8
EQ PS 2 1 PS 3 2 PS 4 3 PS 5 4 PS 6 5 PS 7 6 PS 8 7 PS 8 1
ST .71 PS 2 1
EQ PS 3 1 PS 4 2 PS 5 3 PS 6 4 PS 7 5 PS 8 6 PS 7 1 PS 8 2
ST .00 PS 3 1
EQ PS 4 1 PS 5 2 PS 6 3 PS 7 4 PS 8 5 PS 6 1 PS 7 2 PS 8 3
ST -.71 PS 4 1
EQ PS 5 1 PS 6 2 PS 7 3 PS 8 4
ST -1.00 PS 5 1
OU ALL ME=ML RO RC AD=OFF
```

Hofsess & Tracey (2005, *n* = 206)

```
HOFSESS & TRACEY (2005) EQUAL SPACING, EQUAL COMMUNALITY
DA NI=8 NO=206 MA=KM
KM
1.00
 .20     1.00
 .13      .60     1.00
-.19      .20      .53     1.00
-.36      .14      .29      .54     1.00
-.09     -.52     -.21      .05      .06     1.00
```

Table 6.2 Continued

Hofsess & Tracey (2005, *n* = 206)

−.01	−.41	−.54	−.28	−.10	.51	1.00	
.48	.09	−.12	−.43	−.37	.04	.30	1.00

```
MO NY=8 NE=8 TE=SY,FI LY=FU,FI PS=SY,FR
LA
PA BC DE FG HI JK LM NO
FR TE 1 1 TE 2 2 TE 3 3 TE 4 4 TE 5 5 TE 6 6 TE 7 7 TE 8 8
ST 1.00 LY 1 1 LY 2 2 LY 3 3 LY 4 4 LY 5 5 LY 6 6 LY 7 7 LY 8 8
FI PS 1 1 PS 2 2 PS 3 3 PS 4 4 PS 5 5 PS 6 6 PS 7 7 PS 8 8
ST 1.00 PS 1 1 PS 2 2 PS 3 3 PS 4 4 PS 5 5 PS 6 6 PS 7 7 PS 8 8
EQ PS 2 1 PS 3 2 PS 4 3 PS 5 4 PS 6 5 PS 7 6 PS 8 7 PS 8 1
ST .71 PS 2 1
EQ PS 3 1 PS 4 2 PS 5 3 PS 6 4 PS 7 5 PS 8 6 PS 7 1 PS 8 2
ST .00 PS 3 1
EQ PS 4 1 PS 5 2 PS 6 3 PS 7 4 PS 8 5 PS 6 1 PS 7 2 PS 8 3
ST -.71 PS 4 1
EQ PS 5 1 PS 6 2 PS 7 3 PS 8 4
ST -1.00 PS 5 1
OU ALL ME=ML RO RC AD=OFF
```

Sodano & Tracey (2006, Adult Sample, *n* = 194)

```
SODANO AND TRACEY (2006) EQUAL SPACING EQUAL COMMUNALITY
MODEL
DA NI=8 NO=194 MA=KM
KM
```

1.00							
.22	1.00						
.08	.69	1.00					
.07	.38	.42	1.00				
−.47	.19	.27	.35	1.00			
−.29	−.45	−.28	.03	.25	1.00		
.06	−.43	−.58	−.48	−.19	.23	1.00	
.15	−.22	−.38	−.59	−.28	−.06	.60	1.00

```
MO NY=8 NE=8 TE=SY,FI LY=FU,FI PS=SY,FR
LA
PA BC DE FG HI JK LM NO
FR TE 1 1 TE 2 2 TE 3 3 TE 4 4 TE 5 5 TE 6 6 TE 7 7 TE 8 8
ST 1.00 LY 1 1 LY 2 2 LY 3 3 LY 4 4 LY 5 5 LY 6 6 LY 7 7 LY 8 8
FI PS 1 1 PS 2 2 PS 3 3 PS 4 4 PS 5 5 PS 6 6 PS 7 7 PS 8 8
ST 1.00 PS 1 1 PS 2 2 PS 3 3 PS 4 4 PS 5 5 PS 6 6 PS 7 7 PS 8 8
EQ PS 2 1 PS 3 2 PS 4 3 PS 5 4 PS 6 5 PS 7 6 PS 8 7 PS 8 1
ST .71 PS 2 1
EQ PS 3 1 PS 4 2 PS 5 3 PS 6 4 PS 7 5 PS 8 6 PS 7 1 PS 8 2
ST .00 PS 3 1
EQ PS 4 1 PS 5 2 PS 6 3 PS 7 4 PS 8 5 PS 6 1 PS 7 2 PS 8 3
ST -.71 PS 4 1
EQ PS 5 1 PS 6 2 PS 7 3 PS 8 4
ST -1.00 PS 5 1
OU ALL ME=ML RO RC AD=OFF
```

168 THE SELF IN RELATIONSHIPS

Table 6.3 Reproduced Correlation Matrices for Study 1 Samples

Gaines, Panter, et al. (1997, Study 2, $n = 401$)

Var.	Correlations							
	PA	BC	DE	FG	HI	JK	LM	NO
PA	1.00							
BC	.47	1.00						
DE	.06	.47	1.00					
FG	−.33	.06	.47	1.00				
HI	−.67	−.33	.06	.47	1.00			
JK	−.33	−.67	−.33	.06	.47	1.00		
LM	.06	−.33	−.67	−.33	.06	.47	1.00	
NO	.47	.06	−.33	−.67	−.33	.06	.47	1.00

Hofsess & Tracey (2005, $n = 206$)

Var.	Correlations							
	PA	BC	DE	FG	HI	JK	LM	NO
PA	1.00							
BC	.41	1.00						
DE	.09	.41	1.00					
FG	−.19	.09	.41	1.00				
HI	−.46	−.19	.09	.41	1.00			
JK	−.19	−.46	−.19	.09	.41	1.00		
LM	.09	−.19	−.46	−.19	.09	.41	1.00	
NO	.41	.09	−.19	−.46	−.19	.09	.41	1.00

Sodano & Tracey (2006, Adult Sample, $n = 194$)

Var.	Correlations							
	PA	BC	DE	FG	HI	JK	LM	NO
PA	1.00							
BC	.37	1.00						
DE	.04	.37	1.00					
FG	−.24	.04	.37	1.00				
HI	−.52	−.24	.04	.37	1.00			
JK	−.24	−.52	−.24	.04	.37	1.00		
LM	.04	−.24	−.52	−.24	.04	.37	1.00	
NO	.37	.04	−.24	−.52	−.24	.04	.37	1.00

Note: PA = ambitious-dominant, BC = arrogant-calculating, DE = cold-quarrelsome, FG = aloof-introverted, HI = unassured-submissive, JK = unassuming-ingenuous, LM = warm-agreeable, NO = gregarious-extraverted.

that the estimated correlations were broadly consistent with the pattern that we observed for Wiggins's (1979, p. 399) "simulated" matrix in Chapter 5 (although results from the sample by Gaines, Panter, et al. came closest to approximating Wiggins's "simulation"). Therefore, we concluded that the IAS-R (Wiggins et al., 1988) consistently performed well in terms of geometric properties (i.e., alignment of the eight lower-order traits around a circle or circumplex).

Confirmatory Factor Analyses

Initial confirmatory factor analyses. Subsequently, in order to conduct initial confirmatory factor analyses on the matrices of correlations from the three samples (i.e., Gaines, Panter, et al., 1997, Study 2, p. 616; Hofsess & Tracey, 2005, p. 143; Sodano & Tracey, 2006, Adult Sample, p. 325) in the present Study 1, we used the same templates (i.e., two-factor model with dominance and nurturance as circumplex latent variables; maximum likelihood estimation via LISREL 10.20 [Joreskog & Sorbom, 2019], using the ridge option and ridge constant) that we described in Chapter 5. The syntax files for the three samples are presented in Table 6.4. Results of initial confirmatory factor analyses indicated that, contrary to hypotheses, a two-factor model did *not* provide satisfactory fit for Sample 1 (chi-square = 39.48, df = 24, p < .05; RMSEA = .05; CFI = .96) or Sample 2 (chi-square = 38.52, df = 24, p < .05; RMSEA = .05; CFI = .87), although the fit was marginal for Sample 3 (chi-square = 35.40, df = 24, p < .07; RMSEA = .05; CFI = .90). So far, based on the initial confirmatory factor analyses, the psychometric properties of the IAS-R do not seem to be as well established as previously published studies that relied upon principal component analyses (beginning with Wiggins et al. [1988] and Wiggins [1995]) have led interpersonal circumplex theorists to believe—a discrepancy that Fabrigar et al. (1997) anticipated more than 20 years ago.

Final confirmatory factor analyses. Lastly, in order to conduct final confirmatory factor analyses on the matrices of correlations from the three samples (i.e., Gaines, Panter, et al., 1997, Study 2, p. 616; Hofsess & Tracey, 2005, p. 143; Sodano & Tracey, 2006, Adult Sample, p. 325) in the present Study 1, we used the same templates (i.e., three-factor model with dominance and nurturance as circumplex latent variables, plus "acquiescence" as a noncircumplex latent variable; maximum likelihood estimation via LISREL 10.20 [Joreskog & Sorbom, 2019], using the ridge option and ridge constant) that we described in Chapter 5. The syntax files for the three samples are presented in

170 THE SELF IN RELATIONSHIPS

Table 6.4 Syntax Files Used as Input for Initial Confirmatory Factor Analyses of Lower-Order Subclinical Interpersonal Traits, Study 1 Samples

Gaines, Panter et al. (1997, Study 2, *n* = 401)

```
GAINES ET AL. (1997, STUDY 2) DOM NUR
DA NI=8 NO=401 MA=KM
KM

1.00
 .41    1.00
 .21     .63    1.00
-.20     .22     .54    1.00
-.64    -.18     .04     .49    1.00
-.43    -.64    -.29     .07     .46    1.00
-.13    -.38    -.65    -.43     .12     .37    1.00
 .33    -.06    -.35    -.76    -.38     .01     .49    1.00
```

```
MO NY=8 NE=2 TE=SY,FI LY=FU,FI PS=SY,FI
LA
PA BC DE FG HI JK LM NO
FR TE 1 1 TE 2 2 TE 3 3 TE 4 4 TE 5 5 TE 6 6 TE 7 7 TE 8 8
FR LY 1 1 LY 7 2
FR LY 2 1 LY 8 1 LY 6 2 LY 8 2
FR LY 5 1 LY 3 2
FR LY 4 1 LY 6 1 LY 2 2 LY 4 2
EQ LY 1 1 LY 7 2
EQ LY 2 1 LY 8 1 LY 6 2 LY 8 2
EQ LY 5 1 LY 3 2
EQ LY 4 1 LY 6 1 LY 2 2 LY 4 2
ST 1.00 LY 1 1
ST .71 LY 2 1
ST -.71 LY 4 1
ST -1.00 LY 5 1
ST 1.00 PS 1 1 PS 2 2
OU ALL ME=ML RO RC AD=OFF
```

Hofsess & Tracey (2005, *n* = 206)

```
HOFSESS AND TRACEY (2005) DOM NUR
DA NI=8 NO=206 MA=KM
KM
1.00
 .20    1.00
```

MEASUREMENT OF DOMINANCE AND NURTURANCE I 171

Table 6.4 Continued

Hofsess & Tracey (2005, *n* = 206)

.13	.60	1.00					
−.19	.20	.53	1.00				
−.36	.14	.29	.54	1.00			
−.09	−.52	−.21	.05	.06	1.00		
−.01	−.41	−.54	−.28	−.10	.51	1.00	
.48	.09	−.12	−.43	−.37	.04	.30	1.00

```
MO NY=8 NE=2 TE=SY,FI LY=FU,FI PS=SY,FI
LA
PA BC DE FG HI JK LM NO
FR TE 1 1 TE 2 2 TE 3 3 TE 4 4 TE 5 5 TE 6 6 TE 7 7 TE 8 8
FR LY 1 1 LY 7 2
FR LY 2 1 LY 8 1 LY 6 2 LY 8 2
FR LY 5 1 LY 3 2
FR LY 4 1 LY 6 1 LY 2 2 LY 4 2
EQ LY 1 1 LY 7 2
EQ LY 2 1 LY 8 1 LY 6 2 LY 8 2
EQ LY 5 1 LY 3 2
EQ LY 4 1 LY 6 1 LY 2 2 LY 4 2
ST 1.00 LY 1 1
ST .71 LY 2 1
ST -.71 LY 4 1
ST -1.00 LY 5 1
ST 1.00 PS 1 1 PS 2 2
OU ALL ME=ML RO RC AD=OFF
```

Sodano & Tracey (2006, Adult Sample, *n* = 194)

```
SODANO AND TRACEY (2006) DOM NUR
DA NI=8 NO=194 MA=KM
KM
```

1.00					
.22	1.00				
.08	.69	1.00			
.07	.38	.42	1.00		
−.47	.19	.27	.35	1.00	
−.29	−.45	−.28	.03	.25	1.00

(continued)

172 THE SELF IN RELATIONSHIPS

Table 6.4 Continued

Sodano & Tracey (2006, Adult Sample, n = 194)							
.06	−.43	−.58	−.48	−.19	.23	1.00	
.15	−.22	−.38	−.59	−.28	−.06	.60	1.00

```
MO NY=8 NE=2 TE=SY,FI LY=FU,FI PS=SY,FI
LA
PA BC DE FG HI JK LM NO
FR TE 1 1 TE 2 2 TE 3 3 TE 4 4 TE 5 5 TE 6 6 TE 7 7 TE 8 8
FR LY 1 1 LY 7 2
FR LY 2 1 LY 8 1 LY 6 2 LY 8 2
FR LY 5 1 LY 3 2
FR LY 4 1 LY 6 1 LY 2 2 LY 4 2
EQ LY 1 1 LY 7 2
EQ LY 2 1 LY 8 1 LY 6 2 LY 8 2
EQ LY 5 1 LY 3 2
EQ LY 4 1 LY 6 1 LY 2 2 LY 4 2
ST 1.00 LY 1 1
ST .71 LY 2 1
ST -.71 LY 4 1
ST -1.00 LY 5 1
ST 1.00 PS 1 1 PS 2 2
OU ALL ME=ML RO RC AD=OFF
```

Table 6.5. Results of final confirmatory factor analyses indicated that, consistent with hypotheses, a three-factor model provided satisfactory fit for Sample 1 (chi-square = 30.19, df = 23, NS; RMSEA = .03; CFI = .98) and Sample 2 (chi-square = 25.13, df = 23, NS; RMSEA = .02; CFI = .98), although the model provided marginal fit for Sample 3 (chi-square = 32.79, df = 23, p < .09; RMSEA = .05; CFI = .92). Loadings of the eight lower-order subclinical interpersonal traits on the circumplex factors of dominance and nurturance, plus the noncircumplex factor of "acquiescence," are presented in Table 6.6. So far, based on the final confirmatory factor analyses, the psychometric properties of the IAS-R (Wiggins et al., 1988) seem to be more akin to the psychometric properties of the original IAS (Wiggins, 1979) in terms of yielding *three* substantive latent variables (one of which does not reflect circumplexity) than interpersonal circumplex theorists had come to believe (following Wiggins, 1995)—a convergence that Fabrigar et al. (1997) had anticipated long ago.

Comparing initial versus final confirmatory factor analyses. Although we had not expected the three-factor model to yield significantly better fit than the

MEASUREMENT OF DOMINANCE AND NURTURANCE I 173

Table 6.5 Syntax Files Used as Input for Final Confirmatory Factor Analyses of Lower-Order Subclinical Interpersonal Traits, Study 1 Samples

---

Gaines, Panter, et al. (1997, Study 2, _n_ = 401)

```
GAINES ET AL. (1997, STUDY 2) DOM NUR ACQ
DA NI=8 NO=401 MA=KM
KM
```

1.00							
.41	1.00						
.21	.63	1.00					
−.20	.22	.54	1.00				
−.64	−.18	.04	.49	1.00			
−.43	−.64	−.29	.07	.46	1.00		
−.13	−.38	−.65	−.43	.12	.37	1.00	
.33	−.06	−.35	−.76	−.38	.01	.49	1.00

```
MO NY=8 NE=3 TE=SY,FI LY=FU,FI PS=SY,FI
LA
PA BC DE FG HI JK LM NO
FR TE 1 1 TE 2 2 TE 3 3 TE 4 4 TE 5 5 TE 6 6 TE 7 7 TE 8 8
FR LY 1 1 LY 7 2
FR LY 2 1 LY 8 1 LY 6 2 LY 8 2
FR LY 5 1 LY 3 2
FR LY 4 1 LY 6 1 LY 2 2 LY 4 2
EQ LY 1 1 LY 7 2
EQ LY 2 1 LY 8 1 LY 6 2 LY 8 2
EQ LY 5 1 LY 3 2
EQ LY 4 1 LY 6 1 LY 2 2 LY 4 2
ST 1.00 LY 1 1
ST .71 LY 2 1
ST -.71 LY 4 1
ST -1.00 LY 5 1
FR LY 1 3 LY 2 3 LY 3 3 LY 4 3 LY 5 3 LY 6 3 LY 7 3 LY 8 3
EQ LY 1 3 LY 2 3 LY 3 3 LY 4 3 LY 5 3 LY 6 3 LY 7 3 LY 8 3
ST 1.00 PS 1 1 PS 2 2 PS 3 3
OU ALL ME=ML RO RC AD=OFF
```

Hofsess & Tracey (2005, _n_ = 206)

```
HOFSESS AND TRACEY (2005) DOM NUR ACQ
DA NI=8 NO=206 MA=KM
KM
1.00
```

(continued)

174 THE SELF IN RELATIONSHIPS

Table 6.5 Continued

Hofsess & Tracey (2005, $n = 206$)

.20	1.00						
.13	.60	1.00					
−.19	.20	.53	1.00				
−.36	.14	.29	.54	1.00			
−.09	−.52	−.21	.05	.06	1.00		
−.01	−.41	−.54	−.28	−.10	.51	1.00	
.48	.09	−.12	−.43	−.37	.04	.30	1.00

```
MO NY=8 NE=3 TE=SY,FI LY=FU,FI PS=SY,FI
LA
PA BC DE FG HI JK LM NO
FR TE 1 1 TE 2 2 TE 3 3 TE 4 4 TE 5 5 TE 6 6 TE 7 7 TE 8 8
FR LY 1 1 LY 7 2
FR LY 2 1 LY 8 1 LY 6 2 LY 8 2
FR LY 5 1 LY 3 2
FR LY 4 1 LY 6 1 LY 2 2 LY 4 2
EQ LY 1 1 LY 7 2
EQ LY 2 1 LY 8 1 LY 6 2 LY 8 2
EQ LY 5 1 LY 3 2
EQ LY 4 1 LY 6 1 LY 2 2 LY 4 2
ST 1.00 LY 1 1
ST .71 LY 2 1
ST -.71 LY 4 1
ST -1.00 LY 5 1
FR LY 1 3 LY 2 3 LY 3 3 LY 4 3 LY 5 3 LY 6 3 LY 7 3 LY 8 3
EQ LY 1 3 LY 2 3 LY 3 3 LY 4 3 LY 5 3 LY 6 3 LY 7 3 LY 8 3
ST 1.00 PS 1 1 PS 2 2 PS 3 3
OU ALL ME=ML RO RC AD=OFF
```

Sodano & Tracey (2006, Adult Sample, $n = 194$)

```
SODANO AND TRACEY (2006) DOM NUR ACQ
DA NI=8 NO=194 MA=KM
KM
```

1.00					
.22	1.00				
.08	.69	1.00			
.07	.38	.42	1.00		
−.47	.19	.27	.35	1.00	
−.29	−.45	−.28	.03	.25	1.00

MEASUREMENT OF DOMINANCE AND NURTURANCE I   175

Table 6.5 Continued

Sodano & Tracey (2006, Adult Sample, *n* = 194)							

```
 .06    -.43    -.58    -.48    -.19     .23    1.00
 .15    -.22    -.38    -.59    -.28    -.06     .60    1.00
```

```
MO NY=8 NE=3 TE=SY,FI LY=FU,FI PS=SY,FI
LA
PA BC DE FG HI JK LM NO
FR TE 1 1 TE 2 2 TE 3 3 TE 4 4 TE 5 5 TE 6 6 TE 7 7 TE 8 8
FR LY 1 1 LY 7 2
FR LY 2 1 LY 8 1 LY 6 2 LY 8 2
FR LY 5 1 LY 3 2
FR LY 4 1 LY 6 1 LY 2 2 LY 4 2
EQ LY 1 1 LY 7 2
EQ LY 2 1 LY 8 1 LY 6 2 LY 8 2
EQ LY 5 1 LY 3 2
EQ LY 4 1 LY 6 1 LY 2 2 LY 4 2
ST 1.00 LY 1 1
ST .71 LY 2 1
ST -.71 LY 4 1
ST -1.00 LY 5 1
FR LY 1 3 LY 2 3 LY 3 3 LY 4 3 LY 5 3 LY 6 3 LY 7 3 LY 8 3
EQ LY 1 3 LY 2 3 LY 3 3 LY 4 3 LY 5 3 LY 6 3 LY 7 3 LY 8 3
ST 1.00 PS 1 1 PS 2 2 PS 3 3
OU ALL ME=ML RO RC AD=OFF
```

Table 6.6 Obtained Patterns of Factor Loadings Among Lower-Order Subclinical Interpersonal Traits for Study 1 Samples, Three-Factor Solution

Gaines, Panter, et al. (1997, Study 2, *n* = 401)			
Var.	*Factor*		
	DOM	*NUR*	*ACQ*
PA	.73	.00	.21
BC	.52	-.62	.21
DE	.00	-.78	.21
FG	-.62	-.62	.21
HI	-.78	.00	.21
JK	-.62	.52	.21
LM	.00	.73	.21
NO	.52	.52	.21

(continued)

176 THE SELF IN RELATIONSHIPS

Table 6.6 Continued

Hofsess & Tracey (2005, $n = 206$)

Var.	Factor		
	DOM	NUR	ACQ
PA	.69	.00	.29
BC	.46	−.53	.29
DE	.00	−.65	.29
FG	−.53	−.53	.20
HI	−.65	.00	.29
JK	−.53	.46	.29
LM	.00	.69	.29
NO	.46	.46	.29

Sodano & Tracey (2006, Adult Sample, $n = 194$)

Var.	Factor		
	DOM	NUR	ACQ
PA	.66	.00	.19
BC	.41	-.57	.19
DE	.00	-.70	.19
FG	-.57	-.57	.19
HI	-.70	.00	.19
JK	-.57	.41	.19
LM	.00	.66	.19
NO	.41	.41	.19

Note: Regarding higher-order factors, DOM = dominance, NUR = nurturance, ACQ = acquiescence. Regarding lower-order interpersonal traits, PA = ambitious-dominant, BC = arrogant-calculating, DE = cold-quarrelsome, FG = aloof-introverted, HI = unassured-submissive, JK = unassuming-ingenuous, LM = warm-agreeable, NO = gregarious-extraverted.

two-factor model, direct comparison of the models indicated that the three-factor model yielded significantly better fit after all for Sample 1 (difference in chi-square = 9.29, difference in $df = 1$, $p < .01$) and Sample 2 (difference in chi-square = 13.39, difference in $df = 1$, $p < .01$), whereas the difference in fit was not significant or marginal for Sample 3 (difference in chi-square = 2.61, difference in $df = 1$, NS). Thus, on balance, it appears that Wiggins's (1995) proclamation about the IAS-R (Wiggins et al., 1988) as "acquiescence"-free was premature. Unfortunately, the authors of all three studies that we have just reviewed (i.e.,

Gaines, Panter, et al., 1997, Study 2; Hofsess & Tracey, 2005; Sodano & Tracey, 2006, Adult Sample) accepted Wiggins's proclamation implicitly, if not explicitly (i.e., none of them raised the possibility that an advanced psychometric tool such as confirmatory factor analysis might have allowed them to uncover and statistically control for an "acquiescence" latent variable).

Summary of Results Across the Three Samples for Study 1
Multiple-group circulant correlation analysis. Up to now, we have proceeded on the assumption that we could generalize results of circulant correlation analyses across the three samples (i.e., Gaines, Panter, et al., 1997, Study 2; Hofsess & Tracey, 2005; Sodano & Tracey, 2006, Adult Sample) in the present Study 1. However, we have not formally tested such an assumption. Accordingly, we conducted a multiple-group circulant correlation analysis on the three data sets in question. The multiple-group syntax file, which includes the core of the separate syntax files that we have encountered so far, is presented in Table 6.7. The two major changes for the multiple-group file are as follows: (1) On the Data (DA) line for the first sample (i.e., Gaines, Panter, et al., 1997, Study 2), immediately after the term DA, the number of groups (NG = 3) is inserted; this addition is *not* repeated for the second or third samples. (2) Conversely, for the second and third samples (i.e., Hofsess & Tracey, 2005; Sodano & Tracey, 2006, Adult Sample), the Model line stipulates that the measurement error (Theta Epsilon, or TE), latent-observed (Lambda Y, or LY), and latent variable variance/covariance (Psi, or PS) matrices are held invariant (TE = Invariant, LY = IN, PS = IN) following the lead of the first sample (and details regarding the freed parameters, starting values, and fixed parameters are *not* repeated for the second or third samples). Results of the multiple-group circulant correlation analysis affirmed that an equal-spacing, equal-communality model provided satisfactory fit to the data (chi-square = 83.79, df = 96, *NS*; RMSEA = .00; CFI = 1.00). The reproduced correlation matrix across the three samples is shown in Table 6.8.

Multiple-group confirmatory factor analyses. Similarly, up to now, we have acted on the assumption that we could generalize results of confirmatory factor analyses across the three samples (i.e., Gaines, Panter, et al., 1997, Study 2; Hofsess & Tracey, 2005; Sodano & Tracey, 2006, Adult Sample) in the present Study 1. However, we have not formally tested that assumption. Therefore, we conducted two multiple-group confirmatory factor analyses (one in which a two-factor model with dominance and nurturance as circumplex latent variables was tested, followed by one in which

178 THE SELF IN RELATIONSHIPS

Table 6.7 Syntax Files Used as Input for Multiple-Group Circulant Correlation Analysis of Lower-Order Subclinical Interpersonal Traits, Study 1 Samples

```
GAINES ET AL. (1997, STUDY 2) EQUAL SPACING, EQUAL
COMMUNALITY
DA NG=3 NI=8 NO=401 MA=KM
KM
1.00
 .41   1.00
 .21    .63   1.00
-.20    .22    .54   1.00
-.64   -.18    .04    .49   1.00
-.43   -.64   -.29    .07    .46   1.00
-.13   -.38   -.65   -.43    .12    .37   1.00
 .33   -.06   -.35   -.76   -.38    .01    .49   1.00
```

```
MO NY=8 NE=8 TE=SY,FI LY=FU,FI PS=SY,FR
LA
PA BC DE FG HI JK LM NO
FR TE 1 1 TE 2 2 TE 3 3 TE 4 4 TE 5 5 TE 6 6 TE 7 7 TE 8 8
ST 1.00 LY 1 1 LY 2 2 LY 3 3 LY 4 4 LY 5 5 LY 6 6 LY 7 7 LY 8 8
FI PS 1 1 PS 2 2 PS 3 3 PS 4 4 PS 5 5 PS 6 6 PS 7 7 PS 8 8
ST 1.00 PS 1 1 PS 2 2 PS 3 3 PS 4 4 PS 5 5 PS 6 6 PS 7 7 PS 8 8
EQ PS 2 1 PS 3 2 PS 4 3 PS 5 4 PS 6 5 PS 7 6 PS 8 7 PS 8 1
ST .71 PS 2 1
EQ PS 3 1 PS 4 2 PS 5 3 PS 6 4 PS 7 5 PS 8 6 PS 7 1 PS 8 2
ST .00 PS 3 1
EQ PS 4 1 PS 5 2 PS 6 3 PS 7 4 PS 8 5 PS 6 1 PS 7 2 PS 8 3
ST -.71 PS 4 1
EQ PS 5 1 PS 6 2 PS 7 3 PS 8 4
ST -1.00 PS 5 1
OU ALL ME=ML RO RC AD=OFF
```

```
HOFSESS & TRACEY (2005) EQUAL SPACING, EQUAL COMMUNALITY
DA NI=8 NO=206 MA=KM
KM
1.00
 .20    1.00
 .13     .60   1.00
-.19     .20    .53   1.00
-.36     .14    .29    .54   1.00
-.09    -.52   -.21    .05    .06   1.00
```

MEASUREMENT OF DOMINANCE AND NURTURANCE I 179

Table 6.7 Continued

-.01	-.41	-.54	-.28	-.10	.51	1.00	
.48	.09	-.12	-.43	-.37	.04	.30	1.00

```
MO NY=8 NE=8 TE=IN LY=IN PS=IN
LA
PA BC DE FG HI JK LM NO
OU ALL ME=ML RO RC AD=OFF
```

```
SODANO AND TRACEY (2006) CIRCULANT CORRELATION ANALYSIS OF
IAS-R
DA NI=8 NO=194 MA=KM
KM
1.00
 .22   1.00
 .08    .69   1.00
 .07    .38    .42   1.00
-.47    .19    .27    .35   1.00
-.29   -.45   -.28    .03    .25   1.00
 .06   -.43   -.58   -.48   -.19    .23   1.00
 .15   -.22   -.38   -.59   -.28   -.06    .60   1.00
```

```
MO NY=8 NE=8 TE=IN LY=IN PS=IN
LA
PA BC DE FG HI JK LM NO
OU ALL ME=ML RO RC AD=OFF
```

Table 6.8 Reproduced Correlation Matrix Across Study 1 Samples

Var.	Correlations							
	PA	BC	DE	FG	HI	JK	LM	NO
PA	1.00							
BC	.43	1.00						
DE	.06	.43	1.00					
FG	-.27	.06	.43	1.00				
HI	-.56	-.27	.06	.43	1.00			
JK	-.27	-.56	-.27	.06	.43	1.00		
LM	.06	-.27	-.56	-.27	.06	.43	1.00	
NO	.43	.06	-.27	-.56	-.27	.06	.43	1.00

Note: PA = ambitious-dominant, BC = arrogant-calculating, DE = cold-quarrelsome, FG = aloof-introverted, HI = unassured-submissive, JK = unassuming-ingenuous, LM = warm-agreeable, NO = gregarious-extraverted.

180   THE SELF IN RELATIONSHIPS

a three-factor model adding "acquiescence" as a noncircumplex model was tested) across the three data sets. The multiple-group syntax file, which includes the essence of the separate syntax files that we have encountered so far, is presented in Table 6.9. The same changes to the syntax files that we described for the multiple-group circulant correlation analysis in the preceding paragraph were also applied to the syntax files for the initial and final confirmatory factor analyses of the three data sets. Results of the multiple-group confirmatory factor analyses affirmed that (1) a two-factor model did *not* provide satisfactory fit (chi-square = 124.57, *df* = 96, *p* < .05;

Table 6.9 Syntax Files Used as Input for Multiple-Group Confirmatory Factor Analyses of Lower-Order Subclinical Interpersonal Traits, Study 1 Samples

---

`Two-factor solution`

```
GAINES ET AL. (1997, STUDY 2) DOM NUR
DA NG=3 NI=8 NO=401 MA=KM
KM

1.00
 .41    1.00
 .21     .63    1.00
-.20     .22     .54    1.00
-.64    -.18     .04     .49    1.00
-.43    -.64    -.29     .07     .46    1.00
-.13    -.38    -.65    -.43     .12     .37    1.00
 .33    -.06    -.35    -.76    -.38     .01     .49    1.00
```

```
MO NY=8 NE=2 TE=SY,FI LY=FU,FI PS=SY,FI
LA
PA BC DE FG HI JK LM NO
FR TE 1 1 TE 2 2 TE 3 3 TE 4 4 TE 5 5 TE 6 6 TE 7 7 TE 8 8
FR LY 1 1 LY 7 2
FR LY 2 1 LY 8 1 LY 6 2 LY 8 2
FR LY 5 1 LY 3 2
FR LY 4 1 LY 6 1 LY 2 2 LY 4 2
EQ LY 1 1 LY 7 2
EQ LY 2 1 LY 8 1 LY 6 2 LY 8 2
EQ LY 5 1 LY 3 2
EQ LY 4 1 LY 6 1 LY 2 2 LY 4 2
ST 1.00 LY 1 1
ST .71 LY 2 1
ST -.71 LY 4 1
ST -1.00 LY 5 1
ST 1.00 PS 1 1 PS 2 2
OU ALL ME=ML RO RC AD=OFF
```

MEASUREMENT OF DOMINANCE AND NURTURANCE I 181

Table 6.9 Continued

```
HOFSESS AND TRACEY (2005) DOM NUR
DA NI=8 NO=206 MA=KM
KM
1.00
 .20    1.00
 .13     .60    1.00
-.19     .20     .53    1.00
-.36     .14     .29     .54    1.00
-.09    -.52    -.21     .05     .06    1.00
-.01    -.41    -.54    -.28    -.10     .51    1.00
 .48     .09    -.12    -.43    -.37     .04     .30    1.00
```

```
MO NY=8 NE=2 TE=IN LY=IN PS=IN
LA
PA BC DE FG HI JK LM NO
OU ALL ME=ML RO RC AD=OFF
```

```
SODANO AND TRACEY (2006) DOM NUR
DA NI=8 NO=194 MA=KM
KM
1.00
 .22    1.00
 .08     .69    1.00
 .07     .38     .42    1.00
-.47     .19     .27     .35    1.00
-.29    -.45    -.28     .03     .25    1.00
 .06    -.43    -.58    -.48    -.19     .23    1.00
 .15    -.22    -.38    -.59    -.28    -.06     .60    1.00
```

```
MO NY=8 NE=2 TE=IN LY=IN PS=IN
LA
PA BC DE FG HI JK LM NO
OU ALL ME=ML RO RC AD=OFF
```

Three-factor solution

```
GAINES ET AL. (1997, STUDY 2) DOM NUR ACQ
DA NG=3 NI=8 NO=401 MA=KM
KM
1.00
 .41    1.00
```

(continued)

182 THE SELF IN RELATIONSHIPS

Table 6.9 Continued

Three-factor solution

.21	.63	1.00					
−.20	.22	.54	1.00				
−.64	−.18	.04	.49	1.00			
−.43	−.64	−.29	.07	.46	1.00		
−.13	−.38	−.65	−.43	.12	.37	1.00	
.33	−.06	−.35	−.76	−.38	.01	.49	1.00

```
MO NY=8 NE=3 TE=SY,FI LY=FU,FI PS=SY,FI
LA
PA BC DE FG HI JK LM NO
FR TE 1 1 TE 2 2 TE 3 3 TE 4 4 TE 5 5 TE 6 6 TE 7 7 TE 8 8
FR LY 1 1 LY 7 2
FR LY 2 1 LY 8 1 LY 6 2 LY 8 2
FR LY 5 1 LY 3 2
FR LY 4 1 LY 6 1 LY 2 2 LY 4 2
EQ LY 1 1 LY 7 2
EQ LY 2 1 LY 8 1 LY 6 2 LY 8 2
EQ LY 5 1 LY 3 2
EQ LY 4 1 LY 6 1 LY 2 2 LY 4 2
ST 1.00 LY 1 1
ST .71 LY 2 1
ST -.71 LY 4 1
ST -1.00 LY 5 1
FR LY 1 3 LY 2 3 LY 3 3 LY 4 3 LY 5 3 LY 6 3 LY 7 3 LY 8 3
EQ LY 1 3 LY 2 3 LY 3 3 LY 4 3 LY 5 3 LY 6 3 LY 7 3 LY 8 3
ST 1.00 PS 1 1 PS 2 2 PS 3 3
OU ALL ME=ML RO RC AD=OFF
```

```
HOFSESS AND TRACEY (2005) DOM NUR ACQ
DA NI=8 NO=206 MA=KM
KM
```

1.00							
.20	1.00						
.13	.60	1.00					
−.19	.20	.53	1.00				
−.36	.14	.29	.54	1.00			
−.09	−.52	−.21	.05	.06	1.00		
−.01	−.41	−.54	−.28	−.10	.51	1.00	
.48	.09	−.12	−.43	−.37	.04	.30	1.00

```
MO NY=8 NE=3 TE=IN LY=IN PS=IN
LA
PA BC DE FG HI JK LM NO
OU ALL ME=ML RO RC AD=OFF
```

MEASUREMENT OF DOMINANCE AND NURTURANCE I   183

Table 6.10 Obtained Pattern of Factor Loadings Among Lower-Order Subclinical Interpersonal Traits Across Study 1 Samples, Three-Factor Solution

Var.	Factor		
	DOM	NUR	ACQ
PA	.70	.00	.23
BC	.48	−.59	.23
DE	.00	−.73	.23
FG	−.59	−.59	.23
HI	−.73	.00	.23
JK	−.59	.48	.23
LM	.00	.70	.23
NO	.48	.48	.23

Note: Regarding higher-order factors, DOM = dominance, NUR = nurturance, ACQ = acquiescence. Regarding lower-order interpersonal traits, PA = ambitious-dominant, BC = arrogant-calculating, DE = cold-quarrelsome, FG = aloof-introverted, HI = unassured-submissive, JK = unassuming-ingenuous, LM = warm-agreeable, NO = gregarious-extraverted.

RMSEA = .03; CFI = .96); (2) in contrast, a three-factor model provided satisfactory fit (chi-square = 101.12, df = 95, NS; RMSEA = .02; CFI = .99); and (3) the three-factor model yielded significantly better fit to the data than did the two-factor model (difference in chi-square = 23.45, difference in df = 1, $p < .01$). The matrix of loadings for the three-factor model is presented in Table 6.10.

BONUS: To Ipsatize or Not to Ipsatize Data From the IAS-R(?)

During our review of the literature on published studies in which researchers not only administered the IAS-R (Wiggins et al., 1988) but also reported matrices of correlations among subclinical interpersonal traits, we found one study (i.e., DeYoung et al., 2013, Sample 2) that included a correlation matrix among *ipsatized* scores (in which deviation scores on all [sub]scales are calculated within individuals; Acton & Revelle, 2002), rather than a correlation matrix among raw scores (which has been the case for all of the actual data sets that we have analyzed so far). DeYoung et al.'s (2013, Sample 2) reasoning behind their ipsatization of IAS-R subscale scores (i.e., the raw scores for all

184   THE SELF IN RELATIONSHIPS

of the items within a particular subscale are keyed in the same direction) is at odds with Wiggins's (1995) recommendation that researchers *not* ipsatize IAS-R subscale scores in the absence of evidence concerning an "acquiescence" linear composite within principal component analyses of raw data. Then again, our own confirmatory factor analyses of the three samples in the present Study 1 (i.e., Gaines, Panter, et al., 1997, Study 2; Hofsess & Tracey, 2005; Sodano & Tracey, 2006, Adult Sample) revealed that a noncircumplex "acquiescence" latent variable coexists with the circumplex variables of dominance and nurturance.

The ipsatized matrix of subclinical interpersonal trait correlations for the IAS-R (Wiggins et al., 1988) from the study by DeYoung et al. (2013, Sample 2) is presented in Table 6.11. As was the case for the three samples with nonipsatized matrices that we have analyzed in the present Study 1 (i.e., Gaines et al., 1997, Study 2; Hofsess & Tracey, 2005; Sodano & Tracey, 2006, Adult Sample), we evaluated the geometric properties of the IAS-R data from DeYoung et al. via a circulant correlation analysis (testing the goodness-of-fit regarding an equal-spacing, equal-communality model) using maximum likelihood estimation, ridge option, and ridge constant in LISREL 10.20 (Joreskog & Sorbom, 2019). Afterward, we evaluated the psychometric

Table 6.11 Matrix of Zero-Order Correlations Among Lower-Order Subclinical Interpersonal Traits (Based on Ipsatized Subscale Scores From DeYoung et al., 2013, Sample 2, p. 472)

Var.	Correlations							
	PA	BC	DE	FG	HI	JK	LM	NO
PA	1.00							
BC	.16	1.00						
DE	−.04	.68	1.00					
FG	−.54	.20	.43	1.00				
HI	−.83	−.18	.05	.62	1.00			
JK	−.26	−.82	−.63	−.15	.19	1.00		
LM	.05	−.67	−.86	−.60	−.21	.51	1.00	
NO	.50	−.28	−.51	−.90	−.66	.12	.64	1.00

Note: PA = ambitious-dominant, BC = arrogant-calculating, DE = cold-quarrelsome, FG = aloof-introverted, HI = unassured-submissive, JK = unassuming-ingenuous, LM = warm-agreeable, NO = gregarious-extraverted.

Source: Adapted from "Unifying the Aspects of the Big Five, the Interpersonal Circumplex, and Trait Affiliation," by C. L. DeYoung, Y. H. Weisberg, L. C. Quilty, & J. B. Peterson, 2013, *Journal of Personality, 81*, p. 472. Copyright 2013 by John Wiley & Sons. Reproduced and adapted with permission.

MEASUREMENT OF DOMINANCE AND NURTURANCE I 185

Table 6.12 Syntax File Used as Input for Circulant Correlation Analysis of Lower-Order Subclinical Interpersonal Traits (Ipsatized Matrix), DeYoung et al. (2013, Sample 2)

```
DE YOUNG ET AL. (2013, SAMPLE 2): CCA OF IPSATIZED IAS-R DATA
DA NI=8 NO=294 MA=KM
KM
1.00
 .16    1.00
-.04     .68    1.00
-.54     .20     .43    1.00
-.83    -.18     .05     .62    1.00
-.26    -.82    -.63    -.15     .19    1.00
 .05    -.67    -.86    -.60    -.21     .51    1.00
 .50    -.28    -.51    -.90    -.66     .12     .64    1.00
```

```
MO NY=8 NE=8 TE=SY,FI LY=FU,FI PS=SY,FR
LA
PA BC DE FG HI JK LM NO
FR TE 1 1 TE 2 2 TE 3 3 TE 4 4 TE 5 5 TE 6 6 TE 7 7 TE 8 8
ST 1.00 LY 1 1 LY 2 2 LY 3 3 LY 4 4 LY 5 5 LY 6 6 LY 7 7 LY 8 8
FI PS 1 1 PS 2 2 PS 3 3 PS 4 4 PS 5 5 PS 6 6 PS 7 7 PS 8 8
ST 1.00 PS 1 1 PS 2 2 PS 3 3 PS 4 4 PS 5 5 PS 6 6 PS 7 7 PS 8 8
EQ PS 2 1 PS 3 2 PS 4 3 PS 5 4 PS 6 5 PS 7 6 PS 8 7 PS 8 1
ST .71 PS 2 1
EQ PS 3 1 PS 4 2 PS 5 3 PS 6 4 PS 7 5 PS 8 6 PS 7 1 PS 8 2
ST .00 PS 3 1
EQ PS 4 1 PS 5 2 PS 6 3 PS 7 4 PS 8 5 PS 6 1 PS 7 2 PS 8 3
ST -.71 PS 4 1
EQ PS 5 1 PS 6 2 PS 7 3 PS 8 4
ST -1.00 PS 5 1
OU ALL ME=ML RO RC AD=OFF
```

properties of the IAS-R data from DeYoung et al. via a pair of confirmatory factor analyses (one that was limited to the circumplex factors of dominance and nurturance, followed by one in which a noncircumplex "acquiescence" factor was added), again using LISREL.

The syntax file for the circulant correlation analysis as applied to the ipsatized matrix from DeYoung et al. (2013, Sample 2) is presented in Table 6.12. Results of the circulant correlation analysis indicated that, consistent with hypotheses, an equal-spacing, equal-communality model provided satisfactory fit to the data (chi-square = 24.49, *df* = 24, *NS*; RMSEA = .01; CFI = 1.00). The resulting matrix of reproduced correlations for the data from DeYoung et al. is shown in Table 6.13.

The syntax files for the confirmatory factor analyses as applied to the ipsatized matrix from DeYoung et al. (2013, Sample 2) are presented in

186 THE SELF IN RELATIONSHIPS

Table 6.13 Reproduced Correlation Matrix of Lower-Order Subclinical Interpersonal Traits (Ipsatized Matrix), DeYoung et al. (2013, Sample 2)

Var.	Correlations							
	PA	BC	DE	FG	HI	JK	LM	NO
PA	1.00							
BC	.47	1.00						
DE	−.03	.47	1.00					
FG	−.51	−.03	.47	1.00				
HI	−.85	−.51	−.03	.47	1.00			
JK	−.51	−.85	−.51	−.03	.47	1.00		
LM	−.03	−.51	−.85	−.51	−.03	.47	1.00	
NO	.47	−.03	−.51	−.85	−.51	−.03	.47	1.00

Note: PA = ambitious-dominant, BC = arrogant-calculating, DE = cold-quarrelsome, FG = aloof-introverted, HI = unassured-submissive, JK = unassuming-ingenuous, LM = warm-agreeable, NO = gregarious-extraverted.

Table 6.14. Results of initial confirmatory factor analyses indicated that, contrary to hypotheses, a two-factor model did *not* provide satisfactory fit to the data from DeYoung et al. (chi-square = 39.61, *df* = 24, *p* < .05; RMSEA = .05; CFI = .96). Moreover, contrary to hypotheses, a three-factor model did *not* provide satisfactory fit to the data from DeYoung et al. (chi-square = 39.61, *df* = 24, *p* < .05; RMSEA = .05; CFI = .96); the latter yielded an error message regarding underidentification. Given that the "badness-of-fit" for the two

Table 6.14 Syntax Files Used as Input for Initial and Final Confirmatory Factor Analyses of Lower-Order Subclinical Interpersonal Traits (Ipsatized Data) From DeYoung et al. (2013, Sample 2)

Two-factor solution

```
DE YOUNG ET AL. (2013, SAMPLE 2): CCA FOR IPSATIZED DATA
(DE YOUNG ET AL., 2013) DOM NUR
DA NI=8 NO=294 MA=KM
KM
1.00
 .16   1.00
-.04    .68   1.00
```

MEASUREMENT OF DOMINANCE AND NURTURANCE I 187

Table 6.14 Continued

Two-factor solution							
−.54	.20	.43	1.00				
−.83	−.18	.05	.62	1.00			
−.26	−.82	−.63	−.15	.19	1.00		
.05	−.67	−.86	−.60	−.21	.51	1.00	
.50	−.28	−.51	−.90	−.66	.12	.64	1.00

```
MO NY=8 NE=2 TE=SY,FI LY=FU,FI PS=SY,FI
LA
PA BC DE FG HI JK LM NO
FR TE 1 1 TE 2 2 TE 3 3 TE 4 4 TE 5 5 TE 6 6 TE 7 7 TE 8 8
FR LY 1 1 LY 7 2
FR LY 2 1 LY 8 1 LY 6 2 LY 8 2
FR LY 5 1 LY 3 2
FR LY 4 1 LY 6 1 LY 2 2 LY 4 2
EQ LY 1 1 LY 7 2
EQ LY 2 1 LY 8 1 LY 6 2 LY 8 2
EQ LY 5 1 LY 3 2
EQ LY 4 1 LY 6 1 LY 2 2 LY 4 2
ST 1.00 LY 1 1
ST .71 LY 2 1
ST -.71 LY 4 1
ST -1.00 LY 5 1
ST 1.00 PS 1 1 PS 2 2
OU ALL ME=ML RO RC AD=OFF
```

```
SODANO AND TRACEY (2006) DOM NUR ACQ
DA NI=8 NO=194 MA=KM
KM
```

1.00							
.22	1.00						
.08	.69	1.00					
.07	.38	.42	1.00				
−.47	.19	.27	.35	1.00			
−.29	−.45	−.28	.03	.25	1.00		
.06	−.43	−.58	−.48	−.19	.23	1.00	
.15	−.22	−.38	−.59	−.28	−.06	.60	1.00

```
MO NY=8 NE=3 TE=IN LY=IN PS=IN
LA
PA BC DE FG HI JK LM NO
OU ALL ME=ML RO RC AD=OFF
```

(continued)

188 THE SELF IN RELATIONSHIPS

Table 6.14 Continued

Three-factor solution

DE YOUNG ET AL. (2013, SAMPLE 2): CCA FOR IPSATIZED DATA
(DE YOUNG ET AL., 2013) DOM NUR ACQ

DA NI=8 NO=294 MA=KM

KM

1.00							
.16	1.00						
−.04	.68	1.00					
−.54	.20	.43	1.00				
−.83	−.18	.05	.62	1.00			
−.26	−.82	−.63	−.15	.19	1.00		
.05	−.67	−.86	−.60	−.21	.51	1.00	
.50	−.28	−.51	−.90	−.66	.12	.64	1.00

```
MO NY=8 NE=3 TE=SY,FI LY=FU,FI PS=SY,FI
LA
PA BC DE FG HI JK LM NO
FR TE 1 1 TE 2 2 TE 3 3 TE 4 4 TE 5 5 TE 6 6 TE 7 7 TE 8 8
FR LY 1 1 LY 7 2
FR LY 2 1 LY 8 1 LY 6 2 LY 8 2
FR LY 5 1 LY 3 2
FR LY 4 1 LY 6 1 LY 2 2 LY 4 2
EQ LY 1 1 LY 7 2
EQ LY 2 1 LY 8 1 LY 6 2 LY 8 2
EQ LY 5 1 LY 3 2
EQ LY 4 1 LY 6 1 LY 2 2 LY 4 2
ST 1.00 LY 1 1
ST .71 LY 2 1
ST -.71 LY 4 1
ST -1.00 LY 5 1
FR LY 1 3 LY 2 3 LY 3 3 LY 4 3 LY 5 3 LY 6 3 LY 7 3 LY 8 3
EQ LY 1 3 LY 2 3 LY 3 3 LY 4 3 LY 5 3 LY 6 3 LY 7 3 LY 8 3
ST .32 LY 1 3
ST 1.00 PS 1 1 PS 2 2 PS 3 3
OU ALL ME=ML RO RC AD=OFF
```

models was identical (difference in chi-square = .00, difference in df = 1, *NS*), we concluded that ipsatization raises more questions than it answers regarding the psychometric properties of the IAS-R (see also Cornwell & Dunlap, 1994).

Outside the field of interpersonal psychology, the practice of ipsatizing personality data is highly controversial (for examples of a debate within the *Journal of Occupational and Organizational Psychology* that dates back to the early to mid-1990s concerning this practice, see Bartram, 1996; Closs,

1996; Saville & Wilson, 1991). Nevertheless, within interpersonal psychology, criticism regarding ipsatization of circumplex data is muted at best (e.g., Birtchnell, 2014) and ignored at worst (e.g., Tracey, 2000). Results of our confirmatory factor analyses concerning DeYoung et al.'s (2013, Sample 2) ipsatized data, combined with results of our confirmatory factor analyses regarding the three previous samples (i.e., Gaines, Panter, et al., 1997, Study 2; Hofsess & Tracey, 2005; Sodano & Tracey, 2006, Adult Sample), suggest that interpersonal circumplex theorists would be better off accounting for an "acquiescence" factor by accounting for it as a noncircumplex latent variable in analyses of nonipsatized data (instead of applying ipsatization to raw data and abandoning confirmatory factor analyses; see also Savalei & Falk, 2014). In fact, we concur with Moeller's (2015) advice to researchers who are contemplating the use of ipsatized data from longitudinal samples, which can be readily generalized to cross-sectional samples: "Don't" (p. 1).

Prelude to Chapter 7

Notwithstanding the strong conceptual base (thanks to interpersonal circumplex theory; Wiggins, 1979, 1991, 2003/2005) that serves as the foundation for various iterations of the IAS (Trapnell & Wiggins, 1990; Wiggins, 1979; Wiggins et al., 1988), results of the present Study 1 lead us to conclude that the circularity of lower-order trait intercorrelations from the IAS-R (thus affirming a key geometric property) is better established on empirical grounds than is the underlying factor pattern (thus questioning a key psychometric property, to some extent). Considering that our ultimate goal in the present book is to evaluate the predictive validity (or, perhaps more accurately, *the criterion-related validity*; Nunnally & Bernstein, 1994) of subclinical interpersonal traits as we seek to explain individual differences in accommodation (Rusbult et al., 1991), the results thus far do not bode well for the IAS-R in measuring dominance and nurturance *as predictors* of such an important conflict resolution process (see Rusbult, 1993). Rather than foreclose our options regarding a suitable survey of subclinical interpersonal traits, we remain open to alternative inventories that possess satisfactory construct validity as necessary (though not sufficient) to ensure satisfactory predictive/criterion-related validity (see Fournier et al., 2011).

The consensus view regarding surveys of subclinical interpersonal traits is that the IAS-R (Wiggins et al., 1988) is the gold standard, geometrically and psychometrically speaking (as summarized by Gurtman, 2011). However, some advocates of the IAS-R (e.g., Locke, 2011) have commented upon the presence of several negatively valenced and obscurely worded terms within that inventory. Furthermore, some critics of the IAS-R (e.g., L. S. Benjamin, 2011) have contended that whatever success Wiggins and colleagues have achieved in their quest for optimizing geometric and psychometric properties has come at the cost of real-world face validity. In spite of the continued dominance (no pun intended) of the IAS-R as an index of subclinical interpersonal traits, at least one potential competitor has surfaced—namely, the 32-item IPIP-IPC that was developed by Patrick Markey and Charlotte Markey (2009). Unlike the IAS-R (which consists of trait *adjectives*), the IPIP-IPC consists of trait *statements* that are neither unusually negative in valence nor unusually obscure in terminology (see D. N. Jones & Paulhus, 2011). Using the IPIP-IPC, Markey and Markey (2013) have successfully predicted individuals' relationship quality, reflecting low dominance and high nurturance.

In Chapter 7, we will undertake the same analyses of previously published data concerning the IPIP-IPC (Markey & Markey, 2009) that we undertook regarding the IAS-R (Wiggins et al., 1988) in the present chapter. In particular, we will conduct single-group and multiple-group circulant correlation analyses and confirmatory factor analyses on data sets from Markey and Markey (2009, Study 1, Samples 1 and 2) and Barford et al. (2015), and we will conduct a single-group circulant correlation analysis and confirmatory factor analyses on a bonus data set from DeYoung et al. (2013, Sample 3). In contrast to the IAS-R, the IPIP-IPC rarely has been evaluated with regard to its geometric or psychometric properties by researchers other than the creators of the survey, especially with Ns greater than 1 or 2 (e.g., Dawood & Pincus, 2016). Furthermore, unlike the IAS-R, we are unaware of any previously published study in which researchers have applied confirmatory factor analysis (rather than principal component analysis) to the IPIP-IPC. Thus, our analyses of data from the IPIP-IPC promise to be the most rigorous psychometric analyses to be published concerning that survey (and going beyond Gaines, Panter, et al.'s [1997, Study 2] confirmatory factor analyses of the IAS-R).

7

Measurement of Dominance and Nurturance as Interpersonal Traits II

Synopsis: In the present chapter, we evaluate the geometric and psycho-metric properties of the International Personality Item Pool-Interpersonal Circle (IPIP-IPC) by reanalyzing data sets from journal articles by Markey and Markey (2009, Study 1, Samples 1 and 2) and Barford et al. (2015); we report the results of single-group and multiple-group versions of circulant correlation analyses (i.e., consistent with predictions, an equal-spacing, equal-communality model yields satisfactory fit across the three data sets in general); we report the results of single-group and multiple-group versions of confirmatory factor analyses (i.e., consistent with predictions, two-factor as well as three-factor models excluding versus including a noncircumplex "acquiescence" latent variable along with the circumplex latent variables of dominance and nurturance provide satisfactory fit, with the three-factor model failing to offer a significantly or marginally better fit to the data when compared to the two-factor model); we supplement the aforementioned analyses with a circulant correlation analysis and a pair of confirmatory factor analyses of ipsatized data from DeYoung et al. (2013, Sample 3), finding that (consistent with predictions) an equal-spacing, equal-communality model offers satisfactory fit to the ipsatized data, whereas (contrary to predictions) neither a two-factor nor a three-factor model provides satisfactory fit to the ipsatized data (and the "badness-of-fit" of those models is identical for that data set); and we provide a prelude to Chapter 8, in which we progress beyond the analyses of the present chapter to examine interpersonal traits as predictors of accommodation in close relationships.

In the article that introduced the original Interpersonal Adjective Scales (IAS), Wiggins (1979) cited earlier taxonomy-creating efforts by Norman (1967) and Goldberg (1977) as direct methodological influences, along with Allport and Odbert's (1936) documentation of subclinical

---

The Self in Relationships. Stanley O. Gaines, Jr., Oxford University Press. © Oxford University Press 2023.
DOI: 10.1093/oso/9780197687635.003.0007

194 THE SELF IN RELATIONSHIPS

Study 2

Method

Participants

Samples 1 and 2. In the present Study 2, demographic statistics for Sample 1 (Markey & Markey, 2009, Study 1, Sample 1, $n = 251$) and Sample 2 (Markey & Markey, 2009, Study 1, Sample 2, $n = 250$) were combined in the Markeys' original paper. Thus, across Samples 1 and 2, a total of 501 individuals (216 men, 285 women) served as participants. Markey and Markey (2009, Study 1, Samples 1 and 2) reported an age range from 22 to 90 years of age for their participants. The Markeys did not report descriptive statistics regarding age or ethnic group membership for their participants.

Sample 3. Additionally, in the present Study 2, Sample 3 (Barford et al., 2015) consisted of 206 participants (reported by gender, 26% were men and 76% were women). Barford et al. (2015) reported an age range from 18 to 46 years of age ($M = 20.00$ years, $SD = 4.38$ years) for their participants. In terms of ethnic group membership, Barford et al. did not report descriptive statistics for their participants.

Materials

Sample 1. Participants in the present Study 2, Sample 1 (Markey & Markey, 2009, Study 1, Sample 1) completed the Markeys' 32-item IPIP-IPC, which was designed to measure eight lower-order traits (i.e., ambitious-dominant, arrogant-calculating, cold-quarrelsome, aloof-introverted, unassured-submissive, unassuming-ingenuous, warm-agreeable, and gregarious-extraverted) as blends of two higher-order traits (i.e., the agentic trait of dominance and the communal trait of nurturance). As reported by Markey and Markey (2009, Study 1, Sample 1), results of reliability analyses indicated that the internal consistency was quite varied across the eight subscales (average Cronbach's alpha = .64, though it is not clear how many of the subscales yielded internal consistency coefficients that reached or exceeded the mean; Cronbach's alphas ranged from .51 to .75, although the eight separate internal consistency coefficients were not reported).

Sample 2. Also, participants in the present Study 2, Sample 2 (Markey & Markey, 2009, Study 1, Sample 2) completed the IPIP-IPC (Markey & Markey, 2009). As reported by Markey and Markey (2009, Study 1, Sample 2), results of reliability analyses indicated that the internal consistency varied greatly across the eight subscales (average Cronbach's alpha = .63, though it is not clear how many of the subscales yielded internal consistency coefficients that reached or exceeded the mean; Cronbach's alphas ranged from .50 to .77, although the eight separate internal consistency coefficients were not reported; see J. M. Cortina, 1993, for details regarding .63 as an acceptable alpha coefficient for four-item scales or subscales).

Sample 3. Finally, participants in the present Study 2, Sample 3 (Barford et al., 2015) completed the IPIP-IPC (Markey & Markey, 2009). As reported by Barford et al. (2015), results of reliability analyses indicated that internal consistency was highly varied across the eight subscales (Cronbach's alphas ranged from .42 to .76; separate Cronbach's alphas = .76 for ambitious-dominant, .68 for arrogant-calculating, .42 for cold-quarrelsome, .76 for aloof-introverted, .56 for unassured-submissive, .44 for unassuming-ingenuous, .73 for warm-agreeable, and .77 for gregarious-extraverted).

Procedure

Samples 1 and 2. Markey and Markey (2009, Study 1, Samples 1 and 2) did not provide detailed comments on the procedure for the present Study 2, Samples 1 and 2 (instead, the Markeys referred readers to the earlier publication by Goldberg (1999).

Sample 3. Prior to conducting the present Study 2, Sample 3, Barford et al. (2015) obtained ethics approval from the Psychology Research Committee at their academic institution (a large research university). Participants read and signed an informed consent sheet that explained the purpose of the study in general terms, completed a questionnaire that included the IPIP-IPC (Markey & Markey, 2009) and additional surveys that are not directly relevant to the present book, read a debriefing form that explained the purpose of the study in detail, and received research participant credit for completing the study.

Results and Discussion

Matrices of zero-order correlations among the eight subclinical interpersonal traits that were measured by the IPIP-IPC (Markey & Markey, 2009) among the three samples in the present Study 2 (i.e., Markey & Markey, Study 1, Samples 1 and 2, p. 355; Barford et al., 2015, p. 234) are presented in Table 7.1. First, each of the correlation matrices was entered into a separate circulant

Table 7.1 Matrices of Zero-Order Correlations Among Lower-Order Subclinical Interpersonal Traits, Study 2 Samples[a,b,c]

Markey & Markey (2009, Study 1, Sample 1, p. 355, $n = 251$)

Var.	Correlations							
	PA	BC	DE	FG	HI	JK	LM	NO
PA	1.00							
BC	.43	1.00						
DE	.00	.23	1.00					
FG	−.51	−.14	.39	1.00				
HI	−.64	−.30	.04	.54	1.00			
JK	−.17	−.44	−.43	−.03	.22	1.00		
LM	.01	−.22	−.56	−.30	.01	.54	1.00	
NO	.42	−.10	−.37	−.57	−.42	.12	.36	1.00

Markey & Markey (2009, Study 1, Sample 2, p. 355, $n = 250$)

Var.	Correlations							
	PA	BC	DE	FG	HI	JK	LM	NO
PA	1.00							
BC	.47	1.00						
DE	.05	.34	1.00					
FG	−.41	−.07	.36	1.00				
HI	−.66	−.29	.08	.54	1.00			
JK	−.22	−.45	−.33	.01	.17	1.00		
LM	−.09	−.28	−.53	−.31	−.02	.45	1.00	
NO	.22	−.08	−.45	−.61	−.35	.20	.40	1.00

Barford et al. (2015, p. 234, $n = 206$)

Var.	Correlations							
	PA	BC	DE	FG	HI	JK	LM	NO
PA	1.00							
BC	.36	1.00						
DE	.07	.41	1.00					
FG	−.60	−.12	.30	1.00				
HI	−.70	−.30	−.07	.64	1.00			
JK	−.25	−.45	−.20	.14	.39	1.00		
LM	.12	−.27	−.37	−.30	−.04	.41	1.00	
NO	.46	−.09	−.12	−.59	−.40	.11	.48	1.00

[a,b]Adapted from "A Brief Assessment of the Interpersonal Circumplex: The IPIP-IPC," by P. M. Markey & C. N. Markey, 2009, *Assessment, 16*, p. 355. Copyright 2009 by Sage. Reproduced and adapted with permission.

[c]Adapted from "Mapping the Interpersonal Domain: Translating between the Big Five, HEXACO, and Interpersonal Circumplex," by K. A. Barford, K. Zhao, & L. D. Smillie, 2015, *Personality and Individual Differences, 86*, p. 234. Copyright 2015 by Elsevier. Reproduced and adapted with permission.

Note: PA = ambitious-dominant, BC = arrogant-calculating, DE = cold-quarrelsome, FG = aloof-introverted, HI = unassured-submissive, JK = unassuming-ingenuous, LM = warm-agreeable, NO = gregarious-extraverted.

correlation analysis, in which we tested goodness-of-fit concerning the equal-spacing, equal-communality model that we described in Chapters 5 and 6. Afterward, each of the correlation matrices was entered into a pair of confirmatory factor analyses, in which we tested goodness-of-fit regarding the two-factor (i.e., dominance and nurturance) and three-factor (i.e., dominance, nurturance, and "acquiescence") models that we described in Chapters 5 and 6.

Circulant Correlation Analyses

In order to conduct circulant correlation analyses on the matrices of correlations from the three samples (i.e., Markey & Markey, 2009, p. 355; Barford et al., 2015, p. 234) in the present Study 2, we used the same templates (i.e., equal-spacing, equal communality model; maximum likelihood estimation via LISREL 10.20 [Joreskog & Sorbom, 2019], using the ridge option and ridge constant) that we described in Chapters 5 and 6. The syntax files for the three samples are presented in Table 7.2. Results of circulant correlation analyses indicated that, consistent with hypotheses, an equal-spacing, equal-communality model provided satisfactory fit to the data for Sample 1 (chi-square = 11.14, degrees of freedom [df] = 24, NS; root mean square error of approximation [RMSEA] = .00; comparative fit index [CFI] = 1.00), Sample 2 (chi-square = 12.39, df = 24, NS; RMSEA = .00; CFI = 1.00), and Sample 3 (chi-square = 14.46, df = 24, NS; RMSEA = .00; CFI = 1.00). Furthermore, inspection of reproduced correlation matrices (shown in Table 7.3) revealed that the estimated correlations were broadly consistent with the pattern that we observed for Wiggins's (1979, p. 399) "simulated" matrix in Chapter 5 (the reproduced correlation matrices were highly similar across the three samples). Thus, we concluded that the IPIP-IPC (Markey & Markey, 2009) consistently performed well in terms of geometric properties (i.e., alignment of the eight lower-order traits around a circle or circumplex).

Confirmatory Factor Analyses

Initial confirmatory factor analyses. Afterward, in order to conduct initial confirmatory factor analyses on the matrices of correlations from the three samples (i.e., Markey & Markey, 2009, Samples 1 and 2, p. 355; Barford et al., 2015, p. 234) in the present Study 2, we used the same templates (i.e., two-factor model with dominance and nurturance as circumplex latent variables; maximum likelihood estimation via LISREL 10.20 [Joreskog

198 THE SELF IN RELATIONSHIPS

Table 7.2 Syntax Files Used as Input for Circulant Correlation Analyses of Lower-Order Subclinical Interpersonal Traits, Study 2 Samples

Markey & Markey (2009, Study 1, Sample 1, n = 251)

```
MARKEY & MARKEY (2009, STUDY 1, SAMPLE 1): EQUAL SPACING,
EQUAL COMMUNALITY MODEL
DA NI=8 NO=251 MA=KM
KM
1.00
 .43    1.00
 .00     .23    1.00
-.51    -.14     .39    1.00
-.64    -.30     .04     .54    1.00
-.17    -.44    -.43    -.03     .22    1.00
 .01    -.22    -.56    -.30     .01     .54    1.00
 .42    -.10    -.37    -.57    -.42     .12     .36    1.00
```

```
MO NY=8 NE=8 TE=SY,FI LY=FU,FI PS=SY,FR
LA
PA BC DE FG HI JK LM NO
FR TE 1 1 TE 2 2 TE 3 3 TE 4 4 TE 5 5 TE 6 6 TE 7 7 TE 8 8
ST 1.00 LY 1 1 LY 2 2 LY 3 3 LY 4 4 LY 5 5 LY 6 6 LY 7 7 LY 8 8
FI PS 1 1 PS 2 2 PS 3 3 PS 4 4 PS 5 5 PS 6 6 PS 7 7 PS 8 8
ST 1.00 PS 1 1 PS 2 2 PS 3 3 PS 4 4 PS 5 5 PS 6 6 PS 7 7 PS 8 8
EQ PS 2 1 PS 3 2 PS 4 3 PS 5 4 PS 6 5 PS 7 6 PS 8 7 PS 8 1
ST .71 PS 2 1
EQ PS 3 1 PS 4 2 PS 5 3 PS 6 4 PS 7 5 PS 8 6 PS 7 1 PS 8 2
ST .00 PS 3 1
EQ PS 4 1 PS 5 2 PS 6 3 PS 7 4 PS 8 5 PS 6 1 PS 7 2 PS 8 3
ST -.71 PS 4 1
EQ PS 5 1 PS 6 2 PS 7 3 PS 8 4
ST -1.00 PS 5 1
OU ALL ME=ML RO RC AD=OFF
```

Markey & Markey (2009, Study 1, Sample 2, n = 250)

```
MARKEY & MARKEY (2009, STUDY 1, SAMPLE 2): EQUAL SPACING,
EQUAL COMMUNALITY MODEL
DA NI=8 NO=250 MA=KM
KM
1.00
 .47    1.00
 .05     .34    1.00
-.41    -.07     .36    1.00
-.61    -.29     .08     .54    1.00
-.22    -.45    -.33     .01     .17    1.00
-.09    -.28    -.53    -.31    -.02     .45    1.00
 .22    -.08    -.45    -.61    -.35     .20     .40    1.00
```

Table 7.2 Continued

```
MO NY=8 NE=8 TE=SY,FI LY=FU,FI PS=SY,FR
LA
PA BC DE FG HI JK LM NO
FR TE 1 1 TE 2 2 TE 3 3 TE 4 4 TE 5 5 TE 6 6 TE 7 7 TE 8 8
ST 1.00 LY 1 1 LY 2 2 LY 3 3 LY 4 4 LY 5 5 LY 6 6 LY 7 7 LY 8 8
FI PS 1 1 PS 2 2 PS 3 3 PS 4 4 PS 5 5 PS 6 6 PS 7 7 PS 8 8
ST 1.00 PS 1 1 PS 2 2 PS 3 3 PS 4 4 PS 5 5 PS 6 6 PS 7 7 PS 8 8
EQ PS 2 1 PS 3 2 PS 4 3 PS 5 4 PS 6 5 PS 7 6 PS 8 7 PS 8 1
ST .71 PS 2 1
EQ PS 3 1 PS 4 2 PS 5 3 PS 6 4 PS 7 5 PS 8 6 PS 7 1 PS 8 2
ST .00 PS 3 1
EQ PS 4 1 PS 5 2 PS 6 3 PS 7 4 PS 8 5 PS 6 1 PS 7 2 PS 8 3
ST -.71 PS 4 1
EQ PS 5 1 PS 6 2 PS 7 3 PS 8 4
ST -1.00 PS 5 1
OU ALL ME=ML RO RC AD=OFF
```

Barford et al. (2015, p. 234, n = 206)

```
BARFORD ET AL. (2015): EQUAL SPACING, EQUAL COMMUNALITY MODEL
DA NI=8 NO=206 MA=KM
KM
1.00
 .36   1.00
 .07    .41   1.00
-.60   -.12    .20   1.00
-.70   -.30   -.07    .64   1.00
-.25   -.45   -.20    .14    .39   1.00
 .12   -.27   -.37   -.30   -.04    .41   1.00
 .46   -.09   -.12   -.59   -.40    .11    .48   1.00
```

```
MO NY=8 NE=8 TE=SY,FI LY=FU,FI PS=SY,FR
LA
PA BC DE FG HI JK LM NO
FR TE 1 1 TE 2 2 TE 3 3 TE 4 4 TE 5 5 TE 6 6 TE 7 7 TE 8 8
ST 1.00 LY 1 1 LY 2 2 LY 3 3 LY 4 4 LY 5 5 LY 6 6 LY 7 7 LY 8 8
FI PS 1 1 PS 2 2 PS 3 3 PS 4 4 PS 5 5 PS 6 6 PS 7 7 PS 8 8
ST 1.00 PS 1 1 PS 2 2 PS 3 3 PS 4 4 PS 5 5 PS 6 6 PS 7 7 PS 8 8
EQ PS 2 1 PS 3 2 PS 4 3 PS 5 4 PS 6 5 PS 7 6 PS 8 7 PS 8 1
ST .71 PS 2 1
EQ PS 3 1 PS 4 2 PS 5 3 PS 6 4 PS 7 5 PS 8 6 PS 7 1 PS 8 2
ST .00 PS 3 1
EQ PS 4 1 PS 5 2 PS 6 3 PS 7 4 PS 8 5 PS 6 1 PS 7 2 PS 8 3
ST -.71 PS 4 1
EQ PS 5 1 PS 6 2 PS 7 3 PS 8 4
ST -1.00 PS 5 1
OU ALL ME=ML RO RC AD=OFF
```

200 THE SELF IN RELATIONSHIPS

Table 7.3 Reproduced Correlation Matrices for Study 2 Samples

Markey & Markey (2009, Study 1, Sample 1, $n = 251$)

Var.	Correlations							
	PA	BC	DE	FG	HI	JK	LM	NO
PA	1.00							
BC	.39	1.00						
DE	−.01	.39	1.00					
FG	−.34	−.01	.39	1.00				
HI	−.56	−.34	−.01	.39	1.00			
JK	−.34	−.56	−.34	−.01	.39	1.00		
LM	−.01	−.34	−.56	−.34	−.01	.39	1.00	
NO	.39	−.01	−.34	−.56	−.34	−.01	.39	1.00

P. M. Markey & C. N. Markey (2009, Study 1, Sample 2, $n = 250$)

Var.	Correlations							
	PA	BC	DE	FG	HI	JK	LM	NO
PA	1.00							
BC	.37	1.00						
DE	.01	.37	1.00					
FG	−.33	.01	.37	1.00				
HI	−.55	−.33	.01	.37	1.00			
JK	−.33	−.55	−.33	.01	.37	1.00		
LM	.01	−.33	−.55	−.33	.01	.37	1.00	
NO	.37	.01	−.33	−.55	−.33	.01	.37	1.00

Barford et al. (2015, p. 234, $n = 206$)

Var.	Correlations							
	PA	BC	DE	FG	HI	JK	LM	NO
PA	1.00							
BC	.42	1.00						
DE	.02	.42	1.00					
FG	−.31	.02	.42	1.00				
HI	−.54	−.31	.02	.42	1.00			
JK	−.31	−.54	−.31	.02	.42	1.00		
LM	.02	−.31	−.54	−.31	.02	.42	1.00	
NO	.42	.02	−.31	−.54	−.31	.02	.42	1.00

Note: PA = ambitious–dominant, BC = arrogant–calculating, DE = cold–quarrelsome, FG = aloof–introverted, HI = unassured–submissive, JK = unassuming–ingenuous, LM = warm–agreeable, NO = gregarious–extraverted.

& Sorbom, 2019], using the ridge option and ridge constant) that we described in Chapters 5 and 6. The syntax files for the three samples are presented in Table 7.4. Results of initial confirmatory factor analyses indicated that, consistent with hypotheses, a two-factor model provided satisfactory fit for Sample 1 (chi-square = 14.08, df = 24, NS; RMSEA = .00; CFI = 1.00), Sample 2 (chi-square = 13.62, df = 24, NS; RMSEA = .00; CFI = 1.00), and Sample 3 (chi-square = 18.39, df = 24, NS; RMSEA = .00; CFI = 1.00). Loadings of the eight lower-order subclinical interpersonal traits on the circumplex factors of dominance and nurturance are presented

Table 7.4 Syntax Files Used as Input for Initial Confirmatory Factor Analyses of Lower-Order Subclinical Interpersonal Traits, Study 2 Samples

Markey & Markey (2009, Study 1, Sample 1, *n* = 251)

```
MARKEY & MARKEY (2009, STUDY 1, SAMPLE 1) DOM NUR
DA NI=8 NO=251 MA=KM
KM
 1.00
  .43    1.00
  .00     .23    1.00
 -.51    -.14     .39    1.00
 -.64    -.30     .04     .54    1.00
 -.17    -.44    -.43    -.03     .22    1.00
  .01    -.22    -.56    -.30     .01     .54    1.00
  .42    -.10    -.37    -.57    -.42     .12     .36    1.00
```

```
MO NY=8 NE=2 TE=SY,FI LY=FU,FI PS=SY,FI
LA
PA BC DE FG HI JK LM NO
FR TE 1 1 TE 2 2 TE 3 3 TE 4 4 TE 5 5 TE 6 6 TE 7 7 TE 8 8
FR LY 1 1 LY 7 2
FR LY 2 1 LY 8 1 LY 6 2 LY 8 2
FR LY 5 1 LY 3 2
FR LY 4 1 LY 6 1 LY 2 2 LY 4 2
EQ LY 1 1 LY 7 2
EQ LY 2 1 LY 8 1 LY 6 2 LY 8 2
EQ LY 5 1 LY 3 2
EQ LY 4 1 LY 6 1 LY 2 2 LY 4 2
ST 1.00 LY 1 1
ST .71 LY 2 1
ST -.71 LY 4 1
ST -1.00 LY 5 1
ST 1.00 PS 1 1 PS 2 2
OU ALL ME=ML RO RC AD=OFF
```

(continued)

202 THE SELF IN RELATIONSHIPS

Table 7.4 Continued

Markey & Markey (2009, Study 1, Sample 2, *n* = 250)

```
MARKEY & MARKEY (2009, STUDY 1, SAMPLE 2) DOM NUR
DA NI=8 NO=250 MA=KM
KM
1.00
 .47    1.00
 .05     .34    1.00
-.41    -.07     .36    1.00
-.61    -.29     .08     .54    1.00
-.22    -.45    -.33     .01     .17    1.00
-.09    -.28    -.53    -.31    -.02     .45    1.00
 .22    -.08    -.45    -.61    -.35     .20     .40    1.00
```

```
MO NY=8 NE=2 TE=SY,FI LY=FU,FI PS=SY,FI
LA
PA BC DE FG HI JK LM NO
FR TE 1 1 TE 2 2 TE 3 3 TE 4 4 TE 5 5 TE 6 6 TE 7 7 TE 8 8
FR LY 1 1 LY 7 2
FR LY 2 1 LY 8 1 LY 6 2 LY 8 2
FR LY 5 1 LY 3 2
FR LY 4 1 LY 6 1 LY 2 2 LY 4 2
EQ LY 1 1 LY 7 2
EQ LY 2 1 LY 8 1 LY 6 2 LY 8 2
EQ LY 5 1 LY 3 2
EQ LY 4 1 LY 6 1 LY 2 2 LY 4 2
ST 1.00 LY 1 1
ST .71 LY 2 1
ST -.71 LY 4 1
ST -1.00 LY 5 1
ST 1.00 PS 1 1 PS 2 2
OU ALL ME=ML RO RC AD=OFF
```

Barford et al. (2015, p. 234, *n* = 206)

```
BARFORD ET AL. (2015): DOM NUR
DA NI=8 NO=206 MA=KM
KM
1.00
 .36    1.00
 .07     .41    1.00
-.60    -.12     .20    1.00
-.70    -.30    -.07     .64    1.00
-.25    -.45    -.20     .14     .39    1.00
 .12    -.27    -.37    -.30    -.04     .41    1.00
 .46    -.09    -.12    -.59    -.40     .11     .48    1.00
```

Table 7.4 Continued

```
MO NY=8 NE=2 TE=SY,FI LY=FU,FI PS=SY,FI
LA
PA BC DE FG HI JK LM NO
FR TE 1 1 TE 2 2 TE 3 3 TE 4 4 TE 5 5 TE 6 6 TE 7 7 TE 8 8
FR LY 1 1 LY 7 2
FR LY 2 1 LY 8 1 LY 6 2 LY 8 2
FR LY 5 1 LY 3 2
FR LY 4 1 LY 6 1 LY 2 2 LY 4 2
EQ LY 1 1 LY 7 2
EQ LY 2 1 LY 8 1 LY 6 2 LY 8 2
EQ LY 5 1 LY 3 2
EQ LY 4 1 LY 6 1 LY 2 2 LY 4 2
ST 1.00 LY 1 1
ST .71 LY 2 1
ST -.71 LY 4 1
ST -1.00 LY 5 1
ST 1.00 PS 1 1 PS 2 2
OU ALL ME=ML RO RC AD=OFF
```

in Table 7.5. Thus far, based on the initial confirmatory factor analyses, the psychometric properties of the IPIP-IPC not only are well established in themselves but also seem to be better established than the psychometric properties of the IAS-R (Wiggins et al., 1988) that inspired the development of the IPIP-IPC in the first place.

Final confirmatory factor analyses. Lastly, in order to conduct final confirmatory factor analyses on the matrices of correlations from the three samples (i.e., Markey & Markey, 2009, Samples 1 and 2, p. 355; Barford et al., 2015, p. 234) in the present Study 2, we used the same templates (i.e., three-factor model with dominance and nurturance as circumplex latent variables, plus "acquiescence" as a noncircumplex latent variable; maximum likelihood estimation via LISREL 10.20 [Joreskog & Sorbom, 2019], using the ridge option and ridge constant) that we described in Chapters 5 and 6. The syntax files for the three samples are presented in Table 7.6. Results of final confirmatory factor analyses indicated that, consistent with hypotheses, a three-factor model provided satisfactory fit for Sample 1 (chi-square = 13.85, df = 23, *NS*; RMSEA = .03; CFI = .98), Sample 2 (chi-square = 13.39, df = 23, *NS*; RMSEA = .03; CFI = .98), and Sample 3 (chi-square = 15.36, df = 23, *NS*; RMSEA = .03; CFI = .98). Loadings of the eight lower-order subclinical interpersonal traits on the circumplex factors of dominance and nurturance, plus the noncircumplex factor of "acquiescence," are presented in Table 7.7. Thus far, based on the final confirmatory factor analyses, the psychometric properties of the IPIP-IPC (Markey & Markey, 2009) generally are closer to

Table 7.5 Obtained Patterns of Factor Loadings Among Lower-Order Subclinical Interpersonal Traits for Study 2 Samples, Two-Factor Solution

Markey & Markey (2009, Study 1, Sample 1, *n* = 251)

Var.	Factor		
	DOM	NUR	ACQ
PA	.77	.00	.00
BC	.53	−.45	.00
DE	.00	−.76	.00
FG	−.45	−.45	.00
HI	−.76	.00	.00
JK	−.45	.53	.00
LM	.00	.77	.00
NO	.53	.53	.00

Markey & Markey (2009, Study 1, Sample 2, *n* = 250)

Var.	Factor		
	DOM	NUR	ACQ
PA	.72	.00	.00
BC	.52	−.48	.00
DE	.00	−.74	.00
FG	−.48	−.48	.00
HI	−.74	.00	.00
JK	−.48	.52	.00
LM	.00	.72	.00
NO	.52	.52	.00

Barford et al. (2015, p. 234, *n* = 206)

Var.	Factor		
	DOM	NUR	ACQ
PA	.78	.00	.00
BC	.49	−.52	.00
DE	.00	−.69	.00
FG	−.52	−.52	.00
HI	−.69	.00	.00
JK	−.52	.49	.00
LM	.00	.78	.00
NO	.49	.49	.00

Note: Regarding higher-order factors, DOM = dominance, NUR = nurturance, ACQ = acquiescence. Regarding lower-order interpersonal traits, PA = ambitious-dominant, BC = arrogant-calculating, DE = cold-quarrelsome, FG = aloof-introverted, HI = unassured-submissive, JK = unassuming-ingenuous, LM = warm-agreeable, NO = gregarious-extraverted.

Table 7.6 Syntax Files Used as Input for Final Confirmatory Factor Analyses of Lower-Order Subclinical Interpersonal Traits, Study 2 Samples

Markey & Markey (2009, Study 1, Sample 1, n = 251)

```
MARKEY & MARKEY (2009, STUDY 1, SAMPLE 2) DOM NUR ACQ
DA NI=8 NO=250 MA=KM
KM
1.00
 .47    1.00
 .05     .34    1.00
-.41    -.07     .36    1.00
-.61    -.29     .08     .54    1.00
-.22    -.45    -.33     .01     .17    1.00
-.09    -.28    -.53    -.31    -.02     .45    1.00
 .22    -.08    -.45    -.61    -.35     .20     .40    1.00
```

```
MO NY=8 NE=3 TE=SY,FI LY=FU,FI PS=SY,FI
LA
PA BC DE FG HI JK LM NO
FR TE 1 1 TE 2 2 TE 3 3 TE 4 4 TE 5 5 TE 6 6 TE 7 7 TE 8 8
FR LY 1 1 LY 7 2
FR LY 2 1 LY 8 1 LY 6 2 LY 8 2
FR LY 5 1 LY 3 2
FR LY 4 1 LY 6 1 LY 2 2 LY 4 2
EQ LY 1 1 LY 7 2
EQ LY 2 1 LY 8 1 LY 6 2 LY 8 2
EQ LY 5 1 LY 3 2
EQ LY 4 1 LY 6 1 LY 2 2 LY 4 2
ST 1.00 LY 1 1
ST .71 LY 2 1
ST -.71 LY 4 1
ST -1.00 LY 5 1
FR LY 1 3 LY 2 3 LY 3 3 LY 4 3 LY 5 3 LY 6 3 LY 7 3 LY 8 3
EQ LY 1 3 LY 2 3 LY 3 3 LY 4 3 LY 5 3 LY 6 3 LY 7 3 LY 8 3
ST 1.00 PS 1 1 PS 2 2 PS 3 3
OU ALL ME=ML RO RC AD=OFF
```

Markey & Markey (2009, Study 1, Sample 2, n = 250)

```
MARKEY & MARKEY (2009, STUDY 1, SAMPLE 2) DOM NUR ACQ
DA NI=8 NO=250 MA=KM
KM
1.00
 .47    1.00
 .05     .34    1.00
-.41    -.07     .36    1.00
-.61    -.29     .08     .54    1.00
-.22    -.45    -.33     .01     .17    1.00
-.09    -.28    -.53    -.31    -.02     .45    1.00
 .22    -.08    -.45    -.61    -.35     .20     .40    1.00
```

(continued)

206 THE SELF IN RELATIONSHIPS

Table 7.6 Continued

```
MO NY=8 NE=3 TE=SY,FI LY=FU,FI PS=SY,FI
LA
PA BC DE FG HI JK LM NO
FR TE 1 1 TE 2 2 TE 3 3 TE 4 4 TE 5 5 TE 6 6 TE 7 7 TE 8 8
FR LY 1 1 LY 7 2
FR LY 2 1 LY 8 1 LY 6 2 LY 8 2
FR LY 5 1 LY 3 2
FR LY 4 1 LY 6 1 LY 2 2 LY 4 2
EQ LY 1 1 LY 7 2
EQ LY 2 1 LY 8 1 LY 6 2 LY 8 2
EQ LY 5 1 LY 3 2
EQ LY 4 1 LY 6 1 LY 2 2 LY 4 2
ST 1.00 LY 1 1
ST .71 LY 2 1
ST -.71 LY 4 1
ST -1.00 LY 5 1
FR LY 1 3 LY 2 3 LY 3 3 LY 4 3 LY 5 3 LY 6 3 LY 7 3 LY 8 3
EQ LY 1 3 LY 2 3 LY 3 3 LY 4 3 LY 5 3 LY 6 3 LY 7 3 LY 8 3
ST 1.00 PS 1 1 PS 2 2 PS 3 3
OU ALL ME=ML RO RC AD=OFF
```

Barford et al. (2015, p. 234, $n = 206$)

```
BARFORD ET AL. (2015): DOM NUR ACQ
DA NI=8 NO=206 MA=KM
KM
1.00
 .36     1.00
 .07      .41     1.00
-.60     -.12      .20     1.00
-.70     -.30     -.07      .64     1.00
-.25     -.45     -.20      .14      .39     1.00
 .12     -.27     -.37     -.30     -.04      .41     1.00
 .46     -.09     -.12     -.59     -.40      .11      .48     1.00
```

```
MO NY=8 NE=3 TE=SY,FI LY=FU,FI PS=SY,FI
LA
PA BC DE FG HI JK LM NO
FR TE 1 1 TE 2 2 TE 3 3 TE 4 4 TE 5 5 TE 6 6 TE 7 7 TE 8 8
FR LY 1 1 LY 7 2
FR LY 2 1 LY 8 1 LY 6 2 LY 8 2
FR LY 5 1 LY 3 2
FR LY 4 1 LY 6 1 LY 2 2 LY 4 2
EQ LY 1 1 LY 7 2
EQ LY 2 1 LY 8 1 LY 6 2 LY 8 2
EQ LY 5 1 LY 3 2
EQ LY 4 1 LY 6 1 LY 2 2 LY 4 2
ST 1.00 LY 1 1
ST .71 LY 2 1
ST -.71 LY 4 1
ST -1.00 LY 5 1
FR LY 1 3 LY 2 3 LY 3 3 LY 4 3 LY 5 3 LY 6 3 LY 7 3 LY 8 3
EQ LY 1 3 LY 2 3 LY 3 3 LY 4 3 LY 5 3 LY 6 3 LY 7 3 LY 8 3
ST 1.00 PS 1 1 PS 2 2 PS 3 3
OU ALL ME=ML RO RC AD=OFF
```

Table 7.7 Obtained Patterns of Factor Loadings Among Lower-Order Subclinical Interpersonal Traits for Study 2 Samples, Three-Factor Solution

Markey & Markey (2009, Study 1, Sample 1, n = 251)

Var.	Factor		
	DOM	NUR	ACQ
PA	.78	.00	.09
BC	.53	−.45	.09
DE	.00	−.76	.09
FG	−.45	−.45	.09
HI	−.76	.00	.09
JK	−.45	.53	.09
LM	.00	.78	.09
NO	.53	.53	.09

Markey & Markey (2009, Study 1, Sample 2, n = 250)

Var.	Factor		
	DOM	NUR	ACQ
PA	.73	.00	.10
BC	.52	−.48	.10
DE	.00	−.74	.10
FG	−.48	−.48	.10
HI	−.74	.00	.10
JK	−.48	.52	.10
LM	.00	.73	.10
NO	.52	.52	.10

Barford et al. (2015, p. 234, n = 206)

Var.	Factor		
	DOM	NUR	ACQ
PA	.79	.00	.19
BC	.49	−.53	.19
DE	.00	−.70	.19
FG	−.53	−.53	.19
HI	−.70	.00	.19
JK	−.53	.49	.19
LM	.00	.79	.19
NO	.49	.49	.19

Note: Regarding higher-order factors, DOM = dominance, NUR = nurturance, ACQ = acquiescence. Regarding lower-order interpersonal traits, PA = ambitious-dominant, BC = arrogant-calculating, DE = cold-quarrelsome, FG = aloof-introverted, HI = unassured-submissive, JK = unassuming-ingenuous, LM = warm-agreeable, NO = gregarious-extraverted.

208   THE SELF IN RELATIONSHIPS

the ideal that Wiggins (1995) had envisioned regarding the IAS-R (Wiggins et al., 1988) than one finds concerning the actual performance of the IAS-R (i.e., the added loadings for "acquiescence" are negligible for Samples 1 and 2, although the loadings for "acquiescence" warrant further scrutiny for Sample 3).

Comparing initial versus final confirmatory factor analyses. Consistent with our predictions about the lack of a significant improvement in fit when proceeding from a two-factor model to a three-factor model, direct comparison of the models indicated that adding a noncircumplex "acquiescence" factor did *not* yield significantly or marginally better fit than did a model that was limited to the two circumplex factors of dominance and nurturance for Sample 1 (difference in chi-square = .23, difference in $df = 1$, NS) or Sample 2 (difference in chi-square =.23, difference in $df = 1$, NS), although the addition of an "acquiescence" factor yielded marginally better fit for Sample 3 (difference in chi-square = 3.03, difference in $df = 1$, $p < .10$). Interestingly, none of the authors of the studies in question (i.e., Markey & Markey, 2009, Study 1, Samples 1 and 2; Barford et al., 2015) touted the utility of the IPIP-IPC as a largely "acquiescence"-free measure of subclinical interpersonal traits; more generally, such utility has not been mentioned in *any* publication of which we are aware.

Summary of Results Across the Three Samples for Study 2

Multiple-group circulant correlation analysis. As was the case for the three samples in the present Study 1 (Gaines, Panter, et al., 1997, Study 2; Hofsess & Tracey, 2005; Sodano & Tracey, 2006, Adult Sample), in order to determine whether the results of circulant correlation analyses could be generalized across the three samples in the present Study 2 (i.e., Markey & Markey, 2009, Study 1, Samples 1 and 2; Barford et al., 2015), we tested the goodness-of-fit concerning the equal-spacing, equal-communality model via a multiple-group circulant correlation analysis (via maximum likelihood estimation, ridge option, and ridge constant in LISREL 10.20; Joreskog & Sorbom, 2019) of the three data sets. The multiple-group syntax file, which includes the core of the separate syntax files that we have encountered so far, is presented in Table 7.8. Results of the multiple-group circulant correlation analysis affirmed that an equal-spacing, equal-communality model provided satisfactory fit to the data (chi-square = 43.68, $df = 96$, NS; RMSEA = .00; CFI = 1.00). The reproduced correlation matrix across the three samples is shown in Table 7.9.

MEASUREMENT OF DOMINANCE AND NURTURANCE II   209

Table 7.8 Syntax Files Used as Input for Multiple-Group Circulant Correlation Analysis of Lower-Order Subclinical Interpersonal Traits, Study 2 Samples

```
MARKEY & MARKEY (2009, STUDY 1, SAMPLE 1): EQUAL SPACING,
EQUAL COMMUNALITY MODEL
DA NG=3 NI=8 NO=251 MA=KM
KM
1.00
 .43   1.00
 .00    .23   1.00
-.51   -.14    .39   1.00
-.64   -.30    .04    .54   1.00
-.17   -.44   -.43   -.03    .22   1.00
 .01   -.22   -.56   -.30    .01    .54   1.00
 .42   -.10   -.37   -.57   -.42    .12    .36   1.00
```

```
MO NY=8 NE=8 TE=SY,FI LY=FU,FI PS=SY,FR
LA
PA BC DE FG HI JK LM NO
FR TE 1 1 TE 2 2 TE 3 3 TE 4 4 TE 5 5 TE 6 6 TE 7 7 TE 8 8
ST 1.00 LY 1 1 LY 2 2 LY 3 3 LY 4 4 LY 5 5 LY 6 6 LY 7 7 LY 8 8
FI PS 1 1 PS 2 2 PS 3 3 PS 4 4 PS 5 5 PS 6 6 PS 7 7 PS 8 8
ST 1.00 PS 1 1 PS 2 2 PS 3 3 PS 4 4 PS 5 5 PS 6 6 PS 7 7 PS 8 8
EQ PS 2 1 PS 3 2 PS 4 3 PS 5 4 PS 6 5 PS 7 6 PS 8 7 PS 8 1
ST .71 PS 2 1
EQ PS 3 1 PS 4 2 PS 5 3 PS 6 4 PS 7 5 PS 8 6 PS 7 1 PS 8 2
ST .00 PS 3 1
EQ PS 4 1 PS 5 2 PS 6 3 PS 7 4 PS 8 5 PS 6 1 PS 7 2 PS 8 3
ST -.71 PS 4 1
EQ PS 5 1 PS 6 2 PS 7 3 PS 8 4
ST -1.00 PS 5 1
OU ALL ME=ML RO RC AD=OFF
```

```
MARKEY & MARKEY (2009, STUDY 1, SAMPLE 2): EQUAL SPACING,
EQUAL COMMUNALITY MODEL
DA NI=8 NO=250 MA=KM
KM
1.00
 .47   1.00
 .05    .34   1.00
-.41   -.07    .36   1.00
-.61   -.29    .08    .54   1.00
-.22   -.45   -.33    .01    .17   1.00
-.09   -.28   -.53   -.31   -.02    .45   1.00
 .22   -.08   -.45   -.61   -.35    .20    .40   1.00
```

(continued)

210 THE SELF IN RELATIONSHIPS

Table 7.8 Continued

```
MO NY=8 NE=8 TE=IN LY=IN PS=IN
LA
PA BC DE FG HI JK LM NO
OU ALL ME=ML RO RC AD=OFF
```

```
BARFORD ET AL. (2015) : EQUAL SPACING, EQUAL COMMUNALITY
MODEL
DA NI=8 NO=206 MA=KM
KM
1.00
 .36   1.00
 .07    .41   1.00
-.60   -.12    .20   1.00
-.70   -.30   -.07    .64   1.00
-.25   -.45   -.20    .14    .39   1.00
 .12   -.27   -.37   -.30   -.04    .41   1.00
 .46   -.09   -.12   -.59   -.40    .11    .48   1.00
```

```
MO NY=8 NE=8 TE=IN LY=IN PS=IN
LA
PA BC DE FG HI JK LM NO
OU ALL ME=ML RO RC AD=OFF
```

Table 7.9 Reproduced Correlation Matrix Across Study 2 Samples

Var.	Correlations							
	PA	BC	DE	FG	HI	JK	LM	NO
PA	1.00							
BC	.39	1.00						
DE	.00	.39	1.00					
FG	−.33	.00	.39	1.00				
HI	−.55	−.33	.00	.39	1.00			
JK	−.33	−.55	−.33	.00	.39	1.00		
LM	.00	−.33	−.55	−.33	.00	.39	1.00	
NO	.39	.00	−.33	−.55	−.33	.00	.39	1.00

Note: PA = ambitious-dominant, BC = arrogant-calculating, DE = cold-quarrelsome, FG = aloof-introverted, HI = unassured-submissive, JK = unassuming-ingenuous, LM = warm-agreeable, NO = gregarious-extraverted.

Multiple-group confirmatory factor analyses. Similarly, as was the case for the three studies in the present Study 1 (Gaines, Panter, et al., 1997, Study 2; Hofsess & Tracey, 2005; Sodano & Tracey, 2006, Adult Sample), in order to determine whether the results of confirmatory factor analyses could be generalized across the three studies in the present Study 2 (i.e., Markey & Markey, 2009, Study 1, Samples 1 and 2; Barford et al., 2015), we tested the goodness-of-fit concerning two-factor and three-factor models using multiple-group confirmatory factor analyses (via maximum likelihood estimation, ridge option, and ridge constant in LISREL 10.20; Joreskog & Sorbom, 2019) of the three data sets. The multiple-group syntax files, which include the core of the separate syntax files that we have encountered so far, are presented in Table 7.10. Results of the multiple-group confirmatory factor analyses affirmed that (1) a two-factor model provided satisfactory fit (chi-square = 49.08, df = 96, NS; RMSEA = .00; CFI = 1.00); (2) a three-factor model likewise provided satisfactory fit (chi-square = 46.77, df = 95, NS; RMSEA = .00; CFI = 1.00); and (3) the three-factor model did *not* yield significantly or marginally better fit to the data than did the two-factor model (difference in chi-square = 2.31, difference in df = 1, NS). The matrices of loadings for the two-factor and three-factor models are presented in Table 7.11.

BONUS: To Ipsatize or Not to Ipsatize Data From the IPIP-IPC(?)

Just as DeYoung et al. (2013, Sample 2) report one study in which they ipsatized scores on the eight subscales from the IAS-R (Wiggins et al., 1988) prior to entering the matrix of correlations among lower-order subclinical interpersonal traits into geometric and psychometric analyses, so too did DeYoung et al. (2013, Sample 3) report a separate study (in the same paper) in which they ipsatized scores on the eight subscales from the IPIP-IPC (Markey & Markey, 2009). As far as we know, Markey and Markey have not commented on the ipsatization of subscale scores on the IPIP-IPC. Furthermore, in her master's thesis on the ipsatization of scores on other circumplex measures of personality within the interpersonal domain, Hoessler (2009) did not mention the IPIP-IPC (which was not published until the year that Hoessler completed her thesis). Finally, the results of our confirmatory factor analyses suggest that—even if one believes that it is appropriate to apply the data transformation process of ipsatization to scores on certain circumplex measures in principle—the IPIP-IPC does not strike one as needing such a controversial form of data transformation.

212 THE SELF IN RELATIONSHIPS

Table 7.10 Syntax Files Used as Input for Multiple-Group Confirmatory Factor Analyses of Lower-Order Subclinical Interpersonal Traits, Study 2 Samples

Two-factor solution

```
MARKEY & MARKEY (2009, STUDY 1, SAMPLE 1) DOM NUR
DA NG=3 NI=8 NO=251 MA=KM
KM
1.00
 .43    1.00
 .00     .23    1.00
-.51    -.14     .39    1.00
-.64    -.30     .04     .54    1.00
-.17    -.44    -.43    -.03     .22    1.00
 .01    -.22    -.56    -.30     .01     .54    1.00
 .42    -.10    -.37    -.57    -.42     .12     .36    1.00
```

```
MO NY=8 NE=2 TE=SY,FI LY=FU,FI PS=SY,FI
LA
PA BC DE FG HI JK LM NO
FR TE 1 1 TE 2 2 TE 3 3 TE 4 4 TE 5 5 TE 6 6 TE 7 7 TE 8 8
FR LY 1 1 LY 7 2
FR LY 2 1 LY 8 1 LY 6 2 LY 8 2
FR LY 5 1 LY 3 2
FR LY 4 1 LY 6 1 LY 2 2 LY 4 2
EQ LY 1 1 LY 7 2
EQ LY 2 1 LY 8 1 LY 6 2 LY 8 2
EQ LY 5 1 LY 3 2
EQ LY 4 1 LY 6 1 LY 2 2 LY 4 2
ST 1.00 LY 1 1
ST .71 LY 2 1
ST -.71 LY 4 1
ST -1.00 LY 5 1
ST 1.00 PS 1 1 PS 2 2
OU ALL ME=ML RO RC AD=OFF
```

MARKEY & MARKEY (2009, STUDY 1, SAMPLE 2) DOM NUR

```
DA NI=8 NO=250 MA=KM
KM
1.00
 .47    1.00
 .05     .34    1.00
-.41    -.07     .36    1.00
-.61    -.29     .08     .54    1.00
-.22    -.45    -.33     .01     .17    1.00
-.09    -.28    -.53    -.31    -.02     .45    1.00
 .22    -.08    -.45    -.61    -.35     .20     .40    1.00
```

MEASUREMENT OF DOMINANCE AND NURTURANCE II 213

Table 7.10 Continued

```
MO NY=8 NE=2 TE=IN LY=IN PS=IN
LA
PA BC DE FG HI JK LM NO
OU ALL ME=ML RO RC AD=OFF
```

BARFORD ET AL. (2015) : DOM NUR

```
DA NI=8 NO=206 MA=KM
KM
1.00
 .36   1.00
 .07    .41   1.00
-.60   -.12    .20   1.00
-.70   -.30   -.07    .64   1.00
-.25   -.45   -.20    .14    .39   1.00
 .12   -.27   -.37   -.30   -.04    .41   1.00
 .46   -.09   -.12   -.59   -.40    .11    .48   1.00
```

```
MO NY=8 NE=2 TE=IN LY=IN PS=IN
LA
PA BC DE FG HI JK LM NO
OU ALL ME=ML RO RC AD=OFF
```

Three-factor solution

```
MARKEY & MARKEY (2009, STUDY 1, SAMPLE 1) DOM NUR ACQ
DA NG=3 NI=8 NO=251 MA=KM
KM
1.00
 .43   1.00
 .00    .23   1.00
-.51   -.14    .39   1.00
-.64   -.30    .04    .54   1.00
-.17   -.44   -.43   -.03    .22   1.00
 .01   -.22   -.56   -.30    .01    .54   1.00
 .42   -.10   -.37   -.57   -.42    .12    .36   1.00
```

```
MO NY=8 NE=3 TE=SY,FI LY=FU,FI PS=SY,FI
LA
PA BC DE FG HI JK LM NO
FR TE 1 1 TE 2 2 TE 3 3 TE 4 4 TE 5 5 TE 6 6 TE 7 7 TE 8 8
FR LY 1 1 LY 7 2
FR LY 2 1 LY 8 1 LY 6 2 LY 8 2
FR LY 5 1 LY 3 2
FR LY 4 1 LY 6 1 LY 2 2 LY 4 2
EQ LY 1 1 LY 7 2
```

(continued)

214 THE SELF IN RELATIONSHIPS

Table 7.10 Continued

```
EQ LY 2 1 LY 8 1 LY 6 2 LY 8 2
EQ LY 5 1 LY 3 2
EQ LY 4 1 LY 6 1 LY 2 2 LY 4 2
ST 1.00 LY 1 1
ST .71 LY 2 1
ST -.71 LY 4 1
ST -1.00 LY 5 1
FR LY 1 3 LY 2 3 LY 3 3 LY 4 3 LY 5 3 LY 6 3 LY 7 3 LY 8 3
EQ LY 1 3 LY 2 3 LY 3 3 LY 4 3 LY 5 3 LY 6 3 LY 7 3 LY 8 3
ST 1.00 PS 1 1 PS 2 2 PS 3 3
OU ALL ME=ML RO RC AD=OFF
```

MARKEY & MARKEY (2009, STUDY 1, SAMPLE 2) DOM NUR ACQ

```
DA NI=8 NO=250 MA=KM
KM
1.00
 .47    1.00
 .05     .34    1.00
-.41    -.07     .36    1.00
-.61    -.29     .08     .54    1.00
-.22    -.45    -.33     .01     .17    1.00
-.09    -.28    -.53    -.31    -.02     .45    1.00
 .22    -.08    -.45    -.61    -.35     .20     .40    1.00
```

```
MO NY=8 NE=3 TE=IN LY=IN PS=IN
LA
PA BC DE FG HI JK LM NO
OU ALL ME=ML RO RC AD=OFF
```

BARFORD ET AL. (2015) : DOM NUR ACQ

```
DA NI=8 NO=206 MA=KM
KM
1.00
 .36    1.00
 .07     .41    1.00
-.60    -.12     .20    1.00
-.70    -.30    -.07     .64    1.00
-.25    -.45    -.20     .14     .39    1.00
 .12    -.27    -.37    -.30    -.04     .41    1.00
 .46    -.09    -.12    -.59    -.40     .11     .48    1.00
```

```
MO NY=8 NE=3 TE=IN LY=IN PS=IN
```

MEASUREMENT OF DOMINANCE AND NURTURANCE II   215

Table 7.11 Obtained Pattern of Factor Loadings Among Lower–Order Subclinical Interpersonal Traits Across Study 2 Samples, Two–Factor and Three–Factor Solutions

Two–factor solution

Var.	Factor		
	DOM	NUR	ACQ
PA	.76	.00	.00
BC	.51	−.48	.00
DE	.00	−.73	.00
FG	−.48	−.48	.00
HI	−.73	.00	.00
JK	−.48	.51	.00
LM	.00	.76	.00
NO	.51	.51	.00

Three–factor solution

Var.	Factor		
	DOM	NUR	ACQ
PA	.76	.00	.13
BC	.52	−.48	.13
DE	.00	−.73	.13
FG	−.48	−.48	.13
HI	−.73	.00	.13
JK	−.48	.52	.13
LM	.00	.76	.13
NO	.52	.52	.13

Note: Regarding higher-order factors, DOM = dominance, NUR = nurturance, ACQ = acquiescence. Regarding lower-order interpersonal traits, PA = ambitious–dominant, BC = arrogant–calculating, DE = cold–quarrelsome, FG = aloof–introverted, HI = unassured–submissive, JK = unassuming–ingenuous, LM = warm–agreeable, NO = gregarious–extraverted.

The ipsatized matrix of subclinical interpersonal trait correlations for the IPIP-IPC (Markey & Markey, 2009) from the study by DeYoung et al. (2013, Sample 3) is presented in Table 7.12. As was the case for the three samples with nonipsatized matrices that we have analyzed in the present Study 2 (i.e.,

216 THE SELF IN RELATIONSHIPS

Table 7.12 Matrix of Zero-Order Correlations Among Lower-Order Subclinical Interpersonal Traits (Based on Ipsatized Subscale Scores From DeYoung et al., 2013, Sample 3, p. 472)

Var.	Correlations							
	PA	BC	DE	FG	HI	JK	LM	NO
PA	1.00							
BC	.43	1.00						
DE	−.01	−.03	1.00					
FG	−.52	−.18	.20	1.00				
HI	−.73	−.40	−.01	.50	1.00			
JK	−.42	−.54	−.18	.10	.25	1.00		
LM	−.11	−.39	−.44	−.39	−.04	.21	1.00	
NO	.24	−.12	−.34	−.69	−.44	−.11	.32	1.00

Note: PA = ambitious-dominant, BC = arrogant-calculating, DE = cold-quarrelsome, FG = aloof-introverted, HI = unassured-submissive, JK = unassuming-ingenuous, LM = warm-agreeable, NO = gregarious-extraverted.

Source: Adapted from "Unifying the Aspects of the Big Five, the Interpersonal Circumplex, and Trait Affiliation," by C. L. DeYoung, Y. H. Weisberg, L. C. Quilty, & J. B. Peterson, 2013, *Journal of Personality, 81*, p. 472. Copyright 2013 by John Wiley & Sons. Reproduced and adapted with permission.

Markey & Markey, 2009, Study 1, Samples 1 and 2; Barford et al., 2015), we evaluated the geometric properties of the IPIP-IPC data from DeYoung et al. via a circulant correlation analysis (testing the goodness-of-fit regarding an equal-spacing, equal-communality model) using maximum likelihood estimation, ridge option, and ridge constant in LISREL 10.20 (Joreskog & Sorbom, 2019). Afterward, we evaluated the psychometric properties of the IPIP-IPC data from DeYoung et al. via a pair of confirmatory factor analyses (one that was limited to the circumplex factors of dominance and nurturance, followed by one in which a noncircumplex "acquiescence" factor was added), again using LISREL.

The syntax file for the circulant correlation analysis as applied to the ipsatized matrix from DeYoung et al. (2013, Sample 3) is presented in Table 7.13. Results of the circulant correlation analysis indicated that, consistent with hypotheses, an equal-spacing, equal-communality mode provided satisfactory fit to the data (chi-square = 26.41, *df* = 24, NS; RMSEA = .02; CFI = .99). The resulting matrix of reproduced correlations for the data from DeYoung et al. is shown in Table 7.14.

The syntax files for the confirmatory factor analyses as applied to the ipsatized matrix from DeYoung et al. (2013, Sample 3) are presented in

MEASUREMENT OF DOMINANCE AND NURTURANCE II   217

Table 7.13 Syntax File Used as Input for Circulant Correlation Analysis of Lower-Order Subclinical Interpersonal Traits (Ipsatized Matrix), DeYoung et al. (2013, Sample 3)

```
DE YOUNG ET AL. (2013, SAMPLE 3): EQUAL-SPACING, EQUAL-
COMMUNALITY MODEL FOR IPIP-IPC IPSATIZED DATA
DA NI=8 NO=409 MA=KM
KM
1.00
 .43    1.00
-.01    -.03    1.00
-.52    -.18     .20    1.00
-.73    -.40    -.01     .50    1.00
-.42    -.54    -.18     .10     .25    1.00
-.11    -.39    -.44    -.39    -.04     .21    1.00
 .24    -.12    -.34    -.69    -.44    -.11     .32    1.00
```

```
MO NY=8 NE=8 TE=SY,FI LY=FU,FI PS=SY,FR
LA
PA BC DE FG HI JK LM NO
FR TE 1 1 TE 2 2 TE 3 3 TE 4 4 TE 5 5 TE 6 6 TE 7 7 TE 8 8
ST 1.00 LY 1 1 LY 2 2 LY 3 3 LY 4 4 LY 5 5 LY 6 6 LY 7 7 LY 8 8
FI PS 1 1 PS 2 2 PS 3 3 PS 4 4 PS 5 5 PS 6 6 PS 7 7 PS 8 8
ST 1.00 PS 1 1 PS 2 2 PS 3 3 PS 4 4 PS 5 5 PS 6 6 PS 7 7 PS 8 8
EQ PS 2 1 PS 3 2 PS 4 3 PS 5 4 PS 6 5 PS 7 6 PS 8 7 PS 8 1
ST .71 PS 2 1
EQ PS 3 1 PS 4 2 PS 5 3 PS 6 4 PS 7 5 PS 8 6 PS 7 1 PS 8 2
ST .00 PS 3 1
EQ PS 4 1 PS 5 2 PS 6 3 PS 7 4 PS 8 5 PS 6 1 PS 7 2 PS 8 3
ST -.71 PS 4 1
EQ PS 5 1 PS 6 2 PS 7 3 PS 8 4
ST -1.00 PS 5 1
OU ALL ME=ML RO RC AD=OFF
```

Table 7.15. Results of initial confirmatory factor analyses indicated that, contrary to hypotheses, a two-factor model did *not* provide satisfactory fit to the data from DeYoung et al. (chi-square = 53.22, df = 24, $p < .01$; RMSEA = .05; CFI = .90). Moreover, contrary to hypotheses, a three-factor model did *not* provide satisfactory fit to the data from DeYoung et al. (chi-square = 53.22, df = 24, $p < .01$; RMSEA = .05; CFI = .90); the latter yielded an error message regarding underidentification. Given that the "badness-of-fit" for the two models was identical (difference in chi-square = .00, difference in df = 1, *NS*), we concluded that ipsatization raised more questions than it answered regarding the psychometric properties of the IPIP-IPC (as was true of the IAS-R in Chapter 6).

218 THE SELF IN RELATIONSHIPS

Table 7.14 Reproduced Correlation Matrix of Lower-Order Subclinical Interpersonal Traits (Ipsatized Matrix), DeYoung et al. (2013, Sample 3)

Var.	Correlations							
	PA	BC	DE	FG	HI	JK	LM	NO
PA	1.00							
BC	.27	1.00						
DE	−.06	.27	1.00					
FG	−.39	−.06	.27	1.00				
HI	−.61	−.39	−.06	.27	1.00			
JK	−.39	−.61	−.39	−.06	.27	1.00		
LM	−.06	−.39	−.61	−.39	−.06	.27	1.00	
NO	.27	−.06	−.39	−.61	−.39	−.06	.27	1.00

Note: PA = ambitious-dominant, BC = arrogant-calculating, DE = cold-quarrelsome, FG = aloof-introverted, HI = unassured-submissive, JK = unassuming-ingenuous, LM = warm-agreeable, NO = gregarious-extraverted.

Table 7.15 Syntax Files Used as Input for Initial and Final Confirmatory Factor Analyses of Lower-Order Subclinical Interpersonal Traits (Ipsatized Data) From DeYoung et al. (2013, Sample 3)

Two-factor solution

```
DE YOUNG ET AL. (2013, SAMPLE 3): DOM NUR MODEL FOR IPIP-
IPC IPSATIZED DATA
DA NI=8 NO=409 MA=KM
KM
1.00
 .43   1.00
-.01   -.03   1.00
-.52   -.18    .20   1.00
-.73   -.40   -.01    .50   1.00
-.42   -.54   -.18    .10    .25   1.00
-.11   -.39   -.44   -.39   -.04    .21   1.00
 .24   -.12   -.34   -.69   -.44   -.11    .32   1.00
MO NY=8 NE=2 TE=SY,FI LY=FU,FI PS=SY,FI
LA
PA BC DE FG HI JK LM NO
FR TE 1 1 TE 2 2 TE 3 3 TE 4 4 TE 5 5 TE 6 6 TE 7 7 TE 8 8
FR LY 1 1 LY 7 2
FR LY 2 1 LY 8 1 LY 6 2 LY 8 2
```

MEASUREMENT OF DOMINANCE AND NURTURANCE II 219

Table 7.15 Continued

```
FR LY 5 1 LY 3 2
FR LY 4 1 LY 6 1 LY 2 2 LY 4 2
EQ LY 1 1 LY 7 2
EQ LY 2 1 LY 8 1 LY 6 2 LY 8 2
EQ LY 5 1 LY 3 2
EQ LY 4 1 LY 6 1 LY 2 2 LY 4 2
ST 1.00 LY 1 1
ST .71 LY 2 1
ST -.71 LY 4 1
ST -1.00 LY 5 1
ST 1.00 PS 1 1 PS 2 2
OU ALL ME=ML RO RC AD=OFF
```

Three-factor solution

```
DE YOUNG ET AL. (2013, SAMPLE 3): DOM NUR ACQ MODEL FOR
IPIP-IPC IPSATIZED DATA
DA NI=8 NO=409 MA=KM
KM
1.00
 .43    1.00
-.01    -.03    1.00
-.52    -.18     .20    1.00
-.73    -.40    -.01     .50    1.00
-.42    -.54    -.18     .10     .25    1.00
-.11    -.39    -.44    -.39    -.04     .21    1.00
 .24    -.12    -.34    -.69    -.44    -.11     .32    1.00
```

```
MO NY=8 NE=3 TE=SY,FI LY=FU,FI PS=SY,FI
LA
PA BC DE FG HI JK LM NO
FR TE 1 1 TE 2 2 TE 3 3 TE 4 4 TE 5 5 TE 6 6 TE 7 7 TE 8 8
FR LY 1 1 LY 7 2
FR LY 2 1 LY 8 1 LY 6 2 LY 8 2
FR LY 5 1 LY 3 2
FR LY 4 1 LY 6 1 LY 2 2 LY 4 2
EQ LY 1 1 LY 7 2
EQ LY 2 1 LY 8 1 LY 6 2 LY 8 2
EQ LY 5 1 LY 3 2
EQ LY 4 1 LY 6 1 LY 2 2 LY 4 2
ST 1.00 LY 1 1
ST .71 LY 2 1
ST -.71 LY 4 1
ST -1.00 LY 5 1
FR LY 1 3 LY 2 3 LY 3 3 LY 4 3 LY 5 3 LY 6 3 LY 7 3 LY 8 3
EQ LY 1 3 LY 2 3 LY 3 3 LY 4 3 LY 5 3 LY 6 3 LY 7 3 LY 8 3
ST .32 LY 1 3
ST 1.00 PS 1 1 PS 2 2 PS 3 3
OU ALL ME=ML RO RC AD=OFF
```

220 THE SELF IN RELATIONSHIPS

Prelude to Chapter 8

Results of the present Study 2 suggest that the IPIP-IPC (Markey & Markey, 2009) deserves greater recognition than it has achieved to date within personality psychology. For a survey that performs so well according to rigorous geometric and psychometric standards, the near-total lack of acknowledgment of the IPIP-IPC (except for one passing mention by D. N. Jones & Paulhus, 2011) in the *Handbook of Interpersonal Psychology* (edited by Horowitz & Strack, 2011)—even as the oft-cited yet possibly undercritiqued IAS-R (Wiggins et al., 1988) maintains its dominance (again, no pun intended)—is a head-scratcher. Perhaps the specter of higher-than-desired measurement error that characterizes the IPIP-IPC—a shortcoming that even Markey and Markey (2009) have admitted as they attempted to garner attention for their survey—has deterred personality psychologists from adopting it (especially when critics and supporters alike have noted the strong internal consistencies for all eight subscales of the IAS-R; e.g., see L. S. Benjamin, 2011, versus Gurtman, 2011). By the same token, it is possible that some personality psychologists assume (incorrectly) that strong internal consistency is synonymous with strong construct validity where the IAS-R is concerned (see Nunnally & Bernstein, 1994).

If personality psychologists have tended to minimize the usefulness of the IPIP-IPC (Markey & Markey, 2009), then social psychologists have tended not to demonstrate that they are aware of the existence of that survey. In Chapter 5, we mentioned that the latest editions of *The Oxford Handbook of Close Relationships* (edited by Simpson & Campbell, 2013) and *The Cambridge Handbook of Personal Relationships* (edited by Vangelisti & Perlman, 2018) do not cite Wiggins's (2003/2005) interpersonal circumplex theory; the same critique can be applied regarding the failure of various authors to cite Markey and Markey's (2009) IPIP-IPC within those handbooks of relationship science. As Gaines (2016/2018) contended in *Personality and Close Relationship Processes*, before dismissing the potential variance in relationship-maintaining versus relationship-threatening behaviors that might be explained by "dispositions" (or, more precisely, traits and other relatively stable aspects of personality), many social psychologists and other contributors to relationship scientists would do well to expand their familiarity with theoretical and methodological innovations from personality psychologists and other contributors to interpersonal psychology.

In Chapter 8, we seek to replicate and extend the results of the present Study 2 by applying single-group and multiple-group circulant correlation analyses and covariance structure analyses (incorporating elements of confirmatory factor analyses and path analyses; Kline, 2016) to data from a conference paper by Gaines (2021, Main Studies 1 and 2) concerning dominance and nurturance (as measured via the IPIP-IPC; Markey & Markey, 2009) as predictors of accommodation (as measured via items from previous studies by Rusbult and colleagues, particularly Rusbult et al., 1991) in close relationships. Although we clearly are influenced by Markey and Markey's research on subclinical interpersonal traits, we will chart a different course from the Markeys, who had documented covariance between those interpersonal traits and "interpersonal behaviors" by superimposing interpersonal behaviors onto a circular grid of interpersonal traits (Markey et al., 2013). Instead, our technique echoes Gaines, Panter, et al.'s (1997, Study 2, reduced subsample) analysis of interpersonal traits as predictors of *relational trust* (Rempel & Holmes, 1986), albeit with samples that include more than 10 participants per estimated parameter (see Schumacker & Lomax, 2016).

8

Interpersonal Traits as Predictors of Accommodation

Synopsis: In the present chapter, we evaluate the geometric and psychometric properties of the International Personality Item Pool-Interpersonal Circle (IPIP-IPC) anew by reanalyzing data sets from a conference paper by Gaines (2021, Main Studies 1 and 2); we report the results of single-group and multiple-group versions of circulant correlation analyses (i.e., consistent with predictions, an equal-spacing, equal-communality model yields satisfactory fit across the two data sets in general); we report the results of single-group and multiple-group versions of covariance structure analyses (i.e., consistent with predictions, a two-trait-factor model that includes dominance and nurturance as circumplex latent variables but excludes "acquiescence" as a noncircumplex latent variable yields satisfactory fit across the two data sets in general; and at least in the multiple-group analyses, dominance was a significant negative predictor of accommodation, nurturance was a significant positive predictor of accommodation, and adding "acquiescence" rendered the model uninterpretable); and we offer a prelude to Chapter 9, in which we tie up loose ends, suggest directions for future research, and return to the "grand theory" that is Wiggins's interpersonal circumplex theory of personality and social behavior.

Following Gaines, Panter, et al.'s (1997) research on the psychometric (but not geometric) properties of the Interpersonal Adjective Scales-Revised Version (IAS-R; Wiggins et al., 1988), some personality psychologists adapted Gaines et al.'s confirmatory factor analysis to studies of the circumplexity of "nonevaluative" subclinical interpersonal traits (e.g., Saucier et al., 2001) and the circumplexity of "human values" (e.g., Perrinjaquet et al., 2007). Nevertheless, within interpersonal psychology, pushback against Gaines, Panter, et al.'s technique ensued: Gurtman and Pincus (2000) offered an array of geometric (but not psychometric) analyses in an attempt to counter Gaines et al.'s argument that confirmatory factor analysis should be adopted more widely in studies of interpersonal traits; Acton and Revelle

The Self in Relationships. Stanley O. Gaines, Jr., Oxford University Press. © Oxford University Press 2023.
DOI: 10.1093/oso/9780197687635.003.0008

(2002) concluded (inaccurately) that confirmatory factor analysis was inappropriate for evaluating circumplexity; and Tracey (2000) surmised (also inaccurately) that confirmatory factor analysis was inappropriate when more than two latent variables were measured by a given trait survey. Despite such pushback, we note that results of the present Studies 1 and 2 show convergence between geometric and psychometric analyses *when the IPIP-IPC (Markey & Markey, 2009) is the interpersonal trait survey of choice.*

We hasten to add that perhaps the most far-reaching claim that Gaines, Panter et al. (1997) made regarding results of their Study 2—namely, that a "quasi-circumplex" factor pattern (though failing to consider a noncircumplex "acquiescence" latent variable) led to optimal fit for a model of dominance and nurturance as predictors of relational trust—was based on a subsample of slightly more than 100 participants; an N of approximately 100 was considered to be acceptable at the time (e.g., Loehlin, 1992) but eventually would be deemed lower than desired (with an N of 200 or more participants increasingly cited as the preferred minimum; e.g., Loehlin, 2004). Furthermore, neither supporters nor critics of Gaines et al.'s confirmatory factor analysis addressed the possibility of a "quasi-circumplex" model as part of an optimally fitting model when interpersonal traits are used as predictors of behavioral outcomes—an oversight that might be explained by a gap in Gaines et al.'s conceptual logic (e.g., relational trust is best understood as individuals' *attitude* toward their relationship pairs or dyads, rather than an aspect of individuals' behavior toward their partners; Kelley et al., 2003). More recently, Gaines (2016/2018) has pivoted to interpersonal traits as potential predictors of conflict resolution behaviors (e.g., accommodation; Rusbult et al., 1991).

In the present chapter, we complete the process of heeding Markey and Markey's (2009) call for further inquiry into the statistical properties of their IPIP-IPC as a measure of subclinical interpersonal traits. On the one hand, our focus on establishing geometric and psychometric properties of that survey as a means toward the end goal of predicting individuals' accommodation-relevant responses to partners' anger/criticism (Rusbult et al., 1991) aligns the present Study 3 more closely with Kelley and Thibaut's (1978) major revision of interdependence theory (which, in turn, promoted the concept of *transformation of motivation*) than did Gaines, Panter, et al.'s (1997, Study 2, reduced subsample) study—the latter of which adhered more faithfully to Thibaut and Kelley's (1959) initial formulation of interdependence theory (which, in turn, was a more straightforward extension of social

224 THE SELF IN RELATIONSHIPS

exchange theory; Gaines, 2016/2018). On the other hand, our use of the internal-consistency-challenged IPIP-IPC to measure interpersonal traits may place us at a disadvantage in trying to explain significant variance in accommodation, compared to Gaines, Panter, et al. (who used the high-internal-consistency IAS-R [Wiggins et al., 1988] to measure interpersonal traits as predictors of relational trust; see Rempel & Holmes, 1986).

Goals of Study 3

In Study 3, we built upon hypotheses regarding the geometric and psychometric properties of the IPIP-IPC (Markey & Markey, 2009) that we tested in Study 2: (1) With regard to geometric properties, an equal-spacing, equal-communality model will provide satisfactory fit to the data (i.e., such a circular or circumplex model cannot be rejected when applied to a matrix of correlations among lower-order subclinical interpersonal traits). (2) With regard to psychometric properties, (a) a model that is limited to two circumplex factors (i.e., dominance and nurturance as higher-order axes that are reflected in scores on the eight lower-order traits) will provide satisfactory fit to the data, with nurturance as a significant positive predictor (and dominance as a significant negative predictor) of accommodation, whereas (b) a model that adds a third, noncircumplex factor (i.e., "acquiescence") similarly will provide satisfactory fit on its own but will *not* yield a significant or marginal improvement in fit when compared to the two-factor model. Hypothesis 1 was tested via circulant correlation analysis, while Hypotheses 2a and b were tested via covariance structure analyses, using maximum likelihood estimation in LISREL 10.20 (Joreskog & Sorbom, 2019).

Study 3

Method

Participants
Sample 1. Although demographic statistics were not originally reported for the present Study 3, Sample 1 (conference paper by Gaines, 2021, Main Study 1), a total of 323 participants (124 men, 192 women, and 7 persons who did not report their gender) composed the sample. The mean age of participants

was 23.17 years (SD = 7.70 years). In terms of ethnic group membership, 51.1% of participants classified themselves as White/European descent, 19.8% as Asian descent, 14.9% as Black/African descent, 8.3% as "Mixed," and 1.5% as "Other" (an additional 3.4% of participants did not indicate their ethnic group membership). Among the total sample, 34 individuals did not complete all of the items for the specific surveys that we review in the present book, resulting in a final n of 289 individuals for Sample 1.

Sample 2. In addition, although demographic statistics were not originally reported for the present Study 3, Sample 2 (conference paper by Gaines, 2021, Main Study 2), a total of 440 participants (153 men, 279 women, and 8 persons who did not report their gender) composed the sample. The mean age of participants was 28.99 years (SD = 13.17 years). In terms of ethnic group membership, 51.6% of participants classified themselves as White/European descent, 20.3% as Asian descent, 7.3% as Black/African descent, 6.3% as "Mixed," and 11.1% as "Other" (an additional 3.4% of participants did not indicate their ethnic group membership). Among the total sample, 74 individuals did not complete all of the items for the specific surveys that we review in the present book, resulting in a final n of 366 individuals for Sample 2.

Materials

Sample 1. Participants in the present Study 3, Sample 1 (Gaines, 2021, Main Study 1) completed the aforementioned IPIP-IPC (Markey & Markey, 2009). Each self-descriptive item was scored along a 5-point, Likert-type continuum (1 = very inaccurate, 5 = very accurate). Results of reliability analyses indicated that internal consistency was unusually varied across the eight subscales (Cronbach's alphas ranged from .23 to .72; separate Cronbach's alphas = .62 for ambitious-dominant, .65 for arrogant-calculating, .23 for cold-quarrelsome, .63 for aloof-introverted, .44 for unassured-submissive, .42 for unassuming-ingenuous, .65 for warm-agreeable, and .72 for gregarious-extraverted). The extremely low internal consistency for the cold-quarrelsome subscale was *not* an artifact of negative interitem correlations (all of which were positive, within all eight subscales) or high non-normality of item score distributions (all of which yielded skewness statistics below 1.00 in magnitude and kurtosis statistics below 1.20 in magnitude, within all eight subscales; see Nunnally & Bernstein, 1994, regarding the potentially deleterious effects of negative interitem correlations and high non-normality of item score distributions on Cronbach's alphas). Given the poor internal

226 THE SELF IN RELATIONSHIPS

consistency of the cold-quarrelsome subscale, we will pay particular attention to the effects of the higher-order trait of nurturance (which ostensibly is anchored by the lower-order trait of cold-quarrelsome) on accommodation in Sample 1.

Furthermore, participants in the present Study 3, Sample 1 (Gaines, 2021, Main Study 1) completed a 12-item accommodation survey, based on Rusbult et al. (1991). The accommodation inventory consists of four three-item subscales (i.e., exit, voice, loyalty, and neglect), with each behavioral item scored along a 9-point, Likert type continuum (1 = never do this, 9 = constantly do this). Results of reliability analyses indicated that internal consistency varied dramatically across the four accommodation-related subscales (Cronbach's alphas ranged from .49 to .86; separate Cronbach's alphas = .86 for exit, .62 for voice, .49 for loyalty, and .60 for neglect). For all accommodation-related items, non-normality statistics were very low (skewness below magnitude of 1.00, kurtosis below magnitude of 1.20).

Sample 2. Similarly, participants in the present Study 3, Sample 2 (Gaines, 2021, Main Study 1) completed the IPIP-IPC (Markey & Markey, 2009). Results of reliability analyses indicated that internal consistency was unusually varied across the eight subscales (Cronbach's alphas ranged from .37 to .71; separate Cronbach's alphas = .71 for ambitious-dominant, .69 for arrogant-calculating, .47 for cold-quarrelsome, .65 for aloof-introverted, .44 for unassured-submissive, .37 for unassuming-ingenuous, .61 for warm-agreeable, and .72 for gregarious-extraverted). The extremely low internal consistency for the unassuming-ingenuous subscale was *not* an artifact of negative interitem correlations (all of which were positive, within all eight subscales) or high non-normality of item score distributions (all of which yielded skewness statistics below magnitudes of 1.40 for skewness and 1.30 for kurtosis, within all eight subscales). Given the poor internal consistency of the unassuming-ingenuous subscale, we will pay particular attention to the effects of the higher-order traits of dominance *and* nurturance (with the lower-order unassured-ingenuous trait ostensibly representing the positive pole of agreeableness, which in turn reflects a blend of low dominance and high nurturance) on accommodation in Sample 2.

Lastly, participants in the present Study 3, Sample 2 (Gaines, 2021, Main Study 1) completed the aforementioned 12-item accommodation survey, based on Rusbult et al. (1991). Results of reliability analyses indicated that internal consistency varied considerably across the four accommodation-related subscales, although all of the Cronbach's alphas were acceptable for the small number of items per subscale (Cronbach's alphas ranged from .63 to .89; separate Cronbach's alphas = .89 for exit, .73 for voice, .63 for loyalty, and .65 for neglect). We did not uncover any problems regarding the direction of interitem correlations (all of which were positive, within all four subscales) or non-normality (with the magnitude of non-normality statistics below 1.20 for skewness and 1.10 for kurtosis).

Procedure

In both samples of the present Study 3 (Gaines, 2021, Main Studies 1 and 2), the author obtained ethics approval from the Psychology Ethics Committee at the author's institution (a large research university) prior to conducting the research. The two convenience samples were recruited via posts to social media from separate teams of research assistants. In both samples, participants read and signed an informed consent sheet, explaining the purpose of the study in general; completed a "Personality and Relationships" questionnaire, which included the aforementioned IPIP-IPC (Markey & Markey, 2009) and accommodation scale (Rusbult et al., 1991), along with additional surveys that will not be discussed further in the present chapter (although one of those additional surveys in Study 3, Sample 2 will be discussed in Chapter 9); and read a debriefing sheet, explaining the purposes of the study in greater detail (no incentive was offered in exchange for participation in either sample).

Results and Discussion

Matrices of zero-order correlations among the eight subclinical interpersonal traits that were measured by the IPIP-IPC (Markey & Markey, 2009) and the four accommodation-related behaviors that were measured by the accommodation scale (Rusbult et al., 1991) among the two samples in the present Study 3 (i.e., Gaines, 2021, Main Studies 1 and 2) are presented in Table 8.1. First, the portions of the correlation matrices that were limited to lower-order interpersonal traits were entered into separate circulant correlation analyses, in which we tested goodness-of-fit concerning the equal-spacing, equal-communality model that we described in Chapters 5 through 7. Afterward, each of the correlation matrices was entered into two covariance structure analyses, in which we tested goodness-of-fit regarding models with dominance and nurturance as predictors of accommodation (with

228 THE SELF IN RELATIONSHIPS

Table 8.1 Matrices of Zero-Order Correlations Among Lower-Order Subclinical Interpersonal Traits and Accommodation-Related Behaviors, Study 3 Samples

Gaines (2021, Main Study 1, $n = 289$)

Var.	Correlations											
	PA	BC	DE	FG	HI	JK	LM	NO	EX	VO	LO	NE
PA	1.00											
BC	.46	1.00										
DE	.16	.42	1.00									
FG	−.55	−.14	.09	1.00								
HI	−.52	−.39	−.12	.47	1.00							
JK	−.33	−.43	−.28	.20	.40	1.00						
LM	−.08	−.32	−.41	−.16	.15	.43	1.00					
NO	.49	.13	−.12	−.53	−.30	−.02	.37	1.00				
EX	.13	.10	.08	−.06	−.02	−.14	−.18	−.06	1.00			
VO	−.07	−.13	−.15	−.04	−.05	.13	.18	.11	−.30	1.00		
LO	−.00	−.13	−.06	.01	.03	.12	.02	−.01	.01	.26	1.00	
NE	.05	.04	.07	−.03	.02	−.01	−.13	−.13	.51	−.12	.15	1.00

Gaines (2021, Main Study 2, $n = 366$)

Var.	Correlations											
	PA	BC	DE	FG	HI	JK	LM	NO	EX	VO	LO	NE
	1.00											
	.43	1.00										
	.15	.33	1.00									
	−.50	−.10	.15	1.00								
	−.59	−.27	−.09	.51	1.00							
	−.13	−.19	−.24	.12	.29	1.00						
	.02	−.16	−.31	−.27	.05	.41	1.00					
	.43	−.06	−.03	−.55	−.25	.11	.47	1.00				
	.11	.18	.08	−.01	−.03	.01	−.06	.05	1.00			
	−.11	−.18	−.06	.00	.12	.07	.15	.09	−.19	1.00		
	−.00	−.08	.01	.05	.03	.06	.03	−.02	−.12	.33	1.00	
	.06	.17	.14	.06	.00	.01	−.12	−.13	.52	−.29	.07	1.00

Note: PA = ambitious-dominant, BC = arrogant-calculating, DE = cold-quarrelsome, FG = aloof-introverted, HI = unassured-submissive, JK = unassuming-ingenuous, LM = warm-agreeable, NO = gregarious-extraverted, EX = exit, VO = voice, LO = loyalty, NE = neglect.

INTERPERSONAL TRAITS 229

one model excluding, and the other model including, "acquiescence" as a noncircumplex factor; the path from "acquiescence" to accommodation was fixed at .00 in the second model).

Circulant Correlation Analyses

In order to conduct circulant correlation analyses on the matrices of correlations among the lower-order interpersonal traits from the two samples (i.e., Gaines, 2021, Main Studies 1 and 2) in the present Study 3, we used the same templates (i.e., equal-spacing, equal communality model; maximum likelihood estimation via LISREL 10.20 [Joreskog & Sorbom, 2019], using the ridge option and ridge constant) that we described in Chapters 5 through 7. The syntax files for the two samples are presented in Table 8.2. Results of

Table 8.2 Syntax Files Used as Input for Circulant Correlation Analyses of Lower-Order Subclinical Interpersonal Traits, Study 3 Samples

Gaines (2021, Main Study 1, n = 289)

```
EQUAL-SPACING, EQUAL-COMMUNALITY MODEL FOR GAINES (2021),
MAIN STUDY 1
DA NI=8 NO=289 MA=KM
KM
1.00
 .46    1.00
 .16     .42    1.00
-.55    -.14     .09    1.00
-.52    -.39    -.12     .47    1.00
-.35    -.43    -.28     .20     .40    1.00
-.08    -.32    -.41    -.16     .15     .43    1.00
 .49     .13    -.12    -.54    -.30    -.02     .37    1.00
```

```
LA
PA BC DE FG HI JK LM NO
MO NY=8 NE=8 TE=SY,FI LY=FU,FI PS=SY,FR
FR TE 1 1 TE 2 2 TE 3 3 TE 4 4 TE 5 5 TE 6 6 TE 7 7 TE 8 8
ST 1.00 LY 1 1 LY 2 2 LY 3 3 LY 4 4 LY 5 5 LY 6 6 LY 7 7 LY 8 8
FI PS 1 1 PS 2 2 PS 3 3 PS 4 4 PS 5 5 PS 6 6 PS 7 7 PS 8 8
ST 1.00 PS 1 1 PS 2 2 PS 3 3 PS 4 4 PS 5 5 PS 6 6 PS 7 7 PS 8 8
EQ PS 2 1 PS 3 2 PS 4 3 PS 5 4 PS 6 5 PS 7 6 PS 8 7 PS 8 1
EQ PS 3 1 PS 4 2 PS 5 3 PS 6 4 PS 7 5 PS 8 6 PS 7 1 PS 8 2
EQ PS 4 1 PS 5 2 PS 6 3 PS 7 4 PS 8 5 PS 6 1 PS 7 2 PS 8 3
EQ PS 5 1 PS 6 2 PS 7 3 PS 8 4
OU ALL ME=ML RO RC AD=OFF
```

(continued)

230   THE SELF IN RELATIONSHIPS

Table 8.2 Continued

Gaines (2021, Main Study 2, n = 366)

EQUAL-SPACING, EQUAL-COMMUNALITY MODEL FOR GAINES (2021),
MAIN STUDY 2

DA NI=8 NO=366 MA=KM

KM

1.00							
.43	1.00						
.15	.33	1.00					
−.50	−.10	.15	1.00				
−.59	−.27	−.09	.51	1.00			
−.13	−.19	−.24	.12	.29	1.00		
.02	−.16	−.31	−.27	.05	.41	1.00	
.43	−.06	−.03	−.55	−.25	.11	.47	1.00

MO NY=8 NE=8 TE=SY,FI LY=FU,FI PS=SY,FR
LA
PA BC DE FG HI JK LM NO
FR TE 1 1 TE 2 2 TE 3 3 TE 4 4 TE 5 5 TE 6 6 TE 7 7 TE 8 8
ST 1.00 LY 1 1 LY 2 2 LY 3 3 LY 4 4 LY 5 5 LY 6 6 LY 7 7 LY 8 8
FI PS 1 1 PS 2 2 PS 3 3 PS 4 4 PS 5 5 PS 6 6 PS 7 7 PS 8 8
ST 1.00 PS 1 1 PS 2 2 PS 3 3 PS 4 4 PS 5 5 PS 6 6 PS 7 7 PS 8 8
EQ PS 2 1 PS 3 2 PS 4 3 PS 5 4 PS 6 5 PS 7 6 PS 8 7 PS 8 1
EQ PS 3 1 PS 4 2 PS 5 3 PS 6 4 PS 7 5 PS 8 6 PS 7 1 PS 8 2
EQ PS 4 1 PS 5 2 PS 6 3 PS 7 4 PS 8 5 PS 6 1 PS 7 2 PS 8 3
EQ PS 5 1 PS 6 2 PS 7 3 PS 8 4
OU ALL ME=ML RO RC AD=OFF

circulant correlation analyses indicated that, consistent with hypotheses, an equal-spacing, equal-communality model provided satisfactory fit to the data for Sample 1 (chi-square = 16.58, degrees of freedom [df] = 24, NS; root mean square error of approximation [RMSEA] = .00; comparative fit index [CFI] = 1.00) and Sample 2 (chi-square = 30.63, df = 24, NS; RMSEA = .03; CFI = .96). Furthermore, inspection of reproduced correlation matrices (shown in Table 8.3) revealed that the estimated correlations were broadly consistent with the pattern that we observed for Wiggins's (1979, p. 399) "simulated" matrix in Chapter 5 (the reproduced correlation matrices were highly similar across the three samples). Thus, we concluded that the IPIP-IPC (Markey & Markey, 2009) consistently performed well in terms of geometric properties (i.e., alignment of the eight lower-order traits around a circle or circumplex).

INTERPERSONAL TRAITS 231

Table 8.3 Reproduced Correlation Matrices for Study 3 Samples

Gaines (2021, Main Study 1, $n = 289$)

Var.	Correlations							
	PA	BC	DE	FG	HI	JK	LM	NO
PA	1.00							
BC	.39	1.00						
DE	.04	.39	1.00					
FG	−.31	.04	.39	1.00				
HI	−.48	−.31	.04	.39	1.00			
JK	−.31	−.48	−.31	.04	.39	1.00		
LM	.04	−.31	−.48	−.31	.04	.39	1.00	
NO	.39	.04	−.31	−.48	−.31	.04	.39	1.00

Gaines (2021, Main Study 2, $n = 366$)

Var.	Correlations							
	PA	BC	DE	FG	HI	JK	LM	NO
PA	1.00							
BC	.38	1.00						
DE	.03	.38	1.00					
FG	−.24	.03	.38	1.00				
HI	−.42	−.24	.03	.38	1.00			
JK	−.24	−.42	−.24	.03	.38	1.00		
LM	.03	−.24	−.42	−.24	.03	.38	1.00	
NO	.38	.03	−.24	−.42	−.24	.03	.38	1.00

Note: PA = ambitious-dominant, BC = arrogant-calculating, DE = cold-quarrelsome, FG = aloof-introverted, HI = unassured-submissive, JK = unassuming-ingenuous, LM = warm-agreeable, NO = gregarious-extraverted.

Covariance Structure Analyses

Initial covariance structure analyses. Afterward, in order to conduct initial covariance structure analyses on the matrices of correlations from the two samples (i.e., Gaines, 2021, Main Studies 1 and 2), we expanded upon the templates (i.e., two-factor model with dominance and nurturance as circumplex latent variables; maximum likelihood estimation via LISREL 10.20 [Joreskog & Sorbom, 2019], using the ridge option and ridge constant) that we described in Chapters 5 through 7. Specifically, (1) we added lower-order accommodation-related behaviors to the measurement error

232 THE SELF IN RELATIONSHIPS

or Theta Epsilon (TE) matrix; (2) we added loadings for lower-order accommodation behaviors on the higher-order latent variable of accommodation to the latent-observed or Lambda Y (LY) matrix, fixing the loading
of exit on the higher-order accommodation factor at 1.00 but freeing the
loadings for the other accommodation-related behaviors; (3) we added the
higher-order behavioral pattern of accommodation to the factor variance-
covariance or Psi (PS) matrix, keeping interfactor correlations fixed at .00;
and (4) we added a path coefficient or Beta (BE) matrix with freed paths from
dominance and nurturance to accommodation. The syntax files for the two
samples are presented in Table 8.4.

Results of initial covariance structure analyses indicated that, consistent
with hypotheses, a model with dominance and nurturance as the two trait
factors (with paths from both of those traits to accommodation) provided
satisfactory fit for Sample 1 (chi-square = 40.56, df = 56, NS; RMSEA = .00;
CFI = 1.00) and Sample 2 (chi-square = 60.51, df = 56, NS; RMSEA = .01;
CFI = .98). Loadings of the eight lower-order subclinical interpersonal traits
on the circumplex factors of dominance and nurturance are presented in
Table 8.5; path coefficients from dominance and nurturance are presented
in Figure 8.1. On the one hand, loadings for all eight lower-order traits on
the higher-order dominance and nurturance factors fit a "quasi-circumplex"
pattern as anticipated by Wiggins (1979), and loadings for three of the four
lower-order accommodation-related behaviors on the accommodation
factor fit a traditional factor pattern as anticipated by Rusbult et al. (1991),
with loadings greater than .31 in absolute value, with negative loadings for
exit and neglect, and positive loadings for voice (in contrast, the loadings
for loyalty were positive but were lower than .15 in magnitude). On the
other hand, only one of the paths from interpersonal traits was significant
(i.e., nurturance was a significant positive predictor of accommodation in
both samples; dominance was a marginal negative predictor of accommodation in Sample 2 but was unrelated to accommodation in Sample 1). So far,
results for the path analysis portion of the covariance structure analyses in
the present Study 3 are comparable to the results that Rusbult et al. obtained
regarding the gender-related traits of positive masculinity and positive femininity as predictors of accommodation (i.e., positive femininity as significantly and positively related to accommodation versus positive masculinity
as not consistently related to accommodation).

INTERPERSONAL TRAITS   233

Table 8.4 Syntax Files Used as Input for Initial Covariance Structure Analyses of Lower-Order Subclinical Interpersonal Traits and Accommodation-Related Behaviors, Study 3 Samples

Gaines (2021, Main Study 1, _n_ = 289)

```
TWO TRAIT FACTORS + ONE BEHAVIORAL FACTOR MODEL FOR GAINES
(2021, MAIN STUDY 1) DON NUR PREDICTORS OF ACC
DA NI=12 NO=289 MA=KM
KM
1.00
 .46 1.00
 .16  .42 1.00
-.55 -.14  .09 1.00
-.52 -.39 -.12  .47 1.00
-.33 -.43 -.28 -.20  .40 1.00
-.08 -.32 -.41 -.16  .15  .43 1.00
 .49  .13 -.12 -.54 -.30 -.02  .37 1.00
 .13  .10  .08 -.06 -.02 -.14 -.18 -.06 1.00
-.07 -.13 -.15 -.04 -.05  .13  .18  .11 -.30 1.00
-.00 -.13 -.06  .01  .03  .12  .02 -.01  .01  .26 1.00
 .05  .04  .07 -.03  .02 -.01 -.13 -.13  .51 -.12  .15 1.00
```

```
MO NY=12 NE=3 TE=SY,FI LY=FU,FI PS=SY,FI BE=FU,FI
LA
PA BC DE FG HI JK LM NO EX VO LO NE
FR TE 1 1 TE 2 2 TE 3 3 TE 4 4 TE 5 5 TE 6 6 TE 7 7 TE 8 8
FR TE 9 9 TE 10 10 TE 11 11 TE 12 12
FR LY 1 1 LY 7 2
FR LY 2 1 LY 8 1 LY 6 2 LY 8 2
FR LY 5 1 LY 3 2
FR LY 4 1 LY 6 1 LY 2 2 LY 4 2
EQ LY 1 1 LY 7 2
EQ LY 2 1 LY 8 1 LY 6 2 LY 8 2
EQ LY 5 1 LY 3 2
EQ LY 4 1 LY 6 1 LY 2 2 LY 4 2
ST 1.00 LY 1 1
ST .71 LY 2 1
ST -.71 LY 4 1
ST -1.00 LY 5 1
ST -1.00 LY 9 3
FR LY 10 3 LY 11 3 LY 12 3
ST 1.00 PS 1 1 PS 2 2
FR PS 3 3
FR BE 3 1 BE 3 2
OU ALL ME=ML RO RC AD=OFF
```

(continued)

234 THE SELF IN RELATIONSHIPS

Table 8.4 Continued

Gaines (2021, Main Study 2, *n* = 366)

```
TWO TRAIT FACTORS + ONE BEHAVIORAL FACTOR MODEL FOR GAINES
(2021, MAIN STUDY 2) DON NUR PREDICTORS OF ACC
DA NI=12 NO=366 MA=KM
KM
1.00
 .43  1.00
 .15   .33  1.00
-.50  -.10   .15  1.00
-.59  -.27  -.09   .51  1.00
-.13  -.19  -.24   .12   .29  1.00
 .02  -.16  -.31  -.27   .05   .41  1.00
 .43  -.06  -.03  -.55  -.25   .11   .47  1.00
 .11   .18   .08  -.01  -.03   .01  -.06   .05  1.00
-.11  -.18  -.06   .00   .12   .07   .15   .09  -.19  1.00
-.00  -.08   .01   .05   .03   .06   .03  -.02  -.12   .33  1.00
 .06   .17   .14   .06   .00   .01  -.12  -.13   .52  -.29   .07  1.00
```
```
MO NY=12 NE=3 TE=SY,FI LY=FU,FI PS=SY,FI BE=FU,FI
LA
PA BC DE FG HI JK LM NO EX VO LO NE
FR TE 1 1 TE 2 2 TE 3 3 TE 4 4 TE 5 5 TE 6 6 TE 7 7 TE 8 8
FR TE 9 9 TE 10 10 TE 11 11 TE 12 12
FR LY 1 1 LY 7 2
FR LY 2 1 LY 8 1 LY 6 2 LY 8 2
FR LY 5 1 LY 3 2
FR LY 4 1 LY 6 1 LY 2 2 LY 4 2
EQ LY 1 1 LY 7 2
EQ LY 2 1 LY 8 1 LY 6 2 LY 8 2
EQ LY 5 1 LY 3 2
EQ LY 4 1 LY 6 1 LY 2 2 LY 4 2
ST 1.00 LY 1 1
ST .71 LY 2 1
ST -.71 LY 4 1
ST -1.00 LY 5 1
ST -1.00 LY 9 3
FR LY 10 3 LY 11 3 LY 12 3
ST 1.00 PS 1 1 PS 2 2
FR PS 3 3
FR BE 3 1 BE 3 2
OU ALL ME=ML RO RC AD=OFF
```

Final covariance structure analyses. Lastly, in order to conduct final covariance structure analyses on the matrices of correlations from the two samples (i.e., Gaines, 2021, Main Studies 1 and 2), we built upon the initial (i.e., two-trait-factor) model by adding a noncircumplex "acquiescence" trait factor to

Table 8.5 Obtained Patterns of Factor Loadings Among Lower-Order Subclinical Interpersonal Traits and Accommodation-Related Behaviors for Study 3 Samples, Solution With Two Trait Factors

Gaines (2021, Main Study 1, $n = 289$)

Var.	Factor			
	DOM	NUR	ACC	ACQ
PA	.79	.00		—
BC	.55	−.45		—
DE	.00	−.60		—
FG	−.45	−.45		—
HI	−.60	.00		—
JK	−.45	.55		—
LM	.00	.79		—
NO	.55	.55		—
EX			−.93	
VO			.33	
LO			.01	
NE			−.53	

Gaines (2021, Main Study 2, n = 366)

Var.	Factor			
	DOM	NUR	ACC	ACQ
PA	.80	.00		—
BC	.47	−.42		—
DE	.00	−.58		—
FG	−.42	−.42		—
HI	−.58	.00		—
JK	−.42	.47		—
LM	.00	.80		—
NO	.47	.47		—
EX			−.65	
VO			.40	
LO			.12	
NE			−.75	

Note: DOM = dominance, NUR = nurturance, ACC = accommodation, ACQ = acquiescence, PA = ambitious-dominant, BC = arrogant-calculating, DE = cold-quarrelsome, FG = aloof-introverted, HI = unassured-submissive, JK = unassuming-ingenuous, LM = warm-agreeable, NO = gregarious-extraverted, EX = exit, VO = voice, LO = loyalty, NE = neglect.

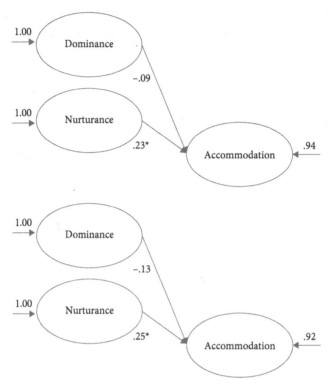

Figure 8.1. Path Coefficients for Dominance and Nurturance as Predictors of Accommodation, Study 3 Samples (Gaines, 2021, Main Study 1, *n* = 289; Gaines, 2021, Main Study 2, *n* = 366). *Note*: All nonerror path coefficients with plus signs are marginal (*p* < .10). All nonerror path coefficients with asterisks are significant (*p* < .05 or lower).

the latent-observed or Lambda Y (LY) matrix and freeing the loadings for all eight lower-order traits on that factor (constraining those loadings to be equal to each other in the process). All other fixed and freed parameters from the initial covariance structure analyses were specified once again in the final covariance structure analyses. The syntax files for the two samples are presented in Table 8.6.

Results of final covariance structure analyses indicated that, consistent with hypotheses, a model with dominance, nurturance, and "acquiescence" as the three trait factors (with paths from both of those traits to accommodation) provided satisfactory fit for Sample 1 (chi-square = 30.52, *df* = 55, *NS*; RMSEA = .00; CFI = 1.00) and Sample 2 (chi-square = 51.51, *df* = 55,

Table 8.6 Syntax Files Used as Input for Final Covariance Structure Analyses of Lower-Order Subclinical Interpersonal Traits and Accommodation-Related Behaviors, Study 3 Samples

Gaines (2021, Main Study 1, *n* = 289)

```
THREE TRAIT FACTORS + ONE BEHAVIORAL FACTOR MODEL FOR GAINES
(2021, MAIN STUDY 1) DON NUR PREDICTORS OF ACC
DA NI=12 NO=289 MA=KM
KM
1.00
 .46  1.00
 .16   .42  1.00
-.55  -.14   .09  1.00
-.52  -.39  -.12   .47  1.00
-.33  -.43  -.28   .20   .40  1.00
-.08  -.32  -.41  -.16   .15   .43  1.00
 .49   .13  -.12  -.54  -.30  -.02   .37  1.00
 .13   .10   .08  -.06  -.02  -.14  -.18  -.06  1.00
-.07  -.13  -.15  -.04  -.05   .13   .18   .11  -.30  1.00
-.00  -.13  -.06   .01   .03   .12   .02  -.01   .01   .26  1.00
 .05   .04   .07  -.03   .02  -.01  -.13  -.13   .51  -.12   .15  1.00
MO NY=12 NE=4 TE=SY,FI LY=FU,FI PS=SY,FI BE=FU,FI
FR TE 1 1 TE 2 2 TE 3 3 TE 4 4 TE 5 5 TE 6 6 TE 7 7 TE 8 8
FR TE 9 9 TE 10 10 TE 11 11 TE 12 12
FR LY 1 1 LY 7 2
FR LY 2 1 LY 8 1 LY 6 2 LY 8 2
FR LY 5 1 LY 3 2
FR LY 4 1 LY 6 1 LY 2 2 LY 4 2
EQ LY 1 1 LY 7 2
EQ LY 2 1 LY 8 1 LY 6 2 LY 8 2
EQ LY 5 1 LY 3 2
EQ LY 4 1 LY 6 1 LY 2 2 LY 4 2
ST 1.00 LY 1 1
ST .71 LY 2 1
ST -.71 LY 4 1
ST -1.00 LY 5 1
ST -1.00 LY 9 3
FR LY 10 3 LY 11 3 LY 12 3
FR LY 1 4 LY 2 4 LY 3 4 LY 4 4 LY 5 4 LY 6 4 LY 7 4 LY 8 4
EQ LY 1 4 LY 2 4 LY 3 4 LY 4 4 LY 5 4 LY 6 4 LY 7 4 LY 8 4
ST 1.00 PS 1 1 PS 2 2 PS 4 4
FR PS 3 3
FR BE 3 1 BE 3 2
OU ALL ME=ML RO RC AD=OFF
```

(continued)

238 THE SELF IN RELATIONSHIPS

Table 8.6 Continued

Gaines (2021, Main Study 2, _n_ = 366)

```
THREE TRAIT FACTORS + ONE BEHAVIORAL FACTOR MODEL FOR GAINES
(2021, MAIN STUDY 2) DON NUR PREDICTORS OF ACC
DA NI=12 NO=366 MA=KM
KM
1.00
 .43  1.00
 .15   .33  1.00
-.50  -.10   .15  1.00
-.59  -.27  -.09   .51  1.00
-.13  -.19  -.24   .12   .29  1.00
 .02  -.16  -.31  -.27   .05   .41  1.00
 .43  -.06  -.03  -.55  -.25   .11   .47  1.00
 .11   .18   .08  -.01  -.03   .01  -.06   .05  1.00
-.11  -.18  -.06   .00   .12   .07   .15   .09  -.19  1.00
-.00  -.08   .01   .05   .03   .06   .03  -.02  -.12   .33  1.00
 .06   .17   .14   .06   .00   .01  -.12  -.13   .52  -.29   .07  1.00
```

```
MO NY=12 NE=4 TE=SY,FI LY=FU,FI PS=SY,FI BE=FU,FI
FR TE 1 1 TE 2 2 TE 3 3 TE 4 4 TE 5 5 TE 6 6 TE 7 7 TE 8 8
FR TE 9 9 TE 10 10 TE 11 11 TE 12 12
FR LY 1 1 LY 7 2
FR LY 2 1 LY 8 1 LY 6 2 LY 8 2
FR LY 5 1 LY 3 2
FR LY 4 1 LY 6 1 LY 2 2 LY 4 2
EQ LY 1 1 LY 7 2
EQ LY 2 1 LY 8 1 LY 6 2 LY 8 2
EQ LY 5 1 LY 3 2
EQ LY 4 1 LY 6 1 LY 2 2 LY 4 2
ST 1.00 LY 1 1
ST .71 LY 2 1
ST -.71 LY 4 1
ST -1.00 LY 5 1
ST -1.00 LY 9 3
FR LY 10 3 LY 11 3 LY 12 3
FR LY 1 4 LY 2 4 LY 3 4 LY 4 4 LY 5 4 LY 6 4 LY 7 4 LY 8 4
EQ LY 1 4 LY 2 4 LY 3 4 LY 4 4 LY 5 4 LY 6 4 LY 7 4 LY 8 4
ST 1.00 PS 1 1 PS 2 2 PS 4 4
FR PS 3 3
FR BE 3 1 BE 3 2
OU ALL ME=ML RO RC AD=OFF
```

_NS_; RMSEA = .00; CFI = 1.00). Loadings of the eight lower-order subclinical interpersonal traits on the circumplex factors of dominance and nurturance (plus the noncircumplex factor of "acquiescence") are presented in Table 8.7; path coefficients from dominance and nurturance are presented

INTERPERSONAL TRAITS 239

Table 8.7 Obtained Patterns of Factor Loadings Among Lower-Order Subclinical Interpersonal Traits and Accommodation-Related Behaviors for Study 3 Samples, Solution With Three Trait Factors

Gaines (2021, Main Study 1, $n = 289$)

Var.	Factor			
	DOM	NUR	ACC	ACQ
PA	.79	.00		.19
BC	.51	−.49		.19
DE	.00	−.63		.19
FG	−.49	−.49		.19
HI	−.63	.00		.19
JK	−.49	.51		.19
LM	.00	.79		.19
NO	.51	.51		.19
EX			−.92	
VO			.33	
LO			.01	
NE			−.53	

Gaines (2021, Main Study 2, $n = 366$)

Var.	Factor			
	DOM	NUR	ACC	ACQ
PA	.80	.00		.23
BC	.46	−.44		.23
DE	.00	−.61		.23
FG	−.44	−.44		.23
HI	−.61	.00		.23
JK	−.44	.46		.23
LM	.00	.80		.23
NO	.46	.46		.23
EX			−.65	
VO			.40	
LO			.12	
NE			−.75	

Note: DOM = dominance, NUR = nurturance, ACC = accommodation, ACQ = acquiescence, PA = ambitious-dominant, BC = arrogant-calculating, DE = cold-quarrelsome, FG = aloof-introverted, HI = unassured-submissive, JK = unassuming-ingenuous, LM = warm-agreeable, NO = gregarious-extraverted, EX = exit, VO = voice, LO = loyalty, NE = neglect.

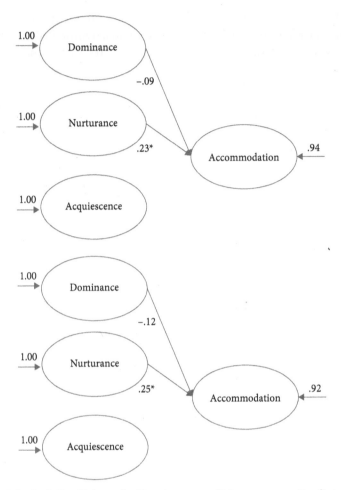

Figure 8.2. Path Coefficients for Dominance and Nurturance as Predictors (plus "Acquiescence" as a Noncircumplex, Noncircumplex Paper) of Accommodation, Study 3 Samples (Gaines, 2021, Main Study 1, $n = 289$). *Note:* All nonerror path coefficients with plus signs are marginal ($p < .10$). All nonerror path coefficients with asterisks are significant ($p < .05$ or lower).

in Figure 8.2. With the exception of the loadings for "acquiescence" (which were slightly below .20 for Sample 1 and slightly above .20 for Sample 3), the factor loadings on traits and behaviors were unchanged in comparison to the results for initial covariance structure analyses. Also, with the exception for the path from nurturance to accommodation in Sample 2 (which was rendered nonsignificant, due to the slight increase in standard error for nurturance), the path coefficients from traits to accommodation were the same across initial and final covariance structure analyses. Thus, for the most part, adding an "acquiescence" factor generally did not affect factor patterns or path coefficients in the final covariance structure analyses.

Comparing initial versus final covariance structure analyses. Contrary to our predictions about the lack of a significant improvement in fit when proceeding from a model with two trait factors to a model with three trait factors, direct comparison of the models indicated that adding a noncircumplex "acquiescence" factor yielded significantly better fit for Sample 1 (difference in chi-square = 10.04, difference in $df = 1$, $p < .01$) and for Sample 2 (difference in chi-square = 10.00, difference in $df = 1$, $p < .01$). Surprisingly, Gaines's (2021, Main Studies 1 and 2) data indicate that the IPIP-IPC (Markey & Markey, 2009) may be plagued by an "acquiescence" factor after all—a possibility that the Markeys (as well as Barford et al., 2015) did not consider.

Summary of Results Across the Two Samples for Study 3

Multiple-group circulant correlation analysis. As was the case for the three samples in the present Study 1 (Gaines et al., 1997, Study 2; Hofsess & Tracey, 2005; Sodano & Tracey, 2006, Adult Sample) and the three samples in the present Study 2 (i.e., Markey & Markey, 2009, Study 1, Samples 1 and 2; Barford et al., 2015), in order to determine whether the results of circulant correlation analyses could be generalized across the two studies in the present Study 3 (i.e., Gaines, 2021, Main Studies 1 and 2), we tested the goodness-of-fit concerning the equal-spacing, equal-communality model via a multiple-group circulant correlation analysis (via maximum likelihood estimation, ridge option, and ridge constant in LISREL 10.20; Joreskog & Sorbom, 2019) of the two data sets. The multiple-group syntax file, which includes the core of the separate syntax files that we have encountered so far, is presented in Table 8.8. Results of the multiple-group circulant correlation analysis affirmed that an equal-spacing, equal-communality model provided satisfactory fit to the data (chi-square = 49.93, $df = 60$, *NS*; RMSEA = .00; CFI = 1.00). The reproduced correlation matrix across the three samples is shown in Table 8.9.

Multiple-group covariance structure analysis. Subsequently, in order to determine whether the results of covariance structure analyses could be generalized across the two samples in the present Study 3 (i.e., Gaines, 2021, Main Studies 1 and 2), we tested the goodness-of-fit regarding two models (one in which a noncircumplex "acquiescence" trait factor was excluded, followed by one in which "acquiescence" was included, as part of the factor

242 THE SELF IN RELATIONSHIPS

Table 8.8 Syntax Files Used as Input for Multiple-Group Circulant Correlation Analysis of Lower-Order Subclinical Interpersonal Traits, Study 3 Samples

---

Gaines (2021, Main Study 1, n = 289)

```
EQUAL-SPACING, EQUAL-COMMUNALITY MODEL FOR GAINES (2021),
MAIN STUDY 1
DA NI=8 NO=289 MA=KM
KM
1.00
 .46    1.00
 .16     .42    1.00
-.55    -.14     .09    1.00
-.52    -.39    -.12     .47    1.00
-.35    -.43    -.28     .20     .40    1.00
-.08    -.32    -.41    -.16     .15     .43    1.00
 .49     .13    -.12    -.54    -.30    -.02     .37    1.00
```

```
MO NY=8 NE=8 TE=SY,FI LY=FU,FI PS=SY,FR
LA
PA BC DE FG HI JK LM NO
FR TE 1 1 TE 2 2 TE 3 3 TE 4 4 TE 5 5 TE 6 6 TE 7 7 TE 8 8
ST 1.00 LY 1 1 LY 2 2 LY 3 3 LY 4 4 LY 5 5 LY 6 6 LY 7 7 LY 8 8
FI PS 1 1 PS 2 2 PS 3 3 PS 4 4 PS 5 5 PS 6 6 PS 7 7 PS 8 8
ST 1.00 PS 1 1 PS 2 2 PS 3 3 PS 4 4 PS 5 5 PS 6 6 PS 7 7 PS 8 8
EQ PS 2 1 PS 3 2 PS 4 3 PS 5 4 PS 6 5 PS 7 6 PS 8 7 PS 8 1
EQ PS 3 1 PS 4 2 PS 5 3 PS 6 4 PS 7 5 PS 8 6 PS 7 1 PS 8 2
EQ PS 4 1 PS 5 2 PS 6 3 PS 7 4 PS 8 5 PS 6 1 PS 7 2 PS 8 3
EQ PS 5 1 PS 6 2 PS 7 3 PS 8 4
OU ALL RO RC AD=OFF
```

Gaines (2021, Main Study 2, n = 366)

```
EQUAL-SPACING, EQUAL-COMMUNALITY MODEL FOR GAINES (2021),
MAIN STUDY 2
DA NI=8 NO=366 MA=KM
KM
1.00
 .43    1.00
 .15     .33    1.00
-.50    -.10     .15    1.00
-.59    -.27    -.09     .51    1.00
-.13    -.19    -.24     .12     .29    1.00
 .02    -.16    -.31    -.27     .05     .41    1.00
 .43    -.06    -.03    -.55    -.25     .11     .47    1.00
```

Table 8.8 Continued

```
MO NY=8 NE=8 TE=SY,FI LY=FU,FI PS=SY,FR
LA
PA BC DE FG HI JK LM NO
FR TE 1 1 TE 2 2 TE 3 3 TE 4 4 TE 5 5 TE 6 6 TE 7 7 TE 8 8
ST 1.00 LY 1 1 LY 2 2 LY 3 3 LY 4 4 LY 5 5 LY 6 6 LY 7 7 LY 8 8
FI PS 1 1 PS 2 2 PS 3 3 PS 4 4 PS 5 5 PS 6 6 PS 7 7 PS 8 8
ST 1.00 PS 1 1 PS 2 2 PS 3 3 PS 4 4 PS 5 5 PS 6 6 PS 7 7 PS 8 8
EQ PS 2 1 PS 3 2 PS 4 3 PS 5 4 PS 6 5 PS 7 6 PS 8 7 PS 8 1
EQ PS 3 1 PS 4 2 PS 5 3 PS 6 4 PS 7 5 PS 8 6 PS 7 1 PS 8 2
EQ PS 4 1 PS 5 2 PS 6 3 PS 7 4 PS 8 5 PS 6 1 PS 7 2 PS 8 3
EQ PS 5 1 PS 6 2 PS 7 3 PS 8 4
OU ALL RO RC AD-OFF
```

patterns that specified circumplex dominance and nurturance factors and paths from dominance and nurturance to accommodation) using multiple-group covariance structure analyses (via maximum likelihood estimation, ridge option, and ridge constant in LISREL 10.20; Joreskog & Sorbom, 2019) of the two data sets. The multiple-group syntax files, which include the core of the separate syntax files that we have encountered so far, are presented in Table 8.10. Results of the multiple-group covariance structure analyses indicated that (1) consistent with hypotheses, a model with dominance and nurturance (but not "acquiescence") as trait factors provided satisfactory fit (chi-square = 105.81, df = 134, NS; RMSEA = .00; CFI = 1.00);

Table 8.9 Reproduced Correlation Matrix Across Study 3 Samples

Var.	Correlations							
	PA	*BC*	*DE*	*FG*	*HI*	*JK*	*LM*	*NO*
PA	1.00							
BC	.39	1.00						
DE	.03	.39	1.00					
FG	−.27	.03	.39	1.00				
HI	−.45	−.27	.03	.39	1.00			
JK	−.27	−.45	−.27	.03	.39	1.00		
LM	.03	−.27	−.45	−.27	.03	.39	1.00	
NO	.39	.03	−.27	−.45	−.27	.03	.39	1.00

Note: PA = ambitious-dominant, BC = arrogant-calculating, DE = cold-quarrelsome, FG = aloof-introverted, HI = unassured-submissive, JK = unassuming-ingenuous, LM = warm-agreeable, NO = gregarious-extraverted.

244 THE SELF IN RELATIONSHIPS

Table 8.10 Syntax Files Used as Input for Multiple-Group Covariance Structure Analyses of Lower-Order Subclinical Interpersonal Traits and Accommodation-Related Behaviors, Study 3 Samples

---

Dominance and nurturance as trait factors

```
TWO TRAIT FACTORS + ONE BEHAVIORAL FACTOR MODEL FOR GAINES
(2021, MAIN STUDY 1) DON NUR PREDICTORS OF ACC
DA NG=2 NI=12 NO=289 MA=KM
KM
1.00
 .46  1.00
 .16   .42  1.00
-.55  -.14   .09  1.00
-.52  -.39  -.12   .47  1.00
-.33  -.43  -.28  -.20   .40  1.00
-.08  -.32  -.41  -.16   .15   .43  1.00
 .49   .13  -.12  -.54  -.30  -.02   .37  1.00
 .13   .10   .08  -.06  -.02  -.14  -.18  -.06  1.00
-.07  -.13  -.15  -.04  -.05   .13   .18   .11  -.30  1.00
-.00  -.13  -.06   .01   .03   .12   .02  -.01   .01   .26  1.00
 .05   .04   .07  -.03   .02  -.01  -.13  -.13   .51  -.12   .15  1.00
```

```
MO NY=12 NE=3 TE=SY,FI LY=FU,FI PS=SY,FI BE=FU,FI
LA
PA BC DE FG HI JK LM NO EX VO LO NE
FR TE 1 1 TE 2 2 TE 3 3 TE 4 4 TE 5 5 TE 6 6 TE 7 7 TE 8 8
FR TE 9 9 TE 10 10 TE 11 11 TE 12 12
FR LY 1 1 LY 7 2
FR LY 2 1 LY 8 1 LY 6 2 LY 8 2
FR LY 5 1 LY 3 2
FR LY 4 1 LY 6 1 LY 2 2 LY 4 2
EQ LY 1 1 LY 7 2
EQ LY 2 1 LY 8 1 LY 6 2 LY 8 2
EQ LY 5 1 LY 3 2
EQ LY 4 1 LY 6 1 LY 2 2 LY 4 2
ST 1.00 LY 1 1
ST .71 LY 2 1
ST -.71 LY 4 1
ST -1.00 LY 5 1
ST -1.00 LY 9 3
FR LY 10 3 LY 11 3 LY 12 3
ST 1.00 PS 1 1 PS 2 2
FR PS 3 3
FR BE 3 1 BE 3 2
OU ALL RO RC AD=OFF
```

Table 8.10 Continued

```
TWO TRAIT FACTORS + ONE BEHAVIORAL FACTOR MODEL FOR GAINES
(2021, MAIN STUDY 2) DON NUR PREDICTORS OF ACC
DA NI=12 NO=366 MA=KM
KM
1.00
 .43  1.00
 .15   .33  1.00
-.50  -.10   .15  1.00
-.59  -.27  -.09   .51  1.00
-.13  -.19  -.24   .12   .29  1.00
 .02  -.16  -.31  -.27   .05   .41  1.00
 .43  -.06  -.03  -.55  -.25   .11   .47  1.00
 .11   .18   .08  -.01  -.03   .01  -.06   .05  1.00
-.11  -.18  -.06   .00   .12   .07   .15   .09  -.19  1.00
-.00  -.08   .01   .05   .03   .06   .03  -.02  -.12   .33  1.00
 .06   .17   .14   .06   .00   .01  -.12  -.13   .52  -.29   .07  1.00
```

```
MO NY=12 NE=3 TE=IN LY=IN PS=IN BE=IN
LA
PA BC DE FG HI JK LM NO EX VO LO NE
OU ALL RO RC AD=OFF
```

Dominance, nurturance, and "acquiescence" as trait factors

```
THREE TRAIT FACTORS + ONE BEHAVIORAL FACTOR MODEL FOR GAINES
(2021, MAIN STUDY 1) DON NUR PREDICTORS OF ACC
DA NG=2 NI=12 NO=289 MA=KM
KM
1.00
 .46  1.00
 .16   .42  1.00
-.55  -.14   .09  1.00
-.52  -.39  -.12   .47  1.00
-.33  -.43  -.28   .20   .40  1.00
-.08  -.32  -.41  -.16   .15   .43  1.00
 .49   .13  -.12  -.54  -.30  -.02   .37  1.00
 .13   .10   .08  -.06  -.02  -.14  -.18  -.06  1.00
-.07  -.13  -.15  -.04  -.05   .13   .18   .11  -.30  1.00
-.00  -.13  -.06   .01   .03   .12   .02  -.01   .01   .26  1.00
 .05   .04   .07  -.03   .02  -.01  -.13  -.13   .51  -.12   .15  1.00
```

(continued)

246 THE SELF IN RELATIONSHIPS

Table 8.10 Continued

```
MO NY=12 NE=4 TE=SY,FI LY=FU,FI PS=SY,FI BE=FU,FI
LA
PA BC DE FG HI JK LM NO EX VO LO NE
FR TE 1 1 TE 2 2 TE 3 3 TE 4 4 TE 5 5 TE 6 6 TE 7 7 TE 8 8
FR TE 9 9 TE 10 10 TE 11 11 TE 12 12
FR LY 1 1 LY 7 2
FR LY 2 1 LY 8 1 LY 6 2 LY 8 2
FR LY 5 1 LY 3 2
FR LY 4 1 LY 6 1 LY 2 2 LY 4 2
EQ LY 1 1 LY 7 2
EQ LY 2 1 LY 8 1 LY 6 2 LY 8 2
EQ LY 5 1 LY 3 2
EQ LY 4 1 LY 6 1 LY 2 2 LY 4 2
ST 1.00 LY 1 1
ST .71 LY 2 1
ST -.71 LY 4 1
ST -1.00 LY 5 1
ST -1.00 LY 9 3
FR LY 10 3 LY 11 3 LY 12 3
FR LY 1 4 LY 2 4 LY 3 4 LY 4 4 LY 5 4 LY 6 4 LY 7 4 LY 8 4
EQ LY 1 4 LY 2 4 LY 3 4 LY 4 4 LY 5 4 LY 6 4 LY 7 4 LY 8 4
ST 1.00 PS 1 1 PS 2 2 PS 4 4
FR PS 3 3
FR BE 3 1 BE 3 2
OU ALL ME=ML RO RC AD=OFF
```

```
THREE TRAIT FACTORS + ONE BEHAVIORAL FACTOR MODEL FOR GAINES
(2021, MAIN STUDY 2) DON NUR PREDICTORS OF ACC
DA NI=12 NO=366 MA=KM

KM
1.00
 .43  1.00
 .15   .33  1.00
-.50  -.10   .15  1.00
-.59  -.27  -.09   .51  1.00
-.13  -.19  -.24   .12   .29  1.00
 .02  -.16  -.31  -.27   .05   .41  1.00
 .43  -.06  -.03  -.55  -.25   .11   .47  1.00
 .11   .18   .08  -.01  -.03   .01  -.06   .05  1.00
-.11  -.18  -.06   .00   .12   .07   .15   .09  -.19  1.00
-.00  -.08   .01   .05   .03   .06   .03  -.02  -.12   .33  1.00
 .06   .17   .14   .06   .00   .01  -.12  -.13   .52  -.29   .07  1.00
```

```
MO NY=12 NE=4 TE=IN LY=IN PS=IN BE=IN
LA
PA BC DE FG HI JK LM NO EX VO LO NE
OU ALL RO RC AD=OFF
```

INTERPERSONAL TRAITS   247

(2) unexpectedly, a model with "acquiescence" added to dominance and nurturance as trait factors led to an underidentified solution that could not be interpreted; and (3) also unexpectedly, we were unable to compare models that excluded versus included "acquiescence."

Interestingly, when we were left with only the two-trait-factor model to generalize across the two samples (i.e., Gaines, 2021, Main Studies 1 and 2), we found that *both* paths from the subclinical interpersonal traits to accommodation were significant. As we had originally predicted, the path from dominance to accommodation was *negative* ($p < .05$), whereas the path from nurturance to accommodation was *positive* ($p < .01$). The multiple-group covariance structure analysis resulted in a slightly lowered standard error for the path from dominance to accommodation, thus making the path coefficient significant. The pattern of loadings for the lower-order subclinical interpersonal traits and accommodation-related behaviors on dominance, nurturance, and accommodation are presented in Table 8.11; the

Table 8.11 Obtained Patterns of Factor Loadings Among Lower-Order Subclinical Interpersonal Traits and Accommodation-Related Behaviors Across Study 3 Samples, Solution with Two Trait Factors

Var.	Factor			
	DOM	*NUR*	*ACC*	*ACQ*
PA	.80	.00		—
BC	.50	−.43		—
DE	.00	−.59		—
FG	−.43	−.43		—
HI	−.59	.00		—
JK	−.43	.50		—
LM	.00	.80		—
NO	.50	.50		—
EX			−.74	
VO			.37	
LO			.08	
NE			−.66	

Note: DOM = dominance, NUR = nurturance, ACC = accommodation, ACQ = acquiescence, PA = ambitious-dominant, BC = arrogant-calculating, DE = cold-quarrelsome, FG = aloof-introverted, HI = unassured-submissive, JK = unassuming-ingenuous, LM = warm-agreeable, NO = gregarious-extraverted, EX = exit, VO = voice, LO = loyalty, NE = neglect.

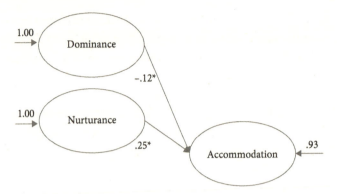

Figure 8.3. Path Coefficients for Dominance and Nurturance as Predictors of Accommodation Across Study 3 Samples (Gaines, 2021, Main Study 2, n = 366). *Note*: All nonerror path coefficients with plus signs are marginal ($p < .10$). All nonerror path coefficients with asterisks are significant ($p < .05$ or lower).

path coefficients from dominance and nurturance to accommodation are presented in Figure 8.3.

Prelude to Chapter 9

Two funny things happened on the way to interpreting results of covariance structure analyses across the two samples within the present Study 3 (i.e., Gaines, 2021, Studies 1 and 2). First, not only was the addition of a noncircumplex "acquiescence" trait factor unnecessary, but also such an addition created problems with parameter estimation that rendered the model uninterpretable in the multiple-group analysis (even though the "acquiescence" loadings had been similar for Sample 1 alone versus Sample 2 alone). Second, despite the small magnitude for the negative path from dominance to accommodation, that path emerged as significant in the multiple-group analysis (undoubtedly aided by the combined sample size as well as the slightly reduced standard error; see Kline, 2015). Oddly enough, these unanticipated twists helped to restore our faith in the IPIP-IPC (Markey & Markey, 2009), which was even more susceptible to measurement error in the present Study 3 than previously published studies would have led us to believe. Overall, in terms of (1) construct validity in its own right and (2) criterion-related validity with respect to accommodation (Rusbult et al., 1991), the IPIP-IPC performed reasonably well in the multiple-group analyses.

The fact that the IPIP-IPC (Markey & Markey, 2009) enabled us to explain significant variance in accommodation (Rusbult et al., 1991) *despite*

INTERPERSONAL TRAITS   249

problems with measurement error leads us to surmise that, if the eight subscales of the IPIP-IPC could be expanded beyond four items apiece (possibly boosting internal consistency), then perhaps covariance between the higher-order interpersonal traits and accommodation can be raised as well (see Nunnally & Bernstein, 1994). In the meantime, those interpersonal circumplex theorists (following Wiggins, 2003/2005) who wish to apply the IPIP-IPC in a descriptive (rather than inferential) manner toward constructing interpersonal trait/conflict resolution behavior profiles for specific individuals within counseling and other applied settings might find it useful to focus on conflict-*escalating* behaviors. Part of the output from LISREL (Joreskog & Sorbom, 2019) that we have not emphasized until now is the set of *factor loading regression weights* that can help researchers determine which variables to interpret versus ignore (see Beauducel & Rabe, 2009); such weights (with magnitudes of .10 or greater considered worth interpreting) in the present Study 3 suggest that exit and neglect should be interpreted alongside the eight lower-order traits, as shown in Table 8.12.

Table 8.12 Factor Loading Regression Weights for Initial Covariance Structure Analyses of Interpersonal Trait and Accommodation Data

Gaines (2021, Main Study 1, n = 289)

Var.	Factor		
	DOM	*NUR*	*ACC*
PA	.25	−.00	−.01
BC	.15	−.13	−.02
DE	.00	−.15	−.02
FG	−.12	−.13	−.01
HI	−.16	.00	.01
JK	−.13	.15	.02
LM	−.00	.23	.03
NO	.16	.16	.01
EX	.02	−.04	−.38
VO	−.00	.01	.08
LO	.00	.00	.00
NE	.01	−.02	−.14

(continued)

250 THE SELF IN RELATIONSHIPS

Table 8.12 Continued

Gaines (2021, Main Study 2, n = 366)

Var.	Factor		
	DOM	*NUR*	*ACC*
PA	.28	−.00	−.01
BC	.13	−.12	−.02
DE	.00	−.15	−.01
FG	−.12	−.12	−.01
HI	−.17	.00	.01
JK	−.11	.13	.02
LM	−.00	.24	.03
NO	.13	.14	.01
EX	.01	−.03	−.15
VO	−.00	.02	.08
LO	−.00	.00	.02
NE	.02	−.04	−.19

Note: DOM = higher-order dominance factor, NUR = higher-order nurturance factor, ACC = higher-order accommodation factor.

In Chapter 9, we tie up loose ends and suggest directions for future research on the self in relationships. Among loose ends, we expand upon our coverage of the present Study 3, Sample 2 (Gaines, 2021, Main Study 2) by examining the extent to which the interpersonal motives of power and intimacy (measured via the Circumplex Scales of Interpersonal Values, or CSIV; Locke, 2000, as reinterpreted by Locke, 2015) can explain variance in accommodation (Rusbult et al., 1991) beyond the variance that the interpersonal traits of dominance and nurturance (Markey & Markey, 2009) can explain. Furthermore, among directions for future research and applications, we comment briefly upon the prospects for further work on interpersonal motives, values, and attitudes (the latter of which we construe as the currently popular dimensions of attachment orientations; Brennan et al., 1998) as manifested accommodation (Rusbult et al., 1991) and other conflict resolution behaviors. Lastly, we return to Wiggins's (2003/2005) interpersonal circumplex theory of personality and social behavior as a "grand theory" that evokes Sullivan's (1953) interpersonal theory of personality and Lewin's (1936) field theory (among other perspectives) in the process of examining the self in relationships.

SECTION V
EPILOGUE

9

The Self in Relationships

Concluding Thoughts

Synopsis: In the present chapter, we consider data specifically from Gaines (2021, Main Study 2)—reanalyzed here as Study 3, Sample 2—regarding the interpersonal motives of power and intimacy as explaining (or failing to explain) variance in accommodation beyond the variance that the interpersonal traits of dominance and nurturance can explain; we offer possible directions for future research and applications concerning interpersonal motives, interpersonal values, and interpersonal attitudes (i.e., attachment orientations); and we provide final thoughts, returning to Wiggins's interpersonal circumplex theory and reinforcing its links to Sullivan's interpersonal theory and Lewin's field theory, while acknowledging the need for diversification of research on the self in relationships.

> Although the basic geometry of interpersonal space is well established and may be analyzed by a variety of methods . . ., the boundary conditions of its applications are less well established. . . . In measuring interpersonal dispositions ("traits"), for example, the fit between the circumplex model and interpersonal theory is so close that one can hardly distinguish the theory from the model. . . . But the precise relations between interpersonal dispositional space and the many circumplex structures obtained for other "spaces," such as interpersonal problems . . ., covert reaction tendencies . . ., and emotions . . ., has only begun to be investigated.
>
> —Jerry S. Wiggins,
> *Paradigms of Personality Assessment* (2003/2005, pp. 87 and 89)

In one of the great ironies within personality psychology, although James's psychology of individual differences (including James's self-theory) is considered to be a functionalist perspective (concerned with the purposes to which consciousness could be put, rather than the structure of consciousness per se), James had a great deal to say about the *structure* of the self in his

The Self in Relationships. Stanley O. Gaines, Jr., Oxford University Press. © Oxford University Press 2023.
DOI: 10.1093/oso/9780197687635.003.0009

two-volume *Principles of Psychology* (1890/2010). In contrast, Allport had considerably less to say about the structure of the self in *Pattern and Growth in Personality* (1961/1963), although the construct of the proprium within Allport's psychology of the individual (including Allport's trait theory) bears a resemblance to the self-concept, as we noted in Chapter 5), than James had said. Subsequently, Wiggins had surprisingly little to say about the structure of the self in *Paradigms of Personality Assessment* (2003/2005), although Wiggins shared Allport's interest in traits as aspects of the self that are relatively accessible to consciousness (keeping in mind that Wiggins acknowledged additional aspects of the self within his interpersonal circumplex theory, as the quote cited above makes clear). Nevertheless, Wiggins's theory directly addresses the self in relationships, to an extent that one does not find in the theories of James or Allport (Gaines, 2016/2018).

Following the evolution of Thibaut and Kelley's (1959; Kelley, 1979; Kelley & Thibaut, 1978) interdependence theory from a theory of N-person intragroup dynamics to a theory of two-person *relationship* dynamics, Kelley (1983, 1997) drew upon the initial version of Wiggins's (1979) interpersonal circumplex theory, which focused on interpersonal traits as potential predictors of interpersonal behavior (Reis et al., 2002). Although Kelley commented primarily upon the agentic trait of dominance as an inconsistent influence on interdependence processes, J. G. Holmes (2002) concluded that the communal trait of nurturance was more central to individuals' relationship maintenance behaviors. Kelley's and J. G. Holmes's respective musings about the impact of interpersonal traits on interdependence processes are congruent with the findings that (1) nurturance was consistently significant (and positive) as a predictor of accommodation, whereas (2) dominance was not so consistently significant (though it *was* consistently negative) as a predictor of accommodation in the present Study 3 (Gaines, 2021, Main Studies 1 and 2). However, the issue of measurement error that plagues the International Personality Item Pool-Interpersonal Circle (IPIP-IPC; Markey & Markey, 2009) leads us to exercise caution in assuming that the findings simply reflect the virtues of our a priori theoretical insight.

In this concluding chapter, we will dig deeper into data from Sample 2 of the present Study 3 (Gaines, 2021, Main Study 2)—in particular, examining the interpersonal motives of power and intimacy (Locke, 2000; reinterpreted by Locke, 2015) alongside the interpersonal traits of dominance and nurturance (Markey & Markey, 2009) as predictors of accommodation (Rusbult et al., 1991) in close relationships. Additionally, as we look toward future

CONCLUDING THOUGHTS 255

research on aspects of the self as reflected in relationship dynamics, we consider the potential for the attachment orientations of anxiety and avoidance (Brennan et al., 1998) to be reinterpreted and remeasured as the interpersonal attitudes toward self (in relation to significant others) and significant others (in relation to the self). Afterward, we address implications of the present studies for clinical and counseling practice regarding interpersonal aspects of personality as influences on conflict resolution processes, as well as the need for research and applications across a wide array of nations (i.e., not limited to the United States and the United Kingdom, where every study of the IPIP-IPC that we have cited was conducted); we end by returning to Wiggins (1991) as standing upon the shoulders of Sullivan (1953) and Lewin (1951/1976) in creating interpersonal circumplex theory.

Interpersonal Motives as Additional Predictors of Accommodation(?)

In Chapter 5, we introduced Wiggins's (1997) circumplex model of interpersonal motives, which eventually was incorporated into the most fully elaborated version of Wiggins's (2003/2005) interpersonal circumplex theory of personality and social behavior. Like the communal trait of nurturance, Wiggins predicted that the communal motive of intimacy would lead individuals to give love/affection and status/respect to other persons. Also, like the agentic trait of dominance, Wiggins hypothesized that the agentic motive of power would lead individuals to give love/affection, but *deny* status/respect, to other persons. Although Wiggins did not make specific predictions regarding the impact of interpersonal motives (or other interpersonal aspects of personality) on accommodation as conceptualized by Rusbult and colleagues (1991), Rusbult's own interpretation of Wiggins's perspective (e.g., Rusbult, 1993) suggests that the need for intimacy will promote accommodation, whereas the need for power will inhibit accommodation. Fortunately, Gaines (2021, Main Study 2) collected data on interpersonal traits (Markey & Markey, 2009) and interpersonal motives (Locke, 2000; reinterpreted by Locke, 2015) from a sufficiently large sample to add tests of these latter two hypotheses (albeit with slight attrition of sample size).

In order to measure lower-order interpersonal motives, Gaines (2021, Main Study 2) used a 32-item version of the Circumplex Scales of Interpersonal Values (CSIV; Locke, 2000), which Locke originally developed

256 THE SELF IN RELATIONSHIPS

as a measure of lower-order interpersonal *values* but ultimately reconstrued as a measure of lower-order interpersonal *motives* (Locke, 2015). Following Locke's reinterpretation (and following personal communication with Locke, August 2, 2019), we revisit Gaines's data from a somewhat reduced sample of 345 participants, using our adaptation of Wiggins's (1997) terminology regarding the eight lower-order motives (i.e., *status, aggression, autonomy, rejection, infavoidance, abasement, solidarity,* and *affiliation*). Overall, internal consistencies were higher for the lower-order interpersonal motive subscales from the CSIV (Cronbach's alphas ranged from .60 to .70; separate Cronbach's alphas = .60 for status, .66 for aggression, .68 for autonomy, .70 for rejection, .61 for infavoidance, .63 for abasement, .62 for solidarity, and .66 for affiliation) that we had obtained for the lower-order interpersonal trait subscales from the IPIP-IPC (Markey & Markey, 2009).

The matrix of zero-order correlations among scores on the lower-order interpersonal motives as measured by the CSIV (Locke, 2000; reinterpreted by Locke, 2015) is presented in Table 9.1. Readers will notice—like the lower-order clinical interpersonal traits that we encountered in Chapter 5, but unlike the lower-order subclinical interpersonal traits that we encountered in Chapters 5 through 8—all of the correlations among lower-order (subclinical) interpersonal motives were *positive,* a fact that is not immediately evident from the matrix that Locke (2000, p. 255) had presented on the basis of *ipsatized* scores (thus creating negative correlations that did not initially exist within

Table 9.1 Matrix of Lower-Order Interpersonal Motive Correlations (Gaines, 2021, Main Study 2, *n* = 345)

Var.	Correlations							
	ST	*AG*	*AU*	*RE*	*IN*	*AB*	*SO*	*AF*
ST	1.00							
AG	.63	1.00						
AU	.54	.70	1.00					
RE	.43	.44	.56	1.00				
IN	.22	.34	.43	.53	1.00			
AB	.32	.10	.16	.33	.54	1.00		
SO	.33	.13	.11	.20	.29	.64	1.00	
AF	.50	.35	.25	.16	.24	.48	.61	1.00

Note: ST = status, AG = aggression, AU = autonomy, RE = rejection, IN = infavoidance, AB = abasement, SO = solidarity, AF = affiliation.

CONCLUDING THOUGHTS   257

Table 9.2 Syntax File for Circulant Correlation Analysis of Actual Data from Gaines (2021, Main Study 2, n = 345), Lower-Order Motives, Equal-Spacing, Equal-Communality Model

```
CIRCULANT CORRELATION ANALYSIS OF CSIV MOTIVE SCALE
CORRELATIONS MAIN STUDY 2
DA NI=8 NO=345 MA=KM
KM
1.00
 .63    1.00
 .54     .70    1.00
 .43     .44     .56    1.00
 .22     .34     .43     .53    1.00
 .32     .10     .16     .33     .53    1.00
 .32     .13     .11     .20     .29     .64    1.00
 .50     .35     .25     .16     .24     .47     .61    1.00
```

```
MO NY=8 NE=8 TE=SY,FI LY=FU,FI PS=SY,FR
LA
ST AG AU RE IN AB SO AF
FR TE 1 1 TE 2 2 TE 3 3 TE 4 4 TE 5 5 TE 6 6 TE 7 7 TE 8 8
ST 1.00 LY 1 1 LY 2 2 LY 3 3 LY 4 4 LY 5 5 LY 6 6 LY 7 7 LY 8 8
FI PS 1 1 PS 2 2 PS 3 3 PS 4 4 PS 5 5 PS 6 6 PS 7 7 PS 8 8
ST 1.00 PS 1 1 PS 2 2 PS 3 3 PS 4 4 PS 5 5 PS 6 6 PS 7 7 PS 8 8
EQ PS 2 1 PS 3 2 PS 4 3 PS 5 4 PS 6 5 PS 7 6 PS 8 7 PS 8 1
EQ PS 3 1 PS 4 2 PS 5 3 PS 6 4 PS 7 5 PS 8 6 PS 7 1 PS 8 2
EQ PS 4 1 PS 5 2 PS 6 3 PS 7 4 PS 8 5 PS 6 1 PS 7 2 PS 8 3
EQ PS 5 1 PS 6 2 PS 7 3 PS 8 4
OU ALL RO RC AD=OFF
```

the data set). The correlation matrix was entered into a circulant correlation analysis, testing the same equal-spacing, equal-communality model that we tested from Chapters 5 through 8; the corresponding syntax file is presented in Table 9.2. Results of the circulant correlation analysis indicated that the model provided satisfactory fit (chi-square = 13.01, degrees of freedom [df] = 24, *NS*; root mean square error of approximation [RMSEA] = .00; comparative fit index [CFI] = 1.00); inspection of the reproduced correlation matrix (shown in Table 9.3) indicated that—again, like the clinical interpersonal traits that we considered in Chapter 5—the reproduced correlations for the subclinical interpersonal motives were all *positive*.

Correlations between lower-order interpersonal motives (Locke, 2000; reinterpreted by Locke, 2015) and accommodation-related behaviors (Rusbult et al., 1991) are presented in Table 9.4. These correlations, as part of a larger matrix that also included the lower-order interpersonal traits

258 THE SELF IN RELATIONSHIPS

Table 9.3 Reproduced Correlation Matrix for Lower-Order Interpersonal Motives (Gaines, 2021, Main Study 2, $n = 345$)

Var.	Correlations							
	ST	AG	AU	RE	IN	AB	SO	AF
ST	1.00							
AG	.59	1.00						
AU	.40	.59	1.00					
RE	.26	.40	.59	1.00				
IN	.15	.26	.40	.59	1.00			
AB	.26	.15	.26	.40	.59	1.00		
SO	.40	.26	.15	.26	.40	.59	1.00	
AF	.59	.40	.26	.15	.26	.40	.59	1.00

Note: ST = status, AG = aggression, AU = autonomy, RE = rejection, IN = infavoidance, AB = abasement, SO = solidarity, AF = affiliation.

(Markey & Markey, 2009) that we covered in Chapter 8, were entered into a pair of covariance structure analyses. Given the sheer number of correlations and the complexity of the corresponding syntax file for these analyses, we report the full contents of output (including the output file that documents the creation of the correlation matrix from raw scores, using the PRELIS portion of LISREL 10.20; Joreskog & Sorbom, 2019) in Appendices 1A through 1C. Results of an initial covariance structure analysis indicated that (1) contrary to hypotheses, when "acquiescence" trait and motive factors were excluded, the model of trait and motive influences on accommodation did *not* yield adequate fit (chi-square = 275.36, *df* = 174, *p* < .01; RMSEA = .04; CFI = .78); (2) consistent with hypotheses, when "acquiescence" trait and motive factors

Table 9.4 Correlations Between Lower-Order Interpersonal Motives and Accommodation-Related Behaviors, Gaines (2021, Main Study 2, $n = 345$)

		Motives							
		ST	AG	AU	RE	IN	AB	SO	AF
Accommodation-related behaviors	EX	.23	.23	.27	.24	.10	.13	.10	.09
	VO	−.11	−.15	−.22	−.07	−.15	−.06	−.03	−.03
	LO	.09	.07	.02	.04	.08	.09	−.02	.04
	NE	.19	.20	.21	.20	.15	.08	.04	−.01

were included, the model of trait and motive influences on accommodation *did* yield adequate fit (chi-square = 146.64, *df* = 172, *NS*; RMSEA = .00, CFI = 1.00); and (3) contrary to hypotheses, inclusion of the "acquiescence" trait and motive factors yielded significantly better fit than did exclusion of those noncircumplex factors (difference in chi-square = 128.72, difference in *df* = 2, *p* < .01).

Loadings of lower-order interpersonal traits, lower-order interpersonal motives, and accommodation on the higher-order factors of dominance, nurturance, need for power, need for intimacy, accommodation, and "acquiescence" (separately for traits and motives) for the data from Gaines (2021, Main Study 2) are presented in Table 9.5. As Table 9.5 indicates, after controlling statistically for "acquiescence," lower-order interpersonal motives as well as lower-order interpersonal traits conform to the expected "quasi-circumplex" patterns with regard to magnitudes (whether zero or nonzero) and directions (whether positive or negative). In turn, path coefficients from dominance, nurturance, need for power, and need for intimacy to accommodation are presented in Figure 9.1. As Figure 9.1 indicates, we obtained clear support for our hypotheses regarding dominance as a significant negative predictor and nurturance as a significant positive predictor; equivocal support for our hypotheses regarding the need for intimacy (which was a marginal positive predictor, due to slightly elevated standard error); and no support for our hypothesis regarding the need for power (which was neither significant nor marginal as a predictor).

Directions for Future Research and Practical Applications

Results of the study from Gaines (2021, Main Study 2), also known as Sample 2 of the present Study 3, are somewhat encouraging with regard to the need for intimacy (though not the need for power) as potentially explaining variance in conflict resolution behaviors. Even with a sample of more than 300 participants and a set of subscales that provide acceptable internal consistency (given the small number of items per subscale), the need for intimacy still fell short of significance as a predictor of accommodation (Rusbult et al., 1991) in Gaines's study. We note that Gaines used Locke's 32-item version of the CSIV, rather than the 64-item version that Locke (2000; reinterpreted by Locke, 2015) used; the 32-item version had been suggested as an option by Locke himself (personal communication, August 2, 2019). However, as

260 THE SELF IN RELATIONSHIPS

Table 9.5 Higher-Order Interpersonal Trait, Interpersonal Motive, and Accommodation Loadings Extracted from Gaines (2021), Main Study 2 (Reduced $n = 345$)

Var.	Factor						
	DOM	NUR	ACQ1	POW	INT	ACQ2	ACC
PA	.80	.00	.22				
BC	.46	−.45	.22				
DE	.00	−.60	.22				
FG	−.45	−.45	.22				
HI	−.60	.00	.22				
JK	−.45	.46	.22				
LM	.00	.80	.22				
NO	.46	.46	.22				
ST				.47	.00	.64	
AG				.40	−.33	.64	
AU				.00	−.48	.64	
RE				−.33	−.33	.64	
IN				−.48	.00	.64	
AB				−.33	.40	.64	
SO				.00	.47	.64	
AF				.40	.40	.64	
EX							−.68
VO							.39
LO							.15
NE							−.67

Note: DOM = higher-order dominance factor, NUR = higher-order nurturance factor, ACQ1 = higher-order acquiescence factor (interpersonal traits only), POW = higher-order power factor, INT = higher-order intimacy factor, ACQ2 = higher-order acquiescence factor (interpersonal motives only), ACC = higher-order accommodation factor.

PA = ambitious-dominant, BC = arrogant-calculating, DE = cold-quarrelsome, FG = aloof-introverted, HI = unassured-submissive, JK = unassuming-ingenuous, LM = warm-agreeable, NO = gregarious-extraverted, ST = status, AG = aggression, AU = autonomy, RE = rejection, IN = infavoidance, AB = abasement, SO = solidarity, AF = affiliation, EX = exit, VO = voice, LO = loyalty, NE = neglect.

we observed in Chapter 8, the 64-item CSIV also is beset by problems with internal consistency. Given that the needs for power and intimacy as measured by the CSIV covary with aspects of interpersonal sensitivities in general (e.g., Hopwood et al., 2011) and rejection sensitivities in particular (e.g., Cain et al., 2017), we believe that further clinical and academic applications of the CSIV to understanding relationship dynamics are warranted.

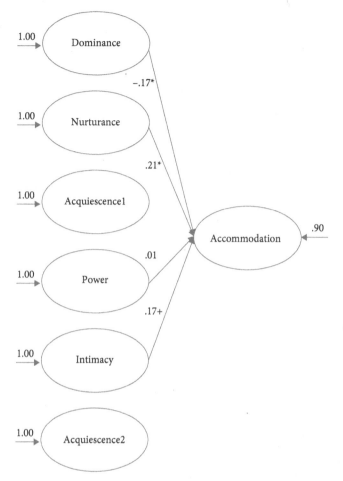

Figure 9.1. Path Coefficients for Interpersonal Traits and Interpersonal Motives as Predictors of Accommodation (Gaines, 2021, reduced *n* = 345). *Note*: All nonerror path coefficients with plus signs are marginal (*p* < .10). All nonerror path coefficients with asterisks are significant (*p* < .05 or lower).

If the CSIV (Locke, 2000) actually measures motives (Locke, 2015) instead of values (Locke, 2011), then how shall academicians and clinicians document interpersonal values in a manner that is consistent with a circumplex model, and would such documentation help relationship scientists understand why some individuals are more versus less likely to engage in accommodation (Rusbult et al., 1991) and other conflict resolution behaviors? At first glance, the Schwartz Value Survey (SVS; S. H. Schwartz, 1992)—which

262 THE SELF IN RELATIONSHIPS

was designed to measure the 10 lower-order "human values" of *achievement, benevolence, conformity, hedonism, power, security, self-direction, stimulation, tradition*, and *universalism*—might seem to be ideal, since (1) the survey is linked to S. H. Schwartz's (1994) *theory of basic human needs* (which holds that the values can be captured within a "modified quasi-circumplex" manner around the axes of *openness to change versus conservation* and *self-enhancement versus self-transcendence*) and (2) all 10 lower-order values ostensibly can be linked to "prosocial" behavior (e.g., S. H. Schwartz, 2010). So far, we are not aware of any attempts to incorporate Schwartz's constructs into Wiggins's (2003/2005) interpersonal circumplex theory, or to integrate Schwartz's constructs with Thibaut and Kelley's (1959) interdependence theory.

Finally, as we alluded in the Preface as well as Chapter 5, it is abundantly clear that secure attachment promotes a variety of "pro-relationship behaviors," whereas forms of insecure attachment (especially attachment avoidance) inhibit those behaviors; yet attachment theorists (following Bowlby, 1969/1997) have not offered a consistent interpretation of where, exactly, attachment orientations can be placed within the pantheon of personality constructs that bear upon the self (Gaines, 2020). However, we have reanalyzed data from a conference paper by Gaines et al. (2013) that support the combination of subscales from the Experiences in Close Relationships survey (ECR; Brennan et al., 1998) and the Relationship Scales Questionnaire (RSQ; Griffin & Bartholomew, 1994b) as a circumplex measure of interpersonal attitudes. We comment upon those new analyses in the Postscript, which we hope will encourage academicians and clinicians to adopt a circumplex perspective on attachment orientations (and, in turn, clarify whether the lack of consistent results for attachment anxiety as a predictor of "pro-relationship" behaviors in previous studies is a function of methodology rather than theory; Gaines, 2016/2018).

Final Thoughts

Returning to the IPIP-IPC (Markey & Markey, 2009), we acknowledge that all of the studies for which we reanalyzed data were conducted in two "Western," English-speaking nations (i.e., the United States and the United Kingdom), which makes us wonder whether that survey—which, as we stated in Chapters 7 through 9, is problematic in terms of internal consistency—might be *more* problematic outside those societal contexts. We are aware of one Japanese-language paper by Hashimoto and Oshio (2019) in which the researchers apparently translated the IPIP-IPC from English to Japanese, although our lack of fluency in Japanese prevents us from ascertaining whether internal consistency surfaced as an issue in that study. Also, we are aware of an earlier Japanese-language paper by Hashimoto and Oshio (2018) that reported a meta-analysis of data from the IPIP-IPC, although we are not in a position to determine which languages or nations were represented in that paper. At any rate, we have not found a single study in which researchers outside the United States or the United Kingdom have reported correlations among the eight lower-order traits, let alone covariance between those traits and "pro-relationship" behaviors (and all of the studies have involved majority-White samples). All in all, we should not overgeneralize results of our reanalyses.

Keeping in mind the need for research that transcends the "East"–"West" dichotomy (as well as the need for research across an expanded array of "Eastern" and "Western" nations), at least we can state with confidence that Wiggins's (2003/2005) interpersonal circumplex theory of personality and social behavior lives to see another day, *when the IPIP-IPC (Markey & Markey, 2009) is used as the measure of interpersonal traits.* Across several studies (i.e., Barford et al., 2015; Gaines, Main Studies 1 and 2 in the present book; Markey & Markey, 2009, Study 1, Samples 1 and 2), the lower-order subclinical interpersonal traits that are measured by the IPIP-IPC display the geometric and psychometric properties that Wiggins's theory would anticipate; and across two of those studies (Gaines, Main Studies 1 and 2), the higher-order subclinical interpersonal traits are reflected in opposing effects on accommodation (Rusbult et al., 1991), whereby dominance is a negative predictor and nurturance is a positive predictor. Ironically, across three studies (Gaines, Panter, et al., 1997, Study 2; Hofsess & Tracey, 2005; Sodano & Tracey, 2006, Adult Sample), Wiggins's own IAS-R (Wiggins et al., 1988) clearly measures a noncircumplex "acquiescence" factor alongside dominance and nurturance, and the IAS-R was not used in predicting accommodation within those studies.

In a chapter from the second edition of the *Handbook of Personality: Theory and Research* (edited by Pervin and John, 1999), Jerry Wiggins and Krista Trobst (1999) provided a panoramic review of the literature on "interpersonal force fields," explicitly connecting the dots from Lewin's (1951/1976) field theory to Sullivan's (1953) interpersonal theory of personality to

Wiggins's (1991) interpersonal circumplex theory of personality and social behavior (among other perspectives). Throughout the present book, we have attempted to trace the progression of conceptualization and measurement of interpersonal aspects of personality through the influence of Lewin's, Sullivan's, and Wiggins's respective theories. We hope that the present book has given academicians and practitioners an in-depth sampling of major conceptual and methodological issues to consider within the interpersonal domain—not just from the standpoints of personality psychology and social psychology, but especially at the crossroads that makes up relationship science, which is indebted largely to these subdisciplines of psychology (plus other subdisciplines, full-fledged disciplines, and multidisciplinary fields). Individually and collectively, our work on the self in relationships is in an exciting yet early stage of development.

Postscript

In the Preface to the present book, we learned about Bartholomew's (1990) conceptualization of four attachment styles (i.e., secure, preoccupied/ anxious-ambivalent, fearful-avoidant, and dismissing-avoidant) as blends of individuals' positive versus negative working models of self and other. Building upon Bartholomew's set of attachment styles, Bartholomew and Horowitz (1991) developed a categorical measure of attachment styles; Gaines et al. (2000) subsequently used that measure in attempting to predict individuals' exit, voice, loyalty, and neglect as distinct yet interrelated responses to partners' anger/criticism as accommodation-related behaviors (Rusbult et al., 1991) in various close relationships. Gaines et al. found that, partially consistent with hypotheses, categorical attachment style was a significant predictor of accommodation in general—and exit in particular—in *romantic* relationships (i.e., securely attached individuals scored lower than did insecurely attached individuals; preoccupied individuals scored lower than did avoidant individuals; and dismissing-avoidant individuals scored lower than did fearful-avoidant individuals). However, Gaines and colleagues did not find any effects of attachment style on the other accommodation-related behaviors in romantic relationships.

Additionally, Bartholomew and Horowitz (1991) created a continuous measure of attachment styles as four separate dimensions; Scharfe and Bartholomew (1995) subsequently used that measure in attempting to predict exit, voice, loyalty, and neglect as accommodation-related responses in marital relationships. Scharfe and Bartholomew found that, partially consistent with hypotheses, secure attachment was positively associated with constructive (i.e., voice and loyalty) responses, whereas fearful-avoidant attachment was positively associated with destructive (i.e., exit and neglect) responses, although results were more consistent for the link between fearful-avoidant attachment and destructive responses than was the case for the link between secure attachment and constructive responses (i.e., the latter link was driven by the positive association between secure attachment and voice, rather than loyalty; see Drigotas et al., 1995, regarding the "peculiarities of loyalty" as a nonbehavior of sorts that is not easily predicted within close

266 POSTSCRIPT

relationships). However, Scharfe and Bartholomew found that preoccupied/anxious-ambivalent and dismissing-avoidant attachment were not consistently related to any of the accommodation-related behaviors.

Compared to Gaines et al.'s (2000) results concerning categorical attachment style, Scharfe and Bartholomew's results regarding continuous attachment styles (Bartholomew & Horowitz, 1991) and accommodation (Rusbult et al., 1991) are easier to interpret in terms of Wiggins's (1991) interpersonal circumplex theory (i.e., as a blend of individuals' positive attitudes toward self and significant others, secure attachment promotes individuals' *giving* of love/affection and status/respect to other persons; conversely, as a blend of individuals' negative attitudes toward self and significant others, fearful-avoidant attachment promotes individuals' *denial* of love/affection and status/respect to other persons; see Gaines, 2016/2018). Nevertheless, the four continuous attachment styles as operationalized by Bartholomew and Horowitz (1991) and employed as predictors of accommodation-related responses by Scharfe and Bartholomew represent only half of the complement of lower-order interpersonal attitudes that we described in Chapter 5. Most notably, the "pure" attachment *orientations* or higher-order axes of anxiety (i.e., the inverse of individuals' positive attitude toward self) and avoidance (i.e., the inverse of individuals' positive attitude toward significant others) as measured by Brennan et al. (1998) are not included.

Following Brennan et al.'s (1998) development of the Experiences in Close Relationships scale (ECR), Wei and colleagues (2007) created the ECR-Short Form as an alternative measure of the "pure" attachment orientations of anxiety and avoidance, which Etcheverry and colleagues (i.e., Etcheverry et al., 2013, Study 2) used subsequently when attempting to predict total scores on accommodation (Rusbult et al., 1991). Having been influenced by Thibaut and Kelley's (1959) interdependence theory in general and Rusbult's (1980, 1983) investment model in particular, Etcheverry et al. predicted that—after controlling for commitment as a mediator—anxiety and avoidance would be unrelated to accommodation. However, Etcheverry and colleagues found that avoidance exerted a direct negative effect on accommodation, as well as an indirect negative effect on accommodation via commitment (i.e., attachment avoidance inhibited commitment; in turn, commitment promoted accommodation). In contrast, Etcheverry et al. found that (consistent with predictions) any effect of anxiety on accommodation was fully mediated by commitment (i.e., attachment anxiety inhibited commitment; in turn, commitment promoted accommodation).

The study by Etcheverry et al. (2013, Study 2) comes closer than do the aforementioned studies by Gaines et al. (2000) or Scharfe and Bartholomew (1995) to the methodology that Gaines (2021, Main Studies 1 and 2) utilized in Study 3 within the present book, at least in terms of conducting covariance structure analyses (see Kline, 2016). However, by essentially limiting themselves to the higher-order axes of attachment anxiety (again, which we interpret as the opposite of individuals' positive attitude toward themselves in relation to significant others) and attachment avoidance (again, which we interpret as the opposite of individuals' positive attitude toward significant others in relation to themselves), Etcheverry and colleagues were not in a position to incorporate a circumplex model of interpersonal attitudes into their covariance structure analyses. Ideally, from our perspective, measuring the full complement of eight lower-order interpersonal attitudes would enable researchers to extract the higher-order interpersonal attitude axes, and keeping the four accommodation-related behaviors separate would allow researchers to extract the higher-order accommodation factor, before examining the effects of interpersonal attitudes/attachment orientations on accommodation (Gaines, 2016/2018).

We cannot know with certainty whether measuring a full circumplex's worth of lower-order interpersonal traits would have enabled Etcheverry et al. (2013, Study 2) to document direct negative effects of attachment anxiety (Wei et al., 2007) on accommodation (Rusbult et al., 1991). Nevertheless, we thought that it would be instructive to reanalyze data from a conference paper by Gaines et al. (2013) that can help establish a blueprint for operationalizing lower-order interpersonal attitudes as manifestations of the higher-order dimensions of individuals' positive attitudes toward themselves in relation to significant others (the opposite of attachment anxiety) and individuals' positive attitudes toward significant others in relation to themselves (the opposite of attachment avoidance). Gaines and colleagues reasoned that one could interpret (1) "negative" items from the anxiety subscale of the original ECR (Brennan et al., 1998) as nonanxious, (2) "positive" items from the dismissing-avoidant subscale of the RSQ (Griffin & Bartholomew, 1994b) as dismissing, (3) "positive" items from the avoidance subscale of the ECR as avoidant, (4) "positive" items from the fearful-avoidant subscale of the RSQ as fearful, (5) "positive" items from the anxiety subscale of the ECR as anxious, (6) "positive" items from the preoccupied/anxious-ambivalent subscale of the RSQ as preoccupied, (7) "negative" items from the avoidance subscale of the ECR as nonavoidant, and (8) "positive" items from the secure subscale of the RSQ as secure.

268   POSTSCRIPT

A total of 183 individuals (61 men, 117 women, and 5 individuals who did not indicate their gender) participated in the study by Gaines et al. (2013). The mean age of participants was 27.25 years (SD = 12.49 years). In terms of ethnic group membership, 60.7% of participants classified themselves as European descent, 9.3% as "Mixed," 12.0% as Asian descent, and 14.8% as African descent (an additional 3.3% of participants did not indicate their ethnic group membership). Data were missing from 11 individuals regarding one or more of the items from the ECR (Brennan et al., 1998) and/or the RSQ (Griffin & Bartholomew, 1994b), leaving a final sample of 172 individuals.

Participants in the study by Gaines et al. (2013) completed the 36-item ECR (Brennan et al., 1998), which was designed to measure attachment anxiety and attachment avoidance. Seventeen items measured attachment anxiety, one item measured the inverse of attachment anxiety, nine items measured attachment avoidance, and nine items measured the inverse of attachment avoidance. Each item was scored according to a 7-point, Likert-type scale (1 = disagree strongly, 7 = agree strongly). Results of reliability analyses indicated that, with the exception of the single-item subscale measuring the inverse of attachment avoidance (for which internal consistency could not be evaluated; Nunnally & Bernstein, 1994), the ECR attachment orientation subscales were internally consistent (Cronbach's alphas = .91 for attachment anxiety, .86 for attachment avoidance, and .81 for the inverse of attachment avoidance).

In addition, participants in the study by Gaines et al. (2013) completed the 30-item RSQ (Griffin & Bartholomew, 1994b), which was designed to measure dismissing-avoidant, fearful-avoidant, preoccupied, and secure attachment styles. Four items measured dismissing-avoidant, four items measured fearful-avoidant, three items measured preoccupied, and five items measured secure (with two reverse-worded items rescored in the direction of secure). The remaining 14 items were filler items for our purposes. Even when one acknowledges that the attachment style scales were relatively short (i.e., five or fewer items; Nunnally & Bernstein, 1994), results of reliability analyses indicated that internal consistency varied widely across the four scales (initial Cronbach's alphas = .58 for dismissing-avoidant, .69 for fearful-avoidant, .38 for preoccupied, and .28 for secure). However, we found that by deleting one item apiece from the dismissing-avoidant, preoccupied, and secure scales, we were able to improve the reliability coefficients to some extent (final Cronbach's alphas = .63 for dismissing-avoidant, .69 for fearful-avoidant, .40 for preoccupied, and .33 for secure).

POSTSCRIPT 269

Prior to conducting the study by Gaines et al. (2013), the lead author received ethics approval from the Psychology Department of the authors' educational institution. The authors collected data from a convenience sample, drawn primarily from the greater London metropolitan area. The participants did not receive any financial or other incentive to take part. Each participant read and signed an informed consent sheet that briefly explained the purpose of the study. Afterward, participants completed a "Self and Social Environment Study" survey that included measures of the attachment orientation subscales and attachment style scales, demographic items, and several additional scales that will not be examined further. Subsequently, participants read a debriefing form that explained the purpose of the study in detail.

Using the PRELIS subroutine within LISREL 10.20 (Joreskog & Sorbom, 2019), we generated a matrix of lower-order attitude correlations; the resulting matrix is contained in the output file that we report as Appendix 2A. Subsequently, the correlation matrix was entered into one circulant correlation analysis (testing the goodness-of-fit concerning an equal-spacing, equal-communality model) and two confirmatory factor analyses (one testing the goodness-of-fit concerning a model with individuals' attitudes toward self and significant others as circumplex higher-order factors but excluding "acquiescence" as a noncircumplex higher-order factor, and one testing the goodness-of-fit concerning individuals' attitudes toward self and significant others joined by "acquiescence") using the main routine in LISREL 10.20. We tested the same hypotheses concerning interpersonal attitudes that we had tested concerning interpersonal traits and interpersonal motives throughout the main text of the present book (i.e., an equal-spacing, equal-communality model will provide adequate fit; a two-factor model without "acquiescence" will provide adequate fit; a three-factor model with "acquiescence" similarly will provide adequate fit but will *not* offer significantly improved fit when compared to the two-factor model).

The syntax file for the circulant correlation analysis is included within the output file that we label as Appendix 2B. Results of the circulant correlation analysis indicated that, consistent with hypotheses, an equal-spacing, equal-communality model provided adequate fit (chi-square = 31.50, degrees of freedom [df] = 24, *NS*; root mean square error of approximation [RMSEA] = .04; comparative fit index [CFI] = .91). The reproduced correlation matrix, which conformed to a "quasi-circumplex" pattern, is presented at the end of the output file.

270 POSTSCRIPT

The syntax files for the initial and final covariance structure analyses are included within the output files that we label as Appendices 2C and 2D. Results of the covariance structure analyses indicated that, consistent with predictions, (1) a two-factor model without "acquiescence" provided adequate fit (chi-square = 29.67, df = 24, NS; RMSEA = .03; CFI = .93); (2) consistent with predictions, a three-factor model with "acquiescence" likewise provided adequate fit (chi-square = 27.98, df = 23, NS; RMSEA = .04; CFI = .94); and (3) consistent with predictions, a three-factor model did *not* yield significantly or marginally improved fit when compared to a two-factor model that was limited to the higher-order circumplex factors of individuals' attitudes toward self and significant others (difference in chi-square = 1.69, difference in df = 1, NS). The matrices of higher-order loadings for the two-factor and three-factor models, which conformed to a "quasi-circumplex" pattern (and yielded appreciable "acquiescence" loadings in the three-factor model), are presented at the end of the respective output files.

Regarding geometric and psychometric properties, the combination of subscales from the ECR (Brennan et al., 1998) and RSQ (Griffin & Bartholomew, 1994b) to create an interpersonal attitude inventory in Gaines et al. (2013) produced a reproduced correlation matrix and matrices of higher-order factor loadings that were comparable to the reproduced correlation matrix and matrices of higher-order factor loadings that we obtained for the IPIP-IPC (Markey & Markey, 2009) when reanalyzing interpersonal trait data from Gaines (2021, Main Studies 1 and 2) and previously published data sets by Barford et al. (2015) and Markey and Markey (Study 1, Samples 1 and 2). Furthermore, our interpretation of results from the ECR/RSQ amalgamation is not as much a matter of repurposing (e.g., the Circumplex Scales of Interpersonal Values [CSIV; Locke, 2000] as a measure of interpersonal motives; Locke, 2015) as it is a matter of clarifying exactly what the ECR and RSQ measure within the interpersonal domain of personality (i.e., attachment orientations as interpersonal attitudes; Gaines, 2016/2018). All things considered, results of our reanalyses concerning data from Gaines et al. (2013) are in keeping with our argument in Chapter 5 that attachment orientations can be incorporated readily within Wiggins's (2003/2005) interpersonal circumplex theory.

Does our attempt to reframe attachment orientations (Brennan et al., 1998; Griffin & Bartholomew, 1994b) as interpersonal attitudes (and, more generally, interpersonal aspects of personality) reflect an interest in supplanting Bowlby's attachment theory (Bowlby, 1969/1997, 1973/1998, 1980/1998) with Wiggins's (1979, 1991, 2003/2005) interpersonal circumplex theory? The short answer to that question is *no*. Unlike Wiggins's theory (which hints that societies play a role in shaping individuals' personalities), Bowlby's theory offers a detailed account of humans' personality and social development (Gaines, 2016/2018). Moreover, unlike Sullivan's (1953, 1954, 1956) interpersonal theory (which, as we have learned throughout the present book, provides much of the conceptual foundation for Wiggins's theory), Bowlby's attachment theory emphasizes *separation anxiety* as central to humans' (and especially young children's) personality and social development (Gaines, 2020). Lastly, unlike Lewin's (1935, 1948/1967, 1951/1976) field theory (which is rather nonspecific regarding the particular motive or motives that matter the most to humans' interpersonal behavior), Bowlby's theory specifies the need for emotional intimacy as a quintessentially (though not uniquely) human motive (see Mikulincer & Shaver, 2007a, 2016).

Ironically, as we alluded to in the Preface to the present book, key attachment theorists such as Hazan and Shaver (1994a) have been criticized for promoting Bowlby's (1969/1997, 1973/1998, 1980/1998) theory as a single, overarching conceptual framework for all of relationship science. For instance, without directly mentioning Thibaut and Kelley's (1959; Kelley, 1979; Kelley & Thibaut, 1978) interdependence theory, Levinger (1994) questioned the viability of attachment theory—which says considerably less about interpersonal interaction (especially within adult relationships) than it does about individual personality—as such an organizing framework. Instead, Levinger cited Kelley et al.'s *Close Relationships* (1983/2002), which included Levinger as a coauthor, as an alternative framework for understanding relationship dynamics. To their credit, Hazan and Shaver (1994b) acknowledged the criticism from Levinger (among others) in the process of welcoming the integration of attachment theory with additional conceptual perspectives within relationship science. In any event, far from advocating the replacement of Bowlby's attachment theory with Wiggins's (1979, 1991, 2003/2005) interpersonal circumplex theory, we endorse the "culinary" approach that Finkel et al. (2017) advocated for the field.

APPENDIX 1A

Output regarding Creation of Correlation Matrix, Gaines (2021), Main Study 3 (Reduced $n = 345$)

```
DATE: 06/25/2022
TIME: 20:29


P R E L I S  10.2 (64 BIT)


BY


Karl G. Jöreskog & Dag Sörbom


This program is published exclusively by
Scientific Software International, Inc.
http://www.ssicentral.com

Copyright by Scientific Software International, Inc., 1981-2018
Use of this program is subject to the terms specified in the
Universal Copyright Convention.
```

The following lines were read from file H:\My Documents\Statistics\ Social Psychological and Personality Science\wpa2014 DOM NUR POW INT ACC for PRELIS.PRL:

!PRELIS SYNTAX: Can be edited

SY='H:\My Documents\Statistics\Social Psychological and Personality Science\wpa2014 DOM NUR POW INT ACC for PRELIS.LSF'

OU MA=KM SM=WPA2014-TRTMOTAC.COR XT

Number of Missing Values per Variable

PATRT	BCTRT	DETRT	FGTRT	HITRT	JKTRT	LMTRT	NOTRT
9	17	14	11	23	18	11	9

Number of Missing Values per Variable

PANEED	BCNEED	DENEED	FGNEED	HINEED	JKNEED	LMNEED	NONEED
17	15	18	21	12	18	17	17

274 APPENDICES

Number of Missing Values per Variable

EXIT	VOICE	LOYALTY	NEGLECT
43	42	47	42

Distribution of Missing Values

Total Sample Size(N) =   440

Number of Missing Values	0	1	2	3	4	5	6	7	8	9	10
Number of Cases	345	28	11	4	32	0	5	1	5	0	1

Number of Missing Values	11	12	13	14	15	16	17	18	19	20
Number of Cases	0	2	0	0	0	0	0	0	0	6

Listwise Deletion

Total Effective Sample Size =   345

Univariate Summary Statistics for Continuous Variables

Variable	Mean	St. Dev.	Skewness	Kurtosis	Minimum	Freq.	Minimum	Freq.
PATRT	10.368	3.310	0.343	-0.219	4.000	10	20.000	2
BCTRT	9.719	3.301	0.372	-0.193	4.000	18	20.000	1
DETRT	10.693	2.829	0.287	-0.120	4.000	2	20.000	1
FGTRT	11.394	3.356	0.065	-0.309	4.000	8	20.000	3
HITRT	12.794	2.801	-0.242	0.124	4.000	2	20.000	3
JKTRT	14.006	2.627	-0.392	0.590	4.000	1	20.000	6
LMTRT	16.313	2.697	-0.762	0.203	7.000	1	20.000	35
NOTRT	13.843	3.579	-0.398	-0.326	4.000	2	20.000	17
PANEED	12.742	3.124	-0.088	-0.411	4.000	1	20.000	4
BCNEED	9.038	3.518	0.484	-0.361	4.000	35	20.000	1
DENEED	9.678	3.214	0.273	-0.157	4.000	18	20.000	1
FGNEED	11.258	3.553	-0.139	-0.621	4.000	10	20.000	3
HINEED	10.458	3.225	0.234	-0.344	4.000	9	19.000	2
JKNEED	14.345	3.080	-0.500	0.103	4.000	1	20.000	10
LMNEED	13.751	3.080	-0.322	0.178	4.000	2	20.000	10
NONEED	14.012	2.923	-0.289	0.067	4.000	1	20.000	10
EXIT	9.128	6.204	0.952	0.204	3.000	96	27.000	8
VOICE	17.148	5.657	-0.355	-0.173	3.000	8	27.000	19
LOYALTY	14.110	5.202	-0.026	-0.068	3.000	13	27.000	5
NEGLECT	12.409	5.353	0.088	-0.588	3.000	20	27.000	1

APPENDICES 275

Test of Univariate Normality for Continuous Variables

	Skewness		Kurtosis		Skewness and Kurtosis	
Variable	Z-Score	P-Value	Z-Score	P-Value	Chi-Square	P-Value
PATRT	2.579	0.010	-0.833	0.405	7.344	0.025
BCTRT	2.780	0.005	-0.708	0.479	8.228	0.016
DETRT	2.169	0.030	-0.374	0.708	4.843	0.089
FGTRT	0.498	0.618	-1.294	0.196	1.922	0.382
HITRT	-1.838	0.066	0.579	0.563	3.714	0.156
JKTRT	-2.925	0.003	1.940	0.052	12.321	0.002
LMTRT	-5.279	0.000	0.845	0.398	28.582	0.000
NOTRT	-2.967	0.003	-1.386	0.166	10.725	0.005
PANEED	-0.680	0.496	-1.885	0.059	4.017	0.134
BCNEED	3.550	0.000	-1.583	0.113	15.108	0.001
DENEED	2.071	0.038	-0.540	0.589	4.579	0.101
FGNEED	-1.066	0.286	-3.384	0.001	12.586	0.002
HINEED	1.782	0.075	-1.488	0.137	5.388	0.068
JKNEED	-3.656	0.000	0.503	0.615	13.621	0.001
LMNEED	-2.428	0.015	0.761	0.447	6.475	0.039
NONEED	-2.185	0.029	0.375	0.708	4.914	0.086
EXIT	6.309	0.000	0.850	0.396	40.523	0.000
VOICE	-2.660	0.008	-0.614	0.539	7.451	0.024
LOYALTY	-0.199	0.842	-0.152	0.879	0.063	0.969
NEGLECT	0.678	0.498	-3.111	0.002	10.138	0.006

Relative Multivariate Kurtosis = 1.097

Test of Multivariate Normality for Continuous Variables

Skewness			Kurtosis			Skewness and Kurtosis	
Value	Z-Score	P-Value	Value	Z-Score	P-Value	Chi-Square	P-Value
40.580	12.379	0.000	482.575	9.800	0.000	249.279	0.000

Correlation Matrix

	PATRT	BCTRT	DETRT	FGTRT	HITRT	JKTRT
PATRT	1.000					
BCTRT	0.409	1.000				
DETRT	0.165	0.350	1.000			
FGTRT	-0.507	-0.083	0.133	1.000		
HITRT	-0.593	-0.257	-0.095	0.510	1.000	
JKTRT	-0.141	-0.196	-0.244	0.107	0.267	1.000
LMTRT	0.003	-0.180	-0.308	-0.274	0.048	0.403
NOTRT	0.438	-0.077	-0.029	-0.564	-0.259	0.106
PANEED	0.265	0.269	0.176	0.040	-0.078	-0.116
BCNEED	0.360	0.314	0.235	0.017	-0.160	-0.259
DENEED	0.172	0.238	0.170	0.195	-0.083	-0.175
FGNEED	0.034	0.055	0.012	0.193	0.118	-0.058

276 APPENDICES

HINEED	0.118	0.103	-0.008	0.085	-0.036	0.024
JKNEED	0.039	0.007	-0.144	0.038	0.037	0.213
LMNEED	0.081	0.005	-0.065	-0.084	-0.012	0.068
NONEED	0.199	0.132	0.060	-0.120	-0.104	-0.019
EXIT	0.134	0.209	0.060	-0.042	-0.067	-0.018
VOICE	-0.105	-0.184	-0.072	-0.020	0.147	0.074
LOYALTY	-0.009	-0.079	0.000	0.050	0.069	0.076
NEGLECT	0.066	0.186	0.133	0.048	-0.011	-0.004

Correlation Matrix

	LMTRT	NOTRT	PANEED	BCNEED	DENEED	FGNEED
LMTRT	1.000					
NOTRT	0.465	1.000				
PANEED	-0.085	-0.030	1.000			
BCNEED	-0.275	-0.029	0.627	1.000		
DENEED	-0.277	-0.216	0.540	0.698	1.000	
FGNEED	-0.169	-0.248	0.431	0.439	0.556	1.000
HINEED	-0.069	-0.114	0.219	0.335	0.428	0.525
JKNEED	0.245	0.029	0.320	0.102	0.161	0.330
LMNEED	0.165	0.083	0.324	0.129	0.113	0.203
NONEED	0.142	0.108	0.499	0.345	0.249	0.158
EXIT	-0.060	0.052	0.229	0.232	0.265	0.124
VOICE	0.143	0.090	-0.106	-0.147	-0.216	-0.072
LOYALTY	0.030	-0.017	0.088	0.068	0.021	0.043
NEGLECT	-0.118	-0.135	0.189	0.202	0.207	0.201

Correlation Matrix

	HINEED	JKNEED	LMNEED	NONEED	EXIT	VOICE
HINEED	1.000					
JKNEED	0.538	1.000				
LMNEED	0.289	0.644	1.000			
NONEED	0.244	0.467	0.607	1.000		
EXIT	0.099	0.129	0.099	0.085	1.000	
VOICE	-0.150	-0.056	-0.028	-0.040	-0.203	1.000
LOYALTY	0.081	0.092	-0.016	0.044	-0.131	0.315
NEGLECT	0.153	0.083	0.043	-0.007	0.502	-0.231

Correlation Matrix

	LOYALTY	NEGLECT
LOYALTY	1.000	
NEGLECT	0.055	1.000

Total Variance = 20.000 Generalized Variance = 0.366191D-03

APPENDICES 277

```
Largest Eigenvalue = 4.186 Smallest Eigenvalue = 0.208

Condition Number = 4.491

Means
            PATRT     BCTRT    DETRT     FGTRT    HITRT    JKTRT
        ---------------------------------------------------------------
            10.368    9.719    10.693    11.394   12.794   14.006
Means
            LMTRT     NOTRT    PANEED    BCNEED   DENEED   FGNEED
        ---------------------------------------------------------------
            16.313    13.843   12.742    9.038    9.678    11.258
Means
            HINEED    JKNEED   LMNEED    NONEED   EXIT     VOICE
        ---------------------------------------------------------------
            10.458    14.345   13.751    14.012   9.128    17.148
Means
            LOYALTY   NEGLECT
        -------------------------
            14.110    12.409
Standard Deviations
            PATRT     BCTRT    DETRT     FGTRT    HITRT    JKTRT
        ---------------------------------------------------------------
            3.310     3.301    2.829     3.356    2.801    2.627
Standard Deviations
            LMTRT     NOTRT    PANEED    BCNEED   DENEED   FGNEED
        ---------------------------------------------------------------
            2.697     3.579    3.124     3.518    3.214    3.553
Standard Deviations
            HINEED    JKNEED   LMNEED    NONEED   EXIT     VOICE
        ---------------------------------------------------------------
            3.225     3.080    3.080     2.923    6.204    5.657
Standard Deviations
            LOYALTY   NEGLECT
        -------------------------
            5.202     5.353

The Problem used 40608 Bytes (= 0.0% of available workspace)
```

APPENDIX 1B

Output regarding Initial Covariance Structure Analysis, Gaines (2021), Main Study 3 (Reduced $n = 345$)

```
DATE:  6/25/2022
TIME:  20:31


L I S R E L  10.2 (64 Bit)


BY


Karl G. Jöreskog & Dag Sörbom


This program is published exclusively by
Scientific Software International, Inc.
http://www.ssicentral.com

Copyright by Scientific Software International, Inc., 1981-2019
Use of this program is subject to the terms specified in the
Universal Copyright Convention.


The following lines were read from file H:\My Documents\Statistics\
Social Psychological and Personality Science\wpa2014 DOM NUR POW INT
ACC without GEN.spl:


WPA2014 COVARIANCE AMONG DOMINANCE, NURTURANCE, POWER, INTIMACY, AND
ACCOMMODATION
DA NI=20 NO=345 MA=KM
KM FI=WPA2014-TRTMOTAC.COR
MO NY=20 NE=5 TE=SY,FI LY=FU,FI PS=SY,FI BE=FU,FI
FR TE 1 1 TE 2 2 TE 3 3 TE 4 4 TE 5 5 TE 6 6 TE 7 7 TE 8 8
FR TE 9 9 TE 10 10 TE 11 11 TE 12 12 TE 13 13 TE 14 14 TE 15 15 TE 16 16
FR TE 17 17 TE 18 18 TE 19 19 TE 20 20
FR LY 1 1 LY 7 2
FR LY 2 1 LY 8 1 LY 6 2 LY 8 2
FR LY 5 1 LY 3 2
FR LY 4 1 LY 6 1 LY 2 2 LY 4 2
FR LY 9 3 LY 15 4
FR LY 10 3 LY 16 3 LY 14 4 LY 16 4
FR LY 13 3 LY 11 4
```

280 APPENDICES

```
FR LY 12 3 LY 14 3 LY 10 4 LY 12 4
EQ LY 1 1 LY 7 2
EQ LY 2 1 LY 8 1 LY 6 2 LY 8 2
EQ LY 5 1 LY 3 2
EQ LY 4 1 LY 6 1 LY 2 2 LY 4 2
EQ LY 9 3 LY 15 4
EQ LY 10 3 LY 16 3 LY 14 4 LY 16 4
EQ LY 13 3 LY 11 4
EQ LY 12 3 LY 14 3 LY 10 4 LY 12 4
ST 1.00 LY 1 1
ST .71 LY 2 1
ST -.71 LY 4 1
ST -1.00 LY 5 1
ST 1.00 LY 9 3
ST .71 LY 10 3
ST -.71 LY 12 3
ST -1.00 LY 13 3
ST -1.00 LY 17 5
FR LY 18 5 LY 19 5 LY 20 5
ST 1.00 PS 1 1 PS 2 2 PS 3 3 PS 4 4
FR PS 5 5
FR BE 5 1 BE 5 2 BE 5 3 BE 5 4
OU ALL ME=ML RO RC AD=OFF
```

PA2014 COVARIANCE AMONG DOMINANCE, NURTURANCE, POWER, INTIMACY, AND ACCOMMODAT

```
            Number of Input Variables 20
            Number of Y - Variables   20
            Number of X - Variables    0
            Number of ETA - Variables  5
            Number of KSI - Variables  0
            Number of Observations   345
```

WPA2014 COVARIANCE AMONG DOMINANCE, NURTURANCE, POWER, INTIMACY, AND ACCOMMODAT

Covariance Matrix

	VAR 1	VAR 2	VAR 3	VAR 4	VAR 5	VAR 6
VAR 1	2.000					
VAR 2	0.409	2.000				
VAR 3	0.165	0.350	2.000			
VAR 4	-0.507	-0.083	0.133	2.000		
VAR 5	-0.593	-0.257	-0.095	0.510	2.000	
VAR 6	-0.141	-0.196	-0.244	0.107	0.267	2.000
VAR 7	0.003	-0.180	-0.308	-0.274	0.048	0.403
VAR 8	0.438	-0.077	-0.029	-0.564	-0.259	0.106
VAR 9	0.265	0.269	0.176	0.040	-0.078	-0.116

VAR 10	0.360	0.314	0.234	0.017	-0.160	-0.259
VAR 11	0.172	0.238	0.170	0.195	-0.083	-0.175
VAR 12	0.034	0.055	0.012	0.193	0.118	-0.058
VAR 13	0.118	0.103	-0.008	0.085	-0.036	0.024
VAR 14	0.039	0.007	-0.144	0.038	0.037	0.213
VAR 15	0.081	0.005	-0.065	-0.084	-0.012	0.068
VAR 16	0.199	0.132	0.060	-0.120	-0.104	-0.019
VAR 17	0.134	0.209	0.060	-0.042	-0.067	-0.018
VAR 18	-0.105	-0.184	-0.072	-0.020	0.147	0.074
VAR 19	-0.009	-0.079	0.000	0.050	0.069	0.076
VAR 20	0.066	0.186	0.133	0.048	-0.011	-0.004

Covariance Matrix

	VAR 7	VAR 8	VAR 9	VAR 10	VAR 11	VAR 12
VAR 7	2.000					
VAR 8	0.465	2.000				
VAR 9	-0.085	-0.030	2.000			
VAR 10	-0.275	-0.029	0.627	2.000		
VAR 11	-0.277	-0.216	0.540	0.698	2.000	
VAR 12	-0.169	-0.248	0.431	0.439	0.556	2.000
VAR 13	-0.069	-0.114	0.219	0.335	0.428	0.525
VAR 14	0.245	0.029	0.320	0.102	0.161	0.330
VAR 15	0.165	0.083	0.324	0.129	0.113	0.203
VAR 16	0.142	0.108	0.499	0.345	0.249	0.158
VAR 17	-0.060	0.052	0.229	0.232	0.265	0.124
VAR 18	0.143	0.090	-0.106	-0.147	-0.216	-0.072
VAR 19	0.030	-0.017	0.088	0.068	0.021	0.043
VAR 20	-0.118	-0.135	0.189	0.202	0.207	0.201

Covariance Matrix

	VAR 13	VAR 14	VAR 15	VAR 16	VAR 17	VAR 18
VAR 13	2.000					
VAR 14	0.538	2.000				
VAR 15	0.289	0.644	2.000			
VAR 16	0.244	0.467	0.607	2.000		
VAR 17	0.099	0.129	0.099	0.085	2.000	
VAR 18	-0.150	-0.056	-0.028	-0.040	-0.203	2.000
VAR 19	0.081	0.092	-0.016	0.044	-0.131	0.315
VAR 20	0.153	0.083	0.043	-0.007	0.502	-0.231

Covariance Matrix

	VAR 19	VAR 20
VAR 19	2.000	
VAR 20	0.055	2.000

282 APPENDICES

Total Variance = 40.000 Generalized Variance = 161539.541

Largest Eigenvalue = 5.186 Smallest Eigenvalue = 1.208

Condition Number = 2.072

WPA2014 COVARIANCE AMONG DOMINANCE, NURTURANCE, POWER, INTIMACY, AND ACCOMMODAT

Parameter Specifications

LAMBDA-Y

	ETA 1	ETA 2	ETA 3	ETA 4	ETA 5
VAR 1	1	0	0	0	0
VAR 2	2	3	0	0	0
VAR 3	0	4	0	0	0
VAR 4	3	3	0	0	0
VAR 5	4	0	0	0	0
VAR 6	3	2	0	0	0
VAR 7	0	1	0	0	0
VAR 8	2	2	0	0	0
VAR 9	0	0	5	0	0
VAR 10	0	0	6	7	0
VAR 11	0	0	0	8	0
VAR 12	0	0	7	7	0
VAR 13	0	0	8	0	0
VAR 14	0	0	7	6	0
VAR 15	0	0	0	5	0
VAR 16	0	0	6	6	0
VAR 17	0	0	0	0	0
VAR 18	0	0	0	0	9
VAR 19	0	0	0	0	10
VAR 20	0	0	0	0	11

BETA

	ETA 1	ETA 2	ETA 3	ETA 4	ETA 5
ETA 1	0	0	0	0	0
ETA 2	0	0	0	0	0
ETA 3	0	0	0	0	0
ETA 4	0	0	0	0	0
ETA 5	12	13	14	15	0

PSI

ETA 1	ETA 2	ETA 3	ETA 4	ETA 5
0	0	0	0	16

THETA-EPS

	VAR 1	VAR 2	VAR 3	VAR 4	VAR 5	VAR 6
	17	18	19	20	21	22

THETA-EPS

	VAR 7	VAR 8	VAR 9	VAR 10	VAR 11	VAR 12
	23	24	25	26	27	28

THETA-EPS

	VAR 13	VAR 14	VAR 15	VAR 16	VAR 17	VAR 18
	29	30	31	32	33	34

THETA-EPS

	VAR 19	VAR 20
	35	36

WPA2014 COVARIANCE AMONG DOMINANCE, NURTURANCE, POWER, INTIMACY, AND ACCOMMODAT

Initial Estimates (TSLS)

LAMBDA-Y

	ETA 1	ETA 2	ETA 3	ETA 4	ETA 5
VAR 1	1.000	- -	- -	- -	- -
VAR 2	0.710	-0.710	- -	- -	- -
VAR 3	- -	-1.000	- -	- -	- -
VAR 4	-0.710	-0.710	- -	- -	- -
VAR 5	-1.000	- -	- -	- -	- -
VAR 6	-0.710	0.710	- -	- -	- -
VAR 7	- -	1.000	- -	- -	- -
VAR 8	0.710	0.710	- -	- -	- -
VAR 9	- -	- -	1.000	- -	- -
VAR 10	- -	- -	0.710	-0.710	- -
VAR 11	- -	- -	- -	-1.000	- -
VAR 12	- -	- -	-0.710	-0.710	- -
VAR 13	- -	- -	-1.000	- -	- -
VAR 14	- -	- -	-0.710	0.710	- -
VAR 15	- -	- -	- -	1.000	- -
VAR 16	- -	- -	0.710	0.710	- -

284 APPENDICES

```
VAR 17        - -         - -         - -         - -      -1.000
VAR 18        - -         - -         - -         - -       0.637
VAR 19        - -         - -         - -         - -       0.024
VAR 20        - -         - -         - -         - -      -0.751
```

BETA

	ETA 1	ETA 2	ETA 3	ETA 4	ETA 5
ETA 1	- -	- -	- -	- -	- -
ETA 2	- -	- -	- -	- -	- -
ETA 3	- -	- -	- -	- -	- -
ETA 4	- -	- -	- -	- -	- -
ETA 5	0.500	0.500	0.500	0.500	- -

Covariance Matrix of ETA
Note: This matrix is diagonal.

ETA 1	ETA 2	ETA 3	ETA 4	ETA 5
1.000	1.000	1.000	1.000	0.520

PSI
Note: This matrix is diagonal.

ETA 1	ETA 2	ETA 3	ETA 4	ETA 5
1.000	1.000	1.000	1.000	0.520

NOTE: R^2 for Structural Equatios are Hayduk's (2006) Blocked-Error R^2

Squared Multiple Correlations for Reduced Form

ETA 1	ETA 2	ETA 3	ETA 4	ETA 5
- -	- -	- -	- -	-1.923

THETA-EPS

VAR 1	VAR 2	VAR 3	VAR 4	VAR 5	VAR 6
1.520	1.597	1.633	1.550	1.520	1.597

THETA-EPS

	VAR 7	VAR 8	VAR 9	VAR 10	VAR 11	VAR 12
	1.633	1.550	1.965	1.859	1.826	1.929

THETA-EPS

	VAR 13	VAR 14	VAR 15	VAR 16	VAR 17	VAR 18
	1.965	1.859	1.826	1.929	1.480	1.789

THETA-EPS

	VAR 19	VAR 20
	2.000	1.707

Behavior under Minimization Iterations

Iter	Try	Abscissa	Slope	Function
1	0	0.00000000D+00	-0.57371597D+00	0.11025675D+01
	1	0.10000000D+01	-0.20044292D+00	0.68422618D+00
	2	0.20000000D+01	0.28384545D+00	0.75769982D+00
	3	0.14138917D+01	0.41837792D-01	0.65111110D+00
2	0	0.00000000D+00	-0.45096206D-01	0.65111110D+00
	1	0.14138917D+01	0.21023284D-01	0.63723386D+00
	2	0.96433214D+00	0.28180490D-02	0.63178873D+00
3	0	0.00000000D+00	-0.78385828D-02	0.63178873D+00
	1	0.96433214D+00	-0.11299457D-01	0.62251845D+00
	2	0.19286643D+01	-0.13954265D-01	0.61025646D+00
	3	0.38573286D+01	-0.15216155D-01	0.58114655D+00
	4	0.77146571D+01	-0.14561215D-03	0.54494340D+00
4	0	0.00000000D+00	-0.75850259D-02	0.54494340D+00
	1	0.77146571D+01	0.58554469D-01	0.74070478D+00
	2	0.88473421D+00	-0.83527594D-03	0.54114673D+00
	3	0.98079238D+00	-0.49113030D-04	0.54110419D+00
5	0	0.00000000D+00	-0.65600257D-02	0.54110419D+00
	1	0.98079238D+00	-0.63512740D-02	0.53477255D+00
	2	0.19615848D+01	-0.61427399D-02	0.52864555D+00
	3	0.39231695D+01	-0.57261030D-02	0.51700475D+00
	4	0.78463391D+01	-0.48931881D-02	0.49617395D+00
	5	0.15692678D+02	-0.32196515D-02	0.46433505D+00
	6	0.31385356D+02	0.22411304D-03	0.44059297D+00
6	0	0.00000000D+00	-0.62175283D-02	0.44059297D+00
	1	0.31385356D+02	0.23346789D-01	0.64994742D+00

	2	0.66005023D+01	-0.18567160D-02	0.41349809D+00
	3	0.84263768D+01	-0.49718674D-03	0.41133814D+00
7	0	0.00000000D+00	-0.51852922D-02	0.41133814D+00
	1	0.84263768D+01	0.20165198D-01	0.45209472D+00
	2	0.17235653D+01	-0.21443041D-02	0.40493577D+00
	3	0.23678140D+01	-0.83806413D-03	0.40396943D+00
	4	0.26095604D+01	-0.31973422D-03	0.40382916D+00
8	0	0.00000000D+00	-0.30235968D-02	0.40382916D+00
	1	0.26095604D+01	0.75798234D-03	0.40086439D+00
	2	0.20864983D+01	-0.32210485D-05	0.40066707D+00
9	0	0.00000000D+00	-0.14316433D-02	0.40066707D+00
	1	0.20864983D+01	0.75425551D-03	0.39997117D+00
	2	0.13665415D+01	0.70859149D-05	0.39969663D+00
10	0	0.00000000D+00	-0.50532956D-03	0.39969663D+00
	1	0.13665415D+01	0.32934061D-04	0.39937458D+00
11	0	0.00000000D+00	-0.22493315D-03	0.39937458D+00
	1	0.13665415D+01	-0.73902174D-04	0.39917020D+00
	2	0.27330829D+01	0.78888470D-04	0.39917340D+00
	3	0.20275138D+01	-0.22377384D-06	0.39914568D+00
12	0	0.00000000D+00	-0.77323732D-04	0.39914568D+00
	1	0.20275138D+01	0.34315876D-04	0.39910213D+00
	2	0.14042949D+01	0.30245467D-07	0.39909143D+00
13	0	0.00000000D+00	-0.28006771D-04	0.39909143D+00
	1	0.14042949D+01	0.55369473D-05	0.39907568D+00
	2	0.11724927D+01	0.19044528D-07	0.39907504D+00
14	0	0.00000000D+00	-0.62539965D-05	0.39907504D+00
	1	0.11724927D+01	-0.96122224D-06	0.39907081D+00
	2	0.23449854D+01	0.43207122D-05	0.39907278D+00
	3	0.13858665D+01	0.80637018D-09	0.39907071D+00
15	0	0.00000000D+00	-0.23986291D-05	0.39907071D+00
	1	0.13858665D+01	-0.97871078D-07	0.39906898D+00
16	0	0.00000000D+00	-0.37204486D-06	0.39906898D+00
	1	0.13858665D+01	-0.22180554D-07	0.39906870D+00
17	0	0.00000000D+00	-0.12059422D-06	0.39906870D+00
	1	0.13858665D+01	-0.77049511D-07	0.39906857D+00
	2	0.27717329D+01	-0.33459115D-07	0.39906849D+00
	3	0.55434658D+01	0.53859109D-07	0.39906852D+00
	4	0.38338220D+01	-0.21681633D-10	0.39906847D+00
18	0	0.00000000D+00	-0.79014302D-07	0.39906847D+00
	1	0.38338220D+01	-0.17728934D-07	0.39906829D+00
	2	0.76676439D+01	0.43620890D-07	0.39906834D+00
	3	0.49417237D+01	-0.66240667D-11	0.39906828D+00
19	0	0.00000000D+00	-0.35092123D-07	0.39906828D+00
	1	0.49417237D+01	0.39777850D-07	0.39906829D+00
	2	0.23162233D+01	0.91127851D-11	0.39906824D+00
20	0	0.00000000D+00	-0.11002846D-07	0.39906824D+00
	1	0.23162233D+01	-0.49538169D-09	0.39906822D+00
21	0	0.00000000D+00	-0.58681600D-08	0.39906822D+00
	1	0.23162233D+01	-0.37100350D-08	0.39906821D+00
	2	0.46324466D+01	-0.15515968D-08	0.39906821D+00
	3	0.92648932D+01	0.27662279D-08	0.39906821D+00
	4	0.62971018D+01	-0.14611119D-12	0.39906821D+00
22	0	0.00000000D+00	-0.44821791D-08	0.39906821D+00

	1	0.62971018D+01	-0.12426112D-08	0.39906819D+00
	2	0.12594204D+02	0.19999222D-08	0.39906819D+00
	3	0.87102919D+01	-0.35078546D-12	0.39906819D+00
23	0	0.00000000D+00	-0.20781585D-08	0.39906819D+00
	1	0.87102919D+01	0.70519643D-08	0.39906821D+00
	2	0.19825984D+01	0.58356808D-13	0.39906818D+00
24	0	0.00000000D+00	-0.34102698D-09	0.39906818D+00
	1	0.19825984D+01	0.14715829D-09	0.39906818D+00
	2	0.13849651D+01	0.39965452D-14	0.39906818D+00
25	0	0.00000000D+00	-0.65451895D-10	0.39906818D+00
	1	0.13849651D+01	-0.11158396D-10	0.39906818D+00
	2	0.27699302D+01	0.43135390D-10	0.39906818D+00
	3	0.16696015D+01	-0.23415589D-16	0.39906818D+00
26	0	0.00000000D+00	-0.14748358D-10	0.39906818D+00
	1	0.16696015D+01	-0.51933981D-12	0.39906818D+00

WPA2014 COVARIANCE AMONG DOMINANCE, NURTURANCE, POWER, INTIMACY, AND ACCOMMODAT

Number of Iterations = 26

LISREL Estimates (Maximum Likelihood)

LAMBDA-Y

	ETA 1	ETA 2	ETA 3	ETA 4	ETA 5
VAR 1	0.803	- -	- -	- -	- -
	(0.081)				
	9.873				
VAR 2	0.464	-0.425	- -	- -	- -
	(0.052)	(0.051)			
	8.922	-8.330			
VAR 3	- -	-0.574	- -	- -	- -
		(0.074)			
		-7.705			
VAR 4	-0.425	-0.425	- -	- -	- -
		(0.051)	(0.051)		
		-8.330	-8.330		
VAR 5	-0.574	- -	- -	- -	- -
		(0.074)			
		-7.705			
VAR 6	-0.425	0.464	- -	- -	- -
	(0.051)	(0.052)			
	-8.330	8.922			
VAR 7	- -	0.803	- -	- -	- -
	(0.081)				
	9.873				
VAR 8	0.464	0.464	- -	- -	- -
	(0.052)	(0.052)			
	8.922	8.922			

288 APPENDICES

VAR 9	- -	- -	0.900 (0.092) 9.774	- -	- -
VAR 10	- -	- -	0.521 (0.052) 10.051	0.273 (0.048) 5.661	- -
VAR 11	- -	- -	- -	0.324 (0.075) 4.308	- -
VAR 12	- -	- -	0.273 (0.048) 5.661	0.273 (0.048) 5.661	- -
VAR 13	- -	- -	0.324 (0.075) 4.308	- -	- -
VAR 14	- -	- -	0.273 (0.048) 5.661	0.521 (0.052) 10.051	- -
VAR 15	- -	- -	- - (0.092) 9.774	0.900	- -
VAR 16	- -	- -	0.521 (0.052) 10.051	0.521 (0.052) 10.051	- -
VAR 17	- -	- -	- -	- -	-1.000
VAR 18	- -	- -	- -	- -	0.525 (0.209) 2.506
VAR 19	- -	- -	- -	- -	0.165 (0.168) 0.985
VAR 20	- -	- -	- -	- -	-0.924 (0.336) -2.747

BETA

	ETA 1	ETA 2	ETA 3	ETA 4	ETA 5
ETA 1	- -	- -	- -	- -	- -
ETA 2	- -	- -	- -	- -	- -
ETA 3	- -	- -	- -	- -	- -
ETA 4	- -	- -	- -	- -	- -
ETA 5	-0.098	0.153 (0.081) -1.203	-0.183 (0.085) 1.811	-0.077 (0.088) -2.073	- - (0.083) -0.929

APPENDICES 289

Covariance Matrix of ETA

	ETA 1	ETA 2	ETA 3	ETA 4	ETA 5
ETA 1	1.000				
ETA 2	- -	1.000			
ETA 3	- -	- -	1.000		
ETA 4	- -	- -	- -	1.000	
ETA 5	-0.098	0.153	-0.183	-0.077	0.501

PSI
Note: This matrix is diagonal.

ETA 1	ETA 2	ETA 3	ETA 4	ETA 5
1.000	1.000	1.000	1.000	0.428
				(0.192)
				2.232

Squared Multiple Correlations for Structural Equations

ETA 1	ETA 2	ETA 3	ETA 4	ETA 5
- -	- -	- -	- -	0.145

NOTE: R^2 for Structural Equatios are Hayduk's (2006) Blocked-Error R^2

THETA-EPS

VAR 1	VAR 2	VAR 3	VAR 4	VAR 5	VAR 6
1.301	1.659	1.765	1.540	1.586	1.709
(0.154)	(0.146)	(0.154)	(0.140)	(0.141)	(0.150)
8.446	11.327	11.447	11.018	11.250	11.388

THETA-EPS

VAR 7	VAR 8	VAR 9	VAR 10	VAR 11	VAR 12
1.413	1.521	1.181	1.623	1.918	1.787
(0.161)	(0.144)	(0.181)	(0.138)	(0.152)	(0.142)
8.752	10.564	6.530	11.783	12.613	12.583

290 APPENDICES

THETA-EPS

VAR 13	VAR 14	VAR 15	VAR 16	VAR 17	VAR 18
1.872	1.588	1.200	1.484	1.491	1.860
(0.149)	(0.135)	(0.183)	(0.142)	(0.220)	(0.157)
12.607	11.728	6.553	10.452	6.779	11.840

THETA-EPS

VAR 19	VAR 20
1.986	1.565
(0.153)	(0.201)
13.018	7.769

Squared Multiple Correlations for Y - Variables

VAR 1	VAR 2	VAR 3	VAR 4	VAR 5	VAR 6
0.331	0.193	0.157	0.190	0.172	0.188

Squared Multiple Correlations for Y - Variables

VAR 7	VAR 8	VAR 9	VAR 10	VAR 11	VAR 12
0.313	0.221	0.407	0.175	0.052	0.077

Squared Multiple Correlations for Y - Variables

VAR 13	VAR 14	VAR 15	VAR 16	VAR 17	VAR 18
0.053	0.179	0.403	0.268	0.251	0.069

Squared Multiple Correlations for Y - Variables

VAR 19	VAR 20
0.007	0.215

Log-likelihood Values

	Estimated Model	Saturated Model
Number of free parameters(t)	36	210
$-2\ln(L)$	11312.771	11037.414
AIC (Akaike, 1974)*	11384.771	11457.414
BIC (Schwarz, 1978)*	11523.139	12264.559

*LISREL uses AIC= $2t - 2\ln(L)$ and BIC = $t\ln(N) - 2\ln(L)$

APPENDICES 291

Goodness-of-Fit Statistics

Degrees of Freedom for (C1)-(C2)	174
Maximum Likelihood Ratio Chi-Square (C1)	275.357 (P = 0.0000)
Browne's (1984) ADF Chi-Square (C2_NT)	297.398 (P = 0.0000)
Estimated Non-centrality Parameter (NCP)	101.357
90 Percent Confidence Interval for NCP	(60.129 ; 150.516)
Minimum Fit Function Value	0.798
Population Discrepancy Function Value (F0)	0.294
90 Percent Confidence Interval for F0	(0.174 ; 0.436)
Root Mean Square Error of Approximation (RMSEA)	0.0411
90 Percent Confidence Interval for RMSEA	(0.0316 ; 0.0501)
P-Value for Test of Close Fit (RMSEA < 0.05)	0.949
Expected Cross-Validation Index (ECVI)	1.007
90 Percent Confidence Interval for ECVI	(0.887 ; 1.149)
ECVI for Saturated Model	1.217
ECVI for Independence Model	1.986
Chi-Square for Independence Model (190 df)	645.301
Normed Fit Index (NFI)	0.573
Non-Normed Fit Index (NNFI)	0.757
Parsimony Normed Fit Index (PNFI)	0.525
Comparative Fit Index (CFI)	0.777
Incremental Fit Index (IFI)	0.785
Relative Fit Index (RFI)	0.534
Critical N (CN)	276.236
Root Mean Square Residual (RMR)	0.146
Standardized RMR	0.0733
Goodness of Fit Index (GFI)	0.921
Adjusted Goodness of Fit Index (AGFI)	0.904
Parsimony Goodness of Fit Index (PGFI)	0.763

WPA2014 COVARIANCE AMONG DOMINANCE, NURTURANCE, POWER, INTIMACY, AND ACCOMMODAT

Fitted Covariance Matrix

	VAR 1	VAR 2	VAR 3	VAR 4	VAR 5	VAR 6
VAR 1	1.945					
VAR 2	0.373	2.055				
VAR 3	- -	0.244	2.094			
VAR 4	-0.341	-0.017	0.244	1.901		
VAR 5	-0.461	-0.266	- -	0.244	1.915	
VAR 6	-0.341	-0.395	-0.266	-0.017	0.244	2.105
VAR 7	- -	-0.341	-0.461	-0.341	- -	0.373
VAR 8	0.373	0.018	-0.266	-0.395	-0.266	0.018
VAR 9	- -	- -	- -	- -	- -	- -
VAR 10	- -	- -	- -	- -	- -	- -
VAR 11	- -	- -	- -	- -	- -	- -
VAR 12	- -	- -	- -	- -	- -	- -
VAR 13	- -	- -	- -	- -	- -	- -
VAR 14	- -	- -	- -	- -	- -	- -

292 APPENDICES

	VAR	VAR	VAR	VAR	VAR	VAR
VAR 15	- -	- -	- -	- -	- -	- -
VAR 16	- -	- -	- -	- -	- -	- -
VAR 17	0.078	0.110	0.088	0.024	-0.056	-0.113
VAR 18	-0.041	-0.058	-0.046	-0.012	0.029	0.059
VAR 19	-0.013	-0.018	-0.015	-0.004	0.009	0.019
VAR 20	0.072	0.102	0.081	0.022	-0.052	-0.104

Fitted Covariance Matrix

	VAR 7	VAR 8	VAR 9	VAR 10	VAR 11	VAR 12
VAR 7	2.057					
VAR 8	0.373	1.952				
VAR 9	- -	- -	1.990			
VAR 10	- -	- -	0.468	1.969		
VAR 11	- -	- -	- -	0.088	2.023	
VAR 12	- -	- -	0.245	0.216	0.088	1.936
VAR 13	- -	- -	0.292	0.169	- -	0.088
VAR 14	- -	- -	0.245	0.284	0.169	0.216
VAR 15	- -	- -	- -	0.245	0.292	0.245
VAR 16	- -	- -	0.468	0.413	0.169	0.284
VAR 17	-0.123	-0.026	0.164	0.116	0.025	0.071
VAR 18	0.065	0.014	-0.086	-0.061	-0.013	-0.037
VAR 19	0.020	0.004	-0.027	-0.019	-0.004	-0.012
VAR 20	-0.114	-0.024	0.152	0.107	0.023	0.066

Fitted Covariance Matrix

	VAR 13	VAR 14	VAR 15	VAR 16	VAR 17	VAR 18
VAR 13	1.978					
VAR 14	0.088	1.934				
VAR 15	- -	0.468	2.010			
VAR 16	0.169	0.413	0.468	2.026		
VAR 17	0.059	0.090	0.070	0.135	1.992	
VAR 18	-0.031	-0.047	-0.037	-0.071	-0.263	1.998
VAR 19	-0.010	-0.015	-0.012	-0.022	-0.083	0.043
VAR 20	0.055	0.083	0.064	0.125	0.463	-0.243

Fitted Covariance Matrix

	VAR 19	VAR 20
VAR 19	2.000	
VAR 20	-0.076	1.993

APPENDICES 293

Fitted Residuals

	VAR 1	VAR 2	VAR 3	VAR 4	VAR 5	VAR 6
VAR 1	0.055					
VAR 2	0.036	-0.055				
VAR 3	0.165	0.106	-0.094			
VAR 4	-0.166	-0.066	-0.111	0.099		
VAR 5	-0.132	0.010	-0.095	0.266	0.085	
VAR 6	0.201	0.199	0.023	0.124	0.023	-0.105
VAR 7	0.003	0.162	0.153	0.067	0.048	0.030
VAR 8	0.065	-0.095	0.237	-0.169	0.007	0.088
VAR 9	0.265	0.269	0.176	0.040	-0.078	-0.116
VAR 10	0.360	0.314	0.234	0.017	-0.160	-0.259
VAR 11	0.172	0.238	0.170	0.195	-0.083	-0.175
VAR 12	0.034	0.055	0.012	0.193	0.118	-0.058
VAR 13	0.118	0.103	-0.008	0.085	-0.036	0.024
VAR 14	0.039	0.007	-0.144	0.038	0.037	0.213
VAR 15	0.081	0.005	-0.065	-0.084	-0.012	0.068
VAR 16	0.199	0.132	0.060	-0.120	-0.104	-0.019
VAR 17	0.055	0.099	-0.028	-0.066	-0.011	0.094
VAR 18	-0.064	-0.126	-0.026	-0.007	0.118	0.015
VAR 19	0.004	-0.061	0.014	0.054	0.060	0.057
VAR 20	-0.006	0.084	0.052	0.026	0.041	0.100

Fitted Residuals

	VAR 7	VAR 8	VAR 9	VAR 10	VAR 11	VAR 12
VAR 7	-0.057					
VAR 8	0.092	0.048				
VAR 9	-0.085	-0.030	0.010			
VAR 10	-0.275	-0.029	0.158	0.031		
VAR 11	-0.277	-0.216	0.540	0.610	-0.023	
VAR 12	-0.169	-0.248	0.186	0.223	0.468	0.064
VAR 13	-0.069	-0.114	-0.072	0.166	0.428	0.437
VAR 14	0.245	0.029	0.075	-0.182	-0.008	0.114
VAR 15	0.165	0.083	0.324	-0.117	-0.179	-0.043
VAR 16	0.142	0.108	0.031	-0.068	0.080	-0.126
VAR 17	0.063	0.078	0.065	0.115	0.240	0.053
VAR 18	0.078	0.076	-0.020	-0.086	-0.203	-0.035
VAR 19	0.010	-0.021	0.115	0.087	0.025	0.055
VAR 20	-0.004	-0.111	0.037	0.095	0.183	0.135

Fitted Residuals

	VAR 13	VAR 14	VAR 15	VAR 16	VAR 17	VAR 18
VAR 13	0.022					
VAR 14	0.450	0.066				
VAR 15	0.289	0.176	-0.010			

294 APPENDICES

```
VAR 16      0.075      0.054      0.139     -0.026
VAR 17      0.040      0.039      0.030     -0.051      0.008
VAR 18     -0.119     -0.009      0.009      0.031      0.060      0.002
VAR 19      0.091      0.107     -0.005      0.067     -0.049      0.271
VAR 20      0.099     -0.001     -0.022     -0.132      0.039      0.011
```

Fitted Residuals

```
              VAR 19      VAR 20
           ------------------------
VAR 19      0.000
VAR 20      0.132       0.007
```

Summary Statistics for Fitted Residuals

```
Smallest Fitted Residual =     -0.277
  Median Fitted Residual =      0.037
 Largest Fitted Residual =      0.610
```

Stemleaf Plot

```
- 2|8865
- 2|20
- 1|8887776
- 1|4333322221111000
- 0|99888877777766666655
- 0|444333332222211111111110000000
0|1111111111112222223333333334444444444
0|5555555555666666666677777888888889999999
1|00000011111222223444
1|56677777888999
2|0001234444
2|67779
3|12
3|6
4|34
4|57
5|4
5|
6|1
```

Standardized Residuals

```
              VAR 1      VAR 2      VAR 3      VAR 4      VAR 5      VAR 6
           -----------------------------------------------------------------
VAR 1       0.435
VAR 2       0.330     -0.352
VAR 3       1.520      0.940     -0.588
```

VAR 4	-1.576	-0.622	-1.033	0.682	
VAR 5	-1.236	0.091	-0.884	2.567	0.586
VAR 6	1.816	1.814	0.198	1.150	0.224	-0.658
VAR 7	0.031	1.440	1.333	0.619	0.447	0.266
VAR 8	0.606	-0.888	2.096	-1.598	0.070	0.809
VAR 9	2.499	2.472	1.603	0.381	-0.741	-1.056
VAR 10	3.417	2.900	2.145	0.163	-1.531	-2.359
VAR 11	1.612	2.166	1.532	1.842	-0.780	-1.578
VAR 12	0.329	0.510	0.108	1.872	1.134	-0.537
VAR 13	1.114	0.950	-0.071	0.817	-0.343	0.222
VAR 14	0.369	0.062	-1.325	0.368	0.353	1.959
VAR 15	0.760	0.047	-0.587	-0.799	-0.117	0.615
VAR 16	1.862	1.199	0.540	-1.137	-0.982	-0.170
VAR 17	0.523	0.913	-0.253	-0.630	-0.107	0.851
VAR 18	-0.601	-1.158	-0.238	-0.070	1.119	0.136
VAR 19	0.036	-0.556	0.131	0.510	0.571	0.519
VAR 20	-0.061	0.768	0.474	0.247	0.385	0.931

Standardized Residuals

	VAR 7	VAR 8	VAR 9	VAR 10	VAR 11	VAR 12
VAR 7	-0.366					
VAR 8	0.840	- -				
VAR 9	-0.776	-0.282	0.065			
VAR 10	-2.542	-0.276	1.446	0.209		
VAR 11	-2.526	-2.019	5.001	5.668	-0.149	
VAR 12	-1.572	-2.373	1.744	2.111	4.386	0.433
VAR 13	-0.639	-1.082	-0.666	1.564	3.974	4.141
VAR 14	2.277	0.281	0.703	-1.715	-0.076	1.074
VAR 15	1.509	0.781	3.013	-1.081	-1.628	-0.397
VAR 16	1.294	1.006	0.276	-0.621	0.729	-1.172
VAR 17	0.577	0.736	0.604	1.080	2.214	0.487
VAR 18	0.717	0.720	-0.186	-0.802	-1.962	-0.332
VAR 19	0.091	-0.197	1.070	0.817	0.233	0.513
VAR 20	-0.040	-1.047	0.345	0.875	1.695	1.280

Standardized Residuals

	VAR 13	VAR 14	VAR 15	VAR 16	VAR 17	VAR 18
VAR 13	0.149					
VAR 14	4.261	0.455				
VAR 15	2.695	1.585	-0.069			
VAR 16	0.669	0.497	1.241	-0.166		
VAR 17	0.379	0.372	0.279	-0.471	0.056	
VAR 18	-1.116	-0.087	0.083	0.279	0.554	0.015
VAR 19	0.848	1.018	-0.042	0.617	-0.463	2.518
VAR 20	0.917	-0.005	-0.209	-1.208	0.354	0.106

296 APPENDICES

```
Standardized Residuals

            VAR 19      VAR 20
        -----------------------
VAR 19     0.002
VAR 20     1.230       0.077


Summary Statistics for Standardized Residuals

Smallest Standardized Residual =   -2.542
  Median Standardized Residual =    0.337
 Largest Standardized Residual =    5.668


Stemleaf Plot

- 2|55
- 2|4400
- 1|7666665
- 1|3222211111000
- 0|99888877766666666555
- 0|44433333222222111111111000000000
  0|111111111111122222223333333344444444444
  0|55555555556666666666777777788888889999999
  1|00111111222233344
  1|55566667788899
  2|0111223
  2|555679
  3|04
  3|
  4|0134
  4|
  5|0
  5|7
Largest Positive Standardized Residuals
Residual for   VAR 10 and    VAR 1   3.417
Residual for   VAR 10 and    VAR 2   2.900
Residual for   VAR 11 and    VAR 9   5.001
Residual for   VAR 11 and   VAR 10   5.668
Residual for   VAR 12 and   VAR 11   4.386
Residual for   VAR 13 and   VAR 11   3.974
Residual for   VAR 13 and   VAR 12   4.141
Residual for   VAR 14 and   VAR 13   4.261
Residual for   VAR 15 and    VAR 9   3.013
Residual for   VAR 15 and   VAR 13   2.695
```

WPA2014 COVARIANCE AMONG DOMINANCE, NURTURANCE, POWER, INTIMACY, AND ACCOMMODAT

Qplot of Standardized Residuals

```
  3.5...........................................
     .                                              . .
     .                                              . .
     .                                          .     .
     .                                           .    .
     .                                            .   .
     .                                             .  x
     .                                              . .
     .                                            .    x
     .                                             .   *
     .                                            .    x
     .                                        .   x   xx
     .                                      .   x x x    .
     .                                    .    x x*      .
 N   .                                  .    xxx         .
 o   .                                 .    xxx          .
 r   .                               .    **x            .
 m   .                              . xxx x              .
 a   .                             . ***                 .
 l   .                            . xx*                  .
     .                           . xx                    .
 Q   .                          . x*x                    .
 u   .                         . *x                      .
 a   .                        . **                       .
 n   .                       . x*x                       .
 t   .                      . **                         .
 i   .                     . x*x                         .
 l   .                    . x*x                          .
 e   .                   . ***                           .
 s   .                  .x*xx                            .
     .                  .xxx                             .
     .                 . x*                              .
     .               xx xx                               .
     .               .x                                  .
     .            x. xx                                  .
     .            x.                                     .
     .          *  .                                     .
     .        x .                                        .
     .                                                   .
     .       .x                                          .
     .                                                   .
     .     .                                             .
     .    .                                              .
     . .                                                 .
 -3.5...........................................
    -3.5                                            3.5
```

Standardized Residuals

298 APPENDICES

WPA2014 COVARIANCE AMONG DOMINANCE, NURTURANCE, POWER, INTIMACY, AND ACCOMMODAT

Modification Indices and Expected Change

Modification Indices for LAMBDA-Y

	ETA 1	ETA 2	ETA 3	ETA 4	ETA 5
VAR 1	0.658	0.057	8.007	1.778	1.163
VAR 2	0.586	0.337	4.915	0.657	2.862
VAR 3	6.786	4.246	1.436	0.013	0.162
VAR 4	9.851	0.205	0.417	0.022	0.169
VAR 5	4.246	0.038	0.032	0.002	0.074
VAR 6	5.447	0.153	0.000	0.403	2.120
VAR 7	0.003	0.658	0.010	1.627	0.161
VAR 8	0.018	1.488	0.548	0.030	0.561
VAR 9	2.129	1.757	0.011	9.694	1.615
VAR 10	8.674	11.506	1.024	3.341	4.062
VAR 11	1.027	17.177	41.595	0.838	19.184
VAR 12	2.478	4.679	5.027	0.022	1.987
VAR 13	0.001	0.432	0.838	17.863	1.898
VAR 14	1.467	5.992	0.033	1.156	0.243
VAR 15	0.092	3.020	3.491	0.011	0.016
VAR 16	1.701	2.308	4.239	0.009	4.295
VAR 17	0.375	1.886	0.082	0.252	- -
VAR 18	0.444	1.119	0.029	0.008	- -
VAR 19	0.324	0.019	2.569	0.226	- -
VAR 20	1.373	0.449	0.003	0.223	- -

Expected Change for LAMBDA-Y

	ETA 1	ETA 2	ETA 3	ETA 4	ETA 5
VAR 1	0.061	0.023	0.272	0.129	-0.182
VAR 2	-0.069	0.053	0.224	0.083	-0.284
VAR 3	0.264	0.161	0.123	-0.012	-0.069
VAR 4	-0.266	0.039	0.063	0.014	0.065
VAR 5	-0.144	0.019	-0.018	0.004	0.043
VAR 6	0.213	-0.036	-0.001	0.065	-0.247
VAR 7	-0.005	-0.066	-0.010	0.127	-0.071
VAR 8	-0.012	0.107	-0.072	-0.017	0.120
VAR 9	0.141	-0.129	0.010	0.317	-0.272
VAR 10	0.286	-0.333	0.092	-0.161	-0.325
VAR 11	0.104	-0.428	0.679	-0.070	-0.723
VAR 12	-0.156	-0.216	0.201	-0.013	-0.231
VAR 13	-0.004	-0.067	0.067	0.443	-0.233
VAR 14	-0.117	0.238	-0.016	0.098	0.079
VAR 15	0.029	0.171	0.191	-0.011	0.026
VAR 16	0.125	0.147	-0.182	-0.008	0.344

VAR 17	0.079	0.191	0.043	0.067	- -
VAR 18	-0.072	0.119	-0.020	-0.010	- -
VAR 19	-0.060	0.015	0.183	0.051	- -
VAR 20	-0.143	-0.088	-0.007	-0.059	- -

Standardized Expected Change for LAMBDA-Y

	ETA 1	ETA 2	ETA 3	ETA 4	ETA 5
VAR 1	0.061	0.023	0.272	0.129	-0.129
VAR 2	-0.069	0.053	0.224	0.083	-0.201
VAR 3	0.264	0.161	0.123	-0.012	-0.049
VAR 4	-0.266	0.039	0.063	0.014	0.046
VAR 5	-0.144	0.019	-0.018	0.004	0.031
VAR 6	0.213	-0.036	-0.001	0.065	-0.175
VAR 7	-0.005	-0.066	-0.010	0.127	-0.051
VAR 8	-0.012	0.107	-0.072	-0.017	0.085
VAR 9	0.141	-0.129	0.010	0.317	-0.193
VAR 10	0.286	-0.333	0.092	-0.161	-0.230
VAR 11	0.104	-0.428	0.679	-0.070	-0.512
VAR 12	-0.156	-0.216	0.201	-0.013	-0.164
VAR 13	-0.004	-0.067	0.067	0.443	-0.165
VAR 14	-0.117	0.238	-0.016	0.098	0.056
VAR 15	0.029	0.171	0.191	-0.011	0.018
VAR 16	0.125	0.147	-0.182	-0.008	0.243
VAR 17	0.079	0.191	0.043	0.067	- -
VAR 18	-0.072	0.119	-0.020	-0.010	- -
VAR 19	-0.060	0.015	0.183	0.051	- -
VAR 20	-0.143	-0.088	-0.007	-0.059	- -

Modification Indices for BETA

	ETA 1	ETA 2	ETA 3	ETA 4	ETA 5
ETA 1	1.641	0.600	8.296	1.121	4.908
ETA 2	0.600	1.641	5.583	0.826	0.111
ETA 3	8.296	5.583	0.102	17.485	14.826
ETA 4	1.121	0.826	17.485	0.102	5.542
ETA 5	- -	- -	- -	- -	- -

Expected Change for BETA

	ETA 1	ETA 2	ETA 3	ETA 4	ETA 5
ETA 1	0.133	0.079	0.290	0.107	-0.808
ETA 2	0.079	-0.133	-0.241	0.093	0.123
ETA 3	0.290	-0.241	0.037	0.513	-1.563
ETA 4	0.107	0.093	0.513	-0.037	-0.976
ETA 5	- -	- -	- -	- -	- -

300 APPENDICES

Standardized Expected Change for BETA

	ETA 1	ETA 2	ETA 3	ETA 4	ETA 5
ETA 1	0.133	0.079	0.290	0.107	-1.142
ETA 2	0.079	-0.133	-0.241	0.093	0.173
ETA 3	0.290	-0.241	0.037	0.513	-2.209
ETA 4	0.107	0.093	0.513	-0.037	-1.379
ETA 5	- -	- -	- -	- -	- -

Modification Indices for PSI

	ETA 1	ETA 2	ETA 3	ETA 4	ETA 5
ETA 1	1.641				
ETA 2	0.600	1.641			
ETA 3	8.296	5.583	0.102		
ETA 4	1.121	0.826	17.485	0.102	
ETA 5	- -	- -	- -	- -	- -

Expected Change for PSI

	ETA 1	ETA 2	ETA 3	ETA 4	ETA 5
ETA 1	0.265				
ETA 2	0.079	-0.265			
ETA 3	0.290	-0.241	0.074		
ETA 4	0.107	0.093	0.513	-0.074	
ETA 5	- -	- -	- -	- -	- -

Standardized Expected Change for PSI

	ETA 1	ETA 2	ETA 3	ETA 4	ETA 5
ETA 1	0.265				
ETA 2	0.079	-0.265			
ETA 3	0.290	-0.241	0.074		
ETA 4	0.107	0.093	0.513	-0.074	
ETA 5	- -	- -	- -	- -	- -

Modification Indices for THETA-EPS

	VAR 1	VAR 2	VAR 3	VAR 4	VAR 5	VAR 6
VAR 1	- -					
VAR 2	0.687	- -				
VAR 3	1.195	1.666	- -			
VAR 4	0.356	0.018	0.023	- -		

VAR 5	1.065	0.166	0.071	4.792	- -	
VAR 6	4.631	2.694	0.070	1.164	0.324	- -
VAR 7	0.085	3.230	1.256	0.395	0.523	1.274
VAR 8	0.377	1.313	5.026	2.300	0.424	0.313
VAR 9	1.687	1.419	0.991	0.144	0.002	0.043
VAR 10	3.975	0.930	1.304	0.000	0.318	1.375
VAR 11	1.936	1.340	0.264	2.211	0.270	0.401
VAR 12	0.192	0.023	0.676	1.714	1.115	0.126
VAR 13	0.706	0.140	0.418	0.530	0.046	0.469
VAR 14	0.003	0.033	1.274	0.738	0.118	2.916
VAR 15	0.004	0.035	0.032	0.438	0.019	0.084
VAR 16	0.100	0.085	0.565	0.948	0.205	0.006
VAR 17	0.000	0.502	0.054	0.093	0.071	0.480
VAR 18	0.054	0.454	0.012	0.013	1.074	0.003
VAR 19	0.214	0.134	0.047	0.206	0.187	0.245
VAR 20	0.013	0.306	0.114	0.038	0.192	0.673

Modification Indices for THETA-EPS

	VAR 7	VAR 8	VAR 9	VAR 10	VAR 11	VAR 12
VAR 7	- -					
VAR 8	1.458	- -				
VAR 9	0.010	0.025	- -			
VAR 10	3.741	0.022	1.632	- -		
VAR 11	2.445	2.872	6.729	25.321	- -	
VAR 12	1.225	3.642	0.540	3.722	15.407	- -
VAR 13	0.085	1.123	3.677	0.588	5.625	11.808
VAR 14	3.540	0.000	0.177	6.750	1.482	0.535
VAR 15	0.939	0.346	5.358	5.601	6.652	1.623
VAR 16	1.554	0.574	0.041	0.679	1.372	5.597
VAR 17	0.134	0.878	0.072	0.165	1.019	0.018
VAR 18	0.305	0.553	0.030	0.204	1.518	0.001
VAR 19	0.005	0.019	0.537	0.304	0.166	0.122
VAR 20	0.015	0.931	0.004	0.148	0.314	1.180

Modification Indices for THETA-EPS

	VAR 13	VAR 14	VAR 15	VAR 16	VAR 17	VAR 18
VAR 13	- -					
VAR 14	12.764	- -				
VAR 15	0.417	4.080	- -			
VAR 16	0.402	0.077	1.973	- -		
VAR 17	0.041	0.144	0.002	0.252	- -	
VAR 18	0.839	0.002	0.093	0.067	1.683	- -
VAR 19	0.513	0.628	0.139	0.005	0.477	7.642
VAR 20	0.359	0.009	0.119	1.874	2.382	0.077

302 APPENDICES

Modification Indices for THETA-EPS

	VAR 19	VAR 20
VAR 19	- -	
VAR 20	3.137	- -

Expected Change for THETA-EPS

	VAR 1	VAR 2	VAR 3	VAR 4	VAR 5	VAR 6
VAR 1	- -					
VAR 2	0.087	- -				
VAR 3	0.106	0.138	- -			
VAR 4	-0.061	0.013	-0.016	- -		
VAR 5	-0.121	0.042	-0.026	0.217	- -	
VAR 6	0.226	0.192	0.029	0.107	0.059	- -
VAR 7	-0.027	0.192	0.137	0.066	0.069	0.123
VAR 8	0.064	-0.114	0.236	-0.168	0.066	0.056
VAR 9	0.120	0.116	0.099	0.035	0.004	-0.020
VAR 10	0.185	0.095	0.114	0.001	-0.054	-0.116
VAR 11	0.136	0.120	0.054	0.148	-0.052	-0.066
VAR 12	0.042	-0.015	-0.084	0.126	0.102	-0.036
VAR 13	0.081	0.038	-0.067	0.071	-0.021	0.071
VAR 14	-0.005	0.018	-0.112	0.080	0.032	0.168
VAR 15	0.006	-0.018	-0.018	-0.062	0.013	0.029
VAR 16	0.029	0.028	0.074	-0.091	-0.042	-0.008
VAR 17	0.001	0.073	-0.024	-0.030	0.026	0.072
VAR 18	-0.023	-0.070	0.012	-0.011	0.103	-0.006
VAR 19	0.046	-0.038	0.023	0.045	0.044	0.052
VAR 20	-0.011	0.057	0.035	0.019	0.043	0.085

Expected Change for THETA-EPS

	VAR 7	VAR 8	VAR 9	VAR 10	VAR 11	VAR 12
VAR 7	- -					
VAR 8	0.129	- -				
VAR 9	0.010	-0.015	- -			
VAR 10	-0.186	-0.014	0.141	- -		
VAR 11	-0.158	-0.169	0.261	0.510	- -	
VAR 12	-0.109	-0.185	0.076	0.194	0.406	- -
VAR 13	-0.029	-0.105	-0.225	0.079	0.249	0.351
VAR 14	0.179	0.000	-0.044	-0.258	-0.126	0.073
VAR 15	0.093	0.056	0.239	-0.250	-0.307	-0.133
VAR 16	0.118	0.071	-0.022	-0.089	-0.120	-0.239
VAR 17	0.038	0.093	0.030	0.040	0.104	-0.013
VAR 18	0.056	0.074	0.018	-0.045	-0.130	-0.002
VAR 19	0.007	-0.014	0.074	0.056	0.044	0.036
VAR 20	0.013	-0.095	-0.007	0.038	0.058	0.109

APPENDICES   303

Expected Change for THETA-EPS

	VAR 13	VAR 14	VAR 15	VAR 16	VAR 17	VAR 18
VAR 13	- -					
VAR 14	0.355	- -				
VAR 15	0.065	0.224	- -			
VAR 16	-0.064	0.030	0.153	- -		
VAR 17	-0.021	0.037	0.005	-0.050	- -	
VAR 18	-0.096	-0.004	0.031	0.026	0.210	- -
VAR 19	0.076	0.080	-0.038	0.007	-0.087	0.303
VAR 20	0.061	0.009	-0.036	-0.135	0.518	0.042

Expected Change for THETA-EPS

	VAR 19	VAR 20
VAR 19	- -	
VAR 20	0.213	- -

Maximum Modification Index is   41.60 for Element (11, 3) of LAMBDA-Y

Covariance Matrix of Parameter Estimates

	LY 1_1	LY 2_1	LY 2_2	LY 3_2	LY 9_3	LY 10_3
LY 1_1	0.007					
LY 2_1	-0.001	0.003				
LY 2_2	0.001	0.000	0.003			
LY 3_2	0.001	0.000	0.000	0.006		
LY 9_3	0.000	0.000	0.000	0.000	0.008	
LY 10_3	0.000	0.000	0.000	0.000	-0.001	0.003
LY 10_4	0.000	0.000	0.000	0.000	0.000	0.000
LY 11_4	0.000	0.000	0.000	0.000	-0.001	0.000
LY 18_5	0.000	0.000	0.000	0.000	0.000	0.000
LY 19_5	0.000	0.000	0.000	0.000	0.000	0.000
LY 20_5	0.000	0.000	0.000	0.000	0.000	0.000
BE 5_1	0.000	0.000	0.000	0.000	0.000	0.000
BE 5_2	0.000	0.000	0.000	0.000	0.000	0.000
BE 5_3	0.000	0.000	0.000	0.000	0.000	0.000
BE 5_4	0.000	0.000	0.000	0.000	0.000	0.000
PS 5_5	0.000	0.000	0.000	0.000	0.000	0.000
TE 1_1	-0.007	0.001	-0.001	-0.002	0.000	0.000
TE 2_2	0.001	-0.001	0.001	0.000	0.000	0.000
TE 3_3	0.001	0.000	0.000	0.003	0.000	0.000
TE 4_4	0.001	0.000	0.002	0.000	0.000	0.000
TE 5_5	0.001	0.000	0.000	0.003	0.000	0.000
TE 6_6	0.001	-0.001	0.001	0.000	0.000	0.000
TE 7_7	-0.007	0.001	-0.001	-0.001	0.000	0.000
TE 8_8	0.002	-0.003	0.000	0.000	0.000	0.000

304 APPENDICES

```
   TE 9_9     0.000     0.000     0.000     0.000    -0.011     0.002
  TE 10_10    0.000     0.000     0.000     0.000     0.002    -0.001
  TE 11_11    0.000     0.000     0.000     0.000     0.001     0.000
  TE 12_12    0.000     0.000     0.000     0.000     0.000     0.000
  TE 13_13    0.000     0.000     0.000     0.000     0.001     0.000
  TE 14_14    0.000     0.000     0.000     0.000     0.002    -0.001
  TE 15_15    0.000     0.000     0.000     0.000    -0.011     0.003
  TE 16_16    0.000     0.000     0.000     0.000     0.003    -0.002
  TE 17_17    0.000     0.000     0.000     0.000     0.000     0.000
  TE 18_18    0.000     0.000     0.000     0.000     0.000     0.000
  TE 19_19    0.000     0.000     0.000     0.000     0.000     0.000
  TE 20_20    0.000     0.000     0.000     0.000     0.000     0.000
```

Covariance Matrix of Parameter Estimates

	LY 10_4	LY 11_4	LY 18_5	LY 19_5	LY 20_5	BE 5_1
LY 10_4	0.002					
LY 11_4	0.000	0.006				
LY 18_5	0.000	0.000	0.044			
LY 19_5	0.000	0.000	0.005	0.028		
LY 20_5	0.000	0.000	-0.034	-0.010	0.113	
BE 5_1	0.000	0.000	0.002	0.001	-0.005	0.007
BE 5_2	0.000	0.000	-0.004	-0.001	0.009	-0.001
BE 5_3	0.000	0.000	0.004	0.001	-0.010	0.001
BE 5_4	0.000	0.000	0.002	0.001	-0.004	0.000
PS 5_5	0.000	0.000	-0.024	-0.007	0.052	-0.002
TE 1_1	0.000	0.000	0.000	0.000	0.000	0.000
TE 2_2	0.000	0.000	0.000	0.000	0.000	0.000
TE 3_3	0.000	0.000	0.000	0.000	0.000	0.000
TE 4_4	0.000	0.000	0.000	0.000	0.000	0.000
TE 5_5	0.000	0.000	0.000	0.000	0.000	0.000
TE 6_6	0.000	0.000	0.000	0.000	0.000	0.000
TE 7_7	0.000	0.000	0.000	0.000	0.000	0.000
TE 8_8	0.000	0.000	0.000	0.000	0.000	0.000
TE 9_9	0.000	0.002	0.000	0.000	0.000	0.000
TE 10_10	0.000	0.000	0.000	0.000	0.000	0.000
TE 11_11	0.000	-0.002	0.000	0.000	0.000	0.000
TE 12_12	-0.001	0.000	0.000	0.000	0.000	0.000
TE 13_13	0.000	-0.002	0.000	0.000	0.000	0.000
TE 14_14	0.000	0.000	0.000	0.000	0.000	0.000
TE 15_15	0.000	0.002	0.000	0.000	0.000	0.000
TE 16_16	0.000	0.000	0.000	0.000	0.000	0.000
TE 17_17	0.000	0.000	0.023	0.007	-0.052	0.003
TE 18_18	0.000	0.000	-0.010	0.000	0.001	0.000
TE 19_19	0.000	0.000	0.000	-0.003	0.000	0.000
TE 20_20	0.000	0.000	-0.008	-0.003	0.045	-0.002

APPENDICES 305

Covariance Matrix of Parameter Estimates

	BE 5_2	BE 5_3	BE 5_4	PS 5_5	TE 1_1	TE 2_2
BE 5_2	0.007					
BE 5_3	-0.001	0.008				
BE 5_4	0.000	-0.001	0.007			
PS 5_5	0.003	-0.004	-0.002	0.037		
TE 1_1	0.000	0.000	0.000	0.000	0.024	
TE 2_2	0.000	0.000	0.000	0.000	-0.002	0.021
TE 3_3	0.000	0.000	0.000	0.000	-0.001	0.000
TE 4_4	0.000	0.000	0.000	0.000	-0.002	0.001
TE 5_5	0.000	0.000	0.000	0.000	-0.002	0.000
TE 6_6	0.000	0.000	0.000	0.000	-0.002	0.001
TE 7_7	0.000	0.000	0.000	0.000	0.007	-0.002
TE 8_8	0.000	0.000	0.000	0.000	-0.003	0.001
TE 9_9	0.000	-0.001	0.001	0.000	0.000	0.000
TE 10_10	0.000	0.000	0.000	0.000	0.000	0.000
TE 11_11	0.000	0.000	0.000	0.000	0.000	0.000
TE 12_12	0.000	0.000	0.000	0.000	0.000	0.000
TE 13_13	0.000	0.000	0.000	0.000	0.000	0.000
TE 14_14	0.000	0.000	0.000	0.000	0.000	0.000
TE 15_15	0.000	0.000	0.000	0.000	0.000	0.000
TE 16_16	0.000	0.000	0.000	0.000	0.000	0.000
TE 17_17	-0.004	0.005	0.002	-0.032	0.000	0.000
TE 18_18	0.000	0.000	0.000	0.002	0.000	0.000
TE 19_19	0.000	0.000	0.000	0.000	0.000	0.000
TE 20_20	0.003	-0.004	-0.002	0.015	0.000	0.000

Covariance Matrix of Parameter Estimates

	TE 3_3	TE 4_4	TE 5_5	TE 6_6	TE 7_7	TE 8_8
TE 3_3	0.024					
TE 4_4	0.000	0.020				
TE 5_5	0.002	0.000	0.020			
TE 6_6	0.000	0.001	0.000	0.023		
TE 7_7	-0.002	-0.002	-0.001	-0.002	0.026	
TE 8_8	0.000	0.000	0.000	0.001	-0.003	0.021
TE 9_9	0.000	0.000	0.000	0.000	0.000	0.000
TE 10_10	0.000	0.000	0.000	0.000	0.000	0.000
TE 11_11	0.000	0.000	0.000	0.000	0.000	0.000
TE 12_12	0.000	0.000	0.000	0.000	0.000	0.000
TE 13_13	0.000	0.000	0.000	0.000	0.000	0.000
TE 14_14	0.000	0.000	0.000	0.000	0.000	0.000
TE 15_15	0.000	0.000	0.000	0.000	0.000	0.000
TE 16_16	0.000	0.000	0.000	0.000	0.000	0.000
TE 17_17	0.000	0.000	0.000	0.000	0.000	0.000
TE 18_18	0.000	0.000	0.000	0.000	0.000	0.000
TE 19_19	0.000	0.000	0.000	0.000	0.000	0.000
TE 20_20	0.000	0.000	0.000	0.000	0.000	0.000

306 APPENDICES

Covariance Matrix of Parameter Estimates

	TE 9_9	TE 10_10	TE 11_11	TE 12_12	TE 13_13	TE 14_14
TE 9_9	0.033					
TE 10_10	-0.003	0.019				
TE 11_11	-0.001	0.000	0.023			
TE 12_12	-0.001	0.000	0.000	0.020		
TE 13_13	-0.001	0.000	0.001	0.000	0.022	
TE 14_14	-0.003	0.001	0.000	0.000	0.000	0.018
TE 15_15	0.015	-0.003	-0.002	-0.001	-0.001	-0.003
TE 16_16	-0.005	0.001	0.000	0.000	0.000	0.001
TE 17_17	0.000	0.000	0.000	0.000	0.000	0.000
TE 18_18	0.000	0.000	0.000	0.000	0.000	0.000
TE 19_19	0.000	0.000	0.000	0.000	0.000	0.000
TE 20_20	0.000	0.000	0.000	0.000	0.000	0.000

Covariance Matrix of Parameter Estimates

	TE 15_15	TE 16_16	TE 17_17	TE 18_18	TE 19_19	TE 20_20
TE 15_15	0.034					
TE 16_16	-0.005	0.020				
TE 17_17	0.000	0.000	0.048			
TE 18_18	0.000	0.000	-0.002	0.025		
TE 19_19	0.000	0.000	0.000	0.000	0.023	
TE 20_20	0.000	0.000	-0.018	-0.001	0.000	0.041

WPA2014 COVARIANCE AMONG DOMINANCE, NURTURANCE, POWER, INTIMACY, AND ACCOMMODAT

Correlation Matrix of Parameter Estimates

	LY 1_1	LY 2_1	LY 2_2	LY 3_2	LY 9_3	LY 10_3
LY 1_1	1.000					
LY 2_1	-0.142	1.000				
LY 2_2	0.121	-0.069	1.000			
LY 3_2	0.095	-0.003	0.006	1.000		
LY 9_3	0.000	0.000	0.000	0.000	1.000	
LY 10_3	0.000	0.000	0.000	0.000	-0.220	1.000
LY 10_4	0.000	0.000	0.000	0.000	0.018	-0.020
LY 11_4	0.000	0.000	0.000	0.000	-0.138	0.063
LY 18_5	0.000	0.000	0.000	0.000	0.000	0.000
LY 19_5	0.000	0.000	0.000	0.000	0.000	0.000
LY 20_5	0.000	0.000	0.000	0.000	0.000	0.000
BE 5_1	0.009	-0.004	0.003	0.003	0.000	0.000
BE 5_2	-0.012	0.003	-0.004	-0.004	0.000	0.000
BE 5_3	0.000	0.000	0.000	0.000	0.045	-0.026
BE 5_4	0.000	0.000	0.000	0.000	-0.029	-0.001
PS 5_5	0.005	0.001	-0.001	-0.001	0.009	0.000
TE 1_1	-0.535	0.174	-0.152	-0.132	0.000	0.000
TE 2_2	0.122	-0.174	0.158	-0.028	0.000	0.000
TE 3_3	0.081	0.027	-0.024	0.290	0.000	0.000

TE 4_4	0.110	0.013	0.329	-0.025	0.000	0.000
TE 5_5	0.094	0.027	-0.024	0.314	0.000	0.000
TE 6_6	0.118	-0.172	0.149	-0.027	0.000	0.000
TE 7_7	-0.513	0.167	-0.147	-0.118	0.000	0.000
TE 8_8	0.140	-0.366	-0.009	-0.032	0.000	0.000
TE 9_9	0.000	0.000	0.000	0.000	-0.663	0.263
TE 10_10	0.000	0.000	0.000	0.000	0.126	-0.167
TE 11_11	0.000	0.000	0.000	0.000	0.054	-0.010
TE 12_12	0.000	0.000	0.000	0.000	0.025	0.017
TE 13_13	0.000	0.000	0.000	0.000	0.055	-0.010
TE 14_14	0.000	0.000	0.000	0.000	0.131	-0.174
TE 15_15	0.000	0.000	0.000	0.000	-0.662	0.267
TE 16_16	0.000	0.000	0.000	0.000	0.219	-0.340
TE 17_17	0.000	0.000	0.000	0.000	0.000	0.000
TE 18_18	0.000	0.000	0.000	0.000	0.000	0.000
TE 19_19	0.000	0.000	0.000	0.000	0.000	0.000
TE 20_20	0.000	0.000	0.000	0.000	0.000	0.000

Correlation Matrix of Parameter Estimates

	LY 10_4	LY 11_4	LY 18_5	LY 19_5	LY 20_5	BE 5_1
LY 10_4	1.000					
LY 11_4	0.020	1.000				
LY 18_5	0.000	0.000	1.000			
LY 19_5	0.000	0.000	0.141	1.000		
LY 20_5	0.000	0.000	-0.476	-0.185	1.000	
BE 5_1	0.000	0.000	0.136	0.051	-0.200	1.000
BE 5_2	0.000	0.000	-0.204	-0.077	0.301	-0.073
BE 5_3	-0.011	-0.013	0.234	0.089	-0.345	0.073
BE 5_4	-0.008	0.000	0.105	0.040	-0.155	0.033
PS 5_5	0.001	-0.001	-0.591	-0.227	0.805	-0.136
TE 1_1	0.000	0.000	0.000	0.000	0.000	-0.024
TE 2_2	0.000	0.000	0.000	0.000	0.000	-0.010
TE 3_3	0.000	0.000	0.000	0.000	0.000	0.001
TE 4_4	0.000	0.000	0.000	0.000	0.000	0.004
TE 5_5	0.000	0.000	0.000	0.000	0.000	-0.006
TE 6_6	0.000	0.000	0.000	0.000	0.000	-0.009
TE 7_7	0.000	0.000	0.000	0.000	0.000	-0.005
TE 8_8	0.000	0.000	0.000	0.000	0.000	0.006
TE 9_9	0.020	0.154	0.000	0.000	0.000	0.000
TE 10_10	-0.037	-0.014	0.000	0.000	0.000	0.000
TE 11_11	-0.001	-0.162	0.000	0.000	0.000	0.000
TE 12_12	-0.139	-0.003	0.000	0.000	0.000	0.000
TE 13_13	-0.001	-0.164	0.000	0.000	0.000	0.000
TE 14_14	-0.036	-0.014	0.000	0.000	0.000	0.000
TE 15_15	0.020	0.153	0.000	0.000	0.000	0.000
TE 16_16	0.067	-0.024	0.000	0.000	0.000	0.000
TE 17_17	0.000	0.000	0.492	0.187	-0.704	0.150
TE 18_18	0.000	0.000	-0.301	-0.011	0.020	-0.019
TE 19_19	0.000	0.000	-0.002	-0.098	0.002	-0.002
TE 20_20	0.000	0.000	-0.185	-0.075	0.664	-0.126

APPENDICES

Correlation Matrix of Parameter Estimates

	BE 5_2	BE 5_3	BE 5_4	PS 5_5	TE 1_1	TE 2_2
BE 5_2	1.000					
BE 5_3	-0.110	1.000				
BE 5_4	-0.049	-0.100	1.000			
PS 5_5	0.202	-0.236	-0.128	1.000		
TE 1_1	0.007	0.000	0.000	-0.003	1.000	
TE 2_2	0.009	0.000	0.000	-0.002	-0.104	1.000
TE 3_3	0.009	0.000	0.000	-0.001	-0.060	-0.016
TE 4_4	0.000	0.000	0.000	0.000	-0.093	0.054
TE 5_5	-0.002	0.000	0.000	0.000	-0.092	-0.017
TE 6_6	0.010	0.000	0.000	-0.002	-0.099	0.045
TE 7_7	0.034	0.000	0.000	-0.005	0.297	-0.098
TE 8_8	0.000	0.000	0.000	0.000	-0.118	0.068
TE 9_9	0.000	-0.082	0.036	-0.011	0.000	0.000
TE 10_10	0.000	0.000	-0.005	0.000	0.000	0.000
TE 11_11	0.000	0.004	-0.002	0.000	0.000	0.000
TE 12_12	0.000	0.000	-0.002	0.000	0.000	0.000
TE 13_13	0.000	0.001	0.000	0.000	0.000	0.000
TE 14_14	0.000	0.007	-0.010	0.000	0.000	0.000
TE 15_15	0.000	-0.028	0.005	-0.006	0.000	0.000
TE 16_16	0.000	0.005	-0.016	0.000	0.000	0.000
TE 17_17	-0.225	0.258	0.116	-0.747	0.000	0.000
TE 18_18	0.029	-0.033	-0.015	0.059	0.000	0.000
TE 19_19	0.002	-0.003	-0.001	0.005	0.000	0.000
TE 20_20	0.189	-0.217	-0.097	0.384	0.000	0.000

Correlation Matrix of Parameter Estimates

	TE 3_3	TE 4_4	TE 5_5	TE 6_6	TE 7_7	TE 8_8
TE 3_3	1.000					
TE 4_4	-0.014	1.000				
TE 5_5	0.097	-0.014	1.000			
TE 6_6	-0.016	0.051	-0.015	1.000		
TE 7_7	-0.075	-0.090	-0.063	-0.097	1.000	
TE 8_8	-0.018	-0.023	-0.019	0.068	-0.114	1.000
TE 9_9	0.000	0.000	0.000	0.000	0.000	0.000
TE 10_10	0.000	0.000	0.000	0.000	0.000	0.000
TE 11_11	0.000	0.000	0.000	0.000	0.000	0.000
TE 12_12	0.000	0.000	0.000	0.000	0.000	0.000
TE 13_13	0.000	0.000	0.000	0.000	0.000	0.000
TE 14_14	0.000	0.000	0.000	0.000	0.000	0.000
TE 15_15	0.000	0.000	0.000	0.000	0.000	0.000
TE 16_16	0.000	0.000	0.000	0.000	0.000	0.000
TE 17_17	0.000	0.000	0.000	0.000	0.000	0.000
TE 18_18	0.000	0.000	0.000	0.000	0.000	0.000
TE 19_19	0.000	0.000	0.000	0.000	0.000	0.000
TE 20_20	0.000	0.000	0.000	0.000	0.000	0.000

APPENDICES 309

Correlation Matrix of Parameter Estimates

	TE 9_9	TE 10_10	TE 11_11	TE 12_12	TE 13_13	TE 14_14
TE 9_9	1.000					
TE 10_10	-0.125	1.000				
TE 11_11	-0.045	0.005	1.000			
TE 12_12	-0.022	0.003	0.001	1.000		
TE 13_13	-0.054	0.004	0.028	0.001	1.000	
TE 14_14	-0.108	0.035	0.004	0.003	0.005	1.000
TE 15_15	0.454	-0.105	-0.054	-0.022	-0.045	-0.130
TE 16_16	-0.199	0.057	0.008	-0.014	0.008	0.060
TE 17_17	0.000	0.000	0.000	0.000	0.000	0.000
TE 18_18	0.000	0.000	0.000	0.000	0.000	0.000
TE 19_19	0.000	0.000	0.000	0.000	0.000	0.000
TE 20_20	0.000	0.000	0.000	0.000	0.000	0.000

Correlation Matrix of Parameter Estimates

	TE 15_15	TE 16_16	TE 17_17	TE 18_18	TE 19_19	TE 20_20
TE 15_15	1.000					
TE 16_16	-0.200	1.000				
TE 17_17	0.000	0.000	1.000			
TE 18_18	0.000	0.000	-0.062	1.000		
TE 19_19	0.000	0.000	-0.005	0.000	1.000	
TE 20_20	0.000	0.000	-0.404	-0.026	-0.002	1.000

WPA2014 COVARIANCE AMONG DOMINANCE, NURTURANCE, POWER, INTIMACY, AND ACCOMMODAT

Covariances

Y - ETA

	VAR 1	VAR 2	VAR 3	VAR 4	VAR 5	VAR 6
ETA 1	0.803	0.464	- -	-0.425	-0.574	-0.425
ETA 2	- -	-0.425	-0.574	-0.425	- -	0.464
ETA 3	- -	- -	- -	- -	- -	- -
ETA 4	- -	- -	- -	- -	- -	- -
ETA 5	-0.078	-0.110	-0.088	-0.024	0.056	0.113

Y - ETA

	VAR 7	VAR 8	VAR 9	VAR 10	VAR 11	VAR 12
ETA 1	- -	0.464	- -	- -	- -	- -
ETA 2	0.803	0.464	- -	- -	- -	- -
ETA 3	- -	- -	0.900	0.521	- -	0.273
ETA 4	- -	- -	- -	0.273	0.324	0.273
ETA 5	0.123	0.026	-0.164	-0.116	-0.025	-0.071

310 APPENDICES

Y - ETA

	VAR 13	VAR 14	VAR 15	VAR 16	VAR 17	VAR 18
ETA 1	- -	- -	- -	- -	0.098	-0.051
ETA 2	- -	- -	- -	- -	-0.153	0.080
ETA 3	0.324	0.273	- -	0.521	0.183	-0.096
ETA 4	- -	0.521	0.900	0.521	0.077	-0.041
ETA 5	-0.059	-0.090	-0.070	-0.135	-0.501	0.263

Y - ETA

	VAR 19	VAR 20
ETA 1	-0.016	0.090
ETA 2	0.025	-0.142
ETA 3	-0.030	0.169
ETA 4	-0.013	0.072
ETA 5	0.083	-0.463

WPA2014 COVARIANCE AMONG DOMINANCE, NURTURANCE, POWER, INTIMACY, AND ACCOMMODAT

First Order Derivatives

LAMBDA-Y

	ETA 1	ETA 2	ETA 3	ETA 4	ETA 5
VAR 1	-0.015	-0.007	-0.086	-0.040	0.019
VAR 2	0.018	-0.014	-0.064	-0.023	0.029
VAR 3	-0.075	-0.040	-0.034	0.003	0.007
VAR 4	0.081	-0.012	-0.019	-0.004	-0.008
VAR 5	0.040	-0.006	0.005	-0.001	-0.005
VAR 6	-0.056	0.009	0.000	-0.018	0.025
VAR 7	0.002	0.015	0.003	-0.037	0.007
VAR 8	0.003	-0.031	0.022	0.005	-0.014
VAR 9	-0.044	0.039	-0.002	-0.089	0.017
VAR 10	-0.088	0.100	-0.025	0.046	0.036
VAR 11	-0.029	0.117	-0.178	0.018	0.077
VAR 12	0.046	0.063	-0.054	0.004	0.025
VAR 13	0.001	0.019	-0.018	-0.117	0.024
VAR 14	0.037	-0.073	0.005	-0.026	-0.009
VAR 15	-0.009	-0.051	-0.053	0.002	-0.002
VAR 16	-0.040	-0.046	0.049	0.002	-0.036
VAR 17	-0.014	-0.029	-0.006	-0.011	0.000
VAR 18	0.018	-0.027	0.004	0.002	0.000
VAR 19	0.016	-0.004	-0.041	-0.013	0.000
VAR 20	0.028	0.015	0.001	0.011	0.000

APPENDICES 311

BETA

	ETA 1	ETA 2	ETA 3	ETA 4	ETA 5
ETA 1	-0.036	-0.022	-0.083	-0.030	0.018
ETA 2	-0.022	0.036	0.067	-0.026	-0.003
ETA 3	-0.083	0.067	-0.008	-0.099	0.028
ETA 4	-0.030	-0.026	-0.099	0.008	0.017
ETA 5	0.000	0.000	0.000	0.000	0.000

PSI

	ETA 1	ETA 2	ETA 3	ETA 4	ETA 5
ETA 1	-0.018				
ETA 2	-0.022	0.018			
ETA 3	-0.083	0.067	-0.004		
ETA 4	-0.030	-0.026	-0.099	0.004	
ETA 5	0.000	0.000	0.000	0.000	0.000

THETA-EPS

	VAR 1	VAR 2	VAR 3	VAR 4	VAR 5	VAR 6
VAR 1	0.000					
VAR 2	-0.023	0.000				
VAR 3	-0.033	-0.035	0.000			
VAR 4	0.017	-0.004	0.004	0.000		
VAR 5	0.026	-0.012	0.008	-0.064	0.000	
VAR 6	-0.060	-0.041	-0.007	-0.032	-0.016	0.000
VAR 7	0.009	-0.049	-0.027	-0.017	-0.022	-0.030
VAR 8	-0.017	0.033	-0.062	0.040	-0.019	-0.016
VAR 9	-0.041	-0.036	-0.029	-0.012	-0.001	0.006
VAR 10	-0.062	-0.029	-0.033	0.000	0.017	0.034
VAR 11	-0.041	-0.033	-0.014	-0.044	0.015	0.018
VAR 12	-0.013	0.004	0.023	-0.040	-0.032	0.010
VAR 13	-0.025	-0.011	0.018	-0.022	0.006	-0.019
VAR 14	0.002	-0.005	0.033	-0.027	-0.011	-0.050
VAR 15	-0.002	0.006	0.005	0.020	-0.004	-0.008
VAR 16	-0.010	-0.009	-0.022	0.030	0.014	0.002
VAR 17	0.000	-0.020	0.007	0.009	-0.008	-0.019
VAR 18	0.007	0.019	-0.003	0.003	-0.030	0.002
VAR 19	-0.014	0.010	-0.006	-0.013	-0.012	-0.014
VAR 20	0.003	-0.016	-0.009	-0.006	-0.013	-0.023

THETA-EPS

	VAR 7	VAR 8	VAR 9	VAR 10	VAR 11	VAR 12
VAR 7	0.000					
VAR 8	-0.033	0.000				

312 APPENDICES

```
VAR 9      -0.003    0.005    0.000
VAR 10      0.058    0.005   -0.034    0.000
VAR 11      0.045    0.049   -0.075   -0.144    0.000
VAR 12      0.033    0.057   -0.021   -0.056   -0.110    0.000
VAR 13      0.008    0.031    0.048   -0.022   -0.066   -0.098
VAR 14     -0.057    0.000    0.012    0.076    0.034   -0.021
VAR 15     -0.029   -0.018   -0.065    0.065    0.063    0.035
VAR 16     -0.038   -0.024    0.005    0.022    0.033    0.068
VAR 17     -0.010   -0.028   -0.007   -0.012   -0.028    0.004
VAR 18     -0.016   -0.022   -0.005    0.013    0.034    0.001
VAR 19     -0.002    0.004   -0.021   -0.016   -0.011   -0.010
VAR 20     -0.003    0.028    0.002   -0.011   -0.016   -0.032
```

THETA-EPS

	VAR 13	VAR 14	VAR 15	VAR 16	VAR 17	VAR 18
VAR 13	0.000					
VAR 14	-0.105	0.000				
VAR 15	-0.019	-0.053	0.000			
VAR 16	0.018	-0.008	-0.037	0.000		
VAR 17	0.006	-0.011	-0.001	0.015	0.000	
VAR 18	0.026	0.001	-0.009	-0.008	-0.023	0.000
VAR 19	-0.020	-0.023	0.011	-0.002	0.016	-0.073
VAR 20	-0.017	-0.003	0.009	0.040	-0.013	-0.005

THETA-EPS

	VAR 19	VAR 20
VAR 19	0.000	
VAR 20	-0.043	0.000

WPA2014 COVARIANCE AMONG DOMINANCE, NURTURANCE, POWER, INTIMACY, AND ACCOMMODAT

Factor Scores Regressions

   W_A_R_N_I_N_G: Fitted Covariance Matrix not positive definite.
            Factor Scores Regressions can not be computed.

WPA2014 COVARIANCE AMONG DOMINANCE, NURTURANCE, POWER, INTIMACY, AND ACCOMMODAT

Standardized Solution

APPENDICES 313

LAMBDA-Y

	ETA 1	ETA 2	ETA 3	ETA 4	ETA 5
VAR 1	0.803	- -	- -	- -	- -
VAR 2	0.464	-0.425	- -	- -	- -
VAR 3	- -	- -	- -	- -	-0.574
VAR 4	-0.425	-0.425	- -	- -	- -
VAR 5	-0.574	- -	- -	- -	- -
VAR 6	-0.425	0.464	- -	- -	- -
VAR 7	- -	0.803	- -	- -	- -
VAR 8	0.464	0.464	- -	- -	- -
VAR 9	- -	- -	0.900	- -	- -
VAR 10	- -	- -	0.273	- -	0.521
VAR 11	- -	- -	- -	- -	0.324
VAR 12	- -	- -	0.273	0.273	- -
VAR 13	- -	- -	0.324	- -	- -
VAR 14	- -	- -	0.273	0.521	- -
VAR 15	- -	- -	- -	- -	0.900
VAR 16	- -	0.521	- -	- -	0.521
VAR 17	- -	- -	- -	- -	-0.708
VAR 18	- -	- -	- -	- -	0.371
VAR 19	- -	- -	- -	- -	0.117
VAR 20	- -	- -	- -	- -	-0.654

BETA

	*ETA 1	ETA 2	ETA 3	ETA 4	ETA 5
ETA 1	- -	- -	- -	- -	- -
ETA 2	- -	- -	- -	- -	- -
ETA 3	- -	- -	- -	- -	- -
ETA 4	- -	- -	- -	- -	- -
ETA 5	-0.138	0.217	-0.258	-0.109	- -

Correlation Matrix of ETA

	ETA 1	ETA 2	ETA 3	ETA 4	ETA 5
ETA 1	1.000	.			
ETA 2	- -	1.000			
ETA 3	- -	- -	1.000		
ETA 4	- -	- -	- -	1.000	
ETA 5	-0.138	0.217	-0.258	-0.109	1.000

PSI
Note: This matrix is diagonal.

ETA 1	ETA 2	ETA 3	ETA 4	ETA 5
1.000	1.000	1.000	1.000	0.855

314 APPENDICES

WPA2014 COVARIANCE AMONG DOMINANCE, NURTURANCE, POWER, INTIMACY, AND ACCOMMODAT

Total and Indirect Effects

Total Effects of ETA on ETA

	ETA 1	ETA 2	ETA 3	ETA 4	ETA 5
ETA 1	– –	– –	– –	– –	– –
ETA 2	– –	– –	– –	– –	– –
ETA 3	– –	– –	– –	– –	– –
ETA 4	– –	– –	– –	– –	– –
ETA 5	-0.098	0.153	-0.183	-0.077	– –
	(0.081)	(0.085)	(0.088)	(0.083)	
	-1.203	1.811	-2.073	-0.929	

Largest Eigenvalue of B*B' (Stability Index) is   0.072

Total Effects of ETA on Y

	ETA 1	ETA 2	ETA 3	ETA 4	ETA 5
VAR 1	0.803	– –	– –	– –	– –
	(0.081)				
	9.873				
VAR 2	0.464	-0.425	– –	– –	– –
	(0.052)	(0.051)			
	8.922	-8.330			
VAR 3	– –	-0.574	– –	– –	
		(0.074)			
		-7.705			
VAR 4	-0.425	-0.425	– –	– –	– –
	(0.051)	(0.051)			
	-8.330	-8.330			
VAR 5	-0.574	– –	– –	– –	– –
	(0.074)				
	-7.705				
VAR 6	-0.425	0.464	– –	– –	– –
	(0.051)	(0.052)			
	-8.330	8.922			
VAR 7	– –	– –	0.803	– –	
			(0.081)		
			9.873		
VAR 8	0.464	0.464	– –	– –	– –
	(0.052)	(0.052)			
	8.922	8.922			

APPENDICES 315

VAR 9	- -	- -	0.900 (0.092) 9.774	- -	- -
VAR 10	- -	- -	0.521 (0.052) 10.051	0.273 (0.048) 5.661	- -
VAR 11	- -	- -	- -	0.324 (0.075) 4.308	- -
VAR 12	- -		0.273 (0.048) 5.661	0.273 (0.048) 5.661	- -
VAR 13	- -	- -	0.324 (0.075) 4.308	- -	- -
VAR 14	- -	- -	0.273 (0.048) 5.661	0.521 (0.052) 10.051	- -
VAR 15	- -	- -	- -	0.900 (0.092) 9.774	- -
VAR 16	- -	- -	0.521 (0.052) 10.051	0.521 (0.052) 10.051	- -
VAR 17	0.098 (0.081) 1.203	-0.153 (0.085) -1.811	0.183 (0.088) 2.073	0.077 (0.083) 0.929	-1.000
VAR 18	-0.051 (0.045) -1.147	0.080 (0.049) 1.635	-0.096 (0.053) -1.820	-0.041 (0.045) -0.903	0.525 (0.209) 2.506
VAR 19	-0.016 (0.021) -0.782	0.025 (0.028) 0.895	-0.030 (0.033) -0.922	-0.013 (0.019) -0.690	0.165 (0.168) 0.985
VAR 20	0.090 (0.076) 1.193	-0.142 (0.080) -1.778	0.169 (0.083) 2.024	0.072 (0.077) 0.925	-0.924 (0.336) -2.747

Indirect Effects of ETA on Y

	ETA 1	ETA 2	ETA 3	ETA 4	ETA 5
VAR 1	- -	- -	- -	- -	- -
VAR 2	- -	- -	- -	- -	- -
VAR 3	- -	- -	- -	- -	- -

316 APPENDICES

VAR 4	- -	- -	- -	- -	- -
VAR 5	- -	- -	- -	- -	- -
VAR 6	- -	- -	- -	- -	- -
VAR 7	- -	- -	- -	- -	- -
VAR 8	- -	- -	- -	- -	- -
VAR 9	- -	- -	- -	- -	- -
VAR 10	- -	- -	- -	- -	- -
VAR 11	- -	- -	- -	- -	- -
VAR 12	- -	- -	- -	- -	- -
VAR 13	- -	- -	- -	- -	- -
VAR 14	- -	- -	- -	- -	- -
VAR 15	- -	- -	- -	- -	- -
VAR 16	- -	- -	- -	- -	- -
VAR 17	0.098	-0.153	0.183	0.077	- -
	(0.081)	(0.085)	(0.088)	(0.083)	
	1.203	-1.811	2.073	0.929	
VAR 18	-0.051	0.080	-0.096	-0.041	- -
	(0.045)	(0.049)	(0.053)	(0.045)	
	-1.147	1.635	-1.820	-0.903	
VAR 19	-0.016	0.025	-0.030	-0.013	- -
	(0.021)	(0.028)	(0.033)	(0.019)	
	-0.782	0.895	-0.922	-0.690	
VAR 20	0.090	-0.142	0.169	0.072	- -
	(0.076)	(0.080)	(0.083)	(0.077)	
	1.193	-1.778	2.024	0.925	

WPA2014 COVARIANCE AMONG DOMINANCE, NURTURANCE, POWER, INTIMACY, AND ACCOMMODAT

Standardized Total and Indirect Effects

Standardized Total Effects of ETA on ETA

	ETA 1	ETA 2	ETA 3	ETA 4	ETA 5
ETA 1	- -	- -	- -	- -	- -
ETA 2	- -	- -	- -	- -	- -
ETA 3	- -	- -	- -	- -	- -
ETA 4	- -	- -	- -	- -	- -
ETA 5	-0.138	0.217	-0.258	-0.109	- -

Standardized Total Effects of ETA on Y

	ETA 1	ETA 2	ETA 3	ETA 4	ETA 5
VAR 1	0.803	- -	- -	- -	- -
VAR 2	0.464	-0.425	- -	- -	- -
VAR 3	- -	-0.574	- -	- -	- -

VAR 4	−0.425	−0.425	− −	− −	− −
VAR 5	−0.574	− −	− −	− −	− −
VAR 6	−0.425	0.464	− −	− −	− −
VAR 7	− −	0.803	− −	− −	− −
VAR 8	0.464	0.464	− −	− −	− −
VAR 9	− −	− −	0.900	− −	− −
VAR 10	− −	− −	0.521	0.273	− −
VAR 11	− −	− −	− −	0.324	− −
VAR 12	− −	− −	0.273	0.273	− −
VAR 13	− −	− −	0.324	− −	− −
VAR 14	− −	− −	0.273	0.521	− −
VAR 15	− −	− −	− −	0.900	− −
VAR 16	− −	− −	0.521	0.521	− −
VAR 17	0.098	−0.153	0.183	0.077	−0.708
VAR 18	−0.051	0.080	−0.096	−0.041	0.371
VAR 19	−0.016	0.025	−0.030	−0.013	0.117
VAR 20	0.090	−0.142	0.169	0.072	−0.654

Standardized Indirect Effects of ETA on Y

	ETA 1	ETA 2	ETA 3	ETA 4	ETA 5
VAR 1	− −	− −	− −	− −	− −
VAR 2	− −	− −	− −	− −	− −
VAR 3	− −	− −	− −	− −	− −
VAR 4	− −	− −	− −	− −	− −
VAR 5	− −	− −	− −	− −	− −
VAR 6	− −	− −	− −	− −	− −
VAR 7	− −	− −	− −	− −	− −
VAR 8	− −	− −	− −	− −	− −
VAR 9	− −	− −	− −	− −	− −
VAR 10	− −	− −	− −	− −	− −
VAR 11	− −	− −	− −	− −	− −
VAR 12	− −	− −	− −	− −	− −
VAR 13	− −	− −	− −	− −	− −
VAR 14	− −	− −	− −	− −	− −
VAR 15	− −	− −	− −	− −	− −
VAR 16	− −	− −	− −	− −	− −
VAR 17	0.098	−0.153	0.183	0.077	− −
VAR 18	−0.051	0.080	−0.096	−0.041	− −
VAR 19	−0.016	0.025	−0.030	−0.013	− −
VAR 20	0.090	−0.142	0.169	0.072	− −

Time used 0.156 seconds

APPENDIX 2A

Output regarding Creation of Correlation Matrix, Gaines et al. (2013, $n = 172$)

```
DATE: 06/15/2021
TIME: 23:36


P R E L I S  10.2 (64 BIT)

BY

Karl G. Jöreskog & Dag Sörbom


This program is published exclusively by
Scientific Software International, Inc.
http://www.ssicentral.com

Copyright by Scientific Software International, Inc., 1981-2018
Use of this program is subject to the terms specified in the
Universal Copyright Convention.


The following lines were read from file H:\My Documents\Statistics\
Work Placements\wpa2012\Attachment orientation data for PRELIS.PRL:

!PRELIS SYNTAX: Can be edited
SY='H:\My Documents\Statistics\Work Placements\wpa2012\Attachment ori-
entation data for PRELIS.LSF'
OU MA=KM XT


Number of Missing Values per Variable

 NEGANX DISMISS POSAVOID FEARFUL POSANX PREOCC NEGAVOID SECURE
 -------------------------------------------------------------------
      1       5        5       5      6      2        5      5

Distribution of Missing Values
Total Sample Size(N) =     183

Number of Missing Values    0    1    2    3    4    5    6    7    8
          Number of Cases  172    3    1    5    0    0    1    0    1


Listwise Deletion
```

320 APPENDICES

Total Effective Sample Size =   172
Univariate Summary Statistics for Continuous Variables

Variable	Mean	St. Dev.	Skewness	Kurtosis	Minimum	Freq.	Maximum	Freq.
NEGANX	4.494	1.972	-0.345	-1.123	1.000	17	7.000	33
DISMISS	11.797	2.452	-0.405	-0.524	5.000	1	16.000	1
POSAVOID	30.099	10.280	0.344	-0.041	9.000	1	62.000	1
FEARFUL	10.913	3.542	0.471	-0.035	4.000	4	20.000	4
POSANX	57.465	18.994	0.127	-0.254	17.000	2	116.000	1
PREOCC	5.453	1.768	0.033	-0.293	2.000	11	10.000	2
NEGAVOID	42.145	9.693	-0.327	-0.067	14.000	1	63.000	1
SECURE	13.977	2.849	-0.274	0.450	4.000	1	20.000	5

Test of Univariate Normality for Continuous Variables

	Skewness		Kurtosis		Skewness and Kurtosis	
Variable	Z-Score	P-Value	Z-Score	Z-Score	Chi-Square	P-Value
NEGANX	-1.860	0.063	-7.125	0.000	54.220	0.000
DISMISS	-2.161	0.031	-1.788	0.074	7.865	0.020
POSAVOID	1.851	0.064	0.040	0.968	3.426	0.180
FEARFUL	2.489	0.013	0.057	0.955	6.200	0.045
POSANX	0.696	0.487	-0.650	0.515	0.907	0.635
PREOCC	0.181	0.857	-0.793	0.428	0.661	0.719
NEGAVOID	0.078	-0.038	0.969	3.112	0.211	-1.764
SECURE	-1.489	0.137	1.221	0.222	3.707	0.157

Relative Multivariate Kurtosis = 1.093

Test of Multivariate Normality for Continuous Variables

Skewness			Kurtosis			Skewness and Kurtosis	
Value	Z-Score	P-Value	Value	Z-Score	P-Value	Chi-Square	P-Value
7.045	4.446	0.000	87.455	3.515	0.000	32.127	0.000

Correlation Matrix

	NEGANX	DISMISS	POSAVOID	FEARFUL	POSANX	PREOCC
NEGANX	1.000					
DISMISS	0.109	1.000				
POSAVOID	-0.134	0.263	1.000			
FEARFUL	-0.160	0.364	0.679	1.000		
POSANX	-0.400	-0.173	0.341	0.244	1.000	
PREOCC	-0.303	-0.231	0.027	0.079	0.574	1.000
NEGAVOID	0.146	-0.227	-0.463	-0.564	0.091	0.148
SECURE	0.390	0.052	-0.424	-0.468	-0.505	-0.373

Correlation Matrix

```
            NEGAVOID      SECURE
          ------------------------
NEGAVOID    1.000
SECURE      0.334         1.000
```

Total Variance = 8.000 Generalized Variance = 0.0568

Largest Eigenvalue = 2.926 Smallest Eigenvalue = 0.255

Condition Number = 3.386

Means

```
          NEGANX   DISMISS  POSAVOID  FEARFUL   POSANX   PREOCC
        -------------------------------------------------------
          4.494    11.797   30.099    10.913    57.465   5.453
```

Means

```
          NEGAVOID    SECURE
        ----------------------
          42.145      13.977
```

Standard Deviations

```
          NEGANX   DISMISS  POSAVOID  FEARFUL   POSANX   PREOCC
        -------------------------------------------------------
          1.972    2.452    10.280    3.542     18.994   1.768
```

Standard Deviations

```
          NEGAVOID    SECURE
        ----------------------
          9.693       2.849
```

The Problem used   10680 Bytes (= 0.0% of available workspace)

APPENDIX 2B

Output regarding Circulant Correlation Analysis, Gaines et al. (2013), $n = 172$)

```
DATE:  6/15/2021
TIME: 18:32


L I S R E L  10.2 (64 Bit)


BY


Karl G. Jöreskog & Dag Sörbom


This program is published exclusively by
Scientific Software International, Inc.
http://www.ssicentral.com

Copyright by Scientific Software International, Inc., 1981-2019
Use of this program is subject to the terms specified in the
Universal Copyright Convention.


The following lines were read from file H:\My Documents\Statistics\
Work Placements\wpa2012\WPA2012 ECR and RQ circulat correlation
analysis.SPL:


ECR AND RSQ TOGETHER IN CIRCUMPLEX, QUASI-CIRCUMPLEX MODEL
DA NI=8 NO=172 MA=KM
KM FI=ATT1CIRC.COR
MO NY=8 NE=8 TE=SY,FI LY=FU,FI PS=SY,FR
FR TE 1 1 TE 2 2 TE 3 3 TE 4 4 TE 5 5 TE 6 6 TE 7 7 TE 8 8
ST 1.00 LY 1 1 LY 2 2 LY 3 3 LY 4 4 LY 5 5 LY 6 6 LY 7 7 LY 8 8
FI PS 1 1 PS 2 2 PS 3 3 PS 4 4 PS 5 5 PS 6 6 PS 7 7 PS 8 8
ST 1.00 PS 1 1 PS 2 2 PS 3 3 PS 4 4 PS 5 5 PS 6 6 PS 7 7 PS 8 8
EQ PS 2 1 PS 3 2 PS 4 3 PS 5 4 PS 6 5 PS 7 6 PS 8 7 PS 8 1
ST .71 PS 2 1
EQ PS 3 1 PS 4 2 PS 5 3 PS 6 4 PS 7 5 PS 8 6 PS 7 1 PS 8 2
ST .00 PS 3 1
EQ PS 4 1 PS 5 2 PS 6 3 PS 7 4 PS 8 5 PS 6 1 PS 7 2 PS 8 3
ST -.71 PS 4 1
EQ PS 5 1 PS 6 2 PS 7 3 PS 8 4
ST -1.00 PS 5 1
OU ALL ME=ML RO RC AD=OFF
```

324 APPENDICES

ECR AND RSQ TOGETHER IN CIRCUMPLEX, QUASI-CIRCUMPLEX MODEL

```
Number of Input Variables  8
Number of Y - Variables    8
Number of X - Variables    0
Number of ETA - Variables  8
Number of KSI - Variables  0
Number of Observations    172
```

ECR AND RSQ TOGETHER IN CIRCUMPLEX, QUASI-CIRCUMPLEX MODEL

Covariance Matrix

	VAR 1	VAR 2	VAR 3	VAR 4	VAR 5	VAR 6
VAR 1	2.000					
VAR 2	0.109	2.000				
VAR 3	-0.134	0.263	2.000			
VAR 4	-0.160	0.364	0.679	2.000		
VAR 5	-0.400	-0.173	0.341	0.244	2.000	
VAR 6	-0.303	-0.231	0.027	0.079	0.574	2.000
VAR 7	0.146	-0.227	-0.463	-0.564	0.091	0.148
VAR 8	0.390	0.052	-0.424	-0.468	-0.505	-0.373

Covariance Matrix

	VAR 7	VAR 8
VAR 7	2.000	
VAR 8	0.334	2.000

Total Variance - 16.000 Generalized Variance = 131.142

Largest Eigenvalue = 3.926 Smallest Eigenvalue = 1.255

Condition Number = 1.769

BEHAVIOR UNDER STEEPEST DESCENT ITERATIONS

ITER	TRY	ABSCISSA	SLOPE	FUNCTION
1	0	0.00000000D+00	-0.27810001D+02	0.44807807D+01
	1	0.10000000D+01	0.15590087D+03	0.68526215D+02
	2	0.15137918D+00	-0.88817842D-15	0.23758531D+01
2	0	0.00000000D+00	-0.35182311D+01	0.23758531D+01
	1	0.15137918D+00	-0.17574309D+01	0.19765404D+01
	2	0.30275836D+00	0.33693419D-02	0.18437762D+01
3	0	0.00000000D+00	-0.30610452D+01	0.18437762D+01
	1	0.30275836D+00	0.15089828D+01	0.16088263D+01
	2	0.20279023D+00	0.72164497D-15	0.15334012D+01
4	0	0.00000000D+00	-0.16880919D+01	0.15334012D+01

APPENDICES   325

	1	0.20279023D+00	-0.46191377D+00	0.13154011D+01
	2	0.40558046D+00	0.76426436D+00	0.13460580D+01
	3	0.27918337D+00	0.00000000D+00	0.12977576D+01
5	0	0.00000000D+00	-0.17899445D+01	0.12977576D+01
	1	0.27918337D+00	0.66756721D+00	0.11410831D+01
	2	0.20334501D+00	0.24980018D-15	0.11157695D+01
6	0	0.00000000D+00	-0.10077912D+01	0.11157695D+01
	1	0.20334501D+00	-0.27368112D+00	0.98547898D+00
	2	0.40669002D+00	0.46042901D+00	0.10044661D+01
	3	0.27915337D+00	0.66613381D-15	0.97510532D+00
7	0	0.00000000D+00	-0.10693638D+01	0.97510532D+00
	1	0.27915337D+00	0.39866266D+00	0.88149108D+00
	2	0.20334546D+00	-0.83266727D-16	0.86638019D+00
8	0	0.00000000D+00	-0.60209337D+00	0.86638019D+00
	1	0.20334546D+00	-0.16350665D+00	0.78853954D+00
	2	0.40669091D+00	0.27508006D+00	0.79988352D+00
	3	0.27915335D+00	0.41633363D-16	0.78234200D+00
9	0	0.00000000D+00	-0.63887953D+00	0.78234200D+00
	1	0.27915335D+00	0.23817651D+00	0.72641320D+00
	2	0.20334546D+00	-0.76327833D-16	0.71738537D+00
10	0	0.00000000D+00	-0.35971402D+00	0.71738537D+00
	1	0.20334546D+00	-0.97685240D-01	0.67088034D+00
	2	0.40669091D+00	0.16434354D+00	0.67765767D+00
	3	0.27915335D+00	-0.18735014D-15	0.66717768D+00
11	0	0.00000000D+00	-0.38169150D+00	0.66717768D+00
	1	0.27915335D+00	0.14229592D+00	0.63376364D+00
	2	0.20334546D+00	0.00000000D+00	0.62837007D+00
12	0	0.00000000D+00	-0.21490716D+00	0.62837007D+00
	1	0.20334546D+00	-0.58360965D-01	0.60058615D+00
	2	0.40669091D+00	0.98185228D-01	0.60463519D+00
	3	0.27915335D+00	0.13530843D-15	0.59837404D+00
13	0	0.00000000D+00	-0.22803736D+00	0.59837404D+00
	1	0.27915335D+00	0.85013122D-01	0.57841119D+00
	2	0.20334546D+00	0.13877788D-15	0.57518886D+00

ECR AND RSQ TOGETHER IN CIRCUMPLEX, QUASI-CIRCUMPLEX MODEL

Parameter Specifications

PSI

	ETA 1	ETA 2	ETA 3	ETA 4	ETA 5	ETA 6
ETA 1	0					
ETA 2	1	0				
ETA 3	2	1	0			
ETA 4	3	2	1	0		
ETA 5	4	3	2	1	0	
ETA 6	3	4	3	2	1	0
ETA 7	2	3	4	3	2	1
ETA 8	1	2	3	4	3	2

326 APPENDICES

```
PSI

            ETA 7      ETA 8
         ---------------------
ETA 7        0
ETA 8        1          0


THETA-EPS

        VAR 1      VAR 2      VAR 3      VAR 4      VAR 5      VAR 6
     --------------------------------------------------------------
          5          6          7          8          9         10


THETA-EPS

        VAR 7      VAR 8
     ---------------------
         11         12
```

ECR AND RSQ TOGETHER IN CIRCUMPLEX, QUASI-CIRCUMPLEX MODEL

Initial Estimates (TSLS)

```
LAMBDA-Y

            ETA 1      ETA 2      ETA 3      ETA 4      ETA 5      ETA 6
         --------------------------------------------------------------
VAR 1      1.000        - -        - -        - -        - -        - -
VAR 2        - -      1.000        - -        - -        - -        - -
VAR 3        - -        - -      1.000        - -        - -        - -
VAR 4        - -        - -        - -      1.000        - -        - -
VAR 5        - -      - - - -      - -        - -      1.000        - -
VAR 6        - -      - - - -      - -        - -        - -      1.000
VAR 7        - -      - - - -      - -        - -        - -        - -
VAR 8        - -      - - - -      - -        - -        - -        - -


LAMBDA-Y

            ETA 7      ETA 8
         ---------------------
VAR 1        - -        - -
VAR 2        - -        - -
VAR 3        - -        - -
VAR 4        - -        - -
VAR 5        - -        - -
VAR 6        - -        - -
VAR 7      1.000        - -
VAR 8        - -      1.000
```

Covariance Matrix of ETA

	ETA 1	ETA 2	ETA 3	ETA 4	ETA 5	ETA 6
ETA 1	1.000					
ETA 2	0.324	1.000				
ETA 3	0.071	0.324	1.000			
ETA 4	-0.269	0.071	0.324	1.000		
ETA 5	-0.391	-0.269	0.071	0.324	1.000	
ETA 6	-0.269	-0.391	-0.269	0.071	0.324	1.000
ETA 7	0.071	-0.269	-0.391	-0.269	0.071	0.324
ETA 8	0.324	0.071	-0.269	-0.391	-0.269	0.071

Covariance Matrix of ETA

	ETA 7	ETA 8
ETA 7	1.000	
ETA 8	0.324	1.000

PSI

	ETA 1	ETA 2	ETA 3	ETA 4	ETA 5	ETA 6
ETA 1	1.000					
ETA 2	0.324	1.000				
ETA 3	0.071	0.324	1.000			
ETA 4	-0.269	0.071	0.324	1.000		
ETA 5	-0.391	-0.269	0.071	0.324	1.000	
ETA 6	-0.269	-0.391	-0.269	0.071	0.324	1.000
ETA 7	0.071	-0.269	-0.391	-0.269	0.071	0.324
ETA 8	0.324	0.071	-0.269	-0.391	-0.269	0.071

PSI

	ETA 7	ETA 8
ETA 7	1.000	
ETA 8	0.324	1.000

THETA-EPS

VAR 1	VAR 2	VAR 3	VAR 4	VAR 5	VAR 6
0.806	0.806	0.806	0.806	0.806	0.806

328 APPENDICES

THETA-EPS

VAR 7	VAR 8
0.806	0.806

Behavior under Minimization Iterations

Iter	Try	Abscissa	Slpe	Function
1	0	0.00000000D+00	-0.67497742D-01	0.12170316D+00
	1	0.10000000D+01	0.51375918D-03	0.91640494D-01
2	0	0.00000000D+00	-0.11020428D-03	0.91640494D-01
	1	0.10000000D+01	-0.12781143D-04	0.91579064D-01
	2	0.20000000D+01	0.83918917D-04	0.91614691D-01
	3	0.11321731D+01	0.40099545D-07	0.91578223D-01
3	0	0.00000000D+00	-0.15278963D-05	0.91578223D-01
	1	0.11321731D+01	-0.14943428D-06	0.91577273D-01
4	0	0.00000000D+00	-0.32993203D-07	0.91577273D-01
	1	0.11321731D+01	-0.31141023D-09	0.91577254D-01
5	0	0.00000000D+00	-0.98212174D-09	0.91577254D-01
	1	0.11321731D+01	-0.14801281D-09	0.91577253D-01
	2	0.22643461D+01	0.68602104D-09	0.91577253D-01
	3	0.13330955D+01	0.54799671D-14	0.91577253D-01
6	0	0.00000000D+00	-0.51981732D-11	0.91577253D-01
	1	0.13330955D+01	0.61247217D-12	0.91577253D-01
	2	0.11925803D+01	0.31807201D-18	0.91577253D-01

ECR AND RSQ TOGETHER IN CIRCUMPLEX, QUASI-CIRCUMPLEX MODEL

Number of Iterations = 6
LISREL Estimates (Maximum Likelihood)

LAMBDA-Y

	ETA 1	ETA 2	ETA 3	ETA 4	ETA 5	ETA 6
VAR 1	1.000	- -	- -	- -	- -	- -
VAR 2	- -	1.000	- -	- -	- -	- -
VAR 3	- -	- -	1.000	- -	- -	- -
VAR 4	- -	- -	- -	1.000	- -	- -
VAR 5	- -	- -	- -	- -	1.000	- -
VAR 6	- -	- -	- -	- -	- -	1.000
VAR 7	- -	- -	- -	- -	- -	- -
VAR 8	- -	- -	- -	- -	- -	- -

APPENDICES 329

LAMBDA-Y

	ETA 7	ETA 8
VAR 1	- -	- -
VAR 2	- -	- -
VAR 3	- -	- -
VAR 4	- -	- -
VAR 5	- -	- -
VAR 6	- -	- -
VAR 7	1.000	- -
VAR 8	- -	1.000

Covariance Matrix of ETA

	ETA 1	ETA 2	ETA 3	ETA 4	ETA 5	ETA 6
ETA 1	1.000					
ETA 2	0.346	1.000				
ETA 3	0.074	0.346	1.000			
ETA 4	-0.297	0.074	0.346	1.000		
ETA 5	-0.395	-0.297	0.074	0.346	1.000	
ETA 6	-0.297	-0.395	-0.297	0.074	0.346	1.000
ETA 7	0.074	-0.297	-0.395	-0.297	0.074	0.346
ETA 8	0.346	0.074	-0.297	-0.395	-0.297	0.074

Covariance Matrix of ETA

	ETA 7	ETA 8
ETA 7	1.000	
ETA 8	0.346	1.000

PSI

	ETA 1	ETA 2	ETA 3	ETA 4	ETA 5	ETA 6
ETA 1	1.000					
ETA 2	0.346	1.000				
	(0.059)					
	5.852					
ETA 3	0.074	0.346	1.000			
	(0.043)	(0.059)				
	1.701	5.852				
ETA 4	-0.297	0.074	0.346	1.000		
	(0.059)	(0.043)	(0.059)			
	-5.011	1.701	5.852			

330 APPENDICES

ETA 5	-0.395	-0.297	0.074	0.346	1.000
	0.082)	(0.059)	(0.043)	(0.059)	
	-4.847	-5.011	1.701	5.852	

ETA 6	-0.297	-0.395	-0.297	0.074	0.346	1.000
	(0.059)	(0.082)	(0.059)	(0.043)	(0.059)	
	-5.011	-4.847	-5.011	1.701	5.852	

ETA 7	0.074	-0.297	-0.395	-0.297	0.074	0.346
	(0.043)	(0.059)	(0.082)	(0.059)	(0.043)	(0.059)
	1.701	-5.011	-4.847	-5.011	1.701	5.852

ETA 8	0.346	0.074	-0.297	-0.395	-0.297	0.074
	(0.059)	(0.043)	(0.059)	(0.082)	(0.059)	(0.043)
	5.852	1.701	-5.011	-4.847	-5.011	1.701

PSI

	ETA 7	ETA 8
ETA 7	1.000	
ETA 8	0.346	1.000
	0.059)	
	5.852	

THETA-EPS

	VAR 1	VAR 2	VAR 3	VAR 4	VAR 5	VAR 6
	1.088	1.128	0.942	0.914	0.917	1.101
	(0.208)	(0.213)	(0.193)	(0.190)	(0.191)	(0.210)
	5.224	5.308	4.878	4.812	4.813	5.250

THETA-EPS

	VAR 7	VAR 8
	0.973	0.961
	(0.196)	(0.195)
	4.956	4.930

Squared Multiple Correlations for Y - Variables

	VAR 1	VAR 2	VAR 3	VAR 4	VAR 5	VAR 6
	0.479	0.470	0.515	0.522	0.522	0.476

APPENDICES 331

Squared Multiple Correlations for Y - Variables

```
   VAR 7     VAR 8
-----------------------
   0.507     0.510
```

Log-likelihood Values

	Estimated Model	Saturated Model
Number of free parameters(t)	12	36
-2ln(L)	2246.223	2214.720
AIC (Akaike, 1974)*	2270.223	2286.720
BIC (Schwarz, 1978)*	2307.992	2400.030

*LISREL uses AIC= 2t - 2ln(L) and BIC = tln(N)- 2ln(L)

Goodness-of-Fit Statistics

Degrees of Freedom for (C1)-(C2)	24
Maximum Likelihood Ratio Chi-Square (C1)	31.503 (P = 0.1398)
Browne's (1984) ADF Chi-Square (C2_NT)	30.898 (P = 0.1567)
Estimated Non-centrality Parameter (NCP)	7.503
90 Percent Confidence Interval for NCP	(0.0 ; 26.192)
Minimum Fit Function Value	0.183
Population Discrepancy Function Value (F0)	0.0436
90 Percent Confidence Interval for F0	(0.0 ; 0.152)
Root Mean Square Error of Approximation (RMSEA)	0.0426
90 Percent Confidence Interval for RMSEA	(0.0 ; 0.0797)
P-Value for Test of Close Fit (RMSEA < 0.05)	0.586
Expected Cross-Validation Index (ECVI)	0.323
90 Percent Confidence Interval for ECVI	(0.279 ; 0.431)
ECVI for Saturated Model	0.419
ECVI for Independence Model	0.762
Chi-Square for Independence Model (28 df)	115.051
Normed Fit Index (NFI)	0.726
Non-Normed Fit Index (NNFI)	0.899
Parsimony Normed Fit Index (PNFI)	0.622
Comparative Fit Index (CFI)	0.914
Incremental Fit Index (IFI)	0.918
Relative Fit Index (RFI)	0.681
Critical N (CN)	234.301
Root Mean Square Residual (RMR)	0.171
Standardized RMR	0.0853
Goodness of Fit Index (GFI)	0.957
Adjusted Goodness of Fit Index (AGFI)	0.936
Parsimony Goodness of Fit Index (PGFI)	0.638

332 APPENDICES

ECR AND RSQ TOGETHER IN CIRCUMPLEX, QUASI-CIRCUMPLEX MODEL

Fitted Covariance Matrix

	VAR 1	VAR 2	VAR 3	VAR 4	VAR 5	VAR 6
VAR 1	2.088					
VAR 2	0.346	2.128				
VAR 3	0.074	0.346	1.942			
VAR 4	-0.297	0.074	0.346	1.914		
VAR 5	-0.395	-0.297	0.074	0.346	1.917	
VAR 6	-0.297	-0.395	-0.297	0.074	0.346	2.101
VAR 7	0.074	-0.297	-0.395	-0.297	0.074	0.346
VAR 8	0.346	0.074	-0.297	-0.395	-0.297	0.074

Fitted Covariance Matrix

	VAR 7	VAR 8
VAR 7	1.973	
VAR 8	0.346	1.961

Fitted Residuals

	VAR 1	VAR 2	VAR 3	VAR 4	VAR 5	VAR 6
VAR 1	-0.088					
VAR 2	-0.237	-0.128				
VAR 3	-0.208	-0.083	0.058			
VAR 4	0.137	0.290	0.332	0.086		
VAR 5	-0.004	0.124	0.267	-0.103	0.083	
VAR 6	-0.006	0.165	0.323	0.005	0.227	-0.101
VAR 7	0.072	0.070	-0.068	-0.267	0.018	-0.198
VAR 8	0.044	-0.022	-0.128	-0.073	-0.208	-0.447

Fitted Residuals

	VAR 7	VAR 8
VAR 7	0.027	
VAR 8	-0.012	0.039

Summary Statistics for Fitted Residuals

Smallest Fitted Residual =   -0.447
Median Fitted Residual =   0.000
Largest Fitted Residual =   0.332

APPENDICES 333

```
Stemleaf Plot
 - 4|5
 - 3|
 - 2|74110
 - 1|3300
 - 0|98772110
   0|1234467789
   1|246
   2|379
   3|23
```

Standardized Residuals

	VAR 1	VAR 2	VAR 3	VAR 4	VAR 5	VAR 6
VAR 1	-0.392					
VAR 2	-1.821	-1.695				
VAR 3	-1.353	-0.572	0.278			
VAR 4	0.890	1.894	2.224	0.415		
VAR 5	-0.027	0.793	1.977	-0.708	0.407	
VAR 6	-0.037	1.003	2.078	0.034	1.465	-0.445
VAR 7	0.464	0.442	-0.445	-1.840	0.119	-1.332
VAR 8	0.281	-0.141	-0.852	-0.484	-1.331	-2.907

Standardized Residuals

	VAR 7	VAR 8
VAR 7	0.131	
VAR 8	-0.078	0.479

Summary Statistics for Standardized Residuals

```
Smallest Standardized Residual =   -2.907
  Median Standardized Residual =    0.003
 Largest Standardized Residual =    2.224
```

```
Stemleaf Plot
 - 2|9
 - 1|887433
 - 0|976544411000
   0|11334445589
   1|059
   2|012
Largest Negative Standardized Residuals
Residual for    VAR 8 and    VAR 6  -2.907
```

ECR AND RSQ TOGETHER IN CIRCUMPLEX, QUASI-CIRCUMPLEX MODEL

334 APPENDICES

Qplot of Standardized Residuals

```
       Qplot of Standardized Residuals
  3.5.........................................................
       .                                                  . .
       .                                                   . .
       .                                                  .
       .                                               .
       .                                             .
       .                                           .
       .                                         .
       .                                       .
       .                                      .
       .                                    .
       .                                  .      x
       .                               .
       .                            .       x
       .                          .       x
 N     .                        .       x
 o     .                      x     x
 r     .                        xx
 m     .                   *
 a     .                   *.
 l     .                x x
       .                 xx
 Q     .                xx
 u     .                *
 a     .              .xx
 n     .              *
 t     .             xx
 i     .            x x
 l     .        x   .x
 e     .        xx  .
 s     .       x     .
       .       x    .
       .       x    .
       .          .
       .         .
       .    x       .
       .          .
       .         .
       .        .
       .       .
       .      .
       .     .
       . .
 -3.5.........................................................
   -3.5                                                    3.5
                 Standardized Residuals
```

APPENDICES 335

ECR AND RSQ TOGETHER IN CIRCUMPLEX, QUASI-CIRCUMPLEX MODEL

Modification Indices and Expected Change

Modification Indices for LAMBDA-Y

	ETA 1	ETA 2	ETA 3	ETA 4	ETA 5	ETA 6
VAR 1	0.979	1.132	0.294	0.331	0.165	0.343
VAR 2	2.907	1.869	0.006	2.037	2.196	1.791
VAR 3	3.830	1.002	0.521	5.103	5.885	3.061
VAR 4	2.956	6.431	4.649	0.172	3.203	3.909
VAR 5	0.218	0.042	0.400	0.031	1.109	1.460
VAR 6	1.441	0.224	5.667	3.666	4.757	0.452
VAR 7	0.189	0.088	0.233	1.489	0.003	0.260
VAR 8	0.802	0.696	0.011	0.376	3.312	6.117

Modification Indices for LAMBDA-Y

	ETA 7	ETA 8
VAR 1	0.055	0.086
VAR 2	0.111	0.745
VAR 3	0.245	2.636
VAR 4	4.802	0.004
VAR 5	0.329	0.551
VAR 6	3.611	10.692
VAR 7	0.189	0.141
VAR 8	0.580	0.086

Expected Change for LAMBDA-Y

	ETA 1	ETA 2	ETA 3	ETA 4	ETA 5	ETA 6
VAR 1	-0.247	-0.163	-0.078	0.085	0.063	0.089
VAR 2	-0.262	-0.345	-0.012	0.206	0.221	0.215
VAR 3	-0.276	-0.149	0.175	0.323	0.334	0.256
VAR 4	0.249	0.357	0.309	0.099	-0.255	-0.277
VAR 5	-0.072	-0.030	0.087	-0.025	0.255	0.178
VAR 6	-0.182	0.076	0.353	0.274	0.325	-0.169
VAR 7	0.062	0.044	-0.074	-0.175	-0.008	-0.076
VAR 8	0.132	0.119	0.015	-0.093	-0.260	-0.351

Expected Change for LAMBDA-Y

	ETA 7	ETA 8
VAR 1	0.034	-0.044
VAR 2	0.050	-0.125
VAR 3	-0.075	-0.232
VAR 4	-0.312	-0.009

336 APPENDICES

VAR 5	0.079	-0.106
VAR 6	-0.286	-0.471
VAR 7	0.106	0.055
VAR 8	-0.111	0.071

Standardized Expected Change for LAMBDA-Y

	ETA 1	ETA 2	ETA 3	ETA 4	ETA 5	ETA 6
VAR 1	-0.247	-0.163	-0.078	0.085	0.063	0.089
VAR 2	-0.262	-0.345	-0.012	0.206	0.221	0.215
VAR 3	-0.276	-0.149	0.175	0.323	0.334	0.256
VAR 4	0.249	0.357	0.309	0.099	-0.255	-0.277
VAR 5	-0.072	-0.030	0.087	-0.025	0.255	0.178
VAR 6	-0.182	0.076	0.353	0.274	0.325	-0.169
VAR 7	0.062	0.044	-0.074	-0.175	-0.008	-0.076
VAR 8	0.132	0.119	0.015	-0.093	-0.260	-0.351

Standardized Expected Change for LAMBDA-Y

	ETA 7	ETA 8
VAR 1	0.034	-0.044
VAR 2	0.050	-0.125
VAR 3	-0.075	-0.232
VAR 4	-0.312	-0.009
VAR 5	0.079	-0.106
VAR 6	-0.286	-0.471
VAR 7	0.106	0.055
VAR 8	-0.111	0.071

Modification Indices for PSI

	ETA 1	ETA 2	ETA 3	ETA 4	ETA 5	ETA 6
ETA 1	- -					
ETA 2	0.965	- -				
ETA 3	0.284	0.017	- -			
ETA 4	0.754	1.275	1.601	- -		
ETA 5	0.053	0.193	1.852	1.119	- -	
ETA 6	0.002	0.357	1.405	0.023	2.683	- -
ETA 7	0.003	0.321	0.222	1.900	0.666	0.347
ETA 8	0.015	0.072	0.245	0.017	1.272	6.285

Modification Indices for PSI

	ETA 7	ETA 8
ETA 7	- -	
ETA 8	0.006	- -

APPENDICES 337

Expected Change for PSI

	ETA 1	ETA 2	ETA 3	ETA 4	ETA 5	ETA 6
ETA 1	- -					
ETA 2	-0.137	- -				
ETA 3	-0.070	-0.018	- -			
ETA 4	0.112	0.150	0.158	- -		
ETA 5	-0.028	0.058	0.171	-0.131	- -	
ETA 6	0.007	0.080	0.156	-0.020	0.215	- -
ETA 7	0.008	0.076	-0.056	-0.172	0.104	-0.079
ETA 8	-0.016	-0.036	-0.062	0.015	-0.141	-0.335

Expected Change for PSI

	ETA 7	ETA 8
ETA 7	- -	
ETA 8	-0.010	- -

Standardized Expected Change for PSI

	ETA 1	ETA 2	ETA 3	ETA 4	ETA 5	ETA 6
ETA 1	- -					
ETA 2	-0.137	- -				
ETA 3	-0.070	-0.018	- -			
ETA 4	0.112	0.150	0.158	- -		
ETA 5	-0.028	0.058	0.171	-0.131	- -	
ETA 6	0.007	0.080	0.156	-0.020	0.215	- -
ETA 7	0.008	0.076	-0.056	-0.172	0.104	-0.079
ETA 8	-0.016	-0.036	-0.062	0.015	-0.141	-0.335

Standardized Expected Change for PSI

	ETA 7	ETA 8
ETA 7	- -	
ETA 8	-0.010	- -

Modification Indices for THETA-EPS

	VAR 1	VAR 2	VAR 3	VAR 4	VAR 5	VAR 6
VAR 1	- -					
VAR 2	0.965	- -				
VAR 3	0.284	0.017	- -			
VAR 4	0.754	1.275	1.601	- -		
VAR 5	0.053	0.193	1.852	1.119	- -	
VAR 6	0.002	0.357	1.405	0.023	2.683	- -
VAR 7	0.003	0.321	0.222	1.900	0.666	0.347
VAR 8	0.015	0.072	0.245	0.017	1.272	6.285

338 APPENDICES

Modification Indices for THETA-EPS

	VAR 7	VAR 8
VAR 7	- -	
VAR 8	0.006	- -

Expected Change for THETA-EPS

	VAR 1	VAR 2	VAR 3	VAR 4	VAR 5	VAR 6
VAR 1	- -					
VAR 2	-0.154	- -				
VAR 3	-0.080	-0.020	- -			
VAR 4	0.129	0.171	0.183	- -		
VAR 5	-0.038	0.066	0.198	-0.152	- -	
VAR 6	0.008	0.102	0.177	-0.023	0.245	- -
VAR 7	0.009	0.086	-0.076	-0.199	0.120	-0.089
VAR 8	-0.018	-0.041	-0.072	0.021	-0.162	-0.381

Expected Change for THETA-EPS

	VAR 7	VAR 8
VAR 7	- -	
VAR 8	-0.011	- -

Maximum Modification Index is 10.69 for Element (6, 8) of LAMBDA-Y

Covariance Matrix of Parameter Estimates

	PS 2_1	PS 3_1	PS 4_1	PS 5_1	TE 1_1	TE 2_2
PS 2_1	0.004					
PS 3_1	0.000	0.002				
PS 4_1	-0.001	0.000	0.004			
PS 5_1	-0.002	0.000	0.002	0.007		
TE 1_1	0.002	0.000	-0.002	-0.003	0.043	
TE 2_2	0.002	0.000	-0.002	-0.003	0.002	0.045
TE 3_3	0.002	0.000	-0.002	-0.003	0.002	0.002
TE 4_4	0.002	0.000	-0.002	-0.003	0.002	0.002
TE 5_5	0.002	0.000	-0.002	-0.003	0.002	0.002
TE 6_6	0.002	0.000	-0.002	-0.003	0.002	0.002
TE 7_7	0.002	0.000	-0.002	-0.003	0.002	0.002
TE 8_8	0.002	0.000	-0.002	-0.003	0.002	0.002

Covariance Matrix of Parameter Estimates

	TE 3_3	TE 4_4	TE 5_5	TE 6_6	TE 7_7	TE 8_8
TE 3_3	0.037					
TE 4_4	0.002	0.036				
TE 5_5	0.002	0.002	0.036			
TE 6_6	0.002	0.002	0.002	0.044		
TE 7_7	0.002	0.002	0.002	0.002	0.039	
TE 8_8	0.002	0.002	0.002	0.002	0.002	0.038

ECR AND RSQ TOGETHER IN CIRCUMPLEX, QUASI-CIRCUMPLEX MODEL

Correlation Matrix of Parameter Estimates

	PS 2_1	PS 3_1	PS 4_1	PS 5_1	TE 1_1	TE 2_2
PS 2_1	1.000					
PS 3_1	0.049	1.000				
PS 4_1	-0.361	0.049	1.000			
PS 5_1	-0.437	0.098	0.490	1.000		
TE 1_1	0.190	0.040	-0.171	-0.173	1.000	
TE 2_2	0.187	0.040	-0.170	-0.162	0.038	1.000
TE 3_3	0.206	0.041	-0.183	-0.184	0.056	0.041
TE 4_4	0.215	0.039	-0.186	-0.187	0.050	0.057
TE 5_5	0.209	0.043	-0.185	-0.181	0.044	0.048
TE 6_6	0.194	0.040	-0.170	-0.164	0.045	0.040
TE 7_7	0.202	0.041	-0.181	-0.182	0.056	0.047
TE 8_8	0.203	0.038	-0.187	-0.185	0.043	0.055

Correlation Matrix of Parameter Estimates

	TE 3_3	TE 4_4	TE 5_5	TE 6_6	TE 7_7	TE 8_8
TE 3_3	1.000					
TE 4_4	0.047	1.000				
TE 5_5	0.061	0.047	1.000			
TE 6_6	0.048	0.058	0.042	1.000		
TE 7_7	0.046	0.053	0.060	0.041	1.000	
TE 8_8	0.053	0.049	0.053	0.056	0.045	1.000

ECR AND RSQ TOGETHER IN CIRCUMPLEX, QUASI-CIRCUMPLEX MODEL

Covariances

340 APPENDICES

Y - ETA

	VAR 1	VAR 2	VAR 3	VAR 4	VAR 5	VAR 6
ETA 1	1.000	0.346	0.074	-0.297	-0.395	-0.297
ETA 2	0.346	1.000	0.346	0.074	-0.297	-0.395
ETA 3	0.074	0.346	1.000	0.346	0.074	-0.297
ETA 4	-0.297	0.074	0.346	1.000	0.346	0.074
ETA 5	-0.395	-0.297	0.074	0.346	1.000	0.346
ETA 6	-0.297	-0.395	-0.297	0.074	0.346	1.000
ETA 7	0.074	-0.297	-0.395	-0.297	0.074	0.346
ETA 8	0.346	0.074	-0.297	-0.395	-0.297	0.074

Y - ETA

	VAR 7	VAR 8
ETA 1	0.074	0.346
ETA 2	-0.297	0.074
ETA 3	-0.395	-0.297
ETA 4	-0.297	-0.395
ETA 5	0.074	-0.297
ETA 6	0.346	0.074
ETA 7	1.000	0.346
ETA 8	0.346	1.000

ECR AND RSQ TOGETHER IN CIRCUMPLEX, QUASI-CIRCUMPLEX MODEL

First Order Derivatives

LAMBDA-Y

	ETA 1	ETA 2	ETA 3	ETA 4	ETA 5	ETA 6
VAR 1	0.023	0.041	0.022	-0.023	-0.015	-0.023
VAR 2	0.065	0.032	0.003	-0.058	-0.058	-0.049
VAR 3	0.081	0.039	-0.017	-0.092	-0.103	-0.070
VAR 4	-0.069	-0.105	-0.088	-0.010	0.073	0.082
VAR 5	0.018	0.008	-0.027	0.007	-0.025	-0.048
VAR 6	0.046	-0.017	-0.094	-0.078	-0.086	0.016
VAR 7	-0.018	-0.012	0.018	0.050	0.002	0.020
VAR 8	-0.035	-0.034	-0.004	0.024	0.074	0.102

LAMBDA-Y

	ETA 7	ETA 8
VAR 1	-0.009	0.011
VAR 2	-0.013	0.035
VAR 3	0.019	0.066
VAR 4	0.090	0.002

VAR 5	-0.024	0.031
VAR 6	0.074	0.133
VAR 7	-0.010	-0.015
VAR 8	0.031	-0.007

PSI

	ETA 1	ETA 2	ETA 3	ETA 4	ETA 5	ETA 6
ETA 1	0.000					
ETA 2	0.037	0.000				
ETA 3	0.021	0.005	0.000			
ETA 4	-0.034	-0.044	-0.051	0.000		
ETA 5	0.008	-0.017	-0.055	0.043	0.000	
ETA 6	-0.002	-0.020	-0.046	0.006	-0.064	0.000
ETA 7	-0.002	-0.022	0.017	0.056	-0.033	0.023
ETA 8	0.005	0.010	0.020	-0.005	0.046	0.097

PSI

	ETA 7	ETA 8
ETA 7	0.000	
ETA 8	0.003	0.000

THETA-EPS

	VAR 1	VAR 2	VAR 3	VAR 4	VAR 5	VAR 6
VAR 1	0.000					
VAR 2	0.037	0.000				
VAR 3	0.021	0.005	0.000			
VAR 4	-0.034	-0.044	-0.051	0.000		
VAR 5	0.008	-0.017	-0.055	0.043	0.000	
VAR 6	-0.002	-0.020	-0.046	0.006	-0.064	0.000
VAR 7	-0.002	-0.022	0.017	0.056	-0.033	0.023
VAR 8	0.005	0.010	0.020	-0.005	0.046	0.097

THETA-EPS

	VAR 7	VAR 8
VAR 7	0.000	
VAR 8	0.003	0.000

ECR AND RSQ TOGETHER IN CIRCUMPLEX, QUASI-CIRCUMPLEX MODEL

Factor Scores Regressions

342 APPENDICES

ETA

	VAR 1	VAR 2	VAR 3	VAR 4	VAR 5	VAR 6
ETA 1	0.421	0.071	0.032	-0.062	-0.078	-0.056
ETA 2	0.074	0.412	0.081	0.031	-0.065	-0.070
ETA 3	0.028	0.067	0.456	0.075	0.027	-0.054
ETA 4	-0.052	0.025	0.073	0.463	0.074	0.026
ETA 5	-0.065	-0.052	0.027	0.074	0.463	0.068
ETA 6	-0.057	-0.069	-0.063	0.031	0.081	0.418
ETA 7	0.026	-0.053	-0.073	-0.059	0.031	0.069
ETA 8	0.068	0.027	-0.057	-0.073	-0.059	0.026

ETA

	VAR 7	VAR 8
ETA 1	0.029	0.077
ETA 2	-0.061	0.031
ETA 3	-0.070	-0.056
ETA 4	-0.056	-0.069
ETA 5	0.029	-0.056
ETA 6	0.078	0.030
ETA 7	0.448	0.074
ETA 8	0.073	0.451

ECR AND RSQ TOGETHER IN CIRCUMPLEX, QUASI-CIRCUMPLEX MODEL

Standardized Solution

LAMBDA-Y

	ETA 1	ETA 2	ETA 3	ETA 4	ETA 5	ETA 6
VAR 1	1.000	- -	- -	- -	- -	- -
VAR 2	- -	1.000	- -	- -	- -	- -
VAR 3	- -	- -	1.000	- -	- -	- -
VAR 4	- -	- -	- -	1.000	- -	- -
VAR 5	- -	- -	- -	- -	1.000	- -
VAR 6	- -	- -	- -	- -	- -	1.000
VAR 7	- -	- -	- -	- -	- -	- -
VAR 8	- -	- -	- -	- -	- -	-

LAMBDA-Y

	ETA 7	ETA 8
VAR 1	- -	- -
VAR 2	- -	- -
VAR 3	- -	- -
VAR 4	- -	- -
VAR 5	- -	- -

```
VAR 6        - -          - -
VAR 7       1.000         - -
VAR 8        - -         1.000
```

Correlation Matrix of ETA

	ETA 1	ETA 2	ETA 3	ETA 4	ETA 5	ETA 6
ETA 1	1.000					
ETA 2	0.346	1.000				
ETA 3	0.074	0.346	1.000			
ETA 4	-0.297	0.074	0.346	1.000		
ETA 5	-0.395	-0.297	0.074	0.346	1.000	
ETA 6	-0.297	-0.395	-0.297	0.074	0.346	1.000
ETA 7	0.074	-0.297	-0.395	-0.297	0.074	0.346
ETA 8	0.346	0.074	-0.297	-0.395	-0.297	0.074

Correlation Matrix of ETA

	ETA 7	ETA 8
ETA 7	1.000	
ETA 8	0.346	1.000

PSI

	ETA 1	ETA 2	ETA 3	ETA 4	ETA 5	ETA 6
ETA 1	1.000					
ETA 2	0.346	1.000				
ETA 3	0.074	0.346	1.000			
ETA 4	-0.297	0.074	0.346	1.000		
ETA 5	-0.395	-0.297	0.074	0.346	1.000	
ETA 6	-0.297	-0.395	-0.297	0.074	0.346	1.000
ETA 7	0.074	-0.297	-0.395	-0.297	0.074	0.346
ETA 8	0.346	0.074	-0.297	-0.395	-0.297	0.074

PSI

	ETA 7	ETA 8
ETA 7	1.000	
ETA 8	0.346	1.000

ECR AND RSQ TOGETHER IN CIRCUMPLEX, QUASI-CIRCUMPLEX MODEL

Total and Indirect Effects

ECR AND RSQ TOGETHER IN CIRCUMPLEX, QUASI-CIRCUMPLEX MODEL

Standardized Total and Indirect Effects

Time used 0.016 seconds

APPENDIX 2C

Output regarding Initial Covariance Structure Analysis, Gaines et al. (2013), $n = 172$

```
DATE: 12/30/2020
TIME: 17:15


L I S R E L  10.2 (64 Bit)


BY


Karl G. Jöreskog & Dag Sörbom


This program is published exclusively by
Scientific Software International, Inc.
http://www.ssicentral.com

Copyright by Scientific Software International, Inc., 1981-2019
Use of this program is subject to the terms specified in the
Universal Copyright Convention.
```

```
The following lines were read from file H:\My Documents\Statistics\
Work Placements\wpa2012\WPA2012 ECR and RQ SELF OTHER.SPL:

ECR AND RQ TOGETHER IN CIRCUMPLEX, QUASI-CIRCUMPLEX MODEL
DA NI=8 NO=172 MA=KM
KM FI=ATT1CIRC.COR
MO NY=8 NE=2 TE=SY,FI LY=FU,FI PS=SY,FI
FR TE 1 1 TE 2 2 TE 3 3 TE 4 4 TE 5 5 TE 6 6 TE 7 7 TE 8 8
FR LY 1 1 LY 7 2
FR LY 5 1 LY 3 2
FR LY 2 1 LY 8 1 LY 6 2 LY 8 2
FR LY 4 1 LY 6 1 LY 2 2 LY 4 2
EQ LY 1 1 LY 7 2
EQ LY 5 1 LY 3 2
EQ LY 2 1 LY 8 1 LY 6 2 LY 8 2
EQ LY 4 1 LY 6 1 LY 2 2 LY 4 2
ST 1.00 LY 1 1 LY 7 2
ST -1.00 LY 5 1 LY 3 2
```

346 APPENDICES

```
ST .71 LY 2 1 LY 8 1 LY 6 2 LY 8 2
ST -.71 LY 4 1 LY 6 1 LY 2 2 LY 4 2
ST 1.00 PS 1 1 PS 2 2
OU ALL RO RC AD=OFF
```

ECR AND RQ TOGETHER IN CIRCUMPLEX, QUASI-CIRCUMPLEX MODEL

```
                Number of Input Variables  8
                Number of Y - Variables    8
                Number of X - Variables    0
                Number of ETA - Variables  2
                Number of KSI - Variables  0
                Number of Observations    172
```

ECR AND RQ TOGETHER IN CIRCUMPLEX, QUASI-CIRCUMPLEX MODEL

Covariance Matrix

	VAR 1	VAR 2	VAR 3	VAR 4	VAR 5	VAR 6
VAR 1	2.000					
VAR 2	0.109	2.000				
VAR 3	-0.134	0.263	2.000			
VAR 4	-0.160	0.364	0.679	2.000		
VAR 5	-0.400	-0.173	0.341	0.244	2.000	
VAR 6	-0.303	-0.231	0.027	0.079	0.574	2.000
VAR 7	0.146	-0.227	-0.463	-0.564	0.091	0.148
VAR 8	0.390	0.052	-0.424	-0.468	-0.505	-0.373

Covariance Matrix

	VAR 7	VAR 8
VAR 7	2.000	
VAR 8	0.334	2.000

Total Variance = 16.000 Generalized Variance = 131.142

Largest Eigenvalue = 3.926 Smallest Eigenvalue = 1.255

Condition Number = 1.769

ECR AND RQ TOGETHER IN CIRCUMPLEX, QUASI-CIRCUMPLEX MODEL

Parameter Specifications

LAMBDA-Y

	ETA 1	ETA 2
VAR 1	1	0
VAR 2	2	3
VAR 3	0	4
VAR 4	3	3
VAR 5	4	0
VAR 6	3	2
VAR 7	0	1
VAR 8	2	2

THETA-EPS

VAR 1	VAR 2	VAR 3	VAR 4	VAR 5	VAR 6
5	6	7	8	9	10

THETA-EPS

VAR 7	VAR 8
11	12

ECR AND RQ TOGETHER IN CIRCUMPLEX, QUASI-CIRCUMPLEX MODEL

Initial Estimates (TSLS)

LAMBDA-Y

	ETA 1	ETA 2
VAR 1	1.000	- -
VAR 2	0.710	-0.710
VAR 3	- -	-1.000
VAR 4	-0.710	-0.710
VAR 5	-1.000	- -
VAR 6	-0.710	0.710
VAR 7	- -	1.000
VAR 8	0.710	0.710

Covariance Matrix of ETA
Note: This matrix is diagonal.

ETA 1	ETA 2
1.000	1.000

348 APPENDICES

```
PSI
Note: This matrix is diagonal.


          ETA 1      ETA 2
         ------------------------
          1.000      1.000


THETA-EPS

          VAR 1      VAR 2      VAR 3      VAR 4      VAR 5      VAR 6
         ------------------------------------------------------------------
          1.575      1.702      1.571      1.437      1.575      1.702


THETA-EPS

          VAR 7      VAR 8
         ------------------------
          1.571      1.437
```

Behavior under Minimization Iterations

```
    Iter  Try  Abscissa          Slope              Function

     1     0   0.00000000D+00   -0.19244193D+00    0.22232301D+00
           1   0.10000000D+01   -0.45987351D-01    0.93649320D-01
           2   0.20000000D+01    0.20667322D+00    0.16842627D+00
           3   0.11820124D+01   -0.63940935D-02    0.88820452D-01

     2     0   0.00000000D+00   -0.45800870D-02    0.88820452D-01
           1   0.11820124D+01    0.74841422D-03    0.86503456D-01
           2   0.10159929D+01   -0.33303814D-04    0.86444259D-01

     3     0   0.00000000D+00   -0.37085944D 03    0.86444259D 01
           1   0.10159929D+01    0.15479128D-04    0.86263840D-01

     4     0   0.00000000D+00   -0.19629452D-04    0.86263840D-01
           1   0.10159929D+01    0.63271619D-06    0.86254183D-01

     5     0   0.00000000D+00   -0.74568069D-06    0.86254183D-01
           1   0.10159929D+01   -0.56406204D-07    0.86253775D-01

     6     0   0.00000000D+00   -0.57929431D-07    0.86253775D-01
           1   0.10159929D+01   -0.97022664D-08    0.86253741D-01
           2   0.20319858D+01    0.38527376D-07    0.86253756D-01
           3   0.12203783D+01   -0.19922858D-12    0.86253740D-01

     7     0   0.00000000D+00   -0.31131598D-08    0.86253740D-01
           1   0.12203783D+01   -0.37333140D-09    0.86253738D-01
           2   0.24407566D+01    0.23666805D-08    0.86253739D-01
           3   0.13866570D+01   -0.10794462D-13    0.86253738D-01

     8     0   0.00000000D+00   -0.20636086D-09    0.86253738D-01
           1   0.13866570D+01    0.64246355D-10    0.86253738D-01
           2   0.10574431D+01    0.49426176D-15    0.86253738D-01
```

APPENDICES 349

ECR AND RQ TOGETHER IN CIRCUMPLEX, QUASI-CIRCUMPLEX MODEL

Number of Iterations = 8

LISREL Estimates (Maximum Likelihood)

LAMBDA-Y

	ETA 1	ETA 2
VAR 1	0.587	- -
	(0.105)	
	5.573	
VAR 2	0.350	-0.558
	(0.069)	(0.075)
	5.046	-7.414
VAR 3	- -	-0.762
		(0.112)
		-6.785
VAR 4	-0.558	-0.558
	(0.075)	(0.075)
	-7.414	-7.414
VAR 5	-0.762	- -
	(0.112)	
	-6.785	
VAR 6	-0.558	0.350
	(0.075)	(0.069)
	-7.414	5.046
VAR 7	- -	0.587
		(0.105)
		5.573
VAR 8	0.350	0.350
	(0.069)	(0.069)
	5.046	5.046

Covariance Matrix of ETA
Note: This matrix is diagonal.

	ETA 1	ETA 2
	1.000	1.000

350 APPENDICES

PSI
Note: This matrix is diagonal.

ETA 1	ETA 2
1.000	1.000

THETA-EPS

VAR 1	VAR 2	VAR 3	VAR 4	VAR 5	VAR 6
1.706	1.681	1.424	1.359	1.415	1.584
(0.213)	(0.213)	(0.217)	(0.210)	(0.217)	(0.204)
7.999	7.883	6.546	6.466	6.523	7.779

THETA-EPS

VAR 7	VAR 8
1.608	1.631
(0.203)	(0.195)
7.904	8.376

Squared Multiple Correlations for Y - Variables

VAR 1	VAR 2	VAR 3	VAR 4	VAR 5	VAR 6
0.168	0.205	0.290	0.314	0.291	0.215

Squared Multiple Correlations for Y - Variables

VAR 7	VAR 8
0.176	0.131

Log-likelihood Values

	Estimated Model	Saturated Model
Number of free parameters (t)	12	36
$-2\ln(L)$	2244.391	2214.720
AIC (Akaike, 1974)*	2268.391	2286.720
BIC (Schwarz, 1978)*	2306.161	2400.030

*LISREL uses AIC= $2t - 2\ln(L)$ and BIC = $t\ln(N) - 2\ln(L)$

APPENDICES **351**

Goodness-of-Fit Statistics

Degrees of Freedom for (C1)-(C2)	24
Maximum Likelihood Ratio Chi-Square (C1)	29.671 (P = 0.1959)
Browne's (1984) ADF Chi-Square (C2_NT)	28.596 (P = 0.2357)
Estimated Non-centrality Parameter (NCP)	5.671
90 Percent Confidence Interval for NCP	(0.0 ; 23.696)
Minimum Fit Function Value	0.173
Population Discrepancy Function Value (F0)	0.0330
90 Percent Confidence Interval for F0	(0.0 ; 0.138)
Root Mean Square Error of Approximation (RMSEA)	0.0371
90 Percent Confidence Interval for RMSEA	(0.0 ; 0.0758)
P-Value for Test of Close Fit (RMSEA < 0.05)	0.665
Expected Cross-Validation Index (ECVI)	0.312
90 Percent Confidence Interval for ECVI	(0.279 ; 0.417)
ECVI for Saturated Model	0.419
ECVI for Independence Model	0.762
Chi-Square for Independence Model (28 df)	115.051
Normed Fit Index (NFI)	0.742
Non-Normed Fit Index (NNFI)	0.924
Parsimony Normed Fit Index (PNFI)	0.636
Comparative Fit Index (CFI)	0.935
Incremental Fit Index (IFI)	0.938
Relative Fit Index (RFI)	0.699
Critical N (CN)	248.700
Root Mean Square Residual (RMR)	0.156
Standardized RMR	0.0786
Goodness of Fit Index (GFI)	0.960
Adjusted Goodness of Fit Index (AGFI)	0.940
Parsimony Goodness of Fit Index (PGFI)	0.640

ECR AND RQ TOGETHER IN CIRCUMPLEX, QUASI-CIRCUMPLEX MODEL

Fitted Covariance Matrix

	VAR 1	VAR 2	VAR 3	VAR 4	VAR 5	VAR 6
VAR 1	2.050					
VAR 2	0.205	2.114				
VAR 3	- -	0.425	2.004			
VAR 4	-0.327	0.116	0.425	1.982		
VAR 5	-0.447	-0.267	- -	0.425	1.996	
VAR 6	-0.327	-0.391	-0.267	0.116	0.425	2.018
VAR 7	- -	-0.327	-0.447	-0.327	- -	0.205
VAR 8	0.205	-0.073	-0.267	-0.391	-0.267	-0.073

352 APPENDICES

```
        Fitted Covariance Matrix


                    VAR 7       VAR 8
              --------------------------
VAR 7           1.952
VAR 8           0.205       1.876



        Fitted Residuals·


                    VAR 1       VAR 2       VAR 3       VAR 4       VAR 5       VAR 6
              ------------------------------------------------------------------------
VAR 1          -0.050
VAR 2          -0.096      -0.114
VAR 3          -0.134      -0.162      -0.004
VAR 4           0.168       0.248       0.253       0.018
VAR 5           0.047       0.094       0.341      -0.181       0.004
VAR 6           0.025       0.160       0.294      -0.037       0.149      -0.018
VAR 7           0.146       0.101      -0.016      -0.236       0.091      -0.057
VAR 8           0.185       0.125      -0.158      -0.078      -0.238      -0.300



        Fitted Residuals


                    VAR 7       VAR 8
              --------------------------
VAR 7           0.048
VAR 8           0.129       0.124



        Summary Statistics for Fitted Residuals


Smallest Fitted Residual =     -0.300
  Median Fitted Residual =      0.021
 Largest Fitted Residual =      0.341



Stemleaf Plot

 - 3|0
 - 2|44
 - 1|866310
 - 0|86542200
   0|225599
   1|022355678
   2|559
   3|4
```

Standardized Residuals

	VAR 1	VAR 2	VAR 3	VAR 4	VAR 5	VAR 6
VAR 1	-0.248					
VAR 2	-0.609	-0.683				
VAR 3	-0.867	-1.000	-0.019			
VAR 4	1.078	1.609	1.631	0.086		
VAR 5	0.284	0.592	2.238	-1.192	0.020	
VAR 6	0.154	0.997	1.898	-0.241	0.951	-0.081
VAR 7	0.956	0.641	-0.104	-1.448	0.608	-0.335
VAR 8	1.230	0.823	-0.983	-0.518	-1.570	-1.983

Standardized Residuals

	VAR 7	VAR 8
VAR 7	0.287	
VAR 8	0.880	1.424

Summary Statistics for Standardized Residuals

```
Smallest Standardized Residual =    -1.983
  Median Standardized Residual =     0.120
 Largest Standardized Residual =     2.238
```

Stemleaf Plot

```
 - 2|0
 - 1|6
 - 1|4200
 - 0|9765
 - 0|3221100
   0|1233
   0|66689
   1|000124
   1|669
   2|2
```

ECR AND RQ TOGETHER IN CIRCUMPLEX, QUASI-CIRCUMPLEX MODEL

```
              Qplot of Standardized Residuals
  3.5.............................................................
      .                                                     . .
      .                                                      .  .
      .                                                   .
      .                                                 .        .
      .                                               .          .
      .                                             .            .
      .                                           .              .
      .                                         .                .
      .                                      .  x               .
      .                                     .                    .
      .                                   .  x                   .
      .                                 .  x                     .
  N   .                               .  x                       .
  o   .                             . x x                        .
  r   .                            .xx                           .
  m   .                           . *                            .
  a   .                         .  xx                            .
  l   .                        . *                               .
      .                      x   x                               .
  Q   .                    .xx                                   .
  u   .                   .*                                     .
  a   .                 . *                                      .
  n   .               . xx                                       .
  t   .              . xx                                        .
  i   .             .xx                                          .
  l   .            x x                                           .
  e   .           *                                             .
  s   .          x                                              .
      .        x.                                                .
      .        x.                                                .
      .                                                          .
      .     .                                                    .
      .    x                                                     .
      .   .                                                      .
      .  .                                                       .
      .  .                                                       .
      . .                                                        .
      . .                                                        .
      . .                                                        .
  -3.5.............................................................
  -3.5                                                        3.5
              Standardized Residuals
```

APPENDICES 355

ECR AND RQ TOGETHER IN CIRCUMPLEX, QUASI-CIRCUMPLEX MODEL

Modification Indices and Expected Change

Modification Indices for LAMBDA-Y

	ETA 1	ETA 2
VAR 1	0.640	0.040
VAR 2	1.093	0.512
VAR 3	7.788	0.056
VAR 4	7.248	4.326
VAR 5	0.056	0.010
VAR 6	1.843	2.690
VAR 7	0.156	0.640
VAR 8	6.478	0.001

Expected Change for LAMBDA-Y

	ETA 1	ETA 2
VAR 1	-0.086	0.028
VAR 2	-0.137	0.094
VAR 3	-0.385	0.026
VAR 4	0.336	-0.260
VAR 5	-0.026	0.013
VAR 6	-0.174	-0.208
VAR 7	0.055	0.082
VAR 8	0.309	-0.004

Standardized Expected Change for LAMBDA-Y

	ETA 1	ETA 2
VAR 1	-0.086	0.028
VAR 2	-0.137	0.094
VAR 3	-0.385	0.026
VAR 4	0.336	-0.260
VAR 5	-0.026	0.013
VAR 6	-0.174	-0.208
VAR 7	0.055	0.082
VAR 8	0.309	-0.004

Modification Indices for PSI

	ETA 1	ETA 2
ETA 1	0.169	
ETA 2	4.187	0.169

356 APPENDICES

Expected Change for PSI

	ETA 1	ETA 2
ETA 1	-0.119	
ETA 2	0.298	0.119

Standardized Expected Change for PSI

	ETA 1	ETA 2
ETA 1	-0.119	
ETA 2	0.298	0.119

Modification Indices for THETA-EPS

	VAR 1	VAR 2	VAR 3	VAR 4	VAR 5	VAR 6
VAR 1	- -					
VAR 2	0.008	- -				
VAR 3	0.014	0.347	- -			
VAR 4	1.198	1.641	0.369	- -		
VAR 5	0.036	0.027	3.724	2.226	- -	
VAR 6	0.030	0.320	1.158	0.047	1.804	- -
VAR 7	0.669	0.539	0.027	1.584	2.167	0.039
VAR 8	0.648	0.610	0.662	0.108	1.225	2.065

Modification Indices for THETA-EPS

	VAR 7	VAR 8
VAR 7	- -	
VAR 8	0.647	- -

Expected Change for THETA-EPS

	VAR 1	VAR 2	VAR 3	VAR 4	VAR 5	VAR 6
VAR 1	- -					
VAR 2	-0.013	- -				
VAR 3	0.016	-0.091	- -			
VAR 4	0.164	0.188	0.092	- -		
VAR 5	0.032	0.024	0.258	-0.225	- -	
VAR 6	0.026	0.094	0.155	-0.031	0.204	- -
VAR 7	0.115	0.111	0.028	-0.185	0.199	0.028
VAR 8	0.115	0.110	-0.116	0.052	-0.158	-0.197

APPENDICES 357

Expected Change for THETA-EPS

	VAR 7	VAR 8
VAR 7	- -	
VAR 8	0.112	- -

Maximum Modification Index is   7.79 for Element (3, 1) of LAMBDA-Y

Covariance Matrix of Parameter Estimates

	LY 1_1	LY 2_1	LY 2_2	LY 3_2	TE 1_1	TE 2_2
LY 1_1	0.011					
LY 2_1	0.000	0.005				
LY 2_2	0.000	0.000	0.006			
LY 3_2	0.001	0.001	-0.001	0.013		
TE 1_1	-0.007	0.000	-0.001	-0.002	0.046	
TE 2_2	0.001	-0.002	0.003	-0.003	-0.001	0.045
TE 3_3	0.002	0.001	-0.003	0.012	-0.002	-0.005
TE 4_4	0.002	0.000	0.007	-0.005	-0.002	0.005
TE 5_5	0.002	0.001	-0.003	0.012	-0.003	-0.004
TE 6_6	0.001	-0.002	0.003	-0.003	-0.001	0.002
TE 7_7	-0.007	0.000	-0.001	-0.002	0.004	-0.001
TE 8_8	0.000	-0.003	0.000	-0.001	0.000	0.001

Covariance Matrix of Parameter Estimates

	TE 3_3	TE 4_4	TE 5_5	TE 6_6	TE 7_7	TE 8_8
TE 3_3	0.047					
TE 4_4	-0.007	0.044				
TE 5_5	0.012	-0.007	0.047			
TE 6_6	-0.004	0.005	-0.005	0.041		
TE 7_7	-0.003	-0.002	-0.002	-0.001	0.041	
TE 8_8	-0.002	-0.001	-0.002	0.001	0.000	0.038

ECR AND RQ TOGETHER IN CIRCUMPLEX, QUASI-CIRCUMPLEX MODEL

Correlation Matrix of Parameter Estimates

	LY 1_1	LY 2_1	LY 2_2	LY 3_2	TE 1_1	TE 2_2
LY 1_1	1.000					
LY 2_1	-0.005	1.000				
LY 2_2	0.033	-0.071	1.000			
LY 3_2	0.057	0.068	-0.165	1.000		
TE 1_1	-0.301	0.026	-0.054	-0.065	1.000	
TE 2_2	0.047	-0.117	0.211	-0.119	-0.025	1.000
TE 3_3	0.090	0.093	-0.185	0.476	-0.042	-0.099
TE 4_4	0.078	-0.001	0.458	-0.200	-0.045	0.106

358 APPENDICES

```
TE 5_5      0.086     0.093    -0.189     0.478    -0.060    -0.089
TE 6_6      0.049    -0.125     0.224    -0.127    -0.031     0.052
TE 7_7     -0.317     0.028    -0.056    -0.068     0.101    -0.031
TE 8_8      0.018    -0.244    -0.023    -0.047    -0.010     0.024
```

Correlation Matrix of Parameter Estimates

	TE 3_3	TE 4_4	TE 5_5	TE 6_6	TE 7_7	TE 8_8
TE 3_3	1.000					
TE 4_4	-0.156	1.000				
TE 5_5	0.248	-0.159	1.000			
TE 6_6	-0.093	0.113	-0.107	1.000		
TE 7_7	-0.064	-0.047	-0.043	-0.027	1.000	
TE 8_8	-0.037	-0.027	-0.037	0.026	-0.011	1.000

ECR AND RQ TOGETHER IN CIRCUMPLEX, QUASI-CIRCUMPLEX MODEL

Covariances

Y - ETA

	VAR 1	VAR 2	VAR 3	VAR 4	VAR 5	VAR 6
ETA 1	0.587	0.350	- -	-0.558	-0.762	-0.558
ETA 2	- -	-0.558	-0.762	-0.558	- -	0.350

Y - ETA

	VAR 7	VAR 8
ETA 1	- -	0.350
ETA 2	0.587	0.350

ECR AND RQ TOGETHER IN CIRCUMPLEX, QUASI-CIRCUMPLEX MODEL

First Order Derivatives

LAMBDA-Y

	ETA 1	ETA 2
VAR 1	0.022	-0.008
VAR 2	0.035	-0.023
VAR 3	0.118	-0.006
VAR 4	-0.096	0.075

```
VAR 5          0.006      -0.004
VAR 6          0.045       0.056
VAR 7         -0.017      -0.022
VAR 8         -0.093       0.001


    PSI

                ETA 1       ETA 2
              ----------------------
ETA 1          0.008
ETA 2         -0.082      -0.008


    THETA-EPS

                VAR 1       VAR 2       VAR 3       VAR 4       VAR 5       VAR 6
              --------------------------------------------------------------------
VAR 1          0.000
VAR 2          0.003       0.000
VAR 3         -0.005       0.022       0.000
VAR 4         -0.043      -0.051      -0.023       0.000
VAR 5         -0.007      -0.007      -0.084       0.058       0.000
VAR 6         -0.007      -0.020      -0.044       0.009      -0.052       0.000
VAR 7         -0.034      -0.028      -0.006       0.050      -0.064      -0.008
VAR 8         -0.033      -0.032       0.033      -0.012       0.045       0.061


    THETA-EPS

                VAR 7       VAR 8
              ----------------------
VAR 7          0.000
VAR 8         -0.034       0.000


ECR AND RQ TOGETHER IN CIRCUMPLEX, QUASI-CIRCUMPLEX MODEL

Factor Scores Regressions

    ETA

                VAR 1       VAR 2       VAR 3       VAR 4       VAR 5       VAR 6
              --------------------------------------------------------------------
ETA 1          0.157       0.100       0.007      -0.182      -0.246      -0.164
ETA 2         -0.005      -0.155      -0.245      -0.182       0.007       0.106
```

360 APPENDICES

```
      ETA

              VAR 7      VAR 8
              ----------------------
ETA 1        -0.005      0.095
ETA 2         0.167      0.095
```

ECR AND RQ TOGETHER IN CIRCUMPLEX, QUASI-CIRCUMPLEX MODEL

Standardized Solution

```
      LAMBDA-Y

              ETA 1      ETA 2
              ----------------------
VAR 1         0.587       - -
VAR 2         0.350      -0.558
VAR 3          - -       -0.762
VAR 4        -0.558      -0.558
VAR 5        -0.762       - -
VAR 6        -0.558       0.350
VAR 7          - -        0.587
VAR 8         0.350       0.350
```

```
      Correlation Matrix of ETA
      Note: This matrix is diagonal.

              ETA 1      ETA 2
              ----------------------
              1.000      1.000
```

```
      PSI
      Note: This matrix is diagonal.

              ETA 1      ETA 2
              ----------------------
              1.000      1.000
```

ECR AND RQ TOGETHER IN CIRCUMPLEX, QUASI-CIRCUMPLEX MODEL

Total and Indirect Effects

ECR AND RQ TOGETHER IN CIRCUMPLEX, QUASI-CIRCUMPLEX MODEL

Standardized Total and Indirect Effects

```
              Time used 0.078 seconds
```

APPENDIX 2D

Output regarding Final Covariance Structure Analysis, Gaines et al. (2013), $n = 172$

DATE: 12/30/2020
TIME: 17:18

L I S R E L 10.2 (64 Bit)

BY

Karl G. Jöreskog & Dag Sörbom

This program is published exclusively by
Scientific Software International, Inc.
http://www.ssicentral.com

Copyright by Scientific Software International, Inc., 1981-2019
Use of this program is subject to the terms specified in the
Universal Copyright Convention.

The following lines were read from file H:\My Documents\Statistics\
Work Placements\wpa2012\WPA2012 ECR and RQ SELF OTHER GEN.SPL:

```
ECR AND RQ TOGETHER IN CIRCUMPLEX, QUASI-CIRCUMPLEX MODEL
DA NI=8 NO=172 MA=KM
KM FI=ATT1CIRC.COR
MO NY=8 NE=3 TE=SY,FI LY=FU,FI PS=SY,FI
FR TE 1 1 TE 2 2 TE 3 3 TE 4 4 TE 5 5 TE 6 6 TE 7 7 TE 8 8
FR LY 1 1 LY 7 2
FR LY 5 1 LY 3 2
FR LY 2 1 LY 8 1 LY 6 2 LY 8 2
FR LY 4 1 LY 6 1 LY 2 2 LY 4 2
EQ LY 1 1 LY 7 2
EQ LY 5 1 LY 3 2
EQ LY 2 1 LY 8 1 LY 6 2 LY 8 2
EQ LY 4 1 LY 6 1 LY 2 2 LY 4 2
ST 1.00 LY 1 1 LY 7 2
ST -1.00 LY 5 1 LY 3 2
```

362 APPENDICES

```
ST .71 LY 2 1 LY 8 1 LY 6 2 LY 8 2
ST -.71 LY 4 1 LY 6 1 LY 2 2 LY 4 2
FR LY 1 3 LY 2 3 LY 3 3 LY 4 3 LY 5 3 LY 6 3 LY 7 3 LY 8 3
EQ LY 1 3 LY 2 3 LY 3 3 LY 4 3 LY 5 3 LY 6 3 LY 7 3 LY 8 3
ST 1.00 PS 1 1 PS 2 2 PS 3 3
OU ALL RO RC AD=OFF
```

ECR AND RQ TOGETHER IN CIRCUMPLEX, QUASI-CIRCUMPLEX MODEL

Number of Input Variables	8
Number of Y - Variables	8
Number of X - Variables	0
Number of ETA - Variables	3
Number of KSI - Variables	0
Number of Observations	172

ECR AND RQ TOGETHER IN CIRCUMPLEX, QUASI-CIRCUMPLEX MODEL

Covariance Matrix

	VAR 1	VAR 2	VAR 3	VAR 4	VAR 5	VAR 6
VAR 1	2.000					
VAR 2	0.109	2.000				
VAR 3	-0.134	0.263	2.000			
VAR 4	-0.160	0.364	0.679	2.000		
VAR 5	-0.400	-0.173	0.341	0.244	2.000	
VAR 6	-0.303	-0.231	0.027	0.079	0.574	2.000
VAR 7	0.146	-0.227	-0.463	-0.564	0.091	0.148
VAR 8	0.390	0.052	-0.424	-0.468	-0.505	-0.373

Covariance Matrix

	VAR 7	VAR 8
VAR 7	2.000	
VAR 8	0.334	2.000

Total Variance = 16.000 Generalized Variance = 131.142

Largest Eigenvalue = 3.926 Smallest Eigenvalue = 1.255

Condition Number = 1.769

ECR AND RQ TOGETHER IN CIRCUMPLEX, QUASI-CIRCUMPLEX MODEL

Parameter Specifications

APPENDICES 363

LAMBDA-Y

	ETA 1	ETA 2	ETA 3
VAR 1	1	0	2
VAR 2	3	4	2
VAR 3	0	5	2
VAR 4	4	4	2
VAR 5	5	0	2
VAR 6	4	3	2
VAR 7	0	1	2
VAR 8	3	3	2

THETA-EPS

VAR 1	VAR 2	VAR 3	VAR 4	VAR 5	VAR 6
6	7	8	9	10	11

THETA-EPS

VAR 7	VAR 8
12	13

ECR AND RQ TOGETHER IN CIRCUMPLEX, QUASI-CIRCUMPLEX MODEL

Initial Estimates (TSLS)

LAMBDA-Y

	ETA 1	ETA 2	ETA 3
VAR 1	1.000	- -	0.178
VAR 2	0.710	-0.710	0.178
VAR 3	- -	-1.000	0.178
VAR 4	-0.710	-0.710	0.178
VAR 5	-1.000	- -	0.178
VAR 6	-0.710	0.710	0.178
VAR 7	- -	1.000	0.178
VAR 8	0.710	0.710	0.178

Covariance Matrix of ETA
Note: This matrix is diagonal.

ETA 1	ETA 2	ETA 3
1.000	1.000	1.000

364 APPENDICES

PSI
Note: This matrix is diagonal.

ETA 1	ETA 2	ETA 3
1.000	1.000	1.000

THETA-EPS

VAR 1	VAR 2	VAR 3	VAR 4	VAR 5	VAR 6
1.650	1.625	1.382	1.270	1.380	1.613

THETA-EPS

VAR 7	VAR 8
1.638	1.518

Behavior under Minimization Iterations

Iter	Try	Abscissa	Slope	Function
1	0	0.00000000D+00	-0.19012976D+00	0.21148277D+00
	1	0.10000000D+01	-0.39410383D-01	0.86725254D-01
	2	0.20000000D+01	0.21952759D+00	0.17217275D+00
	3	0.11522001D+01	-0.53174286D-02	0.83283145D-01
2	0	0.00000000D+00	-0.37920848D-02	0.83283145D-01
	1	0.11522001D+01	0.81411054D-03	0.81545225D-01
	2	0.94855735D+00	-0.17287213D-04	0.81464226D-01
3	0	0.00000000D+00	-0.22958085D-03	0.81464226D-01
	1	0.94855735D+00	-0.12725726D-04	0.81349456D-01
4	0	0.00000000D+00	-0.21038423D-04	0.81349456D-01
	1	0.94855735D+00	-0.28964292D-05	0.81338101D-01
	2	0.18971147D+01	0.15284173D-04	0.81343973D-01
	3	0.10996761D+01	-0.25768328D-08	0.81337882D-01
5	0	0.00000000D+00	-0.10860164D-05	0.81337882D-01
	1	0.10996761D+01	-0.15446868D-06	0.81337200D-01
	2	0.21993521D+01	0.77589893D-06	0.81337541D-01
	3	0.12822550D+01	0.81677735D-10	0.81337186D-01
6	0	0.00000000D+00	-0.74961546D-07	0.81337186D-01
	1	0.12822550D+01	0.16902150D-08	0.81337139D-01
7	0	0.00000000D+00	-0.46376652D-08	0.81337139D-01
	1	0.12822550D+01	-0.38942886D-09	0.81337135D-01
8	0	0.00000000D+00	-0.25229207D-09	0.81337135D-01
	1	0.12822550D+01	0.61311607D-10	0.81337135D-01
	2	0.10315656D+01	-0.15419862D-15	0.81337135D-01
9	0	0.00000000D+00	-0.48075993D-11	0.81337135D-01
	1	0.10315656D+01	0.43020879D-12	0.81337135D-01

APPENDICES   365

ECR AND RQ TOGETHER IN CIRCUMPLEX, QUASI-CIRCUMPLEX MODEL

Number of Iterations = 9

LISREL Estimates (Maximum Likelihood)

LAMBDA-Y

	ETA 1	ETA 2	ETA 3
VAR 1	0.623	- -	0.183
	(0.107)		(0.074)
	5.814		2.480
VAR 2	0.367	-0.547	0.183
	(0.071)	(0.075)	(0.074)
	5.168	-7.315	2.480
VAR 3	- -	-0.755	0.183
		(0.110)	(0.074)
		-6.860	2.480
VAR 4	-0.547	-0.547	0.183
	(0.075)	(0.075)	(0.074)
	-7.315	-7.315	2.480
VAR 5	-0.755	- -	0.183
	(0.110)		(0.074)
	-6.860		2.480
VAR 6	-0.547	0.367	0.183
	(0.075)	(0.071)	(0.074)
	-7.315	5.168	2.480
VAR 7	- -	0.623	0.183
		(0.107)	(0.074)
		5.814	2.480
VAR 8	0.367	0.367	0.183
	(0.071)	(0.071)	(0.074)
	5.168	5.168	2.480

Covariance Matrix of ETA
Note: This matrix is diagonal.

ETA 1	ETA 2	ETA 3
1.000	1.000	1.000

366 APPENDICES

```
PSI
Note: This matrix is diagonal.

             ETA 1      ETA 2      ETA 3
        --------------------------------------
             1.000      1.000      1.000


THETA-EPS

            VAR 1      VAR 2      VAR 3      VAR 4      VAR 5      VAR 6
       ------------------------------------------------------------------
            1.629      1.645      1.396      1.356      1.387      1.558
          (0.219)    (0.214)    (0.214)    (0.207)    (0.214)    (0.205)
            7.433      7.696      6.511      6.539      6.490      7.604


THETA-EPS

            VAR 7      VAR 8
       --------------------------
            1.527      1.579
          (0.209)    (0.200)
            7.305      7.900


Squared Multiple Correlations for Y - Variables

            VAR 1      VAR 2      VAR 3      VAR 4      VAR 5      VAR 6
       ------------------------------------------------------------------
            0.205      0.221      0.302      0.318      0.303      0.231


Squared Multiple Correlations for Y - Variables

            VAR 7      VAR 8
       --------------------------
            0.216      0.161
```

Log-likelihood Values

	Estimated Model	Saturated Model
Number of free parameters(t)	13	36
-2ln(L)	2242.700	2214.720
AIC (Akaike, 1974)*	2268.700	2286.720
BIC (Schwarz, 1978)*	2309.617	2400.030

*LISREL uses AIC= 2t - 2ln(L) and BIC = tln(N) - 2ln(L)

APPENDICES 367

Goodness-of-Fit Statistics

```
Degrees of Freedom for (C1)-(C2)                           23
Maximum Likelihood Ratio Chi-Square (C1)                  27.980 (P = 0.2165)
Browne's (1984) ADF Chi-Square (C2_NT)                    27.204 (P = 0.2474)

Estimated Non-centrality Parameter (NCP)                   4.980
90 Percent Confidence Interval for NCP                    (0.0 ; 22.542)

Minimum Fit Function Value                                 0.163
Population Discrepancy Function Value (F0)                 0.0290
90 Percent Confidence Interval for F0                     (0.0 ; 0.131)
Root Mean Square Error of Approximation (RMSEA)           0.0355
90 Percent Confidence Interval for RMSEA                  (0.0 ; 0.0755)
P-Value for Test of Close Fit (RMSEA < 0.05)              0.680

Expected Cross-Validation Index (ECVI)                    0.314
90 Percent Confidence Interval for ECVI                   (0.285 ; 0.416)
ECVI for Saturated Model                                  0.419
ECVI for Independence Model                               0.762

Chi-Square for Independence Model (28 df)               115.051

Normed Fit Index (NFI)                                    0.757
Non-Normed Fit Index (NNFI)                               0.930
Parsimony Normed Fit Index (PNFI)                         0.622
Comparative Fit Index (CFI)                               0.943
Incremental Fit Index (IFI)                               0.946
Relative Fit Index (RFI)                                  0.704

Critical N (CN)                                         255.475

Root Mean Square Residual (RMR)                           0.154
Standardized RMR                                          0.0776
Goodness of Fit Index (GFI)                               0.962
Adjusted Goodness of Fit Index (AGFI)                     0.940
Parsimony Goodness of Fit Index (PGFI)                    0.615
```

ECR AND RQ TOGETHER IN CIRCUMPLEX, QUASI-CIRCUMPLEX MODEL

Fitted Covariance Matrix

	VAR 1	VAR 2	VAR 3	VAR 4	VAR 5	VAR 6
VAR 1	2.051					
VAR 2	0.262	2.112				
VAR 3	0.033	0.446	1.999			
VAR 4	-0.307	0.131	0.446	1.986		
VAR 5	-0.437	-0.244	0.033	0.446	1.990	
VAR 6	-0.307	-0.368	-0.244	0.131	0.446	2.025
VAR 7	0.033	-0.307	-0.437	-0.307	0.033	0.262
VAR 8	0.262	-0.033	-0.244	-0.368	-0.244	-0.033

368 APPENDICES

Fitted Covariance Matrix

	VAR 7	VAR 8
VAR 7	1.948	
VAR 8	0.262	1.882

Fitted Residuals

	VAR 1	VAR 2	VAR 3	VAR 4	VAR 5	VAR 6
VAR 1	-0.051					
VAR 2	-0.153	-0.112				
VAR 3	-0.167	-0.183	0.001			
VAR 4	0.148	0.232	0.233	0.014		
VAR 5	0.037	0.071	0.308	-0.202	0.010	
VAR 6	0.004	0.137	0.271	-0.052	0.128	-0.025
VAR 7	0.113	0.080	-0.026	-0.257	0.058	-0.114
VAR 8	0.128	0.085	-0.181	-0.100	-0.261	-0.340

Fitted Residuals

	VAR 7	VAR 8
VAR 7	0.052	
VAR 8	0.072	0.118

Summary Statistics for Fitted Residuals

```
Smallest Fitted Residual =    -0.340
  Median Fitted Residual =     0.012
 Largest Fitted Residual =     0.308
```

Stemleaf Plot

```
 - 3|4
 - 2|660
 - 1|8875110
 - 0|553300
   0|114567788
   1|123345
   2|337
   3|1
```

APPENDICES **369**

Standardized Residuals

	VAR 1	VAR 2	VAR 3	VAR 4	VAR 5	VAR 6
VAR 1	-0.252					
VAR 2	-0.979	-0.480				
VAR 3	-1.075	-1.140	0.005			
VAR 4	0.892	1.495	1.505	0.063		
VAR 5	0.265	0.423	1.980	-1.242	0.053	
VAR 6	0.026	0.809	1.768	-0.342	0.787	-0.139
VAR 7	0.736	0.463	-0.170	-1.647	0.374	-0.755
VAR 8	0.917	0.541	-1.293	-0.667	-1.782	-2.145

Standardized Residuals

	VAR 7	VAR 8
VAR 7	0.254	
VAR 8	0.477	1.176

Summary Statistics for Standardized Residuals

```
Smallest Standardized Residual =    -2.145
  Median Standardized Residual =     0.058
 Largest Standardized Residual =     1.980
```

Stemleaf Plot

```
 - 2|1
 - 1|86
 - 1|32110
 - 0|875
 - 0|332100
   0|113344
   0|55578899
   1|2
   1|558
   2|0
```

ECR AND RQ TOGETHER IN CIRCUMPLEX, QUASI-CIRCUMPLEX MODEL

370 APPENDICES

Qplot of Standardized Residuals

(figure: normal quantile-quantile plot of standardized residuals; vertical axis "Normal Quantiles" ranging from -3.5 to 3.5, horizontal axis "Standardized Residuals" ranging from -3.5 to 3.5)

Standardized Residuals

APPENDICES 371

ECR AND RQ TOGETHER IN CIRCUMPLEX, QUASI-CIRCUMPLEX MODEL

Modification Indices and Expected Change

Modification Indices for LAMBDA-Y

	ETA 1	ETA 2	ETA 3
VAR 1	0.709	0.109	0.169
VAR 2	1.096	0.524	0.131
VAR 3	7.361	0.062	0.180
VAR 4	7.490	4.321	0.212
VAR 5	0.062	0.053	0.188
VAR 6	2.000	2.958	0.023
VAR 7	0.253	0.709	0.141
VAR 8	6.833	0.000	2.326

Expected Change for LAMBDA-Y

	ETA 1	ETA 2	ETA 3
VAR 1	-0.090	0.047	0.136
VAR 2	-0.135	0.094	0.109
VAR 3	-0.372	0.027	0.127
VAR 4	0.337	-0.255	-0.147
VAR 5	-0.027	0.031	0.129
VAR 6	-0.179	-0.214	-0.045
VAR 7	0.069	0.086	0.122
VAR 8	0.316	-0.003	-0.504

Standardized Expected Change for LAMBDA-Y

	ETA 1	ETA 2	ETA 3
VAR 1	-0.090	0.047	0.136
VAR 2	-0.135	0.094	0.109
VAR 3	-0.372	0.027	0.127
VAR 4	0.337	-0.255	-0.147
VAR 5	-0.027	0.031	0.129
VAR 6	-0.179	-0.214	-0.045
VAR 7	0.069	0.086	0.122
VAR 8	0.316	-0.003	-0.504

Modification Indices for PSI

	ETA 1	ETA 2	ETA 3
ETA 1	0.142		
ETA 2	4.126	0.142	
ETA 3	0.021	0.414	- -

372 APPENDICES

Expected Change for PSI

	ETA 1	ETA 2	ETA 3
ETA 1	-0.107		
ETA 2	0.289	0.107	
ETA 3	-0.052	-0.229	- -

Standardized Expected Change for PSI

	ETA 1	ETA 2	ETA 3
ETA 1	-0.107		
ETA 2	0.289	0.107	
ETA 3	-0.052	-0.229	- -

Modification Indices for THETA-EPS

	VAR 1	VAR 2	VAR 3	VAR 4	VAR 5	VAR 6
VAR 1	- -					
VAR 2	0.403	- -				
VAR 3	0.027	0.832	- -			
VAR 4	0.801	1.236	0.158	- -		
VAR 5	0.001	0.005	2.957	3.113	- -	
VAR 6	0.001	0.107	0.764	0.132	1.224	- -
VAR 7	0.189	0.229	0.001	2.167	1.506	0.082
VAR 8	0.097	0.232	1.105	0.021	1.942	3.347

Modification Indices for THETA-EPS

	VAR 7	VAR 8
VAR 7	- -	
VAR 8	0.123	- -

Expected Change for THETA-EPS

	VAR 1	VAR 2	VAR 3	VAR 4	VAR 5	VAR 6
VAR 1	- -					
VAR 2	-0.101	- -				
VAR 3	-0.023	-0.144	- -			
VAR 4	0.134	0.164	0.061	- -		
VAR 5	0.006	-0.010	0.234	-0.268	- -	
VAR 6	-0.005	0.054	0.127	-0.053	0.172	- -
VAR 7	0.062	0.073	-0.004	-0.216	0.168	-0.044
VAR 8	0.048	0.069	-0.151	0.023	-0.200	-0.258

APPENDICES   373

Expected Change for THETA-EPS

	VAR 7	VAR 8
VAR 7	- -	
VAR 8	0.053	- -

Maximum Modification Index is   7.49 for Element (4, 1) of LAMBDA-Y

Covariance Matrix of Parameter Estimates

	LY 1_1	LY 1_3	LY 2_1	LY 2_2	LY 3_2	TE 1_1
LY 1_1	0.011					
LY 1_3	0.001	0.005				
LY 2_1	0.000	0.001	0.005			
LY 2_2	0.001	0.000	0.000	0.006		
LY 3_2	0.001	0.000	0.001	-0.001	0.012	
TE 1_1	-0.008	-0.003	0.000	-0.001	-0.002	0.048
TE 2_2	0.001	-0.002	-0.002	0.003	-0.003	-0.001
TE 3_3	0.002	-0.001	0.001	-0.003	0.011	-0.001
TE 4_4	0.001	-0.001	0.000	0.007	-0.004	-0.001
TE 5_5	0.002	-0.001	0.001	-0.003	0.011	-0.002
TE 6_6	0.001	-0.002	-0.002	0.003	-0.003	-0.001
TE 7_7	-0.008	-0.003	0.000	-0.001	-0.002	0.007
TE 8_8	0.000	-0.003	-0.004	-0.001	-0.001	0.000

Covariance Matrix of Parameter Estimates

	TE 2_2	TE 3_3	TE 4_4	TE 5_5	TE 6_6	TE 7_7
TE 2_2	0.046					
TE 3_3	-0.004	0.046				
TE 4_4	0.004	-0.007	0.043			
TE 5_5	-0.003	0.011	-0.007	0.046		
TE 6_6	0.003	-0.003	0.004	-0.004	0.042	
TE 7_7	0.000	-0.002	-0.001	-0.001	-0.001	0.044
TE 8_8	0.002	-0.001	0.000	-0.001	0.002	0.000

Covariance Matrix of Parameter Estimates

	TE 8_8
TE 8_8	0.040

ECR AND RQ TOGETHER IN CIRCUMPLEX, QUASI-CIRCUMPLEX MODEL

374 APPENDICES

Correlation Matrix of Parameter Estimates

	LY 1_1	LY 1_3	LY 2_1	LY 2_2	LY 3_2	TE 1_1
LY 1_1	1.000					
LY 1_3	0.173	1.000				
LY 2_1	0.036	0.160	1.000			
LY 2_2	0.069	0.072	-0.025	1.000		
LY 3_2	0.082	0.049	0.088	-0.109	1.000	
TE 1_1	-0.356	-0.198	0.006	-0.076	-0.082	1.000
TE 2_2	0.032	-0.111	-0.143	0.187	-0.115	-0.011
TE 3_3	0.079	-0.065	0.076	-0.168	0.453	-0.031
TE 4_4	0.065	-0.045	-0.006	0.426	-0.182	-0.033
TE 5_5	0.076	-0.061	0.076	-0.172	0.456	-0.047
TE 6_6	0.034	-0.111	-0.149	0.199	-0.122	-0.011
TE 7_7	-0.373	-0.205	0.008	-0.079	-0.085	0.159
TE 8_8	0.002	-0.189	-0.288	-0.035	-0.055	0.011

Correlation Matrix of Parameter Estimates

	TE 2_2	TE 3_3	TE 4_4	TE 5_5	TE 6_6	TE 7_7
TE 2_2	1.000					
TE 3_3	-0.089	1.000				
TE 4_4	0.099	-0.146	1.000			
TE 5_5	-0.073	0.234	-0.149	1.000		
TE 6_6	0.065	-0.076	0.105	-0.097	1.000	
TE 7_7	-0.010	-0.050	-0.034	-0.032	-0.014	1.000
TE 8_8	0.053	-0.019	-0.011	-0.020	0.054	0.010

Correlation Matrix of Parameter Estimates

	TE 8_8
TE 8_8	1.000

ECR AND RQ TOGETHER IN CIRCUMPLEX, QUASI-CIRCUMPLEX MODEL

Covariances

Y - ETA

	VAR 1	VAR 2	VAR 3	VAR 4	VAR 5	VAR 6
ETA 1	0.623	0.367	- -	-0.547	-0.755	-0.547
ETA 2	- -	-0.547	-0.755	-0.547	- -	0.367
ETA 3	0.183	0.183	0.183	0.183	0.183	0.183

Y - ETA

	VAR 7	VAR 8
ETA 1	- -	0.367
ETA 2	0.623	0.367
ETA 3	0.183	0.183

ECR AND RQ TOGETHER IN CIRCUMPLEX, QUASI-CIRCUMPLEX MODEL

First Order Derivatives

LAMBDA-Y

	ETA 1	ETA 2	ETA 3
VAR 1	0.024	-0.014	-0.006
VAR 2	0.036	-0.024	-0.006
VAR 3	0.116	-0.007	-0.007
VAR 4	-0.099	0.076	0.008
VAR 5	0.007	-0.010	-0.008
VAR 6	0.048	0.059	0.003
VAR 7	-0.021	-0.024	-0.006
VAR 8	-0.096	0.001	0.023

PSI

	ETA 1	ETA 2	ETA 3
ETA 1	0.008		
ETA 2	-0.083	-0.008	
ETA 3	0.002	0.011	0.000

THETA-EPS

	VAR 1	VAR 2	VAR 3	VAR 4	VAR 5	VAR 6
VAR 1	0.000					
VAR 2	0.023	0.000				
VAR 3	0.007	0.034	0.000			
VAR 4	-0.035	-0.044	-0.015	0.000		
VAR 5	-0.001	0.003	-0.074	0.068	0.000	
VAR 6	0.001	-0.012	-0.035	0.015	-0.042	0.000
VAR 7	-0.018	-0.018	0.001	0.059	-0.052	0.011
VAR 8	-0.012	-0.020	0.043	-0.005	0.057	0.076

376 APPENDICES

```
THETA-EPS

          VAR 7      VAR 8
         -----------------------
VAR 7    0.000
VAR 8    -0.013     0.000
```

ECR AND RQ TOGETHER IN CIRCUMPLEX, QUASI-CIRCUMPLEX MODEL

Factor Scores Regressions

ETA

	VAR 1	VAR 2	VAR 3	VAR 4	VAR 5	VAR 6
ETA 1	0.176	0.107	0.010	-0.173	-0.241	-0.157
ETA 2	-0.001	-0.148	-0.239	-0.173	0.009	0.112
ETA 3	0.108	0.093	0.097	0.091	0.095	0.095

ETA

	VAR 7	VAR 8
ETA 1	0.000	0.106
ETA 2	0.186	0.105
ETA 3	0.113	0.112

ECR AND RQ TOGETHER IN CIRCUMPLEX, QUASI-CIRCUMPLEX MODEL

Standardized Solution

LAMBDA-Y

	ETA 1	ETA 2	ETA 3
VAR 1	0.623	- -	0.183
VAR 2	0.367	-0.547	0.183
VAR 3	- -	-0.755	0.183
VAR 4	-0.547	-0.547	0.183
VAR 5	-0.755	- -	0.183
VAR 6	-0.547	0.367	0.183
VAR 7	- -	0.623	0.183
VAR 8	0.367	0.367	0.183

Correlation Matrix of ETA
Note: This matrix is diagonal.

	ETA 1	ETA 2	ETA 3
	1.000	1.000	1.000

PSI
Note: This matrix is diagonal.

ETA 1	ETA 2	ETA 3
1.000	1.000	1.000

ECR AND RQ TOGETHER IN CIRCUMPLEX, QUASI-CIRCUMPLEX MODEL

Total and Indirect Effects

ECR AND RQ TOGETHER IN CIRCUMPLEX, QUASI-CIRCUMPLEX MODEL

Standardized Total and Indirect Effects

Time used 0.047 seconds

Bibliography

Ackerman, R. A., & Donnellan, M. B. (2013). Evaluating self-report measures of narcissistic entitlement. *Journal of Psychopathology and Behavioral Assessment, 35*, 460–474.

Acton, G. S., & Revelle, W. (2002). Interpersonal personality measures show circumplex structure based on new psychometric criteria. *Journal of Personality Assessment, 79*, 456–481.

Acton, G. S., & Revelle, W. (2004). Evaluation of ten psychometric criteria for circumplex structure. *Methods of Psychological Research Online, 9*(1), 1–27. Retrieved September 12, 2019, from http://personality-project.org/revelle/publications/acton.revelle.mpr110_10.pdf

Adler, A. (1925). *The practice and theory of individual psychology*. London: Routledge & Kegan Paul.

Adler, A. (1927). *Understanding human nature*. New York, NY: Greenberg.

Adler, A. (1931). *What life should mean to you*. New York, NY: Capricorn.

Agnew, C. R., & VanderDrift, L. E. (2015). Relationship maintenance and dissolution. In M. Mikulincer & P. R. Shaver (Eds.), *APA handbook of personality and social psychology* (Vol. 3: Interpersonal relations, pp. 581–604). Washington, DC: American Psychological Association.

Ainsworth, M. D. S. (1969). Object relations, dependency, and attachment: A theoretical review of the infant-mother relationship. *Child Development, 40*, 969–1025.

Ainsworth, M. D. S., Blehar, M. C., Waters, E., & Wall, S. (1978). *Patterns of attachment: A psychological study of the Strange Situation*. Hillsdale, NJ: Erlbaum.

Alden, L. E., Wiggins, J. S., & Pincus, A. L. (1990). Construction of circumplex scales for the Inventory of Interpersonal Problems. *Journal of Personality Assessment, 55*, 521–536.

Alicke, M. D., Sedikides, C., & Zhang, Y. (2020). The motivation to maintain favorable identities. *Self and Identity, 19*, 572–589.

Allain-Dupre, B. (2005). What does the child analyst bring to Jungian thought? *Journal of Analytical Psychology, 50*, 351–365.

Allen, J. G. (2012). From attachment to intersubjectivity. *Psychiatry, 75*, 32–39.

Allen, J. P. (2021). Beyond stability: Toward understanding the development of attachment beyond childhood. In R. A. Thompson, J. A. Simpson, & L. Berlin (Eds.), *Attachment: The fundamental questions* (pp. 161–168). New York, NY: Guilford.

Allen, T. A., & DeYoung, C. G. (2017). Personality neuroscience and the Five Factor Model. In T. A. Widiger (Ed.), *The Oxford handbook of the Five Factor Model of personality* (pp. 319–349). New York, NY: Oxford University Press.

Allik, J., & Realo, A. (2017). Universal and specific in the Five-Factor Model of personality. In T. A. Widiger (Ed.), *The Oxford handbook of the Five Factor Model of personality* (pp. 173–190). Oxford, UK: Oxford University Press.

Allport, G. W. (1928). A test for ascendance-submission. *Journal of Abnormal and Social Psychology, 23*, 118–136.

380 BIBLIOGRAPHY

Allport, G. W. (1935). Attitudes. In C. A. Murchison (Ed.), *A handbook of social psychology* (pp. 798–844). Worchester, MA: Clark University Press.

Allport, G. W. (1951). *Personality: A psychological interpretation*. New York, NY: Holt. (Original work published 1937)

Allport, G. W. (1963). *Pattern and growth in personality*. London, UK: Holt, Rinehart and Winston. (Originally published in 1961)

Allport, G. W. (1979). *The nature of prejudice*. Reading, MA: Addison-Wesley. (Original work published 1954)

Allport, G. W., & Odbert, H. S. (1936). Trait-names: A psycho-lexical study. *Psychological Monographs, 47*(211), 1–171.

Alvarez-Segura, M., Echavarria, M. F., & Vitz, P. C. (2015). Re-conceptualizing neurosis as a degree of egocentricity: Ethical issues in psychological theory. *Journal of Religion & Health, 54*, 1788–1799.

American Psychiatric Association. (1952). *Diagnostic and statistical manual of mental disorders*. Washington, DC: American Psychiatric Association.

American Psychiatric Association. (1980). *Diagnostic and statistical manual of mental disorders* (3rd ed.). Arlington, VA: American Psychiatric Press.

Anderson, D. (2021). The soul's logical life and Jungian schisms. *Psychological Perspectives, 64*, 37–53.

Antill, J. K. (1983). Sex role complementarity versus similarity in married couples. *Journal of Personality and Social Psychology, 45*, 145–155.

Antonucci, T. C. (1994). Attachment in adulthood and aging. In M. B. Sperling & W. H. Berman (Eds.), *Attachment in adults: Clinical and developmental perspectives* (pp. 256–272). New York, NY: Guilford.

Aron, A., & Aron, E. N. (1986). *Love and the expansion of self: Understanding attraction and satisfaction*. Washington, DC: Hemisphere.

Aron, A., & Nardone, N. (2012). Self and close relationships. In M. R. Leary & J. P. Tangney (Eds.), *Handbook of self and identity* (2nd ed., pp. 520–541). New York, NY: Guilford Press.

Ashton, M. C., & Lee, K. (2001). A theoretical basis for the major dimensions of personality. *European Journal of Personality, 15*, 327–353.

Ashton, M. C., & Lee, K. (2019). How well do Big Five measures capture HEXACO scale variance? *Journal of Personality Assessment, 101*, 567–573.

Ashton, M. C., & Lee, K. (2020). Objections to the HEXACO model of personality structure—and why those objections fail. *European Journal of Personality, 34*, 492–510.

Azim, H. F. A., & Piper, W. E. (1991). The Quality of Object Relations Scale. *Bulletin of the Menninger Clinic, 55*, 323–343.

Azmitia, M., Ittel, A., & Radmacher, K. (2005). Narratives of friendship and self in adolescence. *New Directions for Child and Adolescent Development, 107*, 23–39.

Back, K. (1992). This business of topology. *Journal of Social Issues, 48*, 51–66.

Bahroun, A. (2018). The psychical fragmentation in the perspectives of Sigmund Freud and Jacques Lacan. *Journal of Suleyman Demirel University Institute of Social Sciences, 3*, 421–431.

Bakan, D. (1966). *The duality of human existence*. Chicago, IL: Rand McNally.

Balsam, R. H. (2018). "Castration anxiety" revisited: Especially "female castration anxiety." *Psychoanalytic Inquiry, 38*, 11–22.

Banaji, M. R., & Prentice, D. A. (1994). The self in social contexts. *Annual Review of Psychology, 45*, 297–332.

BIBLIOGRAPHY 381

Barford, K. A., Zhao, K., & Smillie, L. D. (2015). Mapping the interpersonal domain: Translating between the big five, HEXACO, and interpersonal circumplex. *Personality and Individual Differences, 86*, 232–237.

Baron, H. (1996). Strengths and limitations of ipsative measurement. *Journal of Occupational and Organizational Psychology, 69*, 49–56.

Barone-Chapman, M. (2014). Gender legacies of Jung and Freud as epistemology in emergent feminist research on late motherhood. *Behavioral Sciences, 4*, 14–30.

Bartholomew, K. (1990). Avoidance of intimacy: An attachment perspective. *Journal of Social and Personal Relationships, 7*, 147–178.

Bartholomew, K. (1994). The assessment of individual differences in adult attachment. *Psychological Inquiry, 5*, 23–27.

Bartholomew, K. (1997). Adult attachment processes: Individual and couple perspectives. *British Journal of Medical Psychology, 70*, 249–263.

Bartholomew, K., & Horowitz, L. M. (1991). Attachment styles among young adults: A test of a four-category model. *Journal of Personality and Social Psychology, 61*, 226–244.

Bartholomew, K., & Shaver, P. (1998). Methods of assessing adult attachment: Do they converge? In J. A. Simpson & W. S. Rholes (Eds.), *Attachment theory and close relationships* (pp. 25–45). New York, NY: Guilford Press.

Bartram, D. (1996). The relationship between ipsatized and normative measures of personality. *Journal of Occupational and Organizational Psychology, 69*, 25–39.

Baumeister, R. F. (1997). Identity, self-concept, and self-esteem: The self lost and found. In R. Hogan, J. Johnson, & S. Briggs (Eds.), *Handbook of personality psychology* (pp. 681–710). San Diego, CA: Academic Press.

Baumeister, R. F. (1998). The self. In D. T. Gilbert, S. T. Fiske, & G. Lindzey (Eds.), *Handbook of social psychology* (4th ed., Vol. 1, pp. 680–740). New York, NY: McGraw-Hill.

Baumeister, R. F., & Heatherton, T. F. (1996a). Self-regulation failure: An overview. *Psychological Inquiry, 7*, 1–15.

Baumeister, R. F., & Heatherton, T. F. (1996b). Self-regulation failure: Past, present, and future. *Psychological Inquiry, 7*, 90–98.

Baumeister, R. F., & Stillman, T. F. (2016). Self-regulation and close relationships. In J. V. Wood, A. Tesser, & J. G. Holmes (Eds.), *The self in social relationships* (pp. 139–158). New York, NY: Psychology Press. (Original version published 2008)

Beauducel, A., & Rabe, S. (2009). Model-related factor score predictors for confirmatory factor analysis. *British Journal of Mathematical and Statistical Psychology, 62*, 489–506.

Bem, S. L. (1974). The measurement of psychological androgyny. *Journal of Consulting and Clinical Psychology, 42*, 155–162.Bem, S. L. (1977). On the utility of alternative procedures for assessing psychological androgyny. *Journal of Consulting and Clinical Psychology, 45*, 196–205.

Bem, S. L. (1978). Beyond androgyny: Some presumptuous prescriptions for a liberalized sexual identity. In J. A. Sherman & F. L. Denmark (Eds.), *The psychology of women: Future directions in research* (pp. 1–23). New York, NY: Psychological Dimensions.

Bem, S. L. (1981). Gender schema theory: A cognitive account of sex typing. *Psychological Review, 88*, 354–364.

Bem, S. L. (1982). Gender schema theory and self-schema theory compared: A comment on Markus, Crane, Bernstein, and Siladi's "Self-schemas and gender." *Journal of Personality and Social Psychology, 43*, 1192–1194.

382 BIBLIOGRAPHY

Bem, S. L. (1983). Gender schema theory and its implications for child development: Raising gender-aschematic children in a gender-schematic society. *Signs, 8*, 598–616.

Bem, S. L. (1985). Androgyny and gender schema theory: A conceptual and empirical integration. In T. B. Sonderegger (Ed.), *Nebraska Symposium on Motivation 1984: Psychology and gender* (pp. 76–103). Lincoln, NE: University of Nebraska Press.

Bem, S. L. (1993). *The lenses of gender: Transforming the debate on sexual inequality.* New Haven, CT: Yale University Press.

Bem, S. L. (1995). Working on gender as a gender-nonconformist. In P. Chesler, E. D. Rothblum, & E. Cole (Eds.), *Feminist foremothers in women's studies, psychology, and mental health* (pp. 43–53). London, UK: Haworth.

Bem, S. L. (1998). *An unconventional family.* New Haven, CT: Yale University Press.

Bem, S. L., & Lenney, E. (1976). Sex typing and the avoidance of cross-sex behavior. *Journal of Personality and Social Psychology, 33,* 48–54.

Bem, S. L., & Lewis, S. A. (1975). Sex role adaptability: One consequence of psychological androgyny. *Journal of Personality and Social Psychology, 31,* 634–643.

Benet-Martinez, V., & John, O. P. (1998). Los Cinco Grandes across cultures and ethnic groups: Multi-trait multi-method analyses of the Big Five in Spanish and English. *Journal of Personality and Social Psychology, 75,* 729–750.

Benjamin, J. (2015). Masculinity, complex: A historical take. *Studies in Gender and Sexuality, 16,* 271–277.

Benjamin, L. S. (2011). Structural analysis of social behavior (SASB). In L. M. Horowitz & S. Strack (Eds.), *Handbook of interpersonal psychology: Theory, research, assessment, and therapeutic implications* (pp. 325–342). Hoboken, NJ: John Wiley & Sons.

Bentler, P. M., & Chou, C. (1987). Practical issues in structural modeling. *Sociological Methods and Research, 16,* 78–117.

Berndt, T. J. (1996). Exploring the effects of friendship quality on social development. In W. M. Bukowski, A. F. Newcomb, & W. W. Hartup (Eds.), *The company they keep: Friendship in childhood and adolescence* (pp. 346–365). Cambridge, UK: Cambridge University Press.

Berndt, T. J. (2002). Friendship quality and social development. *Current Directions in Psychological Science, 11,* 7–10.

Berndt, T. J. (2004). Children's friendships: Shifts over a half-century in perspectives on their development and their effects. *Merrill-Palmer Quarterly, 50,* 206–223.

Berndt, T. J., Hawkins, J. A., & Jiao, Z. (1999). Influences of friends and friendship on adjustment to junior high school. *Merrill-Palmer Quarterly, 45,* 13–41.

Bernstein, P. P. (2004). Mothers and daughters from today's psychoanalytic perspective. *Psychoanalytical Inquiry, 24,* 601–628.

Berscheid, E. (1985). Interpersonal attraction. In G. Lindzey & E. Aronson (Eds.), *The handbook of social psychology* (3rd ed., Vol. 2, pp. 413–484). New York, NY: Random House.

Berscheid, E. (1994). Interpersonal relationships. *Annual Review of Psychology, 45,* 79–129.

Berscheid, E. (1999). The greening of relationship science. *American Psychologist, 54,* 260–266.

Berscheid, E. (2010). Love in the fourth dimension. *Annual Review of Psychology, 61,* 1–25.

BIBLIOGRAPHY 383

Berscheid, E., & Reis, H. T. (1998). Attraction and close relationships. In D. T. Gilbert, S. T. Fiske, & G. Lindzey (Eds.), *The handbook of social psychology* (4th ed., Vol. 2, pp. 193–281). Boston, MA: McGraw-Hill.

Bertocci, P. A. (1940). A critique of G. W. Allport's theory of motivation. *Psychological Review, 47*, 501–532.

Bhugra, D., & Bhui, K. (2002). Is the Oedipal complex universal? Problems for sexual and relationship psychotherapy across cultures. *Sexual and Relationship Therapy, 17*, 69–86.

Birtchnell, J. (2014). The interpersonal circle and the interpersonal octagon: A confluence of ideas. *Clinical Psychology and Psychotherapy, 21*, 62–72.

Blascovich, J., & Tomaka, J. (1991). Measures of self-esteem. In J. Robinson, P. Shaver, & L. Wrightsman (Eds.), *Measures of personality and social psychological attitudes* (pp. 161–194). New York, NY: Academic Press.

Blatt, S. J. (2007). A fundamental polarity in psychoanalysis: Implications for personality development, psychopathology, and the therapeutic process. *Psychoanalytic Inquiry, 26*, 494–520.

Blechner, M. J. (2006). Love, sex, romance and psychoanalytic goals. *Psychoanalytic Dialogues, 16*, 779–791.

Blechner, M. J. (2008). The political is psychoanalytic: On same-sex marriage. *Studies in Gender and Sexuality, 9*, 146–154.

Boon, S., & Holmes, J. G. (1990). *Interpersonal trust, attachment, and emotion.* Paper presented at the International Conference of Personal Relationships, Oxford, UK.

Borkenau, P., McCrae, R., & Terracciano, A. (2013). Do men vary more than women in personality? A study in 51 cultures. *Journal of Research in Personality, 47*, 135–144.

Bowlby, J. (1997). *Attachment and loss* (Vol. 1: Attachment). London, UK: Pimlico. (Original work published 1969)

Bowlby, J. (1998). *Attachment and loss* (Vol. 2: Separation: Anxiety and anger). London, UK: Pimlico. (Original work published 1973)

Bowlby, J. (1998). *Attachment and loss* (Vol. 3: Loss: Sadness and depression). London, UK: Pimlico. (Original work published 1980)

Bowlby, J. (2005). *A secure base.* London, UK: Routledge. (Original work published 1988)

Bowlby, J. (2005). *The making and breaking of affectional bonds.* London, UK: Routledge. (Original work published 1979)

Braithwaite, V. A., & Scott, W. A. (1991). Values. In J. P. Robinson, P. R. Shaver, & L. S. Wrightsman (Eds.), *Measures of personality and social psychological attitudes* (pp. 661–753). San Diego, CA: Academic Press.

Brannon, T. N., Taylor, V. J., Higginbotham, G. D., & Henderson, K. (2017). Selves in contact: How integrating perspectives on sociocultural selves and intergroup contact can inform theory and application on reducing inequality. *Social and Personality Psychology Compass, 11*, 1–15.

Brennan, K. A., Clark, C. L., & Shaver, P. R. (1998). Self-report measurement of adult romantic attachment: An integrative overview. In J. A. Simpson & W. S. Rholes (Eds.), *Attachment theory and close relationships* (pp. 46–76). New York, NY: Guilford Press.

Bretherton, I. (1992). The origins of attachment theory: John Bowlby and Mary Ainsworth. *Developmental Psychology, 28*, 759–775.

Britton, R. (2004). Narcissistic disorders in clinical practice. *Journal of Analytical Psychology, 49*, 477–490.

Brooks, R. M. (2013). Accounting for material reality in the analytic subject. *Behavioral Sciences, 3*, 619–633.

384 BIBLIOGRAPHY

Brown, B. B., Feiring, C., & Furman, W. (1999). Missing the love boat: Why researchers have shied away from adolescent romance. In W. Furman, B. B. Brown, & C. Feiring (Eds.), *The development of romantic relationships in adolescence* (pp. 1–18). New York, NY: Cambridge University Press.

Brown, R. (1965). *Social psychology*. New York, NY: Free Press.

Brown, R. (1986). *Social psychology* (2nd ed.). New York, NY: Free Press.

Brown, T. A. (2015). *Confirmatory factor analysis for applied research* (2nd ed.). New York, NY: Guilford.

Bucher, M. A., & Samuel, D. B. (2019). Development of a short form of the Abridged Big Five-Dimensional Circumplex Model to aid with the organization of personality traits. *Journal of Personality Assessment, 101*, 16–24.

Bucher, M. A., & Samuel, D. B. (2020). Developing a short form of the IPIP Abridged Big Five-Dimensional Circumplex (AB5C) congruent with the AB5C circumplex locations. *Journal of Research in Personality, 88*, 1–9.

Bukowski, W. M. (2001). Friendship and the worlds of childhood. *New Directions for Child and Adolescent Development, 91*, 93–105.

Bukowski, W. M., Hoza, B., & Boivin, M. (1994). Measuring friendship quality during pre- and early adolescence: The development and psychometric properties of the Friendship Qualities Scale. *Journal of Social and Personal Relationships, 11*, 471–484.

Bukowski, W. M., & Sippola, L. K. (2005). Friendship and development: Putting the most human relationship in its place. *New Directions for Child and Adolescent Development, 109*, 91–98.

Burnes, B., & Cooke, B. M. (2013). Kurt Lewin's field theory: A review and re-evaluation. *International Journal of Management Reviews, 15*, 408–425.

Burrow, T. (1917). II. Notes with reference to Freud, Jung and Adler. *Journal of Abnormal Psychology, 12*, 161–167.

Bussey, K. (2011). Gender identity development. In S. J. Schwartz, K. Luyckx, & V. L. Vignoles (Eds.), *Handbook of identity theory and research* (pp. 603–628). New York, NY: Springer Science + Business Media.

Byock, S. D. (2015). The inner world of the first half of life: Analytical psychology's forgotten developmental stage. *Psychological Perspectives, 58*, 399–415.

Cain, N. M., De Panfilis, C., Meehan, K. B., & Clarkin, J. F. (2017). A multisurface interpersonal circumplex assessment of rejection sensitivity. *Journal of Personality Assessment, 99*, 35–45.

Calkins, M. W. (1917). The case of self against soul. *Psychological Review, 24*, 278–300.

Campbell, J. D. (1990). Self-esteem and clarity of the self-concept. *Journal of Personality and Social Psychology, 59*, 538–549.

Campbell, L., & Simpson, J. A. (2013). The blossoming of relationship science. In J. A. Simpson & L. Campbell (Eds.), *The Oxford handbook of close relationships* (pp. 3–10). Oxford, UK: Oxford University Press.

Campbell, W. K., Bonacci, A. M., Shelton, J., Exline, J. J., & Bushman, B. J. (2004). Psychological entitlement: Interpersonal consequences and validation of a self-report measure. *Journal of Personality Assessment, 83*, 29–45.

Campbell, W. K., Brunell, A. B., & Finkel, E. J. (2006). Narcissism, interpersonal self-regulation and romantic relationships: An agency model approach. In K. D. Vohs & E. J. Finkel (Eds.), *Self and relationships: Connecting intrapersonal and interpersonal processes* (pp. 57–83). New York, NY: Guilford Press.

BIBLIOGRAPHY 385

Campbell, W. K., & Foster, C. A. (2002). Narcissism and commitment in romantic relationships: An investment model analysis. *Personality and Social Psychology Bulletin, 28*, 484–495.

Campbell, W. K., & Green, J. D. (2016). Narcissism and interpersonal self-regulation. In J. V. Wood, A. Tesser, & J. G. Holmes (Eds.), *The self and social relationships* (pp. 73–94). New York, NY: Psychology Press. (Original work published 2008)

Canevello, A., & Crocker, J. (2015). How interpersonal goals shape intrapsychic experiences: Self-image and compassionate goals and feeling uneasy or at ease with others. *Social and Personality Psychology Compass, 9*, 620–629.

Canevello, A., & Crocker, J. (2017). Compassionate goals and affect in social situations. *Motivation and Emotion, 41*, 158–179.

Carson, R. C. (1969). *Interaction concepts of personality*. Chicago, IL: Aldine.

Casement, A. (2003). Encountering the shadow in rites of passage: A study in activations. *Journal of Analytical Psychology, 48*, 29–46.

Cattell, R. B. (1943). The description of personality: Basic traits resolved into clusters. *Journal of Abnormal and Social Psychology, 38*, 476–506.

Cattell, R. B. (1946). *Development and measurement of personality*. New York, NY: World Book Co.

Cattell, R. B. (1950). *Personality: A systematic, theoretical, and factual study*. New York, NY: McGraw-Hill.

Cattell, R. B. (1956). Second-order personality factors in the questionnaire realm. *Journal of Consulting Psychology, 20*, 411–418.

Cattell, R. B. (1957). *Personality and motivation: Structure and measurement*. Yonkers, NY: World Book.

Cattell, R. B. (1970). *Personality and social psychology: Collected papers of Raymond B. Cattell*. San Diego, CA: Knapp.

Cervone, D. (2005). Personality architecture: Within-person structures and processes. *Annual Review of Psychology, 56*, 423–452.

Champion, L. (2012). Social relationships and social roles. *Clinical Psychology and Psychotherapy, 19*, 113–123.

Chandler, C. K. (1991). The psychology of women: Approaching the twenty-first century. *Individual Psychology, 47*, 482–489.

Chesler, P., Rothblum, E. D., & Cole, E., eds. (1995). *Feminist foremothers in women's studies, psychology, and mental health*. London, UK: Haworth.

Chodorow, N. J. (2004). Psychoanalysis and women: A personal thirty-five-year retrospect. *Annual of Psychoanalysis, 32*, 101–129.

Chodorow, N. J. (2015). From the glory of Hera to the wrath of Achilles: Narratives of second-wave masculinity and beyond. *Studies in Gender and Sexuality, 16*, 261–270.

Chow, P., & Jeffrey, M. (2018). The reliability and validity of the Anima-Animus Continuum Scale. *Education, 138*, 264–270.

Clark, M. S., & Lemay, E. P., Jr. (2010). Close relationships. In S. T. Fiske, D. T. Gilbert, & G. Lindzey (Eds.), *Handbook of social psychology* (5th ed., Vol. 2, pp. 898–940). New York, NY: John Wiley & Sons.

Clarkin, J. F., Levy, K. N., & Ellison, W. D. (2011). Personality disorders. In L. M. Horowitz & S. Strack (Eds.), *Handbook of interpersonal psychology: Theory, research, assessment, and therapeutic interventions* (pp. 383–403). New York, NY: John Wiley & Sons.

Closs, S. J. (1996). On the factoring and interpretation of ipsative data. *Journal of Occupational and Organizational Psychology, 69*, 41–47.

386 BIBLIOGRAPHY

Cochrane, M., Flower, S., MacKenna, C., & Morgan, H. (2014). A Jungian approach to analytic work in the twenty-first century. *British Journal of Psychotherapy, 30,* 33–50.

Cohen, J., Cohen, P., West, S. G., & Aiken, L. S. (2003). *Applied multiple regression/correlation analysis for the behavioral sciences* (3rd ed.). Mahwah, NJ: Erlbaum.

Collins, N. L., Ford, M. B., & Feeney, B. C. (2011). An attachment-theory perspective on social support in close relationships. In L. M. Horowitz & S. Strack (Eds.), *Handbook of interpersonal psychology: Theory, research, assessment, and therapeutic interventions* (pp. 209–231). New York, NY: John Wiley & Sons.

Collins, N. L., & Read, S. J. (1994). Cognitive representations of attachment: The structure and function of working models. In K. Bartholomew & D. Perlman (Eds.), *Advances in personal relationships* (Vol. 5, pp. 53–92). London, UK: Jessica Kingsley.

Colman, W. (1996). Aspects of anima and animus in Oedipal development. *Journal of Analytical Psychology, 41,* 37–57.

Colman, W. (2000). Tyrannical omnipotence in the archetypal father. *Journal of Analytical Psychology, 45,* 521–539.

Colman, W. (2018). Are archetypes essential? *Journal of Analytical Psychology, 63,* 336–346.

Columbus, S., Righetti, F., & Balliet, D. (2020). Situations in close relationships. In L. V. Machia, C. R. Agnew, & X. B. Arriaga (Eds.), *Interdependence, interaction, and close relationships* (pp. 11–36). Cambridge, UK: Cambridge University Press.

Conci, M. (1997). Psychiatry, psychoanalysis and sociology in the work of H. S. Sullivan. *International Forum for Psychoanalysis, 6,* 127–134.

Conci, M. (2009). Bion and Sullivan: An enlightening comparison. *International Forum of Psychoanalysis, 18,* 90–99.

Conci, M. (2013). Sullivan and the intersubjective perspective. *International Forum of Psychoanalysis, 22,* 10–16.

Constantinople, A. (1973). Masculinity-femininity: An exception to a famous dictum? *Psychological Bulletin, 80,* 389–407.

Coolidge, F. L., Moor, C. J., Yamazaki, T. G., Stewart, S. E., & Segal, D. L. (2001). On the relationship between Karen Horney's tripartite neurotic type theory and personality disorder features. *Personality and Individual Differences, 30,* 1387–1400.

Cooper, A. B., & Guynn, R. W. (2006). Transcription of fragments of lectures in 1948 by Harry Stack Sullivan. *Psychiatry, 69,* 101–106.

Cooper, W. E. (1992). William James's theory of the self. *Monist, 75,* 504–520.

Corbett, K. (2008). Gender now. *Psychoanalytic Dialogues, 18,* 838–856.

Cornwell, J. M., & Dunlap, W. P. (1994). On the questionable soundness of factoring ipsative measures data: A response to Saville & Wilson (1991). *Journal of Occupational and Organizational Psychology, 67,* 89–100.

Cortina, J. M. (1993). What is coefficient alpha? An examination of theory and applications. *Journal of Applied Psychology, 78,* 98–104.

Cortina, M. (2020). Harry Stack Sullivan and interpersonal theory: A flawed genius. *Psychiatry, 83,* 103–109.

Cortina, M., & Marrone, M. (2004). Reclaiming Bowlby's contribution to psychoanalysis. *International Forum of Psychoanalysis, 13,* 133–146.Costa, P. T., Jr., & McCrae, R. R. (1985). *The NEO personality inventory manual.* Odessa, FL: Psychological Assessment Resources.

Costa, P. T., Jr., & McCrae, R. R. (1989). *The NEO personal inventory manual supplement.* Odessa, FL: Psychological Assessment Resources.

BIBLIOGRAPHY 387

Costa, P T., Jr., & McCrae, R. (1992). *Revised NEO Personality Inventory (NEO-PI-R) and NEO Five Factor Model (NEO-FFI) professional manual*. Odesa, FL: Psychological Assessment Center.

Costa, P. T., Jr., & McCrae, R. R. (1997). Longitudinal stability of adult personality. In R. Hogan, J. Johnson, & S. Briggs (Eds.), *Handbook of personality psychology* (pp. 269–290). San Diego, CA: Academic Press.

Costa, P. T., Jr., & McCrae, R. R. (2011). The Five-Factor Model, five-factor theory, and interpersonal psychology. In L. M. Horowitz & S. Strack (Eds.), *Handbook of interpersonal psychology: Theory, research, assessment, and therapeutic implications* (pp. 91–104). Hoboken, NJ: John Wiley & Sons.

Costa, P. T., Jr., & McCrae, R. R. (2017). The NEO inventories as instruments of psychological theory. In T. A. Widiger (Ed.), *The Oxford handbook of the Five Factor Model* (pp. 11–37). New York, NY: Oxford University Press.

Costa, P. T., Jr., Terracciano, A., & McCrae, R. R. (2001). Gender differences in personality traits across cultures: Robust and surprising findings. *Journal of Personality and Social Psychology, 81*, 322–331.

Costello, A. B., & Osborne, J. (2005). Best practices in exploratory factor analysis: Four recommendations for getting the most from your analysis. *Practical Assessment, Research, and Evaluation, 10*, Article 7.

Coward, H. (1989). Jung's conception of the role of religion in psychological transformation. *Humanistic Psychologist, 17*, 265–273.

Crane, M., & Markus, H. R. (1982). Gender identity: The benefits of a self-schema approach. *Journal of Personality and Social Psychology, 43*, 1195–1197.

Crocker, J., & Canevello, A. (2015). Relationships and the self: Ecosystem and egosystem. In M. Mikulincer & P. R. Shaver (Eds.), *APA handbook of personality and social psychology* (Vol. 3: Interpersonal relations, pp. 93–116). Washington, DC: American Psychological Association.

Crocker, J., Canevello, A., & Brown, A. (2017). Social motivation: Costs and benefits of selfishness and otherishness. *Annual Review of Psychology, 68*, 299–325.

Crocker, J., Olivier, M. A., & Nuer, N. (2009). Self-image goals and compassionate goals: Costs and benefits. *Self and Identity, 8*, 251–269.

Cross, S. E., Bacon, P., & Morris, M. (2000). The relational-interdependent self-construal and relationships. *Journal of Personality and Social Psychology, 78*, 791–808.

Dawood, S., & Pincus, A. L. (2016). Multisurface interpersonal assessment in a cognitive-behavioral therapy context. *Journal of Personality Assessment, 98*, 449–460.

Deaux, K., & Lafrance, M. (1998). Gender. In D. T. Gilbert, S. T. Fiske, & G. Lindzey (Eds.), *The handbook of social psychology* (4th ed., Vol. 1, pp. 788–827). New York, NY: McGraw-Hill.

Deaux, K., & Snyder, M. (Eds.). (2012). *The Oxford handbook of personality and social psychology*. Oxford, UK: Oxford University Press.

De Cuyper, K., De Houwer, J., Vansteelandt, K., Perugini, M., Pieters, G., Claes, L., & Hermans, D. (2017). Using indirect measurement tasks to assess the self-concept of personality: A systematic review and meta-analyses. *European Journal of Personality, 31*, 8–41.

De Fruyt, F., De Clercq, B., & De Bolle, M. (2017). The five-factor model of personality and consequential outcomes in childhood and adolescence. In T. Widiger (Ed.), *The Oxford handbook of the Five Factor Model* (pp. 507–520). New York, NY: Oxford University Press.

388 BIBLIOGRAPHY

De Pauw, S. S. W. (2017). Childhood personality and temperament. In T. Widiger (Ed.), *The Oxford handbook of the Five Factor Model* (pp. 243–280). New York, NY: Oxford University Press.

De Raad, B., & Mlacic, B. (2017). The lexical foundation of the Big Five Factor Model. In T. A. Widiger (Ed.), *The Oxford handbook of the Five Factor Model* (pp. 191–216). New York, NY: Oxford University Press.

DeRobertis, E. M. (2008). Self matters, but not that way: Humanism and selfishness in America. *Encounter, 21*, 38–42.

DeYoung, C. L., Weisberg, Y. J., Quilty, L. C., & Peterson, J. B. (2013). Unifying the aspects of the Big Five, the interpersonal circumplex, and trait affiliation. *Journal of Personality, 81*, 465–475.

Diener, E. (2000). Subjective well-being: The science of happiness and a proposal for a national index. *American Psychologist, 55*, 34–43.

Digman, J. M. (1990). Personality structure: Emergence of the Five-Factor Model. *Annual Review of Psychology, 41*, 417–440.

Dindia, K., & Canary, D. J. (1993). Definitions and theoretical perspectives on maintaining relationships. *Journal of Social and Personal Relationships, 10*, 163–173.

Donmall, K. (2013). What it means to bleed: An exploration of young women's experiences of menarche and menstruation. *British Journal of Psychotherapy, 29*, 202–216.

Donnelly, K., & Twenge, J. M. (2017). Masculine and feminine traits on the Bem Sex-Role Inventory, 1993–2012: A cross-temporal meta-analysis. *Sex Roles, 76*, 556–565.

Dozier, M., & Bernard, K. (2021). Mechanisms of attachment-based intervention effects on child outcomes. In R. A. Thompson, J. A. Simpson, & L. Berlin (Eds.), *Attachment: The fundamental questions* (pp. 307–315). New York, NY: Guilford.

Drigotas, S. M., Whitney, G. A., & Rusbult, C. E. (1995). On the peculiarities of loyalty: A diary study of responses to dissatisfaction in everyday life. *Personality and Social Psychology Bulletin, 21*, 596–609.

Driver, C. (2013). The "Holy Mother" and the shadow: Revisiting Jung's work on the Quaternity. *Journal of Analytical Psychology, 58*, 347–365.

Duck, S. (Ed.). (1988). *Handbook of personal relationships.* Chichester, UK: John Wiley & Sons.

Eagly, A. H. (1987). *Sex differences in social behavior: A social-role interpretation.* Hillsdale, NJ: Erlbaum.

Eagly, A. H. (2018). The shaping of science by ideology: How feminism inspired, led, and constrained scientific understanding of sex and gender. *Journal of Social Issues, 74*, 1–18.

Eagly, A. H., & Wood, W. (2012). Social role theory. In P. A. M. Van Lange, A. W. Kruglanski, & E. T. Higgins (Eds.), *Handbook of theories of social psychology* (pp. 458–476). Thousand Oaks, CA: Sage.

Eagly, A. H., & Wood, W. (2013). The nature-nurture debates. *Perspectives on Psychological Science, 8*, 340–357.

Eastwick, P. W., Finkel, E. J., & Simpson, J. A. (2019a). Relationship trajectories: A meta-theoretical framework and theoretical applications. *Psychological Inquiry, 30*, 1–28.

Eastwick, P. W., Finkel, E. J., & Simpson, J. A. (2019b). The relationship trajectories framework: Explanation and expansion. *Psychological Inquiry, 30*, 48–57.

Eccles, J. S., & Wigfield, A. (2002). Motivational beliefs, values, and goals. *Annual Review of Psychology, 53*, 109–132.

Eisenberg, N. (2000). Emotion, regulation, and moral development. *Annual Review of Psychology, 51*, 665–697.

BIBLIOGRAPHY 389

Ekstrom, S. (2018). Freud, Jung and the great chain of being. *Journal of Analytical Psychology, 63,* 462–483.

Elise, D. (2002). The primary maternal Oedipal situation and female homoerotic desire. *Psychoanalytic Inquiry, 22,* 209–228.

Emmons, R. A., & Paloutzian, R. F. (2003). The psychology of religion. *Annual Review of Psychology, 54,* 377–402.

Enns, C. Z. (1989). Toward teaching inclusive personality theories. *Teaching of Psychology, 16,* 111–117.

Enns, C. Z. (1994). Archetypes and gender: Goddesses, warriors, and psychological health. *Journal of Counseling and Development, 73,* 127–133.

Epstein, S. (1973). The self-concept revisited: Or a theory of a theory. *American Psychologist, 28,* 404–416.

Erol, R. Y., & Orth, U. R. (2016). Self-esteem and the quality of romantic relationships. *European Psychologist, 21,* 274–283.

Etcheverry, P. E., Le, B., Wu, T.-F., & Wei, M. (2013). Attachment and the investment model: Predictors of relationship commitment, maintenance, and persistence. *Personal Relationships, 20,* 546–567.

Erikson, E. H. (1980). *Identity and the life cycle.* New York, NY: Norton. (Original work published 1959)

Erikson, E. H. (1994). *Identity: Youth and crisis.* New York, NY: Norton. (Original work published 1968)

Erikson, E. H. (1995). *Childhood and society.* London, UK: Vintage. (Original work published 1963)

Ewen, R. B. (1998). *An introduction to theories of personality* (5th ed.). Mahwah, NJ: Erlbaum.

Eysenck, H. J. (1947). *Dimensions of personality.* New York, NY: Methuen.

Eysenck, H. J. (1951). The organization of personality. *Journal of Personality, 20,* 101–117.

Eysenck, H. J. (1957). *The dynamics of anxiety and hysteria: An experimental application of modern learning theory to psychiatry.* Oxford, UK: Praeger.

Eysenck, H. J. (1970). *The structure of human personality* (3rd ed.). London, UK: Methuen. (Original work published 1952)

Eysenck, H. J., & Eysenck, S. B. G. (1964). *Manual of the Eysenck Personality Inventory.* London, UK: University of London Press.

Eysenck, H. J., & Eysenck, S. B. G. (1968). *Manual for the Eysenck Personality Inventory.* San Diego, CA: Educational and Industrial Testing.

Eysenck, H. J., & Eysenck, S. B. G. (1975). *Manual of the Eysenck Personality Questionnaire.* London, UK: Hodder and Stoughton.

Eysenck, H. J., & Himmelweit, H. T. (1947). *Dimensions of personality: A record of research carried out in collaboration with H. T. Himmelweit [and others].* London, UK: Routledge & Kegan Paul.

Fabrigar, L. R., Visser, P. S., & Browne, M. W. (1997). Conceptual and methodological issues in testing the circumplex structure of data in personality and social psychology. *Personality and Social Psychology Review, 1,* 184–203.

Fabrigar, L. R., Wegener, D. T., MacCallum, R. C., & Strahan, E. J. (1999). Evaluating the use of exploratory factor analysis in psychological research. *Psychological Methods, 4,* 272–299.

Farrell, D. (1983). Exit, voice, loyalty, and neglect as responses to job dissatisfaction: A multidimensional scaling study. *Academy of Management Journal, 26,* 596–607.

390 BIBLIOGRAPHY

Farrell, D., & Rusbult, C. E. (1992). Exploring the exit, voice, loyalty, and neglect typology: The influence of job satisfaction, quality of alternatives, and investment size. *Employee Responsibilities and Rights Journal, 5,* 201–218.

Feeney, B. C. (2006). An attachment theory perspective on the interplay between intrapersonal and interpersonal processes. In K. D. Vohs & E. J. Finke (Eds.), *Self and relationships: Connecting intrapersonal and interpersonal processes* (pp. 133–159). New York, NY: Guilford.

Feeney, J. A., & Noller, P. (1996). *Adult attachment.* London, UK: Sage.

Feeney, J. A., Noller, P., & Hanrahan, M. (1994). Assessing adult attachment. In M. B. Sperling & W. H. Berman (Eds.), *Attachment in adults* (pp. 128–151). New York, NY: Guilford Press.

Festinger, L. (1954). Motivation leading to social behavior. In M. R. Jones (Ed.), *Nebraska symposium on motivation* (Vol. 2, pp. 191–218). Lincoln, NE: University of Nebraska Press.

Fincham, F. D., & Beach, S. R. (1999). Conflict in marriage: Implications for working with couples. *Annual Review of Psychology, 50,* 47–77.

Finkel, E. J., & Campbell, W. K. (2001). Self-control and accommodation in close relationships: An interdependence analysis. *Journal of Personality and Social Psychology, 81,* 263–277.

Finkel, E. J., Rusbult, C. E., Kumashiro, M., & Hannon, P. A. (2002). Dealing with betrayal in close relationships: Does commitment promote forgiveness? *Journal of Personality and Social Psychology, 82,* 956–974.

Finkel, E. J., Simpson, J. A., & Eastwick, P. W. (2017). The psychology of close relationships: Fourteen core principles. *Annual Review of Psychology, 68,* 383–411.

Fiske, S. T., & Taylor, S. E. (1984). *Social cognition.* New York, NY: McGraw-Hill.

Fiske, S. T., & Taylor, S. E. (1991). *Social cognition* (2nd ed.). New York, NY: McGraw-Hill.

Fleeson, W. (2012). Perspectives on the person: Rapid growth and opportunities for integration. In K. Deaux & M. Snyder (Eds.), *The Oxford handbook of personality and social psychology* (pp. 33–63). Oxford, UK: Oxford University Press.

Fleeson, W. (2020). Live simply so that others may simply live: Trying to get clarity on the meaning of honesty/humility. *European Journal of Personality, 34,* 524–526.

Fletcher, G. J. O., Simpson, J. A., & Thomas, G. (2000). The measurement of perceived relationship quality components: A confirmatory factor analytic approach. *Personality and Social Psychology Bulletin, 26,* 340–354.

Foa, E. B., & Foa, U. G. (1980). Resource theory: Interpersonal behavior as exchange. In K. J. Gergen, M. S. Greenberg, & R. H. Willis (Eds.), *Social exchange: Advances in theory and research* (pp. 77–94). New York, NY: Plenum.

Foa, U. G., & Foa, E. B. (1974). *Societal structures of the mind.* Springfield, IL: Charles C. Thomas.

Fordham, M. (1977). Maturation of the child within the family. *Journal of Analytical Psychology, 22,* 91–105.

Fortune, C. (2003). The analytic nursery: Ferenczi's "wise baby" meets Jung's "divine child." *Journal of Analytical Psychology, 48,* 457–466.

Fournier, M. A., Moskowitz, D. S., & Zuroff, D. C. (2011). Origins and applications of the interpersonal circumplex. In L. M. Horowitz & S. Strack (Eds.), *Handbook of interpersonal psychology: Theory, research, assessment, and therapeutic interventions* (pp. 57–73). New York, NY: John Wiley & Sons.

BIBLIOGRAPHY 391

Frable, D. E. S. (1997). Gender, racial, sexual, and class identities. *Annual Review of Psychology, 48,* 139–163.

Fraley, R. C., Waller, N. G., & Brennan, K. A. (2000). An item response theory analysis of self-report measures of adult attachment. *Journal of Personality and Social Psychology, 78,* 350–365.

Frank, D. M., & Davidson, L. (2014). The central role of self-esteem for persons with psychosis. *Humanistic Psychologist, 42,* 24–34.

Freedman, M. B. (1985). Symposium: Interpersonal circumplex models (1948–1983). *Journal of Personality Assessment, 49,* 622–625.

Freud, S. (1912). A note on the unconscious in psycho–analysis. In S. Freud, *The standard edition of the complete psychological works of Sigmund Freud* (Vol. XII, pp. 255–266). London, UK: Hogarth.

Freud, S. (1922). *Group psychology and the analysis of the ego.* London: G. Allen & Unwin. (Original work published 1921)

Freud, S. (1924). *A connection between a symbol and a symptom* (Collected papers, Vol. II). London, UK: Leonard and V. Woolf.

Freud, S. (1927). *The ego and the id.* London, UK: Hogarth. (Original work published 1923)

Freud, S. (1933). The anatomy of the mental personality. In S. Freud, *New introductory lectures on psycho-analysis* (pp. 82–112). London, UK: Hogarth. (Original work published 1932)

Freud, S. (1953). On narcissism: An introduction. In J. Strachey (Ed. & Trans.), *The standard edition of the complete psychological works of Sigmund Freud* (Vol. 14, pp. 69–102). London, UK: Hogarth Press. (Original work published 1914)

Freud, S. (1955). *The standard edition of the complete psychological works of Sigmund Freud* (Vol. X: Two Case Histories ["Little Hans" and the "Rat Man"]) (J. Strachey, Ed.). London, UK: Hogarth Press. (Original work published 1909)

Freud, S. (1959). On the sexual theories of children (Vol. 9) (D. Bryan, Trans.). In J. Strachey (Ed.), *The standard edition of the complete psychological works of Sigmund Freud* (pp. 205–235). London, UK: Hogarth Press.

Freud, S. (1961). *Beyond the pleasure principle.* New York, NY: Norton. (Original work published 1920)

Freud, S. (1965). *The interpretation of dreams.* New York, NY: Avon. (Original work published 1900)

Fromm, E. (1941). *Escape from freedom.* New York, NY: Farrar & Rinehart.

Fromm, E. (1956). *The art of loving.* London, UK: George Allen & Unwin.

Fuglestad, P. T., & Snyder, M. (2010). Status and the motivational foundations of self-monitoring. *Social and Personality Psychology Compass, 4,* 1031–1041.

Funder, D. C. (2001). Personality. *Annual Review of Psychology, 52,* 197–221.

Funder, D. C., & Fast, L. A. (2010). Personality in social psychology. In S. T. Fiske, D. T. Gilbert, & G. Lindzey (Eds.), *Handbook of social psychology* (5th ed., Vol. 1, pp. 668–697). New York, NY: John Wiley & Sons.

Furman, W., & Buhrmester, D. (1985). Children's perceptions of the personal relationships in their social networks. *Developmental Psychology, 21,* 1016–1024.

Gaines, S. O., Jr. (2007a). Personality and personal relationship processes: An introduction to the special issue. *Journal of Social and Personal Relationships, 24,* 475–478.

Gaines, S. O., Jr. (2007b). Personality and personal relationship processes: Concluding thoughts. *Journal of Social and Personal Relationships, 24,* 613–617.

392 BIBLIOGRAPHY

Gaines, S. O., Jr. (2018). *Identity and interethnic marriage in the United States.* New York, NY: Routledge. (Original work published 2017)

Gaines, S. O., Jr. (2018). *Personality and close relationship processes.* Cambridge, UK: Cambridge University Press. (Original work published 2016)

Gaines, S. O., Jr. (2020). *Personality psychology: The basics.* London, UK: Routledge.

Gaines, S. O., Jr. (2021). *Toward an interpersonal circumplex theory of personality and social behavior: Interpersonal traits, Interpersonal motives, and interdependence processes.* Paper presented at the online Close Relationships Preconference of the Society for Personality and Social Psychology, February 9, 2021.

Gaines, S. O., Jr., Carr, R., Gardner, S. N., Hodgins, P., Kyeyune, J., & Ruffell, M. (2013, August). *How well do correlations among scores on attachment measures fit ideal-, quasi-, and non-circumplex models?* Paper presented at the 2013 conference of the British Psychological Society Social Psychology Section, Exeter, UK.

Gaines, S. O., Jr., Panter, A. T., Lyde, M. D., Steers, W. N., Rusbult, C. E., Cox, C. L., & Wexler, M. O. (1997). Evaluating the circumplexity of interpersonal traits and the manifestation of interpersonal traits in interpersonal trust. *Journal of Personality and Social Psychology, 73*, 610–623.

Gaines, S. O., Jr., Reis, H. T., Summers, S., Rusbult, C. E., Cox, C. L., Wexler, M. O., Marelich, W. D., & Kurland, G. J. (1997). Impact of attachment style on reactions to accommodative dilemmas in close relationships. *Personal Relationships, 4*, 93–113.

Gaines, S. O., Jr., Work, C., Johnson, H., Youn, M. S. P., & Lai, K. (2000). Impact of attachment style and self-monitoring on individuals' responses to accommodative dilemmas across relationship types. *Journal of Social and Personal Relationships, 17*, 767–789.

Galipeau, S. (2013). *The Red Book* and Jung's typology. *Psychological Perspectives, 56*, 34–49.

Gallo, L. C., Smith, T. W., & Ruiz, J. M. (2003). An interpersonal analysis of adult attachment style: Circumplex descriptions, recalled developmental experiences, self-representations, and interpersonal functioning in adulthood. *Journal of Personality, 71*, 141–181.

Gitre, E. J. K. (2011). The great escape: World War II, neo-Freudianism, and the origins of U.S. psychocultural analysis. *Journal of the History of the Behavioral Sciences, 47*, 18–43.

Goldberg, L. R. (1977). *Language and personality: Developing a taxonomy of trait-descriptive terms.* Invited address to the Division of Evaluation and Measurement at the 86th Annual Convention of the American Psychological Association, San Francisco, August 27, 1977.

Goldberg, L. (1981). Language and individual differences: The search for universals in personality lexicons. In L. Wheeler (Ed.), *Review of personality and social psychology* (pp. 141–165). Beverly Hills, CA: Sage Publications.

Goldberg, L. R. (1993). The structure of personality traits: Vertical and horizontal aspects. In D. C. Funder, R. D. Parke, C. Tomlinson–Keasey, & K. Widaman (Eds.), *Studying lives through time: Personality and development* (pp. 169–188). Washington, DC: American Psychological Association.

Goldberg, L. R. (1999). A broad-bandwidth, public-domain, personality inventory measuring the lower-level facets of several Five- Factor models. In I. Mervielde, I. Deary, F. De Fruyt, & F. Ostendorf (Eds.), *Personality psychology in Europe* (Vol. 7, pp. 7–28). Tilburg, The Netherlands: Tilburg University Press.

Golden, C. R., & McHugh, M. C. (2017). The personal, political, and professional life of Sandra Bem. *Sex Roles, 76*, 529–543.

BIBLIOGRAPHY 393

Goldscheider, F. (2014). Rescuing the family from the homophobes and antifeminists: Analyzing the recently developed and already eroding "traditional" notions of family and gender. *Case Western Reserve Law Review, 64*, 1028–1044.

Goodwin, R. (1991). A re-examination of Rusbult's "Responses to Dissatisfaction" typology. *Journal of Social and Personal Relationships, 8*, 569–574.

Goodwin, R. (2009). *Changing relations: Achieving intimacy in a time of social transition.* Cambridge, UK: Cambridge University Press.

Gordon, R. (1987). Big self and little self: Some reflections. *Journal of Analytical Psychology, 30*, 261–271.

Gottman, J. M., & Levenson, R. W. (1986). Assessing the role of emotion in marriage. *Behavioral Assessment, 8*, 31–48.

Gough, B. (2004). Psychoanalysis as a resource for understanding emotional ruptures in the text: The case of defensive masculinities. *British Journal of Social Psychology, 43*, 245–267.

Graziano, W. G., & Tobin, R. M. (2017). Agreeableness and the Five Factor Model. In T. A. Widiger (Ed.), *The Oxford handbook of the Five Factor Model* (pp. 105–132). New York, NY: Oxford University Press.

Greenberg, J. (2008). Understanding the vital human quest for self-esteem. *Perspectives on Psychological Science, 3*, 48–55.

Greenberg, J., Pyszczynski, T., & Solomon, S. (1986). The causes and consequences of a need for self-esteem: A terror management theory. In R. F. Baumeister (Ed.), *Public self and private self* (pp. 189–212). New York, NY: Springer-Verlag.

Gregg, A. P., Sedikides, C., & Gebauer, J. E. (2011). Dynamics of identity: Between self-enhancement and self-assessment. In S. J. Schwartz, K. Luyckx, & V. L. Vignoles (Eds.), *Handbook of identity theory and research* (Vol. 1, pp. 305–327). New York, NY: Springer.

Griessel, L., & Kotze, M. (2009). The feminine and the masculine in the development of the self in women—A post-Jungian perspective. *Women's Studies, 38*, 183–212.

Griffin, D., & Bartholomew, K. (1994a). Metaphysics of measurement: The case of adult attachment. In K. Bartholomew & D. Perlman (Eds.), *Advances in personal relationships* (Vol. 5: Attachment processes in adulthood, pp. 17–52). London, UK: Jessica Kingsley.

Griffin, D., & Bartholomew, K. (1994b). Models of the self and other: Fundamental dimensions underlying measures of adult attachment. *Journal of Personality and Social Psychology, 67*, 430–445.

Guinote, A. (2017). How power affects people: Activating, wanting, and goal seeking. *Annual Review of Psychology, 68*, 353–381.

Gurtman, M. B. (1992). Trust, distrust, and interpersonal problems: A circumplex analysis. *Journal of Personality and Social Psychology, 62*, 989–1002.

Gurtman, M. B. (1993). Constructing personality tests to meet a structural criterion: Applications of the interpersonal circumplex. *Journal of Personality, 61*, 237–263.

Gurtman, M. B. (1995). Personality structure and interpersonal problems: A theoretically guided item analysis of the Inventory of Interpersonal Problems. *Assessment, 2*, 343–361.

Gurtman, M. B. (2009). Exploring personality with the interpersonal circumplex. *Social and Personality Psychology Compass, 3*, 601–619.

Gurtman, M. B. (2011). Circular reasoning about circular assessment. In L. M. Horowitz & S. Strack (Eds.), *Handbook of interpersonal psychology: Theory, research, assessment, and therapeutic interventions* (pp. 299–311). Hoboken, NJ: John Wiley & Sons.

394 BIBLIOGRAPHY

Gurtman, M. B., & Pincus, A. L. (2000). Interpersonal Adjective Scales: Confirmation of circumplex structure from multiple perspectives. *Personality and Social Psychology Bulletin, 26,* 374–384.

Guttman, L. (1954). A new approach to factor analysis: The radex. In P. F. Lazarsfeld (Ed.), *Mathematical thinking in the social sciences* (pp. 258–348). Glencoe, IL: Free Press.

Hall, C. S., & Lindzey, G. (1970). *Theories of personality* (2nd ed.). New York, NY: Wiley & Sons.

Hall, J., & Taylor, M. C. (1985). Psychological androgyny and the masculinity x femininity interaction. *Journal of Personality and Social Psychology, 49,* 429–435.

Hamman, J. J. (2017). The reproduction of the hypermasculine male: Select subaltern views. *Pastoral Psychology, 66,* 799–818.

Hampson, S. E. (1988). *The construction of personality: An introduction* (2nd ed.). London, UK: Routledge.

Hannon, P. A., Rusbult, C. E., Finkel, E. J., & Kumashiro, M. A. (2010). In the wake of betrayal: Perpetrator amends, victim forgiveness, and the resolution of betrayal incidents. *Personal Relationships, 17,* 253–278.

Hansen, B. (2002). Public careers and private sexuality: Some gay and lesbian lives in the history of medicine and public health. *American Journal of Public Health, 92,* 36–44.

Harris, K., & Vazire, S. (2016). On friendship development and the Big Five personality traits. *Social and Personality Psychology Compass, 10,* 647–667.

Harris, R. J. (2001). *A primer of multivariate statistics* (3rd ed.). New York, NY: Psychology Press.

Hashimoto, Y., & Oshio, A. (2018). Relationship between interpersonal traits and Big Five personality: A meta-analysis. *Japanese Journal of Personality, 26,* 294–296.

Hashimoto, Y., & Oshio, A. (2019). Structure of Japanese interpersonal trait words: An analysis based on the psycho-lexical approach. *Japanese Journal of Personality, 28,* 16–27.

Haslam, N. (1995). Factor structure of social relationships: An examination of relational models and resource exchange theories. *Journal of Social and Personal Relationships, 12,* 217–227.

Hazan, C., & Shaver, P. R. (1987). Romantic love conceptualized as an attachment process. *Journal of Personality and Social Psychology, 52,* 511–524.

Hazan, C., & Shaver, P. R. (1994a). Attachment as an organizational framework for research on close relationships. *Psychological Inquiry, 5,* 1–22.

Hazan, C., & Shaver, P. R. (1994b). Deeper into attachment theory: Reply to commentaries. *Psychological Inquiry, 5,* 68–79.

Helgeson, V. S. (1994). The relation of agency and communion to well-being: Evidence and potential explanations. *Psychological Bulletin, 116,* 412–428.

Helgeson, V. S. (2015). Gender and personality. In M. Mikulincer & P. R. Shaver (Eds.), *APA handbook of personality and social psychology* (Vol. 4: Personality processes and individual differences, pp. 515–534). Washington, DC: American Psychological Association.

Helgeson, V. S., & Fritz, H. L. (1998). A theory of unmitigated communion. *Personality and Social Psychology Review, 2,* 173–183.

Helgeson, V. S., & Fritz, H. L. (2000). The implications of unmitigated agency and unmitigated communion for domains of problem behavior. *Journal of Personality, 68,* 1031–1057.

Henderson, J. L. (1985). The self in review. *Journal of Analytical Psychology, 30,* 243–246.

BIBLIOGRAPHY 395

Hendrick, C. (1988). Roles and gender in relationships. In S. W. Duck (Ed.), *Handbook of personal relationships* (pp. 429–448). New York, NY: John Wiley & Sons.

Hendrick, S. S. (1988). A generic measure of relationship satisfaction. *Journal of Marriage and the Family, 50,* 93–98.

Hill, B. (2015). Uroborus: A review of Jung's thinking on the nature of the psyche and the transformation of libido. *Psychological Perspectives, 58,* 72–94.

Hill, C. T. (2019). *Intimate relationships across cultures: A comparative study.* Cambridge, UK: Cambridge University Press.

Hirsch, I. (2014). Narcissism, mania, and analysts' envy of patients. *Psychoanalytic Inquiry, 34,* 408–420.

Hirsch, P. (2005). Apostle of freedom: Alfred Adler and his British disciples. *History of Education, 34,* 473–481.

Hirschman, A. O. (1970). *Exit, voice, and loyalty: Responses to decline in firms, organizations, and states.* Cambridge, MA: Harvard University Press.

Hoessler, C. (2008). *Social Behavior Inventory: To ipsatize or not to ipsatize, that is the question.* Unpublished master's thesis, Wilfrid Laurier University.

Hoffman, R. M. (2001). The measurement of masculinity and femininity: Historical perspective and implications for counselling. *Journal of Counseling and Development, 79,* 472–485.

Hoffman, R. M., & Pasley, K. (1998). Thinking about the sexes: The relation between cognitions and gender stereotypes. *American Journal of Family Therapy, 26,* 189–202.

Hofsess, C. D., & Tracey, T. J. G. (2005). The interpersonal circumplex as a model of interpersonal capabilities. *Journal of Personality Assessment, 84,* 137–147.

Hofstede, G. (1980). *Culture's consequences: International differences in work-related values.* Newbury Park, CA: Sage.

Hofstee, W. K., de Raad, B., & Goldberg, L. R. (1992). Integration of the Big Five and circumplex approaches to trait structure. *Journal of Personality and Social Psychology, 63,* 146–163.

Hogan, J., & Ones, D. S. (1997). Conscientiousness and integrity at work. In R. Hogan, J. Johnson, & S. Briggs (Eds.), *Handbook of personality psychology* (pp. 849–870). San Diego, CA: Academic Press.

Hogan, R., Johnson, J., & Briggs, S. (Eds.). (1997). *Handbook of personality psychology.* San Diego, CA: Academic Press.

Holmes, J. (2004). *The search for the secure base: Attachment theory and psychotherapy.* Hove, UK: Brunner-Routledge.

Holmes, J. G. (2000). Social relationships: The nature and function of relational schemas. *European Journal of Social Psychology, 30,* 447–495.

Holmes, J. G. (2002). Interpersonal expectations as the building blocks of social cognition: An interdependence theory perspective. *Personal Relationships, 9,* 1–26.

Hopwood, C. J. (2018). Interpersonal dynamics in personality and personality disorders. *European Journal of Personality, 32,* 499–524.

Hopwood, C. J., Ansell, E. B., Pincus, A. L., Wright, A. G., Lukowitsky, M. R., & Roche, M. J. (2011). The circumplex structure of interpersonal sensitivities. *Journal of Personality, 79,* 707–740.

Hopwood, C. J., & Waugh, M. H. (Eds.). (2020). *Personality assessment paradigms and methods: A collaborative reassessment of Madeline G.* New York, NY: Routledge.

Horne, M., Sowa, A., & Isenman, D. (2000). Philosophical assumptions in Freud, Jung and Bion: Questions of causality. *Journal of Analytical Psychology, 45,* 109–121.

396 BIBLIOGRAPHY

Horney, K. (1937). *The neurotic personality of our time*. New York, NY: Norton.

Horney, K. (1939). *New ways in psychoanalysis*. New York, NY: Norton.

Horney, K. (1942). *Self-analysis*. New York, NY: Norton.

Horney, K. (1945). *Our inner conflicts*. New York, NY: Norton.

Horney, K. (1950). *Neurosis and human growth*. New York, NY: Norton.

Horney, K. (1967). *Feminine psychology*. New York, NY: Norton.

Horowitz, L. M., Rosenberg, S. E., Baer, B. A., Ureno, G., & Villasenor, V S. (1988). Inventory of interpersonal problems: Psychometric properties and clinical applications. *Journal of Consulting and Clinical Psychology, 56*, 885–892.

Horowitz, L. M., Rosenberg, S. E., & Bartholomew, K. (1993). Interpersonal problems, attachment styles, and outcome in brief dynamic psychotherapy. *Journal of Consulting and Clinical Psychology, 61*, 549–560.

Horowitz, L. M., & Strack, S. (2011). *Handbook of interpersonal psychology: Theory, research, assessment, and therapeutic interventions*. New York: Wiley.

Hough, L. M., Oswald, F. L., & Ock, J. (2015). Beyond the Big Five: New directions for personality research and practice in organizations. *Annual Review of Organizational Psychology and Organizational Behavior, 2*, 183–209.

Hoyle, R. H. (1987). *Factorial validity of the Multifaceted-Evaluation-of-Self Inventory (MESI)*. Paper presented at the 27th annual meeting of the New England Psychological Association, Amherst, Massachusetts.

Hsu, N., Badura, K. L., Newman, D. A., & Speach, M. E. P. (2021). Gender, "masculinity," and "femininity": A meta-analytic review of gender differences in agency and communion. *Psychological Bulletin, 147*, 987–1011.

Hubback, J. (1978). Reflections on the psychology of women. *Journal of Analytical Psychology, 17*, 152–165.

Huston, T. L. (2009). What's love got to do with it? Why some marriages succeed and others fail. *Personal Relationships, 16*, 301–327.

Ickes, W. (1981). Sex-role influences in dyadic interaction: A theoretical model. In C. Mayo & N. M. Henley (Eds.), *Gender and nonverbal behavior* (pp. 95–128). New York, NY: Springer-Verlag.

Ickes, W. (1985). Sex-role influences on compatibility in relationships. In W. Ickes (Ed.), *Compatible and incompatible relationships* (pp. 187–207). New York, NY: Springer-Verlag.

Ickes, W. (1993). Traditional gender roles: Do they make, and then break, our relationships? *Journal of Social Issues, 49*, 71–85.

Ickes, W., Snyder, M., & Garcia, S. (1997). Personality influences on the choice of situations. In R. Hogan, J. Johnson, & S. Briggs. (Eds.), *Handbook of personality psychology* (pp. 165–195). San Diego, CA: Academic Press.

Jackson, D. L. (2003). Revisiting sample size and number of parameter estimates: Some support for the N:q hypothesis. *Structural Equation Modeling, 10*, 128–141.

Jackson, D. N. (1976). *Jackson Personality Inventory: Manual*. Goshen, NY: Research Psychologists Press.

Jackson, J. J., & Roberts, B. W. (2017). Conscientiousness. In T. A. Widiger (Ed.), *The Oxford handbook of the Five Factor Model* (pp. 133–147). New York, NY: Oxford University Press.

James, W. (1902). *The varieties of religious experience*. Glasgow, UK: Collins.

James, W. (2010). *The principles of psychology* (Vols. 1 & 2). Mansfield Center, CT: Martino Publishing. (Original work published 1890)

Janssen, D. F. (2020). Toward sex consciousness: Adler's gender roles—Part 1: From *sexualrolle* to *geschlechtsrolle*. *Journal of Individual Psychology, 76*, 258–272.

BIBLIOGRAPHY 397

Jarnecke, A. M., & South, S. C. (2017). Behavior and molecular genetics of the Five Factor Model. In T. A. Widiger (Ed.), *The Oxford handbook of the Five Factor Model* (pp. 301–317). Oxford, UK: Oxford University Press.

John, O. P., Donahue, E. M., & Kentle, R. L. (1991). *The Big Five Inventory—Versions 4a and 5a.* Berkeley, CA: University of California.

Jones, D. N., & Paulhus, D. L. (2011). Differentiating the Dark Triad within the interpersonal circumplex. In L. M. Horowitz & S. Strack (Eds.), *Handbook of interpersonal psychology: Theory, research, assessment, and therapeutic interventions* (pp. 249–267). New York, NY: John Wiley & Sons.

Jones, W. H., Couch, L. L., & Scott, S. (1997). Trust and betrayal: The psychology of trust violation. In R. Hogan, J. Johnson, & S. R. Briggs (Eds.), *Handbook of personality* (pp. 466–482). New York, NY: Academic Press.

Jordan, E. (1995). Fighting boys and fantasy play: The construction of masculinity in the early years of school. *Gender & Education, 7,* 69–86.

Jordan, F. (1896). *Character as seen in body and parentage* (3rd ed.). London, UK: K. Paul, Trench, Trubner & Co.

Joreskog, K. G., & Sorbom, D. (1979). *Advances in factor analysis and structural equation models.* Cambridge, MA: Abt Books.

Joreskog, K. G., & Sorbom, D. (1984). *LISREL VI user's guide* (3rd ed.). Mooresville, IN: Scientific Software.

Joreskog, K. G., & Sorbom, D. (1989). *LISREL 7: Users Reference Guide.* Chicago, IL: Scientific Software International.

Joreskog, K. G., & Sorbom, D. (1993a). *LISREL 8: Structural equation modeling with the SIMPLIS command language.* Chicago, IL: Scientific Software International.

Joreskog, K. G., & Sorbom, D. (1993b). *LISREL 8 user's reference guide.* Chicago, IL: Scientific Software International.

Joreskog, K. G., & Sorbom, D. (1993c). *PRELIS 2 user's reference guide.* Chicago, IL: Scientific Software International.

Joreskog, K. G., & Sorbom, D. (2019). *LISREL 10.2* [Computer software]. Lincolnwood, IL: Scientific Software International.

Jowett, A. (2020). LGBTIA-related articles within British Psychological Society journals: A review of the literature from 1941–2017. *Psychology of Sexualities Review, 11,* 9–25.

Jung, C. G. (1955). *Answer to Job.* London, UK: Routledge and Paul.

Jung, C. G. (1956). *Symbols of transformation.* London, UK: Routledge.

Jung, C. G. (1958). *Psyche and symbol: A selection from the writings of C. G. Jung* (V. S. De Laszlo, Ed.). Garden City, NY: Doubleday.

Jung, C. G. (1971). *Psychological types.* London, UK: Routledge. (Original work published 1921)

Jung, C. G. (1972). *The structure and dynamics of the psyche.* Princeton, NJ: Princeton University Press.

Jung, C. G. (1973). *Memories, dreams, reflections.* New York, NY: Vintage Books.

Jung, C. G. (1975). *Aion: Researches into the phenomenology of the self.* London, UK: Routledge. (Original work published 1959)

Jung, C. G. (2009). *The red book (Liber novus: A reader's edition).* New York, NY: Norton.

Kafka, J. S. (2006). The trouble with Sullivan's "malevolent transformation." *Psychiatry, 69,* 11311–11314.

Kanter, J. S. (2013). Helping, healing and interpreting: Sullivan, the interpersonal school and clinical social work. *Journal of Social Work Practice, 27,* 273–287.

398 BIBLIOGRAPHY

Karaban, R. A. (1992). Jung's concept of the anima/animus: Enlightening or frightening? *Pastoral Psychology, 41*, 39–44.

Karniol, R., & Ross, M. (1996). The motivational impact of temporal focus: Thinking about the future and the past. *Annual Review of Psychology, 47*, 593–620.

Karremans, J. C., Pronk, T., & van der Wal, R. C. (2015). Executive control and relationship maintenance processes: An empirical overview and theoretical integration. *Social and Personality Psychology Compass, 9*, 333–347.

Kashdan, T. B., & McKnight, P. E. (2011). Dynamic, contextual approaches to studying personality in the social world. *Journal of Personality, 79*, 1177–1190.

Katz, S. M. (2018). Prologue: Sex, gender, and identity. *Psychoanalytic Inquiry, 38*, 1–10.

Kay, J. (2012). In pursuit of emotional security. *Psychiatry, 75*, 18–21.

Keefe, K., & Berndt, T. J. (1996). Relations of friendship quality to self-esteem in early adolescence. *Journal of Early Adolescence, 16*, 110–129.

Kelley, H. H. (1979). *Personal relationships: Their structures and processes.* Hillsdale, NJ: Erlbaum.

Kelley, H. H. (1983). The situation origins of human tendencies: A further reason for the formal analysis of structures. *Personality and Social Psychology Bulletin, 9*, 8–30.

Kelley, H. H. (1991). Lewin, situations, and interdependence. *Journal of Social Issues, 47*, 211–233.

Kelley, H. H. (1997). The "stimulus field" for interpersonal phenomena: The source for language and thought about interpersonal events. *Personality and Social Psychology Review, 1*, 140–169.

Kelley, H. H., Berscheid, E., Christensen, A., Harvey, J. H., Huston, T. L., Levinger, G., McClintock, E., Peplau, L. A., & Peterson, D. R. (2002). *Close relationships.* New York, NY: Percheron Press. (Original work published 1983)

Kelley, H. H., Holmes, J. G., Kerr, N. L., Reis, H. T., Rusbult, C. E., & Van Lange, P. A. M. (2003). *An atlas of interpersonal situations.* New York, NY: Cambridge University Press.

Kelley, H. H., & Thibaut, J. W. (1978). *Interpersonal relations: A theory of interdependence.* New York, NY: Wiley.

Kempf, E. J. (1921). *Psychopathology.* London, UK: H. Kimpton.

Kernis, M. H. (2003). Toward a conceptualization of optimal self-esteem. *Psychological Inquiry, 14*, 1–26.

Kernis, M. H. (2003). Optimal self-esteem and authenticity: Separating fantasy from reality. *Psychological Inquiry, 14*, 83–89.

Kerr, J. (2014). Is there a self, and do we care? Reflections on Kohut and Sullivan. *Contemporary Psychoanalysis, 50*, 627–658.

Kieffer, C. C. (2004). Self-objects, Oedipal objects, and mutual recognition: A self-psychological reappraisal of the female "Oedipal victor." *Annual of Psychoanalysis, 32*, 69–80.

Kierski, W., & Blazina, C. (2009). The male fear of the feminine and its effects on counseling and psychotherapy. *Journal of Men's Studies, 17*, 155–172.

Kiesler, D. J. (1983). The 1982 Interpersonal Circle: A taxonomy for complementarity in human transactions. *Psychological Review, 90*, 185–214.

Kingery, J. N., Erdley, C. A., Marshall, K. V., Whitaker, K. G., & Reuter, T. R. (2010). Peer experiences of anxious and socially withdrawn youth: An integrative review of the developmental and clinical literature. *Clinical Child and Family Psychology Review, 13*, 91–128.

BIBLIOGRAPHY 399

Klein, M. (1927). Symposium on child analysis. *International Journal of Psychoanalysis, 8*, 339–391.

Klein, M. (1975). *Envy and gratitude and other works, 1946–1963.* London, UK: Hogarth Press and the Institute of Psycho-Analysis.

Kline, R. B. (2016). *Principles and practice of structural equation modeling* (4th ed.). New York, NY: Guilford Press.

Klohnen, E., & John, O. (1998.) Working models of attachment: A theory-based prototype approach. In J. A. Simpson & S. Rholes (Eds.), *Attachment theory and close relationships* (pp. 115–142). London: Guilford.

Knafo, D. (2018). Desiring castration: A reformulation of castration theory illustrated with a transgender case. *Psychoanalytic Inquiry, 38*, 34–50.

Koch, S. (1941). The logical character of the motivation concept: II. *Psychological Review, 48*, 127–154.

Kochendorfer, L. B., & Kerns, K. A. (2020). A meta-analysis of friendship qualities and romantic relationship outcomes in adolescence. *Journal of Research on Adolescence, 30*, 4–25.

Koffka, K. (1935). *Principles of Gestalt psychology.* New York, NY: Harcourt Brace.

Kohler, W. (1976). *The place of value in a world of facts.* New York, NY: Liveright. (Original work published 1938)

Korsbek, L. (2016). Corecovery: Mental health recovery in a dynamic interplay between humans in a relationship. *American Journal of Psychiatric Rehabilitation, 19*, 196–205.

Kradin, R. (2009). The family myth: Its deconstruction and replacement with a balanced humanized narrative. *Journal of Analytical Psychology, 54*, 217–232.

Krausz, E. O. (1994). Freud's devaluation of women. *Individual Psychology, 50*, 298–313.

Kullberg, P. (2019). The bad mother. *Psychological Perspectives, 62*, 4–14.

Kumashiro, M., Finkel, E. J., & Rusbult, C. E. (2002). Self-respect and pro-relationship behavior in marital relationships. *Journal of Personality, 70*, 1009–1049.

Kuper, N., Modersitzki, N., Phan, L. V., & Rauthmann, J. F. (2021). The dynamics, processes, mechanisms, and functioning of personality: An overview of the field. *British Journal of Psychology, 112*, 1–51.

Kurdek, L. A. (2002). On being insecure about the assessment of attachment styles. *Journal of Social and Personal Relationships, 19*, 811–834.

Lacan, J. (1977). *The four fundamental concepts of psycho-analysis* (J. A. Miller, Ed.; A. Sheridan, Trans.). New York, NY: Norton. (Original work published 1973)

LaForge, R., & Suczek, R. (1955). The interpersonal dimension of personality: III. An interpersonal check list. *Journal of Personality, 24*, 94–112.

Laughlin, C. D., & Tiberia, V. A. (2012). Archetypes: Toward a Jungian anthropology of consciousness. *Anthropology of Consciousness, 23*, 127–157.

Laursen, B., & Jensen-Campbell, L. A. (1999). The nature and functions of social exchange in adolescent romantic relationships. In W. Furman, B. B. Brown, & C. Feiring (Eds.), *The development of romantic relationships in adolescence* (pp. 50–74). New York, NY: Cambridge University Press.

Le, B., & Agnew, C. R. (2003). Commitment and its theorized determinants: A meta-analysis of the investment model. *Personal Relationships, 10*, 37–57.

Leaper, C. (2017). Further reflections on Sandra Lipsitz Bem's impact. *Sex Roles, 76*, 759–765.

Leary, M. R., & Baumeister, R. F. (2000). The nature and function of self-esteem: Sociometer theory. In M. P. Zanna (Ed.), *Advances in experimental social psychology* (Vol. 32, pp. 1–62). New York, NY: Academic Press.

400 BIBLIOGRAPHY

Leary, M. R., & Toner, K. (2015). Self-processes in the construction and maintenance of personality. In M. Mikulincer & P. R. Shaver (Eds.), *APA handbook of personality and social psychology* (Vol. 4: Personality processes and individual differences, pp. 447–467). Washington, DC: American Psychological Association.

Leary, T. (1957). *Interpersonal diagnosis of personality*. New York, NY: Ronald.

Lee, K., & Ashton, M. C. (2004). Psychometric properties of the HEXACO Personality Inventory. *Multivariate Behavioral Research, 39*, 329–358.

Lee, K., & Ashton, M. C. (2006). Further assessment of the HEXACO Personality Inventory: Two new facet scales and an observer report form. *Psychological Assessment, 18*, 182–191.

Lee, K., & Ashton, M. C. (2020). Why six factors, why it matters. *European Journal of Personality, 34*, 562–590.

Lei, M., & Lomax, R. G. (2005). The effect of varying degrees of nonnormality in structural equation modelling. *Structural Equation Modeling, 12*, 1–27.

Lenney, E. (1991). Sex roles: The measurement of masculinity, femininity, and androgyny. In J. P. Robinson, P. R. Shaver, & L. S. Wrightsman (Eds.), *Measures of personality and social psychological attitudes* (pp. 573–660). San Diego, CA: Academic Press.

Leonard, R. (1997). Theorizing the relationship between agency and communion. *Theory & Psychology, 7*, 823–835.

Levenson, H. (2011). Time-limited dynamic psychotherapy. In L. M. Horowitz & S. Strack (Eds.), *Handbook of interpersonal psychology: Theory, research, assessment, and therapeutic interventions* (pp. 545–564). New York, NY: Wiley.

LeVine, R. A. (2001). Culture and personality studies, 1918–1960: Myth and history. *Journal of Personality, 69*(6), 803–818.

Levinger, G. (1994). Attachment theory as a paradigm for studying close relationships. *Psychological Inquiry, 5*, 45–47. http://www.jstor.org/stable/1449082

Lewin, K. (1935). *A dynamic theory of personality*. New York, NY: McGraw-Hill.

Lewin, K. (1936). *Principles of topological psychology*. New York, NY: McGraw-Hill.

Lewin, K. (1946). Behavior and development as a function of the total situation. In L. Carmichael (Ed.), *Manual of child psychology* (pp. 791–844). New York, NY: Wiley.

Lewin, K. (1967). *Resolving group conflicts: Selected papers on group dynamics* (Gertrude W. Lewin, Ed., 2nd ed.). New York, NY: Harper & Row. (Original work published 1948)

Lewin, K. (1976). *Field theory in social science: Selected theoretical papers* (D. Cartwright, Ed.). New York, NY: Harper. (Original work published 1951)

Lewin, K. (2013). *The conceptual representation and the measurement of psychological forces*. Mansfield Centre, CT: Martino. (Original work published 1938)

Li, T., & Chan, D. K. (2012). How anxious and avoidant attachment affect romantic relationship quality differently: A meta-analytic review. *European Journal of Social Psychology, 42*, 406–419.

Lindenfeld, D. (2009). Jungian archetypes and the discourse of history. *Rethinking History, 13*, 217–234.

Ling, Y., Zhang, M., Locke, K. D., Li, G., & Li, Z. (2016). Examining the process of responding to Circumplex Scales of Interpersonal Values items: Should ideal point scoring methods be considered? *Journal of Personality Assessment, 98*, 310–318.

Liotta, E. (1997). Animus and creativity in psychotherapy: A position statement. *Journal of Analytical Psychology, 42*, 317–324.

BIBLIOGRAPHY   401

Lips, H. M. (2017). Sandra Bem: Naming the impact of gendered categories and identities. *Sex Roles*, *76*, 627–632.

Locke, K. D. (2000). Circumplex scales of interpersonal values: Reliability, validity, and applicability to interpersonal problems and personality disorders. *Journal of Personality Assessment*, *75*, 249–267.

Locke, K. D. (2011). Circumplex measures of interpersonal constructs. In L. M. Horowitz & S. Strack (Eds.), *Handbook of interpersonal psychology: Theory, research, assessment, and therapeutic implications* (pp. 313–324). Hoboken, NJ: John Wiley & Sons.

Locke, K. D. (2014). Circumplex scales of intergroup goals: An interpersonal circle model of goals for interactions between groups. *Personality and Social Psychology Bulletin*, *40*, 433–449.

Locke, K. D. (2015). Agentic and communal social motives. *Social and Personality Psychology Compass*, *9*, 525–538.

Locke, K. D., Sayegh, L., Penberthy, J. K., Weber, C., Haentjens, K., & Turecki, G. (2017). Interpersonal circumplex profiles of persistent depression: Goals, self-efficacy, problems, and effects of group therapy. *Journal of Clinical Psychology*, *73*, 595–611.

Lockenhoff, C. E., Chan, W., McCrae, R. R., De Fruyt, F., Jussim, L., De Bolle, M., Costa, P. T., Sutin, A. R., Realo, A., Allik, J., Nakazato, K., Shimonaka, Y., Hrebickova, M., Graf, S., Yik, M., Fickova, E., Brunner-Sciarra, M., Leibovich de Figueora, N., Schmidt, V., . . . Terracciano, A. (2014). Gender stereotypes of personality: Universal and accurate? *Journal of Cross-Cultural Psychology*, *45*, 675–694.

Loehlin, J. C. (1992). *Latent variable models: An introduction to factor, path, and structural analysis* (2nd ed.). Hillsdale, NJ: Erlbaum.

Loehlin, J. C. (2004). *Latent variable models: An introduction to factor, path, and structural equation analysis* (4th ed.). Hillsdale, NJ: Erlbaum.

Lorr, M. (1996). The interpersonal circle as a heuristic model for interpersonal research. *Journal of Personality Assessment*, *66*, 234–239.

Lorr, M., & McNair, D. M. (1963). An interpersonal behavior circle. *Journal of Abnormal and Social Psychology*, *67*, 68–75.

Lorr, M., & Strack, S. (1990). Wiggins Interpersonal Adjective Scales: A dimensional view. *Personality and Individual Differences*, *11*, 423–425.

Lucas, R. E., & Dyrenforth, P. S. (2006). Does the existence of social relationships matter for subjective well-being? In K. D. Vohs & E. J. Finkel (Eds.), *Self and relationships: Connecting intrapersonal and interpersonal processes* (pp. 254–273). New York, NY: Guilford Press.

Luchies, L. B., Finkel, E. J., McNulty, J. K., & Kumashiro, M. (2010). The doormat effect: When forgiving erodes self-respect and self-concept clarity. *Journal of Personality and Social Psychology*, *98*, 734–749.

Lund, M. (1985). The development of investment and commitment scales for predicting continuity of personal relationships. *Journal of Social and Personal Relationships*, *2*, 3–23.

MacCallum, R. C., & Austin, J. T. (2000). Applications of structural equation modeling in psychological research. *Annual Review of Psychology*, *51*, 201–226.

MacCallum, R. C., Wegener, D. T., Uchino, B. N., & Fabrigar, L. R. (1993). The problem of equivalent models in applications of covariance structure analysis. *Psychological Bulletin*, *114*, 185–199.

Maccoby, E. E. (2002). Gender and social exchange: A developmental perspective. *New Directions for Child & Adolescent Development*, *95*, 87–106.

402 BIBLIOGRAPHY

MacDonald, G., & Leary, M. R. (2012). Individual differences in self-esteem. In M. R. Leary & J. P. Tangney (Eds.), *Handbook of self and identity* (2nd ed., pp. 354–377). New York, NY: Guilford Press.

MacDonald, S. G. (2001). The real and the researchable: A brief review of the contribution of John Bowlby (1907–1990). *Perspectives in Psychiatric Care, 37,* 60–64.

Maguire, M., & Dewing, H. (2007). New psychoanalytic theories of female and male femininity: The Oedipus complex, language and gender embodiment. *British Journal of Psychotherapy, 23,* 531–545.

Makosky, V. P. (1990). Sandra Lipsitz Bem (1944–). In A. N. O'Connell & N. F. Russo (Eds.), *Women in psychology: A bio-bibliographic sourcebook* (pp. 30–39). New York, NY: Greenwood Press.

Mallinckrodt, B. (1997). Interpersonal relationship processes in individual and group psychotherapy. In S. Duck (Ed.), *Handbook of personal relationships: Theory, research and interventions* (pp. 671–693). New York, NY: John Wiley & Sons.

Malouff, J. M., Thorsteinsson, E. B., Schutte, N. S., Bhullar, N., & Rooke, S. E. (2010). The five-factor model of personality and relationship satisfaction of intimate partners: A meta-analysis. *Journal of Research in Personality, 44,* 124–127.

Mandin, P. (2007). The contribution of system and object-relation theories to an understanding of the therapeutic relationship in social work practice. *Journal of Social Work Practice, 21,* 149–162.

Marcus, B. F. (2004). Female passion and the matrix of mother, daughter, and body: Vicissitudes of the maternal transference in the working through of sexual inhibitions. *Psychoanalytic Inquiry, 24,* 680–712.

Margolis, M. L. (1984). *Mothers and such: Views of American women and why they changed.* Berkeley, CA: University of California Press.

Markey, P., Anderson, J. M., & Markey, C. (2013). Using behavioral mapping to examine the validity of the IPIP-IPC. *Assessment, 20,* 165–174.

Markey, P. M., & Kurtz, J. E. (2006). Increasing acquaintanceship and complementarity of behavioral styles and personality traits among college roommates. *Personality and Social Psychology Bulletin, 32,* 907–916.

Markey, P. M., & Markey, C. N. (2007). Romantic ideals, romantic obtainment, and relationship experiences: The complementarity of interpersonal traits among romantic partners. *Journal of Social and Personal Relationships, 24,* 517–533.

Markey, P. M., & Markey, C. N. (2009). A brief assessment of the interpersonal circumplex: The IPIP-IPC. *Assessment, 16,* 352–361.

Markey, P. M., & Markey, C. N. (2013). The complementarity of behavioral styles among female same-sex romantic couples. *Personal Relationships, 20,* 170–183.

Markus, H. (1977). Self-schemata and processing information about the self. *Journal of Personality and Social Psychology, 35,* 63–78.

Markus, H. (1983). Self-knowledge: An expanded view. *Journal of Personality, 51,* 543–565.

Markus, H. R. (2008). Pride, prejudice, and ambivalence: Toward a unified theory of race and ethnicity. *American Psychologist, 63,* 651–670.

Markus, H., Crane, M., Bernstein, S., & Siladi, M. (1982). Self-schemas and gender. *Journal of Personality and Social Psychology, 42,* 38–50.

Marshall, I. N. (1967). Extraversion and libido in Jung and Cattell. *Journal of Analytical Psychology, 12,* 115–136.

Martens, W. H. J. (2013). Complex dynamics of forgiveness: Psychological, interpersonal, and psychotherapeutic implications. *International Forum of Psychoanalysis, 23,* 82–94.

BIBLIOGRAPHY 403

Martin, A. E., & Slepian, M. L. (2021). The primacy of gender: Gendered cognition underlies the Big Two dimensions of social cognition. *Perspectives on Psychological Science, 16*(6), 1143–1158.

Martinez-Arias, R., Silva, F., Diaz-Hidalgo, M. T., Ortet, G., & Moro, M. (1999). The structure of Wiggins' interpersonal circumplex: Cross-cultural studies. *European Journal of Psychological Assessment, 15*, 196–205.

Marvin, R. S., Britner, P. A., & Russell, B. S. (2016). Normative development: The ontogeny of attachment in childhood. In J. Cassidy & P. Shaver (Eds.), *Handbook of attachment: Theory, research, and clinical applications* (3rd ed., pp. 273–290). New York, NY: Guilford Press.

Maslow, A. H. (1968). *Toward a psychology of being* (2nd ed). New York, NY: Van Nostrand Reinhold.

May, R. (1996). *The meaning of anxiety.* New York, NY: Norton. (Original work published 1950)

McAdams, D. P. (1997). A conceptual history of personality psychology. In R. Hogan, J. Johnson, & S. R. Briggs (Eds.), *Handbook of personality psychology* (pp. 3–39). New York, NY: Academic Press.

McAdams, D. P., & Olson, B. D. (2010). Personality development: Continuity and change over the life course. *Annual Review of Psychology, 61*, 517–542.

McClelland, D. C. (1987). *Human motivation.* New York, NY: Cambridge University Press. (Original work published 1985)

McClintock, C. G. (1972). Game behavior and social motivation in interpersonal settings. In C. G. McClintock (Ed.), *Experimental social psychology* (pp. 271–297). New York, NY: Holt, Rinehart & Winston.

McClintock, C. G., & Liebrand, W. B. (1988). Role of interdependence structure, individual value orientation, and another's strategy in social decision making: A transformational analysis. *Journal of Personality and Social Psychology, 55*, 396–409.

McConnell, A. N. (1990). Karen Horney (1885–1952). In A. N. O'Connell & N. F. Russo (Eds.), *Women in psychology: A bio-bibliographic sourcebook* (pp. 184–196). New York, NY: Greenwood Press.

McCrae, R. R., & Costa, P. T., Jr. (1990). *Personality in adulthood.* New York, NY: Guilford Press.

McCrae, R. R., & Costa, P. T., Jr. (2006). *Personality in adulthood: A five-factor theory perspective* (2nd ed.). New York, NY: Guilford Press. (Original version published 2003)

McCrae, R. R., Costa, P. T., Jr., & Busch, C. M. (1986). Evaluating comprehensiveness in personality systems: The California Psychological Inventory and the Five-Factor Model. *Journal of Personality, 61*, 1–26.

McEnery-West, C. (2019). Beyond the Oedipus complex for women: Rethinking identification and desire. *Psychodynamic Practice, 25*, 356–368.

McKenzie, S. (2006). Queering gender: Anima/animus and the paradigm of emergence. *Journal of Analytical Psychology, 51*, 401–421.

McLaughlin, N. G. (1998). Why do schools of thought fail? Neo-Freudianism as a case study in the sociology of knowledge. *Journal of the History of the Behavioral Sciences, 34*, 113–134.

McNulty, J. K. (2013). Personality and relationships. In J. A. Simpson & L. Campbell (Eds.), *Oxford handbook of close relationships* (pp. 535–552). Oxford, UK: Oxford University Press.

Mead, G. H. (1967). *Mind, self and society from the standpoint of a social behaviorist.* Chicago, IL: University of Chicago Press. (Original work published 1934)

Mels, G. (2019). *LISREL 10 for Windows: Getting started guide.* Skokie, IL: Scientific Software International.

Mercer, J. A. (2003). The Idea of the Child in Freud and Jung: Psychological sources for divergent spiritualities of childhood. *International Journal of Children's Spirituality, 8,* 115–132.

Merchant, J. (2019). The controversy around the concept of archetypes and the place for an emergent/developmental model. *Journal of Analytical Psychology, 64*(5), 701–719.

Mikulincer, M., Gillath, O., Sapir-Lavid, Y., Yaakobi, E., Arias, K., Tal-Aloni, L., & Bor, G. (2003). Attachment theory and concern for others' welfare: Evidence that activation of the sense of secure base promotes endorsement of self-transcendence values. *Basic and Applied Social Psychology, 25,* 299–312.

Mikulincer, M., & Shaver, P. R. (2007). *Attachment in adulthood: Structure, dynamics, and change.* New York, NY: Guilford.

Mikulincer, M., & Shaver, P. R. (2012). Adult attachment orientations and relationship processes. *Journal of Family Theory and Review, 4,* 259–274.

Mikulincer, M., & Shaver, P. R. (2007a). *Attachment in adulthood: Structure, dynamics, and change.* New York, NY: Guilford.

Mikulincer, M., & Shaver, P. R. (2007b). Boosting attachment security to promote mental health, prosocial values, and inter-group tolerance. *Psychological Inquiry, 18*(3), 139–156.

Mikulincer, M., & Shaver, P. R. (2007c). Reflections on security dynamics: Core constructs, psychological mechanisms, relational contexts, and the need for an integrative theory. *Psychological Inquiry, 18*(3), 197–209.

Mikulincer, M., & Shaver, P. R. (2016). *Attachment in adulthood: Structure, dynamics, and change* (2nd ed.). New York, NY: Guilford.

Miller, B. K. (2021). Impact of social desirability and common method variance on two measures of entitlement. *Psychological Reports, 124,* 1845–1862.

Miller, J. D., Price, J., & Campbell, W. K. (2012). Is the narcissistic personality inventory still relevant? A test of independent grandiosity and entitlement scales in the assessment of narcissism. *Assessment, 19,* 8–13.

Millon, T. (1996). *Disorders of personality: DSM-IV and beyond.* New York, NY: Wiley.

Mills, J. (2019). The myth of the collective unconscious. *Journal of the History of the Behavioral Sciences, 55,* 40–53.

Mirsu-Paun, A., & Oliver, J. A. (2017). How much does love really hurt? A meta-analysis of the association between romantic relationship quality, breakups and mental health outcomes in adolescents and young adults. *Journal of Relationships Research, 8,* 1–12.

Mitchell, S. A., & Harris, A. (2004). What's American about American psychoanalysis? *Psychoanalytic Dialogues, 14,* 165–191.

Moeller, J. (2015). A word on standardization in longitudinal studies: Don't. *Frontiers in Psychology, 6,* 1389.

Montoya, R. M., & Horton, R. S. (2020). Understanding the attraction process. *Social and Personality Psychology Compass, 14,* e12526.

Moore, N. (1984). The left hand of darkness: Aspects of the shadow and individuation. *Journal of Analytical Psychology, 29,* 255–275.

Moraglia, G. (1994). C. G. Jung and the psychology of adult development. *Journal of Analytical Psychology, 39,* 55–75.

Moreno, M. (1965). Archetypal foundations in the analysis of women. *Journal of Analytical Psychology, 10,* 173–186.

BIBLIOGRAPHY   405

Morf, C. C. (2006). Personality reflected in a coherent idiosyncratic interplay of intra- and interpersonal self-regulatory processes. *Journal of Personality, 74*, 1527–1556.

Morry, M. M., & Sucharyna, T. A. (2016). Relationship social comparison interpretations and dating relationship quality, behaviors, and mood. *Personal Relationships, 23*, 554–576.

Morse, L., & Cohen, T. R. (2020). The importance of the HEXACO Model in behavioral business ethics: Comment on Ashton & Lee (2020). *European Journal of Personality, 34*, 535–536.

Mufson, L., & Dorta, K. P. (2000). Interpersonal psychotherapy for depressed adolescents: Theory, practice, and research. *Adolescent Psychiatry, 25*, 139–167.

Muise, A., Maxwell, J., & Impett, E. A. (2018). What theories and methods from relationship research can contribute to sex research. *Annual Review of Sex Research, 55*, 540–562.

Munafo, M. R. (2009). Behavioural genetics: From variance to DNA. In P. J. Corr & G. Matthews (Eds.), *The Cambridge handbook of personality psychology* (pp. 287–304). Cambridge, UK: Cambridge University Press.

Murray, H. A. (1938). *Explorations in personality.* New York, NY: Oxford University Press.

Murray, S. L. (2016). Risk regulation in relationships: Self-esteem and the if-then contingencies of interdependent life. In J. V. Wood, A. Tesser, & J. G. Holmes (Eds.), *The self and social relationships* (pp. 3–25). Abingdon, UK: Psychology Press. (Original work published 2008)

Myers, I. B. (1962). *The Myers-Briggs Type Indicator: Manual.* Palo Alto, CA: Consulting Psychologists Press.

Neff, K. (2003). Self-compassion: An alternative conceptualization of a healthy attitude toward oneself. *Self and Identity, 2*, 85–101.

Nelson, M. O. (1991). Another look at masculine protest. *Individual Psychology, 47*, 490–497.

Newbigin, J. (2013). Psychoanalysis and homosexuality: Keeping the discussion moving. *British Journal of Psychotherapy, 29*, 276–291.

Norby, K. (2021). In search of the Self a deux: The narcissistic collusion and impeded individuation. *Journal of Analytical Psychology, 66*, 49–69.

Norman, W. T. (1967). *2,800 personality trait descriptors: Normative operating characteristics for a university population.* Unpublished manuscript, University of Michigan.

Notman, M. T. (2003). The female body and its meanings. *Psychoanalytic Inquiry, 23*, 572–591.

Nunnally, J. C., & Bernstein, I. H. (1994). *Psychometric theory* (3rd ed.). New York: McGraw-Hill.

O'Connell, A. N. (1980). Karen Horney: Theorist in psychoanalysis and feminine psychology. *Psychology of Women Quarterly, 5*, 81–93.

Odajnyk, V. W. (2013). *The Red Book* as the source of Jung's *Psychological Types. Psychological Perspectives, 56*, 310–328.

Olsen, L. A. (1979). Bandura's self system sans Sullivan. *American Psychologist, 35*, 439–441.

Onishi, M., Gjerde, P. F., & Block, J. (2001). Personality implications of romantic attachment patterns in young adults: A multi-method, multi-informant study. *Personality and Social Psychology Bulletin, 27*, 1097–1110.

Oulovsky, P., Kosova, M., Kopecky, R., & Locke, K. D. (2020). Psychometric properties of the Circumplex Scales of Interpersonal Values in the Czech population. *Ceskoslovenska Psychologie, 2*, 155–167.

406 BIBLIOGRAPHY

Overall, N. C., & Sibley, C. G. (2010). Convergent and discriminant validity of the Accommodation Scale: Evidence from three diary studies. *Personality and Individual Differences, 48,* 299–304.

Ozer, D. J., & Reise, S. P. (1994). Personality assessment. *Annual Review of Psychology, 45,* 357–388.

Palan, K. M., Areni, C., & Kiecker, P. L. (1999). Reexamining masculinity, femininity, and gender identity scales. *Marketing Letters, 10,* 357–371.

Paris, B. J. (1994). *Karen Horney: A psychoanalyst's search for self-understanding.* New Haven, CT: Yale University Press.

Park, K. A., & Waters, E. (1988). Traits and relationships in developmental perspective. In S. Duck (Ed.), *Handbook of personal relationships* (pp. 161–176). Chichester, UK: John Wiley & Sons.

Parker, J. G., & Asher, S. R. (1993). Friendship and friendship quality in middle childhood: Links with peer group acceptance and feelings of loneliness and social dissatisfaction. *Developmental Psychology, 29,* 611–621.

Paul, E. L., & White, K. M. (1990). The development of intimate relationships in late adolescence. *Adolescence, 25,* 375–400.

Penner, L. A., Dovidio, J. F., Schroeder, D. A., & Piliavin, J. A. (2005). Prosocial behavior: Multilevel perspectives. *Annual Review of Psychology, 56,* 365–392.

Perrinjaquet, A., Furrer, O., Usunier, J.-C., Cestre, G., & Valette-Florence, P. (2007). A test of the quasi-circumplex structure of human values. *Journal of Research in Personality, 41,* 820–840.

Perry, H. S. (1982). *Psychiatrist of America: The life of Harry Stack Sullivan.* Cambridge, MA: Belknap Press of Harvard University Press.

Perunovic, M., & Holmes, J. G. (2008). Automatic accommodation: The role of personality. *Personal Relationships, 15,* 57–70.

Pervin, L. A., & John, O. P. (Eds.). (1999). *Handbook of personality: Theory and research.* New York, NY: Guilford.

Peterson, J. L., & Zill, N. (1986). Marital disruption, parent-child relationships, and behavior problems in children. *Journal of Marriage and the Family, 48,* 295–307.

Pettigrew, T. F., & Cherry, F. (2012). The intertwined histories of personality and social psychology. In K. Deaux & M. Snyder (Eds.), *The Oxford handbook of personality and social psychology* (pp. 13–32). Oxford, UK: Oxford University Press.

Piedmont, R. L. (1998). *The revised NEO Personality Inventory: Clinical and research applications.* New York, NY: Plenum Press.

Piedmont, R. L., & Rodgerson, T. E. (2017). Cross-over analysis: Using the Five Factor Model and NEO Personality Inventory-3 for assessing compatibility and conflict in couples. In T. A. Widiger (Ed.), *The Oxford handbook of the Five Factor Model* (pp. 423–448). New York, NY: Oxford University Press.

Piekkola, B. (2011). Traits across cultures: A neo-Allportian perspective. *Journal of Theoretical and Philosophical Psychology, 31,* 2–24.

Pillay, P., & Pillay, T. (2017). Freud's treatment of the feminine with reference to his theory of the Oedipus complex and its relation to *Oedipus Tyrannus* and *The Sandman. Gender and Behaviour, 15,* 10436–10451.

Pincus, A. L. (2010). Introduction to the special series on integrating personality, psychopathology, and psychotherapy using interpersonal assessment. *Journal of Personality Assessment, 92,* 467–470.

BIBLIOGRAPHY 407

Pincus, A. L., & Wright, A. G. C. (2011). Interpersonal diagnosis of psychopathology. In L. M. Horowitz & S. Strack (Eds.), *Handbook of interpersonal psychology: Theory, research, assessment, and therapeutic interventions* (pp. 359–382). New York, NY: Wiley.

Pizer, B. (2019). Not me: The vicissitudes of aging. *Psychoanalytic Dialogues, 29*, 536–542.

Plutchik, R. (1980). *Emotion: A psychoevolutionary synthesis.* New York, NY: Harper & Row.

Polat, B. (2017). Before attachment theory: Separation research at the Tavistock Clinic, 1948–1956. *Journal of the History of the Behavioral Sciences, 53*, 48–70.

Powell, K. C. (2004). Developmental psychology of adolescent girls: Conflicts and identity issues. *Education, 125*, 77–87.

Pylkko, P. (2019). Ambiguity and contradiction: The outlines of Jung's dialectics. *Journal of Analytical Psychology, 64*, 823–844.

Pyszczynski, T., Greenberg, J., & Arndt, J. (2012). Freedom versus fear revisited: An integrative analysis of the dynamics of the defense and growth of self. In M. R. Leary & J. P. Tangney (Eds.), *Handbook of self and identity* (2nd ed., pp. 378–404). New York, NY: Guilford Press.

Rae, G. (2020). Questioning the phallus: Jacques Lacan and Judith Butler. *Studies in Gender and Sexuality, 21*, 12–26.

Raj, M., & Wiltermuth, S. S. (2016). Barriers to forgiveness. *Social and Personality Psychology Compass, 10*, 679–690.

Raskin, R., & Hall, C. S. (1979). A narcissistic personality inventory. *Psychological Reports, 45*, 590.

Raskin, R., & Terry, H. (1988). A principal-components analysis of the Narcissistic Personality Inventory and further evidence of its construct validity. *Journal of Personality and Social Psychology, 54*, 890–902.

Redfearn, J. W. T. (1977). The self and individuation. *Journal of Analytical Psychology, 22*, 125–141.

Redfearn, J. W. T. (1983). Ego and self: Terminology. *Journal of Analytical Psychology, 28*, 91–106.

Reis, H. T. (2007). Steps toward the ripening of relationship science. *Personal Relationships, 14*, 1–23.

Reis, H. T., Capobianco, A., & Tsai, F.-F. (2002). Finding the person in personal relationships. *Journal of Personality, 70*, 813–850.

Reis, H. T., Lemay, E. P., & Finkenauer, C. (2017). Toward understanding: The importance of feeling understood in relationships. *Social and Personality Psychology Compass, 11*, e12308.

Reis, H. T., & Shaver, P. R. (1988). Intimacy as an interpersonal process. In S. Duck (Ed.), *Handbook of personal relationships* (pp. 367–389). Chichester, UK: John Wiley & Sons.

Reisner, S. (2001). Freud and developmental theory: A 21st-century look at the origin myth of psychoanalysis. *Studies in Gender and Sexuality, 2*, 97–128.

Rempel, J. K., & Holmes, J. G. (1986). How do I trust thee? *Psychology Today, 20*(2), 28–34.

Rempel, J. K., Holmes, J. G., & Zanna, M. P. (1985). Trust in close relationships. *Journal of Personality and Social Psychology, 49*, 95–112.

Rendon, M. (2008). The vicissitudes of affect in Horney's theory. *International Forum of Psychoanalysis, 17*, 158–168.

Revelle, W. (1995). Personality processes. *Annual Review of Psychology, 46*, 295–328.

Riggio, H. R., Weiser, D., Valenzuela, A. M., Lui, P., Montes, R., & Heuer, J. (2013). Self-efficacy in romantic relationships: Prediction of relationship attitudes and outcomes. *Journal of Social Psychology, 153*, 629–650.

408   BIBLIOGRAPHY

Roberts, S. C. (2020). The unquiet ghosts of Jung's abandoned women: What do we owe Helene, Sabina, and Toni? *Psychological Perspectives, 63*, 329–344.

Robins, R. W., & John, O. P. (1997). The quest for self-insight: Theory and research on accuracy and bias in self-perception. In R. Hogan, J. A. Johnson, & S. R. Briggs (Eds.), *Handbook of personality psychology* (pp. 649–679). New York, NY: Academic Press.

Rogers, C. R. (1961). *On becoming a person: A therapist's view of psychotherapy*. London, UK: Constable.

Rogoza, R., Cieciuch, J., Strus, W., & Baran, T. (2019). Seeking a common framework for research on narcissism: An attempt to integrate the different faces of narcissism within the circumplex of personality metatraits. *European Journal of Personality, 33*, 437–455.

Rorschach, H. (1924). *Manual for Rorschach Ink-blot Test*. Chicago, IL: Stoelting.

Rosen, A. S. (1992). The circle as a model for the interpersonal domain of Swedish trait terms. *European Journal of Personality, 5*, 343–365.

Rosenberg, M. (1965). *Society and the adolescent self-image*. Princeton, NJ: Princeton University Press.

Rosenzweig, S. (1944). Converging approaches to personality: Murray, Allport, Lewin. *Psychological Review, 51*, 248–256.

Rothenberg, R.-E. (2013). The orphan archetype. *Psychological Perspectives, 60*, 103–113.

Rubin, Z. (1973). *Liking and loving: An invitation to social psychology*. New York, NY: Holt, Rinehart, & Winston.

Rudden, M. G. (2018). The castration complex. *Psychoanalytic Inquiry, 38*, 51–58.

Rusbridger, R. (2012). Affects in Melanie Klein. *International Journal of Psychoanalysis, 93*, 139–150.

Rusbult, C. E. (1980). Commitment and satisfaction in romantic associations: A test of the investment model. *Journal of Experimental Social Psychology, 16*, 172–186.

Rusbult, C. E. (1983). A longitudinal test of the investment model: The development (and deterioration) of satisfaction and commitment in heterosexual involvements. *Journal of Personality and Social Psychology, 45*, 101–117.

Rusbult, C. E. (1993). Understanding responses to dissatisfaction in close relationships: The exit-voice-loyalty-neglect model. In S. Worchel & J. A. Simpson (Eds.), *Conflict between people and groups: Causes, processes, and resolutions* (pp. 30–59). Chicago, IL: Nelson-Hall.

Rusbult, C. E., & Agnew, C. R. (2010). Prosocial motivation and behavior in close relationships. In M. Mikulincer & P. R. Shaver (Eds.), *Prosocial motives, emotions, and behavior: The better angels of our nature* (pp. 327–345). Washington, DC: American Psychological Association.

Rusbult, C. E., & Buunk, B. P. (1993). Commitment processes in close relationships: An interdependence analysis. *Journal of Social and Personal Relationships, 10*, 175–204.

Rusbult, C. E., Coolsen, M. K., Kirchner, J. L., & Clarke, J. A. (2006). Commitment. In A. L. Vangelisti & D. Perlman (Eds.), *The Cambridge handbook of personal relationships* (pp. 615–635). Cambridge, UK: Cambridge University Press.

Rusbult, C. E., Drigotas, S. M., & Verette, J. (1994). The investment model: An interdependence analysis of commitment processes and relationship maintenance phenomena. In D. J. Canary & L. Stafford (Eds.), *Communication and relational maintenance* (pp. 115–139). San Diego, CA: Academic Press.

Rusbult, C. E., Johnson, D. J., & Morrow, G. D. (1986a). Impact of couple patterns of problem solving on distress and nondistress in dating relationships. *Journal of Personality and Social Psychology, 50*, 744–753.

BIBLIOGRAPHY 409

Rusbult, C. E., Johnson, D. J., & Morrow, G. D. (1986b). Predicting satisfaction and commitment in adult romantic relationships: An assessment of the generalizability of the investment model. *Social Psychology Quarterly, 49,* 81–89.

Rusbult, C. E., Martz, J. M., & Agnew, C. R. (1998). The Investment Model Scale: Measuring commitment level, satisfaction, quality of alternatives, and investment size. *Personal Relationships, 5,* 357–391.

Rusbult, C. E., Morrow, G. D., & Johnson, D. J. (1987). Self-esteem and problem-solving behaviour in close relationships. *British Journal of Social Psychology, 26,* 293–303.

Rusbult, C. E., & Van Lange, P. A. M. (2003). Interdependence, interaction, and relationships. *Annual Review of Psychology, 54,* 351–375.

Rusbult, C., Verette, J., Whitney, G., Slovik, L., & Lipkus, I. (1991). Accommodation processes in close relationships: Theory and preliminary evidence. *Journal of Personality and Social Psychology, 60,* 53–78.

Rusbult, C. E., Zembrodt, I. M., & Gunn, L. K. (1982). Exit, voice, loyalty, and neglect: Responses to dissatisfaction in romantic involvements. *Journal of Personality and Social Psychology, 43,* 1230–1242.

Rusbult, C. E., Zembrodt, I. M., & Iwaniszek, J. (1986). The impact of gender and sex-role orientation on responses to dissatisfaction in close relationships. *Sex Roles, 15,* 1–19.

Russell, J. A. (2003). Core affect and the psychological construction of emotion. *Psychological Review, 110,* 145–172.

Rybak, C. J., Russell-Chapin, L. A., & Moser, M. E. (2000). Jung and theories of gender development. *Journal of Humanistic Counseling, Education & Development, 38,* 152–161.

Sakaluk, J. K., Fisher, A. N., & Kilshaw, R. E. (2021). Dyadic measurement invariance and its importance for replicability in romantic relationship science. *Personal Relationships, 28,* 190–226.

Salberg, J. (2008). "Who wears the pants here?": Gender as protest. *Studies in Gender and Sexuality, 9,* 274–296.

Santamaria, J. (2018). Has castration anxiety anything to do with psychoanalysis? *Psychoanalytic Inquiry, 38,* 91–105.

Saribay, S. A., & Andersen, S. (2007). Are past relationships at the heart of attachment dynamics? What love has to do with it. *Psychological Inquiry, 18,* 183–191.

Saucier, G., Ostendorf, F., & Peabody, D. (2001). The non-evaluative circumplex of personality adjectives. *Journal of Personality, 69,* 537–582.

Saunders, P., & Skar, P. (2001). Archetypes, complexes and self-organization. *Journal of Analytical Psychology, 46,* 305–323.

Savalei, V., & Falk, C. F. (2014). Recovering substantive factor loadings in the presence of acquiescence bias: A comparison of three approaches. *Multivariate Behavioral Research, 49,* 407–424.

Saville, P., & Wilson, E. (1991). The reliability and validity of normative and ipsative approaches in the measurement of personality. *Journal of Occupational Psychology, 64,* 219–238.

Scharfe, E., & Bartholomew, K. (1995). Accommodation and attachment representations in young couples. *Journal of Social and Personal Relationships, 12,* 389–401.

Schellenberg, J. A. (1978). *Masters of social psychology.* Oxford, UK: Oxford University Press.

Schlegel, R. J., & Hicks, J. A. (2011). The true self and psychological health: Emerging evidence and future directions. *Social and Personality Psychology Compass, 5,* 989–1003.

410 BIBLIOGRAPHY

Schumacker, R. E., & Lomax, R. G. (2016). *A beginner's guide to structural equation modelling* (4th ed.). Mahwah, NJ: Erlbaum.

Schunk, D. H. (1991). Self-efficacy and academic motivation. *Educational Psychologist, 26*, 207–231.

Schwartz, J. P., & Waldo, M. (2003). Interpersonal manifestations of lifestyle: Individual psychology integrated with interpersonal theory. *Journal of Mental Health Counseling, 25*, 101–111.

Schwartz, S. H. (1992). Universals in the content and structure of values: Theory and empirical tests in 20 countries. In M. Zanna (Ed.), *Advances in experimental social psychology* (Vol. 25, pp. 1–65). New York, NY: Academic Press.

Schwartz, S. H. (1994). Are there universal aspects in the structure and content of human values? *Journal of Social Issues, 50*, 19–45.

Schwartz, S. H. (2010). Basic values: How they motivate and inhibit prosocial behavior. In M. Mikulincer & P. R. Shaver (Eds.), *Prosocial motives, emotions, and behavior: The better angels of our nature* (pp. 221–241). Washington, DC: American Psychological Association.

Schwartz-Mette, R. A., Shankman, J., Dueweke, A. R., Borowski, S., & Rose, A. J. (2020). Relations of friendship experiences with depressive symptoms and loneliness in childhood and adolescence: A meta-analytic review. *Psychological Bulletin, 146*, 664–700.

Sedney, M. A. (1981). Comments on medial split procedures for scoring androgyny measures. *Sex Roles, 7*, 217–222.

Segrin, C. G. (2011). Depressive disorders and interpersonal processes. In L. M. Horowitz & S. Strack (Eds.), *Handbook of interpersonal psychology: Theory, research, assessment, and therapeutic interventions* (pp. 425–444). New York, NY: Wiley.

Semmelhack, D., Ende, L., Farrell, K., & Pojas, J. (2011). Womb envy and Western society: On the devaluation of nurturing in psychotherapy and society. *Europe's Journal of Psychology, 7*, 164–186.

Shabad, P. (2020). The forward edge of resistance: Toward the dignity of human agency. *Psychoanalytic Dialogues, 30*, 51–63.

Shahar, G. (2011). Projectuality versus eventuality: Sullivan, the (ambivalent) intentionalist. *Journal of Psychotherapy Integration, 21*, 211–220.

Shaver, P. R., & Brennan, K. A. (1991). Measures of depression and loneliness. In J. P. Robinson, P. R. Shaver, & L. S. Wrightsman (Eds.), *Measures of personality and social psychological attitudes* (pp. 195–289). New York, NY: Academic Press.

Shaver, P. R., & Mikulincer, M. (2011). A general attachment-theoretical framework for conceptualizing interpersonal behavior: Cognitive-motivational predispositions and patterns of social information processing. In L. M. Horowitz & S. Strack (Eds.), *Handbook of interpersonal psychology: Theory, research, assessment, and therapeutic interventions* (pp. 17–35). New York, NY: Wiley.

Shaver, P., & Mikulincer, M. (2012). Attachment processes in relationships: Reply to commentaries. *Journal of Family Theory & Review, 4*, 311–317.

Sherer, M., Maddux, J. E., Mercadante, B., Prentice-Dunn, S., Jacobs, B., & Rogers, R. W. (1982). The Self-Efficacy Scale: Construction and validation. *Psychological Reports, 51*, 663–671.

Silberman, E. K. (2012). Commentary on "Conceptions of Modern Psychiatry": Humanism as an aspect of psychiatry and psychiatrists: Where are we and where are we headed? *Psychiatry, 75*, 22–25.

BIBLIOGRAPHY   411

Simms, L. J., Williams, T. F., & Nus, E. (2017). Assessment of the Five Factor Model. In T. A. Widiger (Ed.), *The Oxford handbook of the Five Factor Model* (pp. 353–379). New York, NY: Oxford University Press.

Simpson, J. A. (1990). Influence of attachment styles on romantic relationships. *Journal of Personality and Social Psychology, 59,* 971–980.

Simpson, J. A. (2007). Psychological foundations of trust. *Current Directions in Psychological Science, 16,* 264–268.

Simpson, J. A., & Campbell, L. (Eds.). (2013). *The Oxford handbook of close relationships.* Oxford, UK: Oxford University Press.

Simpson, J. A., Griskevicius, V., & Kim, J. S. (2011). Evolution, life history theory, and personality. In L. M. Horowitz & S. Strack (Eds.), *Handbook of interpersonal psychology: Theory, research, assessment, and therapeutic implications* (pp. 75–89). Hoboken, NJ: John Wiley & Sons.

Simpson, J. A., Rholes, S. W., & Phillips, D. (1996). Conflict in close relationships: An attachment perspective. *Journal of Personality and Social Psychology, 71,* 899–914.

Sinclair, S., Pappas, J., & Lun, J. (2009). The interpersonal basis of stereotype-relevant self-views. *Journal of Personality, 77,* 1343–1364.

Skar, P. (2004). Chaos and self-organization: Emergent patterns at critical life transitions. *Journal of Analytical Psychology, 49*(2), 243–262.

Skinner, B. F. (1938). *The behaviour of organisms: An experimental analysis.* London: D. Appleton Century Company.

Skowron, B., & Wojtowicz, K. (2021). Throwing spatial light: On topological explanations in Gestalt psychology. *Phenomenology and the Cognitive Sciences, 20,* 537–558.

Smith, E. R., Murphy, J., & Coats, S. (1999). Attachment to groups: Theory and management. *Journal of Personality and Social Psychology, 77,* 94–110.

Smith, W. B. (2007). Karen Horney and psychotherapy in the 21st century. *Clinical Social Work Journal, 35,* 57–66.

Smythe, W. E., & Baydala, A. (2012). The hermeneutic background of C. G. Jung. *Journal of Analytical Psychology, 57,* 57–75.

Snyder, M., & Cantor, M. (1998). Understanding personality and social behavior: A functionalist strategy. In D. T. Gilbert, S. T. Fiske, & G. Lindzey (Eds.), *The handbook of social psychology* (4th ed., Vol. 1, pp. 635–679). Boston, MA: McGraw-Hill.

Snyder, M., & Ickes, W. (1985). Personality and social behavior. In G. Lindzey & E. Aronson (Eds.), *Handbook of social psychology* (3rd ed., Vol. 2, pp. 883–947). New York, NY: Random House.

Snyder, W. U. (1958). Psychotherapy. *Annual Review of Psychology, 9,* 353–374.

Society for the Psychological Study of Social Issues. (2021). *The Kurt Lewin Award.* Retrieved July 6, 2021, from https://www.spssi.org/index.cfm?fuseaction=page.viewpage&pageid=938

Sodano, S. M., & Tracey, T. (2006). Interpersonal traits in childhood: Development of the Child and Adolescent Interpersonal Survey. *Journal of Personality Assessment, 87,* 317–329.

Spence, J. T. (1985). Gender identity and its implications for the concepts of masculinity and femininity. In T. B. Sonderegger (Eds.), *Nebraska Symposium on Motivation 1984* (pp. 59–95). Lincoln, NE: University of Nebraska Press.

Spence, J. T. (1993). Gender-related traits and gender ideology: Evidence for a multifactorial theory. *Journal of Personality and Social Psychology, 64,* 624–635.

412 BIBLIOGRAPHY

Spence, J. T., Deaux, K., & Helmreich, R. L. (1985). Sex roles in contemporary American society. In G. Lindzey & E. Aronson (Eds.), *Handbook of social psychology* (Vol. 2, pp. 149–178). New York, NY: Random House.

Spence, J. T., & Helmreich, R. L. (1974). The Personal Attributes Questionnaire: A measure of sex roles stereotypes and masculinity-femininity. *Journal of Personality and Social Psychology, 64*, 624–635.

Spence, J. T., & Helmreich, R. L. (1978). *Masculinity and femininity*. Austin, TX: University of Texas Press.

Spence, J. T., Helmreich, R. L., & Holahan, C. K. (1979). Negative and positive components of psychological masculinity and femininity, and their relationship to self-reports of neuroticism and acting out behavior. *Journal of Personality and Social Psychology, 37*, 1673–1682.

Spence, J. T., Helmreich, R., & Stapp, J. (1975). Ratings of self and peers on sex role attributes and their relation to self-esteem and conceptions of masculinity and femininity. *Journal of Personality and Social Psychology, 32*, 29–39.

Stafford, L. (2011). Measuring relationship maintenance behaviors: Critique and development of the revised relationship maintenance behavior scale. *Journal of Social and Personal Relationships, 28*, 278–303.

Stafford, L., & Canary, D. J. (1991). Maintenance strategies and romantic relationship type, gender and relational characteristics. *Journal of Social and Personal Relationships, 8*, 217–242.

Stafford, L., Dainton, M., & Haas, S. (2000). Measuring routine and strategic relational maintenance: Scale revision, sex versus gender roles, and the prediction of relational characteristics. *Communication Monographs, 67*, 306–323.

Starr, C. R., & Zurbriggen, E. L. (2017). Sandra Bem's gender schema theory after 34 years: A review of its reach and impact. *Sex Roles, 76*, 566–578.

Steele, H. (2010). Test of time: On re-reading "Psychoanalysis and child care," John Bowlby's lecture delivered in 1956 on the centenary of Sigmund Freud's birth. *Clinical Child Psychology and Psychiatry, 15*, 453–458.

Steele, H., & Steele, M. (1998). Attachment and psychoanalysis: Time for a reunion. *Social Development, 7*, 92–119.

Stein, M. (2008). "Divinity expresses the self . . .": An investigation. *Journal of Analytical Psychology, 53*, 305–327.

Stern, D. B. (2013). Field theory in psychoanalysis, Part I: Harry Stack Sullivan and Madeleine and Willy Baranger. *Psychoanalytic Dialogues, 23*, 487–501.

Stern, D. B. (2015). The interpersonal field: Its place in American psychoanalysis. *Psychoanalytic Dialogues, 25*, 388–404.

Sternberg, R. J. (1986). A triangular theory of love. *Psychological Review, 93*, 119–135.

Sternberg, R. J. (1988). Triangulating love. In R. J. Sternberg & M. L. Barnes (Eds.), *The psychology of love* (pp. 119–138). New Haven, CT: Yale University Press.

Stewart, A. J., & McDermott, C. (2004). Gender in psychology. *Annual Review of Psychology, 55*, 519–544.

Stewart, L. H. (1987). A brief report: Affect and archetype. *Journal of Analytical Psychology, 32*, 35–46.

Strachman, A., & Gable, S. L. (2006). Approach and avoidance relationship commitment. *Motivation and Emotion, 30*, 117–126.

Strack, M., Jacobs, I., & Grosse Holtforth, M. (2013). Reliability of circumplex axes. *SAGE Open, 3*, 1–12.

BIBLIOGRAPHY   413

Strack, S. (1996). Introduction to the special series—Interpersonal theory and the interpersonal circumplex: Timothy Leary's legacy. *Journal of Personality Assessment, 66,* 212–216.

Strack, S., & Horowitz, L. M. (2011). Introduction. In L. M. Horowitz & S. Strack (Eds.), *Handbook of interpersonal psychology: Theory, research, assessment, and therapeutic interventions* (pp. 1–13). New York, NY: John Wiley & Sons.

Strack, S., & Millon, T. (2013). Personalized psychotherapy: A treatment approach based on Theodore Millon's integrated model of clinical science. *Journal of Personality, 81,* 528–541.

Sullivan, H. S. (1948). The meaning of anxiety in psychiatry and in life. *Psychiatry, 11,* 1–13.

Sullivan, H. S. (1949). Multidisciplined coordination of interpersonal data. In S. S. Sargent & M. W. Smith (Eds.), *Culture and personality* (pp. 175–212). New York, NY: Viking.

Sullivan, H. S. (1953). *The interpersonal theory of psychiatry.* New York, NY: Norton.

Sullivan, H. S. (1954). *The psychiatric interview.* New York, NY: Norton.

Sullivan, H. S. (1956). *Clinical studies in psychiatry.* New York, NY: Norton.

Sullivan, H. S. (1962). *Schizophrenia as a human process.* New York, NY: Norton.

Sullivan, H. S. (1965). *Conceptions of modern psychiatry.* New York, NY: Norton. (Original work published 1947)

Sullivan, H. S. (1971). *The fusion of psychiatry and social science.* New York, NY: Norton. (Original work published 1964)

Sullivan, H. S. (1972). *Personal psychopathology.* New York, NY: Norton. (Original work published 1966)

Sutin, A. R. (2017). Openness. In T. A. Widiger (Ed.), *The Oxford handbook of the Five Factor Model* (pp. 83–104). New York, NY: Oxford University Press.

Swann, W. B., Jr. (1983). Self-verification: Bringing social reality into harmony with the self. In J. Suls & A. G. Greenwald (Eds.), *Psychological perspectives on the self* (Vol. 2, pp. 33–66). Hillsdale, NJ: Erlbaum.

Swann, W. B., Jr. (1987). Identity negotiation: Where two roads meet. *Journal of Personality and Social Psychology, 53,* 1038–1051.

Swann, W. B., Jr., & Bosson, J. K. (2010). Self and identity. In S. T. Fiske, D. T. Gilbert, & G. Lindzey (Eds.), *Handbook of social psychology* (5th ed., Vol. 1, pp. 589–628). Hoboken, NJ: John Wiley & Sons.

Tabachnick, B. G., & Fidell, L. S. (2009). *Using multivariate statistics* (6th ed.). Boston, MA: Allyn and Bacon.

Tackett, J. L., & Lahey, B. B. (2017). Neuroticism. In T. A. Widiger (Ed.), *The Oxford handbook of the Five Factor Model* (pp. 39–56). New York, NY: Oxford University Press.

Tafarodi, R. W., & Swann, W. B., Jr. (1995). Self-liking and self-competence as dimensions of global self-esteem: Initial validation of a measure. *Journal of Personality Assessment, 65,* 322–342.

Tafarodi, R. W., & Swann, W. B. (2001). Two-dimensional self-esteem: Theory and measurement. *Personality and Individual Differences, 31,* 653–673.

Taylor, E. (2010). William James and the humanistic implications of the neuroscience revolution: An outrageous hypothesis. *Journal of Humanistic Psychology, 50,* 410–429.

Teglasi, H., Simcox, A., & Kim, N. Y. (2007). Personality constructs and measures. *Psychology in the Schools, 44,* 215–228.

TePaske, B. A. (2017). Gender equations: Experiences of the syzygy on the archetypal spectrum. *Psychological Perspectives, 60,* 317–332.

414 BIBLIOGRAPHY

Terman, L. M., & Miles, C. C. (1936). *Sex and personality: Studies in masculinity and femininity*. New York, NY: McGraw-Hill.

Tesser, A. (2000). On the confluence of self-esteem maintenance mechanisms. *Personality and Social Psychology Review, 4*, 290–299.

Thibaut, J. W., & Kelley, H. H. (1959). *The social psychology of groups*. New York, NY: Wiley.

Thompson, B. (2004). *Exploratory and confirmatory factor analysis: Understanding concepts and applications*. Washington, DC: American Psychological Association.

Thompson, R. A., Berlin, L. J., & Simpson, J. A. (2021). Assembling the puzzle: Interlocking pieces, missing pieces, and the emerging picture. In R. A. Thompson, J. A. Simpson, & L. Berlin (Eds.), *Attachment: The fundamental questions* (pp. 391–426). New York, NY: Guilford.

Tracey, T. J. G. (2000). Analysis of circumplex models. In H. E. A. Tinsley & S. D. Brown (Eds.), *Handbook of applied multivariate statistics and mathematical modelling* (pp. 641–663). San Diego, CA: Academic Press.

Tracey, T. J. G., Rounds, J. B., & Gurtman, M. B. (1996). Examination of the general factor with the interpersonal circumplex structure: Application to the Inventory of Interpersonal Problems. *Multivariate Behavioral Research, 31*, 441–466.

Trapnell, P. D., & Paulhus, D. L. (2012). Agentic and communal values: Their scope and measurement. *Journal of Personality Assessment, 94*, 39–52.

Trapnell, P. D., & Wiggins, J. S. (1990). Extension of the Interpersonal Adjective Scales to include the Big Five dimensions of personality. *Journal of Personality and Social Psychology, 59*, 781–790.

Tubert-Oklander, J. (2007). The whole and the parts: Working in the analytic field. *Psychoanalytic Dialogues, 17*, 115–132.

Turner, J. L., Foa, E. B., & Foa, U. G. (1971). Interpersonal reinforcers: Classification, interrelationship, and some differential properties. *Journal of Personality and Social Psychology, 19*, 168–180.

Twenge, J. M. (1997). Changes in masculine and feminine traits over time: A meta-analysis. *Sex Roles: A Journal of Research, 36*, 305–325.

Ullman, J. B. (2006). Structural equation modeling: Reviewing the basics and moving forward. *Journal of Personality Assessment, 87*, 35–50.

Urban, E. (2008). The "self" in analytical psychology: The function of the "central archetype" within T Fordham's model. *Journal of Analytical Psychology, 53*, 329–350.

VanderDrift, L. E., & Agnew, C. R. (2020). Interdependence perspectives on relationship maintenance. In B. G. Ogolsky & J. K. Monk (Eds.), *Relationship maintenance: Theory, process, and context* (pp. 15–28). Cambridge, UK: Cambridge University Press.

Van Dijken, S., van der Veer, R., van Ijzendoorn, M., & Kuipers, H.-J. (1998). Bowlby before Bowlby: The sources of an intellectual departure in psychoanalysis and psychology. *Journal of the History of the Behavioral Sciences, 34*, 247–269.

Vangelisti, A. L., & Perlman, D. (Eds.). (2018). *The Cambridge handbook of personal relationships* (2nd ed.). New York, NY: Cambridge University Press.

Van Lange, P. A. M. (1999). The pursuit of joint outcomes and equality in outcomes: An integrative model of social value orientation. *Journal of Personality and Social Psychology, 77*, 337–349.

Van Lange, P. A. M., & Balliet, D. (2015). Interdependence theory. In M. Mikulincer & P. R. Shaver (Eds.), *APA handbook of personality and social psychology* (Vol. 3: Interpersonal relations, pp. 65–92). Washington, DC: American Psychological Association.

Van Lange, P. A. M., Rusbult, C. E., Drigotas, S. M., Arriaga, X. B., Witcher, B. S., & Cox, C. L. (1997). Willingness to sacrifice in close relationships. *Journal of Personality and Social Psychology, 72*, 1373–1395.

Van Tuinen, M., & Ramanaiah, N. V. (1979). A multimethod analysis of selected self-esteem measures. *Journal of Research in Personality, 13*, 16–24.

Vaughn Becker, D., & Neuberg, S. L. (2019). Archetypes reconsidered as emergent outcomes of cognitive complexity and evolved motivational systems. *Psychological Inquiry, 30*, 59–75.

Viner, R. (1996). Melanie Klein and Anna Freud: The discourse of the early dispute. *Journal of the History of the Behavioral Sciences, 33*, 4–13.

Vohs, K. D., & Finkel, E. J. (Eds.). (2008). *Self and relationships: Connecting intrapersonal and interpersonal processes*. New York, NY: Guilford.

Von Raffay, A. (2000). Why it is difficult to see the anima as a helpful object: Critique and clinical relevance of the theory of archetypes. *Journal of Analytical Psychology, 45*, 541–560.

Von Salisch, M. (1997). Emotional processes in children's relationships with siblings and friends. In S. Duck (Ed.), *Handbook of personal relationships: Theory, research and interventions* (pp. 61–80). Chichester, UK: Wiley.

Wake, N. (2008). Sexuality, intimacy and subjectivity in social psychoanalytic thought of the 1920s and 1930s. *Journal of Community & Applied Social Psychology, 18*, 119–130.

Wake, N. (2019). Homosexuality and psychoanalysis meet at a mental hospital: An early institutional history. *Journal of the History of Medicine and Allied Sciences, 74*, 34–56.

Walsh, R., Teo, T., & Baydala, A. (2014). *A critical history and philosophy of psychology: Diversity of context, thought, and practice*. Cambridge, MA: Cambridge University Press.

Watson, D., & Clark, L. A. (1997). Extraversion and its positive emotional core. In R. Hogan, J. Johnson, & S. Briggs (Eds.), *Handbook of personality psychology* (pp. 767–792). San Diego, CA: Academic Press.

Watson, D., Clark, L. A., & Tellegen, A. (1988). Development and validation of brief measures of positive and negative affect: The PANAS scales. *Journal of Personality and Social Psychology, 54*, 1063–1070.

Waugaman, R. M. (2012). Sullivan and his polarizing legacy. *Psychiatry, 75*, 26–31.

Wei, M., Russell, D. W., Mallinckrodt, B., & Vogel, D. L. (2007). The Experiences in Close Relationships Scale (ECR)–Short Form: Reliability, validity, and factor structure. *Journal of Personality Assessment, 88*, 187–204.

Weidmann, R., Ledermann, T., & Grob, A. (2016). The interdependence of personality and satisfaction in couples: A review. *European Psychologist, 21*, 284–295.

Weitz, L. J. (1976). Jung's and Freud's contributions to dream interpretation: A comparison. *American Journal of Psychotherapy, 30*, 289–293.

Wesley, D. (2019). The divine child. *Psychological Perspectives, 62*, 446–454.

West, S. G., & Finch, J. F. (1997). Personality measurement: Reliability and validity issues. In R. Hogan, J. A. Johnson, & S. R. Briggs (Eds.), *Handbook of personality psychology* (pp. 143–164). San Diego, CA: Academic Press.

Westen, D. (1992). The cognitive self and the psychoanalytic self: Can we put our selves together? *Psychological Inquiry, 3*, 1–13.

Westkott, M. C. (1986). *The feminist legacy of Karen Horney*. New Haven, CT: Yale University Press.

416 BIBLIOGRAPHY

Westkott, M. C. (1990). On the new psychology of women: A cautionary view. *Feminist Issues, 10*, 3–18.

Widiger, T. A. (2010). Personality, interpersonal circumplex, and DSM-5: A commentary on five studies. *Journal of Personality Assessment, 92*, 528–532.

Widiger, T. A. (Ed.). (2017). *The Oxford Handbook of the Five Factor Model*. Oxford, UK: Oxford University Press.

Wieselquist, J., Rusbult, C. E., Foster, C. A., & Agnew, C. R. (1999). Commitment, pro-relationship behavior, and trust in close relationships. *Journal of Personality and Social Psychology, 77*, 942–966.

Wiggins, J. S. (1979). A psychological taxonomy of trait-descriptive terms: The interpersonal domain. *Journal of Personality and Social Psychology, 37*, 395–412.

Wiggins, J. S. (1980). Circumplex models of interpersonal behavior. In L. Wheeler (Ed.), *Review of personality and social psychology* (Vol. 1, pp. 265–293). Beverly Hills, CA: Sage.

Wiggins, J. S. (1991). Agency and communion as conceptual coordinates for the understanding and measurement of interpersonal behavior. In W. M. Grove & D. Ciccetti (Eds.), *Thinking clearly about psychology* (Vol. 2: Personality and psychopathology, pp. 89–113). Minneapolis, MN: University of Minnesota Press.

Wiggins, J. S. (1995). *Interpersonal Adjective Scales professional manual*. Lutz, FL: Psychological Assessment Resources.

Wiggins, J. S. (1997). Circumnavigating Dodge Morgan's interpersonal style. *Journal of Personality, 65*, 1069–1086.

Wiggins, J. S. (2005). *Paradigms of personality assessment*. New York, NY: Guilford. (Original work published 2003)

Wiggins, J. S., & Broughton, R. (1985). The Interpersonal Circle: A structural model for the integration of personality research. In R. Hogan & W. H. Jones (Eds.), *Perspectives in Personality* (pp. 1–47). Greenwich, CT: JAI Press.

Wiggins, J. S., & Broughton, R. (1991). A geometric taxonomy of personality scales. *European Journal of Personality, 5*, 343–365.

Wiggins, J. S., & Holzmuller, A. (1978). Psychological androgyny and interpersonal behavior. *Journal of Consulting and Clinical Psychology, 46*, 40–52.

Wiggins, J. S., & Holzmuller, A. (1981). Further evidence on androgyny and interpersonal flexibility. *Journal of Research in Personality, 15*, 67–80.

Wiggins, J. S., Phillips, N., & Trapnell, P. (1989). Circular reasoning about interpersonal behavior: Evidence concerning some untested assumptions underlying diagnostic classification. *Journal of Personality and Social Psychology, 56*, 296–305.

Wiggins, J. S., Steiger, J. H., & Gaelick, L. (1981). Evaluating circumplexity in personality data. *Multivariate Behavioral Research, 16*, 263–289.

Wiggins, J. S., & Trapnell, P. D. (1997). Personality structure: The return of the Big Five. In R. Hogan, J. Johnson, & S. Briggs (Eds.), *Handbook of personality psychology* (pp. 737–765). San Diego, CA: Academic Press.

Wiggins, J. S., Trapnell, P., & Phillips, N. (1988). Psychometric and geometric characteristics of the Revised Interpersonal Adjective Scales (IAS-R). *Multivariate Behavioral Research, 23*, 517–530.

Wiggins, J. S., & Trobst, K. K. (1997). Prospects for the assessment of normal and abnormal interpersonal behavior. *Journal of Personality Assessment, 68*, 109–125.

Williamson, M. (2004). The importance of fathers in relation to their daughters' psychosexual development. *Psychodynamic Practice, 10*, 207–219.

BIBLIOGRAPHY 417

Wilson, T. D., & Dunn, E. W. (2004). Self-knowledge: Its limits, value, and potential for improvement. *Annual Review of Psychology, 55,* 493–518.

Wilt, J., & Revelle, W. (2017). Extraversion. In T. A. Widiger (Ed.), *The Oxford handbook of the Five Factor Model* (pp. 57–81). New York, NY: Oxford University Press.

Winter, D. G. (1997). Allport's life and Allport's psychology. *Journal of Personality, 65,* 723–731.

Winterheld, H. A., & Simpson, J. A. (2018). Personality in close relationships. In A. L. Vangelisti & D. Perlman (Eds.), *The Cambridge handbook of personal relationships* (2nd ed., pp. 163–174). New York, NY: Cambridge University Press.

Wollman, N. (1982). Jung and Freud compared on two types of reductionism. *Journal of Analytical Psychology, 27,* 149–161.

Wood, J., Tesser, A., & Holmes, J. G. (Eds.). (2016). *The self in social relationships.* New York, NY: Psychology Press. (Original version published 2008)

Wood, W., & Eagly, A. H. (2002). A cross-cultural analysis of the behavior of women and men: Implications for the origins of sex differences. *Psychological Bulletin, 128,* 699–727.

Wood, W., & Eagly, A. H. (2010). Gender. In S. T. Fiske, D. T. Gilbert, & G. Lindzey (Eds.), *Handbook of social psychology* (5th ed., Vol. 1, pp. 629–667). New York, NY: Wiley.

Woodhill, B., & Samuels, C. (2004). Desirable and undesirable androgyny: A prescription for the twenty-first century. *Journal of Gender Studies, 13,* 15–42.

Woods, C. M., & Edwards, M. C. (2007). Factor analysis and related methods. *Handbook of Statistics, 27,* 175–201.

Wothke, W. (1993). Nonpositive definite matrices in structural modeling. In K. A. Bollen & J. S. Long (Eds.), *Testing structural equation models* (pp. 256–93). Newbury Park, CA: Sage.

Wright, A. G. C. (2017). Factor analytic support for the Five Factor Model. In T. A. Widiger (Ed.), *The Oxford handbook of the Five Factor Model* (pp. 217–242). New York, NY: Oxford University Press.

Wright, A. G., Pincus, A. L., & Lenzenweger, M. F. (2010). Modeling stability and change in borderline personality disorder symptoms using the Revised Interpersonal Adjective Scales-Big Five (IASR-B5). *Journal of Personality Assessment, 92,* 501–513.

Wright, A. G. C., Pincus, A. L., & Lenzenweger, M. F. (2012). An empirical examination of distributional assumptions underlying the relationship between personality disorder symptoms and personality traits. *Journal of Abnormal Psychology, 121,* 699–706.

Wrightsman, L. S. (1991). Interpersonal trust and attitudes toward human nature. In J. P. Robinson, P. R. Shaver, & L. S. Wrightsman (Eds.), *Measures of personality and social psychological attitudes* (pp. 373–412). San Diego, CA: Academic Press.

Young-Bruehl, E. (2009). Women and children first! *Modern Psychoanalysis, 34,* 52–74.

Young-Bruehl, E., & Wexler, L. (1992). On "psychoanalysis and feminism." *Social Research, 59,* 454–483.

Yovetich, N. A., & Rusbult, C. E. (1994). Accommodative behavior in close relationships: Exploring transformation of motivation. *Journal of Experimental Social Psychology, 30,* 138–164.

Zayas, V., Shoda, Y., & Ayduk, O. N. (2002). Personality in context: An interpersonal systems perspective. *Journal of Personality, 70,* 851–900.

Zerbe, K. J. (1990). Through the storm: Psychoanalytic theory in the psychotherapy of anxiety disorders. *Bulletin of the Menninger Clinic, 54,* 171–183.

Zinkin, L. (2008). Your Self: Did you find it or did you make it? *Journal of Analytical Psychology, 53,* 389–406.

Index

For the benefit of digital users, indexed terms that span two pages (e.g., 52–53) may, on occasion, appear on only one of those pages.

Note: Tables and figures are indicated by *t* and *f* following the page number

abasement (AB), 129–30, 255–56, 258, 260
abnormality, continuum from normality to, 126–27
accommodation, 9. *See also* automatic accommodation
    acquiescence and, 234–47, 235*t*, 239*t*, 240*f*, 244*t*, 247*t*, 257–59, 261*f*
    dominance, nurturance, and, 231–32, 233*t*, 235*t*, 241–48, 244*t*, 248*f*
    following partners' anger/criticism narcissism as reflected in, 45–48
    self-esteem and, 41–45
    interpersonal motives and, 255–59, 260, 261*f*
    and the need for intimacy, 255, 259–60, 261*f*, 279–317
    Rusbult on, 9, 11–12, 41–42
    self-esteem and subclinical narcissism as differentially related to, 48–50
accommodation-related behaviors and positive masculinity and femininity, 82–85
accommodative dilemma, 9
achievement, need for, 14–15, 261–62
acquiescence
    accommodation and, 234–47, 235*t*, 239*t*, 240*f*, 244*t*, 247*t*, 257–59, 261*f*
    higher-order acquiescence factors (ACQ1 and ACQ2), 260*t*
    noncircumplex acquiescence factor/ dimension (ACQ), 142, 143–44, 145*t*, 146*t*, 150–53, 175*t*, 183*t*, 183–84, 204*t*, 207*t*, 208, 215*t*, 270
    Interpersonal Adjective Scales (IAS) and, 159–60
    as trait factor, 236–47, 237*t*, 239*t*, 244*t*, 248

active vs. passive responses to dissatisfaction, 8–9, 40–41, 42, 79–80
actual self and real self, 92
adaptation, modes of. *See* functions/ modes of adaptation
Adler, Alfred. *See also* individual psychology
    styles of life typology, 69–70 (*see also* inferiority complex)
affection
    giving (vs. denial of), 79, 111
    indiscriminately seeking, 70–71
affiliation (AF), 129–30, 255–56, 258, 260
agency and communion, Bakan's superordinate constructs of, xiv– xv, 120, 131–33
agentic traits, xii–xiii, 110*f*, 110–11, 143–44
aggression (AG), 71, 127, 129–30, 255–56, 258, 260. *See also* power
    Freud on, 62
agreeableness. *See also* "Big Five" traits; circumplex theory of personality and social behavior; lower-order clinical interpersonal traits; lower-order subclinical interpersonal traits
    automatic accommodation and, 116– 17, 118–19
    and pro-relationship behaviors, 114–15
Alden, L. E., 128–29, 129*f*
Allport, Gordon W., 13–14, 105, 154– 55, 253–54
aloof-introverted (FG). *See* lower-order clinical interpersonal traits; lower-order subclinical interpersonal traits

420 INDEX

alternatives to the relationship,
  perception of, 10
ambitious-dominant (PA). *See* lower-
  order clinical interpersonal
  traits; lower-order subclinical
  interpersonal traits
ambivalent attachment. *See* preoccupied/
  anxious-ambivalent attachment
analytical psychology, Jung's, 93
  "Big Five" traits and, 104–6
  gender and, 92–93
  gendered self-concept and, 117–18
  Horney and, 92–93
  legacy of, 117–18
androgyny, psychological, 73–74
  Bem's conceptualization and
    measurement of, 73–75, 77
  controversies surrounding, 75–77
  Bem's gender schema theory and, 73–
    75, 76, 77, 81–82, 117–18, 132
  beyond, 82–85
  gender aschematicity and, 73–75
  and pro-relationship behaviors, 77–78
  and responses to relationship
    dissatisfaction, 81–82
anger/criticism, partners'
  accommodation following (*see*
    accommodation)
  constructive vs. destructive responses
    to, 8–9, 42–43, 79–82, 83–
    84, 265–66
  narcissism as reflected in
    accommodation following, 45–48
Anima and Animus (archetypes), 97–101
  defined, 98
anima and animus complexes, 100–1
  defined, 93
Anima-Animus Continuum Scale
  (AACS), 101
anxiety, 85–86
  avoidance and, xii–xiii
  types of, 69–70, 85–86 (*see also*
    attachment anxiety; castration
    anxiety; interpersonal anxiety)
  existential anxiety, 38
  separation anxiety, 28–29, 270–71
anxiety reduction motive
  fulfillment of, leading to high self-
    esteem, 27–29

Horney on, 54–55, 69, 92–93
anxious-ambivalent attachment. *See*
  preoccupied/anxious-ambivalent
  attachment
"approach" and "avoidance" motives, 7–8
archetypes. *See also specific archetypes*
  defined, 93
arrogant-calculating (BC). *See* lower-
  order clinical interpersonal
  traits; lower-order subclinical
  interpersonal traits
attachment anxiety, xii, 117, 267, 268.
    See also preoccupied/anxious-
    ambivalent attachment
attachment avoidance, xi–xii, 117, 268.
    See also dismissing-avoidant style;
    fearful-avoidant attachment
attachment security, ix–x, 28, 262
attachment styles/orientations, 117, 265–
  68. *See also specific styles*
  attachment theory and, ix–xii, 117,
    262, 270–71
  as interpersonal attitudes, x–xiv, 117,
    267, 270–71
  interpersonal circumplex theory and,
    266, 270–71
  measures of, x, 117, 265–66, 268–69
    (*see also* Experiences in Close
    Relationships Scale)
  and the self, xi–xii, xiii, 262
attachment theory, Bowlby's, 4–5, 28–29,
    32–33, 270–71
  attachment styles/orientations and, ix–
    xii, 117, 262, 270–71
attitudes, 49–50. *See also specific topics*
  Jung on, 102, 103
  vs. traits, xiii–xiv
automatic accommodation, 91–92
  agreeableness and, 116–17, 118–19
  conscientiousness and, 116–17
autonomy (AU), 129–30, 255–56, 258, 260
avoidance. *See* attachment avoidance;
    dismissing-avoidant style; fearful-
    avoidant attachment; infavoidance;
    socially avoidant

Bakan, David
  The Duality of Human Existence,
    131, 132

superordinate constructs of agency and communion as conceptualized by, 120, 131–33
Bartholomew, K., 265–66
basic anxiety, 69–70
Baumeister, R. F., 5–6, 30–31, 112–14
Bem, Sandra L. *See also* androgyny; gender schema theory
  feminism and, 72–73, 75, 77, 85, 86–87
  on her own marriage, 77
  Horney and, 72–73, 76, 84–87
  The Lenses of Gender, 72–73, 75–77, 85–87, 90
  and positive masculinity and femininity, 73–74, 78–79, 83
Bem Sex Role Inventory (BSRI), 73–74, 76, 113
  development, 72–73, 74
  McCrae/Costa's version of factor-analytic theory and, 108–10
  scoring procedures, 75–76
betrayal by partners
  forgiveness following, 9, 50–52
  self-esteem following, 50–52
between-person conflict resolution behaviors, conceptualizing, 8–9
"Big Five" traits. *See also* "heritability" of traits
  and conflict resolution, 91–92, 117–19
  dominance, nurturance, and, 119
  interpersonal circumplex theory and, 110f, 110–12, 115–16, 119
  Jung's analytical psychology and, 104–6
  McCrae and Costa on gender, heredity, and, 118–19
  measures of, 103
  The Oxford Handbook of the Five Factor Model, 87–88, 104–5, 107
  and pro-relationship behaviors, 49–51, 111–12, 114–16
Blechner, M. J., 57–58
Bowlby, John. *See also* attachment theory
  on expression of negative emotions, 3–4
  on separation anxiety, 28–29

calculating. *See* lower-order clinical interpersonal traits; lower-order subclinical interpersonal traits
Campbell, W. K., 46–48

Carson, R. C., 126–27
castration anxiety
  female, 62–63, 64
  Horney vs. Freud on, 62–64, 65–66
Cattell, Raymond, 105–6
change, openness to. *See* openness to change
Child, Mother, and Father archetypes, 95–97, 100–1
Chow, P., 101
chumship, 33, 34, 53–54, 59
circumplexity and higher- and lower-order traits, 153–54
circumplex model of interpersonal motives, 129–30, 130f
circumplex model of interpersonal traits, Leary's, 78–79, 126–28, 153–54, 191–92
circumplex model of lower-order clinical interpersonal traits, 128–29, 129f
circumplex model of lower-order subclinical interpersonal traits, 127–28, 128f, *See also* lower-order subclinical interpersonal traits
circumplex model of maladaptive interpersonal traits, Alden's, 128–29, 129f
Circumplex Scales of Interpersonal Values (CSIV), 255–56, 257t, 259–62
circumplex theory of personality and social behavior, interpersonal, 120, 153–54. *See also* circumplex model of lower-order subclinical interpersonal traits
  agency, communion, and, xiv–xv
  attachment orientations and, 266, 270–71
  "Big Five" traits and, 110f, 110–12, 115–16, 119
  evolution from a model of traits to a theory of personality and social behavior, 127–31
  geometrics, 133–41
  Jung's *Psychological Types* and, 125–26
  maladaptive trait version, 128–29, 129f
  and moving toward vs. against others, 71
  origin, 79

422 INDEX

circumplex theory of personality and
social behavior, interpersonal
(*cont.*)
overview, 126–31
and positive masculinity and femininity,
78–80, 81, 109–11, 110*f*
psychometrics, 141–43
combining circumplex and
noncircumplex factors, 143–44,
145*t*, 146*t*
lower-order clinical interpersonal
trait intercorrelations, 150–53,
151*t*, 152*t*
lower-order subclinical interpersonal
trait intercorrelations, 145–50,
147*t*, 149*t*
Rusbult and, 81–83
Timothy Leary and, 78–79, 127
close relationship, definition and
characteristics of a, ix
cognitive consistency theories, 31
cognitive functions (Jung). *See* functions/
modes of adaptation
cold (CO), 128–29, 139*t*, 141*t*, 152*t*
cold-quarrelsome (DE). *See* lower-
order clinical interpersonal
traits; lower-order subclinical
interpersonal traits
commitment (to relationship). *See also*
investment model of commitment
processes
and conflict resolution processes, 11–12
defined, 10
factors influencing, 10
measures of, 38–39
narcissism and, 46–47, 48–49
Rusbult on, 10–12
commitment factors, 84
commodities, tangible and intangible, 79
communal traits, xii–xiii, 110*f*, 110–11,
143–44. *See also* equal-spacing,
equal-communality model
communion
Bakan's superordinate constructs of
agency and, xiv–xv, 120, 131–33
unmitigated, 132
complexes. *See also specific complexes*
from collective archetypes to
personal, 100–1

defined, 93
compliant behavior, 70–71
confirmatory factor analysis, nature
of, 142–43
conflict, 7. *See also specific topics*
conflict resolution
"Big Five" traits and, 91–92, 117–19 (*see
also* "Big Five" traits)
commitment and, 11–12
interpersonal anxiety and
gender-related traits and, 85–86
self-esteem and, 52–53
responses to (*see* exit-voice-loyalty-
neglect (EVLN) typology)
conflict resolution behaviors, 91–92
investment model and, 10–11
conscientiousness. *See also* "Big Five" traits
and pro-relationship behaviors, 115–16
Consistency Seeker mode, 113–14
constructive vs. destructive responses to
partners' anger/criticism, 8–9, 42–
43, 79–82, 83–84, 265–66
cooperation in friendships, 59
coping strategies (Horney). *See* neurotic
responses/coping strategies
Cortina, Mauricio, 28–29
Costa, Paul T., Jr., 124. *See also* McCrae/
Costa's version of factor-
analytic theory
criticism. *See* anger/criticism
cultural factors in personality, 54, 86–87
Bem and, 86–87, 108
Horney on, 54, 61–62, 68, 86–87, 90
McCrae and Costa on, 108, 109
Sullivan on, 57

dark side of archetypes, 94–95, 96, 97
defense mechanisms. *See* security
operations
dependent behavioral tendency, 70–71
depression
and interpersonal functioning, 32, 33
loneliness and, 33
self-esteem and, 32–33
destructive vs. constructive responses to
partners' anger/criticism, 8–9, 42–
43, 79–82, 83–84, 265–66
detached behavioral tendency, 70–71
dismissing-avoidant style, x, 268, 319–21

dispositions, xiv. *See also* traits
terminology, xiii–xiv, 220
dominance (DOM), 145*t*, 146*t*, *See also*
lower-order clinical interpersonal
traits; lower-order subclinical
interpersonal traits; submission
dominance and nurturance, xiv–xv. *See
also* positive masculinity and
femininity
accommodation and, 231–32, 233*t*,
235*t*, 241–48, 244*t*, 248*f*
maladaptive versions, 128–29, 129*f*
terminology, 129–30
as trait factors, 231–48, 233*t*–39*t*, 244*t*
domineering (DO), 70–71, 128–29, 139*t*,
141*t*, 152. *See also* aggression
drives. *See* instincts and archetypes

ego psychology, xi
Electra complex, 65
emotional intimacy, 7–8, 32. *See also*
intimacy
Empirical Me, 25–26
environment
defined, 6, 24–25
vs. genetics (*see* "heritability" of traits)
equal communality, 135–36
equal-spacing, equal-communality model,
165–69, 217*t*, 229–30, 256–57
Gaines's, 229*t*, 242*t*, 257*t*
goodness-of-fit, 161, 163–64, 177, 185,
193, 195–97, 208, 216, 224, 227–
29, 241, 269
Hofsess and Tracey's, 166*t*, 178*t*
hypothetical data from Gurtman's,
137*t*, 140*t*, 140–41 (*see also*
Gurtman, M. B.)
Markey and Markey's, 198*t*, 209*t*
Ewen, R. B., 126–27
existential anxiety, 38
exit-voice-loyalty-neglect (EVLN)
typology, 8–9, 39
Expanded Personality Attributes
Questionnaire (EPAQ), 109–
10, 132
expansive solution (neurotic
response), 70–71
Experiences in Close Relationships Scale
(ECR), x, 267–68

ECR-Short Form, 266
RSQ and, 262, 267, 268, 270
ECR and RSQ together in
circumplex, quasi-circumplex
model, 323–43
exploitable (EX), 128–29, 139*t*, 141*t*, 152*t*
exploratory factor analysis, nature of, 142
extraversion. *See* circumplex theory of
personality and social behavior;
introversion/extraversion
Eysenck, Hans J., 104–6

factor-analytic trait theory
Cattell's version of, 105–6
Eysenck's version of, 104–6
false self, 92–93. *See also* ideal self
family-related archetypes, 95–97
fearful-avoidant attachment, ix–x, xi,
265–66, 267, 268, 319–21. *See also*
attachment styles/orientations
female genital anxieties, 62–63, 64
Feminine Psychology (Horney), 58,
61, 68–69
Bem's *The Lenses of Gender* and, 72–
73, 86–87
femininity and, 66–68
masculinity and, 66–67
feminine psychology, Horney's. *See
also Feminine Psychology*;
Horney, Karen
Adler's individual psychology and, 60–
62, 64, 66, 69–70
Bem's gender schema theory and, 72–73
legacy of, 85–86
meanings of masculinity and femininity
in, 66–68
femininity. *See also specific topics*
defining, 66–68
positive aspects (*see* positive
masculinity and femininity)
femininity complex in men, 65–66
feminism. *See also* Horney, Karen
Sandra Bem and, 72–73, 75, 77,
85, 86–87
field theory, Lewin's, 53
as a conceptual starting point, 5–6
five-factor model of traits, 105–6, 107. *See
also* "Big Five" traits
Foe, Edna B., 79

424 INDEX

Foe, Uriel G., 79
forgiveness following betrayal by partners, 9, 50–52
Foster, C. A., 46–47
Freud, Sigmund, 61–62, 64
  interpersonal anxiety and, 62–63 (*see also* castration anxiety)
  Kurt Lewin and, 15
  "masculine psychology," 54–55, 56–57, 64–67
  on Oedipus complex, 62, 65
  on penis envy, 58, 63–64
  sexism, 61–62, 64, 65–66
friendship. *See also* chumship
  Sullivan on, 53–54, 59
friendship quality, 36
  meaning of the term, 35–36
  measuring, 35–36
  self-esteem and
    in adults, 37–38
    in children, 34–35
Fritz, H. L., 132
Fromm, Erich, 72
functional autonomy of motives, 13
functions/modes of adaptation (Jung), 102–3, 126

gender aschematicity, 75, 76
  defined, 73
  vs. gender schematicity, 73, 75
  psychological androgyny as evidence of, 73–75
gendered self-concept, 85–86, 89–90, 91–93
  agreeableness and, 118–19
  factor-analytic trait theory and, 112–14, 118–19
  vs. gender identity, 112–13, 114, 118–19
  Jung's analytical psychology and, 117–18
gender identity, 113. *See also* multifactorial gender identity theory
"gender-plus" factor-analytic trait theory
  gendered self-concept and, 112–14
  toward a, 109–12
gender-related archetypes, 97–100
gender-related traits, 54–55.
    See also androgyny;

circumplex theory of personality and social behavior; feminine psychology; positive masculinity and femininity
  culture vs. biology and, 108
  gender-role attitudes and, 80–81, 113
  interpersonal anxiety, conflict resolution, and, 85–86
  Janet Spence on, 113
  and pro-relationship behaviors, 77–78, 84–85
gender roles. *See* sex roles
gender schema, defined, 73
gender schema theory, Bem's, 72–73, 74–75, 84–85. *See also* Bem, Sandra L.
  androgyny and, 73–75, 76, 77, 81–82, 117–18, 132 (*see also under* androgyny)
  from Horney's feminine psychology to, 72–73
  legacy of, 85–86, 87
  McCrae/Costa's factor-analytic trait theory and, 91–92, 108–9
gender schematic nations, 74
genital anxieties. *See* castration anxiety; female genital anxieties
global self-esteem, xi–xii, 49–50
  attachment styles and, xii–xiii
  definition and nature of, xi–xii, xiii
  self-respect and, 44–45
goals, 12
  defined, 12
  transformation of, 14 (*see also* transformation of motivation)
gregarious-extraverted (NO). *See* lower-order clinical interpersonal traits; lower-order subclinical interpersonal traits
Gurtman, M. B., 134*t*–51*t*, 135–41, 144–53

Helgeson, V. S., 132
"heritability" of traits, 118, 130–31
  increasing emphasis on, 106–7
  McCrae/Costa's factor-analytic trait theory vs. Bem's gender schema theory and, 108–9
higher-order interpersonal traits, 110–11, 260. *See also* communal traits

Hofsess, C. D. *See under* equal-spacing, equal-communality model

Holmes, J. G., 116–17, 254

Holzmuller, A. *See* circumplex theory of personality and social behavior

homosexuality. *See also* sexual orientation
Sullivan on, 37, 45–46, 57–58

Horney, Karen. *See also* feminine psychology; *Feminine Psychology*
Bem and, 72–73, 76, 84–87 (*see also* multifactorial gender identity theory)
on cultural factors, 61–62, 68, 86–87, 90
evolution in her theory over time, 68–70
interpersonal anxiety and, 28, 54–55, 58, 62–63, 69–72, 85–86, 92–93 (*see also* castration anxiety; neurotic responses/coping strategies)
Neurosis and Human Growth, 70–71, 90–91, 92
on neurotic responses, 70–71
New Ways in Psychoanalysis, 61, 65, 66–68, 69–70, 85–86, 90
on power, 67, 69–71, 90–91

Horowitz, L. M., 265–66

humanism, 72, 92–93

Ickes, W., 78, 126

id, ego, and superego, 93

ideal self and real self, 90–91, 92–93

identity
defined, 112–13, 114
vs. self-concept, 112–13

individual, the
Jung on the concept of, 123–24
psychology of, 13–14, 105

individual psychology, Adler's, 60–62, 64, 66, 69–70
Horney's feminine psychology and, 60–62, 64, 66, 69–70
as questioning male-oriented sexism in society, 60–62

individuation, 92–93
animus and, 98–99
Self and, 95, 96

infavoidance (IN), 129–30, 255–56, 258, 260

inferiority complex, 64, 66, 69–70

inferiority feelings of women, 64, 66, 90–91

ingenuous. *See* lower-order clinical interpersonal traits; lower-order subclinical interpersonal traits

instincts and archetypes, conflicts between, 101–2

interdependence theory, Kelley and Thibaut's, 8, 11, 13–14, 15, 49–50
Rusbult and, 12, 14–15, 40–42, 82–83, 84

interethnic relationships, 7

intergroup conflict, 7

intergroup relations, 54

internal representation systems, 100

International Personality Item Pool-Interpersonal Circle (IPIP-IPC), 192–93, 194–97, 208, 220, 223–24, 225–26, 227–30, 241, 248–49, 262–63
IAS-R and, 189–90, 191–92, 193, 197–208, 211, 222–24
to ipsatize or not to ipsatize data from, 211–17, 216t–18t
measurement error, 254

Interpersonal Adjective Scales (IAS), 159–60, 191–92

Interpersonal Adjective Scales-Revised version (IAS-R), 153–54, 159–61, 162–72, 189–90, 263
IPIP-IPC and, 189–90, 191–92, 193, 197–208, 211, 220, 222–24
to ipsatize or not to ipsatize data from, 183–89, 184t–86t

interpersonal anxiety, 18
Bem's gender schema theory and, 86
conflict resolution and, 53
Freud and, 62–63 (*see also* castration anxiety)
Horney and, 28, 54–55, 58, 62–63, 69–72, 85–86, 92–93 (*see also* castration anxiety; neurotic responses/coping strategies)
self-esteem and, 18–19, 27–30, 52–53
Sullivan on, 18–19, 25, 27–29, 52–53, 54–55, 59

426 INDEX

interpersonal circumplex model of traits, Leary's. *See* circumplex model of interpersonal traits

interpersonal circumplex theory of personality and social behavior. *See* circumplex theory of personality and social behavior

interpersonal force field, 26, 263–64

interpersonal intimacy, 32. *See also* intimacy

interpersonal motives, 255–59, 260. *See also* lower-order interpersonal motives; motives
- and accommodation, 255–59, 260, 261*f*
- circumplex model of, 129–30, 130*f*
- status (ST) and, 129–30, 255–56, 258, 260

interpersonal theory of personality, Sullivan's, 26–27, 33
- Horney's feminine psychology and, 58, 59, 60
- Kurt Lewin and, 26
- legacy of, 52–53

interpersonal values, 255–56, 261–62. *See also* Circumplex Scales of Interpersonal Values

intimacy, 14–15, 38–39
- communal motive of, 129–30, 255
- measures of, 38–39
- need for, 3–4, 7–8, 14–15, 259–60, 279–317
  - and accommodation, 255, 259–60, 261*f*, 279–317
  - preteen emergence of the, 32–33
  - Sullivan on, 32, 53–54
  - types of, 32

introversion/extraversion, 103–4, 110–11. *See also* lower-order clinical interpersonal traits; lower-order subclinical interpersonal traits
- as attitudes, 89–90, 102, 103
- defined, 102–3
- measures of, 103
- psychic energy as reflected in, 101–3

intrusive (IT), 128–29, 129*f*, 139*t*, 141*t*, 152*t*

investment model of commitment processes, 10, 12, 14–15, 38–39, 46–47

investment model variables as influences on conflict resolution behaviors, 10–11

investment size, 10

ipsatizing personality data, 188–89. *See also under* International Personality Item Pool-Interpersonal Circle; Interpersonal Adjective Scales-Revised version

Jackson Personality Inventory (JPI), 41

James, William, 25–26, 253–54

Jeffrey, M., 101

John, O., xii–xiii

Jordan, Furneaux, 102–3

Jung, Carl Gustav. *See also* Anima and Animus
- on individuality, 123–24
- on psychological types, 126–27
- writings, 96–97, 99–100
  - *Aion: Researches into the Phenomenology of the Self*, 94–95
  - *Memories, Dreams, Reflections*, 99–100
  - *Psychological Types*, 94–95, 101–5
  - *The Red Book*, 103–4

Jungian cognitive functions. *See* functions/modes of adaptation

Karaban, R. A., 98–99

Kay, J., 28–29

Kelley, H. H. *See* interdependence theory

Kempf, Edward J., 52

Klohnen, E., xii–xiii

Kumashiro, M. A.
- on pro-relationship behaviors, 42, 44–45, 50–52

Leary, M. R., 38

Leary, Timothy. *See also* circumplex model of lower-order subclinical interpersonal traits
- Jung and, 126–27
- Sullivan and, 26, 79, 127

Lewin, Kurt, 5, 7–8, 24. *See also* field theory
- on conflict, 7

A Dynamic Theory of Personality,
6, 24–25
on environment, 13–14, 24–25
Freud and, 15
on psychological field/life space, 7
on self-consciousness, 6
on self-control, 14
Sullivan's interpersonal theory of
personality and, 26
libido
from archetypes to desexed
"libido," 101–3
nature of, 101–2
life space, 5, 7, 26. *See also*
psychological field
defined, 5
Little Hans, Freud's case of, 65–66
locomotion, 24–25
loneliness, 33
loving, ways of, 72. *See also* affection
lower-order clinical interpersonal
traits, 150–53
intercorrelations among, 139, 139*t*, 150
lower-order clinical interpersonal
values, 255–56. *See also*
Circumplex Scales of
Interpersonal Values
lower-order interpersonal motives, 255–
58, 256*t*, 259
lower-order interpersonal traits, 120, 145*t*,
145–48, 259
intercorrelations among, 133,
134*t*, 227–30
lower-order subclinical
interpersonal traits
circumplex model of, 127–28, 128*f*
factor loadings, 215*t*, 235*t*, 239*t*,
247*t*, 260*t*
intercorrelations among, 133–41, 134*t*,
136*t*, 216*t*, 218*t*, 228*t*, 231*t*, 243*t*
internal consistency, 225–26
loyalty (response to conflict resolution).
See exit-voice-loyalty-neglect
(EVLN) typology
Luchies, L. B., 50–52

maladaptive interpersonal traits,
circumplex model of, 128–29, 129*f*

maladaptive traits, 126, 127, 128–29, 129*f*,
See also specific traits
male privilege, 61, 64
Markey, C. N. *See under* equal-spacing,
equal-communality model
Markey, P. M. *See under* equal-spacing,
equal-communality model
Markus, Hazel R., 74–75
masculine protest, 60–61
"masculine psychology" of Freud, 54–55,
56–57, 64–67. *See also* Freud,
Sigmund
masculinity. *See also specific topics*
defining, 66–67
nature of, 67
positive aspects (*see* positive
masculinity and femininity)
masculinity complex in women, Horney
vs. Freud on, 63–65
masculinity-femininity dichotomy,
criticism of, 60, 117–18
May, Rollo, 69–70
McCrae, Robert R., 124
McCrae/Costa's version of factor-
analytic theory
evolution of, 106–7
from Jung's analytical psychology
to, 104–6
legacy of, 118–19
McKenzie, S., 98–99
Millon, Theodore, 153
Mother and Father archetypes, 95–
97, 100–1
motives, 11–14. *See also* interpersonal
motives; transformation of
motivation
defined, 12
functional autonomy of, 13
goals and, 12, 14
individual differences in, 11–12, 14–15
moving toward vs. against vs. away from
others, 70–71
multifactorial gender identity theory,
Spence's, 109–10, 118–19
McCrae/Costa's theory and, 109–
12, 114
self-concept and, 112, 113–14
Murray, Henry A. *See* personology

428 INDEX

Myers-Briggs Type Indicator (MBTI), 103, 104–5

narcissism. *See also under* accommodation
and accommodation following partners' anger/criticism, 45–48
commitment and, 48–49
defined, 18–19
extraversion and, 104
self-enhancement bias and, 30
self-esteem and, 18–19, 30–31, 48–50, 92
Sullivan and, 25–26, 27, 45–46, 47
Narcissistic Personality Inventory (NPI), 46–48
neglect (response to conflict resolution). *See* exit-voice-loyalty-neglect (EVLN) typology
neurotic anxiety, 69–70, 85–86
neuroticism, 115. *See also* "Big Five" traits
and pro-relationship behaviors, 115
neurotic responses/coping strategies, Horney's, 70–71
nonassertive (NA), 128–29, 139*t*, 141*t*, 152*t*
normality to abnormality, continuum from, 126–27
nurturance (NUR), 145*t*, 146*t*, *See also* dominance and nurturance; overly nurturance; positive masculinity and femininity

O'Connell, A. N., 90–91
Oedipus complex, 62, 65
openness to change, 105
vs. conservation, 261–62
openness to experience, 107. *See also* "Big Five" traits
and pro-relationship behaviors, 115–16
orientations, perceptual. *See* attitudes
otherishness motivation, 12
Overall, N. C., 43–44
overly nurturance (NA), 128–29, 139*t*, 141*t*, 152*t*

partners behaving badly. *See also* anger/ criticism

responses to, 10 (*see also* accommodation)
passion
introversion/extraversion and, 102–3
lack of, 102–3
passive vs. active responses to dissatisfaction, 8–9, 40–41, 42, 79–80
penis envy
Freud on, 58, 63–64
Horney on, 58, 61, 64
womb envy and, 58, 61–62
Perceived Relationship Quality Components inventory (PRQC), 36, 38–39
perception of alternatives to the relationship, 10
perceptual orientations. *See* attitudes
Perry, Helen Swick, 52
person, Kurt Lewin's construct of, 5
personality, defined, 113–14
Personality and Close Relationship Processes (Gaines), xv–xvi, 141–42, 220
personality traits. *See* traits
personified self, 29
personology, 14–15
physical intimacy. *See also* intimacy
desire for, 32
positive masculinity and femininity, xiv–xv, 72–73. *See also* dominance and nurturance
accommodation-related behaviors and, 82–85
interpersonal circumplex theory and, 78–80, 81, 109–11, 110*f*
among nonclinical populations, 72–73
and responses to relationship dissatisfaction, 78–82
Sandra Bem and, 73–74, 78–79, 83
power
gender and, 67, 90, 91, 112
Horney on, 67, 69–71, 90–91
power (value/agentic motive), 14–15, 129–30, 254–55, 259–62, 261*f*

preoccupied/anxious-ambivalent attachment, xi, 265–67, 319–21. *See also* attachment styles/orientations
automatic accommodation and, 117
principal component analysis, nature of, 142
projective tests, 124, 125–26
pro-relationship behaviors, 42, 44–45, 111
"Big Five" traits and, 49–51, 111–12, 114–16
extraversion and, 103–4
gender-related traits and, 77–78, 84–85
Kumashiro on, 42, 44–45, 50–52
self-respect and, 44–45, 50–51
psychic determinism, 13–14
psychocultural analysis movement, 54
Psychological Entitlement Scale (PES), 47–48
psychological field, 7, 17–18. *See also* life space
psychological types
Jung on, 126–27
rigidity in adhering to a single type, 126
Psychological Types (Jung), 94–95, 101–5
psychology of the individual, Allport's, 13–14, 105
Pure Ego, 25–26

quarrelsome. *See* lower-order clinical interpersonal traits; lower-order subclinical interpersonal traits
quasi-circumplex model, 143–44, 150–53, 223. *See also under* Experiences in Close Relationships Scale: RSQ and
quasi-circumplex patterns, 148–49, 223, 232, 261–62, 269, 270

real self
actual self and, 92
ideal self and, 90–91, 92–93
reciprocity of tangible and intangible commodities, 79
rejection (RE), 129–30, 255–56, 258, 260
relational maintenance, 39–40. *See also* relationship maintenance

relational schemas, xiii–xiv
relational self-concept, xiii–xiv
relational trust, 9, 35, 38–39
relationship dissatisfaction. *See* relationship satisfaction; responses to relationship dissatisfaction
relationship maintenance, 39–40, 104
from relationship quality to, 38–40
relationship quality, 38–39
in children's friendships and adolescents' and adults' romances, 35–37
meanings and uses of the term, 36–37, 38–39
self-esteem and, 37–38
relationship satisfaction, 10, 38–39, 43–44. *See also* responses to relationship dissatisfaction
Relationship Scales Questionnaire (RSQ), 268. *See also* Experiences in Close Relationships Scale: RSQ and
resigned solution (neurotic response), 70–71
resource exchange theory, xiv–xv, 79
respect. *See also* self-respect; status
to others, 79, 111
responses to relationship dissatisfaction, 8–9. *See also* exit-voice-loyalty-neglect (EVLN) typology
active vs. passive, 8–9, 40–41, 42, 79–80
defined, 8–9, 41–42
positive masculinity and femininity and, 78–82
psychological androgyny and, 81–82
responses to partner-nonspecific dissatisfaction, 10–11
self-esteem and, 40–41
Rosenberg Self-Esteem Scale (RSES), 40–41, 44, 45, 50–51
Rusbult, Caryl E., 39–40. *See also* investment model of commitment processes; responses to relationship dissatisfaction; *specific topics*
on accommodation, 9, 11–12, 41–42

430 INDEX

Rusbult, Caryl E. (*cont.*)
  on commitment, 10–12
  on forgiveness, 9
  initial research: Study 4 (1991), 42–43
  interdependence theory and, 12, 14–15,
    40–42, 82–83, 84
  interpersonal circumplex theory
    and, 81–83
  on responses to relationship
    dissatisfaction and conflict
    resolution, 8–9
    (*see also* exit-voice-loyalty-neglect
    (EVLN) typology)
  self-control and, 8–9

schemas
  defined, 73
  relational, xiii–xiv
schizophrenia, Sullivan and, 29–30,
  37, 57–58
Schwartz, S. H., 261–62
Schwartz Value Survey (SVS), 261–62
Scientist mode, 113–14
secure attachment, xi. *See also* attachment
  security
secure base, 3–4
security. *See also* attachment security
  felt, 18–19
  as value, 261–62
security operations, 25, 26–27
security priming, 28–29
self, xi. *See also specific topics*
  defining, xi, 5–6, 24–25, 114
self-actualization theorists, 92–93
Self archetype, 93–96
self-as-known construct, 25–26
self-centeredness factors, 83
self-competence, 45
self-concept, 61–62. *See also* gendered
  self-concept
  Baumeister and, xiii, 6, 31, 114
  defined, xiii, 6, 112–14
  field theory and, 6
  nature of, 118
  relational, xiii–xiv
  Sullivan on relationships and, 31, 37–38
  as unifying construct within "gender-
    plus" factor-analytic trait
    theory, 112–15

self-concept clarity, 51
self-consciousness, 6
self-control
  accommodation and, 9
  of behavior following within- and
    between-person conflict, 7–8
  Bowlby and, 4–5
  development of, 3–4
  forgiveness and, 9
  goals and, 14
  Kurt Lewin on, 8, 14
  relationships and, 4–5, 9
  Rusbult and, 8–9
  tension and, 17–18
self-effacing solution (neurotic
  response), 70–71
self-enhancement bias, 30
self-enhancement vs. self-
  transcendence, 261–62
self-esteem. *See also* global self-esteem
  accommodation and, 41–45, 48–50
  affective dimension, 45
  definitions, 6
  depression and, 32–33
  and forgiveness following
    betrayal, 50–52
  and friendship quality
    in adults, 37–38
    in children, 34–35
  fulfillment of anxiety reduction motive
    and, 27–29
  interpersonal anxiety and, 18–19, 27–
    30, 52–53
  and interpersonal functioning, 30–32
  and intrapersonal functioning, 29–30
  meanings and scope of the term, 25
  narcissism and, 18–19, 30–31, 48–
    50, 92
  Rosenberg Self-Esteem Scale (RSES),
    40–41, 44, 45, 50–51
  self-respect and, 44–45, 50–52
  social, xi–xii, xiii, 41, 42–43
  terminology and use of the term, 50–51
self-interest, 13–14
  need for, 12, 13–14
selfishness motivation, 12
self-liking, 45
self-perception, modes/metaphors
  of, 113–14

INDEX 431

self-realization, 92–93, 95, 98–99. *See also* individuation
self-respect
  defined, 44–45
  measuring, 44–45
  self-esteem and, 44–45, 50–52
self-schema, 73
self-schema theory, 74–75
separation anxiety, 28–29, 270–71
sexism, 58
  Adler's individual psychology as questioning society's, 60–62
  in Freud's theory, 61–62, 64, 65–66
sex-role orientation, 78–79, 82
sex roles. *See also* Bem Sex Role Inventory
  conformity vs. nonconformity to, 66–67
  gender-role attitudes, 80–81, 109–10, 113
sex-typed partners/sex-typed pairings, 78
sex-typing, 74–76
sexual orientation. *See also* homosexuality
  and relationship dissatisfaction, 82
shadow, 94–95. *See also* dark side of archetypes
Sibley, C. G., 43–44
Snyder, M., 127
social interest, need for, 69
socially avoidant (SO), 128–29, 139*t*, 141*t*, 152*t*
social motives, 15. *See also* interpersonal motives
social role theory, 109
social self-esteem/social competence, xi–xii, xiii, 41, 42–43
  defined, xi–xii
sociometer theory, 38
solidarity (SO), 129–30, 255–56, 258, 260
Spence, Janet Taylor, 113, 117–18, 132. *See also* multifactorial gender identity theory
  Sandra Bem and, 74–75, 113
status (ST). *See also* respect
  giving vs. denying other people, 79, 255, 266
  interpersonal circumplex theory and, 266
  interpersonal motives and, 129–30, 255–56, 258, 260
  terminology, 129–30
styles of life typology, Adler's, 69–70. *See also* inferiority complex

subclinical traits. *See* circumplex model of lower-order subclinical interpersonal traits; lower-order subclinical interpersonal traits
sublimation of motivation, 13–14
submission, 127–28
  dominance and, 127, 154–55
  unassured-submissive (HI) (*see* lower-order clinical interpersonal traits; lower-order subclinical interpersonal traits)
submissive/compliant behavior, 70–71
Sullivan, Harry Stack, 126–27. *See also* interpersonal theory of personality
  Conceptions of Modern Psychiatry, 28–29, 35, 37, 52–54, 57–58, 59
  on friendship, 53–54, 59 (*see also* chumship)
  on homosexuality, 37, 45–46, 57–58
  on interpersonal anxiety, 18–19, 25, 27–29, 52–53, 54–55, 59
  narcissism and, 25–26, 27, 45–46, 47
  Personal Psychopathology, 45–46, 52, 53–54
  schizophrenia and, 29–30, 37, 57–58
  Timothy Leary and, 26, 79, 127
superiority, 47–48
  striving for, 60–61
superiority complex, 66
syzygy, 98

tangible and intangible commodities, reciprocity of, 79
terror management theory, 27–28, 38
Tesser, A., 6
Thibaut, J. W. *See* interdependence theory
Tracey, T. J. G. *See under* equal-spacing, equal-communality model
trait factor(s)
  acquiescence as, 236–47, 237*t*, 239*t*, 244*t*, 248
  dominance and nurturance as, 231–48, 233*t*–39*t*, 244*t*
traits, 102, 103–4. *See also specific topics*
  and Allport's psychology of the individual, 13
  meaning and scope of the term, xiii–xiv
  terminology, xiii–xiv, 220
transformational tendencies, 116–17

432 INDEX

transformation of motivation, 13–14
  forgiveness and, 51–52
  meanings of the term, 13–14
  origin and use of the term, 13
true self and false self, 92–93. *See also* ideal
  self and real self

unassuming-ingenuous (JK). *See* lower-
  order clinical interpersonal
  traits; lower-order subclinical
  interpersonal traits
unassured-submissive (HI). *See* lower-
  order clinical interpersonal
  traits; lower-order subclinical
  interpersonal traits
unmitigated agency, negative masculinity
  as a form of, 132
unmitigated communion
  Helgeson and Fritz's theory of, 132
  negative femininity as a form of, 132

values, interpersonal, 255–56, 261–62.
  See also Circumplex Scales of
  Interpersonal Values

vindictive (VI), 128–29, 139*t*, 141*t*, 152*t*
voice (response to conflict resolution). *See*
  exit-voice-loyalty-neglect (EVLN)
  typology

warm-agreeable (LM). *See* lower-
  order clinical interpersonal
  traits; lower-order subclinical
  interpersonal traits
Waugaman, Richard M., 57–58
Westkott, Marcia C., 70–71, 90–91
Widiger, Thomas A.
  *The Oxford Handbook of the
  Five Factor Model*, 87–88,
  104–5, 107
Wiggins, Jerry S., 263–64. *See also*
  circumplex theory of personality
  and social behavior
  Paradigms of Personality Assessment, xv,
  129–31, 141–42, 253
withdrawal, 70–71. *See also* neurotic
  responses/coping strategies
womb envy, 58, 61–62, 65–66
World-Soul, 93–94